Textbook on Criminology

Textbook on
Criminology

Fifth edition

Katherine S. Williams

Lecturer in Law, University of Wales, Aberystwyth

OXFORD
UNIVERSITY PRESS

OXFORD
UNIVERSITY PRESS

Great Clarendon Street, Oxford OX2 6DP

Oxford University Press is a department of the University of Oxford.
It furthers the University's objective of excellence in research, scholarship,
and education by publishing worldwide in

Oxford NewYork

Auckland Bangkok Buenos Aires Cape Town Chennai
Dar es Salaam Delhi Hong Kong Istanbul Karachi Kolkata
Kuala Lumpur Madrid Melbourne Mexico City Mumbai Nairobi
Paris São Paulo Shanghai Taipei Tokyo Toronto

Oxford is a registered trade mark of Oxford University Press
in the UK and certain other countries

Published in the United States
by Oxford University Press Inc., New York

British Library Cataloguing in Publication Data
Data available

Library of Congress Cataloging in Publication Data
Data available

ISBN 13: 978-0-19-926440-7
ISBN 10: 0 19 926440 6

5 7 9 10 8 6

Typeset in ITC Stone Serif and ITC Stone Sans
by RefineCatch Limited, Bungay, Suffolk
Printed in Great Britain by
Ashford Colour Press Limited, Gosport, Hants

OUTLINE CONTENTS

DETAILED CONTENTS

9 Mental disorder and criminality   208

10 Intelligence and learning   237

11 The sociology of criminality   267

16 Criminology and realism 419

17 Positivist explanations of female criminality 447

18 Feminist theories 469

19 Terrorism and state violence 493

20   Governance, risk and globalisation theories   522

21   Envoi   543

ACKNOWLEDGEMENTS

Special thanks to my father, John, who lent continuous support and made helpful suggestions for improvement, and also to my mother, Mair, who helped with the typing.

Thanks and apologies also to Alex, Siân and Dewi who kept me sane.

1

Introduction

This book is intended to introduce students to the broad study of criminology. Stated thus the project sounds very simple, but the breadth of the disciplines and theories involved in the study of the subject renders it rather more elusive. It seems logical to begin with an explanation of what criminology is. Criminology includes the study of: the characteristics of the criminal law; the extent of crime; the effects of crime on victims and on society; methods of crime prevention; the attributes of criminals; and the characteristics and workings of the criminal justice system.

In earlier times there was a greater belief in the supernatural and in the effects of God on good behaviour and the Devil on bad behaviour. This gave rise to methods of resolving disputes like trial by battle and of deciding guilt or innocence as trials by ordeal. These were perfectly understandable and logical if there was a reasonably wide acceptance of the premise that God would watch over the good and see that they got their reward—God would protect the innocent and see to it that the guilty were punished. It is a perfect example of how comprehension of certain social phenomena, such as crime, depends upon the important concepts of the day. In a more sceptical society, and as the importance of science and empirical enquiry increased, these views of criminality and criminal justice became less accepted. People became more and more interested in 'why' certain things occurred. It is not possible to prove or disprove the existence or effects of metaphysical or divine factors. Especially with the rise of rationalism through the eighteenth century, belief in heavenly or ethereal explanations declined and criminal justice moved on to set its bases on 'fact'.

Much of the modern work purports to be factual and claims to be scientific. It records information, often in statistics; uses the results of studies or tests; and embodies the conclusions drawn from such results. Even in this scientific era there is a place for speculation. Most scientific study begins with an idea of why something happens or works, and criminology is no different. The main difference between the old metaphysical ideas and those of today is that the modern theories lend themselves more readily to ideas of 'proof', or as Popper would put it, are capable of disproof. In criminological study the change is sometimes more apparent than real because the range of influences to be considered is wide and includes such intangibles as the effect of the environment on an individual's behaviour. Thus although modern criminology claims to be more scientific, that claim needs to be treated with care: some theories remain incapable of proof.

Part of the problem is that inherent in the nature of the subject are many concepts which are difficult to define and hard to measure. Even the central idea of what is a crime and who is a criminal has no single definitive answer. In fact, a number of the more recent theories are concerned with a consideration of why some behaviours are defined as criminal whilst others which may also be damaging are not, and why certain individuals are convicted of crimes whilst others who have also committed offences are allowed to escape conviction. Such approaches centre on the workings of the official systems of control rather than on trying to explain why people commit crimes. Their central reference is the definitions of the behaviour rather than the reasons for that behaviour. But, as we shall see, definitions which appear to be objective may turn out to have subjective elements: in this area of study the elusive nature of objectivity is a recurrent obstacle. Definitions always need careful scrutiny, but they are also indispensable. They are, for example, important to efforts to establish or explain why crime is committed or what should be done about it. For example, many researchers do not work within the legal definitions of crime, tied in with technicalities of defences, but rather consider what causes are behind a particular type of behaviour or what might help to prevent that behaviour. What the researcher accepts as criminal may be presented as objective but might in fact have subjective elements drawn, perhaps unconsciously, from the researcher's view of the world and how to improve it. Subjectivity is likely to be present throughout the study of criminology, including the present book, and its effects should always be considered.

Criminologists must take care to remember that their experimental material is human and that any testing will have effects on people. For this reason most of the scientific 'testing' is actually based on observation and use of available or collected data rather than experiments in any laboratory sense. However, in the area of punishment and treatment any effect given to theories has a very direct, and in some cases, unpleasant effect on those convicted of offences (some theorists would also treat those who might commit crimes) and their rights to be dealt with humanely must never be forgotten. These considerations are particularly relevant in late modern societies where crime and its control have taken on an almost overwhelming significance. Crime has become a central factor in politics; it has a widespread effect on the daily lives and behaviour of people (locking homes and cars, checking for valuables, use of credit cards, wariness on the streets); it is a pervasive theme in both the media and fiction (books, film and television); and it gives rise to emotional and often misinformed discussions and judgments. In this environment the 'scientific' study of the subject is sometimes overlooked and policy can be based on irrational foundations, not now of divine or devilish origin, but still worrying. At the very least, in late modernity the reasoning and connections on crime become socially complex.

The present text contains a collection of theoretical and factual material. When dealing with what claims to be factual or objective proof of an idea it is important to be very wary. Some of the difficulties with such information have been mentioned above: a few need further consideration. First, just because one idea has more studies which uphold it does not mean it is correct: each of those studies may be based on a false premise or be flawed through being subjective or through an unscientific work base. Similarly, although one theory may appear 'true' this might be misleading, as it may be limited by the knowledge available at the time—once we thought the world flat; our knowledge has since been extended and we now think we know it is a globe; knowledge may one day move us on again. Such shifts are more common in the case of criminology, partly because we are dealing with less solid proof than is available to other sciences and much of a proof may depend on attitudes. Indeed, in this area shifts in interpretation are necessary and desirable since they are affected by a constantly changing social and institutional environment. Most of the ideas put forward to explain criminality are based on some reasonably plausible premise. They can usually call upon some 'facts' to 'prove' that they explain criminality. Since no-one can encompass all possible data, which is literally limitless, the 'facts' are necessarily selective. At the same time, since in dealing with complex human issues there is never likely to be just one single cause, the process necessarily involves giving more weight to some factor or factors than to others. And since some, if not most, of these factors are likely to be impervious to measurement, an exercise of judgement is entailed. In assessing their significance, readers will be influenced by their own view of the world, which may also be shaped by the disciplines from which they approach the subject and by their preconceptions of the subject matter. Although it is necessary to warn about the perils of subjectivity and to indicate the limits to the scientific basis of the subject, it needs also to be remembered that what this book is reporting represents the fruits of a great deal of study by many fine minds over a long period of time. In the nature of the subject, certainty is rarely on offer, but it is hoped to extend understanding.

Criminology is a subject with a fairly long and varied history. Our study will begin at the end of the nineteenth century and will consider theories which have gained credence over the past century or so. There have been many approaches to the subject drawn from many different disciplines. The student of the subject is likely therefore to be confronted with a range of ideas drawn from numerous discourses. The object of the book is to attempt to bring together the main currents and to act as a basic introduction to each and to provide a survey of the existing state of our knowledge in each area. Such a survey is particularly useful because there is no single accepted approach or answer to the problem of who commits crimes. Although the subject matter is largely set out in the various disciplines, it is hoped that students might be encouraged to consider the subject as a whole and from each discipline apply those parts which might be most useful.

It is perhaps necessary to recognise that over the period studied there are two important aspects to many theories, and certainly to the policies used by States in addressing crime. First, are offenders acting entirely out of choice or free will and can thus be blamed and called to account for their actions? This provides a logic in making crime 'costly' in terms of the punishment to be faced for breach of the rules in order to deter. Or, secondly, are offenders less volitional in that their choices are limited through structural or social factors which tend to exclude or marginalise some groups or individuals? If so, then addressing criminality might be a matter of addressing or ameliorating such structural issues as employment, education and racial exclusion. This could be done either through grand schemes such as welfare programmes or through more individual approaches such as support for individual offenders. For most States the more comfortable theory to accept is the 'volitional' or 'free-choice' of the individual as this blames offenders and society is still good and unblemished. This approach tends to be embraced most frequently by the press, the public and politicians, whereas 'structural' theories are most accepted by academics and theorists. The comfortable volitional approach belittles the real question concerning 'how offenders think' and ignores the possibly more important question of 'why offenders think that way or make those choices'. Possibly the most important limiting factor with the theories concerning individual choice is precisely that they stop at blame and punish; they do not search for either the reasons behind people's choices or any underlying causes. In modern policy this is perhaps the most unsatisfactory element, the willingness to stop where societal reaction is comfortable and not to ask the difficult questions.

Inevitably, a book of this kind which is trying to survey as large a part as possible of the literature and its origins and at the same time to put it into both its historical and contemporary contexts, will entail a great deal of enforced categorisation. No doubt other writers might organise all this somewhat differently. It is therefore necessary to say something briefly about how the present work has been ordered.

It is necessary to begin the study by indicating the basic constituents of the central subject, crime. One essential prerequisite is to place definitions on some of the major terms, and so Chapter Two looks at the definition of crime and how it is differently interpreted.

Crime is a subject about which nearly everyone has views. This is not a trivial consideration because criminology is not the property of the experts. Indeed, generally held views are important because notions of crime and how it and criminals should be dealt with are matters of public policy. Chapter Three considers some of the influences which shape public perceptions and in so doing places special importance on the media. Chapter Three goes on to consider some of the most problematic misconceptions about crime.

Perception of the problems caused by crime and the fear of it are largely shaped by popular impressions of how common it is, of—so to speak—the amount of crime that is about. This interacts with the influence of the media, e.g., every year when crime statistics are published all the papers carry features and stories about the amount and kinds of crime. The journalists' treatment is, however, necessarily selective and occasionally misleading. It is thus of crucial importance to the study of criminology both to know the sources of statistics, official and other, and to have some clear understanding of the use and limitations of this information. This area is considered in Chapter Four.

Beside needing to know about the amount of crime and the numbers of criminals, it is also important to have some information about victims of crime. Chapter Five considers the victim, the effects on victims and whether victims can be 'blamed' for their own victimisation. It also considers whether criminology and criminal law processes are sufficiently concerned with the victim.

The book then moves on to the various explanations and theories that have been developed over the years to account for the characteristics of criminals or of criminality. It is based around three main types of theory. First, those which argue that criminality is caused by forces beyond the control of the individual. This characterises many of the chapters in this section, particularly the earlier ones, and is based on a positivist idea that behaviour is predetermined. It appears in biological and psychological as well as sociological disciplines and tries to explain what causes criminality. Although often illuminating, it is essentially limited as it ignores the human factor of choice. One might say that entering a pool of water causes someone to become wet but that explanation does not explain why the person fell into or chose to enter the pool. The second group of theories allows for free choice in taking part in crime and therefore recognises a basic human trait: the ability of people to think and choose what is perceived as their own best interests. This is the basis of so-called classical theory. It has more recently been given extra weight by adding the possibility that people can by social process be influenced to believe that law-abiding behaviour is best for them and for society. This characterises a number of the learning and control theories. The third body of theories is less interested in crime and criminals than in the way society decides what and who to control and how it goes about these functions. These ideas grew up in the 1960s and are called the 'New Criminologies'.

There is a rough chronology about this in the sense that the type of general explanations which were initially developed are first treated before proceeding, in each area, to the more modern developments. The actual sequence is outlined below.

Chapters Six and Seven consider the effects of physical and biological factors on criminality and are largely deterministic. Chapters Eight, Nine and Ten then deal with the connection between psychological and mental factors and criminality. Most of these are deterministic in character. Parts of these, especially of Chapter Ten, also consider the effects of learning and socialisation on criminality. They involve a willingness to take part in criminal behaviour which introduces an element of choice or at least opens up the subject to such possibilities. Chapter Eleven goes on to discuss the effects of the environment on criminality. It considers factors such as ecology, poverty, unemployment and lower-class culture. Many of these are built upon in Chapter Twelve, where the effects of some social structures are considered and special attention is paid to juvenile criminality. Both of these chapters are largely positivist in approach. Chapter Thirteen leaves more to free will and is concerned with the way society might persuade individuals to be law-abiding. It looks at the social structures which may help law-abiding behaviour: by implication if they are absent criminality might well arise. Chapters Fourteen and Fifteen take a very different approach, either attributing criminality to the official control mechanisms or questioning the efficacy of the present definitions of criminality and the way in which we choose to control those who live in society. The ideas set out in Chapter Sixteen use elements drawn from all three approaches and relate these to what these writers regard as the real problems of crime and the practicalities of solving them. Chapters Seventeen and Eighteen deal with female offending. Although the author is unconvinced that different explanations are relevant to explain male and female criminality and believes that much of the earlier chapters apply equally to males and females, many criminologists have considered it necessary to look for differing explanations, often because they perceive that the two groups act differently. It would not be correct to ignore these other explanations but it is hoped that the reader will not thereby dismiss the earlier ideas from any relevance in considering female criminality. Indeed, possibly the most important role of feminist criminologies has been to force the practical and theoretical consideration of the 'others' by the discipline as a whole Chapter Nineteen considers the subjects of terrorism and State violence. Although here the explanations for criminality may appear to be very different they can help to put other theories in perspective. Explanations often assume that terrorism and State violence are both 'volitional', in the sense that the perpetrators choose to take part in the activity, but it is also necessary to recognise that volition is only the start of understanding and to look behind the choice to uncover the root causes. After this Chapter Twenty returns to more general considerations. In particular it draws on the interest of criminologists in recent developments in governance, technical change, and risk.

The student may feel disappointed that relatively little emerges in the form of settled conclusions. Instead the intention has been to indicate the present state of a continuing debate and to point, where appropriate, to those interpretations and proposals which currently command the most general acceptance. Given what has been said about the complexities of criminology, the difficulties of suppressing subjectivity and even prejudice, the disputes over definitions and the resistance of many of the key concepts to precision and measurement, definite conclusions and certainties are probably inappropriate. The book is intended to give a broad over-view to the scope of criminology, to the ideas which have influenced the area covered by the subject, and to the practical uses to which these have been, or might be, put. In the course of the work a wide range of authorities has been drawn on; they have necessarily been treated rather briefly. If this encourages students to turn to the original texts a major object of the book will have been achieved.

QUESTIONS

1 What is criminology?
2 Can its study claim to be objective?

2

Definitions, terminology and the criminal process

2.1 Introduction

Criminology is concerned with crime: to understand the materials every criminologist should thus have a good grounding in the criminal law. This chapter can only act as a very brief introduction to that field and students should have recourse to one of the more detailed texts on this subject (see for example Smith and Hogan (2002); *Blackstone's Criminal Practice* (published annually); Allen (2003). In this chapter some of the technical terms will be briefly explained and some of the theories about the sources and limits of criminal laws will be considered.

2.2 The judicial process

In England and Wales the legal system consists of two separate sets of hierarchies of courts. One set (together with the police, the Crown Prosecution Service, the court officers and the penal institutions) enforces the criminal law on behalf of the State. The other set enforces the civil law between and on behalf of aggrieved individuals in society. Criminal law, irrespective of what its aim or purpose should be, is punitive. It punishes any act or omission forbidden by the criminal law.

There are differences in the aims and procedures of criminal as opposed to civil courts, but it is difficult to define what is criminal, especially since most acts or omissions which are crimes, or at least serious crimes, will also (simultaneously) be civil wrongs (i.e., torts). Criminal cases require proof 'beyond all reasonable doubt' whereas civil cases only require a 'balance of probabilities'. Many activities may be torts which are not also crimes. Generally, any act or omission may give rise to two consequences, one criminal and the other tortious (i.e., civil). One act or omission may result in an individual being prosecuted and punished by the State and also in the person injured bringing a claim (i.e., suing) in the civil courts for compensation called damages. Only in the former will the police and prosecuting authorities be involved and the liberty of the individual be in jeopardy. In the latter, only that person's, or his insurers', wallet will be in any danger.

2.3 **Formal sources of criminal law**

Textbooks on the legal system of England and Wales state that there are various sources of law: custom, the judiciary (common law), the prerogative (of the Crown), legislation and directives from the institutions of the European Community. As far as the principles of criminal law dealt with in this book are concerned, an appreciation of only two of these creative sources of legal rules is required: common law and legislation. Common law consists of the rules established by the decisions of judges. These decisions in our system become precedents which are binding on, and therefore must be applied by, courts lower in the hierarchy than the one which made the decision. Legislation consists of statutes or Acts of Parliament and delegated legislation (rules made by persons or bodies other than Parliament but authorised to do so by Parliament). Following devolution, the respective governing bodies in Scotland and Northern Ireland can both legislate and pass secondary legislation, and the Welsh Assembly can pass secondary legislation in certain defined fields. Here we will concern ourselves with the Parliament in Westminster which deals with most criminal matters for England and Wales. English and Welsh criminal law is made up of rules contained in statutes and precedents, in court precedents (the common law) and in the judicial interpretations of those statutes, which interpretations become the law unless and until Parliament or a higher court alters any such judicial interpretation.

In most instances Parliament lays down the conduct which is to be criminalised and also sets out the maximum and, for a growing number of offences, the minimum—penalties and sometimes whether there are any special powers, for example of search or arrest, which should attach to the detection of this type of conduct. The courts through the judges (legal matters) and the jury (matters of fact) set the limits in any particular case. In this phase the judges are very important, because in most cases various elements such as what are the limits of mental intention or of particular defences arise, which are questions of common law for the judge to rule upon. It is then for the jury to decide what factually occurred. The judges can thus play a very powerful role in the outcome of any trial, and do this without appearing to be making any decisions and claiming that they are merely applying the will of Parliament. For offences which are considered to be less serious (mainly non-indictable cases) the process may be carried out by magistrates under the legal guidance of clerks to the court.

The above lays out the formal sources of the law but does not consider where these laws arise or why they are chosen. There are numerous theories on the sources of the laws themselves. Some believe that they are derived from torts or wrongs done to the individual and that those which were most serious or which were perceived as having consequences for the State also became crimes. Moral standards have also been given as a source of our criminal laws. Others believe that they are the product of customs or mores which society found or finds particularly important. In all cases they are supposed to alter and be repealed as society decides that they are no longer of import. Unfortunately, they often are left sitting on the statute books or in the common law long after their usefulness has been outlived, only because no-one bothers to repeal them. Such oversight can give rise to problems and to anomalies.

Most of these ideas are based on a consensus idea of society, that is, that society functions as an integrated structure whose members agree on the norms, rules and values which are to be uniformly respected: the criminal law is then merely the embodiment of what the members in a society disapprove of and find most unacceptable. This idea breaks down from time to time. More recently, two other ideas have emerged about the sources of the criminal law. The first contends that rather than acting as a consensus, society is made up of a series of conflicting and competing groups—the conflict theory. Under this idea the criminal law is said to be built on what is important to the wealthy and powerful in the society, and particularly protects them against those who might try to usurp their position. At the same time, some of the proponents of conflict theory assert that the criminal law often fails to criminalise activities from which these groups may gain even if others in society suffer (these ideas will be further considered in Chapter Fifteen). The last idea is also a more recent interpretation and is again based on the hypothesis that the criminal law is built up by those in political and legal power. In this case, however, it is not claimed that the law arises only to protect their interests; rather that it represents the preferred definition of these privileged groups as to where the line should be drawn, and they may make their decision depending upon their values, norms or morals as well as on their position in society (see Chapter Fourteen).

Criminology has totally different origins. Its aim is to ascertain the causes of crime, to pre-empt or prevent crime by 'treating' its perceived causes, to study the effects of crime on society, and to analyse societal reactions to crime. Consequently, its source is a combination of theory and empirical research. Its aim is to be more scientific than forensic.

2.4 Underlying influences

The common law system of England and Wales is adversarial not inquisitorial, and generally it does not permit the judiciary to consider and rule on points (or give interpretations of the meanings of statutes) which are not in issue on the facts of the case brought before the court (in civil law by a party, and in criminal law generally by or on behalf of the State) or arising on an appeal. The courts cannot take the initiative and clarify criminal law principles *ad hoc*. They must wait until the obscure or difficult points come before them. Even then the court's ruling will be authoritative only on the particular point in issue. As a consequence, the courts frequently consider an issue relating to criminal liability in one case without reference to the effect such a decision may have on other parts of the criminal law because that effect is not in issue. Because the judiciary cannot consider and rule on points which are not in issue on the facts of the case before the court, such areas of potential conflict between the rules and principles of criminal law may only be resolved where an individual case raises such issues simultaneously or where the point in conflict is raised specifically in a subsequent case or on appeal. Considerable time may pass before any of these events occur. Meanwhile academics may be critical and pressure may grow amongst the public for Parliament to change or clarify the law by legislation.

The courts, however, sometimes voluntarily undertake the creation of principles of criminal law. For example, at one time the rule was that where an accused intended his conduct to produce certain consequences (such as the death or serious injury of another) or he foresaw as a matter of high probability the occurrence of those consequences he could, if his conduct caused the death of another, be convicted of murder. It has now been determined that foresight of consequences is in law neither an alternative nor an equivalent of intention. Nevertheless, the judiciary tell us that foresight of such consequences may still lead to an irresistible inference that those very consequences were in fact intended by an accused. A jury may, therefore, come to the conclusion as a matter of evidence or fact that if an accused foresaw certain consequences resulting from his actions, he intended to bring them about, but a jury is no longer compelled because of a rule of law to come to that conclusion.

Sometimes the judiciary create or change law which remains part of the realm of common law (i.e., those areas of our law not legislated but traditionally derived from court decisions) by an express pronouncement or reformulation of a rule of substantive law. A good example is in the cases concerning conspiracy to corrupt public morals and conspiracy to outrage public decency. Although academics may debate the point, it would appear that the judiciary in those instances clearly created new criminal offences. Sometimes, however, the judiciary alter the law by more arcane methods. In the example noted above relating to murder, the courts had classified an element of the offence as a rule of substantive law which permitted but one conclusion, and later reclassified that element as a matter of adjectival law, in other words as a matter of evidence or fact for a jury to determine from its own conclusions. Such a development illustrates the subtle ways in which the judiciary may work a reformulation of the criminal law; it should thus be of great interest to, but rarely appears to have been taken into consideration by, criminologists. It should be clear that the judiciary are contracting or expanding the net within which persons may be made liable for particular offences whenever they expand or contract the definition of intention (by saying that foresight is or is not included) or the definition of recklessness (by saying that failure to consider a risk either is or is not included), or if they impose an objective test as opposed to a subjective test for *mens rea* (the mental state of the accused in respect of the elements of the offence). Likewise, if the judiciary declare an offence to be one of strict liability as opposed to one requiring proof of *mens rea*, they are widening the net and increasing the possibility of persons being found guilty of that particular offence. This is seldom, if ever, referred to by criminologists despite the fact that it must have some bearing at least on the way criminal statistics are perceived.

The reasons why the judges seek to change our criminal law in such a covert way are partly social and partly political. Today the constitutional position of the judiciary is such that they must avoid being seen overtly to create new offences or to widen the ambit of existing criminal liability. This function is now, in theory at least, the responsibility of Parliament, but in reality the judges always have played a part, either directly in developing the common law, or by the process of interpreting the will of Parliament in pronouncing on the meaning of statutes. What affects the judges' views, amongst other things, may well be what they perceive, rightly or wrongly, to be socially desirable or what they consider a danger to society, its culture, its ethos, its Judaeo-Christian morals and its liberal-democratic tradition.

Their views may in turn be affected by whether or not they perceive crime generally, or particular crimes, to be on the increase. There is no doubt that the judges play a very significant role in our society. Two things should be evident, first that at various stages in the criminal process (prosecution, adjudication and sentence) there are many gaps in the guide-lines or rules and much discretion is left in the first instance to the prosecutors and in the latter instances to the judiciary. The beliefs and attitudes of judges about criminals and crime, and about public policy (which is a guise for public opinion or more often public acceptability) become very important. If their views are too idiosyncratic or flexible they may not attain proportionality by way of punishment and equality of treatment or justice between offenders, and may create uncertainty because there would be no predictability. On the other hand, if their views are too stereotyped or ultra-conservative or radical, they may detract from the second constitutional function of the judge, which is to protect our traditional freedom and liberties. If they show evidence of prejudice for or against the ways of life or traditions of particular groups of people, again they may attack the constitutional rights of citizens and residents of Britain. Some discussion of the importance and effects of this judicial power is made in Chapters Fourteen and Fifteen, where it is shown that it is only relatively recently that criminologists have acknowledged the importance of the judiciary and their opinions. Since October 2000 their discretion, in every case, must be shaped by the Human Rights Act 1998, under which they are required to bear in mind the rights of the individual as defined in the European Convention on Human Rights when they interpret any law, whether statutory or common law. This may curtail some of the more extreme decision-making.

A criminologist should be aware of the factors and policies which mould the criminal law causing the creation, and constant reshaping, of criminal offences. Also needed is an appreciation of the nature of, and reasons for, the criminal law and of the judicially controlled mechanisms for its reformulation. A realisation of the influences and policies behind the judicial or parliamentary mind, which in a constantly changing society are themselves necessarily unstable, gives an understanding of the impetus for change in the criminal law and an explanation of its fluidity. An understanding is also required of the motivation of individuals and pressure groups (including the prosecutors, the magistracy and the judiciary), since these are seeking to change or to prevent change in the law. Such motives can range from direct vested interest to a deep belief that it is in the best interests of society as a whole, essential for the protection of individuals or a class, or an unwarranted detriment to freedom. These are some of the basic skills and qualities which it would be desirable to find in a criminologist: simply to specify them is enough to indicate that they represent a sort of ideal.

2.5 Defining a crime

2.5.1 Formal legalistic definition

It is difficult to define what is criminal or to distinguish a crime from a tort. One cannot even declare that crimes are always more serious in their effects either on the individual or on society. For example, the negligent manufacture and marketing of a product which turns out to be dangerous may be far more injurious to both individuals and society than the theft of a pencil, yet the former would normally only constitute a tort whereas the latter is criminal. There are similarities: each is a wrong, each is a breach of a legal obligation or rule. What, then, is the difference? Although it is circular, the best definition and the best distinguishing feature is that only if the breach of a legal rule (the wrong) has criminal consequences attached to it, will it be a criminal offence. An offence or a crime, then, is a wrong to society involving the breach of a legal rule which has criminal consequences attached to it (i.e., prosecution by the State in the criminal courts and the possibility of punishment being imposed). This gives a legalistic view of a crime but fails to impart the types of activity which may fall under that head. Above all, it must be re-emphasised that it is a circular definition—a crime is something the law calls a crime and uses criminal prosecutions and sanctions to deal with. Despite these shortcomings with the definition, it is essential that one never forgets that no matter how immoral, reprehensible, damaging or dangerous an act is, it is not a crime unless it is made such by the authorities of the State.

2.5.2 Basic elements of most crimes

Most criminal laws forbid certain types of behaviour, and therefore before a person can be convicted, it must be proved that he or she acted in a fashion proscribed by law: this is generally known as the *actus reus* of an offence. Some defences go to the very core of the action and claim that part of the *actus reus* was missing. For example, the offence of assault requires that an individual unlawfully injures another: a claim that an injury was caused as the result of self defence is thus claiming that the action has not been completed, i.e., it renders the injury lawful. Another example arises in the offence of rape, which involves sexual intercourse with a woman without her consent; if the man claims that she consented he is claiming that part of the *actus reus* is absent. In both cases the defence goes to the heart of the action. Other defences may admit the action but ask that it be excused because of, for example, duress or certain types of mistake. In stealing, someone intentionally deprives another person of property and thus clearly commits an offence: but if that offence is committed because a third party forced it at gunpoint, the offender could plead lack of choice.

Generally, omitting to do something will not amount to the *actus reus* of an offence. For example, if I decide to watch a young child drowning in inches of water and do nothing to save its life, I am not guilty of any criminal offence though clearly my inaction is morally indefensible. Basically, the law usually only punishes individuals for positive conduct and not for inaction. There are, however, some notable exceptions. In a few instances the law requires certain types of behaviour, for example, failure to submit the accounts of a limited company is a crime. In others, there may be a duty to act. This duty may arise through statute, for example, the duty to report road accidents to the police; or it may arise out of a person's job or out of holding public office, for example, a police officer has a duty to prevent an assault; or it may arise out of the obligation to care for a dependant.

The second important element which is required in most cases is a mental state. There must be a state of mind with respect to the *actus reus*: this is called the *mens rea*, that is an intention to act in the proscribed fashion or to bring about the unacceptable ends, or in some cases reckless indifference to causing a particular harm. It is important to distinguish *mens rea* from motive. If I decide to kill a close relative, such as my grandmother, because she is helpless and begs me to put her out of her misery, some might argue that my motive is honourable and under-standable. But if I premeditate my action and intend its consequences, my conduct is murder just as if I had shot an enemy with hatred in my heart. Both are murder; the motive does not alter the fact that the crime has been committed. Motive, however, may be taken into account in sentencing or in carrying out the sentence. In the above example, the court has to pass a life sentence on all murderers, but the time actually spent in prison may vary depending on the conduct of the prisoners and possibly also on the motive for the crime, as this may touch on the possibility of the offence being repeated. In cases where the court has a discretion, it may decide to punish the person whose motive was good less severely than where the motive was greed, hatred etc. Foucault (1988) has claimed that all too often the law gets caught up with motive rather than with intent. He also questions the idea that motive should be used at the sentencing stage, although most would have more sympathy for a merciful killing than for a cold-blooded killing, and most would prefer to see the former sentenced less severely than the latter.

There are some defences which question the *mens rea* of an offence, such as a plea of insanity, diminished responsibility and automatism, all of which are discussed in Chapter Nine.

In some cases the *mens rea* of an offence may be established if the individual intended to do wrong, though a greater harm than intended occurs as a result of the actions. For example, if I intentionally hit someone it is an assault, and I could be convicted of that crime, but if the person is particularly weak and dies as a result of the injury, then I may be convicted of manslaughter or, if it can be proven that I intended to cause grievous bodily harm, murder. Although I did not intend to kill, the death is the direct result of a crime which I did intend. Although most lawyers tend to claim that 'crime', '*mens rea*' and '*actus reus*' are carefully defined and object-ively applied, and thus lead to just decisions, a number of critical legal theorists have begun to question this and look at the sociological conditions and the histor-ical or anthropological context in which the law is made and used (Norrie, 2001; Kelman, 1981; Lacey and Wells, 1998; Lacey 2001).

Some offences do not require any *mens rea*, as to all or some of the *actus reus*, on behalf of the offender. These offences are known as strict liability offences. Many strict liability offences are set by Parliament and are sometimes referred to as 'state of affairs' offences or as absolute liability offences. They often fall into the area of public welfare offences or regulatory offences, and regulate potentially dangerous activities, like motoring, or they protect people against other dangers of modern life. In these cases, all that needs to be proven is that the state of affairs existed and the crime is complete; it is no defence to say that one did not intend this state of affairs or even that one was unaware of it. Examples of this arise in many road traffic violations (e.g., driving with defective brakes, or more generally the use of defective and dangerous motor vehicles); possession of dangerous objects or sub-stances such as firearms or controlled drugs (where all that is necessary is know-ledge of possession, not that the thing possessed is a controlled drug); public health legislation such as the sale of food containing extraneous matter; or control of pollution. These types of activities fall into the category of strict liability to force people to exercise higher standards of care to ensure that offences are not committed, especially when their activities could present a danger to the public. Furthermore, because they often involve an omission, for example failure to renew the tyres on a vehicle, it would be difficult to prove the *mens rea* as to all or some of the *actus reus*.

Lastly, for all crimes there is a legally prescribed punishment. The punishment is usually set out in terms of a maximum and the actual punishment in any particular case is left to the discretion of the judge, although increasingly there are guidelines, usually set by the Court of Appeal, to help assess the seriousness of the case and the weight to give to its various aspects. In a growing number of cases there is a minimum punishment. For example, murder carries a life sentence, drunk driving the loss of a driving licence, and there is now a minimum sentence for repeat offenders of certain serious crimes under the Powers of Criminal Courts (Sentencing) Act 2000, part V, chapter III. In addition, both the defence and the prosecution can now appeal the sentence, and the Court of Appeal can lay down guidelines for sentencing.

2.5.3 **What actions are criminalised?**

Why certain acts or omissions are declared criminal and others are not is a difficult question. So are the questions: what aggravating factors warrant being made the subject of a separate offence? and which mitigating factors should be recognised as defences? As with the terminology (see 2.8), there is an element of fashion involved in attempts to answer these fundamental issues, but the underlying rationale is largely governed by the traditional ethos and ethics of the society. In our case this relates mainly to the largely white, male-oriented, Judaeo-Christian tradition and the conservatism that accompanies the desire for stability, order and predictability. Morality and notions of blameworthiness based on harm may explain the formulation of the early fundamental crimes (murder, theft etc.) but do not necessarily fully explain the modern social welfare, moral improvement and traffic offences created by statute. No one philosophy or cause can adequately explain why differing forms of activity are deemed criminal. Morality, economics, politics, power, public administration, public order and public safety all play a part. Also, there is an interrelationship with the equally complex question: why do people commit crimes? If defining crime is problematic, explaining why people participate in these activities is even more elusive. As we shall see, attempts to provide explanations have to confront such fundamental issues as: does crime occur because man is inherently evil; or because of socio-economic conditions; or because of physical or mental illness; or because of genetic, inherited defects; or are there other factors or combinations of factors which are responsible? Such questions form the core of this book and are considered in Chapters Six to Eighteen. They represent an attempt to get away from studying the principles of criminal law and the theories of criminology in a vacuum, and to enquire about their aim and purpose; whether these ends are achieved; and whether claims made by criminologists and others are substantiated by sound research. It is not claimed that such an approach gives, or can give, clear-cut conclusions, but it is strongly contended that it is essential for anyone seeking understanding of a hugely complex field.

2.5.3.1 *Consensus approach*

This assumes that the activities which are criminalised are firmly based on the generally agreed mores for conduct. The criminal law thus seeks to identify and control the types of behaviour which the community finds unacceptable: in this way it helps to preserve public order. Perhaps the most universally assumed aim of the criminal law, and that which is said to be the strongest unifying element in the consensus theory is that of averting harm. Mill accepted that the State could always intervene in the liberty of personal conduct to prevent one individual harming another. This basic liberal ideal has guided the consensus theory in its main aim, the prohibition of crimes which are *mala in se*, harmful in themselves. This includes activities which attack the person such as assault, murder and rape as well as acts which attack property or the possession or ownership of property such as theft, arson or intentional damage. Feinberg (1985, 1988) would also include the prevention of offences. Many of these offences are criminalised in most societies and there is often claimed to be a general consensus about their prohibition. Much more difficult are the questions of how much harm is necessary to trigger the use of the term 'crime' and who assesses whether there is consensus.

A modern portrayal of a consensus theory should take account of autonomy. Within this Lacey and Wells (1998, p. 105) explained the criminal law:

as a set of norms backed up by the threat and imposition of sanctions, the function of which is to protect the autonomy and welfare of individuals and groups in society with respect to a set of basic goods, both individual and collective.

In terms of autonomy the law should create an environment in which individual choices are maximised except where they might impact upon the autonomy of another individual. This requires a minimalist version of the harm principle whereby the criminal law 'should only be used as a last resort or for the most reprehensible types of wrongdoing' (Jareborg (1995)) and individuals need as much autonomy as possible whilst guaranteeing a similar freedom to others. Raz (1986) argues that in order for individuals to be autonomous they need to be independent and free from coercion and manipulation. Neither the State nor the law should interfere with that freedom nor should it be curtailed by the actions of other individuals. It is here that the State should instigate criminal laws to protect individuals from one another. Autonomy and harm can also be used to justify protection of the State, such as tax evasion, although here the links are more tenuous—autonomy requires that the State works to create the conditions necessary for choices to be realistic; without revenue this would be difficult so that some citizens would suffer reduced autonomy and therefore harm. In addition, autonomy is undermined by feelings of insecurity so that it might be necessary to criminalise activities which cause such offence as to put others in fear (for example, racial hatred). Von Hirsch and Jareborg (1991) noted that for individual victims four generic interests might be in need of protection: physical integrity, privacy, autonomy and freedom from humiliation or degrading treatment. This would be supported by recourse to human rights as the source of criminal law and would pave the way for crimes which recognise the State as perpetrator. Schwendinger and Schwendinger (1970) went further, claiming that all violations of basic human rights were acts of criminality whether included in the criminal law or not. Here many States would be included as perpetrators of crimes rather than as the force that defines and enforces them, and human rights then become standards that must be defended by the criminal law.

The all-embracing concept of rights moves towards defending against the abuse of power wherever that power resides. Here all criminal acts would be viewed as the unacceptable use of power which removes the right of victims to enjoy their rightful amount of power, their humanity (see Henry and Milovanovic (1996)). They split harms into two. Firstly, harms of reduction which remove from someone something they presently enjoy (be that a status, a feeling or something physical). Secondly, harms of repression or oppression which prevent or limit future achievements or desired ends. Central to this criminality would be oppression be it of gender, race, class or other status and any acts of hate whether these acts are perpetrated by individuals, organisations or the State. They are designed largely to protect the weak from oppression. Most States do not protect these types of behaviour through criminal law so this stance is important to act as a contrast to the present consensus view of harm.

A very modern analysis of the need for crime is to answer the problems faced by citizens as members of the 'risk society'. Key proponents of this are Giddens (1994) and Beck (1992, 1998 and 2000), who have both referred to a concept of 'manufactured uncertainty' where everyone in society is forced to live with large risks. Most of these risks are caused by successful advances in science and technology whose effects are difficult to assess. Note here that a risk society is not necessarily more dangerous than anything faced in the past. Rather it means that the risks are now manufactured in that technology has altered the natural world so extensively and in so many areas of our lives that there is almost no aspect of modern life which is unaltered. This means that we cannot predict from the past what the risks may be in the future and therefore risk becomes more profound and for many more debilitating. Individuals assume and expect the State, through politicians, to minimise future risks for everyone and provide compensation, or require companies to compensate, when they fail in this responsibility. In the area of crime, risks and uncertainties give rise to feelings of insecurity which may be very debilitating, interfering with autonomy and thereby harming the lives of individuals. There is therefore an argument to include risk or insecurity (Vail et al. (1999)) as a reason for creating criminal laws. This might include the control of the mentally disordered and supervision of disorderly juveniles in the criminal laws. Risk will also be an important aspect of crime control in later chapters, and a survey of recent trends will be made in Chapter Twenty.

Some consensus theorists would accept a role for the criminal law in protecting individuals from themselves, from taking dangerous substances, participating in dangerous activities or regulating the way we participate in such activities (requiring protective clothing in some jobs or wearing seat belts in cars). A number of liberals, although largely agreeing with Mill and the autonomy theories, have sympathy for this argument: '. . . paternalism—the protection of people against themselves—is a perfectly coherent policy' (Hart (1963)).

Consensus theorists thus recognise that protecting the safety and integrity of the individual is not the only aim of the criminal law. They accept that there are numerous aims: maintenance of public order; raising revenue (e.g., the laws punishing those who evade income tax); regulating business (e.g., they punish the charging of excessive prices and they punish unhygienic and unsafe practices); protecting employees; conserving the environment; preserving heritage; and enforcing morality. It is interesting that the significance of this last function—the upholding of morality—has changed in recent years. In a pluristic, multicultural society Devlin's 1965 view of the criminal law as centrally necessary to prevent the moral disintegration of society is on the wane—although this has not shifted much political rhetoric away from a stress on protecting morals. Overall the basic effect of these various aims of the criminal law is to maintain society in its present form and to ensure its smooth functioning.

Today in this country there are literally thousands of offences created by statute which are designed to enforce certain standards in the practice of otherwise lawful activities. The rules relating to road traffic, to public hygiene, rules about health and safety at work and rules governing the entry into and conduct of certain businesses or professions are examples. These rules are generally enforceable by way of criminal sanction. Unlike the traditional common law notions of crime, these newer statutory offences generally punish omissions as well as positive acts.

Furthermore, they are more often than not created as offences of strict liability for which an accused may be held liable without any proof of a blameworthy state of mind with regard to one or more element of the *actus reus*. This last innovation has produced practical advantages but it means that if a minor prohibited act, omission or event occurs for which a person is responsible, that person may be guilty. Guilt does not necessarily depend, as it must in other offences, on state of mind. People may be deemed guilty irrespective of what they intended, thought or believed. Consensus theories accept this as necessary to the smooth running of society and also as a way of permitting activities which may cause harm, whilst minimising the danger. Generally, the ordinary man or woman in society does not consider persons convicted of these sorts of offences, including traffic violations, 'criminals', that term being popularly reserved to express moral condemnation for the acts of murderers, rapists, thieves and the like; yet these regulatory or social welfare type offences can cause no less suffering and harm. Should society and the law treat such offenders as being as blameworthy and reprehensible as the traditional 'criminals'? Why is there a consensus that they should not?

Finally, there are offences the sole purpose of which is the enforcement of morality. As indicated above the justification for these has tended to be brought more into question. Should the criminal law be concerned with matters of private morality if the conduct does no harm to society or to the participants? The abrogation or repeal of such laws would delete a mass of criminal statistics and prevent large numbers of people being labelled criminals. It would not mean that these acts and their perpetrators would be acceptable, because they may still be considered anti-social by the majority of the community. Clearly, repeal would be to those persons' advantage, but it could also be to the advantage of the community generally. Law enforcement agencies may, for example, then be able to concentrate their resources in the prevention or pursuit of serious criminal offenders: the muggers, rapists, fraudsters, robbers, those who cause grievous bodily harm, and the like. Are the criminal offences relating to alcohol, gambling, pornography, bigamy, blasphemy, bestiality, criminal libel, conspiracy to corrupt public morals, conspiracy to outrage public decency and possibly also controls on drugs outmoded and unreasonable restrictions on our liberty? Would individuals and society be at risk if current laws on these matters were abolished? If these laws are essential to our society, why are adultery, fornication and seduction not criminal? Many argue that criminalising issues of 'pure morality' or what might be termed 'transactional crime' where all the parties consent is divisive and would thus undermine the claim that the criminal law represents a concensus which includes broad agreement over the morals of society. Occasionally, popular demands lead to legislation to withdraw certain conduct from the ambit of the criminal law. One of the best examples is the public debate following the Wolfenden Committee Report (1957) which led to Parliament passing the Sexual Offences Act 1967, which declared that homosexual acts between consenting adult males (then over age 21, altered to 16 by s. 1 of the Sexual Offences (Amendment) Act 2000) in private were no longer a crime.

The limit of the criminal law is a topic which has taxed lawyers, criminologists, sociologists, philosophers and others for many years. It is necessarily complicated by the wide range of problems which the criminal law is expected to address. Sharp disagreements over what the law should, and should not, include thus reflect not only the enduring mysteries of the human condition, but also the variety and subjectivity of the aims and functions of the criminal law. A further set of nuances is explored in the next subsection.

2.5.3.2 *Modern sociological approaches*

The above approaches generally assumed that there was something about the nature of an act itself or its consequences which made it unacceptable. The present approach will consider whether the crime consists not in the act itself, but simply in it being defined as criminal. The implication is that crime is constructed by the society or group. This idea has given rise to a number of explanations of criminality (discussed in Chapters Fourteen and Fifteen) but here we are concerned with how this might have affected the definitions of crimes. Virtually all societies are too large for everyone to define the rules which are thus constructed by some group or groups. Acceptance of this as a sociological fact has led to various interpretations of the ways in which such crimes are defined.

The first of these is the conflict school which views the constructs of modern society as fluid and claims that new issues are resolved, or old ones redefined, by the resolution of conflict (Dahrendorf (1959)). In this analysis society is not built on harmony and consensus but rather is constructed of competing groups who struggle for power. Conflicts between workers and employers; between the sexes or the races; between religions; between political groupings. Each of these conflicts is resolved by the more powerful group enforcing its views and using the law as its weapon. In criminal terms this is done through controlling their opponents' behaviour, by calling it illegal. On this view the criminal law is constructed to protect the interests of powerful groups. Neither individuals nor their behaviour is inherently criminal: the social order has constructed the proscribed areas of behaviour (see Quinney (1970) and Turk (1969)). It is further argued that the law is applied more vigorously to the less powerful than to others, making criminality almost by definition the normal response of the powerless or disadvantaged to their position in life. Conflict theorists also claim that public opinion is manipulated by the same powerful groups so that the proscribed behaviour becomes widely accepted. This might explain why certain actions are either not criminal or are treated very leniently (for a fuller discussion of conflict see Chapter Fifteen and for some illustrations see Chapter Three).

A more chronological approach to conflict theory, based on Marx, studied crime as a wider subject, including the relationships between crime, criminal, victim and State. The areas of behaviour which are defined as criminal are those necessary to a capitalist society. Under these the upper classes can exploit the weak, put them in physical danger, and transgress their human rights either with total impunity or with only very light punishment (for a full discussion see Chapter Fifteen). This very politicised attack led some to question the *status quo* and to confront the possibility that the criminal law was designed to control certain types of behaviour for reasons other than the general well-being of those in the society. The anti-capitalist slant alienated many.

More recently the critical school of thought has splintered into Marxist and more conservative sections. Most of the latter group still provide socialist perspectives but do not accept the Marxist alternative to the *status quo*. They retain the attack on early theories but do not accept that the criminal system emerges solely out of the capitalist domination of society. They see power as just one element—others include culture, personality, prejudice and even chance—in determining the social order. They agree that the criminal law tends to define the activities of those who are dominant as legitimate and those of the weak as less acceptable, but the reasons are not always capitalistic. Many activities are deconstructed to discover interactions and to understand and analyse behaviour. Law may be constructed by the powerful and in their interest, but this may often be with the blessing of the weaker in society. These writers have a wider view of the concept of crime. They look not only at the criminals and their behaviour, and the State and its need for a definition of criminal, but also at society's constructs of social control, and at the views, actions and input of the victims.

Each of these theories sees crime as an artificially constructed social reality: it is made by particular people to protect the interests of some over those of others. The thesis is that the criminal law is intended to enforce conformity with the norms of those with the dominant interest in a given society (Ashworth (1995) and Bauman (2000)). To illustrate the point, even violent behaviour is not always viewed and treated the same way. Criminal violence is created by those who make and enforce the law rather than by the nature of the behaviour. In the media and general discussions on the level of violence it is usually only this officially constructed area of behaviour that is considered. Thus most of the controls on violence only protect against violence on the street. Until recently domestic violence was not taken seriously and the law still permits parents (and other carers) to treat children in ways which if committed against an adult, would be a crime. Only in the last 20 years has excessive violence against partners or children been accepted as an activity needing strong enforcement measures to punish and control it. Assaults committed by law enforcers themselves are rarely prosecuted whereas similar acts by others might well culminate in imprisonment. Corporations and governments may take decisions they know or suspect will result in death or injury and yet will not necessarily face criminal prosecution: asbestos, thalidomide; use of soldiers to test mustard gas or the effects of atomic bomb radiation. The criminal law does not protect against all the dangers we face, nor even against all the worst dangers (e.g., food, air, environment).

A few analysts of crime definitions raise the still more fundamental issue of whether the criminal laws embody social advantage. Zemeologists suggest much more would be gained by looking at harm and correcting harm wherever it arises (inadequate health care, unemployment, poverty, natural disasters etc.). In criminalising too much energy is expended on searching out and blaming the offender rather than concentrating on correcting the underlying problem. Community safety is presently a matter of controlling criminal tendencies and those who undermine order; this may be to the detriment of some. For example, Williams et al. (2000) note that CCTV though being claimed as a weapon against crime is in effect often used to exclude certain groups from some places usually to protect business interests. Zemeology would suggest that community safety should be concerned with the harm inflicted by the effects (physical, psychological or financial) of social exclusion, poverty etc. Many of these harms and the needs to which they give rise remain ignored whilst society concentrates on crime as the main area of insecurity. Zemiologists contend that the criminal law should be broadened to take account of all harmful behaviours. This is very similar to the abolutionists who question, first, the utility of a punitive approach, suggesting that it may be more likely to lead to more harmful/criminal behaviour rather than less, and then also question the need for categories of behaviour labelled criminal. The argument is not that the concept of criminal behaviour should be abolished but rather, as with zemiologists, that it should be viewed and resolved along with other social problems (see van Swaaningen (1997) and (1999)).

2.5.4 Particular cases

In the above discussion a number of theories were briefly mentioned which might help students of criminology to understand the complexity of the subject and to see that the factors on which it is based are not necessarily objectively defined and universally accepted. A further major force shaping the criminal law is political opportunism or expediency which often responds to a matter which is of transient public concern or which the media whips into a popular issue (see Chapter Three). In this context the motive does not necessarily fit any of the above theories. It is important to keep this problem in mind through some of the discussions which arise later. Before we leave the subject of the definition of crimes we will look at some areas which give substance to these difficulties.

2.5.4.1 Victimless crime

The concept of victimless crime picks up on one of the central elements of the consensus theory of crime.

It has been suggested that victimless crime arises when a few basic principles are met. First, there must be a consensual participation of all the people involved in the activity. Secondly, no participant complains to the police. Thirdly, the participants generally believe that they are not harmed by the activity, although others may disagree with their assessment. Finally, most of these offences involve the willing exchange, among adults, of desired goods or services.

Each author who writes in this area has a slightly different view of what activities fall within this concept, but the following are frequently included: drunkenness and related offences; sale and use of prohibited substances; vagrancy and begging;

gambling; prostitution (or rather the offence of soliciting); various adult consensual sexual offences such as bestiality. Some also include abortion, bigamy, private fighting, bribery, flashing between adults and obscenity and pornography between adults. There are some clear inconsistencies in this area; for example, why is bigamy illegal whereas both adultery and living with a person of the opposite sex as if married are legal? Why are the use and sale of some substances which may be considered harmful to the user, such as heroin, made unlawful whilst sale and use of others, such as tobacco, is legal? Why are soliciting in public, setting up a brothel, kerb-crawling and living off immoral earnings illegal whilst prostitution itself, although unlawful, is not criminal?

Whether and how these activities are regulated varies very widely from State to State. They vary on habitual and cultural grounds, but most frequently they vary on moral grounds, and most of these have a basis in authority. It appears that the legality or illegality of these activities depends mostly upon the morality and the economic interests of the groups with the most political power in the State.

Many elements in society now call for these offences to be decriminalised. Some have been *de facto* decriminalised in that they are either not policed and/or when discovered their perpetrators are not prosecuted (e.g., possession and use of small amounts of soft drugs). Others have been *de jure* decriminalised, such as homosexuality. Many people who argue for their decriminalisation do so on the basis that criminalising them has failed to control the problem and in some cases it may have exacerbated the difficulties. Many of those, including some in the police and other enforcement agencies, who question the use of the criminal law to control drug-taking, do so on this basis. Non-criminal methods, such as programmes to help drug addicts, may be more appropriate.

A case for decriminalisation has also been argued on wider cost-benefit grounds. These can be summarised under six broad heads. First, the police and court time spent in dealing with these offences is, it is suggested, an inefficient use of these expensive resources. Secondly, that the type of police investigations required to control this behaviour is often unsavoury and degrading to the police officers, whilst, thirdly, criminalising the behaviour causes a black market to open up allowing large profits to be made. In addition, law enforcement officers are exposed to bribes, some of which could be very tempting. Fifthly, that in order to obtain these substances or services the individual has to turn to criminals, and may become cut off from law-abiding citizens and learn further criminal behaviours. Sixthly, if the substance is illegal and there is a market, then the providers of that service or item are taking a risk providing it, and will require a high price which may force the customers to perform crimes in order to obtain the necessary money. Each of these suggests that the cost of criminalising and policing these types of offences is excessive, and that society should therefore find some other way of controlling them, if control is warranted.

As an example of some of the issues one might look specifically at drugs. Britain and many other Western States (especially the US) have been waging a 'War on Drugs' campaign. The basic tenet of this policy is that drug use should be stamped out by criminalising every facet of drug use and through vigilant application of those criminal laws. At the Conservative Party Conference in 2000 the Shadow Home Secretary, Ann Widdecombe, even suggested that those caught in possession of illegal drugs should receive an automatic £100 fixed penalty for the first offence and stated that 'from the possession of the most minimal amount of soft drugs right up the chain to the large importer, there will be no hiding place. There will be zero tolerance'. This policy was dropped after the police objected to its introduction but it is indicative of the fervent belief by many that firm application of criminal laws will solve the problem. The situation is not this simplistic. Most police forces now accept that 'zero tolerance' on drugs is not a policy which they can sustain and they use cautions for possession of recreational amounts of drugs whilst still trying to use the law against the sellers and pushers. However, even this may not be socially positive. Many of those who sell drugs are just small-time users. The person supplying in school is likely to be a classmate or older sibling so that a crackdown is an attack on one's friends and family not 'the other' evil pushers portrayed in many media images. Many addicts in fact pay for their habit by buying more than they need and then mixing it with other substances before selling it on to others. It is often these extra substances which cause the drug-related deaths and illnesses rather than the drugs themselves. Furthermore the clamour for drugs probably sustains much other criminal activity. Our prisons certainly contain many addicts. The most frightening factor is the power possessed by the drugs barons who have an interest in retaining the 'War on Drugs' as it keeps drug prices buoyant and therefore gives them high profits. They have enough financial power to suborn institutions of the State. In such a situation contemplating supplying addicts with heroin (this reduced drug addiction in Switzerland), legalising and controlling the sale of drugs (tried to a limited extent in the Netherlands) may not seem completely impossible or ridiculous ideas.

Before leaving the area of victimless crimes, it is worth noting that there is now a realisation that crimes do not fall neatly into victimless and predatory offences. If the term 'victimless' means consensual participants there are some offences where all those who participate are consenting. In the case of drugs there are producers, importers, dealers and sellers and each of these generally consents to his or her crime, although people may unwittingly carry the drugs, hidden in their luggage or in a vehicle (a particular problem for international lorry drivers). There are other clusters of offences of a primarily predatory nature, such as assault, where the victim does not normally consent. Lastly there are clusters of offences which have both consensual and predatory elements. Property offences are often of this sort. The initial theft or burglary is predatory with a definite victim, but it is followed by much consensual activity in receiving and dealing in stolen property. Many of the predatory offences would be unlikely to occur without the consensual offence which occurs later. Conceptualising offences as victimless can thus sometimes be counter-productive when they may be organically connected with a predatory crime. In assessing victimless offences and considering them for decriminalisation it is therefore necessary to be aware of the wider context and their possible connections with predatory offences.

2.5.4.2 *Control of the powerful*

Lack of control over the powerful has often been a complaint of conflict and critical criminologists. As will be seen in Chapter Three, it is the powerful who are often involved in white-collar crimes (which this author considers are crimes they commit for their own gain) and in corporate crimes (which are committed by employees in a corporation for the good of the corporation) and crimes committed by governments (which are considered in Chapter Nineteen). Many argue that the criminal sanctions in these areas are too narrow and inadequate to control the dangerous activities of these people and bodies. In this section we will briefly consider how the criminal law controls corporations in the way it is defined and enforced, and whether there are better methods of control.

In order for the State to control the dangerous or harmful activities of corporations these activities need to be both defined as criminal and properly enforced. This may seem straightforward since the dangers are often known and their causes are clear; yet the activity may not be defined as criminal, nor the corporation made liable. In part this is defended on the grounds that corporations provide wealth for society and have a social utility in a way which is not recognised in, for instance, burglars. More tendentious is the argument that enforced State control will push up production costs, and corporations will threaten to locate new production lines in States where regulation is not so strict. The implication is that the State must choose between these possible costs of over-regulation, and the possible harmful effects for the community of under-regulation. Conflict and critical theorists argue that the corporations use their political and economic powers to ensure that they are not threatened by either the definition of criminal activities or their enforcement. They also see that the situation has, to an extent, worsened with the statutory reduction in union powers and call for tougher criminal laws, more effective controls and harsher sanctions. Against this, it is argued that corporations are now too complex and their creators and controllers too ingenious to be controlled effectively by criminal law structures and by punishments designed to deal with individual transgressions. Other approaches have been suggested.

A number of authors (Braithwaite (1993); DiMento (1993); and van de Bunt (1994)) have suggested a middle ground of reasonably strict criminal laws, but then aiming to influence corporate behaviour by a discriminating use of prosecutions. The call for restraint by enforcement agencies is partly based on the belief that most employees have an obligation to the general society as well as the organisation. There are three parts to the equation leading to corporate social responsiveness: first employees at all levels and therefore the organisation must be aware of the possible harm a particular action will cause; secondly the employees and therefore the corporation must realise the social unacceptability of the conduct; and finally they need to be aware of the possible criminal sanctions, the negative consequences for them, which might ensue if they proceed. These conditions are necessary for responsible decision-making in the organisation, but they may not be sufficient if the bonds of employees to the corporation, or their identity within it, become more important than their commitment to the outside world. Braithwaite is sanguine that the consciences and professional ethics of employees will constitute an essential enforcement factor in preventing corporate criminality, increasing the likelihood that serious breaches of regulation will be uncovered. These writers would thus leave some regulation to the corporations themselves, or to the social conscience of employees within them.

One implication, as van de Bunt argues, is that the job of the regulatory body is to inform corporations of their duties, make them aware of the norms with which they must comply, talk with them about the most effective means of compliance and give reasonable weight to real problems and constraints on compliance whilst not accepting excuses for non-compliance. Therefore regulatory agencies are

consultants first, advising on how to comply, and police officers second, only prosecuting where all else fails. Such a system can work only if there is a strong criminal
law and fierce sentencing on its transgression. Without this enforcers have no
leverage to persuade corporations to act.

Critics of such a strategy attack it as being permissive of breach, too accepting of
the problems claimed to be faced by businesses and too prone to a cosy solution
between business and regulator. It is predicated on a view that corporations are
basically conforming organisations which can be trusted to act responsibly. There
could be contradiction between this and the basic ethos of business to make a
profit. As Bauman (1994) notes, business is ruled by 'instrumental rationality'
whereby the ends justify the means. As long as greater profits are achieved moral
indifference is accepted, even encouraged. Employees should do as they are told
and allow the ethical questions to be considered, if at all, by others. These arguments were given much credibility during the stock market boom of the 1990s and
the revelations when this collapsed in the early 2000s. Businesses certainly wish
and aim to control as much of their working environment as possible, a consideration which grows in significance as corporations grow in size enabling them to
exercise such control more effectively, through pressure on government and workers. Some would therefore argue that what is necessary is to make it more expensive
to breach than to comply, and urge an approach which involves both civil and
criminal law: that is, realistic and effective criminal sanctions which are harmful to
the corporation; and civil payments in compensation to workers and their families.

Pearce and Tombs (1992) combine these ideas. They see a need to require a
change to corporate structure such that criminal actions become simpler—marking out those responsible for worker safety, pollution control and product safety—
and thus making any necessary prosecutions easier, cheaper and more likely to
succeed. In the Hatfield train crash, although it is clear the company, Railtrack, had
knowledge of the faulty line, a corporate manslaughter charge would probably fail
under the existing law (2003). Despite these difficulties both Balfour Beaty and
Network Rail, the successor to Railtrack, face corporate manslaughter charges, and
six ex-employees of these companies face manslaughter charges because of the
difficulty of clearly blaming any one person. Pearce and Tombs's suggestion would
be very useful in such cases. It would also make the corporation perform some of
the work for the enforcers, as has been done in relation to financial responsibility
by s. 89 of the Insolvency Act 1986. The Company Directors (Health and Safety) Bill
2003 would make the prosecution of individual directors simpler and the government has promised a Corporate Manslaughter Bill in the near future. But beyond
more, and more certain, prosecutions they also call for closer policing (to detect
breaches), more pressure on firms (to alter practices), and willingness to challenge
financial reasons given for non-compliance. Increases in production costs could,
theoretically at least, be minimised by social pressure on shareholders to accept
lower or steadier returns on their investment, and to take responsibility for the
long-term viability of the company. Here again strict regulation may help: without
it those who transgress can increase profits by harming others, but with strong
regulation there will be a profit in conformity. For most of this to operate there
might need to be statutory criminal laws which place clear responsibility on corporations and an interpretation of these which permits criminal responsibility to
be imputed to corporations and/or their senior officers.

It may be difficult or impossible effectively to punish certain targets at all. No State has the powers fully to control corporations either by reforming them or their main actors, or by incapacitating their unacceptable behaviours; nor would such activities be either economically viable or desirable as they would bankrupt firms and leave many innocent people unemployed. If it is thus necessary to note that not all can or should be controlled, it is also necessary to recognise that deterrence can be strengthened by the targeting of some corporations and individuals. In addition to these criminal justice approaches it may be possible to affect behaviours by public questioning of the activities of powerful operators within a corporation, who may not themselves have taken part in the criminal activity but who could have prevented it: these individuals might be shamed into preventing future activities by threatening to expose their moral responsibility for the activity. This may be optimistic. While it is true that the dubious, and often fraudulent, practices common in the 1990s boom and which were exposed when it collapsed *c.*2000 led to much public debate about standards of corporate government, there has been little in terms of effective regulation. The criminal justice system can expose them through careful questioning of witnesses but would need support. In particular, as suggested in the next chapter, the media may be better placed to perform such functions and professional and other regulatory bodies may also be used (though the massive Enron collapse in the US showed that accountants could be complicit in providing misleading information). Full investigation by professional bodies such as that relating to accountants, or by a judicial inquiry rather than by criminal justice agencies, may be more effective. Fisse and Braithwaite (1993) suggest that what may be needed is a much wider accountability model, an holistic problem-solving approach, whereby all systems are utilised to try to achieve the desired outcome of more responsible corporate activity. This may mean using civil actions either as well as or instead of criminal means where these may be more effective at reaching the desired ends—a more responsible trading system. Lastly, what may work best is to force the law-abiding sections of the corporation to investigate and deal internally with the criminal elements. This may not punish the wrongdoing, but it can effectively prevent its continuation.

The discussion of victimless crime and corporate crime illustrates the large and complex issues involved in defining the criminal law and in its enforcement. It illustrates the problem of trying to consider the criminal law in a vacuum without studying its relationship with other aspects of society, and without discovering or considering the reasons for the criminal nature of the activity. The examples can also indicate that the law does alter and respond over time, but such adjustment is normally slow, extending the anguish and suffering of those who feel discriminated against.

2.5.5 Definitions and usage

Definitions become still more complicated when sociological considerations of crime or rule-breaking are included. One of the first aspects to grasp is that without law—the criminal law—there would be no (defined) crime and no (defined) criminals. Criminalising an act usually takes place only because some people want to do that act and others wish to prevent them. On this reading an act is not controlled by use of the criminal law because the nature of the act is essentially criminal, but because those whose job it is to formulate such matters within a society define it or name it as criminal. The acts which are criminalised are acts which some people wish to do; it is thus unlikely that any criminal law will totally prevent a particular activity. The more realistic object is to control its frequency and to punish when it occurs; in this way the State (society) has exhibited its disapproval.

If the act itself is not considered to be inherently wrong, everyone will have his or her own conception of acceptable limits of behaviour, based partly on his or her present circumstances and upbringing. Even if individuals recognise an activity as they may still be willing to accept its occurrence or even to participate in it. For example, some may be willing to accept theft of limited amounts from large institutions though not from individuals; employees often steal from employers and view their activities as 'perks' of the job or as minor fiddles. Others may have more permissive attitudes to sexual matters than those which are permitted in the criminal law. A few might even attract some sympathy in breaking even the most fundamental laws of murder or stealing: killing to release someone from appalling pain, especially when it is at that person's request, or a person stealing food when their children are hungry. In other cases where generally serious crimes are committed the participant may claim the moral high ground by stating that the killing or other crime was necessary in pursuit of a political ideal: considering themselves as freedom fighters, forced to perform these activities out of political necessity, in order to correct intolerable situations. They will be more generally viewed as terrorists, who will stop at nothing and be seen as totally amoral (even evil). Outside their immediate society, the way in which their acts will be judged often depends on the acceptance or otherwise of their political aims. This issue is further explored in Chapter Nineteen.

More generally, others, indignant at behaviour of which they disapprove, argue that the law should be altered to make it criminal (as Chapter Three shows, the press often feeds on and fuels these attitudes): others call for decriminalisation, particularly in areas of life they consider private (see the discussion above concerning victimless crime). When these problems are taken into account 'consensus' looks more difficult to claim or achieve.

The perception of people is often coloured by their position in relation to the particular activity. For example, the drug user (his or her family and friends), drug addict (his or her family and friends), police officer, psychologist, doctor, magistrate, judge, academic lawyer and sociologist may view the use of various drugs in very different ways. Some argue for legalisation and control merely through medical/therapeutic channels; others accept criminalisation of drug dealing though not of use, preferring the treatment approach for the latter; others want full criminalisation. Personal assessments also condition reasons for varying positions: economic; moral; political; or paternalistic.

These differences between individuals and groups are significant and act as important indicators of the societal tolerance of behaviour over time and the need to change criminal laws. However, the democratic need to accommodate differences should not obscure another central feature of the relationship between democracy and law: in a democracy the law would lose its legitimacy if it was not perceived as reflecting most people's ideas of morality or which activities are in need of control. If this disjuncture became widespread the trust in the criminal justice system and ultimately, possibly, in the State would dissolve.

The contrived nature of criminal law should be borne in mind when considering theories on why people participate in these activities. The theories often suggest that such people are 'different' or even 'abnormal', or that they have been less 'moral' in the way in which they have allowed their free will and choice to rule their activities. If the activities are not manifestly unacceptable then ideas of 'normal' and 'moral' become less firmly and clearly acceptable. Explanations therefore need to keep in mind the activities of the State in criminalising and enforcing certain activities.

2.6 Enforcement of criminal laws

Before progressing to define a criminal, it might be useful to consider the effects of the workings of the enforcement agencies. This work is carried out by a plethora of organisations which together make up the criminal justice system. The main agencies involved are: the police; the Crown Prosecution Service; the courts; prisons; the probation service; and social services. This list is not exhaustive—the Inland Revenue, Customs and Excise, Factories Inspectorate, fraud squads etc. all have investigation powers and sometimes also prosecution powers. Fines and similar sorts of punishments may be administered by court officials. Although not part of the official system, lawyers (both solicitors and barristers) are an essential part of its workings and are generally considered as part of the criminal justice system. Outside the official system are many private agencies, particularly private security firms. This is now a very big business: the numbers employed as private security guards are greater then those in the official police forces. They are employed in the private sector covering tasks such as credit investigation, information services, private investigations, transport for prisoners, private security patrols, and as bailiffs; in the early 1990s Group Four, one of the larger firms, began to operate the first private prison, Wolds Remand Prison. Nine of the 130 prisons are now (2003) privately operated and there are competitions for two more. Increasingly the State is using these private agencies to fulfil its obligations to its citizens in the criminal justice system. This may be seen as sensible economic management, but does it address the needs of society and does it help to solve the crime problem? Many argue it does not and see this move as the State refusing to face its responsibilities and relying on private firms which have their own economic and other objectives to place above the good of society (for further discussion see Chapters Sixteen and Twenty).

As the above makes clear, the criminal justice system is large and complex. It has many goals or aims, though its ultimate goal is generally said to be to make society safer for its citizens. More specific and generally accepted aims include:

- enforcing the criminal law and so exhibiting society's disapproval of criminal activity through catching, convicting and punishing criminals on a principled basis;
- protecting the public by preventing and deterring crime; by advising citizens on how to avoid victimisation; by making crime commission both more difficult and more likely to be detected through control, surveillance and design

of public space; by attempting to rehabilitate offenders; and by incapacitating those who might otherwise prove to be a danger to the public;

- protecting society through maintaining law and order;
- helping victims;
- efficient and fair application of the law, ensuring the proper treatment of suspects, defendants, those held in custody and witnesses, and ensuring that the innocent are acquitted and the guilty punished in a fair and equitable manner, all of which should help to promote respect both for the law and for the criminal justice system;
- ensuring that each aspect of the system is accountable to society.

Each of the agencies mentioned above plays its part in trying to achieve these aims. Thus the police investigate and help to prevent crime and maintain order. They are usually the link between the public and the system, playing a key role in advising victims and the public on such issues as crime prevention. The Crown Prosecution Service prepares cases for trial and decides which cases are too weak to justify proceeding. In the near future it will also take over the charging of suspects, presently done by the police (see the Criminal Justice Act 2003, Part 4). The courts are intended to ensure the efficient and fair application of law by protecting the rights of all parties and making decisions as to bail or remand, guilty or not guilty and on what types of sentence to pass. The probation service provides information on many defendants so that correct decisions concerning bail and sentencing can be made, but its largest single role is intended to be rehabilitative, working with offenders on community orders and with those released from custody. While hoping to rehabilitate and deter some people, the main role of prisons and other custodial institutions now appears to be the humane detention of individuals refused bail and offenders sentenced to custodial orders. The private security firms and others acting outside the system may have the above aims in mind but their position may be complicated by their overriding loyalty to their shareholders which can cause problems for the criminal justice system (see below).

The above suggests that the aims and activities of the system are not in dispute, but this is too simplistic a picture since the aims may conflict with each other. Possible contradictions between the two main aims (due process and crime control) will be discussed here, while others (rehabilitative, bureaucratic, denunciation and degradation, and power) will be outlined only. Due process and crime control are given prominence because the whole criminal justice system turns around balancing these two conflicting value systems, one of which prioritises justice and protecting the innocent (due process) while the other centres on swift prosecution and early punishment (crime control).

Due process maintains that the purpose of the criminal justice system is to require the State to prove the guilt of a defendant beyond reasonable doubt in a public trial as the condition for the imposition of a sentence. It is based upon an idealised form of the rule of law. This recognises the State's duty to protect the community from crime and criminals by requiring agencies of the State to seek out and to punish the guilty, but to ensure that only the guilty are punished by requiring the State to prove the guilt of those it wishes to accuse. If an innocent person is convicted it is viewed as a double failure, being both a breach of his or her rights as well as a failure to protect society because the guilty person has escaped conviction and punishment. Central to this idea is the presumption of innocence—that is that every suspect and accused is presumed innocent until proven guilty and no-one should have to incriminate him or herself—the defendant's right to a fair trial, equality before the law and justice being seen to be done. A due process model requires and enforces rules governing the powers of the police and the admissibility and utility of evidence. Due process notes the power of the State in the application of criminal laws and, to prevent misuse of this position of power by agents of the State, requires checks and balances to protect the interests of suspects and defendants.

The due process model recognises the possibility of error in any State system of adversarial justice. Due process theorists understand that the authorities may be convinced that they have arrested and charged the right person but recognise that there may have been an error: a witness may mis-remember, may twist his or her recollection or may just wish to appear helpful and caring and so feign memory or over-exaggerate its accuracy; suspects may be willing to confess because they feel under pressure, whether or not pressure is intended; officials may 'twist' evidence because they are sure they have the guilty person etc. Recognising the fallibility of humans and the possibility of error, due process theorists stress the need for formal procedures to reduce the risks: all processes should be controlled by formal rules governing the powers of the police and the admissibility and utility of evidence. These rules should be applied even where it may lead to an offender escaping justice because the approach requires that the criminal justice system does not profit by illegalities. If one of the enforcement agencies breaks the process rules and in so doing obtains evidence which proves beyond reasonable doubt that that individual committed the offence in question, be it shop lifting or murder, strict application of the due process system would exclude that evidence from the court as being unfairly obtained. The rationale for this is neatly encapsulated by Zander in his dissenting opinion in the Runciman Report (1993) when he says that allowing such evidence:

... would I believe encourage serious wrongdoing from some police officers who might be tempted to exert force or fabricate or suppress evidence in the hope of establishing the guilt of the suspect, especially in a serious case where they believe him to be guilty . . .. The integrity of the criminal justice system is a higher objective than the conviction of any individual. (pp. 234–5)

Even so, errors can still occur: the possibility of a re-trial in light of new evidence must therefore be kept open.

If, within these constraints, the State is believed and proves a person guilty, it can then punish the individual or other guilty party to the extent which reflects that party's responsibility and the severity of the offence. Note that the finding of guilt does not necessarily mean that the individual is guilty—it does not even mean that a crime has been committed—it merely denotes that 12 people believed one set of facts over another.

A strict due process approach recognises that some guilty people will go free and unpunished; this is considered necessary to prevent wrongful conviction and punishment. The value judgement which is being asserted here is that the arbitrary or excessive use of State power is a worse evil.

Even if one accepts the ideals of due process it is not a panacea: it can be misused and can disintegrate into a type of legal formalism where the technical details of the rules are applied but the underlying intentions ignored, so perverting any idea of justice. It also needs to be made explicit that due process, or any approach which prioritises suspects and defendants, tends to ignore or give less priority to the interests of victims or of society at large.

A quite different approach results if the stress is placed instead on the need to control the level of crime—if, within the constraints imposed by the need for evidence of guilt, the central function of the criminal justice system is seen to be the repression and punishment of criminal conduct. In this way society can express its disgust for criminal activities, and this communal expression then tends to strengthen the moral standards and cohesion within society. From this standpoint it is desirable that there should be as few fetters as possible on the authorities in pursuing criminals. Here the criminal justice system must be seen to be strong, providing a high rate of conviction and low acquittal rate, and harsh and certain punishment. A high acquittal rate makes it look as if the criminal justice agencies are not performing their functions correctly or are inefficient, either in not catching the right people or in not providing sufficient evidence so that too many criminals are getting away with it. The effect would be a failure to deter others from indulging in criminal activity.

To prevent this the crime control model prioritises efficiency and getting results: to catch, convict and punish the offender is paramount. Inherent in crime control models is the idea that once the police and prosecutor believe in the guilt there is almost a 'presumption of guilt'. This model places great faith in the police and Crown Prosecution Service as professionals, who would accuse and bring to court only those who they are confident are guilty. The model is less respectful of legal controls which exist to protect the individual defendant; these are seen as practical obstacles which need to be overcome in order to get on with crime control and punishment. The trial becomes more ritualistic, with an expected outcome of conviction based on the presumed reliability of the police (or other enforcement agency) in identifying the true offender. There is, at best, a much-reduced presumption of innocence at trial since the presumption of innocence only really rules the way in which the court process is conducted—guilt is the expected outcome. In this approach the balance between due process and crime control has been shifted towards the latter: the central element is seen to be the control of crime which requires a high rate of apprehension and conviction of criminals and quick results. If occasionally some innocent individuals are sacrificed to the ultimate aim of crime control this may be a necessary evil. However, it needs to be emphasised that such errors are intended to be kept to a minimum through the careful application of justice by the agents of the law, whose professionalism ensures that they apprehend the guilty and allow the innocent to go free.

Once guilt is pronounced punishment begins and should be sure, unpleasant, and sufficient to recognise the seriousness of the offence. It should also reflect the extent of blame attaching to the offender, since there is a presumption that all people are responsible for their behaviour. Any failure to punish severely might be seen as weakness and a failure to uphold standards of behaviour.

In the crime control model the interests of victims and society are thus given priority over those of suspects and defendants. The justification is that swifter processing makes the system appear more efficient and that this will deter greater criminality—if you offend you are likely to be caught and punished, therefore it is not worth it. In seeking to achieve this aim the model is willing to convict the innocent (though not in large numbers). Formal procedures are kept to an absolute minimum and their breach should not lead to the exclusion of evidence which is otherwise thought reliable—the guilty should never be acquitted on a technicality. The primary aim of crime control is to punish the guilty and deter crime as a means of reducing crime and creating a safer society.

A very different approach is taken by those with a rehabilitative aim, which is more individualised and asks, at each stage of the process, how best to deal with this person. Criminal activity is the catalyst for official intervention usually designed to help, or even 'treat', the offender whose free will and responsibility are seen as limited. This is based upon ideas that offenders may not be wholly responsible for their acts, which arise, at least in part, due to individual or social factors (see Chapters Six to Twelve).

A fourth model, the bureaucratic, derives from classical Weberian sociology and its intention is the management of both crime and criminals by such means as the standardisation of procedures, political neutrality, precision and efficiency. Lengthy periods before trial, extended trials and claims of miscarriages of justice all undermine trust in the administration of justice and lead to less confidence being placed in the system and less respect for the law. All agencies in the criminal justice system should keep clear records and be able to substantiate allegations with clear documentation; this minimises conflict and so reduces expense. In the bureaucratic model the success of the system is tested by how well it achieves internally set targets such as response times for incidents, percentage of cases in which there is a guilty plea or a finding of guilt, or the time it takes to get a case through court, regardless of the effects this has on such wider problems as levels of criminal activity, public safety, and levels of rehabilitation of offenders. In its extreme form managerial efficiency is seen as an end in itself, rather than as a means to create a better society. The agencies of criminal justice can be said to succeed even if levels of crime are rising as long as they have properly performed their bureaucratic function. The approach provides a powerful political tool for avoiding responsibility and is utilised, to a greater or lesser degree, by most governments in the Western world.

The fifth approach centres on the denunciation and degradation of criminals and derives from the sociology of Émile Durkheim. Stigmatisation and the reinforcement of social cohesion are the central features. To stigmatise offenders (and even defendants) is to set them out as separate from the other, law-abiding, members of the community, who are thus made to feel like a more cohesive group. The public shaming of individuals is meant to persuade them of the stupidity of their actions and to reassure others of their own virtue. Furthermore, the use of media coverage to disseminate information is valuable since it leads to wider denunciation and knowledge of the processes and consequences of unacceptable behaviour. Braithwaite in 1988 suggested that a reasonable level of shaming was necessary to permit proper rehabilitation—an understanding of the consequences and a feeling of shame for having made others suffer is necessary for one to decide not to act in that way again—what he terms re-integrative shaming.

Questioning of the interests served by crime and crime control is central to the final model to be considered here—the power model—which derives largely from

Marxism, post-Marxist critical theory and post-modern theory. Each of these tends to attack criminal laws and the criminal justice system for maintaining the position of the powerful in society, a power which might be based on class, wealth, race or sex. The system is seen as one the central intention of which is to maintain order and the *status quo* rather than to enforce the criminal law to protect the whole of society. The attack is that most official crime control is just about order, controlling the weak to the advantage of the strong. This may be done in a number of ways: for example, by having very clear and set rules which are then implemented in ways that ensure a discriminatory outcome; or by having loose rules within which there is a wide area of discretion which may then be exercised in a discriminatory manner. In simplistic terms, theorists in this area point to the way in which criminal law and its enforcement often tend to exclude some, painting them as welfare-dependent, undeserving, generally irresponsible and different from the other good citizens who are self-reliant and law-abiding. The majority are thus enticed into supporting a system the main object of which is to preserve the position of the ruling group or groups.

It is necessary to add to these a rights model. The concepts of rights in all aspects of our lives are increasing so that it is now necessary to consider their place in the criminal justice system. Under the Human Rights Act 1998 British courts are now obliged to take the rights guaranteed under the European Convention on Human Rights (ECHR) into account in their decision-making (it requires that Articles 2–12 and 14 of the Convention, Articles 1–3 of the First Protocol and Articles 1 and 2 of the Sixth Protocol should be given weight in the British courts). This does not give rights under the European Prison Rules (a detailed code of standards set up under the Council of Europe). In applying the Convention rights the courts in Britain must take account of the extensive judgments and opinions of the European Court of Human Rights, the former Commission of Human Rights and the Committee of Ministers.

A rights discourse is important to the criminal justice process because it guarantees the individual protection even when that protection is inconvenient to those in authority or it interferes with efficiency or other goals of the criminal justice system. They are necessary because they respect the person being accused, because they recognise his or her autonomy. A rights perspective should also prioritise the rights of victims although not to the detriment of defendants. It is also important to recognise that the rights which appear in the ECHR are very much minimum standards which our judges could build upon and which many other States would now regard as too low in certain respects. A rights model does have the advantage of preventing the State and its representatives (such as the police) from using its powers in an unjust way merely for convenience, political advantage etc. The Human Rights Act has already led to extensive retraining of the police, judges, magistrates, prosecutors and other public servants to try to curtail violations of rights which, presumably, were occurring before the Act was passed. It has therefore already had a beneficial effect and hopefully will continue to check the unacceptable use of power. A more all embracing use for human rights is to see them as a guiding principle. The rights to be protected are always going to be in conflict: society's right to expect the guilty will be convicted; protecting the innocent from conviction; preventing arbitrary and oppressive treatment or punishment; protecting victims and potential victims; maintaining law and order;

guaranteeing safety to all to allow them freedom to enjoy their lives. The conflicts need to be resolved: under a rights ideology the aim would be for the system, wherever possible, to respect rights and freedoms, not because they are required to by law but because their *raison d'être* is to increase the freedom of all—suspects, offenders, victims and the general public.

These various models are sufficient to illustrate how the system can be pulled in different, and possibly inconsistent, directions. The criminal justice system of England and Wales does not conform to any one approach, and there is much debate as to which approach is paramount.

This is a continuous and continuing debate. For example, Herbert Packer (1968) argued that in England and Wales—as he had earlier found in the US—although the legal rules and the apparent values of the criminal justice system appeared to conform with the due process approach, in practice the crime control approach was most often used. He suggested that similar findings would be made in most common law jurisdictions. Certainly the system in England and Wales, like any adversarial system, starts with the due process presumption that a person is innocent until proven guilty; but what an adversarial system actually does is to say that a person will be treated as innocent unless the evidence is sufficient, beyond reasonable doubt, to prove guilt. In effect, then, a trial never establishes innocence; it either purports to establish guilt, or finds that there was insufficient evidence to prove guilt or that the jury (or magistrates) were unwilling to convict. In this legal environment it might be said that the crime control approach is prevalent in that a trial can never establish innocence. Doreen McBarnett (1978) on looking at the British system claimed that law, values and practice all take on a crime control approach, while McConville and Baldwin (1981) found that the practice in Britain is geared towards conviction and crime control. Bottoms and McClean (1976) and Robert Reiner (1992) came to a similar conclusion, but suggested that the reason was not ideological but rather that the participants in the criminal justice system were simply led by the application of rules. Saunders and Young (2003) add that despite legal provisions for some due process rights, enforcement bodies such as the police find ways round this, so preserving a crime control dimension.

It can thus be seen that, although the professed intentions give weight to due process, some commentators see the outcomes of the system in England and Wales as being closer to the crime control approach. Which approach wins out is indicative both of the way in which society controls behaviour and of the insight it gives to the weighting of the aims set out above, and of the way in which criminal behaviour is viewed within our society. How many innocent people are we willing to see convicted, or how many guilty people are we willing to see go free? In an ideal world the answer to each would be none, but neither that nor a perfect balance between due process and crime control is likely to be achieved. An official tendency to lean one way or the other will have an impact on the way in which justice is experienced by a society. The issue is obviously of high importance, and a recurring theme in the discussions of the numerous studies outlined in this work centres on the question: where should the balance be between the demands for crime control and those for justice and humanity?

Although most of the above models centre around the narrow aspects of controlling and punishing crime, it is essential to retain the wider view of the criminal justice system as being necessary to provide a public service, aimed at promoting public safety, protecting the weak and vulnerable, providing justice for all, promoting and encouraging civilised behaviour, and a safer society. A criminal justice system must treat victims, defendants and criminals with respect; a system which excludes individuals and makes them the subject of fear and suspicion even after their punishment is served is one where continued criminal behaviour is almost guaranteed. The simplistic idea that crime will be solved and society made safer if more criminals are harshly punished may not be the most successful or efficient approach. It may not even be the best way of responding to the needs of victims and redressing the wrongs done to them. Impacting on the real problem of crime means addressing the wider aspects mentioned above, which can sometimes involve new criminal justice solutions such as mediation, but in other cases the need may be for earlier, very different solutions such as town planning, helping the disadvantaged overcome difficulties, providing opportunities for all. Some of these possibilities will be explored in later chapters, but for the moment it needs only to be recognised that crime reduction and a safe society cannot simply be provided by criminal justice agencies. Criminal justice is basically about the society in which one lives: a healthy society treats all its citizens with respect and punishes only when necessary to redress a balance; its criminal laws are to restrain activities which reduce the freedom of others, not to interfere with individual freedom; its end is to increase the freedom of all citizens. Such a high ideal can only be the product of a responsible, holistic and reasoned approach to crime.

2.7 The criminal

Who is a criminal? Most people would probably argue that a criminal is a person who commits a crime. By this idea, everyone in almost any modern State is a criminal, as most of us have breached a law at one time or another. In a technical legal sense a person is not a criminal until he or she has been convicted by a court of law of having committed a criminal offence.

For criminology it is sometimes important and useful to be able to use the idea of a criminal more widely than the very technical legal concept would permit. If the purpose is to understand why individuals are willing to participate in certain forms of behaviour, the looser idea of someone having performed an act which appears to be a crime may be more useful, regardless of whether or not that person has been caught and convicted. Most of the theorists referred to in this book take this wider, less precise, less technical and in some ways less correct meaning of the word criminal. Some also use the word delinquent, which is even more imprecise. First, it may be used to designate a young criminal and can therefore take on either the technical legal meaning or the wider criminological meaning. It is also frequently used to denote a young person who performs acts which some members of society find unacceptable, but which have not been criminalised. It has to be said that theorists are not always clear how they are using the term, and this causes even greater problems. The reader should be aware of these facts in reading this and other texts.

The wider use of the word 'criminal' or 'delinquent' raises the question: how long should the term 'criminal' be used to describe a person who has committed a crime? In a technical legal case this is often decided by statute, for example, after a certain period of time most convictions become spent for most purposes. Where the term is used in the wider criminological sense there are no such rules. If the term is being used in a social sense as a stigma, the exact meaning and the time it will last are impossible to predict.

Use of the official term 'criminal' is very limiting and excludes most of those who commit offences: from Home Office figures only 2 per cent of offences result in a conviction. In fact many who commit offences are excluded by most definitions: of every 100 offences committed, the Home Office estimates that only 41 are reported; the police record only 23 (see Chapter Four for an explanation of this); five are cleared up; three result in a caution; and only two result in a conviction. This not only shows the limit in using official labels of criminality, but also indicates the narrow effects that the criminal justice system is likely to have, particularly one based on harsh punishments.

2.8 Terminology and classification

What is currently in vogue in terminology, as in fashion, changes from time to time. The words 'crime' and 'offence' are synonymous, but generally 'crime' is used only in relation to serious offences such as rape or murder, which are technically called indictable offences (see below). Throughout the book an individual who has been charged with and prosecuted, but not yet convicted, for a criminal offence is referred to as the 'accused' or the 'defendant'.

An accused may be tried and found not guilty (i.e., acquitted), or that person may be found guilty (i.e., convicted) and sentenced. In some instances (see below) a person who has been convicted may appeal either against the severity of the sentence imposed, or against the conviction seeking to have it quashed. In these instances the individual concerned may be referred to as the appellant or accused.

2.8.1 Felonies and misdemeanours

The terminology for the classification of offences has changed with time. It is necessary to be aware of some of the old terms in order to understand the older, reported English cases and some of the texts, old and new. American texts also generally use the old terminology. Criminal offences used to be categorised at common law either as felonies or as misdemeanours. Felonies were those crimes which had as their penalty on conviction the forfeiture of land and goods, and if Parliament had declared a crime to be a felony without benefit of clergy (originally exemption of clergymen from criminal process before a secular judge, but later extended to cover the first offence of all those who could read), then the penalty was death as well as forfeiture of property to the State. The Forfeiture Act 1870 abolished forfeiture for felony. A misdemeanour was any offence not amounting to a felony; these were regarded as less serious offences and never incurred the death penalty or forfeiture of property. They were punished by fines or imprisonment at the court's discretion. The distinction between the gravity of these two categories of offences and their differing consequences had all but disappeared in Britain by the time they were formally abolished by s. 1 of the Criminal Law Act 1967. That Act, by s. 2, put in place of those old categories a new classification—arrestable and non-arrestable offences.

2.8.2 **Arrestable and non-arrestable offences**

The definition of an arrestable offence was first contained in s. 2 of the Criminal Law Act 1967, which concentrated upon the procedural consequences of a crime. It has been incorporated into and expanded by the Police and Criminal Evidence Act 1984. Where an individual has committed an arrestable offence, a police officer or a member of the public may arrest him without a warrant. This classification encompasses all offences for which the penalty upon conviction is fixed by law (e.g., the mandatory life sentence in case of murder) or for which a person of 21 years of age or over (not previously convicted) may be sentenced to imprisonment for a term of five years or more. In addition, s. 24(2) and (3) of the Police and Criminal Evidence Act 1984 declare numerous specific offences to be arrestable offences even though the prescribed penalty on conviction is less than five years' imprisonment. An arrestable offence which is a 'serious arrestable offence' as defined in s. 116 of that Act has enhanced powers of arrest for the police attached to it. The majority of arrestable offences will be indictable offences (see 2.8.3). In addition, s. 25 of the Act gives the police a general power to arrest for any non-arrestable offence, no matter how petty, provided one of the general arrest conditions specified in s. 25(3) is satisfied. For example, the name of the relevant person is unknown to, and cannot be readily ascertained by, the constable, making the service of a summons impracticable or inappropriate. This new general power of arrest permits arrest without warrant for summary and otherwise non-arrestable offences if one of the general arrest conditions is satisfied. But, broadly speaking, arrestable offences are in the main indictable, i.e., serious, offences.

2.8.3 **Indictable and summary offences**

Another classification of criminal offences is by reference to the modes by which offences may be tried. Criminal offences are either tried summarily before a magistrates' court (less serious types) or are tried on indictment in the Crown Court (the more serious types). At least 95 per cent of all cases are heard in the magistrates' court.

Summary trial, i.e., before magistrates, takes place with regard to offences which are so minor that they must be so tried, or offences for which the magistrates, at a mode of trial hearing (under s. 19 of the Magistrates' Courts Act 1980), have decided can be heard summarily and the defendant has accepted that decision. (These offences are known as offences triable either way.) A list of such offences is contained in the Magistrates' Court Act 1980; statutes may also specifically provide that the offences contained therein must or may be tried summarily. A magistrates' court is comprised of two or more lay magistrates, i.e., individuals who are neither salaried nor in most cases legally qualified. In some cases a magistrates' court may comprise a single stipendiary magistrate (a professional salaried judge who is legally qualified).

Trials on indictment in the Crown Court take place in relation to offences where an accused may elect such a trial (and has so chosen), when the magistrates choose to send a 'triable either way' case to the Crown Court, or where the offence can only be tried in the Crown Court because of its seriousness. (The system for determining where a case will be tried is, however, set to alter under Part 6 of the Criminal Justice Act 2003). Trials on indictment are so named because the trial is commenced by a document known as a bill of indictment which sets out the offence and its particulars with which the accused is charged. A Crown Court trial is before a judge and jury, although Part 7 of the Criminal Justice Act 2003 provides for trial by judge only in certain circumstances. The trial of an accused is preceded by an initial investigation of the accused's potential criminal liability by magistrates who, if convinced that an accused has a case to answer, commit him to the Crown Court for trial. This process is known as committal proceedings.

2.9 **Appeals**

An accused convicted by a magistrates' court of an offence may appeal by way of a full rehearing of the case to the Crown Court. In this instance the Crown Court consists of lay magistrates and a judge as chairman (usually a circuit judge but with no jury). Any further appeal can only be on a point of law and can be from either the Crown Court following a rehearing as noted above, or from the magistrates' court direct. The appellate court in such instances is the Divisional Court of the Queen's Bench Division, which comprises two or more High Court judges. There is a final appeal from the Divisional Court to the House of Lords. Such appeals are restricted to instances where a point of law of general public importance is raised and where either court has given leave to appeal.

Where an accused has been convicted of an offence following a trial before the Crown Court (i.e., before judge and jury) he may appeal to the Court of Appeal, Criminal Division on a point of law, and ultimately to the House of Lords upon the restricted ground that the point of law concerned is of general public importance and leave has been given by either court because it is an issue that should be settled by the House of Lords. Under the Criminal Appeal Act 1995 the Criminal Cases Review Commission can refer any convictions from a jury trial (indictment) where it feels that there is a 'real possibility' that the verdict would not be upheld.

The prosecution may appeal against an accused's acquittal in all cases except where the accused has been acquitted by a jury's verdict where appeal is limited under Part 10 of the Criminal Justice Act 2003.

2.10 **Limits of prosecution**

Each of the limitations listed below acts as a bar or barrier to prosecution, but that is not to say that no crime has been committed. Criminal conduct will have occurred and a victim often will have been harmed, but for various policy reasons the State chooses not to prosecute.

Unlike civil wrongs, there is generally no limitation period for criminal offences. Prosecutions can be brought against an accused at any time, even years after the act or omission has been committed. Parliament, however, may by statute provide exceptions in specific instances to that general rule (e.g., s. 127 of the Magistrates' Courts Act 1980 provides that all summary prosecutions must be brought within six months of the commission of the offence, again unless a specific statute provides to the contrary).

Certain persons are in effect absolutely immune from prosecution (e.g., the monarch, foreign sovereigns and their emissaries, members of diplomatic staff and persons working for international organisations). Others receive a limited immunity (e.g., the administrative and technical staff of an embassy are only immune for acts or omissions done in the course of their duties; visiting armed forces are given a very technical and limited immunity).

Certain children in effect receive immunity from criminal prosecution in the form of a presumption of incapacity to commit crimes. Age can furnish a defence in that the law maintains that no child under 10 years of age can be guilty of an offence (see the Children and Young Persons Act 1933, s. 50 as amended; in Scotland the relevant age is 8). Although this still applies, s. 11 of the Crime and Disorder Act 1998 permits a local authority to apply for a child under 10 to be placed under the supervision of a social worker if the child commits an act which would be a crime if the child had been over 10. Over the age of 10 children are assumed to have mental capacity.

Almost all prosecutions are brought on behalf of the Crown, which is a synonym for the State, and generally they are instituted in the name of the monarch or an officer of the Crown such as the Attorney-General or the Director of Public Prosecutions. For less serious offences the prosecution may be brought by the Crown Prosecution Service in the name of the police, or the actual police officer, or by a representative of a local authority, or by a representative of a government department, such as the Inland Revenue, the Health and Safety Executive or Customs and Excise. A few prosecutions can be brought by a private citizen. In some of these cases a limitation of sorts arises in that the permission or leave of the Attorney-General, or the Director of Public Prosecutions, or the Home Secretary or some other Minister is sometimes required. Without the necessary approval specified in the particular statute from whichever of those representatives of the Crown, the trial cannot proceed, and if commenced the proceedings are deemed void. Examples of prosecutions requiring such approval are incest, homosexual offences, theft of or unlawful damage to a spouse's property and offences under the Official Secrets Act 1911. In most instances private prosecutions are permitted under s. 6 of the Prosecution of Offenders Act 1985, but such actions are in fact rare and in practice most prosecutions are brought by the Crown Prosecution Service on behalf of the police.

Appeals aside (see above) there is a principle of criminal law that if a competent court finds in favour of an accused and acquits him, the prosecution cannot re-open that issue in another trial involving either the same accusation or another necessarily dependent on the issue already adjudged in the accused's favour: double jeopardy. This principle is severely eroded by the power to retry cases, if in the public interest, provided for under Part 10 of the Criminal Justice Act 2003.

Jurisdiction can be a further limitation to prosecution. In the main, English criminal law is concerned with where an offence is committed. If it occurs within the territorial boundaries of England or Wales, or on or over the territorial sea of those countries, then the offence is triable in either England or Wales irrespective of the nationality of the accused. There are exceptions to this general rule in that certain offences (like piracy) are tried here no matter where in the world the offence occurred. British ships and aircraft are considered by the law to be British territory; consequently offences committed on board such vessels, no matter where in the world they are, may be tried in England or Wales, again irrespective of the accused's nationality. Certain statutes, the best example of which is the Offences against the Person Act 1861, ss. 9 and 57, provide that British citizens who commit certain offences abroad may be tried in England and Wales. Lastly, an individual liable to be tried in England and Wales who flees or escapes to another country may be retrieved by the formal procedure of extradition, provided there is an extradition treaty in existence between Britain and the country in which the fugitive has sought refuge or, by virtue of a special extradition arrangement where there is no general extradition treaty.

2.11 **Evidence**

In criminal prosecutions the law applies the maxims: 'The party that alleges must prove' and 'The accused is presumed innocent until proved guilty'. To obtain a conviction, the prosecution must prove all the constituent elements of the substantive offence in question beyond reasonable doubt. Although in theory this concept has never been attacked or altered, it has been diluted by ss. 34–7 of the Criminal Justice and Public Order Act 1994, which allow inferences to be drawn from the failure of a suspect or an accused to answer questions or to mention facts when questioned by those (police or others) properly charged with the duty of investigating offences: this does not include private persons or bodies, such as store detectives. Likewise, if a defence is raised the prosecution must disprove it beyond reasonable doubt. In the very few rare instances where the burden of proof relating to a defence is imposed on the accused, then the law specifies that the accused need only prove on a balance of probabilities (the usual civil standard) rather than beyond reasonable doubt.

2.12 **Punishment**

There are various theories concerning the purpose of punishment ranging from retribution, through prevention, deterrence and education to rehabilitation. In this country the criminal courts have available to them a number of punishments which they may impose following conviction, ranging from deprivation of liberty to absolute and conditional discharges. The death penalty was abolished for murder by the Murder (Abolition of Death Penalty) Act 1965. Except in the case of murder, for which a mandatory sentence of life imprisonment is automatically imposed, there are as a general rule no minimum sentences prescribed. However, the Powers of Criminal Courts (Sentencing) Act 2000, part V, chapter III, imposes normal minimum sentences for repeat offenders: life for certain serious sexual and violent offenders; seven years for certain drug offences; and three years for domestic burglary. The Crime (Sentences) Act 1997 also abolishes automatic remission. The effect has been a steady rise in the prison population to an average of 73,661 in 2003 (almost 20,000 more than in mid-1996 and still rising).

Generally, the maximum sentence imposable is specified and it is left to the judge's discretion, having considered all the circumstances, what term of imprisonment to impose short of the maximum. The length of the prison sentence is usually commensurate with the seriousness of the offence (Powers of Criminal Courts (Sentencing) Act 2000, ss. 79(2) and 80(2)). Section 80(2) empowers a court to imprison a person convicted of a violent or sexual offence for longer than the seriousness of the case requires (but not exceeding the maximum) if it is necessary for the protection of the public. In a number of instances the offender may serve a shorter sentence but the judge is now expected to explain the effect of a sentence (Practice Direction (Custodial Sentences: Explanations) [1998] 1 WLR 278). In the case of offences for which there is now a minimum for a second offence, judges may indicate seriousness by increasing sentences for first-time offenders. One means of reducing the likelihood of unjustified judicial discretion would be to move towards the universal use of a computerised sentencing information system such as that which is shortly to be introduced into the Scottish High Court of Justiciary. Their system has been researched since 1993 and has been tested and perfected over some seven years. The system should be provided to all High Court judges by the end of 2002. It will be updated monthly and will allow textual communication between judges. It provides information concerning aspects which may affect sentencing decisions and shows the sentences used in particular sets of circumstances so it provides a norm against which a judge can test his or her decision-making whilst not actually fettering discretion in any particular case (for more information see Hutton and Tata (2000); Tata and Hutton (1998); Hutton (1996); Tata, Hutton and Wilson (1996); Hutton (1995)). The Home Office is just putting out tenders for a feasibility study of a similar system to be used in England and Wales. Clearly as there are only about 30 judges in the Scottish High Court whereas the system in England and Wales would have to service over 2000 judges and incorporate many more cases it may be some time before there is a usable system available. Such a system may allow conformity in approach to be achieved but this does not necessarily guarantee better justice since the approach itself may be flawed. Furthermore, it may allow more careful political and other control which again may decrease actual justice as politicians may have short-term personal political gains in mind rather than the longer-term ideal of justice.

Apart from prisons there are remand homes, attendance and detention centres and approved schools. Those accused who are either mentally unfit to plead or found not guilty on grounds of insanity will be detained in a mental institution at Her Majesty's pleasure (until certified safe for release). Where the circumstances warrant it, the judge may impose a suspended sentence or give a conditional or an absolute discharge. Where the convicted person may be punished by the imposition of a fine (whether or not in conjunction with a term of imprisonment), generally the maximum fine imposable is prescribed, leaving it to judges' discretion to fix the actual amount. Sections 130 to 134 of the Powers of Criminal Courts (Sentencing) Act 2000 permit all criminal courts to award compensation to individuals who have suffered loss as a result of the convicted person's criminal activity.

QUESTIONS

1 Who or what determines what is criminal?
2 In what sense do judges make criminal law?
3 How far are the two main aims of the criminal justice system (due process and crime control) compatible?

REFERENCES

Allen, Michael, J. (2003), *Textbook on Criminal Law*, 7th edn, Oxford: Oxford University Press.

Ashworth, A. (1995), *Principles of the Criminal Law*, 7th edn, London: Sweet & Maxwell.

Bauman, Zygmunt (1994), *Alone Again: Ethics after Certainty*, London: Demos.

Bauman, Z. (2000), 'Social Uses of Law and Order', in Garland, D. and Sparks, R., *Criminology and Social Theory*, Oxford: Oxford University Press.

Beck, U. (1992), *Risk Society: Towards a New Modernity*, translated by Mark Ritter, London: Sage.

Beck, U. (1998), 'Politics of Risk Society', in J. Franklin (ed.), *The Politics of Risk Society*, Cambridge: Polity Press.

Beck, U. (2000), *World Risk Society*, Cambridge: Polity Press.

Blackstone's Criminal Practice, published annually, ed. Peter Murphy, London: Blackstone.

Bottoms, A.E. and McClean, J.D. (1976), *Defendants in the Criminal Process*, London: Routledge & Kegan Paul.

Braithwaite, John (1988), *Crime Shame and Reintegration*, Cambridge: Cambridge University Press.

Braithwaite, John (1993), 'Transnational Regulation of the Pharmaceutical Industry', in Gilbert Geis and Paul Jesilow (eds), *Annals of the American Academy of Political and Social Science*, Newbury Park, CA: Sage Periodicals Press.

Dahrendorf, Ralf (1959), *Class and Conflict in Industrial Society*, London: Routledge.

DiMento, Joseph, F. (1993), 'Criminal Enforcement of Environmental Law', in Gilbert Geis and Paul Jesilow (eds), *Annals of the American Academy of Political and Social Science*, Newbury Park, CA: Sage Periodicals Press.

Feinberg, J. (1985), *The Moral Limits of the Criminal Law*, vol. 2, *Offense to Others*, New York: Oxford University Press.

Feinberg, J. (1988), *The Moral Limits of the Criminal Law*, vol. 4, *Harmless Wrongdoing*, New York: Oxford University Press.

Fisse, Brent and Braithwaite, John (1993), *Corporations, Crime and Accountability*, Cambridge: Cambridge University Press.

Foucault, Michel (1988), 'The Dangerous Individual', in Lawrence D. Kritzman (ed.), *Foucault: Politics, Philosophy and Culture*, transl. by Alan Sheridan and others, New York: Routledge.

Giddens, A. (1994), *Beyond Left and Right*, Cambridge: Polity Press.

Hart, H.L.A. (1963), *Law, Liberty and Morality*, Oxford: Oxford University Press.

Henry, S. and Dragan, M. (1996), *Constitutive Criminology: Beyond Postmodernism*, Thousand Oaks, CA: Sage.

Home Affairs Committee of the House of Lords (1993), *Third Report, Domestic Violence*, vol. 1, London: HMSO.

Hutton, N. (1995), 'Sentencing, Rationality and Computer Technology', *Journal of Law and Society*, vol. 22, pp. 549–70.

Hutton, N. (1996), *A Sentencing Information System for the Scottish High Court*, Edinburgh: Scottish Office Central Research Unit, Scottish Office.

Hutton, N. and Tata, C. (2000), 'The Judicial Role in the Balance between Two Visions of

Justice in Sentencing', in Sean Doran and John Jackson (eds), *The Judicial Role in Criminal Proceedings*, Oxford: Hart Publishing.

Jareborg, N. (1995), 'What Type of Crime Law Do We Want?', in Snare, A. (ed.), *Beware of Punishment: on the Utility or Futility of Criminal Law* (Scandinavian Studies in Criminology, vol. 14). Oslo.

Kelman, M. (1981), 'Interpretative Construction in the Substantive Criminal Law', *Stanford Law Review*, vol. 33, p. 591.

Kershaw, C., Budd, T., Kinshott, G., Mattinson, J., Mayhew, P. and Myhill, A. (2000), *The 2000 British Crime Survey: England and Wales* (Home Office Statistical Bulletin 18/00), London: Home Office.

Lacey, N. (2001), 'In Search of the Responsible Subject', *Modern Law Review*, vol. 64, p. 350.

Lacey, N. and Wells, C. (1998), *Reconstructing Criminal Law: Texts and Materials*, 2nd edn, London: Butterworths.

McBarnett, Doreen (1978), 'False Dichotomies in Criminal Justice Research', in John Baldwin and A. Keith Bottomley (eds), *Criminal Justice: Selected Readings*, London: Martin Robertson.

McConville, Michael and Baldwin, John (1981), *Courts, Prosecution and Conviction*, Oxford: Clarendon Press.

Mill, J.S. (1974) (first published 1859), *On Liberty*, Middlesex: Penguin Books.

Norrie, A. (2001), *Crime, Reason and History*, 2nd edn, London: Butterworths.

Packer, Herbert (1968), *The Limits of the Criminal Sanction*, Stanford, CA: Stanford University Press.

Pearce, Frank and Tombs, Steve (1992), 'Realism and Corporate Crime', in Roger Matthews and Jock Young (eds), *Issues in Realist Criminology*, London: Sage.

Quinney, Richard (1970), *The Social Reality of Crime*, Boston, MA: Little Brown.

Raz, Joseph (1986), *The Morality of Freedom*, Oxford: Clarendon Press.

Reiner, Robert (1992), *The Politics of the Police*, 2nd edn, London: Harvester Wheatsheaf.

Runciman Report (1993), *The Royal Commission on Criminal Justice*, Cm 2263.

Saunders, A. and Young, R. (2003), 'From Suspect to Trial', in M. Maguire, R. Morgan and R. Reiner, *The Oxford Handbook of Criminology*, 3rd edn, Oxford: Oxford University Press.

Schwendinger, H. and Schwendinger, J. (1970), 'Defenders of Order or Guardians of Human Rights?', *Issues in Criminology*, vol. 5, p. 123.

Smith, J.C. and Hogan, Brian (2002), *Criminal Law*, 10th edn, London: Butterworths.

Tata, C. and Hutton, N. (1998), 'Sentencing Support for Judges: A Second Generation of Information Systems', *Overcrowded Times*.

Tata, C., Hutton, N. and Wilson, J.N. (1996), 'Representations of Knowledge and Discretionary Decision-Making by Decision-Support Systems: the Case of Judicial Sentencing', *Journal of Information Law and Technology*, 1996 issue 2, **http://www.elj.warwick.ac.uk/jilt/ArtifInt/2tata/default.htm**.

Turk, Austin, T. (1969), *Criminality and Legal Order*, Chicago, IL: Rand McNally.

Vail, J., Wheelock, J. and Hill, M. (1999), *Insecure Times: Living with Insecurity in Contemporary Society*, London: Routledge.

van de Bunt, H.G. (1994), 'Corporate Crime', *Asset Protection and Financial Crime*, vol. 2(1), p. 11.

van Swaaningen, R. (1997), *Critical Criminology: Visions from Europe*, London: Sage.

van Swaaningen, R. (1999), 'Reclaiming Critical Criminology: Social Justice and the European Tradition', *Theoretical Criminology*, vol. 3(1), p. 5.

Von Hirsch, A. and Jareborg, N. (1991), 'Gauging Criminal Harms: A Living Standard Analysis', *Oxford Journal of Legal Studies*, vol. 11, p. 25.

Wolfenden Committee Report (1957), *Report of the Committee on Homosexual Offences and Prostitution*, Cmd 247, London: HMSO.

3

Public conceptions and misconceptions of crime

3.1 Introduction

This chapter will review popular ideas of criminality and how these are affected by the media. It will then illustrate the limitations of public conceptions with two brief case studies which outline specific areas of criminal activity which are not popularly perceived as criminal, namely, 'white-collar crime' and 'corporate crime'. Later chapters will discuss related issues such as the effect of the media on the amount of crime that is committed (e.g., whether it causes crime) and on perceptions of criminal types which are not usually in the public mind (such as female criminals).

The way people perceive crime and criminals is important to criminologists for a number of reasons. First, it is vital for new students to this area to be aware of any prejudices, preconceptions or opinions which they may hold. The mere awareness of these can often prevent those views interfering with an objective approach. It will allow students to evaluate the usefulness of such views in the light both of extra information and of other, possibly conflicting, views. Secondly, the public's attitude to crime and criminals is used by certain theorists to explain why people might commit crimes, see for example, labelling in Chapter Fourteen. Thirdly, the perception of crime as being 'wrong' or 'abhorrent' may be questioned when one looks at crime in its wider sense rather than looking just at the acts most commonly associated with the idea of crime (see also Chapter Two where the relationship between crime and morality was discussed). Lastly, perceptions of crime are all important when it comes to looking at punishment. If perceptions, although inaccurate, determine or even influence punishment the result may be unfairness and inefficiency.

3.2 Popular and media perceptions of crime

The word 'crime' generally evokes images of murder, rape, drug abuse, drug trafficking, terrorism, aggravated assault, aggravated burglary, armed robbery, arson, theft or similar dramatic acts. The 'criminal' is often perceived as thoroughly 'bad' or an out and out villain: not the sort of person one knows and is friendly with—an unknown and feared creature. Often, if one does know a person who has been convicted, that person is perceived differently; not a true criminal but rather someone basically good who has perhaps been led astray by others. Or their crime is an activity which is not considered as truly criminal: driving offences or petty dishonesty offences for example. Actions, indeed, which one might even have committed oneself without being apprehended.

Images of criminals are particularly interesting as most of us will know someone who has offended, even if they have not been caught and officially labelled a criminal. Offending is common, especially for men: one-third of males have a conviction for a relatively serious offence (standard list offence) by the time they are 46 (Prime et al. 2001); and, many more people commit offences and are never caught. Moreover, many offenders commit more than one offence; a quarter of males and a tenth of females admit committing five or six offences. This might suggest a habit of offending, but for most this is a brief phase which will pass and which the young person will grow out of. The ideal is to try to prevent their offending in the first place or, where this is not possible, to limit the damage they cause. All this should make us confront the possibility that many of those who commit offences are not others but rather ourselves and those we know, even if we, or they, have no overt contact with the criminal justice system.

With this in mind it is particularly difficult to assess how these perceptions are constructed, still less how they are maintained, but some understanding of these issues is useful. Our awareness of any social phenomenon is clearly affected by all our personal experiences. Contact with crime may come directly as criminal or victim, or in contact with the police, or indirectly through police information, family, friends, work, education, the community or the media. It is difficult to assess the effect each of these may have on public opinion.

It is, however, safe to assert that one of these sources, the media, plays some role in forming people's perceptions of crime. One eloquent confirmation of this is implicit in the much greater attention paid to the media in recent times by all the main interested bodies. Not just the Home Office and the police, but the professional associations and trade unions as well as the many pressure groups all work hard to influence media coverage which they see as influencing public attitudes. How great is its effect is more debatable. Media take various forms (newspapers, television etc.) and are made up of a number of aspects—news, editorials and documentaries, each of which is assumed to be largely non-fiction. There are also stories, drama and films which are largely fictitious. Here most attention will be paid to the non-fiction areas, particularly news reporting. News provides us with an important point of contact with the rest of society. In evaluating its effect on popular perceptions of crime it becomes important to consider where most of the information comes from and how representative it is of actual criminality.

To illustrate our points attention will be concentrated on newspapers although, allowing for differences of style and technique, many of the points would broadly apply to radio and television. There are several broad styles or forms of presentation which journalists use in the reporting of crime. The most direct is the straightforward giving of factual accounts, where the information is documented and presented as reliable. This is in sharp contrast to a sensationalist mode, presenting crime, usually a specific crime, in graphic terms which are expected both to attract readers and to rouse strong emotions of anger, revenge or fear. This approach is mainly, though not exclusively, associated with the more popular tabloid press while the broadsheets are more likely to use a more analytical approach. Analysis should not, however, be assumed to represent impartiality: the broadsheets, like the tabloids, each reflect a particular political stance which will tend to be reflected in their reporting, and particularly in their explanations of and cures for crime. Most newspapers have a conservative take on crime, some more than others, and most are basically supportive of the criminal justice system and criminal justice agencies.

Journalists largely have the same access to criminal data as most other individuals, but they have a professional motive to make use of these sources. Most crime stories come to them from official sources such as the police, the courts and the Home Office. Some may originate from unofficial sources such as victims, witnesses or informants. Generally, information from these latter sources must be checked against official sources before printing or presenting. The more official the source, the more credible the account, and the more likely it is to be reported as fact rather than allegation. The seeming objective nature of facts lends further weight to the report. Rarely does the criminal's own view or interpretation appear in the media, and when it does the reference will tend to be more anecdotal than factual. There is an increasing tendency, however, for groups—even those critical of the establishment—to be given a voice (Lawrence (2000)).

The newspapers themselves sift this information, choosing only those areas which are 'newsworthy'. The distortion of information arises from the commercial and highly competitive nature of newspapers and their fight to obtain a wider readership which is generally achieved by titillating their patrons and/or by stimulating their lives with sensational information. Crime reports, particularly of violent and/or sexual crimes, sell newspapers, which gives the media a powerful incentive to give most prominence to the more graphic cases of criminal behaviour. Lord Shawcross's introduction to the Press Council Report (1977) is still apposite:

an avid appetite in the readership, leading for the most part humdrum and uneventful lives, to know about what goes on in the more exciting world. In reporting crime or violence in a sensational way the media may well be giving that section of the public the sort of food they want. But the appetite grows with the eating.

Why are certain items reported while others remain in the dark? Clearly it would be impossible to report every item, so some selection is necessary, but how do the press decide which crimes are newsworthy?

Reporters are not generally interested in the most common crimes involving those people who are most usually the victims of crime, but concentrate rather on more serious crimes or on ones whose victims are particularly vulnerable or 'newsworthy'. Moreover, they present these crimes in a deliberately shocking, blunt, or brutal manner, and emphasise the contrast with what is implied to be a quiet and law-abiding community. To achieve this the papers simplify events, sensationalise them with shock headlines, and present the story as good threatened by evil, or law and order threatened by crime and chaos. Reports will be presented in a dramatic and unusual way so as to capture the readers' imagination; for example, reporting of rape focuses on dramatic attacks by strangers in public places, whereas women are more likely to be raped in private by someone they know. In 1996 over 90 per cent of reported cases fell into this category (see Harris and Grace (1999)). Furthermore, once an individual is convicted, the papers often print as factual, sensational information concerning that individual or the crime, irrespective of the accuracy of that information; often the criminal has no reputation to be protected and so the papers have no fear of a prosecution. In this way the 'story' is supposedly rendered more interesting to the public.

In general the media is most drawn towards acts which are visible and spectacular, especially if they have sexual or political connotations and lend themselves to presentation in pictures. The clear implication is that the violence most likely to receive coverage in the press is that which involves sudden physical injury to seemingly innocent strangers, preferably committed in public. So, the escapades of football hooligans outside football grounds are particularly newsworthy, as are those of muggers, vandals, rioters and terrorists. If there is also a controversial political content, its interest is enhanced. For example, racial attacks are particularly newsworthy where the majority race is threatened. Such broad and permanent characteristics should not be taken to imply that the list of what is newsworthy is static—until fairly recently, the newspaper coverage of child- and baby-battering was rare; now it is reported fairly frequently. This may reflect an increase in such offences, or it may simply portray a change in what is judged to be newsworthy. There are still some areas of violence which are rarely reported, such as injuries or deaths at work resulting from unsafe working conditions, and illness caused by pollution. On the other hand, some sexual and/or violent crimes (e.g., paedophilia and terrorism) seem always to have a high value in news reporting.

Another factor involved in deciding whether an item is newsworthy or not is the vulnerability of the victim. If the victim is very old or very young, or female (especially if photogenic), there is particular interest. Violent acts committed by individuals, for example women, who are generally thought of as passive are also newsworthy. The conflict is often given more dramatic impact by being simplified into clashes between opposing factions: young versus old; hooligans or rioters versus police; black versus white. The criminal is often labelled as a psychopath, a beast, a madman or just a bored yobbo. In these ways the crime and the criminals are simplified, and the intricacies necessary to provide a full picture are almost never provided. The crimes mentioned above may be far from typical, but are presented as if they were the usual activity of most criminals. The criminals themselves are perceived as violent, immoral and a threat to society, being depicted as people who attack the normal harmony of our existence.

The press are also used to voice political messages concerning crime and criminal justice issues and indeed create their own political message. This divided and politicised reporting and representation of crime in Britain seems to date from the start of the 1970s. Hall et al. (1978) note that in 1970 the then Prime Minister, Edward Heath, through speeches and press articles, constructed a series of 'folk devils' (such as criminals, scroungers, trades unions and marauding youths). He and the media portrayed these groups as in need of legal control in order to guarantee an ordered and crime-free society. This media portrayal of 'folk devils' and the need for their control has continued, indeed those who should be controlled has expanded to include terrorists, 'subversives', single mothers, de-institutionalised mentally ill, the homeless, and asylum seekers. The press are very ready to disseminate political attacks on crime and call for harsher policies on law and order because they are both easily understood by, and appeal to readers. Furthermore they feed on and are fed by fear and unease which is likely to enhance sales.

Normality would be boring to read about, so the papers naturally pick out the unusual. This leads to seeing things in extremes, so that young people are either drugtaking, sexually permissive and partaking in wanton violence, or they are sav-ing lives, taking part in Outward Bound courses, or performing great charitable works. To gain newsworthy status it is therefore necessary to fall outside many people's experiences. But being unusual does not necessarily guarantee a place in the newspapers. The story must normally also contain an element of human inter-est, which often arises by violating what most people see as being acceptable. The reporting then takes on a stereotypical style, using basic ideas of what it sees as moral and portraying the criminal acts as wholly alien to that morality. Ideally therefore crime reporting is about disruption to or violation of the lives of indi-viduals or about broader disorder. This basic crime information is then woven into a story which ideally has bad villains and good victims so the moral stance is clear and we all know which side we should be on. Sometimes the law enforcement agencies are portrayed as heroes, sometimes as working hard but as yet unsuccess-ful, very occasionally they fail or have added to the problem and may be depicted in a negative light. If ever they are depicted as villains it is usually only as indi-viduals, the system may be failing but this will rarely be depicted as intentional.

What has been said above has assumed a bias in media news reporting, albeit a bias which in part arises more or less unavoidably out of what is generally seen as constituting 'news': 'dog bites man is not news; man bites dog is'. Thus what we have described as 'bias' in newspapers is inherent in their own functions (informa-tive, entertaining, making money etc.) and is not necessarily a criticism. But for our purposes it does raise the question: are the types of crime most commonly reported the ones which are actually most commonly committed? Is crime reporting representative of the amount and type of crime committed?

The bias in the press on the type of crime considered worth reporting has a long history. For example, both Rochier (1973) and Cumberbatch and Beardsworth (1976) discovered an over-emphasis on crimes of violence. This over-emphasis has been consistently found in research over the last 30 years. Thus Tumber (1995) shows that most coverage was given to violence against the person and to sexual offences. Beckett and Sasson (2000) noted the particular rise in the reporting of sexual offences.

Schlesinger et al. (1995) in a study of the whole range of the national press demonstrated both the proportion of coverage given to different types of crime and the variations between different sections of the press. They found that most cover-age in all types of newspapers was given to violence, although there are interesting differences in the coverage by different newspapers. Non-sexual violence occurred in a quarter of the cases mentioned in the 'quality press' as against 45.9 per cent of those in the tabloid press; the corresponding figures for sexual offences were 7 per cent and 11 per cent. These percentages, and the differences between types of newspaper, remained much the same for non-sexual violence when attention was limited to front-page coverage. But for sexual offences there was now a dramatic difference: in the 'quality' papers these accounted for 2.8 per cent of all front-page treatment of crime; in the tabloids it was 22.7 per cent. They noted that television coverage was also varied both in substance and style. Of the national channels ITV came closest to the tabloid coverage, but local bulletins were even more clearly of this type, being most likely to focus on violent crime.

Also of interest is the focus of programmes such as *Crimewatch UK*. Again their intention is to entertain viewers, which means that they both use powerful visual images such as reconstructions and focus on crimes of violence and stranger on stranger sexual attacks. Offences such as complex frauds and corporate offences are more difficult to visualise and so are rarely depicted unless it is also possible to show very vulnerable victims. This focus is also necessary because the point of these programmes is to encourage viewers to help the police so they have to encourage viewers to identify with the victim and the police and to be reviled by the offender and, usually, his crimes.

Although certain subject matter has always been prevalent the exact nature does alter over time. Domestic violence would hardly have featured in the early 1970s whereas it is regularly in the media today. An even more marked change can be seen in the reporting of paedophilia and child pornography over the last 30 years. In the early 1970s this almost never appeared, especially not under the heading of paedophilia (Williams (2003)).

Selection by the media over what they should cover is literally inescapable and is a necessary part of their role both to entertain and to inform. But in attempting to assess the effects of the media on public perceptions of crime the scale and the nature of the selection has to be borne in mind. Two brief illustrations can serve to suggest the significance of this. An early study of the Scottish press (Ditton and Duffy ((1983)) compared the official crime statistics for the Strathclyde region over a month with the reports on crime in six newspapers produced in the area. Of 47,970 offences either made known to the police or recorded as court proceedings only 120 (0.25 per cent) were reported in the paper. A similar study of local Birmingham Papers (Susan Smith (1984)) illustrated the nature of the selection: more than half (52.7 per cent) of the space given by newspapers to crime stories involved personal offences which represented less than 6 per cent of recorded crime; whilst burglary and theft not involving direct contact accounted for 83.9 per cent of recorded crimes, but were given only 3.8 per cent of the newspaper space given to crime. For the newspapers, looking to 'human interest' stories to interest and entertain their readers, this is both natural and sensible: but to the extent that general perceptions of the scale and nature of crime are formed by the media it needs to be borne in mind that the picture is necessarily distorted.

A further finding of these studies was that in the 1990s crime reporting, particularly in the 'quality' papers and on television, tended to move more towards an analysis of what is being done about the problem of crime (a similar though less marked trend is seen in the tabloids though it started later). The media seems to believe that their readers are more interested in the wider issues of solving the crime problem because such information touches more clearly on their own lives and well-being; the public wants to know what is being done to tackle burglaries or violence on the streets. These papers may therefore utilise more column inches in considering the performance of the professional crime control agencies of the criminal justice system than in discussing individual criminal activity. The coverage will often entail a 'debate' in which there is a competition between the acceptability and rationality of the actions of the criminal justice system and the emotionally powerful anguish of a vulnerable victim (or victims) who may feel they have been failed by or even injured by the system (see Anderson (1995)). This preoccupation with crime and the criminal justice system is, on the one hand understandable, and on the other becoming obsessive for many people. Over the past 30 years or so crime has become a more common experience amongst many, especially in the middle classes, who previously had little direct contact. During this period their property has become more accessible to the criminal though increased availability of vehicular transport, and their increasing ownership of portable goods makes them more attractive targets. Furthermore the visible signs of disorder on the streets have increased, including graffiti and vandalism as well as the presence of large numbers of youths who, even if not rude or dangerous, swagger and sometimes look threatening, drug dealing etc. Their everyday experience of crime or rather their feeling that they might realistically experience crime has increased. All this makes them interested in what is being done to improve their safety and to remove or decrease the dangers. The media feed this personally experienced unease through reports of dangerous and violent crimes and then provide critical comment on the alleged failures of the system of criminal justice. Much press coverage in fact calls for ever greater controls of what are viewed as problems and crimes.

Fictional accounts, particularly television, cinema and video presentations, are also relevant. Most of us are subjected to such representations from an early age and are probably more interested in them and watch them for longer periods than our exposure to news or other non-fiction criminal information. They are arguably the most effective medium of mass communication. If the news presentations have an effect on our perceptions, attitudes are equally likely to be formed by the impact of fiction. In Chapter Ten the effect of media on criminality will be considered; here we are concerned only with its effect on perceptions of crime.

Fiction is full of representations of crime, criminals, victims and enforcement agencies. Such images are so common that we take them for granted. What is more difficult is to understand the images and the effects they have on our understanding of the world. Like the news media they tend to over-represent sensational crimes which makes for good drama, but they do not represent what are most people's real experience of crime. However, they are even more complex than the news reports: they are imbued with other meanings, a moral representation. There is an even greater bias towards criminality than non-fiction: it is one of the commonest themes of dramas, films and serials, especially soap operas. And like non-fiction accounts, sex and sensationalism are heavily over-represented. In a recent study Reiner et al. (2001) note a marked change in the media representation of crime over the past 50 years. They claim that in the immediate post-war (Second World War) period crime stories both fictional and non-fictional presented a consensus view of society, which accepted the differing status of individuals and groups as well as the need for, and actions of, authority. They claim that victims were seen as being good and in need of protection, that criminals were caught and made to pay for their wrongdoing (or helped to change their ways) and the criminal justice system was good, and effective. In the late 1960s until almost 1980 they see a massive shift. Authority and the criminal justice system and its employees are not now depicted as necessarily good. The acceptability and effectiveness of the system and of criminal laws are questioned. Society is portrayed as full of conflicts and the law enforcement officials and the victims are often no better than the criminals. In fact victimisation is depicted as a more complex issue and the offenders may well be portrayed as the real victims. Much is made of the possibility and need for reforming the system and such a project is portrayed as possible. Reiner et al. argue that this change encapsulates a move from an unquestioning acceptance of those in the criminal justice system as professional and therefore necessarily good, to seeing them as no different from anyone else and therefore as needing to prove their worth daily and with results. It also depicts crime as a problematically defined legal concept. Having said that they do conclude that despite these enormous changes it is still true that the vast majority of media representations continue to conclude in favour of the system even if along the way they question certain facets of it. In this way the media continue to support socially acceptable behaviour and to accept social control as a good and a necessary part of communal living. This, largely conservative, depiction is likely to continue as shareholders and advertisers take a more in-depth interest in the programmes they are associated with and use their influence. This happened, for example, when Becks Brewery withdrew funding from *Queer as Folk* (1998) after explicit portrayal of gay sexual intercourse in the first episode. Despite this overall conservatism some representations retain a confrontational element.

Allegations of a bias in both crime reporting and fictional representations would therefore seem to be towards the more sensational crimes of violence and possibly also of sex. Given that such bias exists, what is its effect, if any, on the public's perceptions of crime?

3.3 Effects of media on public perceptions of crime

It should not be assumed that television necessarily influences people's perception of crime, particularly that it might do so in specific ways. That we view fictional crime programmes for entertainment not enlightenment is a common argument and obviously has some substance; but more as a caution against exaggeration than as a total dismissal of the effects of the media. At the least, it seems plausible that many fictional accounts encourage fears and insecurity. And it is interesting that it is often difficult to tell the difference between fiction and the crime reconstruction that takes place in a programme such as *Crimewatch UK*. Here the non-fiction programme employs the techniques of fiction programmes so as to grab the imagination and appear more entertaining, thereby using our preoccupation with fictional depiction of fear as a weapon in crime detection.

As a generalisation it could be suggested that the media affect public opinion in one of three ways:

(a) by mass manipulation,

(b) by a commercial '*laissez-faire*', or

(c) by the 'consensual paradigm'.

Those who argue that the media seek mass manipulation envisage the public as a gullible mass into which the media can pour chosen information in order to mould that society's opinions. The theorists who support this thesis generally see the press as dangerous because of the possibility of political manipulation.

Those who argue for commercial '*laissez-faire*' say that the media offer a variety of differing views allowing the public a choice of opinions. They would argue that a person is not just a void into which ideas can be poured and accepted without question, but rather that an individual's attitudes already exist and so he or she will choose the paper or programme which best reinforces that view. Of course they see it is possible to alter some of these views, but the ease with which this may be done is inversely proportional to the importance of a particular view to the person. Against this those who support the 'consensual paradigm' theory would argue that there are not many views portrayed in newspapers, largely because they are all owned and run by a few people.

Garland (2000) suggests another approach to the explanation of the role of the media in relation to recent trends towards more punitive developments in crime control. He argues that these do not originate with the media. They arise from changes in social structures and everyday experience which the media reflect, disseminate and then use to justify punitive remedies. He suggests that behind these developments were several cultural changes. Thus he asserts that, since the 1960s, there has been a decline in political clout of welfare professionals partly because their ability to deliver a safer society was seriously questioned; politicians took over the role of how best to punish and to solve the crime problem; and wielded this power in answer to popular fears. In addition, as already mentioned, the combination of more portable electronic valuables and thieves with cars and vans meant that crime became a growing problem for the middle classes, although this did not alter the basic fact that most crime was committed by the poor against the poor. At the same time the spread of vandalism, graffiti and incivility gave a general feeling that crime was not far away whilst the 1960s policy of concentrating on serious offending and neglecting more minor offences also encouraged an uneasy atmosphere. Finally the emergence of a widespread drugs culture and its associated violence evoked a fear that was fed by much lurid media coverage.

It is in this already fertile arena that Garland sees the media have had an effect. They have responded to the increased interest in crime by producing more and more fictional and non-fictional portrayals of crime. As noted above, these often question the integrity and/or competence of the system to deal with the crime problem. The media coverage does not cause the change in mindset but rather reinforces widespread experience and feelings, making it easier to accept media calls for legal and political action to address the 'problem' with punitive action.

Reiner et al. (2001) suggest a more complex and fragmented effect of media, particularly fictional media. They found that each generation tended to be positively affected by the media of their youth and this most shaped their perceptions and their views on the criminal justice system and the society today. Older people spoke with approval of idealised clear moral and justice positions displayed in their youth; younger generations welcomed the more complex moral issues and questioning of authority through rights and alternative viewpoints. Gender differences were also discovered. Women perceived themselves as potential victims, young women used media stories to help them assess and learn to deal with risk. Men rarely perceived risks to themselves as potential victims, older men tended to identify with the authority figures, younger men were more ambivalent not seeing clear moral differences between the two. Clearly though the message is of a marked media effect on perceptions of crime and criminal justice system.

Against this one of the most recent large-scale pieces of research throws some doubt on the extent to which the media influences views and opinions. Gillespie and McLaughlin (2002) suggest that media representations (fictional and non-fictional) do not have a strong impact either on people's knowledge of the criminal justice system or on their views and attitudes, especially towards sentencing. Most informants had a punitive attitude towards crime and this arose whether they were subjected to a lot or only a little media coverage. The individuals who were most affected were those who regularly watched soap operas where the crime details were affected by the depth of character and personal circumstances of both the victim and the offender. But even here the often less punitive attitudes to particular cases did not necessarily affect the overall punitive values of the individual. Many individuals felt strongly that the media could be used to alter views towards a less punitive stance but that this form of social engineering would be unacceptable. Of course this does not prove that the media does not have an influence, it may suggest that the influence comes to the fore even in quite low exposures. It might also be explained by the fact that the media feed on what they see as public opinion to sell their goods so that they support rather than alter prejudices in order to make money.

Furthermore, this research is somewhat at odds with the work of Simmons (2002) and Fletcher and Allen (2003). Each of these suggests links between types of papers read and understanding of the crime rate. In the 2003 survey 43 per cent of tabloid readers but only 26 per cent of broadsheet readers thought the national crime rate had increased a lot. This finding arose against a backdrop of a 17 per cent reduction in crime since 1999. Chadee (2001) in a discussion of the synthesis of three extensive studies concluded that the media, especially television and newspaper reports are a major source of information on crime and influence the readers'/viewers' perceptions of crime.

All of this suggests that the media have some effect on perceptions of crime and beliefs about what should be done to solve the 'problem'. In this environment it would clearly be helpful if we could discern how the press affects public opinion. Equally clearly this is an elusive goal, but some guidance can be obtained from the attempts that have been made. For example, as already indicated, Susan Smith (1984) studied the effects of media reportage of crime on the inhabitants of a small area in Birmingham. Her survey suggested that 52 per cent derived their main source of information about crime from the media, 35.8 per cent from hearsay or the supposed experience of friends and neighbours, 3.2 per cent from their own experience and only 1.3 per cent from the police. The study suggested that those who had gleaned most of their information from the media were more likely to believe that local crime consisted mainly of personal violence or vice, and more likely when considering crime generally to think of it in terms of personal or violent incidents.

The study therefore lent some support to the view that there was a clear link between the public's opinion of crime and the media reporting of crime. It also suggested another possible relationship—that between hearsay and public opinion. It may be that information gained from hearsay provides more balanced information than the press and so allows the public to fill in the gaps left by press reporting. Schlesinger et al. (1995), in what they admit to be a very limited study, found a relationship between the types of media to which individuals were exposed, those reading tabloid papers and watching a large amount of television (especially ITV), and their level of fear of victimisation. The link was particularly marked so far as fear of violent attacks was concerned. The researchers suggest that the media may be reinforcing personal fears and insecurities and may build on life experiences. Hough (2002) would support this claim but, perhaps optimistically, suggests that the cycle of fear and punitive views might be broken by a more factually sound presentation of information and a more balanced political presentation based on information from practitioners and academics rather than the 'spin' presently used to feed this ill informed public clamour. All this is highly conjectural, but at least the studies establish reasonably firmly that press reporting of crime creates a broad public awareness of crime which is substantially different from any contained in the official statistics and, as will become apparent in Chapter Four, is different again from actual criminal activity.

A related problem (Sparks (1992)) is that the fictional representation of crime depicts ordinary citizens as victims or helpless onlookers, unable to enforce the criminal law or counter crime. Stopping criminality and corruption is left to heroes (and very occasionally heroines). The images are steeped in strong feelings, which hugely simplify the complex social reality. Of course this simplicity is probably partly what renders them enjoyable but, if they do affect our perceptions of crime (and there is no firm proof that they do) then this simplicity may render their effects actually, or potentially, dangerous.

While much in this area is conjectural, there is some positive support for the initial hypothesis. The media, or at least the press, do distort crime reporting and the public do, to some extent, rely upon that information to form their picture of crime and criminals, and of the possibility of either affecting themselves.

This perception of crime has a number of undesirable side effects such as increasing moral indignation, causing public panic, or individual fear of crime. All of which may cause people to modify their lives so as to take account of these, e.g., by staying in at night, which may be sensible if the perceptions are true but may be totally unnecessary if they are exaggerating the problem. The increased fear is likely to lead to greater feelings of insecurity and a desire to withdraw to the perceived safety of home, all of which represents a loss of freedom. Even those who are only moderately influenced in this way can have their lives and social interactions affected. By playing on anxieties for commercial purposes both fictional and non-fictional portrayals of crime may be increasing fear and decreasing feelings of citizenship, safety and social community. Possibly most serious is the effect such perceptions may have on the criminal justice system by causing the public to support, or appear to support, severe sentences, so making certain reforms of the penal system more difficult to carry out, even if these may in fact improve the situation. Newspapers often carry stories in which they purport to be outraged by what they consider to be lenient sentences for particular offences. They rarely complain of sentences which may be too punitive. In this way they portray our criminal justice system as over-sympathetic to the criminal, and render the introduction of less punitive sentences or alternative sentences very difficult, if not impossible.

The perception the public seems to have of the sentencing structure, and certainly that portrayed by most popular newspapers, is that sentencing is too lenient. Information from successive British Crime Surveys since 1995 have discovered that a large proportion of the public believe that sentencing is too lenient, they frequently and consistently underestimate the severity of sentences and yet believe that they are getting accurate information about the criminal justice system (see, e.g., Mirrlees-Black (2001). This is particularly galling when studies stretching back as far as the early 1980s have consistently contradicted this.

Moreover, when individuals are themselves asked to choose appropriate sentences they pick ones which are the same, or more lenient, than those which the judges actually pass. The public believed that the courts were more lenient than they actually are.

Despite these findings the media continue to affect the law, penal sanctions and the criminal justice system. This is well documented in many sources. For example, Koch (1998) after extensive access to government departments and politicians concluded that Home Office decisions and policies were based not on detailed research and reasoned discussion but on what the politicians believed the readers of the tabloid press would support (especially readers of *The Sun*). She portrayed these decisions as irrational and highly politicised, designed as vote winners rather than genuine solutions to the problem of crime. Here press coverage which may influence public opinion is being used by politicians to assess what the public are thinking. Similar types of analysis can be seen in Williams's (2003) consideration of the passing of the laws against child pornography.

It seems reasonable to conclude that the media seem, on occasions at least, to affect perceptions of crime: but equally it needs to be noted that the way this occurs is complex. Motivation is also difficult. Many theorists believe that crime depiction in the media is deliberately skewed towards a particular bias which distorts reality, and that this holds for both fiction and non-fiction. Fictional representations are likely to be especially misleading; and some would argue that their effects are more powerful because they are deliberately imbued with morals and sentiments intended to engage the reader's (or viewer's) feelings, reactions and understanding. And perceptions, wherever they originate, are significant because they have fairly strong effects on the lives of individuals and on their reactions to crime and harmful behaviours. An indication of the significance of this can be obtained by looking at a couple of areas where activity which is undoubtedly criminal has traditionally been given little coverage or condemnation.

3.4 Two less visible areas of crime

3.4.1 Introduction

Two areas of crime which, to date, have had little media coverage and which are not topics that most people think of when they consider what is crime, are white-collar and corporate crime. Today both have a well-established place in criminology text books (see, e.g., Croall (1992), Nelken (1994), and Bologna (1993), but until the late 1980s the former was not something generally recognised or readily perceived by the general public to be criminal in the United Kingdom. Corporate crime remains relatively unrecognised as crime even today, despite many national and international events that should have altered the general public perceptions. In brief, both types of crime are given relatively little media coverage, and corporate crime (because of its magnitude, possibly because of powerful lobbying factions and for other legal reasons) is still rarely, if ever, dealt with in the media as crime. This may well be set to change, especially in relation to the environment and food safety where there is now a heightened public awareness.

Both categories of crime, therefore, fit very appropriately into a discussion of the relation between the public perception of crime and the ways in which crime is reported in the media. Clearly, strong grounds exist to support the view that there is a connection, but equally it is clear that proving this in an unequivocal manner is difficult. The media treatment of white-collar and corporate crime lends further evidence, albeit circumstantial, to the case for a connection.

3.4.2 White-collar crime

What is white-collar crime? Edwin H. Sutherland was the first to bring this topic to the forefront of criminological study. He did this in works such as *White-Collar Criminality* (1940) and *White-Collar Crime* (1949). His work in this area is still the best known and continues to be both highly regarded and controversial. Most introductions to this subject begin with Sutherland's study (see, e.g., Coleman and Moynihan (1996), pp. 8–10).

Carson (1970) broadly summed up Sutherland's thesis as follows:

. . . the behaviour of persons of respectability and upper socio-economic class frequently exhibits all the essential attributes of crime but it is only very rarely dealt with as such. This situation emerges (Sutherland claims), from a tendency for systems of criminal justice in societies such as our own to favour certain economically and politically powerful groups and to disfavour others, notably the poor and the unskilled who comprise the bulk of the visible criminal population. (p. 384)

Sutherland's definition of white-collar crime consists of four criteria, namely:

(a) A crime—this is an obvious element but is often forgotten. These crimes are often committed but no criminal sanction is incurred because of its white-collar nature. It may escape prosecution and harsh sentencing because there has been no general public perception of such behaviour as criminal, nor have the media generally treated it as such and so the politicians have no interest in it: indeed, many of those administering the criminal justice system act as if these were 'not really criminal offences' (see, e.g., Croall (1992), ch. 5).

(b) Committed by a person of respectability—someone with no convictions for non white-collar crimes; and

(c) Of high social status—Sutherland included this to call attention to a vast area of criminal behaviour which is generally overlooked, and to prove his theory of 'Differential Association' (see 10.2.3). However, this element is not essential and white-collar crimes can include any offence committed at work by any of the hundreds of thousands of white-collar workers. One could go even wider and include all offences committed at work although this would more correctly be labelled 'occupational crime'.

(d) In the course of his/her occupation—If white collar workers or those of higher class commit murder, burglary or other 'ordinary crimes' they are not included here. Typical of the types of crime usual to this category are: over-charging, charging for unnecessary work, pilfering, misuse of the employer's computer, telephone, photocopier and other equipment or facilities, false accounting, time fiddling, false allowance claims, bribery, the use of fictitious or over-valued collateral, embezzlement and insider dealing. Certain crimes, however, are commonly included in this category, for example tax evasion, which are not authentic white-collar crime, at least not in terms of Sutherland's definition. These activities, although associated with work, are not committed in the course of an occupation, but are included by many commentators.

Many writers have included a fifth element, namely:

(e) A violation of trust—Some commentators add 'a violation of trust' to the definition. A more useful distinction can be made between job-related crimes committed for the corporation, and those committed against it. The easiest way to do this is to remove the former category (i.e., where employees commit crimes for the benefit of the company or corporation) and label it 'corporate crime'. Then white-collar or occupational crime may be used to describe the remainder; where the employer does not gain. This would include crimes such as embezzlement and theft from the employer (company, firm or individual) and from other employees. It is difficult to fit into this distinction some recent research (e.g., Nelken (2002)) which examines the links between white-collar crime and organised crime. Despite any such reservations, however, it is hoped that enough has been given in this section to indicate the essence of white-collar crime in order to consider both its media image and the way in which the system deals with it.

3.4.2.1 *White-collar crime and its enforcement*

In legal terms the social class of the offender is irrelevant, it is the nature of the offence and the mental intention which are of importance. Almost all white-collar offences are financial offences and involve frauds. Some frauds are wider than the white-collar crimes discussed above, they involve cheque or credit card frauds committed by people outside the workplace. These are dealt with under the same legal and enforcement provisions as other frauds and are the frauds about which most people are aware because they involve direct and obvious victimisation of the general public. Other frauds involve actions such as embezzlements from companies (very often those for whom the offender works), insider dealing (which can be committed by the directors or the secretarial and other staff) and deceptions to obtain money by false pretences which could be committed by a person in work or by others (collecting money from senior citizens whilst claiming to be from the gas board). Most frauds are for fairly small amounts and committed by offenders who are not rich and famous. These frauds are dealt with by local police and Crown Prosecution Service, but their complexity makes them expensive to investigate and prosecute both in terms of finance and labour. A police force which focused on fraud would be seen to have poor overall performance in terms of cost and efficiency. Furthermore the general invisibility of fraud means that there is less political, and popular or media pressure on chief constables to deal with it. For these reasons fraud tends to have a low priority and low profile in most forces outside London.

Beyond these common frauds there is a smaller number of very different white-collar offences where the sums involved are very high, where the victims may not know of their victimisation, and where clever and calculated investments or deals are used to line the pockets of a few, already very rich individuals. Such cases are dealt with by the Serious Fraud Office (set up under the Criminal Justice Act 1987). It deals with cases where there is at least £5 million at risk, but in effect it rarely accepts frauds which involve less than £6 million. It enjoys extended powers in order to carry out investigations and bring cases to trial. For example under s. 2 of the Criminal Justice Act 1987, the Director of the Serious Fraud Office was given powers to require a person under investigation, or any other person whom he or she has reason to believe has relevant information, to produce documents and to provide an explanation of them even where the information may be incriminating to that person or to another person. These powers were necessary partly to protect employees who might be willing but frightened to give evidence, but were also intended, and have been used, to force information to be provided to help with investigations, though there is protection against self-incrimination. This clearly marked an intention to deal with these kinds of offences and possibly suggested that they were at last being treated seriously by the authorities. Even so the success rate in terms of convictions in cases brought to trial has been very low.

Despite the extended powers bringing these cases to trial is very expensive. The complexity of the cases means that trials tend to be very lengthy (three to 18 months) and the information is very complex for jurors to understand. There have been a number of acquittals, and even on conviction there seems to be little possibility of imprisonment; where imprisonment does ensue it has in practice been for a short period. The lenient sentences are especially unfortunate because they can plausibly be interpreted as a reluctance by judges to send their own kind to prison even when they have let the side down. All the enforcement problems make it very difficult for there to be any bargaining for guilty pleas. The accused has nothing to lose from a full case as he or she is unlikely to be convicted and if convicted unlikely to be severely sentenced. Change seems dubious because, apart from any social discrimination, these crimes do not induce fear in the community and the media condemnation—though growing—is still muted. Indeed, some argue that the issue of high-level fraud should not be pressed very hard because a strong economy needs to encourage enterprise: but whether a strong society can be built by tolerating injustice is a wider issue (for a more detailed discussion see Nelken (2002)).

3.4.2.2 *Media coverage of white-collar crime*

As noted above much media coverage of crime is largely drawn from official sources and they do not always include areas of white-collar crime in the main official statistics. Furthermore other organisations such as banking regulators and financial services tribunals may be involved in the control of this area and these organisations are less well known and understood. Having said that the broadsheets, especially the *Financial Times*, carry a large number of stories concerning problems which may affect the 'City' or the stock market. Few of these reach the more popular press though instances of cybercrime, some of which are also white-collar offences, abound. As with other crimes many reports tend to try to isolate a bad and greedy villain and locate a good, innocent victim. For this reason they often home in on the individual who might have been central to the crime but ignore both the individuals higher up the company who may also gain (in some instances it may, indeed, have been their idea), and the employers and regulators whose lax supervision let it happen. Frequently, however, the newspapers, television companies and reporters lack the drive, understanding and resources necessary for the more investigative journalism required to uncover many of these stories. Even where these are present they often have to take account of how they will be received by their advertisers and whether their readership and viewers will be sufficiently interested or able to follow the often intricate information, especially as these stories may lack moral clarity or the clear message of pain and damage present in most media reporting of crimes.

This lack of media interest or censure does influence the public and politicians to see this as less serious and possibly as one of the prices of capitalism. In consequence resources for enforcement and regulation remain fairly low.

3.4.3 **Corporate crime or organisational crime**

Corporate crime is difficult to define partly because it covers such a wide range of offences (see Slapper and Tombs (1999)), and is complicated by a problem of terminology being variously called corporate, business or organisational crime. Here it will be defined as: an illegal act of omission or commission, punishable by a criminal sanction, which is committed by an individual or group of individuals in the course of their work as employees of a legitimate organisation, and which is intended to contribute to the achievement, goals or other objectives thought to be important to the organisation as a whole or some sub-unit within it, and which has a serious physical or economic impact on employees, the general public, consumers, corporations, organisations and governments.

The first part of this definition makes it clear that the concern is with criminal acts rather than just unlawful acts. An activity may be unlawful in civil or administrative law without being criminal or illegal. 'Illegal' only includes acts or omissions declared by the law to be criminal in that society, as opposed to civil wrongs.

The definition covers omissions as well as commissions, and may include both intentional and unintentional harms. The mere fact that machinery in a factory is dangerous may be sufficient to prove a crime even if those in charge of the factory did not intend to injure anyone, or even did not know it was dangerous. They ought to know, and have a duty to ensure it is safe. Similarly, if a drug company distributes a product before adequately testing it, if that product is harmful they may be liable to criminal prosecution even if they neither intended harm nor knew of the danger: they are liable as long as in distributing it they break a criminal regulation. In each case a prosecution could occur even though no-one is actually hurt but merely because the criminal law is breached. Some theorists have argued that such crimes are actually worse than intentional crimes, as they show a general disregard for humanity and could lead to the injury of numerous victims, whereas an intentional crime is usually directed towards one victim (for a further discussion of this idea see Box (1983)).

The definition does not concentrate on economic goals but allows a wider understanding of organisational goals. It also recognises that the impact of such crime upon victims may well be, and often is, physical rather than economic (e.g., environmental dumping), and that the victims may be corporations, organisations and even governments. Such victims may result from tax evasion, bribing governmental officials, industrial espionage, illegal mergers and takeovers, trademark or patent violations, insider dealing, fraudulent advertising, and so on. Their inclusion is therefore necessary.

Is corporate crime important? Is it surprising that many people do not consider corporate crime as crime? Arguably it is surprising, because of the extensive harm corporate crime causes to the community generally. But the relative lack of public concern is more understandable when consideration is given to the information made available to the public in a readily accessible and digestible form. Corporate crime receives very little exposure in the media or, if it is covered, it is often confined to the 'city' pages or portrayed as a disaster or accident rather than a crime.

Corporate crime can be a cause of injury, or even death. Death does occur in the course of, and as a result of, legitimate corporate activities such as exploration, mining and machine failure. Sometimes, however, the corporate activities which resulted in deaths or serious injuries are illegitimate in that the corporation has shown wanton disregard for, or been reckless or negligent of, the health and safety of its employees or its customers. Corporations often disregard the interests of society as a whole in pursuit of their corporate goals, so they may dump toxic waste, emit dangerous fumes into the atmosphere, fit faulty equipment to products such as cars, and expose employees or others to dangers.

The problem is substantial. In 2000–1 the Health and Safety Executive and Local Authorities reported 444 work related deaths (149 were members of the public, see **http://www.corporateaccountability.org/ststs_deaths.htm**)and27,935non-fatal major injuries (see **http://www.corporateaccountability.org/ststs_majors.htm**). Much of the work on enforcement of corporate safety standards is carried out by regulatory bodies such as the Health and Safety Commission, the Health and Safety Executive, Local Authorities, Environmental Health Departments and the Marine and Coastguard Agency. These bodies often consider that their primary role is to encourage and aid organisations to achieve high safety standards, prosecutions may therefore be a secondary consideration. They might therefore place enforcement notices on companies (requiring them to come up to safety standards within a particular period) rather than prosecute. These regulatory agencies may bring prosecutions under regulatory provisions such as those in the Health and Safety at Work Act 1974 but do not generally act in traditional crime areas such as manslaughter. They often lack the training necessary to investigate such criminal transgressions and are severely under-resourced making such work difficult to carry out. The police also lack the expertise to carry out investigations of workplace deaths. Furthermore, it is very difficult to get a conviction in corporate manslaughter cases. Safety is legally the responsibility of the company and companies cannot be prosecuted for manslaughter; only real people can face such charges. Directors do not have individual responsibility for safety, therefore unless one can prove a 'controlling mind' behind the action or the failure to act a conviction is impossible. Proving individual responsibility is generally only possible in small companies where the director/owner is or ought to be aware of all the rules and of the breaches. All prosecutions of directors of major companies have failed. This may be set to change. Over the past ten years there have been numerous discussions about a corporate killing bill. In 2000 the Home Office issued a consultation paper entitled *Reforming the Law on Involuntary Manslaughter* and in May 2003 the Home Secretary, David Blunkett promised to publish a bill which would make corporate manslaughter a crimes by the end of the year (this did not appear in the Queen's Speech on 26 November 2003). Even if this happens it is probable that it will merely be a discussion document and is unlikely to become law for a few years. However, there has been some movement to alter the situation. First, in two recent cases involving the regulatory offences the Court of Appeal has issued guidelines. In *R v F. Howe and Son (Engineers) Ltd* (1998) [1999] 2 Cr App R (S) 37 it suggested fines were too low and set out issues to take into consideration: whether the breach was deliberate and with a view to profit; how far short of the safety standards it fell; the degree of risk; whether it was a one off incident; whether a death had occurred; and the effect of the fine on the business. In *R v Friskes Petcare (UK) Ltd* (2000) Cr App R (S) 401 the Court suggested that before the case begins the prosecutor should set out aggravating circumstances and the company should set out mitigating circumstances so allowing the guidelines in *Howe* to be more carefully applied (see **htpp:// www.hse.gov.uk/enforce/off00-01.pdf**; the most up to date report is the Health and Safety Offences and Penalties 2002–2003, see **http://www.hse.gov.uk/ enforce/off02-03.pdf**.) The Health and Safety at Work (Offences) Bill 2003, would have made alterations to the Health and Safety at Work Act (1974); it would have raised fines, made prison an option and made it possible to try more offences in the crown court. A second bill, Company Directors' (Health and Safety) Bill (2003) would have made it easier to prosecute company directors for transgressions of Health and Safety. It required companies to appoint a health and safety director and imposed duties on this director and others in relation to health and safety. This should have made it easier to prosecute company directors for the failure of their company to protect its workers. Neither Bill was passed into law.

There are economic losses as well. Fraud on the grand scale can go as far as raising the possibility of destabilising the economic framework by using corporate structures. This is certainly a possibility in the particular cases of international banking or State manipulation. At a less grandiose level some of the economic losses are suffered by other companies, for example through industrial espionage, price-fixing and patent violation. Others are suffered by the public, for example through corporate tax evasion. In the end it is generally the public who are the final losers, and most authors would agree that the losses suffered as a result of corporate crime far outweigh those suffered as a result of economic street crimes such as robbery, theft, larceny and motor vehicle theft.

Lastly, there is the possibility of almost unquantifiable environmental damage even when, as it should be for this purpose, consideration is limited to corporate acts which are criminal, i.e., the illegal cleaning of oil tanks at sea or the dumping of toxic pollutants in rivers. Slapper and Tombs (1999) and Tombs and Whyte (2003) present clear evidence that the economic, physical and social impact of corporate crimes far outweighs that of other criminal activities.

Again in relation to economic and other non-safety areas of corporate crime the enforcement is often conducted by regulatory bodies such as the Department of Trade and the Serious Fraud Office who work more in the areas of prevention and proactive enforcement of standards than in the prosecution of offences. This approach is partly due to a lack of finances and the excessive costs of such prosecutions which rarely result in convictions. When they do the fines are insufficient to dissuade perpetrators and anyway give out the message that everything can be bought and prison sentences are rarely used. Again perpetrators are unlikely to be convicted and even if they are they will normally only be fined so the deterrence element is not strong. Some commentators such as Slapper and Tombs (1999) and Tombs and Whyte (2003) question the effectiveness of this approach and see its ever widening use as part of the globalisation, decentralisation and reduction of accountability discussed in Chapter Twenty. Others such as Braithwaite (1995) see open self-regulation where large firms set their own standards and are then held to them as the only way forward.

3.4.3.1 *Perceptions of corporate crime*

Corporate crime is therefore a real social problem and represents a definite danger to society. Yet corporate crime, like white-collar crime, is not usually among the first to spring to mind when crime is being considered. Why not? They are no less morally reprehensible, and in terms of suffering inflicted or damage caused they are as bad, and often because of their magnitude, worse than conventional, run-of-the-mill crimes committed by individuals.

The media are at least partially responsible for this situation. When a murder is committed and reported in the papers, it is clearly reported as a life criminally taken by another. But when life is lost as the result of a corporate crime, it is often reported as a disaster or an 'act of God' rather than as the result of human culpability. In this way, these activities are not perceived to be the result of criminal acts or omissions but as unfortunate accidents. Of course, this perception is not simply due to the media. Corporate crime does not often have an immediate and obvious direct impact on individuals so there is no real and general fear of it, and thus no clamour for its control. Fictional entertainment, in books and on the screen, is full of classic criminal activities or cops and robbers stories but few of these feature corporate crime, the same is true of films. In the non-fiction area there are some documentaries where these issues are aired, particularly if they can point to the perpetrators but such coverage is again far less than in that given over to other criminal activities. A similar picture is found in most newspapers. Tombs and Whyte (2001) analysed crime stories in five daily newspapers and four Sunday papers over a six-week period, they discovered that although conventional crime was heavily reported (911 stories) corporate crime was not (237 stories). In tabloid papers the difference was about 20 conventional crime stories to one corporate crime; general broadsheets had a ratio of 4:1 whereas the liberal broadsheets had a 2:1 ratio. The only paper to have more corporate crime was the *Financial Times* which had four such stories to each conventional crime story. Corporate crime stories tended to be hidden well inside the paper, in financial or business sections and not on the front page. Most important was the fact that many corporate crime stories were not presented as crime stories but more as financial or business reports.

This lack of or difference in reporting probably shapes our views of these offences and offenders. This situation is particularly lamentable as publicity, by providing information, can discourage corporate crime. Certainly, in some of these infractions publicising the breaches of particular companies would have a powerful enforcing effect. The corporations rely on consumers for their well-being; consumers can take legal action in civil courts for damage done to themselves; or can boycott, or threaten to boycott, goods which offend regulations; or can write letters, individually or collectively, drawing the problems to the attention of the corporation. The corporations involved are usually basically legal and responsible, wish to retain a positive corporate image and profile, and will wish to avoid a bad press or possible boycott if they ignore the original letter or letters. To be effective the consumer pressure needs to be well organised. Braithwaite (1993) gives examples of the power of such action in altering the behaviour of major pharmaceutical companies. This can be illustrated from a non-criminal field where publicity has largely persuaded drugs companies to provide cheaper HIV-Aids drugs to poor countries (see Stewart (2003)). Corporations are interested in their public image and the media could, by drawing attention to problems, do much to persuade companies to work within the regulations and, possibly, to even more acceptable standards.

Interestingly, where perceptions of crime could do most for enforcement they have a low media profile; where their most effective result is to increase fear of victimisation by reporting of street crime, often in a distorted and startling way, they proliferate.

3.5 Media hype and folk devils

In stark contrast to the previous section there are areas of criminal activity which are over-emphasised and focused upon in the media, possibly leading to distorted perceptions, illogical fears and to laws which may not deliver safety. The two areas that best illustrate this are reporting on paedophilia and on terrorism. First it is necessary to consider the concept of 'folk devils'.

Press fascination or obsession with crime probably began to arise in the 1970s, Hall et al. (1978) noted that in 1970 the Prime Minister, Edward Heath, talked of the need to control classes of person (such as criminals, scroungers, the unions and marauding youths) by strict laws and heavy handed enforcement of order to deliver a crime free society. Hall et al. (1978) famously referred to this as the forming of 'folk devils'.

In order to obtain the political power to use strict law and order policies it was necessary to have popular backing for such a solution. In order to obtain this backing it was necessary not only to convince the public that these folk devils were bad but also to create a feeling of moral panic associated with them. Here politicians found the press willing conspirators; crimes (especially violent and sexual crimes) sell newspapers. The press could produce stories which fed on and are fed by fear and panic; they could also produce documentaries and dramas on the theme of crime and be sure of an interested audience. The level of press coverage of crime stories has increased from about 10 per cent of stories in the 1940s, 1950s and 1960s to about 20 per cent or more in the 1970s, 1980s and 1990s (Reiner (2001)) so the press did respond to the call for them to be involved in the dissemination of 'folk devils' and moral panics. Over time new categories have been added and become feared: terrorists, paedophiles, 'subversives', single mothers, the homeless, sex offenders, child molesters, asylum seekers.

As well as this additional level of reporting the type of reporting changed dramatically. This is graphically illustrated by Reiner (2001). He compares reporting of crimes in 1945 with those in 1989. He reports that in the *Daily Mirror* on 19 January 1945 there is a two-page spread concerning a killing by a couple. The two-page spread carries many photographs and banner headlines but he is struck by what is absent: '. . . no account of the details of the murder itself, of the injuries suffered by the victim, or any fear he might have suffered'. On 27 February 1945 this paper reported on a case of child abuse. It carried her photo and detailed her injuries but in a very matter of fact way. The story then focused on the problems suffered by the offender and reasons for trying to understand him. Reiner then contrasts these against a story in *The Times* on 25 November 1989 where a girl was attacked and killed by her mother's boyfriend (there are pictures of all three). It details the girl's injuries and states that she '. . . died from a combination of pain, shock and exhaustion after a vengeful beating'. Reiner states that 'The story graphically details the fear and suffering of the girl, and undermines any excuse of "bad temper" offered on behalf of the accused.' He is made fully responsible for her death, the only other 'baddies' are the social services who failed to intervene. Reiner concludes:

These stories illustrate vividly the changes implied by the statistical data. Crime stories fifty years ago took for granted that crime was wrong independently of whether suffering was inflicted on sympathetic victims. The burden of the story was to make the perpetrator comprehensible, often thereby invoking a degree of compassion on their behalf. This fitted well with the rehabilitative conception of the purpose of punishment that was explicitly argued for in many stories . . . After the mid-1970s crime was increasingly presented as a widespread menace threatening everyone, and stories became increasingly victim-centred. Offenders became demonised as dangerous predators whose vicious actions called for harsh but justified retribution on behalf of the vulnerable innocents they savaged.

This clearly illustrates a very marked change in press coverage of crimes over time and illustrates the way in which the press willingly played their part in the creation of a moral panic over certain groups and over certain activities. The 'spin' in the media and for politicians changed dramatically. This use of the press has at times led to the press leading government and police on law and order. So there are aspects of law which have grown wholly out of media hype: press reports concerning dogs attacking humans, particularly the young and elderly culminated in the Dangerous Dogs Act 1991, following which reports of attacks subsided as if the law had solved the problem; reports on new age travellers and the problems and ills they caused was a large factor in the laws to control this way of life (in the Criminal Justice and Public Order Act 1994); dislike of fines which really caused the middle classes to consider their behaviour were attacked so causing the unit fine system introduced in the Criminal Justice Act of 1991 to be withdrawn again in 1993 after just nine months in operation.

However, where it suits their political objectives, those in power have fed the media with constructions of 'folk devils' or 'moral panics' and so helped to lead public opinion. As Hall (1980) states:

By . . . first informing public opinion; then, disingenuously, consulting it, the tendency to 'reach for the Law', above, is complemented by a popular demand to be governed more strictly, from below. Thereby, the drift towards law and order, above, secures a degree of popular support and legitimacy amongst the powerless, who see no other alternative' (1980, p. 4).

Paedophilia and terrorism have seen both these scenarios. Importantly both are reported as wholly unacceptable and yet within each there is an element of sleight of hand. In both the UK and the US reporting on the activities of paedophiles can be dated from the 1970s which was in fact when the word 'paedophile' first began to be included in popular or standard dictionaries. In the UK it came to media interest because of the campaigning of some paedophiles fighting for their 'right' to enjoy sexual relations with children. This campaign led to other organisations campaigning against this and brought the activity to the attention of the media. Here one can see the beginnings of both a 'moral panic' involving the attack on the innocence of the nation's children and paedophiles as a 'folk devil'—a separate group of people believed to be different from 'normal' people and who posed grave dangers for children and for society in general. Since that time paedophiles have periodically been the centre of media reports (see Williams (2003)) but the present moral panic surrounding them began in 1996 with a major Belgian case involving Marc Dutroux who predated on numerous children. Following this were a number of revelations of paedophilia in children's homes and then the abduction, *rape and killing* of Sarah Payne in 2000. The *News of the World* (23 July 2000) used this event to launch a campaign calling for child sex offenders to be locked up for life. As part of their campaign they published photographs and information concerning 49 paedophiles and threatened to publish a list of 100,000 others, this led to vigilante action against many of those depicted and even to attacks on paediatricians as people were unsure of the difference between them and paedophiles. Many other papers and organisations such as the Association of Chief Police Officers attacked their campaign as being counter-productive. However, the government, in response to the clear public outrage, published proposals to toughen sentences for certain child sex offences. Later the *News of the World* (30 July 2000) began a second campaign calling for parents to be informed of a sex offender in their area and for life to mean life—this was dubbed the call for 'Sarah's Law' to mimic laws already available in most states in the US (called Megan's Laws). Paedophiles are now one of the most reviled and feared 'folk devils'. However, largely as a result of these media campaigns most people view paedophiles as predatory criminals whereas most sexual abuse of children is committed by members of the family or close friends.

Before moving to look at terrorism it is possibly instructive to look at the destructive side of our fascination with paedophilia, Adler (2001a) and (2001b) argues that having laws and a strong societal condemnation of an activity increases the desire to perform the act and so puts children at greater risk. She also argues (2001a) and (2001b) that having the law, and presumably the media focused on the sexualisation of children leads to children being socially constructed as sexual, more people see the sexual potential in the child and therefore more may be drawn to act. Certainly the vast increase in viewing of child pornography since it was made available via the web suggests there may be something in this—people desire children and feel released to enjoy that desire through the anonymity and believed safety of their own computer. Children as objects of sex are on the increase not just in law or in the discussion of paedophilia but also more generally in society. The viewing of children as possible sex objects can be seen from the banning of cameras in some school activities such as nativity plays and sports days (Silverman (2002)). But more worrying is the fact that the market economy is busy enticing ever younger children into more sexually explicit clothing. Young children, especially girls, are being enticed by advertisers to become sensation seekers, to dress in erotic and sexual ways, often very revealing of their bodies. They are being used by advertisers to sell products, often in sensual and sometimes even sexual ways (see the Calvin Klein advertisements that were withdrawn in 1995). Society has a very schizophrenic approach to this whole area: on the one hand we are being encouraged to protect children from the potential abuse of others' erotic fantasies (the 'beasts' that are paedophiles); on the other, as a society we are encouraging our children to aspire to a sexual persona and to become sensation seekers from a very young age. Both sides having been promoted by the media.

A similar dichotomy is evident in the media approach to terrorism (the general topic of terrorism is more fully treated in Chapter Nineteen). In the UK terrorists have long been 'folk devils' but until recently terrorists were Irish or only operated outside the UK. Since 11 September 2001 this view has altered. In the US until 11 September 2001 paedophiles were the most reviled group in the US. In fact following the terrorist attacks in New York and elsewhere certain Baptist evangelists in the US dubbed Mohamed a paedophile partly in order to ensure that Muslims and their faith became hated and feared, a paedophile being the most dangerous individual prior to the terrorist attacks. The attacks in New York and elsewhere led to media calls for the State to protect us more carefully and suggested that the State should have done more. So in the UK and the US terrorists are now both hated and feared, this has released governments to launch a 'war on terrorism' and, particularly in the US, to take powers to the State, removing rights from citizens, which would have been inconceivable before that date (see Chapter Nineteen). In particular the acceptance of the limbo for prisoners in Guantanimo Bay is aided by the muted condemnation of the total removal of their rights and unclear status. The press help to build a moral panic and fear such that rights can be eroded and some might say States move closer to tyrannical actions.

The natural outrage against the terrorist attacks should not obscure the likelihood that some of the perpetrators find their motivation in their reaction to what they perceive as Western oppression or injustice. If this does not justify the attacks it might help to explain them. It can also be plausibly argued that many Western States have backed tyrannical regimes or terrorist groups if it served their political interests. Yet the press fail to draw this to the attention of the public, the assumption is always that democratic regimes are clean and not associated with terrorism; 'we' are good and 'they' are bad.

More important in media terms is the fact that publicity is the lifeblood of terrorism. Terrorists want their message to be disseminated and their attacks may be designed to ensure that they receive maximum coverage. The media can, to some extent, determine who will be included in the category of terrorist. Thus in the USA the anti-abortion fighters who used terrorist tactics were until the early 1990s, generally condemned, but were not labelled as terrorists. Since the early 1990s their activities have been classed as terrorism. More generally the media can decide whether to treat particular acts of violence (by the State, by 'freedom fighters' etc.) as examples of terrorism. Such decisions usually embody a value judgement and depend on which side of a conflict the media (or particular sectors of it) sympathises with—this can be seen clearly in relation to the Israeli/Palestinian conflict.

These two brief examples suggest that to debate and discuss crime or its solution in a setting of fear and moral panic is likely to have negative consequences and is unlikely to provide intelligent and well-balanced solutions. The media offers a disservice to society whenever it over-sensationalises its coverage of many common crimes and when it ignores or underplays the problems as is the case with white-collar and corporate crime. What is necessary to a healthy and safer society is more balanced reporting and dissemination of information and ideas about crime and its solutions.

SUGGESTED READING

Beckett, K. and Sasson, T. (2000), *The Politics of Injustice*, Thousand Oaks: Pine Forge.

Criminal Justice Matters, vol. 43, 'Crime and the Media'.

Hope, T. and Sparks, R. (eds) (2000), *Crime, Risk and Insecurity*, London: Routledge.

Stensen, K. and Sullivan, R. (eds) (2000), *Crime, Risk and Justice*. Cullompton: Willan, part III.

QUESTIONS

1   Are public perceptions of crime mostly derived from the media?
2   What are the main deficiencies of media coverage of crime?
3   What significant areas of crime are generally little covered by the media? Why and with what consequences?

REFERENCES

Adler, A. (2001a), 'The Perverse Law of Child Pornography', *Columbia Law Review*, p. 209.

Adler, A. (2001b), 'Inverting the First Amendment', 149, *University of Pennsylvania Law Review* vol. 149, p. 921.

Anderson, D.C. (1995), *Crime and the Politics of Hysteria. How the Willie Horton Case Changed American Justice*, New York, NY: Times Books.

Beckett, K. and Sasson, T. (2000), *The Politics of Injustice*, Thousand Oaks, CA: Pine Forge.

Box, Steven (1983), *Power, Crime and Mystification*, London: Tavistock.

Braithwaite, John (1993), 'Transnational Regulation of the Pharmaceutical Industry', in Gilbert Geis and Paul Jesilow (eds), *Annals of the American Academy of Political and Social Science*, Newbury Park: Sage Periodicals Press.

Braithwaite, J. (1995), 'Corporate Crime and Republican Criminological Praxis', in F. Pearce and L. Snider (eds), *Corporate Crime*, Toronto: University of Toronto Press, pp. 48–72.

Chadee, D. (2001), 'Fear of Crime and the Media: From Perceptions to Reality', in *Criminal Justice Matters*, vol. 43, pp. 10–11.

Chibnall, Steven (1977), *Law and Order News. An Analysis of Crime Reporting in the British Press*, London: Tavistock.

Coleman, C. and Moynihan, J. (1996), *Understanding Crime Data*, Buckingham: Open University Press.

Croall, Hazel (1992), *White Collar Crime*, Buckingham: Open University Press.

Cumberbatch, C. and Beardsworth, A. (1976), 'Criminals, Victims and Mass Communications', in E. Viano (ed.), *Crimes, Victims, and Society*, Lexington, KY: DC Heath.

Ditton, Jason and Duffy, James (1983), 'Bias in the Newspaper Reporting of Crime News', *British Journal of Criminology*, vol. 23, p. 159.

Ericson, R.V. (ed.) (1995), *Crime and the Media*, Aldershot: Dartmouth.

Fletcher, G. and Allen, J. (2003), 'Perceptions of and Concern About Crime in England and Wales', in J. Simmons and T. Dodd (eds), *Crime in England and Wales 2002/2003*, Home Office Statistical Bulletin 07/03, London: Home Office. **http://www.homeoffice.gov.uk/ rds/pdfs2/hosb703.pdf.**

Garland, D. (2000), 'The Culture of High Crime Societies', *Brit. J. Criminol*; vol. 40, pp. 347–75.

Gillespie, M. and McLaughlin, E. (2002), 'Media and the Shaping of Public Attitudes', *Criminal Justice Matters*, vol. 49, pp. 8–9 and 23.

Hall, S. (1980), *Drifting into a Law and Order Society*, London: Cobden Trust.

Hall, S., Critcher, C., Jefferson, T., Clarke, J. and Roberts, B. (1978), *Policing the Crisis*, Basingstoke: Macmillan.

Harris, J. and Grace, S. (1999), *A Question of Evidence?: Investigating and Prosecuting Rape in the 1990s*, Home Office Research Study 196. A Research, Development and Statistics Directorate Report. London: Home Office. **http://www.homeoffice.gov.uk/rds/pdfs/hors196.pdf**.

Health and Safety Executive (1997a), *Health and Safety Commission Annual Report (1996/97)*, London: Health and Safety Executive.

Health and Safety Executive (1997b), *Workplace Injuries in Small and Large Manufacturing Workplaces 1994/5–1995/96 Statistical Tables*, London: Health and Safety Executive.

Health and Safety Offences and Penalties 2000–2001, London: Health and Safety Executive.

Home Office (1995), *Criminal Careers of those Born Between 1953 and 1973*, Home Office Statistical Bulletin, London: HMSO.

Home Office (2000), *Reforming the Law on Involuntary Manslaughter: the Government's Proposals*, London: Home Office.

Hope T. and Sparks, R. (eds) (2000), *Crime, Risk and Insecurity*, London: Routledge.

Hough, M. (2002), 'Populism and Punitive Penal Policy', in *Criminal Justice Matters*, vol. 49 pp. 4–5.

Hough, M. and Mayhew, P. (1983), *The British Crime Survey: First Report*, Home Office Research Study No. 76, London: HMSO.

Hough, M. and Mayhew, P. (1985), *Taking Account of Crime: Findings From the Second British Crime Survey*, Home Office Research Study No. 85, London: HMSO.

Koch, B. (1998), *The Politics of Crime Prevention*, Aldershot: Ashgate.

Law Commission, No. 237, Part V.

Lawrence, R.G. (2000), *The Politics of Force: Mass Media and the Construction of Police Brutality*, Berkley, CA: University of California Press.

Levi, Michael (1991), 'Sentencing White-Collar Crime in the Dark? Reflections on the Guinness Four', *Howard Journal of Criminal Justice*, vol. 30, p. 257.

Mirrlees-Black, C. (2001), *Confidence in the Criminal Justice System: Findings from the 2000 British Crime Survey*. Home Office Research, Development and Statistics Directorate; research findings No. 137, London: Home Office. **http://www.homeoffice.gov.uk/rds/pdfs/r137.pdf**.

Nelken, D. (2002), 'White-Collar Crime', in M. Maguire, R. Morgan and R. Reiner, *The Oxford Handbook of Criminology*, 3rd edn, Oxford: Oxford University Press.

Nelken, D. (ed.) (1994), *White-collar Crime*, Aldershot: Dartmouth.

Occupational Safety and Health Report (1987), *Annual Statistical Report*, London: HMSO.

Press Council Report (1977), London: Press Council.

Prime, J., White, S., Liriano, S. and Patel, K., (2001), 'Criminal careers of those born between 1953 and 1978' Home Office Statistical Bulletin 04/01, London: Home Office. **http://www.homeoffice.gov.uk/rds/pdfs/hosb401.pdf**

Reiner, R. (2001), 'The Rise of Virtual Vigilantism: Crime Reporting Since World War II', *Criminal Justice Matters*, vol. 43, pp. 4–5.

Reiner, R., Livingstone, S. and Allen, J. (2001), 'Casino Culture: Media, and Crime in a Winner-loser Society', in K. Stenson and R.R. Sullivan (eds), *Crime, Risk and Justice*, Cullompton: Willan Publishing.

Rochier, R. (1973), 'The selection of Crime News by the Press', in S. Cohen and J. Young (eds), *The Manufacture of News*, London: Constable.

Schlesinger, P., Tumber, H. and Murdock, G. (1995), 'The Politics of Crime and Criminal Justice', in R. Ericson (ed.), *Crime and the Media*, Aldershot: Dartmouth.

Silverman. J. (2002), 'Is this a Pornographic Photograph?', *Guardian*, 18 December 2002.

Simmons, J. (2002), *Crime in England and Wales 2001/2002*, Home Office Statistical Bulletin 07/02, London: Home Office. **http://www.homeoffice.gov.uk/rds/pdfs2/hosb702.pdf**.

Slapper, G. and Tombs, S. (1999), *Corporate Crime*, London: Longman.

Smith, Susan (1984), 'Crime in the News', *British Journal of Criminology*, vol. 24, p. 289.

Sparks, Richard (1992), *Television and the Drama of Crime: Moral Tales and the Place of Crime in Public Life*, Buckingham: Open University Press.

Stensen, K. and Sullivan, R. (eds) (2000), *Crime, Risk and Justice*, part III, Cullompton: Willan.

Stewart, H. (2003), 'Deal Reached over Cheap Drugs', *Guardian*, 1 September 2003.

Sutherland, Edwin H. (1940), 'White-Collar Criminality', *American Sociological Review*, vol. 5, pp. 1–12.

Sutherland, Edwin H. (1949), *White Collar Crime*, New York: Dryden Press.

Tombs, S. and Whyte, D. (2001), 'Reporting Corporate Crime Out of Existence', *Criminal Justice Matters*, vol. 43, p. 22.

Tombs, S. and Whyte, D. (2003), *Unmasking The Crimes of the Powerful*, London: Peter Lang.

West Midlands Health and Safety Advice Centre (1994), see Bergman.

Williams, K.S. (2004), 'Child Pornography: Does it Protect Children?', Forthcoming.

Work Hazards Group (1987), *Death at Work*, London: WEA.

4

The extent of crime: a comparison of official and unofficial calculations

4.1 Official statistics

4.1.1 Introduction

Almost all discussions of the level of crimes in any area start with a consideration of the official criminal statistics. These are the statistics gathered by the police, the courts and the punishment establishments. Court records have been kept since medieval times and until very recently it was to these that people turned for information concerning the crime rate. In 1778 Jeremy Bentham suggested that these should be centrally collected and used to measure the moral health of the country. Gradually, information concerning the imprisonment of individuals, and later the crimes reported to the police, began to be kept. The methods of recording were generally localised, making comparison difficult. It was not until 1856 that tables showing crimes known to the police were first included in the official statistics for England and Wales (then called the *Judicial Statistics*), and only since 1876 have such offences been systematically collected and collated. It was much later that these figures became used as the main indicators of the crime levels in the country. Now the police statistics are almost universally taken as the best official indicators of the level of crime. The court and other statistics will naturally record a substantially lower level of crime, since many crimes are either not solved or not taken to court. The police and court statistics for England and Wales are collected and published annually as the *Criminal Statistics*. Quarterly bulletins present supplementary information. (For the raw statistics see **http://www.homeoffice.gov.uk/rds//statsprog1.html**, for Quarterly updates see **http://www.homeoffice.gov.uk/rds/hosbpubs1.html**, and for analysis on statistical information see **http://www.homeoffice.gov.uk/rds/hosbpubs1.html**).

This chapter is mainly concerned with the statistics collected by the police as these relate to the measure of crime of which the authorities are aware. In England and Wales the police record serious offences about which they are aware, but this does not represent all crimes committed in the country. In fact, the statistics collected by the police are a poor indication of the full extent of criminal activity in the country. There are a number of reasons for this, which can be studied in some detail in recent accounts of the nature and limitations of criminal statistics (see, e.g., Coleman and Moynihan (1996); and Walker (1995)): the immediate purpose, however, is simply to make a few broad points about the deficiencies of police statistics as indicators of the overall level of criminal activity. First, although the police detect some crimes for themselves, for example drugs-related offences, driving offences, public order offences or street brawls, football hooliganism and offences against unoccupied property, the majority of offences come to light because they are reported by the victim or victims. In both instances some crimes may never come to light. There will be cases where the police do not discover crimes which fall into the category of those most likely to be detected by them, and there will be many offences which victims fail to report to the police. Secondly, the police may not record all the activities which are reported to them, or may not record them as crimes, e.g., they may be recorded as lost goods instead of stolen. In any event recorded statistics only cover 'notifiable offences': these are virtually the same as indictable offences so all summary offences go unrecorded (see Chapter Two). Thirdly, there are many crimes which are not controlled by the police but which fall under the auspices of some other authority such as the Customs and Excise. The official statistics are a better reflection of society's attitudes towards crime and criminals than an objective measure of criminal behaviour.

4.1.2 Reasons for reporting and non-reporting of offences

As mentioned above, there are many crimes which are never reported to the police, and these often remain wholly undetected by officials. There are various reasons why some are not so reported:

1. The victim may be unaware that a crime has been perpetrated. This is especially likely if the crime is one against a large corporation, such as shoplifting and pilfering by the staff, or if there are a number of victims, none of whom realises they have been victimised. Similarly, the victim may be unaware that what has occurred is a crime. This is especially a problem with offences committed against children.

2. The victim may participate willingly, or there may be no victim, so that no-one is likely to report the activity, e.g., many sexual offences, illegal abortions, prostitution, drugs offences, obscene publications.

3. The victim may be unable to report the offence. This occurs, for example, in most offences against children or other offences against relatively weak victims where the victims may be threatened (e.g., with loss of a job) to prevent revelation. Problems of this type occur also with illegal immigrants, who are afraid of reporting offences committed against them as it may result in their being deported.

4. The victim may consider that the offence is too trivial to bother reporting it to the police.

5. The victim may not wish to participate in the time-consuming procedures to which reporting may give rise.

6. The victim may be worried about other consequences of reporting, such as not being believed or having to face very personal and attacking questions in court. There may also be a fear of reprisals.

7. The victim may not want to see the offender punished because he is a child or a relative, friend, employee or employer.

8. The victim may not have any confidence in the criminal justice system.

9. The victim may consider that, in the circumstances, the official system is inappropriate, possibly because the property is returned or some form of

compensation is forthcoming, or because the victim is not altogether blameless or wishes certain activities to remain secret.
10. The victim may conclude that he or she has nothing to gain from reporting the offence.
11. The victim may feel that the offence should not be illegal.

The British Crime Surveys (BCS) represent an important means of countering some of these problems and also providing an additional authoritative source of crime statistics. The surveys take a sample of the population and interview them on their experience as victims of crime. One result is to uncover a great many crimes which are not reported to, or recorded by, the police. These findings will be partly used in this chapter to supplement other statistical sources, but we need to bear in mind that they, too, have limitations as an accurate record of the level of crime. They record all crimes told by adult victims to one of their interviewers. But this necessarily excludes; crimes against children; crimes against corporate victims; crimes against public sector property; and, of course, murders. If crime as indicated by the BCS is substantially greater than suggested by police statistics it is still far less than the actual figure, if that could be known. With that important caveat the BCS represent a substantial addition to our knowledge of the extent of crime.

For example, in successive *British Crime Surveys* (BCS) since 1984, the reason most often given for non-reporting of crimes was that the crime was too trivial to report (between 40 and 55 per cent); whilst next was that victims felt that the police would not have been able to do anything (between 23 per cent and 36 per cent). Recent BSCs found that offences which had the most serious consequences for the victim were most likely to be reported (two-thirds were reported as against a quarter of the least serious cases). This still meant that in 2001 almost 1.3 million of the most serious offences went unreported, a large number when one considers that only 2.2 million offences involving similar seriousness were reported to the police.

The degree to which crimes are or are not reported to the police also varies with the type of offence. Murders tend to have high rates of reporting. People often report their loved ones as missing; the police normally search for them; it is difficult to dispose of bodies; and discovered bodies are nearly always reported to the police. But even in the case of murder there is not 100 per cent reporting. The actual victim is clearly unable to report the offence, and sometimes discovery may depend on chance, as the case of Shipman showed. Harold Shipman, a family doctor, was finally convicted on 31 January 2000 of murdering 15 of his female patients, but the first report into the case said he had murdered at least 215 patients (2003). He also allowed others to die in extreme pain and then used the drugs prescribed for them to kill some of his victims. His crimes remained hidden for many years and only came to light by chance. Normally, however, a very high proportion of murders as the most serious of crimes, are reported. Crimes to property have become increasingly likely to be reported, probably largely due to increased insurance. In 1972 approximately 78 per cent of burglaries involving loss were reported; this rose to 90 per cent by 1987, but fell back to 77 per cent in 1999 (BSC, 1988 and 2000). Actual burglaries involving loss increased only 17 per cent, whilst recorded offences increased 127 per cent (nearly 8 times more). Insurance policies make it a normal condition of payment that the offence should have been reported. The reporting seems also to have affected recoveries. In 1972 only 19 per cent of property stolen as a result of burglaries was recovered through insurance, whereas in 1987, 58 per cent was so recovered (figures drawn from the BCS (1988)). Other offences are, for various reasons, rarely reported. For example, child sexual or other child abuse, domestic violence, rape (although recently the rate of reporting has increased due to better police response to and treatment of the victims, but it still remains a little-reported crime) and other sexual offences, driving offences, drugs related offences, fraud, blackmail and corporate crime. The 1998 survey showed that a low reporting rate was normal when the victim knows the offender, and this, along with a fear of reprisals, helped to explain the lowish reporting rates in both domestic violence (26 per cent) and acquaintance violence (34 per cent).

4.1.3 Police recording of crimes

The police have a statutory obligation to record crimes. There are a number of rules for the collecting of criminal statistics by the police, but the basic criteria for recording an incident as a crime are:

(a) there must be *prima facie* evidence, in the eyes of the police, that a notifiable offence has been committed (notifiable offences are basically the more serious offences such as violence against the person and serious property offences, and include all those which are indictable, see Chapter Two);

(b) the case must be sufficiently serious to merit police attention—i.e., any identified offender should in the normal course be prosecuted, cautioned or dealt with in some other formal way.

Clearly, these criteria allow different interpretation by different forces, different divisions within the same force and even different police officers. The police could not operate if they had to record and deal with every minor infraction of which they became aware: operational requirements demand selectivity. Each force has some discretion about how to operate in their area, and therefore to deploy their resources. Similarly, each police officer has to use discretion in performing his or her duties, resulting in further imprecision. Reports of crimes may be disbelieved, deemed trivial or not criminal. None of this is surprising, nor does it indicate that police officers are not performing their jobs; it is necessary for the smooth running of the force. However some crimes are intentionally excluded ('cuffed' meaning they disappear up the cuffs of the officer to whom they are reported) in order to avoid extra work or to improve clear up rates.

From the above it should become apparent that there are two ways in which the police recording of crimes may affect the figures. First, the rules for classifying and counting these incidents might change, and secondly, these rules and the incidents have to be interpreted by police officers when faced with a recording decision. Therefore, variations in the recorded statistics over time or place may reflect the way in which they are compiled more than the phenomenon they are intended to record.

The most important source of discrepancy comes in the rules for the recording of crimes by the police. The rules are set by internal force regulations, which can lead to differences between forces, and by Home Office directives concerning how criminal statistics are recorded. In 1998 the counting rules were altered so that a number of summary offences were moved into the notifiable offences list, most notable being common assault and assault on a police officer. The result was an apparent large rise in crimes of violence against the person when there may have been little or no change in behaviour. Since 2000 the Home Office has been working to alter the recording of crimes statistics (Simmons (2000)). It has been working towards two goals: to make the counting more consistent over all 43 police forces and to introduce a more victim-centred approach to crime reporting. All forces were supposed to have introduced these by the end of March 2002. The full effects have yet to be assessed but preliminary findings suggest that they will produce an apparent increase of about 3–7 per cent in recorded crime (Simmons (2001)).

Another statistical problem with police recording is that after an offence is classified in one way, this classification will generally not be altered, even if it later transpires that the offender is only convicted of a lesser offence. The only exception to this is the murder statistics, where if the offender is only convicted of manslaughter the figures can be altered at a later date. Similarly, incidents which may once have appeared as accidental deaths may later, on forensic or other evidence, be defined as murders and then again the statistics may be altered. These considerations necessarily affect the accuracy of the figures for any particular year.

Individual police officers can also affect the crime statistics by the way they make their decisions to record an incident as an offence or not. If an activity is reported to the police as a crime they may decide not to record it as such; a reported theft may be treated as lost property if the circumstances suggest that theft is unlikely. Or the police may decide that it is not a case which warrants reporting. For example, if it is not sufficiently serious, the police may still investigate but it will only be officially recorded if it comes to court. Again, the police may decide that the offence was committed too long ago to warrant investigation and therefore not record it (for further details see Coleman and Bottomley (1986)).

A further factor that appears to affect the level of recorded offences is the number of police officers. The fewer officers, the lower the officially recorded crime rates. This may be coincidence but may also account for some of the rise in recorded crime in the 1980s when police numbers were rising and might account for some of a later decline in recorded offences when police numbers have been declining. However, the relationship is not mechanical: since 2000 police numbers have been rising and recorded crime dropping. It may be this is due to a greater police workload through pro-active policing, the management of risk etc. (see Chapter Twenty).

According to Home Office (1999), the results of all these factors are quite considerable:

Table 4.1

Of every	100	offences committed:
only	45.2	are reported,
only	24.3	are recorded,
only	5.5	are cleared up,
only	0.8	result in a police caution,
only	2.2	result in a conviction,
only	0.3	result in a custodial sentence.

4.1.4 **Other official effects on crime statistics**

The final way in which the official *Criminal Statistics* may be inaccurate arises because many types of crime are controlled by bodies other than the police. The records of these bodies are not usually recorded in the *Criminal Statistics* unless they are brought to court, in which case they appear in the court records. Examples of such criminal activity are tax evasion, which is controlled and recorded by the Inland Revenue; VAT evasion and smuggling or related offences, controlled and recorded by the Customs and Excise; and breaches of factories legislation controlled and recorded by the Factories Inspectorate. The number of offences in this category may be very high, although the number of prosecutions and of convictions is often very low.

4.2 **Comparative problems with official statistics**

In the following sections other methods of assessing the extent of criminal behaviour will be considered, the most useful of which are crime surveys. It is necessary to note that the information on crime surveys is dependent on the methods used and the accuracy of the recording, and that comparisons between surveys in different countries need extreme caution. Despite these problems, comparisons can be interesting and constructive, especially when they are gleaned from research such as the highly respected International Crime Victimisation Survey (ICVS), which is alive to the problems of comparison and tries to reduce or eliminate their effects. The 1996 ICVS was a victim survey carried out in 11 Western industrialised countries (Mayhew et al. (1997)). The 2000 survey was carried out in 17 industrial countries (van Kesteren et al. (2000)) whilst Barclay et al. (2001) also provide a comparison of recorded crime in 32 countries. As they point out, differences in legal, administrative and statistical procedures make comparisons of absolute numbers hazardous but examination of trends should be more reliable. In this context, and restricting comparison to the average experience of all European Union Member States, the record of England and Wales between 1995 and 1999 is at one level encouraging: total recorded crime fell more rapidly than in the EU as a whole (by 10 per cent against 1 per cent); as did domestic burglaries (31 against 14 per cent); whilst thefts of motor vehicles, which rose 7 per cent in the EU, fell 27 per cent in England and Wales, and drug trafficking offences showed similar trends (a 31 per cent rise in the EU, but a 6 per cent fall in England and Wales). As is usual with crime statistics, however, the picture is more mixed than this would suggest. In particular violent crime rose faster than in the EU as a whole (by 20 per cent against 11 per cent), while a more recent ICVS study showed that in 1999 the percentage of victims for contact crime and burglary was higher in England and Wales than in any of the 17 countries considered except Australia (van Kestoren et al. (2000)). The number of persons in prison per 100,000 population was also higher in England and Wales in 1999 than in all the other EU Member States, except Portugal.

4.3 The dark figure of crime

From the above it should be evident that the criminal statistics do not represent all criminality which occurs in England and Wales. The criminal activity which falls outside this area is often referred to as the 'dark figure of crime'. Many criminologists have tried to assess the size of the dark figure. There are three methods used. First, estimates (or guesses). Many people have tried to estimate the real level of criminality in Britain, either for a particular offence or for crime in general. The estimates differ enormously, but all agree that a great deal of criminal activity (many estimate well over 50 per cent) goes undetected. Nothing further need be said about this approach, but the two other methods—self-report studies and victim surveys—need additional comment.

4.3.1 Self-report studies

In these, subjects are asked whether they have ever committed any particular type of offence. The survey can take the form of a questionnaire, in which respondents are asked to tick which offences they have committed and to record the frequency with which they have committed them; or of an interview, in which they may be asked about these activities in greater detail. Most of these studies require respondents to provide details of their social characteristics, such as class, race, religion, sex, age and certain other factors which sociologists may have used to explain criminality. This is because this research method is mostly used to test hypotheses about the reason for crime rather than to assess how much crime is actually committed. Nonetheless, self-report studies do record levels of criminal statistics above the official figures and so may be useful in assessing the dark figure, at least in respect of particular offences.

However, their use raises a number of problems. First, and most important, is the problem of validity. Are the subjects telling the truth? Theoretically, cross-checking is possible with family and friends, peer group members, and/or with official statistics, the police, teachers, employers and others in authority over the subject. Or lie detectors could be used. Such checks can never be exact or definite, and are often impractical.

Validity is also suspect because subjects may forget crimes they have committed; have rationalised them so that they do not consider them as crimes; wrongly characterise something as criminal when in fact it is not, or when they would in law have a legitimate defence; or, of course, they may do the opposite.

Finally, the sample is often not representative of the population as a whole. For example, nearly all actual self-report studies have been carried out on adolescents. These studies can be used for a discussion of the extra amount of juvenile crime; for testing the correctness of explanations of juvenile crime; or for assessing which groups of juveniles commit crime; but not more generally. Moreover, many of the studies have been carried out on young people in school. In thus missing truants and drop-outs, some say that they have excluded the two groups most likely to be criminal.

If one wishes to compare the results of self-report studies, a problem arises because each researcher chooses different crimes to include in their samples. Clearly, no research could include all crimes committed by juveniles, but the lack of uniformity complicates the comparison of results. This is especially true if the object is to test theories about why offences are committed when the types of crimes chosen may make it likely that certain groups will admit to more (or less) crime, which will slant the results.

Although they cast some light on the extent of the dark figure of crime, the main use of self-report studies is as a means of testing theories of criminality. In some cases these two uses are joined. For example, self-report studies have consistently shown that trivial offences are far more common amongst all social classes than official statistics suggest. Therefore they indicate a much higher actual rate of criminality than is indicated in the official statistics and more criminal behaviour than many of the theories would have us believe. Such qualifications are especially damaging for theories which predict that crime is related to some special physical (for example, increased testosterone, see Chapter Seven), mental (for example, a psychoanalytical problem, see Chapter Eight) or social (for example, class differences or strain, see Chapters Eleven and Twelve) characteristic, rather than related to the likelihood of being caught and punished, as is suggested for example in control theories (see Chapter Thirteen). Furthermore, self-report studies indicate that the serious crime rates for different social classes are not as great as the official statistics would have us believe: the dark figure seems to indicate less of a class split in criminality. Self-report surveys were given a new, wider and interesting lease of life when, in the 1992 BCS, those between the ages of 16 and 19 were asked about their own offending, and those between 16 and 59 were asked about misuse of drugs. Questions concerning youth crime now appear in the Youth Lifestyle Survey which surveys 12 to 30 year olds in England and Wales. The questions concerning drugs have been repeated in subsequent BCSs. The most recent analysis of the data is Aust et al. (2002). These studies have reinforced much of the work which had been carried out on drug use and the information has been used to advise government policy in the area.

Added to this self-reported information concerning those who commit crimes is the Offenders Index. This Home Office index contains information concerning all court appearances and therefore all convictions since 1963. In recent years this index has been analysed (see Prime et al. (2001)) to assess the levels of convictions of various groups and looked at age, life-style and sex differentials of offenders. It found that a third of males born in 1953 had a criminal record by the time they were 46 compared to only 9 per cent of women. This shows that for men at least offending is not restricted to the lower classes or to the young. The figures also show that repeat offending, or at least repeat convictions only arise in 8 per cent of the male population.

4.3.2 **Victim or crime surveys**

4.3.2.1 *Introduction*

These are the most frequently used and claim to be the most reliable indicators of the true level of criminality in a society. Victim surveys, or crime surveys as they are often called, measure rates of victimisation by questioning a randomly selected sample of the population about their experiences as victims of selected crimes. The results can be used to make fairly reliable estimates of the extent of those particular crimes in the society studied, and if similar surveys are carried out over intervals of time, then crime trends (for these offences) can be discerned. It is important to note that these surveys do not record the true level of crime in the State; they only help to estimate the level of particular crimes. Victim studies can never give a true picture of crimes such as those which do not have clearly identifiable victims, for example, pollution, violation of safety codes, dangerous products. Most crime surveys only study crimes against the person and/or property of private adult individuals. Even within this remit they are not well placed to measure consensual offences such as those involving drugs and consensual sexual offences. Corporate victims, such as companies, businesses, shops, clubs, schools and public services, are less often studied because victimisation is more likely to go unnoticed and no one person is likely to be aware of all offences committed. For example, fare evasion and shop-lifting may occur but go undetected; employees may commit crimes, particularly fraud or theft, and be well placed to hide their criminality; and companies may violate laws which have other companies as their unknowing victims. Crimes against children are also usually excluded.

Within these limitations crime surveys are a fairly good measure for individual victims and for the crimes they actually cover. They can also be useful in assessing whether any increases or decreases reflected in official crime statistics are genuine or whether they arise because people are reporting the incidents in an increasing or decreasing number of cases. In the case of crimes such as robbery and rape, which are thought to be relatively rare, both official statistics and BCS are bad indicators of the real levels in society, although the BCS is probably slightly more accurate.

A virtue of crime surveys is that most of them do not only count crimes. Most, including the BCSs (see below), collect additional information about crime, the victim, and the police. Official statistics provide very little information about victims, offences and offenders. Although many police forces have been trying to increase their information, crime surveys still collect, for the crimes which they cover, more of this extra information than do the police and other officials. Such surveys give a better idea of the groups of the population which are most at risk and why this extra risk arises, and can assess whether the high risk groups are also those who fear crime (these questions will be addressed in Chapter Five). Crime surveys can record both reported crimes and unreported crimes, and discern the differences between them and suggest why some offences are not reported (see above, section 4.1.2). They can look at public attitudes to the police and to preventing and dealing with crimes. They can study special areas such as crime committed against workers, or such special groups as ethnic minorities or the young. In these and other ways, therefore, crime surveys are a very valuable tool.

Crime surveys are not new. Sparks (1982) has discovered a reference to this idea in eighteenth-century Denmark. However, the modern use of them grew up in the 1960s in the United States, and the first modern national survey was carried out in 1972, again in the United States. The surveys relected a growing and widespread scepticism with the official statistics. National Crime Surveys have now been conducted in many countries. In Britain since 1972 the General Household Survey has intermittently recorded levels of victimisation of residential burglary. The first BCS covered crimes in England and Wales; a separate report covered Scotland. Since then there have been many BCSs, which are now conducted annually. There have also been a number of local surveys such as Kinsey's 1985 Merseyside study, the Nottingham study in 1985 by Farrington and Dowds, the Sheffield study carried out by Bottoms, Mawby and Walker and reported in 1987, the two Islington crime studies (Jones et al. (1986); Crawford et al. (1990)), the 1989 Hammersmith and Fulham study (Painter, Lea, Woodhouse and Young) and the Aberystwyth crime survey (Koffman (1996) which is one of the first to look at the levels of crime in more rural areas). The national surveys give an overall idea of the extent of crime, whereas the more localised surveys can pin-point problems of a particular area and can also be used to discover whether small environmental, particularly housing, differences affect criminality. Importantly, local studies have been more radical and have served to alter the BCSs over the years (Maguire (2002)).

As well as national and local surveys there are now, as indicated above, international crime surveys. Particular care must be taken in interpreting these as the figures will hide strong cultural differences between the victims in each State, between the law enforcement agencies, and in definitions of criminality in the various jurisdictions. International studies will not form part of the discussion in the rest of this work.

4.3.2.2 *How are surveys conducted?*

As an example of how these are conducted, the basic methodology of the BCS will be described. All surveys are based on a sample of the population. The larger and the more representative the sample the greater the accuracy of the results, but such surveys are more expensive to conduct; there is always a trade-off between expense and accuracy. In recent BCS one person over 16 was selected for interview in each of about 40,000 households in England and Wales. The sample was raised from 19,000 to permit analysis on the basis of police force areas as well as at a national level. Households were chosen from the Postal Address File by a system of random sampling. More inner city areas are chosen than would strictly have been included in such a sample. Already several problems arise. By choosing the sample according to households, the homeless, those living in temporary accommodation, and those living in institutions are completely excluded. This may bias the sample away from the least well off in society, who may also be most likely to be victimised. In addition, the inclusion of high levels of inner city constituencies is likely to give rise to high crime rates being discovered. Most surveys from 1988 have included a booster sample of ethnic minorities to discover their victimisation and their attitudes to, and experiences of, the police.

Each participant in the survey fills out a main questionnaire which includes some questions on attitudes, but the main aim of which is to discover whether the individual (in the case of assaults, robberies, thefts from the person, other personal thefts and sexual offences) or any member of the household (in the case of car thefts, other theft, vandalism of household property and domestic burglary) had been the victim of a crime in the last 12 months. The questionnaire is couched in everyday language such as, 'in the last 12 months has anyone done X to you?', where X is a layman's way of describing a crime, such as, 'has anyone got into your house without your permission, in order to steal?'. All respondents also complete a questionnaire about their personal details, and in more recent studies give information on their attitudes towards local crime or fear of crime. Those respondents who had been victimised are asked to fill out detailed information on the incidents (up to a limit of six) indicating where the incident took place; what happened; the offenders; whether the incident was reported to the police; satisfaction with the police and information concerning victim support. All studies then ask further questions of some or all of their respondents which are designed to record extra elements, such as fear of crime, contact with and attitudes to the police, and self-reporting offending. Each survey also asked about a few particular matters. So, for example, the 1998 survey included questions covering road rage, attitudes to juvenile offenders and knowledge of victim support. Since 1992 those between 16 and 59 have been asked about their own drug taking.

The results obtained from all the various questionnaires are then 'multiplied up' to give a crime rate which represents the whole population with which the survey is concerned.

The defects of any type of survey carried out in this way include:

(a) Respondents may forget about crimes, particularly the less serious ones, which gives an undue weight to serious crime and reduces the usefulness of the survey as an indicator of the real level of criminality in our society.

(b) Respondents may be mistaken about when the incident occurred. They may therefore include incidents which occurred before or after the relevant dates, or may exclude items which occurred within them.

(c) Respondents may remember an incident but not wish to reveal it to the interviewer. For example, if it was a sexual offence which the respondent finds embarrassing or difficult to talk about, or if an offence was committed by a member of the family or a close friend. To try to counter this problem computer-assisted self-interview forms have been introduced for issues such as domestic violence and sexual attacks, but even so much of this behaviour is probably missed.

(d) The respondent may not understand the question and therefore fail to report incidents.

(e) The respondent may not consider that a particular incident falls within the terms of a question.

(f) The respondent may invent an offence, possibly to appear interesting, to obtain the sympathy of the interviewer or to 'help' the interviewer.

(g) The respondent may purposely omit offences so as to speed up the process and get rid of the interviewer. This is particularly likely if they know that they will be asked for further particulars of offences.

(h) The surveys record that better-educated respondents are more able to recall relevant events, and this may give the survey a bias.

(i) The surveys record that middle-class respondents are more ready to define certain types of incidents as assaults, again giving the appearance of a relatively higher rate for this class than is actually the case.

(j) The British Crime Surveys always exclude those in institutions whose experience of crime may be very different from the rest of the population. They also exclude victimless crimes, and crimes against organisations, the State and children as well as motoring offences. Nor do they specifically ask about crimes committed by organisations. Some of the local surveys are better in these respects.

From the above it is obvious that certain inaccuracies are inevitable in these surveys. On balance, the inaccuracies are thought to undercount offences rather than overcount them.

4.3.2.3 *What crimes do crime surveys count?*

In 4.1.3 it was stated that police did not record all crimes. What do these surveys usually do? As was stated in 4.3.2.1, crime surveys only research into and record a small number of crimes, those against clearly identifiable victims and their property. Within these categories, however, they may include offences which would be too trivial to be recorded by the police. Unlike the police (see 4.1.3), the surveys record all crimes which are reported to them. This suggests that the survey counts are more accurate than the police count. Such a conclusion assumes that crime is a concrete and definite term, but the concept of a crime can vary from individual to individual. For this reason it is important that any survey or official figures should stick to a legalistic idea of crime. In Chapter Two above, crime was defined as a wrong to society involving the breach of a legal rule which has criminal consequences attached to it (i.e., prosecution by the State in the criminal courts and the possibility of punishment being imposed). Both police and survey counts depart from this strict rule but in different ways.

As was seen above, the police tend not to record crimes which they consider too trivial to require a prosecution, a police caution or other formal response, or those with insufficient evidence that a crime has occurred: they tend towards recording only those crimes which *would* be punished. They generally do not record: if they do not believe the victim; if it is unclear whether it is a crime or an accident (e.g., stolen property or lost property); if moral consensus is weak (for example, some forces do not prosecute or record possession of small quantities of certain drugs which are only for personal use).

Crime surveys tend to approach the problem in different ways depending upon the reason for the survey. The BCS believe all reports of crime, and count all incidents which fall within the letter of the criminal law: they record all offences which *could* be punished. Therefore the BCS contain crimes which are very trivial, and record as assaults and threats some incidents which, although falling within that idea, are not 'notifiable offences'.

Some incidents such as burglaries or thefts of, or from, cars will be considered as crimes by the general public, police and surveys alike. Other incidents such as some domestic troubles or family fights; scuffles in pubs, clubs or football grounds; fights outside such establishments; fights at school; incidents on sports fields; and minor criminal damage are technically criminal but may not be reported to the police, and even if reported they may not be recorded. However, if reported to the BCS, they will always be recorded. Some of the extra crimes recorded by the BCS may be fairly minor, but many are very serious indeed. In order to compare the BCS with official statistics, the surveys have a list of about three-quarters of their data set, called the 'comparable subset' which covers the information most frequently used.

4.3.2.4 *Size of the 'dark figure' as indicated by the BCS*

The BCS indicate a much higher level of crime than is recorded by the police. In those offence categories covered on the 2002/2003 BCS and which can be directly compared with police figures, the BCS estimated 9.5 million offences whereas the police recorded only 2.3 million. The implication is that, if the BCS are relied upon, the police figures record less than one quarter of all offences.

If it seems worrying that the recorded figures are a significant underestimate of actual criminality, some perspective is gained from the 1998 BCS summarised in Table 4.2.

In this context it is important to note that aggregates produced by the BCSs, which portray victimisation as a fairly rare occurrence, only portray national trends and gloss over the different expectations in, for example, inner-city areas and rural areas. Those living in the inner city have a higher expectancy of being victimised. In the Hammersmith and Fulham study, 40 per cent of women who lived in the area were frightened to go out after dark due to fear of crime, and one household in two had experienced serious crime within the previous 12 months. Fear of crime was high; dissatisfaction with the police was similarly high; and after unemployment, crime was the most important public issue facing the residents.

It is clear that each of the BCSs usefully sheds some light on the dark figure of crime—how large it is, what sort of crimes are included. Beyond this these surveys add to our understanding of crime because they are carried out regularly, allowing trends in crime and victimisation to be assessed. One of the most prominent claims made over the last three decades of the twentieth century was that crime has risen by record amounts, making it a major political issue, with politicians vying for position in solving the 'crime problem'. All records of crime, including both official statistics and the BCS, showed some increase. However, careful analysis of the trends indicated by the BCSs suggests that the increase may be less dramatic than has been claimed. One reason for this view can be seen in the trends in the proportion of crime which was reported (see BCS 2000, at p. 13). The strong indication is that a higher percentage of offences were being reported to the police,

Table 4.2

Overall risk	Types of groups or households most at risk
Only 5.6 per cent of households had a burglary	• Head of household: under 24; single parent; unemployed; private renter; income below £5,000. • Property: high physical disorder; inner city; council area; in flats; on main road.
Only 15.7 per cent of vehicle-owning households suffered a vehicle-related theft	• Head of household: unemployed; under 24; single parent; income below £30,000; private renter. • Property: inner city; high physical disorder; in flats; council area; on main road;
Only 4.7 per cent of individuals experienced a violent crime	• Person is: male 16–24; single parent; unemployed; private renter; female 16–24; income below £5,000. • Household is: in high physical disorder; inner city; in flats; council area.

implying that some of the apparent increase in crime is in fact due to an increase in its reporting. There is a variety of factors which lend further plausibility to such a conclusion: more coverage by insurance necessitating reporting; greater confidence in police action; increased ease in reporting due to larger numbers of private telephones and better access to working public telephones and possibly more mobile phones; higher owner-occupation; increased sensitivity to crime; and, importantly, the suggestion of the BCS that victims may now be less tolerant towards anti-social behaviour and criminal activity.

More recently this trend appears to have started to reverse, both the BCS and official statistics record that from about 1995 crime has been declining. Neither the rise nor the decline are as marked in the BCS data as in official statistics but the fact that they show some correlation suggests that the changes are real. Despite this fact the official statistics sometimes show dramatic changes in particular areas which are used to justify new laws and punishments which, if more reliance were placed on the BCS figures might not be justified. Is the present downward trend real? It may not be. Both sets of figures may be lulling us into a false sense of security about a declining crime rate as the incidence of more hidden consensual crime may be increasing and offences against non-individual targets may be increasing. There is some reason to believe this may be the case. The government's own figures recognise that problem drug-use has increased from 1995 onwards, from about 200,000 to 250,000. Many of these users commit other offences which may not turn up in either set of statistics. These users shoplift and sell to other users to support their habits. These offences are very likely to remain hidden from the police and are never reported to the BCS as all individual participants are consensual and commercial enterprises are not included. So it may be that the trend is not down but across to more invisible offences which are less likely to result in a conviction.

The BCS can also be used to assess the validity of claims about trends in crime based on single years of the official statistics. Usually these take the form of a government claiming to have achieved a reduction in some categories of crime which other statistical sources do not detect, or which hide an overall increase.

Lastly the BCS may be used to indicate changes in policy on the part of the authorities. For example, the rate of vandalism registered in successive BCS has remained almost level (with perhaps a slight decrease in household, as against vehicle, vandalism) although the overall crime statistics have doubled: more vandalism crimes must be being recorded. Interestingly, as will be seen in Chapter Sixteen, the increased perception of the seriousness of offences, particularly those of vandalism, is in line with the authorities having accepted some of the policies of right realists which suggests that policing is being seen as a public order, rather than just a law enforcement, issue. It also indicates less tolerance by members of the public.

Although victim surveys suffer from inaccuracies of their own, they are nonetheless useful for testing actual levels of offending and are even more important for measuring trends in both rates of victimisation and rates of the reporting of crime.

4.3.3 **Proposed new statistical measures**

In order to try to attain a better system the Home Office carried out a review of statistics (Simmons (2000)). This led to the change in recording practices referred to above but also recommended that the collection and use of statistical material should be 'modernised'.

The argument is that the present system is wedded to nineteenth-century aims and gives only a crude understanding of the problems of crime and the effectiveness of the system in countering them. The suggestion is to secure fuller information and, even more, for a 'more flexible view of information—one where we first define the problems requiring solution and then develop the information needed to better understand those problems' (Simmons (2000) ii). The official statistics derived from police activities would be abandoned and replaced by a broad annual picture drawn from a variety of sources and agencies, and which would be used to assess the operation of the criminal justice system. This new system of 'Crime Indexes' would focus on crimes reported by the public or activities, even if not criminal, about which the public are most concerned and would ignore areas of activity that are rarely reported by victims. Simmons looks forward to a time when victims' feelings of a problem are believed and the police do not intervene to assess whether it is a crime or whether it is serious: if the public report an incident it is serious; so, presumably, if they do not it is not. He also considers that the public should be supported in reporting incidents of disorder as well as crime and that these should be recorded and appear in the indexes.

The indexes are to break with the legal categorisation of offences so as to record social information about offences: when, where and how they were committed; whether by strangers or by someone known to the victim; was the victim an individual or a commercial enterprise; what the victim believes might be the motives of the offender; and the victims' assessment of the seriousness of the incident. The assertion is that this would allow the figures to be used to make a real evaluation of how well the authorities, police, other criminal justice system agencies, local government, central government etc. are delivering on their promises of crime reductions and would then be used to assess where resources should be focused.

At present (2003) these are simply proposals. But it needs to be registered that there are strong grounds for misgivings. Whatever advantage may be attached to such an approach the stress on flexibility will produce a fractured set of figures which would make it more difficult to identify and measure general trends. The closer link to aspects of behaviour which seem to concern the public (or sections of it) would necessarily weaken the connection with precise legal definitions of crime. In addition the reliance on victim reports might well mask such real problems as drug abuse and its associated criminality, white collar and corporate crime—presumably with the implication that resources be directed away from these. There is no necessary and direct relationship between victim reports and the seriousness of, or harm caused by, crime in general. Nor are the expected gains in the accountability of the system guaranteed: for example, the inclusion of beliefs about motives and seriousness raises problems of subjectivity when different persons will perceive the same activity in sharply differing ways. Finally, since all this detailed information is supposed to be relayed directly to the Home Office both from the police and other agencies, significant issues concerning data protection and the collection of personal data by the State need to be addressed.

The proposals are firmly in line with current Home Office policy and with the way in which the State, local partnerships and the criminal justice system seem to be moving—towards a victim led process with targets set, and 'problems' and 'risks' (real or apparent) to be addressed. This shift of interest over crime was discussed in Chapter Two, and the concerns with more specific crime reduction strategies and the emerging stress on risk will be explored in Chapter Twenty. Here suffice it to say that these proposals fit within this new social positioning of crime and criminology. One consequence is that much less weight will be given to offender information, but without this it is difficult to see how much of the crime problem could be genuinely addressed. A system focused on victims and managerialism seems better suited for coping with, rather than solving, problems. It is true that, as will be seen in Chapter Twenty, the balance of the work of the criminal justice system has been moved in the direction of crime management rather than solutions, but that tendency will be given a powerful further impetus by these proposals. Before that much more consultation and analysis is required to ensure that the claimed benefits will be attained and that the possible disadvantages have been assessed and, possibly overcome.

4.4 Conclusion

Official statistics give a distorted picture of criminality in Britain. The more involved the incident becomes with the criminal justice system, the less representative it is of the offence type. The least reliable statistics to use for an idea of the size of the crime problem, or the types of crimes committed, or the types of people who commit crimes, are the prison statistics. These are probably a better indication of the types of incidents which, and persons who, are institutionalised, rather than bearing upon crime more generally. Awareness of the various deficiencies which have been discussed is particularly important because criminologists necessarily use official statistics in support of their theories. An additional problem is that the statistics are probably a better measure of why people are caught and prosecuted than of why they commit crimes which is the central interest of criminolgists. The most obvious example of this is the use of official statistics to prove a class bias in criminality—usually that crime is more prevalent amongst the poor than the rich. As already shown, self-report studies suggest that the bias is not as strong as is indicated by official statistics, and if certain white-collar offences (see Chapter Three) were included then possibly there would be even less of a discrepancy. These problems with criminal statistics and with any estimate of the full crime problem should be borne in mind when studying the arguments of theorists about the reason for criminality (see Chapters Six to Eighteen).

For the crimes included, a better assessment of levels of criminality can be obtained from the BCS and it is also a better measure of trends but only for the offences measured. By any assessment both are rather crude measures and it may be time to search for new methods although the Simmons (2000) proposal is not wholly convincing as a better alternative, since it would not collect the data which may be useful to the resolution of crime as opposed to the management of crime and risk.

SUGGESTED READING

Annual and quarterly publications of crime statistics. See **http://www.homeoffice.gov.uk/rds/ statsprog1.html**, and **http://www.homeoffice.gov.uk/rds/hosbpubs1.html**.

British Crime Surveys. **http://www.homeoffice.gov.uk/rds/pdfs2/r182.pdf** (2002/3 survey).

Coleman, C. and Moynihan, J. (1996), *Understanding Crime Data*, Buckingham: Open University Press.

Maguire, M. (2002), 'Crime Statistics', in M. Maguire, R. Morgan and R. Reiner, *The Oxford Handbook of Criminology*, 3rd edn, Oxford: Oxford University Press.

Simmons, J. (2000), *Review of Crime Statistics: A Discussion Document*, London: Home Office. **http://www.homeoffice.gov.uk/docs/review.pdf**.

REVISION BOX *Types of statistics, their uses and limitations*

	Sources of statistics	Main uses	Main drawbacks
Official Crime Statistics	Police—mostly the police record of crimes reported to them and which they considered worthy of recording.	To assess performance of the criminal justice system. As an indicator of policy and funding.	Inaccurate: not all crimes are reported and not all reported crime is recorded. Apparent trends maybe misleading and a poor guide for policy.
Offender Surveys	Researchers— responses by individuals about their own criminal activity. Some questions have been included in the BCS, especially those relating to drug taking.	Mostly to test theories about the causes of crime and give more reliable guide of who commits crime. Official figures only give those caught and prosecuted. Better information on racial and social mix of offenders.	Too narrow to measure actual crime levels: usually only conducted on juveniles and for a small number of offenders.
Victim Surveys, BCS	Home Office— collection and analysis of answers to detailed questionnaires about rates of victimisation over the previous 12 months. Information on the offenders and views of victims on issues linked to crime.	To test accuracy of official crime statistics, and particularly trends. Increases breadth and texture of information on crime and its incidence. As a measure of the success and acceptability of the criminal justice system.	Only applies to a limited number of offences so cannot measure total level of offending. Mostly, omits: hidden areas of victimisation such as sexual offences and domestic violence; victimisation of children; companies; public services; organised crime; consensual offenders; homeless and those in institutions.

QUESTIONS FOR REVISIONS

1 What do the official statistics for recorded crime record? And what do they leave out?
2 What are offender surveys and victim surveys and do they fill the deficiencies of official statistics of crime?

REFERENCES

Aust, R., Sharp, C. and Goulden, C. (2002), *Prevalence of drug use: key findings from the 2001/ 2002 British Crime Survey*. Home Office Research Findings No. 182, London: Home Office. **http://www.homeoffice.gov.uk/rds/pdfs2/r182.pdf**.

Barclay, G., Tavares, C., and Siddique, A. (2001), *International Comparisons of Criminal Justice Statistics*, London: Home Office.

BCS, see British Crime Survey.

Bottoms, A.E., Mawby, R.I. and Walker, Monica, A. (1987), 'A Localised Crime Survey in Contrasting Areas of a City', *British Journal of Criminology*, vol. 27, p. 125.

Coleman, C. and Moynihan, J. (1996), *Understanding Crime Data*, Buckingham: Open University.

Crawford, A., Jones, T., Woodhouse, T. and Young, J. (1990), *Second Islington Crime Survey*, Middlesex: Middlesex Polytechnic, Centre for Criminology.

First Report on the Shipman Case (2003), *Death Disguised*, London: HMSO.

Hough, M. and Mayhew, P. (1983), *The British Crime Survey: First Report*, Home Office Research Study No. 76, London: HMSO.

Hough, M. and Mayhew, P. (1985), *Taking Account of Crime: Findings From the Second British Crime Survey*, Home Office Research Study No. 85, London: HMSO.

Jones, T., Maclean, B. and Young, J. (1986), *The Islington Crime Survey: Crime Victimisation and Policing in Inner City London*, Aldershot: Gower.

Kaufmann, L. (1996), *Crime Surveys and Victims of Crime*, Cardiff: University of Wales Press.

Kershaw, C., Budd, T., Kinshott, G., Mattinson, J., Mayhew, P. and Myhill, A. (2000), *The 2000 British Crime Survey: England and Wales*, Home Office Statistical Bulletin 18/00, London: Home Office.

Kinsey, R. (1985), *Merseyside Crime and Police Surveys: Final Report*, Edinburgh: Centre for Criminology, University of Edinburgh.

Maguire, M. (2002), 'Crime Statistics', in M. Maguire, R. Morgan and R. Reiner, *The Oxford Handbook of Criminology*, 3rd edn, Oxford: Oxford University Press.

Mayhew, Pat, Elliot, David and Dowds, Lizanne (1989), *The British Crime Survey: Third Report*, Home Office Research Study No. 111, London: HMSO.

Mayhew, Pat, Mirrlees-Black, Catriona and Aye Maung, Natalie (1994), *Trends in Crime: Findings from the 1994 British Crime Survey*, Research Findings No. 14, Home Office Research and Statistics Department, London: HMSO.

Mayhew, Pat and Van Dijk, Jan J.M. (1997), *Criminal Victimisation in Eleven Industrialised Countries: Key Findings from the 1996 International Crime Victims Survey*, London: Home Office.

Mirrlees-Black, Catriona, Mayhew, Pat and Percy, Andrew (1996), *The 1996 British Crime Survey for England and Wales*, Home Office Statistical Bulletin, Issue 19/96.

Mirrlees-Black, Catriona, Budd, Tracey, Partridge, Sarah and Mayhew, Pat (1998), *The 1998 British Crime Survey*, Home Office Statistical Bulletin Issue 21/98, London: Home Office.

Painter, K., Lea, J., Woodhouse, T. and Young, J. (1989), *Hammersmith and Fulham Crime and Policy Survey*, Middlesex: Middlesex Polytechnic, Centre for Criminology.

Prime, J., White, S., Liriano, S. and Patel, K. (2001), *Criminal careers of those born between 1953 and 1978*. Home Office Statistical Bulletin 4/01, London: Home Office. **http://www.home office.gov.uk/rds/pdfs/hosb401.pdf**.

Simmons, J. (2000), *Review of Crime Statistics: A Discussion Document*, London: Home Office. **http://www.homeoffice.gov.uk/docs/review.pdf**.

Simmons, J. (2001), *An Initial Analysis of Police Recorded Crime Data to End of March 2001 to Establish the Effects of the Introduction of the ACPO National Crime Recording Standard*, London: Home Office Website. **http://www.homeoffice.gov.uk/rds/pdfs/1201analysis.doc**.

Sparks, R.F. (1982), *Research on Victims of Crime: Accomplishments, Issues and New Directions*, Rockville, MD: National Institute of Mental Health, Centre for Studies of Crime and Delinquency, US Department of Health and Human Services.

Van Dijk, J.M., Mayhew, Pat and Killias, Martin (1991), *Experience of Crime across the World: Key Findings of the 1989 International Crime Survey*, 2nd edn, Deventer: Kluwer Law and Taxation Publishers.

Van Kesteren, J., Mayhew, P. and Nieuwbeerta, P. (2000), *Criminal Vicitmisation in Seventeen Industrialised Countries*, The Hague: WODC.

Walker, M. (ed.) (1995), *Interpreting Crime Statistics*, Oxford: Clarendon Press.

5

Victims, survivors and victimology

5.1 Introduction

A generation ago it would have been difficult to have found any criminological agency (official, professional, voluntary or other) or research group working in the field of victims of crime, or which considered crime victims as having any central relevance to the subject apart from being a sad product of the activity under study—criminality. To officials the victim was merely a witness in the court case, to researchers either the victim was totally ignored or was used as a source of information about crime and criminals. Until very recently there was a striking lack of information about victims, and even now the knowledge is sketchy, limited to certain crimes and often to certain types of victim. This ignorance is astonishing when one considers that the criminal justice system would collapse if victims were to refuse to cooperate. Some victims have found that their treatment by the officials in the criminal justice system—the police, lawyers, court officials, judges and compensation boards—to be too stressful, demeaning, unfair, disregarding of their feelings, rights, needs and interests. Sometimes they see the system as a second victimisation which can be more unpleasant than the original crime. In such cases they may well choose not to report or to cooperate in the future; their experiences may also affect their friends and family, and even the general public, spreading a general reluctance to cooperate. This syndrome is best known in rape cases but it also exists in other areas.

Various reasons might be suggested for this neglect of victims. In the early twentieth century many criminologists followed a positivist idea of crime, which involved the idea that an individual's criminal behaviour was determined by certain social or biological forces which they could neither control nor understand. In this model the criminal is seen largely as a victim. The notion of offender as victim implies his or her relative lack of responsibility for their criminality, and tends to focus attention on their need for help rather than on the needs of the actual victim. As was seen in Chapter Three the media colluded in this representation. Early Marxist or left wing criminology often saw the criminal as the victim, but in these writings the victimisation is through the use of power in labelling the offender, and in the bias of the way the law operates. The effect is again to make the literal victim invisible. Marxist theories may also serve to distance the victim from study by arguing that crime is an expression of political opposition to capitalism. In all these approaches the criminal and not the crime or its consequences is studied (for further discussions in each of these areas see Chapters Six to Eighteen). Part of the reason for this is that in Britain most of the funding for criminological research comes from central government, which was interested only in the problem of crime and not with the problems of vulnerability. In consequence, the attention of such research centred on the criminals rather than the victims. It is thus not surprising that much of the early interest in victims in Britain came from non-government funded research, from victim support schemes, and from feminist writers on rape, sexual assaults and violence against women and children. Much current critical analysis still comes from these sources. More recently, central government has become interested in victims, to the substantial exclusion of offenders, and more money has been made available. The focus on victims has led to offenders being seen mostly in their relation to victims: not to be understood or rehabilitated, but blamed, made responsible and given harsher sentences.

As a result interest in victims has increased and today it is central to the subject, to professionals, to officials and to the public. The media have given increased attention to the victim, and political responses include improved compensation awards which courts can both offer and make more important than such sentences as the fine; new funds available to agencies who offer help and support to victims, especially to Victim Support Schemes (VSS); and the use of screening and video-recordings for evidence given by vulnerable witnesses (Youth Justice and Criminal Evidence Act 1999 Part II). In addition Part 8 of the Criminal Justice Act 2003 would allow the use of video links to help the efficiency or effectiveness of a trial allowing children to give evidence by video-link or video recording (see, e.g., the Criminal Justice Act 1988, s. 32 as amended by the Criminal Justice Act 1991, s. 54). The police have also reacted positively, for example, they now occasionally provide rape suites and arrange screening for witnesses in identification parades. Unfortunately such provision is not universal. Some have argued the victim's place in the criminal justice system has been over-strengthened, upsetting the balance between the State and the offender where a crime is seen as an attack against the State or the society as a whole, and not just an attack on the victim.

There was some early work on 'victimology' which centred on the extent and way in which crime may be said to be 'precipitated' by the behaviour or lifestyle of the victim (Mendelsohn (1947)), or by some people being prone to attack (von Hentig (1948)). This early work has had a partial revival in recent years when, in certain controversial cases, particularly rape cases, it has been suggested that victimisation is precipitated or even caused by the victim. As one judge put it in 1989: 'As gentlemen of the jury will understand, when a woman says no, she doesn't always mean it.' In these accounts the criminal is portrayed as almost as much a victim as the victim herself. There has also been study of what victims can do to prevent crimes, suggesting again that the victim may in some way cause or precipitate criminal acts. This fits with the recent general trend to make individuals more responsible for the safety of themselves, their dependants and their property and is central to some of the questions asked of victims in the British Crime Surveys.

At the beginning of the 1970s there emerged in the US a number of groups concerned with: restitution or compensation for victims; the welfare of victims; groups of victims of particular crimes such as survivors of concentration camps, prisoners of war (especially Vietnam); the relatives of the victims of drunk drivers; the often hidden victimisation of women and children; and the victimisation of mental health practitioners. Although these groups were drawn from different backgrounds and had differing interests, they generally agreed on two issues: that punishments should be harsher; and that criminals should be made to pay. If the two could be merged through restitution, compensation or reparation, all the better. It was possibly more than coincidental that these groups were growing at a time when the belief that a criminal could be rehabilitated within, or by, the criminal justice system was dying: their stance was largely one of revenge. But they also argued that victims had certain rights which they could expect to be met, and needs which should somehow be addressed. These were taken up internationally by the United Nations in its 1985 charter for victims' rights entitled *Declaration on the Basic Principles of Justice for Victims of Crime and Abuse of Power*. This charter first specified ways in which victims should have access to judicial and adminis-trative procedures, be treated fairly and have their views considered; secondly, encouraged restitution (or compensation) by offender to victim; thirdly, encour-aged government funded compensation where the victim was poor; and finally suggested ways in which the victim may need assistance to recover from the ordeal. More recently the UN published *a Handbook on Justice for Victims*, 1999. The Coun-cil of Europe similarly addressed the problems of victims' rights and produced the European Convention on the Compensation of Victims of Violent Crime (1983, this entered into force in Britain on 1 June 1990) and guidelines, *Recommendation on the Position of the Victim in the Framework of Criminal Law and Procedure*, 1985 (Council of Europe Recommendation No. R(85)11 of the Committee of Ministers to Member States). The Convention deals with compensation for the victims and the guidelines deal with the treatment of victims by State agents such as the police and courts, and the assistance which victims need.

In Britain, as in much of the rest of Europe, most of the focus has been on providing practical services to victims rather than on addressing their rights in a criminal justice or legalistic way (although the Human Rights Act 1998 might change this in future). Much of the work so far has been done by VSS, which started in 1974 in Bristol to fill a gap in provision for those involved with crime. It was started by the National Association for the Care and Resettlement of Offenders, on the assumption that victims too had needs which were not being met. These needs soon became very apparent and the VSS grew very quickly. Almost all of its work was initially done by volunteers, but as the numbers of serious cases needing long-term support grows it has been being forced towards professionalism. VSS has largely avoided any political arguments on the position of victims in the British system. Other important victim agencies in Britain are the Rape Crisis Centres (RCC) and shelter homes or refuges. These deal with survivors of sexual abuse and violence perpetrated against women. They provide them with three types of sup-port; advice and information; help in resolving practical difficulties; and emotional support in helping to deal with the offence. Similarly, the 1996 Home Office book-let entitled 'Victim's Charter' is only a statement of what should be good practice on the part of the criminal justice organisations; it does not give the victim any legal rights. This seems likely to continue through the present revision process (Home Office (2000a) and (2003)).

This chapter will act as an introduction to an interesting, still developing and dynamic area of study. Its focus on a rather narrow conception of victimisation, should not obscure the possibility of criminals also being victims. As the United Nations *Declaration on the Basic Principles of Justice for Victims of Crime and Abuse of*

Power makes clear, far more victimisation occurs as a result of the actions of governments and of business institutions than ever arises from what are defined as crimes under national laws, and furthermore that much traditional criminal victimisation is caused by social victimisation often resulting from the actions of governments and businesses. Thus when the authorities use the plight of victims to sustain or back up particular criminal justice and sentencing policies it is necessary to enquire behind their motives and question who will be the real winners if such policies are accepted and become law. In addition, before embarking on a consideration of the plight of victims of crime, it must be remembered that this will include a consideration only of those who suffer from what the State has defined as criminal behaviour and, as the last two chapters should have made clear, this is sometimes a fairly arbitrary group of activities. Lastly, the press, as is clear from the last chapter, have their own idea of 'victim', particularly 'deserving victim', and use their immense influence to convince others of that idea. All of which reinforces the initial caveat that the definition used here is necessarily restricted.

5.2 The extent of the problem

One of the first ways in which the extent of the problem became known was as a side product of the crime surveys described in the last chapter. In these surveys people are asked whether they have fallen victim to certain crimes over a fixed period. As already indicated, and will be confirmed below, they showed that crime and victimisation were more widespread than had hitherto been believed, while demonstrating that not everyone was equally in danger of victimisation. As their value as indicators of information about victims became more obvious, so more questions were included to discern the position of victims, their satisfaction or otherwise with the criminal justice system, and the feelings and fears of the general public about crime. Different surveys, by including different questions, consider discrete areas of these puzzles. This chapter will be mainly concerned with the British Crime Surveys (BCS), each of which contains important questions about victims and victimisation. Other surveys will also be considered where these provide more detailed information on a particular area (see Chapter Four): a more general assessment of victim surveys is provided by Zedner (1997), pp. 580–6.

Before further consideration is given to such surveys, one of their main limiting factors must be recalled. Victim surveys study only personal victimisation and largely street crimes. Therefore, 'victimless' crimes are excluded from study, as are many crimes committed at work where the employer or company is the victim or where another company, the general public, a government body or other body is victimised by a company. One survey which redressed this balance was the second Islington crime survey (Pearce (1990)) which included questions concerning victimisation of individuals by corporations and businesses and found high levels of such victimisation. Victimisation of individuals as consumers, tenants and workers was perceived to be more extensive than their victimisation in street crimes. The design and approach of most of the surveys tend to exclude victimisation which takes place in private, or between friends or relations, especially domestic violence, and to miss sensitive crime areas such as rape and sexual assault even where these are between strangers. Finally, in almost all such surveys it is adults who are questioned: the extent and type of criminality against children is not understood or documented, and the effects of crime on children are also largely ignored. This is changing. Apart from the inclusion of those aged 16 in more recent BSCs, there have been several highly publicised cases of the abuse of children in care homes and by nuns and priests.

With these limitations in mind, some interesting and useful information is forthcoming. Certain groups (e.g., those living in the inner cities, the young, ethnic minorities) will suffer far higher victimisation. Apart from the uneven distribution, those who suffer most are those who can least afford the loss and to whom even a small loss may be devastating. Recent studies have also categorically shown that 'victimisation predicts further victimisation', thus what is happening is not so much an increase in the total number of people becoming victims, but for victims to suffer more than once (Shaw and Pease (2000)).

What the figures cannot record are the practical and emotional consequences which often accompany victimisation. Among the practical difficulties might be having to cope without a car, or without some other object, time spent in giving evidence or completing insurance claims. For those suffering a physical crime, practical problems might include loss of earnings, pain, inability to perform certain tasks either in the short term or at all. Emotional problems might include anger, frustration, annoyance, depression, fear, loss of confidence, stress, difficulties in sleeping or other health problems. These emotional consequences were more common and strongest among those who suffered a personal attack or a burglary.

Nor can the figures record the severity of the crime to the victim. A burglary or robbery may involve a few pennies or thousands of pounds. Crimes range from being a minor inconvenience to great personal suffering, even totally ruining a person's life. But the figures do show that victimisation is widespread.

5.3 Who is at risk and why?

The general risks of victimisation disguise the greater real risks for some groups. Individuals within certain groups may fall victim to many offences in a year whereas others in different subgroups may never, or only very rarely, experience a crime. Furthermore, a person's lifestyle may affect the likelihood of victimisation. Successive BCS found that those most at risk of robbery were young males who live in inner cities or other densely populated areas and who go out a lot in the evening. The stark figures concerning victimisation overestimate the likelihood of criminality occurring to many in society, but underestimate the probability for those who are prone to victimisation.

Successive British Crime Surveys have shown that the risk of victimisation varies between types of community and is related to personal characteristics. Amongst the factors associated with the risk are the type of area people live in, their financial resources, their household structure and their lifestyles. Analysing the information into stranger violence and acquaintance violence also produces interesting differences especially on a sex basis. In every group the most important connector is still youth, the 16–29 age group carried with it the highest risk. But in acquaintance violence other high-risk factors, for both men and women, were: being unmarried; having children under 12; and living in an area where the rate of incivilities was high. Against this the rates for stranger violence differed for men and women. For men, age and lifestyle variables (drinking, going out frequently etc.) were important; for women only area of residence and marital status were important, but when cases of mugging were removed from the victimisation of women, lifestyle and age again became strong risk factors (most muggings involving women are of older married women). The nature of the risk also varies for men and women. Men were the victims of 83 per cent of assaults by strangers: women were the victims in 70 per cent of all domestic assaults.

It is admitted that the surveys do not adequately assess crimes of violence against women, particularly rape or crimes committed against them in their own homes by friends or relatives. Some women may not see offences committed in the home as criminal or may not feel able to reveal them, perhaps because their assailant is in the same room when the interview is being conducted, or because they are embarrassed. From other evidence it is known that women suffer a large amount of violence, much of which is committed in their own homes by people known to them. In fact the 1998 survey found that a quarter of all violent crime was domestic and a further 43 per cent involved people who were acquainted in some other way (British Crime Survey (1998)). Such violence is often perceived as less 'criminal' than offences committed on the street and by strangers (see Stanko (1988)). Police and society often treat the latter more seriously than the former even if the physical effects are the same.

An exception is violence against street workers, mostly women, which is both endemic and not yet taken seriously by the authorities. In fact many of the offences which are ignored involve violence against women (Campbell and Kinnell (2000–2001)). Using government figures, Wong (2000–2001) shows that 'one in four women experience domestic violence in their lives (Mirrlees-Black (1999)), seven out of ten women under 30 worry about being raped (British Crime Survey 1998) and every week two women are killed by their current or former partners' (official statistics).

Although 8,400 cases of rape were reported in 2000, this only represents about 15 per cent of all occurrences. Of those reported only about 10 per cent get to trial and only about 3 per cent of those result in a conviction. The growing group seems to be 'acquaintance rape' and the victims of this are often fairly young (Harris and Grace (1999), Women's Unit (1999)). Myhill and Allen (2002) found that almost 1 per cent of women had been sexually victimised in the previous year and almost 0.5 per cent had been raped, this would mean that 61,000 women were raped in 2000. They also estimated that about 750,000 women had been raped at least once since age 16.

In crimes of violence repeat victimisation is common. About a third suffer more than one incident and 16 per cent suffer three or more incidents compared with 19 per cent and 7 per cent respectively for burglary. Violence is also the largest growing area of victimisation.

Clearly the system is failing victims of violence, particularly women. The reasons are likely to be complex but as Stanko (2000–2001) points out it is likely to be related to the fact that we tend to simplify violence into statistics or types and do not take sufficient notice of the detail surrounding the violence the 'who, what, when, where are critical social and demographic features of social relations to begin to sketch out why violence happens, what it means to the parties involved, what social resources these parties use to manage its impact, and which institutional support might be available to minimise its impact'. In brief it is essential to understand the social context of violence as well as the individuals involved in the situation to be able to respond to it and reduce it.

5.3.1 Victimisation in and out of the workplace

Victimisation in the workplace is becoming more common and yet it attracts little interest. In 2000 the British Crime Survey estimated that 17 per cent of all violent incidents occurred in or around the workplace and Budd (1999) calculated that there were 1.2 million incidents of violence at work in 1997. The problem is therefore enormous. Hopkins (2000–2001) used figures from the retail sector to suggest that employees are more at risk of violence in the workplace than individuals outside that environment. However, when looking at the whole picture Budd (1999) suggests that this is not the case, though it may be that they are more at risk for the time they spend at work than they are in the outside environment. Within the workplace the dangers vary: in smaller businesses, service-sector workers (especially pubs, fast-food outlets and bookmakers) are most at risk, closely followed by the retail industry (Hopkins 2000–2001). Within the retail industry in particular, much of the violence is racially motivated (Ekblom and Simon (1988)). However, the wider picture is very different showing that police officers, social workers, probation officers, and security guards are most at risk of violence at work. Other high-risk groups are workers in health, transport (public and private), welfare, and such retail civil servants as benefit staff (see Budd (1999)).

The reporting of such incidents is low. Gill (1999) has suggested that 1 in 9 shop workers had been attacked in the previous year but many failed to report fearing that they might be blamed or because they thought they might have contributed to the situation. In 1998 he discovered that only 12.2 per cent of incidents of verbal abuse at work had been reported.

The effects are, however, substantial. Budd (1999) estimates that three-quarters of victims are emotionally affected by the incident and the BCS 1998 estimated that 3.3 million work hours were lost as a result of this violence. In the long run, of course, this means that any extra costs will be passed on to customers or that the firms will cease to trade, or cease to trade in that location which then has knock-on effects for the wider society. In the public sector it means that provision of such services becomes more costly and recruitment is adversely affected. There is also evidence that crimes against small to medium-sized businesses are very high (Gill, (1998 and 1999) and Wood et al. (1997)). It is clear that much victimisation is suffered in the workplace and that this has extreme consequences for society. Employers are under a duty to regulate the danger through the Health and Safety at Work etc. Act 1974 but the scale indicates that there is a need for more guidance and for employers to adopt positive strategies to reduce the danger to staff.

5.3.2 **Ethnic minorities**

Successive British Crime Surveys have indicated that both Afro-Caribbeans and Asians suffer more victimisation than whites. This finding is true over many of the crime areas studied. Part of the discrepancy is explicable by locational and demographic differences between whites, Afro-Caribbeans and Asians. Both Afro-Caribbeans (70 per cent) and Asians (40 per cent) are more likely than whites (17 per cent) to live in the highest crime risk inner city areas, and to be more transient and less residentially stable. They tend to have lower household incomes. They have a larger proportion of young people and higher rates of unemployment. Asians tend to fall in between whites and Afro-Caribbeans on all these lifestyle differences, and they also tend to have more stable family backgrounds than either whites or Afro-Caribbeans. Asians were more socially tied to the family, rarely going out at night. However, even having taken this into consideration, the risk to these ethnic minority groups still tends to be higher than for whites.

Interestingly, Afro-Caribbeans were more likely than Asians and significantly more likely than whites to be victimised by other Afro-Caribbeans. This appears to back up the assertion often made that crime is more often intra-racial than it is inter-racial, and that black criminality is a problem mostly because it victimises other blacks rather than because of the small victimisation of whites which may occur (see Roshier (1989)). As a general statement it is, however, misleading to present crime as largely intra-racial. There is no doubt that both ethnic minority groups, but particularly the Asians, see much of the victimisation as being racially motivated. An analysis of all the BCS since 1988 suggests that the offences most often seen as racially motivated are assaults, threats and incidents of vandalism. The racial nature of much of the criminality against racial minorities is borne out in many other studies and has been well documented both here and in the States.

There is much evidence that many members of the ethnic minorities suffer name calling, rubbish or excreta dumped on their premises, urine through the letter box, racist graffiti on their premises, damage to property, being spat at, having missiles such as milk bottles or rotten fruit thrown at them, and being punched or kicked (see Houts and Kassab (1997), Phillips and Sampson (1998 and *Criminal Justic Matters* 2002)). For some, everyday life is frightening, never knowing when the next attack may descend. Families, particularly the women and children, end up almost as prisoners in their own homes, but even here they do not feel safe. Normal activities such as shopping or visiting friends can be hazardous.

The most telling factor in racial victimisation is the institutionalised racism highlighted by the MacPherson report (1999) into the death of Stephen Lawrence. The report found that racism was endemic within the force and led to the police failing to perform their functions properly in this and probably in other cases. Lawrence was killed in south London on 22 April 1993. The police consistently failed to treat his death as a racist murder or to follow up lines of evidence that might have solved the crime. At the inquiry they tried to undermine the evidence from the family. Only very late in the day did the Metropolitan Police Commissioner, Sir Paul Condon, intervene and apologise for their failures. The MacPherson report was damning of the Met and saw institutional racism as endemic in official criminal justice agencies. The report defined a racist incident as one which is perceived as such by the victim or any other person (recommendation number 12). This means that both black-on-white and white-on-black incidents are similar and removes the essential power differential or dynamic from the problem. However, it has provided a very wide concept of racism which allows authorities to ensure they share information in as many cases as possible so as to eradicate the problem. Interestingly in many of its conclusions the report was not new, the Scarman Report (1981) covered similar ground but, unlike in the early 1980s, in 1999 senior politicians and senior figures in the public services such as the police were willing to take the MacPherson Report seriously. There were 70 recommendations. Sixty of them referred to the police; many of these also applied to other criminal justice agencies (the Local Government Association identified 30 that apply to them). The remaining 10 applied to other agencies such as the Crown Prosecution Service, local authorities, education authorities and others. There were four areas addressed by the recommendations:

- the inadequacies of the Metropolitan Police investigation;
- racism and institutional racism in all public services;
- more effective measures to deal with racial harassment and attacks; and
- the eradication of racism among children and young people.

Even as the very public Lawrence case was moving towards an inquiry other high-profile incidents were unfolding. In Cardiff on 19 August 1997 two black teenagers, Marcus Walters and Francisco Borg, were the victims of a racist attack which was witnessed by at least three police officers and caught on CCTV. Yet it was the black youths who were subjected to a violent arrest in which CS gas was used, and were charged. Some nine months later, following much pressure, the charges were dropped. Their white attackers were eventually charged and convicted but neither the police nor the Crown Prosecution Service was particularly vigilant in ensuring this outcome.

More recently in 2000, and after the MacPherson Report, Robert Stewart bludgeoned to death his cell mate Zahid Mubarek on the eve of his release from Feltham Young Offenders' Institution. It seems that Stewart had made clear his racial hatred and yet the prison authorities did nothing to ensure that he could not inflict harm on anyone from an ethnic minority. The Bradford Riots of 2001 showed institutional racism was still present. Asian youths rioted violently on the streets of Bradford causing much damage to property and serious injuries to the police and others. Understandably there was anger at the actions of a few but less understanding of the frustration and feelings of exclusion which spawned the violence. The desire on the part of the authorities was to punish the perpetrators: equal weight needed to be given to the resolution of the problems not just in Bradford but elsewhere (Commission for Racial Equality (2002)).

This institutional racism leads at best to a flagrant disregard for the rights and needs of ethnic minorities and a failure to protect them, and at worst to an official victimisation of these groups or members of these groups. Mere inaction on the part of the authorities, particularly the police, can lead to greater fear, and feelings of being abandoned by the system which should protect them. This may result in the ethnic community rallying together and protecting each other but this carries a danger of vigilantism. A preferable approach would be for problems which emanate from within a community to be addressed by those within it. In a positive desire to recognise and respect cultural differences some police areas have allowed a certain amount of this self-policing to take place. However, this approach can also lead to greater problems as noted by Siddiqui (2000–2001). She writes about problems noted by cases brought to the Southall Black Sisters of police unwillingness to address domestic violence in ethnic minority communities. This failure leads black women to suffer grave deprivation of rights, liberty and violence from which it is extremely difficult for them to escape because of cultural, linguistic, economic and other problems. The police failure to respond, even if based on a desire to respect cultural difference, allows this suffering to continue.

Following the very public and damning MacPherson Report and other high-profile incidents there have been changes. In particular:

- The Crime and Disorder Act 1998 introduced new racially aggravated offences for which higher maxima are applicable than for their non-racially aggravated equivalents.

- Police services have been brought within the scope of the Race Relations Act 1976.

- There have been changes in actions, certainly on the part of the police. In the year ending March 1999 racial incidents recorded by the police were up by two-thirds on the previous 12 months (from 13,900 to 23,000) and then seem to have stabilised at around that figure. This shows a real change in attitude from the denial of racist crime that was apparent in the 1980s and for most of the 1990s.

There is still a long way to go. Some police areas where ethnic minorities suffer have failed to respond positively. Many officers are in denial that there is a problem whilst some senior staff seem to be complacent that strategies have been designed which should help to counter the problem so feel they have dealt with the issue and can move on. There is a danger in this, and it is unlikely that the racial victimisation of ethnic minority communities has been fully recognised, understood, or even fully accepted.

5.3.2.1 *Hate crimes*

There is an argument that the authorities should also be looking at hate crimes and prejudice more widely. Clearly hate crimes vary in seriousness—from genocide, ethnic cleansing and serial killing at one end to name calling and harassment at the other. They all degrade the individual simply because of the group to which they are seen to belong: perpetrators of hate crimes see their victims as a type 'them' not 'us'—rather than as individuals with rights and feelings. If this is very clearly felt in racial crimes as can be seen from the previous section it is also evident in other areas of difference; religious difference, or differences within religions; against women (especially in the areas of domestic violence and sexual offences); in sexual differences such as homosexuality (often homophobia is recognised as a hate crime by official agencies), transsexuals etc.; against travellers; against those with disabilities (or who are differently able); against asylum seekers and refugees.

There has rightly been much focus on racial hatred and discrimination which needs to be tackled and solved. However, this is only part of the problem/equation. There is a need to address all forms of violence based on dislike of a group. There is also a need to look at the wider culture: as Moran (2002) suggests in a homophobic society a homophobic crime is not defined as a hate crime.

There are other related problems—we should not categorise all offences between two groups as acts of hate. Two recent studies (Ray and Smith (2002) and Kielinger and Stanko (2002)) concluded that the concept of hate crime was too simplistic to explain most of the violence in their studies. The connection between hate and crime is often complex and may also be associated with resentment, fear and possibly also exclusion on the part of the perpetrator as well as the victim. Merely to label these crimes does not deal with the problem, there is a need to address the difficulties arising in the communities, or more often the community (they usually share much in common) from which both perpetrator and victim are drawn. Furthermore, once discovered, convicted and punished the perpetrator may feel that they are themselves on the receiving end of hatred, from society, particularly if they are punished more severely for the act.

All this raises difficult questions. Should there be legal definitions such as that in the Crime and Disorder Act 1998 which only recognises racially motivated crimes or should they be dealt with under a broad head of hate crime or even just as normal crimes? There is much debate about the effectiveness of the law to deal fairly with these issues: broadening out the idea of hate crime has many knock-on effects on rights and freedoms. It also gives the police the power to intervene on grounds associated with expression, thought and beliefs and might therefore cause more problems of feelings of discrimination than they solve. In any event passing laws and forming policies to counteract these crimes and feelings of racial or other institutional discrimination does not get rid of it.

5.3.3 Other groups at risk

Some crimes and victims are rarely assessed by the BCS and yet have been calculated to be large problems for certain sectors of the population. Sexual and domestic violence against both women and children falls into this category. The group least studied, at least until very recently, is that of child victims. Before 1992 child victims had never been the subject of a BCS, which only questioned those over 16. The plight of children was brought to the fore mainly through the work of feminist writers who often included them in studies of women as victims or survivors. More recently children have been the centre of a few studies. The areas which have received most emphasis have been child physical abuse and child sexual abuse. As yet there has not been much study of the effects of more ordinary crime on children and the effects of indirect victimisation.

Child physical and sexual abuse became the subject of much media coverage in the late 1980s and 1990s. It was claimed that these crimes were increasing but it may be that, although they have always occurred, only now are they being recognised. The levels of these offences are difficult to assess. Like rape and other sexual and physical abuse of women, they rarely come to light and are rarely studied. These offences also raise problems of definition. They are often not legally defined separately from offences committed on adults or, at least, are not all legally defined together.

For example, should any definitions only cover actual violence and neglect or should they also deal with psychological abuses which may be much more difficult to pin-point and to fit into any form of criminal behaviour? Such psychological abuses are probably best left out of the present discussion whilst still noting that they may occur and have great effects upon the children involved. Child physical abuse is a prevalent occurrence; both sexes suffer it and both perpetrate it. It can also fall outside the family, or at least outside the immediate family. It only requires a relationship of care, which may be one in which the abuser is a baby-sitter, child minder, nanny, teacher or a friend of the family into whose care the child has been entrusted. This aspect has been given great prominence by some very public revelations of abuse in some official children's homes and by a few Catholic priests and nuns. When these relationships are also included, the instances are even more widespread.

Child sexual abuse is also difficult to define. Russell (1984) helpfully splits it into two distinct types of behaviour, namely, extra-familial child sexual abuse and incestuous child abuse. Both include any form of sexual contact or attempted sexual contact, but in extra-familial abuse the victim must be under 14 (or 18 if the offence is rape), whereas incestuous abuse goes up to 18. In San Francisco, Russell conducted one of the clearest and most detailed assessments of the extent of such offences and discovered that 31 per cent (two-thirds of whom were under 14) experienced extra-familial sexual abuse, and 16 per cent (three-quarters of whom were under 14) suffered incestuous sexual abuse. Paediatricians support the existence of these sorts of levels. One abuser perpetrates sexual acts against more than one victim and that all children, or at least all children of the same sex (usually female), within the family are likely to be victimised.

Child sexual abuse has normally been portrayed either as a violent street offence or as taking place in the child's own home and with members of its family, but recent police work has uncovered large numbers of child abusers or paedophiles. The first official estimate of the scale of the paedophile problem in England and Wales was conducted by the Home Office in 1997. It found that there were 110,000 men who had been convicted of offences against children (*Guardian*, 19 June 1997). Such criminals, all of whom have so far been found to be male, work in rings or networks passing on videos of their experiences and even sharing the victims, often young boys, between them. More recently concerns have been expressed at the use of the Internet for these purposes, for example 7,000 names and addresses of those who had viewed child pornography on a particularly vicious child pornography site had been passed to the UK police in 2002 (Russell (2002)). Many of those so far investigated were not previously labelled as having a sexual interest in children suggesting that paedophilia is more widespread than previously believed. Very often the criminal activity begins because the first abuser is a friend of the child's family, but some children are bribed with offers of sweets or other inducements into trusting these men, and now computer chat rooms are also used. These are the least studied and least suspected types of criminal sexual behaviour. In the late 1980s special police work was started in this area, and a number of rings have been discovered and their members prosecuted and gaoled.

In both child physical and sexual abuse, figures now show that a large and grave problem exists which is still little recognised. Little is done for the children who suffer this violence, which very often comes from those closest to them—parents or step-parents. Children may also be very badly affected by other offences committed against them. Unfortunately, the spotlight which has been placed on child victims of sexual and violent crimes has not carried over into the less dramatic victimisation of children: the routine, but not trivial, acts of violence committed against children both by adults and by other children (especially bullying); acts of theft committed against them, and such acts as harassment. In these cases their victimisation, though often ignored, can cause great emotional distress. They need to be addressed.

Lastly, there are the indirect victimisations which may occur. Children may be aware of, or actually witness, crimes, especially those committed by one member of the family against another or by one peer against another. They may be affected by household crimes such as burglary which affect the whole family. None of these may in themselves constitute specific crimes against the children, but they can be distressing to the child and could have lasting detrimental effects. The children are often the ones who take longest to recover from the violation.

From this it is clear that victimisation is a more common and everyday experience for some groups than for others; that some suffer more from certain crimes; and some are more adversely affected than others. The likelihood of victimisation can be understood only in this context.

5.3.4 **What is a victim?**

The preceding sections have centred on what has been described as positivist victimology—the identification of factors that lead to criminal victimisation, some of which may be attributable to the victims themselves. Much of this focus comes from an assumption that victim is a term to be used for clear individual suffering or is defined by law and dealt with by the criminal justice agencies. Even within this certain types are prioritised—largely those commonly known as street crimes. The feminist movement of the 1970s and 1980s forced attention on to new areas of criminal concern such as rape, domestic violence, child abuse and sexual harassment. These served the purpose of moving attention at least in part to the private home sphere instead of just the street and to recognition of many perpetrators as relatives or acquaintances not strangers. Of course, men can also be domestic victims, but the extent of this is very unclear. There are, however, other versions of victim and harm, such as victimisation by and of businesses where, for example, few view insurance fraud as a victimisation.

In addition, the increased attention which has been given in recent decades to issues of human rights has highlighted the extent to which State actions has violated these. The consequence has been the emergence of surveys of victimisation by agents of the State (see, for example, Ruggiero (1999a and b) and (2000), Scraton (1999) and James (1999).

More recently again there has been study of a new field of zemiology. People working in this area concentrate on the effects, and particularly the social harm, caused by actions (Hillyard and Tombs (2001)). They study all social harm whether it has 'physical, psychological or financial consequences for an individual, family or community' (Hillyard and Tombs (2001), at p. 11). This permits the widest possible concept of victim and allows the assessment of levels of harm from such general causes as poverty and social exclusion, thus making the potential number of victims very large.

All of this suggests that the concept of 'victim' is not as simple as the previous sections have assumed. Even taking account of differing views of what activities should be recognised as giving rise to victims such as domestic violence, date rape, rape in marriage or State violence; or differing views of what constitutes harm (a concept outside present definitions of crime), we have still not fully explored the depths and complexities of the concept of 'victim'. Who decides which individuals are victims? Is it merely an attribute which is simply used to label someone who suffers from criminal activity or does the individual have any power over its use? I might fall 'victim' to criminal activity but choose not to report it to the police, it may be too trivial or perpetrated by a member of my family or a myriad of other reasons but should I still be labelled a victim? The whole ethos of victim surveys assumes that anyone who is on the receiving end of a crime is necessarily a victim, that it is merely a case of counting them in but those conducting the BCS survey have often noticed that many 'victims' of non-reported crimes considered their victimisation to be too trivial to bother with, they did not really consider themselves as 'victims', not real 'victims'. BCS researchers have also noted that how people classify events and their own 'victimisation' often depends on class and status. The middle-classes are more likely to report incidents that the working-classes do not bother with. Even those who suffer severe physical attacks may eschew the term: many women's groups, particularly those working with women who have been raped or suffered domestic violence, find that women often do not wish the term 'victim' to be used to describe them; women often choose the word 'survivor'. Others may choose the term 'plaintiff' or 'claimant'. This may look like semantics but there are reasons why this may be important. The term 'victim' carries with it all sorts of connotations, some positive others not. On what is often seen as the positive side it suggests:

- The individual is blameless of the activity which has occurred;
- That they are deserving of sympathy and should be absolved;
- That they deserve attention and help;
- That they deserve compensation;
- That they have a right to expect that their transgressor be fully punished;
- It even often suggests that the person is good; this is very heavily used by the press where the innocent, good and almost saintly victim is juxtaposed to the evil criminal;
- Honesty (although victims of property offences often exaggerate the level of loss partly to enhance an insurance claim);
- Moral superiority;
- That their view of crime and what should be done about it should be given precedence over the views of others, even professionals in the system;

On what may be seen as the negative side it suggests:

- Weakness and inability to protect oneself;
- A loss of control, both at the time of the offence and in being able to do anything about it;
- Submission, first to the offence and then to the criminal justice system;
- Passivity (this can increase feelings of fear in the future);
- That risk of claiming the position of victim which is not then vindicated by the magistrate/jury and thus made to feel aggrieved;

- That even if the claim is recognised the perpetrator may not be found or the accused may not be convicted and so there is no feeling of justice or retribution, no-one on whom one can place the anger;

One might invest a lot into feeling for the victim and asking others to recognise you as such and then another may appear and claim that status so shaking your moral and social standing—this happened in 2001 when police officers who attended at Hillsborough football stadium in 1999 when many fans, mostly Liverpool fans, died were compensated for the trauma they had suffered and the surviving families were outraged that the 'victimisation' of the officers was being recognised over their own 'victimisation'.

'Victim' is thus a loaded term. Many of these aspects of victimisation will not be felt immediately and many others will no doubt emerge in various cases. As the concept of victim gets more used and abused by the press, politicians (often to bring in more severe punishment or to prove they care) and others for their own ends it becomes more difficult to carve out what it can and should mean and where truth and reality lie. The term is now so powerful and politicised that Garland (2001) at p. 143 sees the 'victim' as the central justification for 'measures of penal repression'. Is it possible to concentrate on the criminal event as defined in law to carry the connotation of victim or do we need to know how much harm it caused the 'victim/survivor'? Should we concentrate on how they feel or on some objective assessment of their harm? Should we also take account of their actions, to see if they should bear any blame and what we might mean by that term? Rock (2002) even suggests that the media and other images of what it is to be a victim and how they should feel and represent themselves are so strong that the victims cannot even know if what they feel is real or is induced by these images. For this reason he recommends first, that as a society we need to look more carefully at the criminal act which gives rise to the event of someone being labelled a criminal, and also to examine carefully what we mean when these terms are used.

These are interesting developments but most of the rest of the chapter will take a fairly positivistic view of the definition of victim although in Chapter Twenty there will be consideration of some of these issues and their connection with crime and crime control.

REVISION BOX *Victims of crime*

Categories of most likely groups and places of victims

1 Those living in Inner Cities.
2 Young males.
3 Most victims of assault by strangers are men.
4 Most victims of domestic assault are women.
5 Assaults of the workplace: especially in service sector (pubs, bookmakers, retail); and public sector (against police, social workers, hospital staff).
6 Ethnic groups.
7 Children (physical and sexual abuse).

5.4 Who fears crime?

Fear of crime has been perceived as an increasing phenomenon. As was seen in Chapter Three, many people are influenced by the media portrayal of crime which bears little relation to the actual situation. Some radical and left-wing criminologists such as Harman (1982) questioned the very existence of a crime problem, suggesting it had been manufactured by right-wing newspapers and politicians to control the working class and blacks by portraying them as the perpetrators. Other left-wing writers, such as Kinsey, Lea and Young (1986), recognised that there is a crime problem but attacked the way in which this was used as an excuse to control society and maintain social order (see Chapters Thirteen and Sixteen).

Whatever the reason for the media portrayal, or the use to which the fear it manufactures is put, it undoubtedly makes people fear that they may be victimised. Many alter their lifestyles to reduce this possibility. The reality is that serious crime is less common than is portrayed by the media. In this regard, what criminologists, police officers and others in the criminal justice field regard as irrational fear is then often seen as more of a problem for many than is crime itself. One recent Home Office response is to adopt a target to reduce, by March 2002, the level of fear of burglary, car crime and violence to below that of 1998. The BCS shows there has been some success.

In fact all the BCS have studied this aspect and discovered that two groups—women and the elderly—were particularly vulnerable to the fear of crime, although the victimisation rates for these groups were actually found to be relatively low.

Thus although women were (outside the house) less likely to be victims than men, every BCS shows women having more fear of crime. The fear of crime amongst women was, as recent surveys indicate, particularly marked in relation to violence and personal safety (Brogden and Nijhar (2000)). Much the same was true of the elderly (particularly elderly women) who are less concerned about burglary and car crime but very anxious about being out at night though this is questioned by Chaddee and Ditton (2003). Hough (1995) indicated two very rational grounds for such fear: outside and at night was judged to be high risk; and those who were most vulnerable in size, confidence, or ability to defend themselves, were the most fearful. This explanation of fear of crime by women and the elderly is largely substantiated in detailed studies by Pantazis (2000) and Killias and Clerici (2000).

The group consistently exhibiting least fear is young men, and yet the group which is most likely to be victimised consists of young, working-class males who inhabit inner cities and who spend a lot of their time in public places, particularly pubs and clubs. One exception, confirmed in the BCS for 2000, where young males do have more fear of crime is in car-related theft. Their cars—older, kept on the street, and possibly uninsured—are more vulnerable, while the young are also financially less able to replace them.

Since 1994 differences between the concerns of various ethnic groups have been noted and have increased. This trend was confirmed by the BCS for 2000, which, for example, showed that only 5 per cent of whites were very concerned about racially motivated attacks against 28 per cent of blacks and 33 per cent of Asians. Similar differences show up in those who are 'fairly worried'—7 per cent of whites against 23 per cent of blacks and 27 per cent of Asians. Within Asian and black groups women suffer most fear, about 40 per cent of Asian women and 33 per cent of black women were 'very worried' about such attacks.

The 2000 and 2002 surveys link a number of other factors with high levels of fear of crime: bad health; partly skilled or unskilled occupation; low-income household; living in council or housing association accommodation; living in inner-city areas; experience of victimisation; living in areas with high levels of physical disorder (as assessed by the interviewer). Respondents who perceived that they lived in areas with high levels of disorder (teenagers hanging around, vandalism and drug use) also have more fear of crime; and those living in areas where they perceived the community to lack cohesion were more fearful.

The early BCS studies claimed that the fear of crime often reflected the interviewee's perception of their likelihood of falling victim but that their perception of risk was unrealistic, and conclude that fear of crime was, to this extent, irrational. The fear itself was thus thought to be a problem over and above that which would be justified by actual crime levels. This was a convenient official interpretation since it suggests that it is an irrational fear which exaggerates the significance of crime. Such a cosy view would have to confront much inconvenient evidence.

The question needs to be asked: is the level of fear to which these and other surveys give witness actually as illogical, irrational and ill-founded as some reports and criminologists suggest? (See Holloway and Jefferson (2000).) It could be that those who fear crime conduct their lifestyles to reduce their likelihood of falling victim to a criminal act. Their fear would thereby contribute to their low victimisation, which would suggest that it is not as irrational as the figures might suggest.

There are other possible grounds for doubting whether the fear is 'illogical or irrational'. The Islington Crime Survey (1986) discovered higher rates of female crime than had usually been recorded. They found that 20 per cent of women knew someone who had been sexually assaulted or molested in the previous 12 months, and that women were 40 per cent more likely to be victims of non-sexual assault than are men. This survey and its follow-up (Crawford et al. (1990)) demonstrated that the women had a firm grasp about their likelihood of becoming victims. These figures on female victimisation tie in closely with work carried out by other criminologists such as Dobash and Dobash (1992) and Stanko (1990) and Boran (2003). If these figures are accurate then possibly women's fear is not so irrational. Many of the chapters reproduced in Rock (1994) indicate a more rational basis for fear of crime and this is supported by the more careful analysis of fear in the later BCSs. In addition Walklate (2001) and Pantazis (2000) found that when women and the elderly are attacked they often suffer greater physical, psychological and economic harm than do the young or men. This too may contribute to making their fear of crime more rational.

Lastly, many women are subjected to sexual and other harassments. Although these may fall short of actual crimes, they add to their fear and feeling of vulnerability. This is very similar to the experiences of ethnic minorities who also tend to fear crime. In addition, women, the elderly and people who are from one of the ethnic minority groups tend to be relatively powerless physically, financially and socially, and this adds to their vulnerability. These insecurities amongst the poorest groups are specifically stressed by Pantazis (2000), while Farrall et al. (2000) mention the possibility of psychological anxieties inducing fear.

Much of the research noted above ignores the effects of secondary victimisation. It also ignores structural aspects of fear, produced by the social environment and/or feelings of marginalisation. The general patriarchal nature of our society tends to be made invisible even though many women's lives are controlled by male violence. Sliding over these aspects can make victimisation appear to be illogical: their recognition makes the fear more rational.

There are other aspects to this equation which have been pointed out most carefully by the left realists (see Chapter Sixteen), who recognise that fear includes emotional responses, as well as social and cultural expectations. These can be rendered illogical by definition, but that does not render them less real. Left realists also argue that the rational calculation of risk is simply not possible for the average person. Fear may indeed have as much to do with the unknown as with actual risk, making myths as important as are the facts, and general feelings of insecurity as important as real dangers. Essentially, what the left realists are arguing is that the rationality or irrationality of fear cannot be objectively assessed: what is important is the reality of the fear and the effect this has on a person's life, limiting enjoyment and their spheres of activity. In addition to the left realist theory examined in Chapter Sixteen, this idea is considered in more depth in Chapter Twenty.

Fear also has social and structural causes—related to vandalism, boarded-up buildings, noisy neighbours, teenagers hanging around, poor street lighting and a feeling of powerlessness to alter these negative factors. There is now a realisation that fear is a real experience which needs to be addressed, and that both crime and fear of crime reduce the quality of life in a State. Such awareness can produce policy conflicts: thus many of the crime prevention schemes raise the public's awareness of the risks and so tend to increase rather than decrease fear of crime, even where the programme may lead to some decrease in actual crime. The awareness also calls in question some of the more prurient elements of press reporting which tend to feed on the interest/fear of criminality to sell news and to entertain.

Successive BCSs have noted that the effect of the fear of crime on the quality of life is greater than the effect of crime itself Reduction of fear of crime has become a major police objective. However, as Tulloch (2000) notes, to achieve this 'initiatives aimed at reducing fear of crime must move beyond identifying levels of perceived risk and fear to a consideration of how these constructs are linked to aspects of personal definition and social identity' (p. 466). Thus for the elderly it might be linked to seeing youths as 'other' and as threatening whereas for young males the risk is seen as coming from other young males, often in different ethnic or other groups, and for young females it is related to any unknown young males. The fear relates to the quality of life when, to avoid the danger, the individuals abandon or adjust their behaviour and habits.

Perhaps the irrationality which really needs addressing is: why are young men not more fearful of victimisation when they are seemingly the highest risk group? Are they really fearless, or just frightened of admitting their fear to the researcher, or even of articulating it to themselves? Is any lack of fear part of the image of their male virility and street credibility? Should someone try to raise their fear, or at least their appreciation of their own vulnerability, to help them protect themselves? At present these are neglected issues. Perhaps policy-oriented assessments of fear could clarify the meaning of the concept and its effect (Gabriel and Greve (2003) and Lee (2001)).

5.5 Support and services for victims

Victims have to compete with all other disadvantaged or unfortunate groups for the aid that they may require. Therefore groups working for the victims must both state their case and point out why their particular demands should be met. The plight of victims received recognition from both the Council of Europe (in its 1983 Convention and its 1985 guidelines) and the United Nations (in their 1985 Declaration) and these rights and interests have been included in the work of the International Criminal Court (see Amnesty International (1999)). These international bodies include similar lists of victims' needs: the need to be treated with respect and dignity; to be allowed access to the mechanisms of justice and to legal processes which will provide them with redress for the harm done; offenders should make restitution for the harm done to victims, their families or dependants, and such restitution should be possible as a sentencing option in criminal cases; information for victims concerning the progress of the case; allowing the views of victims to be considered where their personal interests are affected (as long as the accused is not prejudiced); assisting victims through the legal process; use of informal dispute resolution such as mediation where appropriate; and material, medical, psychological and social assistance for victims through governmental and community-based means (these are taken from the UN document). In 1990 in the United Kingdom the *Victims Charter* was published which largely set out, in general terms, the existing arrangements for victims and this charter was updated in 1996 and is presently undergoing a substantial revision (Home Office (2001) and (2003)). It includes items under most of the heads covered by the international documents, but interestingly it omits any mention of informal dispute resolution. In 1990 the charter spoke (rather misleadingly) in terms of 'rights'; in 1996 it referred (more realistically) to 'standards of service'. The main limiting factor is that there is no means of enforcement so that it does not give victims any legal rights (see Reeves and Mully (2000)) though it does represent an official recognition of the interests of victims and provides victims' organisations with a powerful tool to lobby Parliament. Its strength lies in the provision of welfare-based support rather than rights in the criminal justice system. This perpetuates the way in which the needs of victims were anyway being addressed in Britain, by two very different approaches: first, officially through the criminal justice system; and, secondly, unofficially through a largely voluntary network of support schemes, most notably the VSS. In both approaches the victim is generally provided with opportunities rather than rights.

5.5.1 Victims in the criminal justice process

Until the establishment of a true police force in the middle of the last century, often the victim was the most important element in the bringing to justice of any criminal. The police slowly took over the prosecuting function of the victim. Today, private prosecutions are possible but rare and only arise where the State refuses to prosecute. It is usually the State, originally through the police and now through the Crown Prosecution Service, which carries out most of these functions. The victim's role has been reduced largely to one of reporting offences and giving evidence if so requested. Although these are essential to the system, they do not furnish the victim with any decision-making power. Some would argue that this reduces the feeling that the victimisation has been atoned: the prosecution seems to have little to do with them or what occurred and far more to do with State or police policy. Until the 1960s this feeling was enhanced by the lack of compensation or restitution for the victim. Although there was some, fairly minimal, legislative provision for compensation it was rarely used, and the victim had no right to compensation. In recent years, and especially since 1997 and after much political pressure, there have been several important advances. All agencies are now expected to consider victims and are monitored on how well they have responded (see, e.g., H.M. Inspectorate of Probation (2000)).

Apart from feeling ignored by the criminal justice system, victims often feel they are being used by the courts. They are expected to report to the police but are not always made to feel comfortable in doing this; for most victims the police station remains a fairly uninviting environment. This reduces the effectiveness of crime control, as it increases the offender's chances of getting away undetected. If victims are asked to identify offenders they are often not screened and may, through fear of facing the offender, fail to identify him or her. When called to give evidence, they are rarely permitted to relate their experiences in their own words but are forced to answer questions which may actually misrepresent their account of what occurred. Furthermore if they refuse to cooperate they may be prosecuted because they would thereby be obstructing the course of justice. The proceedings are indeed mostly adapted to the needs of the State, which has also been victimised in that its peace and its rules have been broken. The State has an interest in social control of offenders and therefore has a right to require anyone to give evidence. To alleviate some of the stress caused by these difficulties, Crown Court Witness Services are now available to offer support, but these on their own cannot redress the difficulties which are inherent in an adversarial system. Prosecution, conviction and sentence can help victims feel less vulnerable and help them come to terms with the event but Hoyle and Sanders (2000) suggest that the difficulties of the system can lead some victims to withdraw their complaints from the system and so limit this cathartic effect and also prevent the effective operation of the criminal justice system.

5.5.1.1 *State compensation*

There have been some improvements. The first compensation scheme was set up in 1963 when New Zealand introduced a State compensation scheme, supposedly removing the need for the victim to rely upon the offender being wealthy. Britain followed a year later with a State compensatory scheme for victims of violent crime.

This scheme was non-statutory and was only formalised in legislation in the Criminal Justice Act 1988. Under it, victims have no rights to compensation and payment is at the discretion of the Criminal Injuries Compensation Board (CICB). Indeed, the system was set up without any consultation of victims, and there was no real evidence that victims of violence wanted to be compensated by the State. It originated more from a wish to forestall possible complaints of lenient punishments at a time when criminal justice was pursuing a rehabilitative ideal, whilst it was also seen as an extension of the welfare principle of State support of those in need which was strong at the time. It was never considered as part of a wider idea for victims' rights.

One of the most important qualities necessary to qualify for compensation is that the victim be adjudged 'innocent', in other words, that the claim is not fraudulent and that in suffering the injury the victim was not at fault. This condition generally excludes cases where the victim may have participated in the violence. Any payment is reduced by an assessment of the amount for which the victim can be said to be responsible or to have contributed to the injury. It is important to note that compensation is not means tested, nor is it set to meet a particular need. It is set by the amount of injury the CICB assesses the victim to have suffered and not by the help which that person may need. The system compensates only those who suffer due to criminal violence, and therefore excludes those who suffer physical injury following other crimes, e.g., after breaches of the factories legislation or as a result of driving offences. The criminal is not permitted to gain from any payment; therefore claims in cases of domestic violence will be countenanced only if the parties are now living apart and look unlikely to co-habit in the future. The Criminal Injuries Compensation Act 1995 set out a statutory tariff for injuries ranging from £1,000 to £250,000 plus an additional payment against expenses and for loss of earnings or earnings capacity (but only if at least 28 weeks were lost).

The scheme is therefore limited in the help it offers, the people who qualify, and the way in which they qualify. None the less, it is a recognition of the suffering of the victim. One of the largest problems arises out of public ignorance of its existence. There is no automatic mechanism in the criminal justice system to inform them of the possibility of compensation even if they would have a good case. Under the Victims Charter the police are expected to inform victims, but only as a matter of good practice and not as a legal requirement.

Many argue that rather than the State helping the victim, the offender should be ordered to do so. In this context reparation as well as compensation has been considered, each being a means of repaying the victim for the wrong suffered. This 'payment' may be in the form of restitution of the objects stolen; monetary payment for harm done (as in compensation orders); work done for the victim (direct reparation); or work for the victims of other offenders (indirect reparation). A very indirect form of reparation exists in the form of Community Punishment Orders where the offender performs a useful task for the public at large, not for victims in particular.

Actual recompence might be useful for some victims and compensation from the offenders is now an important element in the criminal justice system. The change began with the Criminal Justice Act 1972. This Act provided that in addition to dealing with the offender in any other way, the court may require the payment of compensation for any 'personal injury, loss or damage' resulting from the offence (the provisions are now set out in the Powers of Criminal Courts (Sentencing) Act 2000, ss. 130 to 134)). The orders were only permitted in addition to other sentences, partly to indicate that they were not intended as a substitute for punishment, nor as a way of allowing rich offenders to buy their way out of the normal consequences of their conviction. As Scarman LJ (as he then was) explained, the purpose of the compensation order was to provide the victim with:

... a convenient and rapid means of avoiding the expense of resorting to civil litigation when the criminal clearly has means which would enable the compensation to be paid. (*R v Inwood* (1975) 60 Cr App R 70)

This clear separation of the purpose of the compensation order remained until the Criminal Justice Act 1982 enacted that a compensation order could be made instead of (or in addition to) any other sentence of the court. This was the first time compensation was seen as an alternative to punishment. Whatever the intention, the offender often perceives compensation as if it were punishment and is as resentful of it as of any fine. To the offender the result is the same, and is especially resented if the compensation is paid to a person who is far better off than the offender.

Where the court considers that both a fine and a compensation order would be appropriate, but that the offender has insufficient funds for both, then the court should give preference to the compensation order. Courts must give reasons for not ordering compensation for injury, loss or damage. Unfortunately many victims still fail to receive compensation largely because courts are not provided with sufficient information to assess the level of damage, and victims have no right of audience on this matter. Despite general approval of the system of making offenders pay, many victims get frustrated with having to wait for their compensation to be paid in instalments.

Traditionally there was a problem with obtaining information concerning the level of loss suffered but since 2001 (see Home Office (2001b and 2001c)) all victims are invited to make a Victim Personal Statement (VPS) in which they can state not just the level of damage or injury they have suffered but also what the offence has meant to them. It is the impact of the crime which is important not the victim's opinions concerning sentencing, (for discussion of the pilot projects for these see Hoyle et al. (1999)). The completion of these statements is entirely voluntary and victims can still provide the court with just the information necessary to making a compensation order. Where offenders opt to make a VPS they are told that its contents will be made available to all criminal justice agencies including probation and prisons. Victims are also told that the information is just one factor which will be taken into account in sentencing, discretion and responsibility for sentencing remains with the judge/magistrates (*R v Hayes The Times*, 5 April 1999). In 2001 the Lord Chief Justice, in a practice direction, stated that the views of the victim or those close to them are not important, the only factor considered is the actual impact of the offences on them. The fact that these are voluntary and that some victims may be forgiving whilst others are not raises some problems concerning fairness and justice in sentencing generally. It is hoped that courts will not be unduly influenced by these statements making sentencing too disparate for similar offences.

For victims the two most difficult aspects of compensation orders are: offenders being permitted to pay orders over extended periods; and offenders failing to complete the order. State payment of the compensation order and later recovery of the funds from the offender would help to alleviate both of these. There are also more subtle problems: compensation focuses on harm to a specific victim and is therefore more akin to civil damages (it often falls below these) and lacks any penal element and there is insufficient account taken of the offender's culpability, of their action against the wider society, nor is there any preventative element to the adjudication. Furthermore, it is dependant on a particular offender being caught, convicted and being able to pay. The State compensation scheme (above) is some help in filling the gaps but only for crimes of violence. Despite these shortcomings it does go some way to recognising the place of the offender in the criminal justice system.

5.5.1.2 *Restorative justice*

The core element to restorative justice is to return things to the way they were, as if the crime had not occurred. Clearly in reality this is impossible but it is intended to represent the ideal that offenders should make good the harm they did to the victim and to society as a whole, they should work towards mending not merely physical but also psychological harms and breaches in relationships and bonds in society which their crime has caused. The route by which we have arrived at the use of restorative justice in the UK has been circuitous and involved a number of differing policies and initiatives. Understanding this route not only helps to grasp how restorative justice is used in the UK today but also to understand the rise of 'victims' within the system to their present position of dominance at least rhetorically and for political ends.

Some of the earliest moves involved the system itself taking more account of the victim through ideas such as compensation orders (see above) and also of reparation—the return of property taken during a criminal offence. These were fairly crude reparation schemes. The Community Service Order (introduced in 1973 and now called Community Punishment Orders) is intended to add some refinement by requiring the offender to put something back into society through performing a job for the community.

Victim groups continued to look for alternative solutions which might better serve the victim. In the 1970s they worked to redress the balance in the system towards the victim by giving the victim more control through the use of mediation. Successful mediation resolves the situation often without the use of the courts, and sometimes without the use of any part of the official criminal justice system. The parties, offender and victim, retain absolute control over events. They meet, supervised by a trained mediator, to discuss their differences and hopefully resolve their grievances and remove or reduce the hostility between them. It is the parties who resolve the issues, the mediator does not direct or decide anything. Mediation schemes take on many guises and arise at different points in the system, some obviate any official involvement others arise either before any court hearing or after this but before sentence and some arise after sentencing and even after the offender is in custody. Clearly these differing schemes have different intended outcomes. Such schemes have proved to have some success but they are generally limited to less serious offences (Hudson (1998)).

More recently again have been full restorative justice schemes, usually based on community justice schemes historically used by some indigenous groups in New

Zealand (Maori justice) and North America (Native American Sentencing Circles) and informed by theoretical analysis of writers such as Braithwaite (1988 and 2003), Umbreit (2001) and Weitekamp and Kerner (2002). This has brought a wave of new orders/practices in many countries around the world as well as many research projects to assess their worth and books and articles considering all aspects of the subject (see, e.g., Von Hirsch et al. (2003), Johnstone (2003), Strang (2002) Strang and Braithwaite (2002), Walgrave (2002), Johnstone (2001), Miers (2001)).

Restorative justice is based on the idea of requiring offenders to confront their criminal activity and the consequences of their crime. It does this by taking a personal and emotionally charged approach which is often absent in court processes and using it to encourage feelings of responsibility on the part of the offender. Theoretical analysis suggests that by relying on respect and relationships between the offender and those who care for him or her and for whom he or she cares, constructive use can be made of reintegrative shaming to reduce crime or other harmful activities. The system therefore diverts offenders away from an official court appearance towards a system based on consent and where offenders are encouraged to take responsibility for their own behaviour to an extent which is not possible in a court-room. It draws together offenders and those important to them, victims and their supporters (including Victim Support) and other interested parties which may include probation officers, social services, education or schools, drug outreach workers, voluntary workers or other persons who may have an interest from a societal or community perspective. The offender explains the offence and what he or she feels should be done. The victim then describes the effects of the crime, emotional physical and financial. Others may add to these, the whole system is based on the story and justice is approached by what is necessary to that particular set of events rather than as a set response to a category of case. The hope is that this causes the offender and their family or friends to feel shame, prompts an apology and opens up the possibility of accepting the offender back into the community. This may be by means of an agreed plan of action which may involve the offender in certain responsibilities (reparation or community work) and the community in certain responsibilities to the offender (help in finding employment, help in dealing with problems such as drink or drug habits, or marital difficulties). Versions of this can also be used for corporate violations where the victim is either another corporation, an individual or the community (Young (2002)). From this it certainly appears that the victim would be central to the scheme but in 2000–1 victims attended fewer than 7 per cent of panels Newburn (2001) and Miers et al. (2001). This may show shortcomings in the systems operated, possibly victims have not been told or the schemes are not fully explained to them but it might be a positive in that victims are not being coerced into participating. What is clear is that victims are not central to the systems in the UK (see Hoyle (2002)). If victims are not present their case and interests might be represented by someone else such as a member of Victim Support. This also means that the process can be used for offenders of victimless crimes and corporate crimes without identifiable victims where the problems for the community might be explained.

Possibly the greatest strength of any system is that it draws on those most affected by the crime: the criminal; the victim; and the community to draw up and agree an outcome which they feel most appropriate in the circumstances. In most instances the agreement is then enforced and monitored by the police or other officials in the system. These factors render it very different from mediation.

Although there has been a lot of interest both academic and practical some of the essential questions are still being considered. For example should restorative justice replace present punishment systems or systems of justice altogether? Some such as Braithwaite (2003) and Walgrave (2003) suggest that it could. Others suggest that it could be used to resolve problems caused by criminal and other harms in society; this is often suggested by abolitionists such as de Haan (1990). Another conception is that it should be carefully built into the criminal justice or punishment system by being given a specific place within the tariff (see Dignan (2003) and Daly (2003)) or that it should only work alongside the present systems (see Bottoms (2003)). How can we best ensure that in an informal approach the rights of the parties concerned are not ignored, particularly rights of the accused, offenders and victims? Clearly one way would be to require a full trial and finding of guilt before embarking on the system and ensure that the court be involved in the process (see Duff (2003)). Should it be used in cases without victims or with many victims (see Young (2001)) or should it be confined to particular types of cases and the process and rights and responsi-bilities be different depending on the type of case? Can it be implemented without a broadening of the criminal justice system, that is without drawing new types of cases into the net? Can it really be used to reduce sentencing and prison numbers? Can it reduce re-offending? Can it empower victims and/or the community and to what extent can and should each be empowered? Will it result in differential justice depending on the anger or forgiveness of the victim and is that important?

This type of policy is very attractive in todays political climate: it appears to prioritise victims at a time when that is presented as important; it is cheaper than the present systems; it seems to be at least as effective in preventing re-offending and few negative aspects have yet been found. There are still many unresolved questions.

5.5.1.3 Evidence and information

The criminal justice system sees victims as important sources of evidence: in the past this was the only way in which they were recognised by the system. Although this has altered many victims feel that the changes are not sufficiently radical. For a long time there has been a reduction in sentence for pleading guilty and part of the reason for this has traditionally been said to be that it relieves the victim of the trauma of giving evidence. There are other reasons, important for the system, related to cost and efficiency whilst victims are not even consulted when a lesser offence is entered as the guilty plea. Perhaps victims should be consulted when a caution is considered, or when a bail decision is being made, whilst the probation system has already been expected to consult on some decisions and the new Victims' Charter is expected to extend this requirement and to place the require-ment on other agencies (Home Office (2002)). In setting court dates the availability and convenience of victims and other witnesses is supposed to be considered. However the fact of giving evidence is still traumatic. For some time there have been special provisions in the case of children, the removal of wigs and gowns and the use of video evidence or video-links. More recently in part II of the Youth Justice and Criminal Evidence Act 1999 vulnerable witnesses more generally are protected through screening in court or giving evidence in camera, by live video-link or recorded on video (see Ashworth (2000)). Part VIII would allow some of these methods to be used in order to permit more efficient and/or effective trials, e.g., for the taking of expert testimony. These types of provision could go a long way to reducing the trauma of giving evidence but they need to become more widely accepted by the criminal justice professionals and more finances need to be put into their funding. As they become more accepted they may become more widely available to all victims and witnesses.

There are also more informal changes to try to make the process easier, explaining what to expect and who sits where etc. in court and therefore less of a shock for victims and other witnesses. Some work has also been done to separate victims and accused and his or her family whilst waiting for trial. In addition many victims feel that they are not kept informed about progress.

Victims need information about the criminal justice process in general, about where they may obtain help, about their rights, about ways they may improve their lot (through CICB or otherwise), and about the progression of their own case. Such information could be provided by insisting that the police give every victim an information sheet and by requiring them to keep victims informed of progress in their case. Although recent guidelines have called for the victim to be given information about aid agencies and the progress of the case, sentencing and the release of the alleged offender, these are not requirements: the victim has no right to be told. There is one exception, in the case of serious sexual or violent offences the Probation Service is now required to inform a victim of the release of the offender (National Standards for the Supervision of Offenders in the Community 2000). These mechanisms to keep the victims informed have not been entirely successful, partly because they are expensive to administer and the two agencies most involved, the police and probation, have been given no extra funds for this purpose.

However, despite the real experience of victims being only partially improved, the importance of victims to the system is now fully recognised, and government and most official criminal justice bodies have committees to represent their interests. The Home Office has a division entitled Procedures and Victims Unit and the system, or parts of it, are frequently considered from a victim-centred viewpoint. Certainly no alterations to the system occur until the victim perspective has been fully considered. The criminal justice agencies and other organisations which touch on victims have an interdepartmental Victims Steering Group which is intended to ensure that the second Victims Charter is implemented and to comment on proposals from government. In addition the use of reintegrative shaming techniques and reparative justice for young offenders which results from the Crime and Disorder Act 1998 gives the victim a central role. More may be achieved through the use of the Human Rights Act 1998, depending on how the courts weigh up the often opposing interests and rights of victim and criminal. Despite all this recent action it remains the case that many of the initiatives which have increased the welfare of victims have occurred in the voluntary sectors, briefly described in the next section.

5.5.2 Victims and the voluntary sector

If help is to be offered it is important to assess the needs of victims. This task is not easy, as individuals differ. But Maguire (1985) identified a number of needs which can be summarised into three broad areas. First, victims need information, which, in the absence of positive action, means that the voluntary agencies are often the main and sometimes the only source. Unfortunately, they cannot help with information concerning particular cases. Secondly, there may be a need for practical help in completing insurance claims, repairing property, transport to hospital or court etc. Most of these needs arise immediately after the crime and generally abate shortly thereafter. Thirdly, victims may need emotional support. The extent of this is impossible accurately to assess, but on a conservative basis several hundred thousand people suffer from traumatic distress every year in England and Wales. For many the problem will be short lived, but for some, post-traumatic stress disorders may persist for extended periods of two years or more. These are usually associated with rape, kidnapping and other serious offences (even some victims of serious property offences). This may overstate the case, but clearly distress suffered by victims is a serious problem and one which in Britain has long been virtually ignored by the State. Nor has the official criminal justice system, until very recently, given victims any knowledge about its rationale or method of operation, or given much consideration to the position and role of victims. Maguire and Kynch (2000) reported that 40 per cent of victims had needs which were not met by anyone. Eighteen per cent wanted someone to talk to; 14 per cent wanted information from the police; 13 per cent protection from further victimisation; and 9 per cent advise on security. Victims needs cannot be easily predicted. Some victims of very serious offences have few needs whilst those whose victimisation looks relatively trivial have far greater needs. Some victims can ask and express their needs articulately whilst others are unable to do so. The voluntary sector has addressed these problems through two main types of agency. One type deals only with the problems of violence towards women and the other with victims more generally.

The feminist movement has been very active in helping female victims. They refer to them as survivors, as this gives the women a more positive and less passive view of their position. Feminist organisations have been especially useful in helping the survivors of domestic violence and rape or other sexual offences. They have also been supportive of child survivors (victims), either along with the women who suffer domestic violence, or more broadly in support groups such as the incest support group.

The help given to survivors of domestic violence is usually in the form of a place in a refuge, many of which are attached to the National Federation of Women's Aid. Shelter homes or refuges were set up as safe havens for women who were being criminally battered or whose children were being assaulted by people living with them, generally their husbands and/or lovers. These provide very practical help by giving the victim a roof over her head and a place to care for her children, outside the violence of the home and with the help and support of other women in the same predicament. Domestic violence is a major problem in Britain Stanko (2000) estimates that the police receive 570,000 calls a year and in the year up to 31 August 2002 Women's Aid National 24 Hour Helpline received 56,566 calls (Women's Aid (2002)) and 54,000 women and children stay in refuges in England and Wales every year (Women's Aid (2000)).

Many survivors of rape feel that the criminal justice system does not meet their needs; the woman often feels as victimised by the police and court processes as she does by the initial act of violence. Sometimes women are even blamed for their own attacks. In response to the plight of these women the first Rape Crisis Centre (RCC) was opened in 1976 in London, and there are now many such centres in Britain. RCC operate by means of telephone 'hotlines' or drop-in centres. They allow women to make their own decisions about, e.g., reporting to the police or visiting a psychiatrist or other health professional. Each local unit is largely autonomous though there is now a Rape Crisis Federation. They are generally intended as places where women survivors can talk with supportive women. The centres offer emotional support as well as legal and medical information.

Both refuges and RCC also play a political and educational role. They try to inform the public about the reality of rape and domestic violence. They try to change the law, social attitudes and social policy towards these problems. This politicisation has probably led to their being under-funded as far as government financing is concerned. What these organisations and some feminist writers have done is to attack the idea that the home is necessarily a safe place, to widen the concepts of 'victim' and 'criminal' and by highlighting previously 'invisible' social problems, open up avenues for dealing with these issues.

The much wider range of general victims, most of whom have suffered property offences gain help from Victim Support Schemes (VSS) which are the part of the voluntary sector which has received any substantial central support. The VSS organisation was less political, especially at the outset. It did not try to alter the criminal justice system, nor did it attack that system. Originally it offered short-term help to victims on a good neighbour principle: it now offers more long-term help on the same basis. In fact in 1979 its low political profile was reinforced when it became a charity, limiting its scope for campaigning or political agitation. The approach has gained the support of the police, from whom the VSS obtain information concerning victims who may need help. This less political approach also made the organisation's schemes more palatable to central government, which since the mid-1980s has awarded it an increasing annual budget to support this work. The provision of aid has had a profound effect. The VSS has always relied on the cooperation of the police in informing them of victims, and many schemes now operate a direct referral system. This involves the police informing them of the victims of all appropriate crimes.

There are really two parts to the service: the general community-based victim support volunteer who helps and supports the victim in many practical ways; and the Witness Service. In the early 1980s VSS introduced a Witness Service into the Crown Court, and a similar service is now available in magistrates' courts. Initial resistance on the part of criminal justice departments due to fears that the service might interfere with evidence has long since been overcome and the service is seen as a vital resource. Staff, both volunteer and paid, are fully trained and work to strict codes of practice and professional standards. These two elements of victim support and Witness Service work hand in hand. The initial referral by the police (or victim) results in a letter or phone call from a VS volunteer who can give practical and emotional support to the victim. First there will be advice about the police investigative procedures and support for any part the victim has to play in this procedure (the volunteer may accompany the victim to an identity parade or to the station when the victim has to make a statement). In serious or complex cases this support and advice will run through the whole period of the preparation of the case and the trial. A volunteer can also help with practical matters such as completing insurance forms or arranging for any necessary repairs to be done. If the victim is to meet the offender through some sort of reparation or mediation system, support of the VS volunteer is essential. The volunteer should be involved in the preparation of the victim for the experience, accompany the victim to the meeting and be present throughout. The volunteer's participation should ensure that the experience is positive for the victim. If a case is to go to court and be contested, the victim (and all other witnesses) will be informed about the Witness Service who help to prepare them for the trial. The Service may show them around the courtroom, talk about their role as witnesses and how to ask for help during the trial. They therefore prepare the victim, and other witnesses, for the ordeal of giving evidence in court but they never mention or discuss the actual evidence in any particular trial. Having provided this support the community-based volunteer may accompany the victim to court on the day and sit with the victim until called, but cannot prepare the victim for what will happen in the courtroom. Volunteers work for one or other arm of the service but they are kept fairly separate.

The third important function of VSS is to advise on the impact new initiatives may have on victims and help to formulate local plans. VSS is supported on all multi-agency partnerships set up under the Crime and Disorder Act 1998 where they can give invaluable help and advice. They are also invited to work on government advisory groups where the interests of victims may be affected. For example, in 1997 and 1998 they worked closely on the Interdepartmental Working Group on Special Provision for Vulnerable and Intimidated Witnesses. Here the organisation now promotes the ideal of rights for victims, an ideal not yet achieved. The organisation, however, wishes to prevent victims being forced to take decisions about how offenders should be dealt with and thus preserve the situation where the State is responsible for the final decisions. This they perceive as necessary to ensure that weak victims are not intimidated. In the author's opinion it is also necessary to protect a weak offender from an angry and powerful victim, especially one who has been empowered through being given a voice in the media.

The service certainly provides an invaluable support for victims and survivors. As the government has relied more and more on VSS to provide, cheaply and effectively, the services which it feels that a responsible State should ensure is available to victims, the organisation has gained confidence in pushing for the interests of victims. Real progress is being made partly because of this situation and partly because it is politically expedient for government to ensure that victims are given greater consideration and rights.

5.6 Victim precipitation and lifestyle

There seems to be a 'common-sense' or commonly accepted idea or conception of a victim. One is that a victim is vulnerable, so that the victim of a street robbery (or mugging) is often thought of as being elderly, usually female. A victim of rape is generally female (although men can now legally be raped but only by other men), usually young, and must have fought vigorously to defend herself. Although legally her male attacker may be her husband, partner or other acquaintance, many only recognise her as a victim if her attacker is a stranger to her. She must also be 'respectable', otherwise she is deemed to have no honour to protect. Insurance companies often refuse to insure homes unless certain security measures are taken and may refuse to pay out if the victim of a theft has not been diligent in protecting their property. A victim, in common ideology, is therefore seen as someone who has not contributed to the criminality in any way; they are helpless and wholly innocent. This idea of an innocent victim is important in deciding whether compensation should be paid; whether and to what extent the criminal should compensate or perform reparation to the victim; whether victims should be believed; and lastly, it might also affect the criminal's sentence by the court after conviction. These perceptions are central to the criminal justice system.

5.6.1 Victim precipitation

Ideas of what constitutes a victim have long been a part of the discussion of whether victims precipitate the offence against themselves. At times it may be unclear who is acting and who is being acted upon, and at others, the eventual victim may actually precipitate the activity which results in the victimisation, for example, by being the first to resort to violence. The idea of the precipitation of the offence is particularly strong where cases of violence and rape are concerned.

These are examples of the danger involved in taking the concept of victim precipitation too literally. Can it illuminate the phenomenon of criminality without moving responsibility from criminal to victim? Probably not. Even stating that the crime happened here and now against this victim because the victim did or said something suggests that if the criminal had not been so stimulated, the crime would not have occurred. Victim precipitation is therefore a fairly dangerous concept, which leads to victim blaming. According to Miers (1992), victim blaming, or at least placing more responsibility on all citizens to avoid victimsation, is one of the dangers inherent in the enhanced position given to victims under modern responses to the victim movement.

Certainly many government strategies aimed at crime prevention over the last 30 years have involved potential victims taking responsibility for their own safety or that of their property, e.g., the slogan 'Together we can crack it', calling on people to keep cars locked and valuables out of sight and to secure their homes, not to let children out of sight etc. (see Garland (1996) and (2000)). This, if taken further, could lead to victim blaming by the system or, possibly as damaging and more likely, victims feeling that they should bear responsibility for the crime. The whole official policy of 'responsibilisation' may therefore be very negative if it causes victims to feel not only anger and upset at the offender but also guilt at their failure to prevent their own victimisation.

5.6.2 Victim lifestyles and criminality

The claim is made that different lifestyles, particularly how much time is allocated to leisure activities, affect the probability of being in places where crime is likely, at times when crime is likely, and with people who are likely to commit those crimes. It might also lead to leaving property accessible for others to take advantage.

The BCSs have discovered that individuals who tend to have an increased risk of victimisation are: male; under 30 years old; single, widowed or divorced; spend several evenings a week out; drink heavily; and assault others. The last three of these are obviously lifestyle variables. They relate to activities which increase the likelihood of such people being victims. The basis for viewing these behavioural factors in this way is obvious enough. For personal victimisation to occur, there needs to be a meeting between criminal and victim. Thus for street crime the element of going out more frequently will clearly increase the likelihood of such meetings. Similarly as many such offences take place in the evening, particularly in or around drinking establishments or between those who have been drinking, going out in the evening and frequenting drinking establishments will increase the likelihood of victimisation. And property offences are more likely to occur if the property is left empty, open, or not protected by locks or alarms.

The first three of the variables in the above example are demographic, but they too are related to lifestyle. In most cultures, certain lifestyles are thought normal for given groups, and are therefore more or less socially encouraged or discouraged within such groups. Western cultures usually encourage young single men to socialise widely, and therefore the normal and encouraged lifestyle for this group within society is also the one which exposes them to most risk from street crimes. It is also the same group who commit most of this type of criminality.

An important reservation is that the lifestyle victimisation criteria so far discussed hold only for street crime or for crime committed on personal property. They totally ignore the private victimisation, referred to above in the areas of domestic violence and of sexual violence committed within relationships of family ties or of trust. Victims of these offences may find that they are safer outside the home rather than in it. They also ignore the fact that certain groups are sought out to be victimised. These are thus likely to suffer relatively high rates of victimisation, whether they remain in the home or venture out onto the street. Racial minorities are especially prone to such treatment.

Six factors have been suggested (Sparks (1982)) for identifying such victims: vulnerability; opportunity; attractiveness; facilitation; and impunity. *Vulnerability* arises either from some personal attribute (being weak, mentally or physically; being old or being young), or from conditions beyond the control of an individual (social status, economic position or environment). *Opportunity* reflects both simple availability (such as valuables left unguarded) and being created by the behaviour (lifestyle) of the victim. Opportunities are also created, or changed, by technology (computer crime) and social habits. The increase in mobile phone thefts from people walking the streets combines both trends. *Attractiveness* could describe the degree of temptation; the criminal calculating whether the potential gain is worth the cost of attainment. Thus the less the risk and the more the gain, the greater the attraction. *Facilitation* arises out of the neglect to counter a special risk, such as failing to fit locks in an area of high burglary. *Precipitation* is particularly relevant to cases of interpersonal violence and rape, as discussed above. Finally, *impunity*, is meant to indicate situations where the victim is unlikely to complain or unlikely to be believed. This often covers sexual offences against women or children; cases against known criminals, illegal immigrants, racial minorities and (male and female) prostitutes; corporate offending where there may be no single victim; and crimes committed by the agents of the State.

Implicit in most of these categories is the notion that victims carry some responsibility for crimes, and should adjust their actions and behaviour to avoid putting themselves or their property at risk. To a degree this is reasonable but it can easily be pushed to a level where it becomes very restrictive on the liberty of the potential victim.

5.7 Conclusion

Recently the interests of victims have gained a prominence in both media and political rhetoric. This shift has usually been associated with a call for greater 'law and order'. Some argue that the interests of victims have been hijacked to serve the needs of media entertainment and political power (for some discussion of this see Mawby and Walklate (1994), (especially pp. 13–21) and Elias (1993)). It is thus necessary to ask how many of the changes which are claimed to be in the interests of victims actually serve those interests? To respond to such a question some assumptions about the needs, interests and desires of victims have to be made. Here it is assumed that victims wish to be afforded dignity and have assurances that their lives will not be blighted by victimisation in the future. They may also wish to see the perpetrator dealt with. With this in mind, a number of new initiatives and suggested changes will be considered.

One prominent recent change is in increased powers of the police and other criminal justice agencies. The policy began under the Police and Criminal Evidence Act 1984 and has continued in enactments like the Criminal Justice and Public Order Act 1994, the Crime and Disorder Act 1998, the Criminal Justice and Police Act 2001, and in the Criminal Justice Act 2003, which have vastly increased the powers criminal justice agencies have in the way of protection for individuals. To some degree these have reduced the rights of suspects and defendants, while there are some doubts as to how far these enhanced powers and new criminal laws have increased the rights or interests of victims. Powers which do not respect the rights of suspects and defendants may well lead to miscarriages of justice—wrongful convictions, which not only breach the rights of the person convicted but are also clearly contrary to the interests of victims and of justice (see also the discussion concerning the crime control model in Chapter Two).

There is a plethora of crime prevention and control initiatives: neighbourhood watch (using individuals to keep an eye on each other, see above); closed circuit television (using cameras to watch the public); the suggested carrying of identity cards; bans on guns and tighter controls on the sale of knives; designing cities and towns in ways which might reduce crime (see Chapter Eleven); increasing aware-ness of the individual's responsibility to protect his or her own goods and person. More recent attempts to persuade communities to take responsibility and be active in criminal justice initiatives have been adopted by the Crime and Disorder Act 1998 (the issue is further discussed in Chapter Sixteen), while various other preven-tion initiatives seem to draw citizens more and more into the control of crime. Such initiatives could be said to benefit victims and society if they actually reduce crim-inal activity, but the crime figures suggest that this has not yet occurred on any great scale. Each initiative needs to be considered in it own right, taking into account not only possible advantages to potential victims and society but also such negative effects for individuals and society as intrusions into privacy and the increased responsibilities placed on victims or potential victims (victim blaming). It needs to be asked: do the possible advantages outweigh the reduction in freedom?

There are also calls for increased information for, and participation by, victims in the process, often in decisions as to bail, diversion, and levels of sentence. Britain has, as indicated above, increased information and ensured that the victim's experience of the criminal justice system is made smoother. However, such provision still largely depends on where the victim is located since agencies in some localities are better equipped to serve victims, while much depends on the personalities of the officials in a particular case.

If the provision of information has improved, little has yet been done to increase the participation of victims in the criminal justice process. Schemes such as reparation, mediation and restorative justice, which might most effectively move in that direction, have not been widely used. The introduction of victims' personal statements permits sentencers to have more information on the consequences of the offence. This has, rightly, not allowed the opinions of victims to affect sentencing, but factual information on consequences can be used in court.

However, even these statements are not without difficulties; some victims may exaggerate levels of loss and suffering, and if these become increasingly used by courts, victims may be called to answer questions as to the level of damage suffered. Nonetheless most accept that the use of VPS is positive both for victims and for society.

Most prominent in political and media initiatives has been the concept of tougher sentencing. The core of the crime control or law and order lobby is that one must force offenders to take responsibility for their actions and, as part of this, to face heavier sentences in the hope that these will incapacitate some offenders for a limited period of time and will deter others. In the 1990s this was the main focus of initiatives culminating in the Crime (Sentences) Act 1997, the most important provisions of which introduce mandatory minimum sentences for repeat burglars, drug dealers, violent and sexual offenders, and are now largely included in Part V chapter III of the Powers of the Criminal Courts (Sentencing) Act 2000. Whether this type of crime initiative 'works' is at best debatable. Harsh punishments are powerful political rhetoric and make good media hype, but they may well make bad criminal justice policy and may not serve the interests either of victims or of the rest of society.

Another victim-led initiative which is seen by many as a further punitive element, is embodied in the Sex Offenders Act 1997 as amended by the Criminal Justice and Court Services Act 2000 under which a register is kept of certain categories of sex offenders; registration continues for periods of five, seven, ten years or life, depending on the length of the sentence imposed for their offence. The register permits the authorities to keep sex offenders under surveillance so, it is hoped, rendering it less likely that they will re-offend. The police are entrusted with keeping the register. Despite intense media pressure to pass what they dub as 'Sarah's law', which would allow either wider access to the register or for residents to be informed if a sex offender comes to the neighbourhood, there are no plans to provide this. Such information might make communities feel safer, but previous offenders must have some right of settlement; and the emotive nature of the issue can lead to a mob law, as was evidenced when neighbours set fire to the home of an alleged paedophile and burnt to death a child who was inside (*Guardian*, 19 February 1997), and again in the summer of 2000 when the *News of the World* published photographs of paedophiles: in the consequent mob violence some who simply looked like the photographs were attacked, as was—because of linguistic confusion—a medical paediatrician. A register, particularly if the information is widely disseminated, may in fact be counterproductive as it might lead to what Braithwaite (1988) terms 'disintegrative shaming', where the criminal is not only punished but is also considered to be a criminal for life, beyond forgiveness and not worthy of being welcomed back into society—an outcast. The register may then become a self-fulfilling prophecy whereby such individuals become more and more dangerous and necessarily re-offend.

Such a result would be counter-productive to society. The registers allow authorities the opportunity to keep an eye on previous offenders. The police and probation are then supposed to assess the risk posed by each offender and manage the levels of risk such that the public are safer, see especially ss. 67–9 of the Criminal Justice and Court Services Act 2000. Nothing in the procedure requires probation to try to reduce the risk posed by the offender through programmes unless that is a separate part of their sentencing. They only have to keep an eye on them and manage the risk. As little extra funding has been allocated to this work it seems reasonable to suppose that fulfilment of this requirement will be patchy at best and generally fairly minimal. Even were it to include programmes to reduce risk levels there are still many sex offenders who have never been prosecuted. However, as the public have been led to believe that they are safer as a result of the policy, they may lower their own safety precautions. When these provisions probably provide little if any extra safety this might mean an overall lowering of protection, particularly for children. Again the prominence given by politicians and the press to victims has been used to take greater powers to the State on the claim of increasing safety and security. Yet the end result may at best be unlikely and at worst a lowering of safety.

As was noted in Chapter Two, those who define crime and control the criminal justice agencies narrow the concepts of offenders and crime. These are then still further narrowed by what the media choose to depict as crime. The same process is true for victims: we have a narrow and controlled view of those who suffer harm and who are entitled to the concerns that go with the title of 'victim'. Victims of corporate or government offences or atrocities are rarely recognised as such. They are generally marginalised: they are not usually represented by victim groups, nor do they obtain the support offered by organisations such as VSS. Nor, indeed, do they get much notice in this book. However, it should at least be registered that they must be included in any consideration of how to respond to victimisation, while feminist writers point out that the conceptions of victimisation which are most frequently given recognition fail fully to understand the concept of 'victim' for women and other groups who suffer discrimination. Much feminist work in this area has opened up areas for recognition as crimes and has given the 'victims' some status—especially in the areas of child abuse (particularly child sexual abuse), rape and domestic violence. Such concerns have also started to break down the reluctance felt by the crime control agencies for entering the private domain, while demonstrating the resilience of many victims to survive their position. This too should be respected, forcing recognition that victims are a diverse group with different needs.

Paradoxically, one approach which might meet these requirements is to consider providing guaranteed and universal rights for victims. Great care would be needed to ensure that such rights do not interfere with the rights necessary to the suspect or defendant. The aim would be for a rights strategy which would go much further than the provision of legal powers towards ensuring that rights, legal and social, are enjoyed by all in a society. Many believe this wide rights base might reduce criminality more effectively (Elias (1993), ch. 8; and see also Chapter Eleven of this volume). In such a rights-based society, discrimination would be reduced and equality as citizens would be actively promoted. Ideally this would be the effect of the Human Rights Act 1998, but government would need to be more proactive to ensure it delivers such protection. In any event, moves to protect the rights of victims do not always succeed: the Youth Justice and Criminal Evidence Act 1999, s. 41, was intended to restrict questions about the sexual history of a rape complaint, but in court it was claimed that this breached the Article 6 (fair trial) right of the defendant. The defendent wanted to ask the victim about recent consensual sexual activity between them. The House of Lords dismissed his claim that s. 41 breached Article 6 of the ECHR since s. 41(3)(c) permitted the judge to admit the evidence where the relevance of the issue of consent was so strong that its exclusion might jeopardise a fair trial (*R* v *A* (No. 2) [2001] 2 WLR 1546).

Victims are now an integral part of criminological study. Their importance in the criminal justice system is increasing, but they still lack basic powers and rights or interests which will be legally protected within that system. It is important that the study of the victim does not take over from the study of the criminal, and so allow the criminal to escape culpability and social condemnation. If the needs of victims must be kept in perspective, they must also be taken more seriously by those in authority, not least because without their cooperation the system quite literally could not operate.

SUGGESTED READING

Crawford, A. and Goodey, J. (eds) (2000), *Integrating a Victim Perspective Within Criminal Justice: International Debates*, Aldershot: Dartmouth.

Hale, C. (1996), 'Fear of Crime: A Review of the Literature', *International Review of Victimology*, 4, p. 79.

Hoyle, C. and Young, R. (2002), *New Visions of Crime and Victims*, Oxford: Hart Publishing.

It is essential to visit Home Office sites to understand the extent to which victims are involved in the system. See for example: **http://www.homeoffice.gov.uk/ http://www.homeoffice.gov.uk/justice/index.html http://www.homeoffice. gov.uk/rds/index.htm**.

QUESTIONS

1 Why, over recent decades, have victims come to figure more prominently in the study of criminology?

2   Which groups are most likely to be victims of crime? Are these the groups which most fear crime?

3   What assistance does the criminal justice system afford to victims?

REFERENCES

Amnesty International (1999), *United Nations International Criminal Court: Ensuring an Effective Role for Victims*, **http://www.amnesty.org/ailib/aipub/1999/IOR/I4001099.htm.**

Ashworth, A. (1986), 'Punishment and Compensation: Victims, Offenders and the State', *Oxford Journal of Legal Studies*, vol. 6, p. 86.

Ashworth, A. (2000), 'Victims' Rights, Defendants' Rights and Criminal Procedure', in A. Crawford and J. Goodey (eds), *Integrating a Victim Perspective Within Criminal Justice*, Aldershot: Ashgate Dartmouth

Austin, C. (1988), *The Prevention of Robbery at Building Society Branches*, Crime Prevention Unit Paper No. 14, London: Home Office.

Aye Maung, N. and Mirlees-Black, C. (1994), *Racially Motivated Crime*, Home Office Research and Planning Unit, Paper 82, London: HMSO.

BCS, see British Crime Survey.

Boran, Anne (ed.) (2003), *Crime Fear or Fascination?*, Chester: Charter Academic Press.

Bottoms, A. (2003), 'Some Sociological Reflections on Restorative Justice', in A. von Hirsch, J. Roberts, A. E. Bottoms, K. Roach and M. Schiff, *Restorative Justice and Criminal Justice: Competing of Reconcilable Paradigms?*, Oxford: Hart Publishing.

Braithwaite, John (1988), *Crime, Shame and Reintegration*, Cambridge: Cambridge University Press.

Braithwaite, J. (2003), 'Principles of Restorative Justice', in A. von Hirsch, J. Roberts, A.E. Bottoms, K. Roach and M. Schiff (eds), *Restorative Justice and Criminal Justice: Competing of Reconcilable Paradigms?*, Oxford: Hart Publishing.

British Crime Survey 1992, see Mayhew et al. (1993).

British Crime Survey 1994, see Mayhew et al. (1994).

British Crime Survey 1998, see Mirrlees-Black et al. (1998).

British Crime Survey 1998, see Kershaw et al. (2000).

Brogden, M. and Nijhar, P. (2000), *Crime, Abuse and the Elderly*, Cullompton: Willan Publishing.

Budd, T. (1999), *Violence at Work: Findings from the British Crime Survey*, Research and Statistical Unit Occasional Paper, London: Home Office.

Campbell, R. and Kinnell, H. (2000–2001), ' "We Shouldn't Have to Put Up with This": Street Sex Work and Violence', *Criminal Justice Matters* vol. 42, p. 12.

Chadee, D. and Ditton, J. (2003), 'Are Older People Most Afraid of Crime?: revising Ferraro and LaGrange in Trinidad', *Brit. J. Criminol.*, vol. 43, p. 417.

Commission for Racial Equality (2002), *A Plan for Us All: Learning from Bradford, Oldham and Burnley*, London: Commission for Racial Equality.

Council of Europe (1983), *European Convention on the Compensation of Victims of Violent Crime*, European Treaties Series No. 116.

Crawford, Adam (1995), 'Appeals to Community and Crime Prevention', *Crime, Law and Social Change*, vol. 22, p. 97.

Criminal Justice Matters (2002), Issue 48.

Daly, K. (2003), 'Mind the Gap: Restorative Justice in Theory and Practice', in A. von Hirsch, J. Roberts, A.E. Bottoms, K. Roach and M. Schiff (eds), *Restorative Justice and Criminal Justice: Competing of Reconcilable Paradigms?*, Oxford: Hart Publishing.

De Haan, W. (1990), *The Politics of Redress*, London: Unwyn Hyman.

Dignan, J. (2003), 'Towards a Systematic Model of Restorative Justice: Reflections on the Concept, its Context and the need for Clear Constraints', in A. von Hirsch, J. Roberts,

A.E. Bottoms, K. Roach and M. Schiff (eds), *Restorative Justice and Criminal Justice: Competing of Reconcilable Paradigms?*, Oxford: Hart Publishing.

Dobash, R.E. and Dobash, R.P. (1992), *Women, Violence and Social Change*, London: Routledge.

Duff, A. (2003), 'Restoration and Retribution', in A. von Hirsch, J. Roberts, A.E. Bottoms, K. Roach and M. Schiff (eds), *Restorative Justice and Criminal Justice: Competing of Reconcilable Paradigms?*, Oxford: Hart Publishing.

Ekblom, P. and Simon, F. (1988), 'Crime and Racial Harassment in Asian-run Small Shops', *Police Research Group Crime Prevention Paper Series*, No. 15, London: HMSO.

Elias, R. (1993), *Victims Still*, London: Sage.

Farrall, S., Bannister, J., Ditton, J. and Gilchrist, E. (2000), 'Social Psychology and the Fear of Crime', *British Journal of Criminology*, vol. 40, p. 399.

Gabriel, U. and Grieve, W. (2003), 'The Psychology of Fear of Crime. Conceptual and Methodological Perspectives', *Brit. J. Criminol.*, vol. 43, p. 600.

Garland, David (1996), 'The Limits of the Sovereign State: Strategies of Crime Control in Contemporary Society', *British Journal of Criminology*, vol. 36, pp. 445–71.

Garland, David (2000), 'The Culture of High Crime Societies: Some Preconditions of Recent "Law and Order" Policies', *British Journal of Criminology*, vol. 40, pp. 347–75.

Garland, D. (2001), *The Culture of Control: Crime and Social Order in Contemporary Society*, Oxford: Oxford University Press.

Gill, M. (1998), 'The Victimisation of Businesses: Indicators of Risk and the Direction of Future Research', *International Review of Victimology*, vol. 6, p. 17.

Gill, M. (1999), 'Crimes, Victims and the Workplace', *Criminal Justice Matters*, vol. 35, p. 12.

H.M. Inspectorate of Probation (2000), *The Victim Perspective: Ensuring the Victim Matters*, London: Home Office.

Harman, C. (1982), 'The Law and Order Show', *Socialist Review*, vol. 1.

Harris, J. and Grace, S. (1999), *A Question of Evidence? Investigating and Prosecuting Rape in the 1990s*, London: Home Office.

Hillyard, P. and Tombs, S. (2001), 'Criminology, Zemiology and Justice', Paper presented to the Socio Legal Studies Association in Bristol, April 2001.

Holloway, W. and Jefferson, T. (2000), 'The Role of Anxiety in Fear of Crime', in T. Hope and R. Sparks (eds), *Crime, Risk and Insecurity*, London: Routledge.

Home Office (2001a), *A Review of the Victim's Charter*, London: Home Office. **http://www.homeoffice.gov.uk/docs/revictch.pdf.**

Home Office (2001b), *The Victim Personal Statement Scheme: Guidance Note for Practitioners or those Operating the Scheme*, London: Home Office. **http://www.homeoffice.gov.uk/docs/guidenote.pdf.**

Home Office (2001c), *The Victim Personal Statement Scheme: A Guide for investigators*, London: Home Office. **http://www.homeoffice.gov.uk/docs/guideinvestig.pdf.**

Home Office (2003), *A New Deal for Victims and Witnesses: National Strategy to Deliver Improved Services 2003*. Home Office Communication Directorate. London: Home Office **http://www.cjsonline.org/library/pdf/18890_victims_and_witness_strategy.pdf.**

Hopkins, M. (2000–2001), 'Abuse and Violence against Small Businesses', *Criminal Justice Matters*, vol. 12, p. 34.

Hough, M. (1995), *Anxiety about Crime: Findings from the 1994 British Crime Survey*, Home Office Research Study No. 147, London: Home Office Research and Statistics Directorate.

Hough, M. and Mayhew, P. (1983), *The British Crime Survey: First Report*, Home Office Research Study No. 76, London; HMSO.

Hough, M. and Mayhew, P. (1985), *Taking Account of Crime: Findings From the Second British Crime Survey*, Home Office Research Study No. 85, London: HMSO.

Houts, S. and Kassab, C. (1997), 'Rotter's Social Learning Theory and Fear of Crime: Differences by Race and Ethnicity', *Social Science Quarterly*, vol. 78, p. 122.

Hoyle, C. (2002), 'Restorative Justice and the "Non-Participating" Victim', in C. Hoyle and R. Young (eds.) *New Visions of Crime and Victims*, Oxford: Hart Publishing.

Hoyle, C., Morgan, R. and Sanders, A. (1999), *The Victim's Charter—An Evaluation of Pilot Projects* Home Office Research Findings No. 107, 1999—ISSN 1364–6540 (**http://www.homeoffice.gov.uk/rds/index.htm**).

Hoyle, C. and Sanders, A. (2000), 'Police Response to Domestic Violence: From Victim Choice to Victim Empowerment?', *British Journal of Criminology*, vol. 40, p. 14.

Islington Crime Survey 1986, see Jones, T., Maclean, B. and Young, J. (1986).

Johnstone, G. (2001), *Restorative Justice: Ideas, Values, Debates*, Cullompton: Willan Publishing.

Johnstone, G. (2003), *Restorative Justice Reader: Texts, Sources, Context*. Cullompton: Willan Publishing.

Jones, T., Maclean, B. and Young, J. (1986), *The Islington Crime Survey: Crime Victimisation and Policing in Inner City London*, Aldershot: Gower.

Kershaw, C., Budd, T., Kinshott, G., Mattinson, J., Mayhew, P., and Myhill, A. (2000), *The British Crime Survey 2000*, Home Office Statistical Bulletin Issue 18/00, London: HMSO.

Kielinger, V. and Stanko, B. (2002), 'What Can We Learn From People's Use of the Police?' *Criminal Justice Matters*, vol. 48, p. 4.

Killias, M. and Clerici, C. (2000), 'Different Measures of Vulnerability in their Relation to Different Dimensions of Fear of Crime', *British Journal of Criminology*, vol. 40, p. 437.

Kinsey, R., Lea, J. and Young, J. (1986), *Losing the Fight Against Crime*, Oxford: Basil Blackwell.

Lee, M. (2001), 'The Genesis of "Fear of Crime"', *Theoretical Criminology*, vol. 5(4), p. 467.

Lloyd, S., Farrell, G. and Pease, K., *Preventing Repeated Domestic Violence; the Results of a Demonstration Project in Merseyside Police 'C' Division*, Home Office Crime Prevention Paper, London: HMSO.

Lord Chief Justice (2001), *Practice Direction: Victim Personal Statements*, London: Court Service.

Mackay, R.E. and Moody, S.R. (1994), *Neighbourhood Disputes in the Criminal Justice System*, Edinburgh: Scottish Office Central Unit, HMSO.

Macpherson, Sir William (1999), *The Stephen Lawrence Inquiry: Report of an Inquiry by Sir William Macpherson of Cluny*, London: HMSO.

Maguire, Mike (1985), 'Victims Needs and Victims Services', *Victimology*, vol. 10, p. 539.

Maguire, M. and Kynch, J. (2000), *Public Perceptions and Victims' Experiences of Victim Support: Findings from the 1998 British Crime Survey*. Home Office Occasional Paper, London: Home Office.

Mawby, R.I. and Walklate, S. (1994), *Critical Victimology*, London: Sage.

Mayhew, Pat, Elliot, David and Dowds, Lizanne (1989), *The British Crime Survey: Third Report*, Home Office Research Study No. 111, London: HMSO.

Mayhew, Pat, Aye, Maung, Natalie and Mirrlees-Black, Catriona (1993), *The 1992 British Crime Survey*, Home Office Research Study No. 132, London: HMSO.

Mayhew, Pat, Mirrlees-Black, Catriona and Aye Maung, Natalie (1994), *Trends in Crime: Findings from the 1994 British Crime Survey*, Research Findings No. 14, Home Office Research and Statistics Department, London: HMSO.

Mendelsohn, B. (1947), 'New Bio-psychosocial Horizons: Victimology', *American Law Review*, vol. 13, p. 649.

Miers, D. (1989), 'Positivist Criminology: A Critique', *International Review of Victimology*, vol. 1(1), p. 3.

Miers, David (1992), 'The Responsibilities and the Rights of Victims of Crime', *Modern Law Review*, vol. 55, p. 482.

Miers, D., Maguire, M., Goldie, S., Sharpe, K., Hale, C., Netten, A., Uglow, S., Doolin, K., Hallam, A., Enterkin, J. and Newburn, T. (2001), *An Exploratory Evaluation of Restorative Justice Schemes*, Home Office Crime Reduction Research Series, 9, Home Office: London

Miers, L. (2001), *An Exploratory Evaluation of Restorative Justice Schemes*, London: Home Office.

Mirlees-Black, C. (1999), *Domestic Violence: Findings From a New British Crime Survey Self Compilation Questionnaire*, London: Home Office.

Mirrlees-Black, Catriona, Mayhew, Pat and Percy, Andrew (1996), *The 1996 British Crime Survey: England and Wales*, Home Office Statistical Bulletin Issue 19/96, London: HMSO.

Mirrlees-Black, Catriona, Budd, Tracey, Partridge, Sarah and Mayhew, Pat (1998), *The 1998 British Crime Survey*, Home Office Statistical Bulletin Issue 21/98, London: HMSO.

Mirrlees-Black, C., Mayhew, P. and Percy, A. (1996), *The 1996 British Crime Survey: England and Wales*, London: Home Office Research and Statistics Division.

Moran, L. (2002), 'Homophobic Violence as Hate Crime', *Criminal Justice Matters*, vol. 48, p. 8.

Morgan, Jane, Winkel, Frans and Williams, Katherine (1994), 'Protection and Compensation for Victims of Crime', in Phil Fennell, Chris Harding, Nico Jörg and Bert Schwarts (eds), *The Europeanisation of Criminal Justice*, Oxford: Oxford University Press.

Myhill, A. and Allen, J. (2002), *Rape and Sexual Assault of Women: The Extent and Nature of the Problem, Findings from the British Crime Survey*. Home Office Research Study 237, London: Home Office. **http://www.homeoffice.gov.uk/rds/pdfs2/hors237.pdf**.

National Standard for the Supervision of Offenders in the Community (2000), Home Office, London: HMSO.

Newburn, T., Crawford, A., Earle, R., Sharpe, K., Goldie, S., Campbell, A. Masters, G., Hale, C., Saunders, R, Uglow, S. and Netten, A. (2001), *The Introduction of Referral Orders into the Youth Justice System: Second Interim Report*. RDS Occasional Paper No. 73, London: Home Office. **http://www.homeoffice.gov.uk/rds/pdfs/occ73-justice2.pdf**.

Pantazis, C. (2000), ' "Fear of Crime", Vulnerability and Poverty', *British Journal of Criminology*, vol. 40, p. 414.

Phillips, C. and Sampson, A. (1998), 'Preventing Repeat Racial Victimisation: An Action Research Project', *British Journal of Criminology*, vol. 38, p. 124.

Ray, L., Smith, D., and Wastell, L. (2000–2001), 'Understanding Racist Violence', *Criminal Justice Matters*, vol. 42, p. 28.

Ray, L. and Smith, D. (2002), 'Racist Violence as Hate Crime', *Criminal Justice Matters*, vol. 48, p. 6.

Reeves, H. and Mulley, K. (2000), 'The New Status of Victims in the UK: Opportunities and Threats', in A. Crawford and J. Goody (eds), *Integrating a Victim Perspective Within Criminal Justice*, Aldershot: Ashgate Dartmouth.

Roberts, A.R. and Roberts, B.S. (1990), 'A Mode for Crisis Intervention with Battered Women and their Children' in A.R. Roberts (ed.), *Helping Crime Victims* London: Sage.

Rock, Paul (1988), 'Governments, Victims and Policies in Two Countries', *British Journal of Criminology*, vol 28, p. 44.

Rock, P. (1994), *Victimology*, Aldershot: Dartmouth.

Rock, P. (2002), 'On Becoming a victim', in C. Hoyle and R. Young (eds), *New Visions of Crime and Victims*, Oxford: Hart Publishing.

Roshier, Bob (1989), *Controlling Crime*, Milton Keynes: Open University Press.

Ruggiero, V. (2000), *Crime and Markets*, Oxford: Oxford University Press.

Russell, Dianna (1984), *Sexual Exploitation*, Beverly Hills, CA: Sage.

Russell, J., 'Safe Indoors', *Guardian*, 18 November 2002.

Scarman, Lord (1981), *The Brixton Disorders, 10–12 April 1981*, Cmnd 8427, London: HMSO.

Shaw, M. and Pease, K. (2000), *Preventing Repeat Victimisation in Scotland: Some Examples of Good Practice*, Edinburgh: Scottish Executive Central Research, Central Research Unit.

Siddiqui, H. (2000–2001) 'Domestic Violence and Black/Minority Women: Enough is Enough', *Criminal Justice Matters*, vol. 42, p. 14.

Sparks, R.F. (1982), *Research on Victims of Crime: Accomplishments, Issues, and New Directions*, Rockville, Md: National Institute of Mental Health, Centre for Studies of Crime and Delinquency, US Department of Health and Human Services.

Stanko, B. (2000–2001), 'Murder and Moral Outrage: Understanding Violence', *Criminal Justice Matters*, vol. 42, p. 4.

Stanko, B. (2000), 'The Day to Count: A Snapshot of the Impact of Domestic Violence in the UK', *Criminal Justice*, vol. 1, p. 2.

Stanko, Elizabeth, A. (1988), 'Hidden Violence Against Women', in Mike Maguire and John Pointing (eds), *Victims of Crime: A New Deal*, Milton Keynes: Open University Press.

Stanko, Elizabeth, A. (1990), 'When Precaution is Normal: a Feminist Critique of Crime Prevention', in L. Goldthorpe and A. Morris (eds), *Feminist Perspectives on Criminology*, Buckingham: Open University Press.

Strang, H. (2002), *Repair or Revenge: Victims and Restorative Justice*, Oxford: Clarendon Press.

Strang, H. and Braithwaite, J. (2002), *Restorative Justice and Family Violence*, Cambridge: Cambridge University Press.

Tulloch, M. (2000), 'The Meaning of Age Differences in the Fear of Crime: Combining Quantitative and Qualitative Approaches', *British Journal of Criminology*, vol. 40, p. 451.

Umbreit, M. (2001), *The Handbook of Victim/Offender Mediation: An Essential Guide to Practice and Research*, San Francisco: Josey Bass.

United Nations (1985), *Declaration on the Basic Principles of Justice for Victims of Crimes and Abuse of Power*, A/RES/40/34.

Vachss, Alice (1993), *Sex Crimes*, New York: Random House.

von Hentig, H. (1948), *The Criminal and his Victim*, New Haven, CT: Yale University Press.

von Hirsch, A., Roberts, J., Bottoms, A.E., Roach, K. and Schiff, M. (eds), (2003), *Restorative Justice and Criminal Justice: Competing of Reconcilable Paradigms?*, Oxford: Hart Publishing.

Walgrave, L. (2002), *Restorative Justice and the Law*, Cullompton: Willan Publishing.

Walgrave, L. (2003), 'Imposing Restoration Instead of Inflicting Pain', in A. von Hirsch, J. Roberts, A.E. Bottoms, K. Roach and M. Schiff (eds), *Restorative Justice and Criminal Justice: Competing of Reconcilable Paradigms?*, Oxford: Hart Publishing.

Walklate, S. (2001), 'The Victim's Lobby', in M. Ryan, S. Savage and D. Wall (eds), *Policy Networks in Criminal Justice*, Basingstoke: Palgrave.

Weitekamp, E.G.M. and Kerner, H.-J. (2002), *Restorative Justice: Theoretical Foundations*, Cullompton: Willan Publishing.

White Paper (1990), *Crime, Justice and Protecting the Public*, London: HMSO.

Wilson, J.Q. and Kelling, G. (1982), 'Broken Windows: The Police and Neighbourhood Safety' *The Atlantic Monthly*, March 1982, 29–38.

Women's Unit (1999), *Living without Fear: An Integrated Approach to Tackling Violence against Women*, London: Cabinet Office.

Wong, K. (2000–2001), 'New Projects to Deal with Violence against Women', *Criminal Justice Matters*, vol. 42, p. 17.

Wood, J., Wheelwright, G., Burrows, J. (1997), *Crime against Small Business: Facing the Challenge*, Leicester: Small Business Centre.

Wright, M. (1992), 'Victims, Mediation and Criminal Justice', *Cambridge Law Review*, 187.

Young, R. (2001), 'Just Cops Doing "Shameful" in Business?: Police-Led Initiatives in Restorative Justice and the Lessons of Research', in I. A. Morris and G. Maxwell (eds), *Restorative Justice for Juveniles*, Oxford: Hart Publishing.

Young, R. (2002), 'Testing the Limits of Restorative Justice: The Case of Corporate Victims', in C. Hoyle and R. Young (eds), *New Visions of Crime and Victims*, Oxford: Hart Publishing.

Zedner, L. (1997), 'Victims', in M. Maguire, R. Morgan, and R. Reiner (eds), *The Oxford Handbook of Criminology*, Oxford: Clarendon Press.

6

Influences of physical factors and
genetics on criminality

6.1 Introduction

The aim of this chapter is to consider, from both an historical and a contemporary viewpoint, the assertion that there are biological explanations for crime. In the past, theories which advanced this type of explanation tended to adopt the stance that crime was a sickness or illness which afflicted individual criminals, and was the result of some biological disfunction or disorder. Many contemporary criminologists have doubted these biological, particularly genetic, explanations of crime. They perceive such ideas as an admission of hopelessness and untreatability which carry with them the inference that the public will demand the removal of these individuals from society for good, an approach of 'lock them up and throw away the keys'. These fears are, to an extent, understandable as some of the past research favoured this conclusion (see, for example, 6.4).

Modern biologists consider that genes are relevant because they have a strong influence on brain function and therefore, it is believed, on behaviour and criminality. Since all human beings (except identical twins) are genetically unique this can help explain differences in behaviour by individuals who have been subjected to similar environmental and social influences. However, most modern researchers do not view the part played by biology in any explanation of criminality as indicating an illness or a dysfunction; rather it suggests the possibility of a slightly different configuration of normal genes giving rise to a temperament which is more receptive to antisocial types of behaviour. Furthermore, many do not view such differences as immutable, recognising instead that biological and genetic differences can be altered. Some of the results, they accept, may be unpleasant but assert that this should not prevent the scientific investigation of the phenomenon of crime. The claim is that science should be allowed to seek for truth and leave it to the politicians and moral philosophers to decide how to deal with the results. In any event, there is an awareness that biology and genetics cannot be an answer in themselves. Modern biologists generally acknowledge the importance of environmental and social influences on criminal behaviour and suggest that they should be studied in parallel with genetics—they call this a biosocial perspective by which they recognise that biological characteristics will not determine whether an individual will take part in criminal behaviour but they may increase its likelihood (Fishbein (2001)).

Any interaction of the 'ologies' (particularly criminology, sociology, biology and psychology) poses problems. One of the main difficulties lies in the nature of the different types of research involved. Despite being one of the less exact 'sciences', biological research tends to be more precise than its sociological and psychological counterparts in that the variables studied are generally more exact. For example, an individual only has so much adrenalin in the body at any one time, and this level can be precisely measured. On the other hand, a sociologist may be attempting to measure or assess parental discipline, which will involve the researcher in more subjective and necessarily less exact conclusions. This may lead to problems when comparing the relative importance of each type of research.

For example, exact calculations based on precisely measurable data, such as the amount of a certain chemical in the body, may appear to show a stronger correlation between one variable and criminality than that which exists between a more imprecise variable, such as parental discipline, and criminal behaviour.It does not necessarily follow from this that the former is really more important than the latter, or is a better guide to predicting criminality. It may simply be that the element of say, parental discipline, has not been, and cannot be, measured and presented so clearly and in isolation from other social factors. Similarly, even if criminality is shown to be linked to, say, genetics, this, as already indicated, does not mean that genes are the sole cause of criminality. It may be that an individual has inherited the potential to act in a criminal manner, but whether or not that potential is realised may depend upon the interaction of the physical and social environment with those individual traits.

If it is appreciated that neither biological nor social explanations offer anything like a complete solution, but that their interaction may provide a more balanced perspective, then it may be possible to arrive at a better understanding of crime and its prevention. In any event, the interaction between biological and social factors is clearly very complex. What is said about biological theories in this chapter should therefore be read with an awareness that they may also need to be considered in a social context.

6.2 Lombroso and after

It could be said that biological explanations for crime began with the phrenologists in the eighteenth and early nineteenth centuries (for full history, see Fink (1985)). Their claim of a relationship between the size and shape of the skull, the brain and social behaviour was for a time very fashionable. Although these ideas have virtually no significance for modern criminology they did focus attention on the individual criminal. This was a link which was made more explicitly and effectively by Lombroso.

Lombroso (1835–1909) after a medical education spent most of his working life at the University of Turin in his native Italy. In 1876 he published *L'Uomo Deliquente* (The Criminal Man) which then ran to 252 pages; by its fifth and final edition in 1897 it held 1,903 pages. Lombroso is worth mentioning here because on the basis of his work he has been called the father of modern criminology. This is a reasonable claim because of the major shift he effected in the approach to issues of crime and the criminal. He aimed to replace the then dominant abstract, religious or philosophical study of crime with a more scientific approach requiring direct empirical evidence and its careful analysis.

His claim as the founder of modern criminology thus rests on the, for his time, remarkable weight of scientific observation and statistical analysis. Nonetheless his actual findings have been more or less totally rejected partly because of fundamental methodological flaws and partly because his analysis rested on a dubious assumption. Briefly, the most serious shortcoming of his empirical evidence arose from a failure to match his prison sample of criminals with a representative group from the same racial and social background, whilst the work also assumes the existence of a distinct anthropological type—the 'born criminal'—who is likely, or even bound, to commit crime. He initially claimed that his observations on the criminals in his studies showed that they exhibited a wide range of physical features—such as peculiar size or shape of head, excessive length of arms—and that anyone who possessed five of these characteristics was 'a born criminal'.

In his later work Lombroso (1906) included many other variables which could impinge on criminality: climate, rainfall, grain prices, sex and marriage customs, education, religious and government structures. On the one hand the multiplication of variables threatened to swamp the original thesis (though the stress was always on the physical): on the other hand these extensions increased his reputation as the father of modern criminology because they now encompassed the three major strands of most contemporary works—biology, psychology and environment.

The particulars of Lombroso's theories, especially that of equating a propensity to commit crime with physical make-up have long been discredited as too simplistic. This must not blind today's students to the importance of Lombroso's work. Part of his legacy was to establish the basis for a positivist school of criminological study with its requirement of a 'scientific' foundation for knowledge through the careful collection of measurable and verifiable data, submitted to stringent analysis, and subjecting any assumptions to empirical verification. One consequence of positivist approaches in criminology is to suggest either that the individual has some inherent predisposition to criminality, or that the environment (broadly defined) forces him towards criminality. In either case the element of free individual choice is reduced. Lombroso's scientific credentials were also boosted by his early use of Darwin's evolutionary theory. Although his main use was ill founded in that he argued that the physical characteristics of his criminals represented atavism, an evolutionary throwback, the fact of appealing to new advances in scientific thought was more important.

Some of the more practical potential consequences of Lomboso also merit brief attention. Thus in its crudest form of the 'born criminal', it could influence attitudes to punishment. Earlier classical writings (see Beccaria (1964, first published 1776)) urged that the punishment should fit the crime: a positivist approach could argue that if the individual was inherently criminal a much larger sentence could be justified to prevent future offences and to protect society. The early twentieth-century's fascination with eugenics also led some to argue that long imprisonment would also help prevent 'born criminals' from passing on their characteristics to a new generation. (see Garland (1985)). From a slightly different standpoint—if it was thought that those with criminal propensities could be 'reformed'—the positivist arguments for longer sentencing could also be supported. The logical conclusions of both the reform and eugenics arguments was that society should not wait for a crime to be committed; if 'born criminals' were physically identifiable why not detain them until they are 'cured', or subject them to drug treatment or sterilisation to pre-empt their criminal propensity and/or prevent passing it to the next generation? Such chilling possibilities mostly serve to indicate the dangers of mis-using theories.

One natural extension of Lombroso's approach was into *Somatotyping* which purports to relate the behaviour and constitution of a person to the shape of their body. This was best systemised by William Sheldon (1949) who identified three basic body types: endomorphic (soft, rounded, fat); mesomorphic (hard, muscular, athletic); and ectomorphic (thin, weak, frail), each with its associated personality traits (e.g., friendly, sociable for endomorphic). In a study comparing young male delinquents with a control group of students he concluded that most delinquents tended towards mesomorphy. Later more sophisticated studies to test this finding (Gluecks, 1950 and Cortes and Gatti, 1972) found some support for such an association but, more crucially, found that delinquency was related to a combination of biological, environmental and psychological factors.

Lombroso and somatotypist theorists considered that biological traits were a useful means of identifying criminals or potential criminals. There are some contemporary claims to make similar use of one of the central areas of modern science, genetics. More generally, as we shall see (Chapters Eight to Thirteen), in both cases many studies and much evidence point towards the need to include social and psychological aspects: but these additions are not necessarily incompatible with the overall positivist approach.

6.3 Genetic factors

6.3.1 Introduction

In recent years the study of genetics has become one of the fastest moving and most significant areas of modern science. The exercise of such techniques as genetic engineering, already commercially used for cereals and vegetables, and for cloning, of farm animals and body parts, raise possibilities which are at once exciting and frightening. They raise major moral issues. Most of the work relating genetics to human characteristics has so far been more concerned with linking genetics with particular diseases, rather than with criminal behaviour, but the recent genetic advances clearly have possible implications for criminology and some of them will be indicated later (see 6.3.6). It is first necessary to survey the various attempts which have previously been made to examine a genetic basis for crime and criminal behaviour.

6.3.2 Inherited genetic factors: family studies

The early attempts to prove a genetic link with criminality were unsophisticated. They usually involved studying the family trees of known criminals. The most famous of these was undertaken by Richard Dugdale (1877). The Jukes were a New York family who were infamous for criminality, prostitution and (apparent) poverty. Dugdale postulated that all three factors were related and were fixed, so that criminality would always run in the family. It was true that in the Jukes family there was a very high proportion of criminals, but that does not prove any link between criminality and genetic or inherited factors. Such a close family similarity might be explained by similar environmental factors acting on all members of that family, or by arguing that all had learnt the ideas and methods of criminality from one another, making it difficult for any member to remain non-criminal. Goring (1913) was another early writer who rejected physical and environmental factors to claim that criminal tendencies were basically inherited. He studied convicts and found that the correlation between father and son—and between brothers—for criminality was very similar to that for physical traits such as eye colour and stature. Goring's argument is that the important factor is not the physical features but the contents of the genetic material passed on from the parents. If the parents were criminal, they would pass the tendency on to their children exactly as they might pass on any other trait (Goring (1913), pp. 365–7).

The similarity in behaviour between parents and children could not, he said, be environmental because the correlation was too closely related to other clearly hereditary factors, such as physical appearance. Further, the coefficient was found to be no higher in crimes such as stealing, where one might expect fathers to act as examples for their sons and so teach them, than for sex crimes where one would expect the father to try to hide his involvement so the example would not be present. He also discovered that where parents were removed from the home when the child was still very young (usually the removal was the result of imprisonment), the child was as likely if not more likely to turn to criminality than if the parents were removed at a later stage. He accordingly claimed that a longer period of contact did not increase the criminality, which was the result of hereditary factors, and from this he drew the conclusion that people with those inherited characteristics should have their reproduction regulated. This is a frightening conclusion, particularly when it is drawn from research that is so weakly based.

Briefly: Goring considered only convicts without a control group; made no attempt to measure the influence of the environment; only considered the possibility of transmitting criminal techniques by parents—not the likelihood of their transmitting criminal values; and was unable to account for the apparent failure of the inherited characteristics to show up in the females in the families.

This is not to say that Goring's approach should simply be dismissed. Indeed, a recent unexpected finding from the Cambridge Study in Delinquent Development (an ongoing longtitudinal study set up in the 1960s) lends some weight to the claim that criminality runs in families. Of 397 families in the study half of the convictions were attributed to just 23 families and three-quarters of convicted mothers and fathers have a convicted child. Despite the seemingly heavy suggestion that therefore genetics and crime are closely correlated it is important to recognise that family members also enjoy close social and environmental similarities and therefore the behavioural correspondence may be equally or more explicable on these grounds. All that can be safely gleaned from these studies is that there are close behavioural similarities within families: it is more difficult to draw strong conclusions as to the causes. For a general discussion see Rowe and Farrington (1997).

6.3.3 **Twin studies**

Does heredity or environment cause criminality? Theorists realised that if you could hold one of these variables constant, then similarities in criminality would suggest that crime was related to the constant, whereas differences would suggest a connection with the variables. The only way they saw of doing this was to study twins. There are two sorts of twins—monozygotic (MZ) or identical twins, who are from a single egg and single sperm and therefore genetically identical, and dizygotic (DZ) or non-identical twins, who are born from two eggs simultaneously fertilised by two sperm (i.e., they share only 50 per cent of their genes) and so are no more similar than ordinary brothers and sisters. The claim was that, if identical twins act in identical ways, their behaviours could be the result of identical inheritance, but any difference in behaviour would have to be the result of the environment. If criminality was caused by genetics, then if one MZ twin was criminal then the other would also be criminal, i.e., they would depict concordant behaviour patterns, whereas there need be no such relationship between DZ twins whose behaviour would be different or discordant. If criminality was related to the environment, then both MZ and DZ twins would show similar concordance rates.

Early studies of this sort suggested that criminality was closely related to genetics (see Lange (1929)). The MZ twins did show greater rates of concordance than did the DZ twins. Even so, it is important to note that the MZ twins also showed some discordance and that the DZ twins showed some concordance: clearly, criminality could not be wholly explained by genetics. Some part had to be played by other factors, such as the environment. In any event, most of these early studies suffered from very basic research problems. In particular, in most of the studies at least one of the twins was drawn either from prison or from a psychiatric clinic, giving an unrepresentative cross-section of the twin population.

Two well-known twin studies by Christiansen (1968 and 1974) and Dalgaard and Kringlen (1976) were more firmly based.

Christiansen drew his twins from the official twin register of Denmark, and collected information on some 6,000 pairs of twins born between 1881 and 1910 and who lived up to the age of 15. He then separated them into MZ and DZ twins, and finally used the Penal Register to discover whether either or both twins had been convicted. In the MZ or identical group he found that for males there was a 35.8 per cent concordance rate, i.e., if one male MZ twin was convicted of a criminal offence the likelihood that the other twin would also be convicted was 35.8 per cent; for male DZ twins the corresponding figure was only 12.3 per cent. For females the differences were even more marked: 21.4 per cent for MZ twins but only 4.3 per cent for DZ twins. It has been claimed that these figures show a significant role is played by inherited factors. It does portray a possible connection, but care must be taken. Christiansen himself recognised that no study had yet provided conclusive evidence of the complete dominance of either genetics or environment. He recognised that none of his results could be interpreted as indicating that heredity played a predominant part in the causation of crime, but stated that it is an *a priori* hypothesis that heredity and environment always interact in a dynamic fashion to bring about and shape criminal behaviour.

Dalgaard and Kringlen studied 139 pairs of Norwegian male twins and discovered a 25.8 per cent concordance rate in MZ twins as compared with only 14.9 per cent in DZ twins. Dalgaard and Kringlen suggested that the results might be explained by the close similarities in upbringing in the case of identical twins. To test this idea, they grouped all the twins according to their mutual psychological closeness. They discovered that more of the MZ twins were close than were the DZ twins, and that among those who were psychologically close there was no difference in their concordance rates by zygosity. They therefore concluded that this wiped out the apparent involvement of genetics in criminality, leaving the environment as the only appreciable influence. On the evidence they present, this conclusion seems at least as doubtful as would be a simple acceptance of heredity.

A later different twin study gave rather different results which can be used to uphold both social and genetic reasons for criminality. Rowe (1990) refers to the Ohio twin study which he and Rodgers conducted (Rowe and Rodgers 1989). They collected information from self-report questionnaires on personal delinquency, temperament, perceptions of family environment, and association with delinquent peers from 308 sets of twins in schools in the Ohio State area and included 265 sets of same-sex twins and 43 opposite-sex twins, as well as a small non-twin-sibling control group. They concluded that genetic influences partly determine the similarity of behaviour of same-sex and monozygotic twins. They recognised that interaction between siblings could cause initially discordant siblings to become concordant in their levels of delinquency. Therefore genetics can explain some of the concordance but sibling and twin interaction also play a large part in shaping behavioural patterns. Rowe claims that some of the disparities found in other twin studies can be explained by a failure to recognise fully the importance of interaction between siblings.

None of the above studies is decisive as to the significance of heredity for criminality, mainly because twins are brought up together as a general rule, and as Rowe (1990) notes, this makes it virtually impossible to reach any firm conclusion as to the role of genetics alone. It is still possible that a predisposition to crime could be genetically transmitted. Attempts to test this hypothesis have been based on studies of adoption, which permit a better delineation between genetics and environment.

6.3.4 **Adoption studies**

The intention is to discover whether there is a correlation between biological parental, particularly paternal, criminality and the adoptee's criminality. The tests are based on the adoptee having been removed from the criminal influence of its natural parent at an early age. If such a relationship is found, the argument is that it indicates a correlation between criminality and genetics. Whereas if family environmental elements are most important there will be no such correlation, and, instead, a link to the behavioural patterns of the adoptive parents will be discovered. Adoption studies are considered particularly important because they isolate one factor, genetics, from the other, environmental influences.

Hutchings and Mednick (1977) studied all Copenhagen male adoptions where the adopting parents were not related to the child and where the adoptee was born between 1927 and 1941. They discovered that boys with criminal biological fathers were more likely to be criminal than those with law-abiding fathers. Further, they found that those with criminal adoptive fathers were also more likely to be criminal than those with law-abiding adoptive fathers, but that the effects of a criminal biological father were more noticeable than a criminal adoptive father (22 per cent and 12 per cent respectively). This finding suggested that genetics were in this respect more important than environment. Lastly, they found the most significant effects when both the biological fathers and the adoptive fathers were criminal. In these cases, the effect upon the rate of criminality of the adoptee was quite marked, at 36 per cent. In 1984 they replicated their research in a wider study which encompassed all non-familial adoptions in Denmark between 1924 and 1947 (Mednick et al. (1984)). In this wider study they found a similar though slightly less strong correlation between biological parents (note this study compared parents rather than just fathers) and their adoptee children (20 per cent). The relationship between adoptive parents and their adopted children was 15 per cent. Again they found the most significant results when both biological and adoptive parents were criminal (25 per cent).

From these results, Hutchings, Mednick and Gabrielli have claimed that criminality is related to genetics. It is important to note, however, that adoption agencies try to place children in homes situated in similar environments to those from which they came. If environmental forces are significant, this would tend to exaggerate the apparent genetic effects because their environment will remain relatively unchanged: but it may still be the upbringing and not the genetic material which causes criminality. In addition the claims have been questioned by Gottfredson and Hirschi (1990), who begin by observing that in the wider study, against expectations, the genetic correlation was reduced rather than increased. That is, the comparison was no longer with fathers and children but by including mothers had become a comparison between adoptive parents and children: if the important factor was genetic, Gottfredson and Hirschi claim this alteration should have strengthened the link. But in fact the link was weakened. Furthermore, they noted that although the number of adoptions studied rose by 3,403 cases, the actual number of cases in the category of criminal biological parents only rose from 58 to 85. From this Gottfredson and Hirschi concluded that:

the true genetic effect on the likelihood of criminal behaviour is *somewhere between zero and the results finally reported by Mednick, Gabrielli and Hutchings*. That is, we suspect that the magnitude of this effect is minimal.

The link between criminality, genetics and the environment is essential to the work of Walters (1992) who analysed 38 of the significant family, twin and adoption studies. He concluded that there was a small, though not insignificant, correlation between genetics and crime (11 to 17 per cent); that the common environmental element (that suffered or enjoyed by others in the same conditions) seemed to be 24 to 32 per cent; and the remaining 51 to 65 per cent is attributable to specific environmental influences (experiences unique to a particular individual), and to error. He notes that the better designed and more recent gene–crime studies were less supportive of a link between genetics and crime than were the earlier and less well designed studies. Despite this he concludes that one should not ignore a genetic link when studying reasons for criminality and suggests that the genetic and environmental and sociological elements combine in contributing to delinquent and criminal activity. This approach would be supported by many of the biosocial theorists (see Ellis and Hoffman (1990) and Fishbein (2001)).

6.3.5 Race, crime and genetics

As was seen in Chapter Four, there is broad agreement that there is a large and relatively stable correlation between race and crime: in the UK Afro-Caribbeans consistently have the highest conviction rates for crime; whites are the next most likely criminal group; followed at some distance by Asians. Many theorists have suggested sociological reasons for the differences although, as was also mentioned in Chapter Four, some of the variation may be explained by prejudiced crime enforcement rather than by difference in crime committal, although Smith (1997 at p. 101) concludes the actual offending rate is substantially higher among black people than among other groups. In contrast to the considerable body of socio-logical work linking race to crime, there have been few recent attempts to connect the racial differences in crime to genetic difference. Whitney (1990) argues that such research is long overdue because of what she regards as strong suggestive evidence for a link. A number of studies (Latter 1980; Rushton 1985; Rushton 1988; Rushton and Bogaert 1987) suggest that there is an Afro-Caribbean—white—Asian ordering of differentiation between races with regard to certain testable genetic traits. As there is a similar breakdown of crime rates, she argues that there is enough evidence to support the need for research to assess whether genetics can provide a partial explanation for the criminality. Clearly her hypothesis will be supported if it is accepted that there is a genetic basis for some of the indi-vidual differences in criminality (still a contentious issue, see 6.3.4 above). Whitney is not alone: Wilson and Herrnstein (1985) and Herrnstein and Murray (1994) make similar, though circumstantial, claims for a link between crime, race and genetics.

Whitney recognises the sensitivity of her suggestions but considers that science should not shrink from discovering the truth merely because it may be misused by society. Even so, the apparent rationality of Whitney's argument should not obscure two facts: first, that such studies are scientifically questionable as we do not yet possess the information necessary to perform them: and secondly that information linking racial genetic differences to crime could prove to be very dan-gerous and might lead to increased discrimination with potentially very serious consequences. This should never be forgotten. With little of obvious positive value to be gained from any conclusions, the justification for pursuing this line of research must be questionable. Until the way in which the possible genetic differ-ence operates is more fully understood the very powerful negative effects which might arise should be very clearly considered by scientists, politicians and lawyers. Furthermore, Tonry (1997), having collated research from nine countries on the criminal behaviour of immigrant ethnic minority groups as compared to that of members of the indigenous resident communities, concludes that, whilst some ethnic minorities are over-represented in the crime statistics in every State, the high crime-rate groups were not consistently from one racial minority. So whilst it may be that in the UK Afro-Caribbeans commit more crime than do whites or Asians, in other States other immigrant and minority groups fill this spot. He notes a correl-ation between the high offending groups and various social and economic dis-advantages, as well as to elements such as subcultural norms; the aid States provide to the settlement of immigrants; and reasons for the migration that might affect their behaviour patterns and ability to settle. All of Tonry's research suggests that social rather than genetic explanations would be more likely to explain any differences.

6.3.6 **Can genetics explain crime?**

In recent years the advances in genetic science have given rise to widespread claims that not only human physical characteristics, but also aspects of human behaviour derive from genetic sources. In this context it is thus unsurprising to find claims, not necessarily by the scientists themselves, that aspects of criminality can be accounted for by genetic factors. Here two strands of this tendency will be examined: the first drawn from speculation based on analogies with theories of animal behaviour; the second deduced from the expansion of scientific knowledge about genes.

6.3.6.1 *Theories of animal behaviour*

The first approach is exemplified in the work of Ellis (1990a), who looked to processes of natural selection operating on genetic evolution to explain both some aspects of criminal behaviour and some of the major characteristics of the criminal justice system. In terms of behaviour, the argument is that some criminal activities—especially rape, assault, child abuse and property offences—are related to powerful genetic forces. Thus it is contended that forcible rape could have evolved from the part of the male makeup which aims to mate with many females in order to guarantee the gene line, and from the natural resistance of females to this as it interferes with their control over choosing sex partners with suitable genetic characteristics. To support this speculation Ellis points to numerous studies revealing forcible copulation in many non-human species; to the fact that most rapes are on females in the fertile age group; and to the further observation that the risk of pregnancy from rape is quite high. Similarly he argues that assault often occurs as part of the ritual of finding and retaining a sex partner, involving fighting off rivals and controlling partners.

The link between natural selection and child abuse drew its speculative basis from findings of animal studies that such behaviour occurred where the parents were unable to rear all their young, where one of the parents abandoned its parental duties, where the offspring had a low probability of being reproductively viable, and where there was a lack of close genetic connection between the offspring and the abusing parent (adoption or replacing defeated or deceased parent). Ellis then proposed a connection between the large category of property-based crime with a characteristic feature of gene-based evolutionary theory. The evolutionary claim is that every species aims to ensure the survival of its offspring, and one way of doing so is by (females) mating with (male) partners who are best able to provide the resources necessary for survival. The speculative claim is that many property crimes, as well as much violent crime, result from a genetic drive to attract and retain a mate. A supporting argument is that such a theory would explain why such crimes are apparently most commonly committed by those males with a low ability to provide, especially those in the lower social and economic groups.

It is clear that none of this offers any proof of genetic connections with crime and criminality: it is rather providing suggestive hypotheses drawn on the analogy of presumed explanations of animal behaviour. Much the same stricture applies to the attempt by Ellis (1990b) to explain aspects of the criminal justice system in similarly evolutionary terms. This draws mostly upon studies of primate groups where the dominant males patrol the groups to protect females and offspring, to control the rest of the group, and to protect their own mating interests. The hypothesis is that human control systems, and particularly that of criminal justice, reflect similar evolutionary imperatives. The exercise of control by the dominant group obviously favours the perpetuation of the *status quo* and hence safeguards the existing social structure and those individuals and groups already in positions of power. Even if the genetic and evolutionary impulses which are presumed to be behind these control systems have plausibility (but not proof) for primate groups, their explanatory power for accounting for complex human systems of criminal justice seems much more tenuous.

6.3.6.2 *Genetic influences*

The second strand relating genetics to criminality also contains elements of speculation. However, in sharp contrast to those considered above, these aspects arise more from the current limitations of scientific knowledge rather than from the inherent problems involved in basing imaginative leaps on dubious analogies. This second strand reflects the giant strides recently taken in the science of genetics. As little as a generation ago textbooks on genetics had little to say on humans, although, as already indicated in the first part of this chapter, this had not prevented strong assertions about the significance of human inheritance in determining the tendency of individuals towards criminal behaviour. Now that we have the full map of the human genome we know that the pattern is very complicated. But it seems clear that there is no simple 'criminal gene'. Certain genes will, in time, become associated with certain feelings or impulses, e.g., aggression. If this is the case then these will suggest a predisposition to behaviour patterns involving aggression. Carey and Gottesman (1996) predict a number of loci which affect temperament, motivation, cognition etc., all of which may make it more likely that an individual will perform a criminal or unacceptable act. This does not mean that there will be a predisposition to criminality; the two can never be linked in such a crude fashion. Many will find outlets for this type of impulse in perfectly legal ways: through physical and often competitive sports; through very physical work; through occupations where violence or at least aggression may be encouraged, e.g., boxing and the armed forces; through aggressively competitive business practices. The link with aggression or any other factor alone gets us no closer necessarily to a reason for a criminal outlet for that feeling. However, if such a link is discovered, there are some guaranteed uses which will be made of the information:

- Lawyers will argue the link in court, stating that the criminality was the result of a predisposition and not the chosen action of the offender. This might lead to two contradictory arguments. First, the offender should not face harsh, blaming and determinate sentences but should be treated as an individual and helped, presumably through less invasive interventions. Many of the researchers in this field would support this type of intervention. For example, Fishbein (1996 and 2001) accepts that genetics does not render the trait immutable. The environment in which the individual lives may control the genetic predisposition or there may be drugs or other treatments available.

- Alternatively if it is not possible to control their urges, they are more dangerous and should be removed from society, not to be punished but to reduce the risk to others; a form of humane containment would then be necessary. Much of our present crime control strategy concerns risk management and control (see Chapter Twenty) and in this political climate if treatment is unavailable or cannot be guaranteed and the danger posed is great then the call will be for indefinite confinement. This has already been seen in relation to paedophiles. Some argue that the calls could go still further (see Spallone (1998)) to allow selective breeding, genetic manipulation of individuals or foetuses, or execution of those with certain genetic links.

Either of these would be an unscientific and unacceptable use of such a link. The possibilities need to be further considered.

Apart from the sheer intellectual excitement of such advances, the developments in genetics are having major practical implications. It is clear, for example, that the propensity to contract many diseases is strongly affected by inheritance; and the particular genes related to particular diseases are being identified. Such features can have large social implications; already there are suggestions that insurance companies (and credit institutions) might wish to examine the genetic characteristics of potential clients. Not surprisingly, attention—and research—has tended to concentrate on such links with health, particularly since the genetic origins of some diseases prompt the possibility of genetic cures. Prudent geneticists are, however, much more cautious in claiming or expecting that human behaviour is primarily an inherited characteristic—that our genes determine how we act.

Nonetheless, given the enormous potential implications of work in this field, it is not surprising that projections about its results have reflected on the possibility of using genetic engineering to manipulate human behavioural, as well as physical, characteristics. The relevance of such trends for theories of criminal behaviour is obvious, although little work directly relating genetic make-up to criminal behaviour has yet been carried out. If criminals can plausibly claim that they have no control over their actions which are the result of their genetic inheritance, both the practical and ethical bases of criminal justice systems would be substantially undermined.

The implication is that advances in genetics could foster a new determinism, more soundly based not only than the biological determinism sponsored by Lombroso's earlier experiments, but also than the economic determinism derived from Marx. Recent developments in this scientific field have given new life and liveliness to the ancient philosophical debate of Nature (inheritance) versus Nurture (environment): many would also claim that the result has been to shift the balance towards Nature.

More pertinently, many geneticists would say that it is imprudent to claim too much knowledge for this area: rapid as the advances have been, there is still only limited understanding about the ways in which inheritance of characteristics takes place even in relatively simple organisms. One major finding that is now generally established and accepted is that acquired characteristics are not inherited. This is not to deny that the offspring of musicians may not be above-average musically, or that the offspring of criminals may not be somewhat more likely to commit criminal offences; but the reason for this is not fully explained in genetic inheritance.

Families share the same environment as well as the same genes. Even characters which are inherited 'involve', as one authority expresses it:

gene and environment acting together. It is impossible to sort them into convenient compartments. An attribute such as intelligence is often seen as a cake which can be sliced into so much 'gene' and so much 'environment'. In fact, the two are so closely blended that trying to separate them is more like trying to unbake the cake. (Jones (1993), p. 171)

Where there is so much uncertainty, even over characters which can be measured, extra caution is needed in looking to genetics for explanations of such ambiguous concepts as criminal behaviour. None the less, the discovery that some traits of personality, such as aggressiveness, have a genetic component greatly strengthens the possibility that some criminal behaviour can be explained by a genetic susceptibility being then triggered by environmental factors. Sight of the influence of environmental factors must not be lost. Most geneticists would agree with Jones that genetics will probably only ever be a partial and complex element in explaining criminal behaviour. Its insights should be used to inform the debate, not to control it.

6.3.7 An assessment of genetic factors

None of these studies conclusively proves that either 'Nature' or 'Nurture' are the only factors involved in criminality. It seems that each plays some part, but that it is impossible to ascertain their relative importance at this stage. The problem has been further exacerbated by the now fairly widely accepted claims that a foetus is affected by its environment before birth, so that even claims that a new-born child portrays a distinct personality is not proof that that personality was simply genetically inherited. What can be said with some certainty is that the evidence of these studies is insufficient to found a claim that genetics provides a complete explanation for criminality. The most that can be claimed is that some members of society, because of their physical or psychological make-up, which to some extent may be a genetic endowment, are more prone to criminality if other environmental factors are also present.

Furthermore, there is as yet no adequate biological explanation as to what exactly is being inherited. There is much research into this area but the topic is new and, although developing quickly, the precision of the information is insufficient to provide an explanation. Although the human genome has been mapped, its enormous complexities have been little explored. There has certainly been very little research into how genetic information might affect the propensity to criminality. Yet unless geneticists can explain how inheritance affects criminality, there is no acceptable way to help limit criminality except through controlling the environment so that fewer individuals are tempted to, or have the opportunity for, criminality. Even that carries the assumption that we know which aspects of the environment give rise to criminal behaviour.

What the biological theorists claim now (see 6.3.3 to 6.3.6) is not that criminality is inherited but rather that we inherit certain biological predispositions. In claiming this the researchers are not saying that there is a link between a specific gene and criminality or antisocial behaviour. Indeed, it is unlikely that a single gene pair could ever produce the complex traits which are generally associated with criminality. Instead genetic links may arise from the interrelationship of many genes each producing a relatively small effect. Therefore criminal behaviour, if it is related to genetics, may arise from particular combinations of normal genes rather than from defective genetic structures. Many physical traits are the result of poly-genetic groupings and it is therefore likely that behaviour results from such complex interrelationships. Geneticists point out that: the formation of the central nervous system is dictated by genetics; that the central nervous system is the organ which dictates human behaviour including criminal behaviour; therefore, there must be a link between genetics and criminality. It is not claimed that any polygenetic group-ings force an individual into criminal behaviour but rather that some may pre-dispose them to certain types of behaviour. What is not explained is how this predis-position is expanded and developed into antisocial or criminal activity in some individuals, but is subdued or channelled into non-criminal activities in others. The above studies do suggest a connection between crime and genetics, but thus far this information is of limited practical use as we do not understand how it operates.

6.4 Conclusion

Biological theories have been out of vogue for some time. Most people would now find Lombroso's ideas concerning appearance and physical traits crude and laugh-able, yet Bull and McAlpine (1998) suggest that most people have stereotypes of the facial appearance of criminals and worryingly suggest that these might affect judgments of guilt and innocence in criminal trials. On reading the earlier theorists and some of their suggestions for change, it is easy to understand how this distaste for biological theories arose. In the older writings, the argument is often that the biological reason is the only reason for criminality. These biological and genetic explanations have been seen as proving that a criminal is untreatable, lending plausibility to the idea that society might turn towards sterilisation of the carriers of these genetic or biological disorders to breed a less antisocial society. Other sug-gested remedies, such as locking them away for good or utilising the death penalty, raised similar ethical questions (for a further discussion, see 10.1.7).

Today it is unusual for such Draconian measures to be countenanced, but new ideas may bring with them implications which are equally unpalatable. Recent genetic work could certainly produce highly intrusive possibilities for the future. Scientists are trying to understand and link specific genetic structures with types of behaviour. Some of the behaviour may be antisocial or criminal. As yet this research is not far enough advanced to draw any conclusions, but the possible implications are disturbing. If firm links are drawn between types of behaviour and genes, this could lead to calls for selective breeding or genetic engineering to eradicate unwanted genes and unwanted behaviour. Such selection could be carried out in a number of different ways—sterilisation of those with unwanted genes; mass exe-cution of these same groups of people; or by laws specifying legal and illegal breed-ing groups. Lastly, it may be possible to perform surgery on a very young foetus (under 14 days) and remove the unwanted genetic material before returning the foetus to its mother. Some of the issues in this area will be regulated by the Human Fertilisation and Embryology Act 1990. Most of these possibilities should be unacceptable in a democratic society, and yet if the evidence was sufficiently strong the arguments for such measures could be extremely persuasive. We need to be aware that modern and seemingly objective scientific research could give results which could be used in wholly unacceptable ways.

Rose (2000) is less concerned about the possible consequences. He considers it unlikely that the effect of the present genetic discoveries will lead to eugenics or the belief that any conduct is predetermined by biology: there will always be room for choice and thus blame but the new penological response will be more focused than the old eugenics. Individuals who have transgressed can and presumably should be punished but if they are found to have a genetic susceptibility, this should be dealt with and treated so that they are no longer a danger to themselves, their families or their communities. In his discussion this seems to be compulsory treatment though presumably it may be voluntary. Further than this Rose suggests that a positive response would be to diagnose these possible propensities, identify individual sufferers before they transgress and intervene to prevent criminality by effective treatment. This he postulates as an acceptable and measured response despite earlier having noted that there is no guaranteed link between these possible propensities and criminal behaviour. Again treatment is presented as though it would be compulsory and the benefits to both individual and society are assumed. The only advantage over the old eugenics is in the targeting of individuals not groups: it still involves altering individuals where this may prove unnecessary and is clearly in violation of rights. For many the future Rose presents is as dangerous in essence as the old eugenics even if it would affect fewer people: it is arguably as morally unacceptable and is indicative of the dangers associated with this type of progress.

Biological research is not, of course, mostly being conducted to solve the problems caused by criminal behaviour. Its applications to this area can thus be ambiguous. For example, up to the present some of this research has had a far more positive part to play in crime control in the guise of genetic or DNA fingerprinting. The structure of each individual's DNA is very distinctive, and the possibility of two being the same is very low. For this reason it has been used in a number of cases of rape and murder in Britain and other Western countries, although its reliability has been questioned (see Alldridge et al. (1994)). The analyses can be obtained from samples of hair, nails or from body fluids. If such materials are found at the scene of a crime, they can be matched up with possible suspects in order to solve a crime. Even here, however, there are potential dangers. For example, a future discovery could be that certain patterns of DNA are more prevalent among criminals than non-criminals. Such information could be used to control the lives of people, possibly even before they commit any crimes, or to control their right to have children. The dangers of this become even greater when one considers that a databank of DNA fingerprints is being constructed by the police to help in future cases. The DNA databank is to be expanded to hold DNA material from almost anyone from whom a sample is taken in connection with the investigation of an offence (Criminal Justice and Police Act 2001, s. 82). The danger is already growing and only awaits interpretation.

The lesson would seem to be that while criminologists cannot and must not obstruct biological research, they should be watchful to ensure that any discoveries made are used in humane, acceptable and positive ways. They need to question carefully any strong assertions of close links between genetics and crime. Thus, for example, it is known that most criminals start offending in their teens and alter their offending patterns or become law abiding by their mid-twenties. Why would the genetic predisposition cause and then stop causing criminal behaviour? Even more importantly, they should be vigilant in ensuring that such knowledge is never used for negative or unacceptable intrusions. The need is the greater since the power of science on political and social decision-making can no longer be ignored.

SUGGESTED READING

Ciba Foundation Symposium 194 (1996), *Genetics of Criminal and Antisocial Behaviour*, Chichester: Wiley.

Ellis, L. and Hoffman, H. (eds) (1990), *Crime in Biological, Social and Moral Contexts*, New York: Praegar. Various chapters. Most are of clear use to this aspect and to that covered in Chapter Seven of this book.

Mednick, S. and Christiansen, K.O. (eds) (1977), *Biosocial Bases of Criminal Behaviour*, New York: Gardner Press. Various chapters. Most are of clear use to this aspect and to that covered in Chapter Seven of this book.

REVISION BOX

The importance of the early aspects of this area of study are threefold:

1   The work of Lombroso and his followers marked a move from what has become thought of as the classical school of criminology generally portrayed as arguing that crime resulted from the free will and hedonism of the individual (Beccaria and Bentham) towards the positivist school of criminology (criminal activity being determined, for these early positivists, by features within the individual's mind or body: for later positivists by social or environmental features).

2   Lombroso has been called the father of modern criminology largely because of his scientific rather than philosophical or juridical methodology. Unlike earlier positivist writers, Lombroso searched for empirical facts to confirm his theories and used scientific methodologies in the collection of data. Although this methodology had been growing in importance throughout the nineteenth century, his is the first major body of work to be based entirely in this approach. His grounding in and use of Darwinism was also exceptional for this period and makes his work more memorable and durable. His scientific methodology has been used by most criminologists in the past 100 years or so.

3   The policy consequences of these researchers. The theories were heavily based on Darwin's idea of the survival of the fittest. At its widest the theory was used by many to argue against social welfare programmes as these might artificially perpetuate the survival of the less 'fit' in society. In criminal policy it led to calls for the elimination of the 'born criminal' (eugenics) or at least their permanent removal from society to protect others from the dangers of these biologically determined criminals together with sterilisation policies so that they could not pass on their propensity to offspring.

Impact of more recent biological theories:

1   Today biology is not seen as determining behaviour rather it is seen as interacting with social and environmental factors to give rise to particular behaviours: biosocial theory. Here learning and societal conditioning is important but seen to occur at a different rate for each individual, even individuals who are subject to the same exposure to learning. The rate or effectiveness with which behaviour is learnt may well be decided by biological differences or propensities which cannot be altered although it may be possible to change their effects on behaviour.

2   There is a general recognition that we will never discover a 'criminal gene' but an acceptance that there are many genes which can affect behaviour (possibly as many as 5,000) some of which may be particularly relevant to criminal activity, e.g., ones associated with aggression. The way in which these develop and the opportunities which open up for their legitimate use will be part of what will be used to decide whether criminality is chosen as a form of behaviour.

3   As this is not seen as deterministic and much will depend on the development of facets of the personality which are attributed to the genes then one may be able to alter behaviour through treatment. These ideas and policy options will be addressed later.

4   There is a recognition that biology is never the only and usually is probably not the major element shaping behaviour; there is room for learning, social and environmental factors as well as free will.

QUESTIONS FOR REVISIONS

1   Is it likely that sports heroes, such as footballers, have similar gene patterns to violent offenders such as football hooligans? What more might you want to know before answering this?

2   Can biosocial theories ever explain white-collar and corporate crimes (those of the powerful) or are they only of any use as explanations of the more traditional 'antisocial behaviours' (more street level crimes often committed by the less well off)?

3   Why do many view biological or biosocial explanations as dangerous and wish to suppress studies in this direction?

4   Is there any practical point in studying the links between criminal behaviour and genetics?

5   Does the history of biological and genetic links with crime teach us more about the dangers inherent in policy applications in this field than it does about the causes of criminal behaviour?

REFERENCES

Beccaria, Cesare (1964), *Of Crimes and Punishments* (first published 1776 as *Dei delitti e delle pene*) (6th edn), trans. by Fr. Kenelm Foster and Jane Grigson with an introduction by A.P. D'Entreves, London: Oxford University Press.

Bull, R. and McAlpine, S. (1998), 'Facial Appearance and Criminality', in A. Memmon, A. Vriji and R. Bull, *Psychology and Law: Truthfulness, Accuracy and Credibility*, Maidenhead: McGraw-Hill.

Carey, G. and Gottesman, I.I. (1996), 'Genetics and Anti-Social Behaviour: Substance versus Soundbites', *Politics and the Life Sciences*, vol. 15, p. 88.

Christiansen, K.O. (1968), 'Threshold of Tolerance in Various Population Groups Illustrated by Results from the Danish Criminological Twin Study', in A.V.S. de Reuck and R. Porter (eds), *The Mentally Abnormal Offender*, Boston, MA: Little Brown.

Christiansen, K.O. (1974), 'Seriousness of Criminality and Concordance among Danish Twins', in Roger Hood (ed.), *Crime, Criminology and Public Policy*, London: Heinemann.

Cortes, Juan, B. and Gatti, Florence, M. (1972), *Delinquency and Crime: A Biopsychological Approach*, New York: Seminar Press.

Dalgaard, Steffen Odd and Kringlen, Einar (1976), 'A Norwegian Twin Study of Criminality', *British Journal of Criminology*, vol. 16, p. 213.

Dawkins, R. (1976), *The Selfish Gene*, Oxford: Oxford University Press.

Dawkins, R. (1982), *The Extended Phenotype*, Oxford: Oxford University Press.

Dugdale, Richard (1877), *The Jukes: A Study in Crime, Pauperism, Disease and Heredity*, Putnam: New York: reprinted (1977), New York: Arno.

Ellis, Havelock (1900), *The Criminal*, 2nd edn, New York: Scribner.

Ellis, Lee (1990a), 'The Evolution of Violent Criminal Behaviour and its Nonlegal Equivalent', in Lee Ellis and Harry Hoffman (eds), *Crime in Biological, Social, and Moral Contexts*, New York: Praeger.

Ellis, Lee (1990b), 'The Evolution of Collective Counterstrategies to Crime: from the Primate Control Role to the Criminal Justice System', in Lee Ellis and Harry Hoffman (eds), *Crime in Biological, Social, and Moral Contexts*, New York: Praeger.

Ellis, Lee and Hoffman, Harry (eds) (1990), *Crime in Biological, Social, and Moral Contexts*, New York: Praeger.

Fink, Arthur, E. (1985) (first published in 1938), *Causes of Crime*, London: Greenwood.

Fishbein, D. (1996), 'Prospects for the Application of Genetic Findings to Crime and Violence Prevention', *Politics and Life Sciences*, vol. 15, p. 91.

Fishbein, D. (2001), *Biobehavioural Perspectives in Criminology*, Belmont, CA: Wadsworth Publishing.

Garland, David (1985), *Punishment and Welfare: A History of Penal Strategies*, Aldershot: Gower.

Glueck, Sheldon and Glueck, Eleanor (1950), *Unravelling Juvenile Delinquency*, New York: Commonwealth Fund.

Goring, Charles Buchman (1913), *The English Convict: A Statistical Study*, London: HMSO.

Gottfredson, Michael, R. and Hirschi, Travis (1990), *A General Theory of Crime*, Stanford, CA: Stanford University Press.

Herrnstein, R. J. and Murray, C. (1994), *The Bell Curve*, New York: Free Press.

Hutchings, Barry and Mednick, Sarnoff, A. (1977), 'Criminality in Adoptees and Their Adoptive and Biological Parents: A Pilot Study', published in Sarnoff A. Mednick and Karl O. Christensen (eds), *Biosocial Bases of Criminal Behaviour*, New York: Gardner Press.

Jones, S. (1993) *The Language of the Genes*, London: HarperCollins.

Lange, Johannes (1929), *Verbrechen als Shicksal: Studien an Kriminellen Zwillingen*, trans. by Charlotte Haldane, (1930), *Crime as Destiny*, New York: Charles Boni.

Latter, B.D.H. (1980), 'Genetic Differences within and between Populations of the Major Human Subgroups', *American Naturalist*, vol. 116, p. 220.

Lombroso, Cesare, *L'Uomo Delinquente*, first published (1876), 5th and final edn (1897), Torino: Bocca.

Lombroso, Cesare (1906), *Crime: Causes et Remèdes*, 2nd edn, Paris: Alcan.

Mednick, Sarnoff, A., Gabrielli, T., William, F. and Hutchings, Barry (1984), 'Genetic Influences on Criminal Convictions: Evidence from an Adoption Cohort', *Science*, vol. 224, p. 891.

Rose, N. (2000), 'The Biology of Culpability: Pathological Identity and Crime Control in a Biological Culture', *Theoretical Criminology*, vol. 4, p. 5.

Rowe, David, C. (1990), 'Inherited Dispositions toward Learning Delinquent and Criminal Behaviour: New Evidence', in Lee Ellis and Harry Hoffman (eds), *Crime in Biological, Social, and Moral Contexts*, New York: Praeger.

Rowe, David, C. and Rodgers, J.L. (1989), 'Behaviour Genetics, Adolescent Deviance, and "d": Contributions and Issues', in G.R. Adams, R. Montemayor and T.P. Gullotta (eds), *Advances in Adolescent Development*, Newbury Park, CA: Sage Periodical Press, pp. 38–67.

Rowe, D.C. and Farrington, D.P. (1997), 'The Familial Transmission of Criminal Convictions', *Criminology*, vol. 35, p. 177.

Rushton, J.P. (1985), 'Differential K theory: the Sociobiology of Individual and Group Differences', *Personality and Individual Differences*, vol. 6, p. 441.

Rushton, J.P. (1988), 'Race Differences in Behaviour: a Review and Evolutionary Analysis', *Personality and Individual Differences*, vol. 9, p. 1009.

Rushton, J.P. and Bogaert, A.F. (1987), 'Race Differences in Sexual Behaviour: Testing and Evolutionary Hypothesis', *Journal of Research in Personality*, vol. 21, p. 529.

Sheldon, William, H. (1949), *Varieties of Delinquent Youth*, New York and London: Harper.

Smith, D.J. (1997), 'Ethnic Origins, Crime, and Criminal Justice in England and Wales', in Michael Tonry (ed.), *Ethnicity, Crime, and Immigration: Comparative and Cross-National Perspectives*, London: University of Chicago Press.

Spallone, P. (1998), 'The New Biology of Violence: New Geneticisms for Old?', *Body and Society*, vol. 4(4), p. 47.

Tonry, M. (1997), 'Ethnicity, Crime and Immigration', in Michael Tonry (ed.), *Ethnicity, Crime, and Immigration: Comparative and Cross-National Perspectives*, London: University of Chicago Press.

Walters, Glenn D. (1992), 'A Meta-analysis of the Gene-Crime Relationship', *Criminology*, vol. 30, p. 595.

Whitney, Glayde (1990), 'On Possible Genetic Bases of Race Differences in Criminality', in Lee Ellis and Harry Hoffman (eds), *Crime in Biological, Social, and Moral Contexts*, New York: Praeger.

Wilson, J.Q. and Herrnstein, R.J. (1985), *Crime and Human Nature*, New York: Simon & Schuster.

Wolfgang, Marvin, E. (1960), 'Cesare Lombroso', in Herman Mannheim (ed.), *Pioneers in Criminology*, London: Stevens & Son.

Yaralian, P.S. and Raine, A. (2001), 'Biological Approaches to Crime', in R. Paternoster and R. Bachman (eds), *Explaining Criminals and Crime*, Los Angeles: Roxbury.

7

Influences of biochemical factors and of the
central and autonomic nervous systems on
criminality

7.1 Biochemical factors

7.1.1 Introduction

Hormones, the secretions of the endocrine gland, were first discovered and artificially copied in laboratories before 1890. The interest in the effects of these substances grew and their significance to the personality began to be studied (see
Berman (1921)). Eventually, interest turned towards the effects of hormonal imbalance on criminal activity but researchers have found it difficult to discover any
causal link between hormonal activity and criminality or other behaviour because
hormones have only an indirect effect on behaviour. Hormones may act as a catalyst for behaviour or may provide a biological environment favourable to other
causal factors, but they have rarely been found to be connected to criminality.

There are a few exceptions to this, most of which involve an imbalance in the sex
hormones. A factor which affects women is the unusually large hormonal changes
which occur just before and during menstruation, often referred to as premenstrual
tension (PMT) and menstrual tension (MT). These have been accepted as factors
which can mitigate the sentence in some cases (see 17.2.4). The other main exception seems to be in the relationship between the level of the male sex hormone,
testosterone, and criminality, particularly violent criminality (see below, 7.1.2).
Although courts have accepted these as explaining criminal acts in particular cases
the link may not be causal but simply something which predisposes an individual
to particular behaviour in a specific context.

The preponderant opinion amongst criminologists that hormone imbalances do
not effect criminality has occasionally been disregarded in the criminal law. These
discrepancies have not led to any public dissension. For example, criminal law and
society generally accept that the recognised defence of infanticide (Infanticide Act
1938, s. 1) is an acceptable and, prior to the abolition of the death penalty, a very
necessary defence against one category of murder charge. It is a recognition that a
mother who kills her child within 12 months of giving birth to it should be given
some allowance, either because her mind was disturbed by reason of having given
birth or because of lactation consequent on the birth. This would seem to be a
recognition that hormone imbalance can be a cause of criminal behaviour. However, it might also be interpreted as a simple recognition that the death penalty for
such crimes had become unacceptable (at the time death was the penalty for all
murders), making the chemical imbalance a plausible excuse for humane leniency
in such a case whilst retaining a severe penalty for all other murders. This would be

consistent with the view that hormonal imbalance does not produce criminal conduct (see Shah and Roth (1974), p. 122), a view which has perhaps been instrumental in preventing premenstrual or menstrual tension from being generally recognised by the criminal courts or Parliament as a full defence. If used at all, it tends to be as a reason for reducing the sentence of the court (see 17.2.4).

Although it is a relatively new area, the initial research suggests some connection between biochemical factors and criminality. This chapter will consider its use as a tool to explain crime and possibly to prevent or control criminal activity. Work in this area is once again gaining political interest, and financial backing. How much this has to do with biological causes of criminality and how much is to do with a desire to locate the reasons for social problems, such as crime, in the individual rather than in society, is something which will be considered in the conclusion.

7.1.2 **Testosterone**

Testosterone has been popularly related to the most aggressive and antisocial crimes such as rape and murder. The claim is that the male sex hormone, plasma testosterone, adversely affects the central nervous system causing aggressive behaviour. The exact meaning of aggressive or violent behaviour is rarely defined in these studies, but most of the writers are interested in interpersonal violence such as rape, murder and assault. Here, only a general introduction to some of the central research in this area will be undertaken and some of the more interesting results presented.

Studies on animals indicated that testosterone, the male hormone, was related to the aggressive behaviour of monkeys. They also indicated that testosterone levels varied with environmental condition. Thus Keverne, Meller and Eberhart (1982) discovered that males held in separate cages had very similar testosterone levels, and that when each was individually introduced to a single female the increases in testosterone were of a similar size, but that when they were introduced into a mixed social grouping the high ranking, dominant monkeys produced large quantities of testosterone but the low ranking monkeys produced only very small quantities. When they were returned to separate cages there was again no difference in the testosterone levels of high and low ranking monkeys. If there seems to be a close relationship between the environment and the hormonal balance in some monkeys, as yet this is not fully understood. It is not clear whether the obvious association between aggression and testosterone in monkeys is proof of biological causation or not.

In humans the same male hormone exists and is thought to have similar effects. In studies on humans, men's testosterone levels are measured and then a psychological rating scale is used to measure aggression and social dominance. In some studies, aggressive male criminals are tested and their past records of aggressive behaviour are considered along with the other factors. In most men the testosterone levels probably do not significantly affect levels of aggression (for example, see Persky, Smith and Basu (1971), and Scarmella and Brown (1978)). In studies of proven violent male prisoners the results suggest that testosterone levels had an effect on aggressive and sexual behaviour, but even these results were not as strong as might be expected from the animal studies (see for example Kreuz and Rose (1972), and Ehrenkranz, Bliss and Sheard (1974)).

One factor which some have argued limits the usefulness of these studies on humans is that they do not separate out differing forms of aggression. They usually consider only actual bodily violence, whereas human aggression is frequently verbal. Furthermore, within both verbal and physical aggression or violence there is a distinct difference between persons who wantonly seek out or cause violent situations and those who defend themselves if violence is forced upon them. Lastly, the complexity of human personality requires attention to be paid to elements such as social dominance, sensation seeking, assertiveness, extroversion and sociability as well as aggression. Dan Olwens (1987) and Daisy Schalling (1987) have each conducted studies which address some of these problems. Dan Olwens's study was conducted on young men with no marked criminal career. Daisy Schalling's study was conducted on a group of young male inmates with a control group of males of a similar age.

Dan Olwens first found a clear connection between testosterone and both verbal and physical aggression. He then noticed a distinction between provoked and unprovoked aggressive behaviour. Provoked aggressive behaviour, which tended to be verbal more often than physical, was a response to unfair or threatening behaviour by another; any other aggression would be unprovoked. His research using a group of boys suggested that provoked violence was directly associated with levels of testosterone. In these boys, the provocation resulted in heightened testosterone production and so more aggressive behaviour. The testosterone production was directly related to the aggression, but was only produced in response to environmental circumstances. The relationship between testosterone and unprovoked violence and antisocial behaviour was indirect and more complex, tending to act on the level of tolerance. Olwens also found a weak but indirect relationship between testosterone and general antisocial behaviour and concluded that testosterone was only one of many factors affecting aggression, and possibly only a minor one.

Daisy Schalling discovered that high testosterone levels in young males were associated with verbal aggression but not with actual physical aggression or fighting. This, she said, portrayed a desire, on behalf of the high testosterone boys, to protect their status by threats. The low testosterone level boys would tend not to protect their position, preferring to avoid conflict and remain silent. High testosterone boys tended to shun monotony; to enjoy physical and competitive sports; to be more extrovert and sociable; and cared less about conventional rules and attitudes. Schalling thus portrays high testosterone boys as assertive, self-assured, sociable, and liable to become angry when aroused.

These findings are largely consistent with Olwens's finding that high testosterone levels in males cause low levels of tolerance, making them easily provoked and more likely to respond aggressively. Neither study suggests that there is a direct link between aggression and testosterone, but simply that if the correct social circumstances arise, especially a provocative situation, then those with an ability to secrete high levels of testosterone are most likely to resort to violence or aggression. The ability to secrete a high quantity of testosterone is a biological characteristic. Whether large amounts of testosterone are secreted depends upon the situations in which the individual finds himself. If that situation is provocative, it may lead to aggression and criminality may arise; if it is merely the setting for physical activity, e.g., sport, the high testosterone might be secreted but have its effects in more positive and acceptable ways. It is still unclear how the testosterone level interacts with social factors.

High levels of testosterone have also been related to crime generally and to sexual aggression. Ellis and Coontz (1990) note that testosterone peaks during puberty and early twenties, which correlates with the highest crime rates, and they claim that socio-environmental researchers have failed to explain why this distribution exists across almost all societies and cultures. They claim that this is persuasive support for a biological explanation. The evidence for such a connection, is, however, very tenuous and does not arise from direct experimental data: a similar criticism can be made of the claim that testosterone is linked with sexual crime. Sexual assaults by males, particularly rape, tend to be committed by men at an age when their sex hormones are very strong. This is not sufficient to prove a causal relationship, and generally rapists and non-rapists have not been found to have very different levels of testosterone but the most violent rapists have very high levels of the hormone (see Rada et al. (1983)). Despite these findings there is no evidence that there is any causal relationship between the behaviour and the level of testosterone. The assumption of such a link was, however, used in the twentieth century to justify legalised castration for sex offenders. The policy was tried in such countries as Denmark (1920), Germany (1933), Norway (1934), Estonia (1937) and Sweden (1944) (amongst others). Thousands of such operations were conducted, but it was never proved that such methods would reduce levels of sexual aggression. More recently antiandrogen drugs such as cyproterone acetate and medroxyprogesterone acetate are offered to aggressive sex offenders as an alternative to castration. These drugs have been found to reduce some of the effects of testosterone and have proved to be fairly effective in certain cases (see Walker et al. (1984), p. 440 and Rubin (1987), p. 248). In this way, the causative link is, to an extent, implied although Walker considered that the drugs were of real use only in high doses and when other positive environmental conditions exist: the individual volunteers for treatment; lack of substance abuse; there is a sexually consenting partner. Certainly none of the studies or the treatments explains the link, and in the absence of any convincing explanation its practical significance is limited, particularly as it may be that social and environmental factors trigger the testosterone levels which are being claimed as the cause of the criminality. If this is the case it might be better to address these rather than the levels of testosterone. Either way any solutions involve intrusions into individual liberty which would require social and political decisions.

Ellis and Coontz (1990) try to provide a partial explanation for the effects of testosterone. As mentioned above they note that the age and sex rates for criminality have about the same variation as levels of testosterone, and claim that this shows a possible causative link with both property crimes and aggressive behaviour against victims. They explain that the androgen testosterone has a strong presence in the male foetus before birth and is central to the formation of the sex of the child. At this stage it passes into the brain where they claim it affects development. The effects are strongest in male foetuses as the levels of testosterone are much higher. Female androgens might have similar effects, but as they do not pass into the brain this does not occur. Ellis and Coontz claim that testosterone in the brain at this early stage and again later produces three main effects, each of which they see as related to criminality.

First, it controls reticular arousability and thus the way in which external stimuli will be passed on to the brain. They link this low reticular arousal with criminality (see 7.1.3 and 7.3.1, below), because people needing very high levels of stimulation will act to start the necessary stimulation which might include criminal behaviour. Conversely, such people will be less responsive to negative stimulation, which in others would deter such behaviours.

Secondly, the limbic system which controls emotions such as rage, love-hate, jealousy, envy and religious fervour can be affected by testosterone levels in the brain. Problems with the limbic area may cause sudden and unpredictable emotions to arise, even in response to normal occurrences. These have been linked with epilepsy and epileptic seizures, and the proof for their relation to testosterone is that these conditions are far more common in men. Ellis and Coontz then draw on research which links criminality to epilepsy and epileptic tendencies to suggest a link between testosterone and criminality (see 7.3.2, below).

Thirdly, they point to a suggested link between domination of a particular brain hemisphere and criminality. Heavy reliance on the hemisphere that is least open to reason, logic and linguistic statements and most closely related to the limbic system is claimed to be related to criminality (see 7.3.3.2, below). Reliance on this hemisphere is more common in males than females: proof of this arises from the fact that there are more left-handed or ambidextrous men than women.

These three factors they put forward as an indication that criminal behaviour which involves a victim, but particularly aggressive behaviour, is more likely amongst those whose brains have been or are being affected by high levels of androgens, particularly testosterone. If correct, this moves us a step closer to explaining a causal link, if one exists, between criminality and testosterone, but it does no more than that. Probably the most that can be said is that the relationship between testosterone and crime, particularly aggressive crime, is sufficiently strong to merit further study.

Even if such study indicated a positive link, what should be done with the results? Should all male criminals be placed on antiandrogen drugs, or even all aggressive male criminals? Although these drugs are generally reversible and benign, they can produce potentially serious side effects in some people. In addition, there would be a marked reduction in offspring among those subjected to these drugs and they are therefore a form of control on birth levels to these individuals: such interference should never be lightly treated.

7.1.3 Adrenalin

The relationship between adrenalin and aggressive behaviour is a similar area of study to that involving testosterone. Each involves the relationship between a hormonal level and aggressive antisocial behaviour. In the case of adrenalin, Olwens (1987) found a negative relationship between adrenalin and aggression. Adrenalin levels are outwardly shown by the level of cortical arousal. Cortical arousal is a psychological state which usually involves all the outward portrayals of fear or excitement—high blood flow leading to more moisture on the skin, general alertness etc. It is this which is measured by a lie detector, as most people have a 'fear' of being discovered lying. A low level of adrenalin and a low cortical arousal are often found in those with an habitually aggressive tendency. Hare (1982) also found that, when threatened with pain, criminals exhibited both fewer signs of stress and heightened cortical arousal than did other people. Furthermore, Mednick et al. (1982) found that certain criminals, particularly violent criminals, take stronger stimuli to arouse them, and recover more slowly to their normal levels than do non-criminals. Mednick et al. linked rapid recovery to an ability to learn from unpleasant stimuli, including punishment, suggesting that criminals, particularly violent criminals, are less able to learn acceptable behaviour from either negative or positive stimuli.

Each of these studies links cortical arousal to adrenalin. Such a link is unsurprising. Eysenck (1959), researching into cortical arousal, argued that an individual with a low cortical arousal is easily bored, becomes quickly disinterested in things, and craves exciting experiences which will suspend this state of disinterest. For such subjects, normally stressful situations are not disturbing; rather they are exciting and enjoyable, something to be savoured and sought after. This alone would not necessarily be sufficient to enhance the use of aggression: instead those who enjoy high stimulation may turn to sport, exciting jobs or other outlets. The choice will depend on social and environmental influences rather than on biology. At the other end of the spectrum, subjects with high cortical arousal generally avoid stressful aggressive or arousing situations.

Baldwin (1990) suggests that the link between age and crime rates can be partially explained by considering arousal rates and certain other biological aspects. He notes that all individuals enjoy stimulation at some level and that children quickly become used to stimuli which formerly frightened them and seek other, more exciting inputs. Of course if a stimulus gives unpleasant results the individual will usually learn to avoid the behaviour but the more pleasant the experience the more quickly the child will become used to it and, certainly if he or she enjoys high arousal, will wish to move on to more stimulating behaviours. The enjoyment of high stimulation will be fed if there are rewards and no painful experiences from the activities. He concludes that biology may predispose to enjoyment of exciting behaviour, but socialisation and environment will dictate the type of activity learned: which might be either sport or other legal and exciting activities, or crime and delinquency. All this raises the question whether the production of adrenalin is biologically or environmentally dictated. If the levels of adrenalin may be linked with criminality, are these causally linked or are the levels of adrenalin and criminality both caused by other factors?

7.1.4 **Neurotransmitters**

Substances such as serotonin, dopamine and norepinephrine all transmit signals between neurons in the brain. In animal studies, each of these substances has been linked to violent or aggressive behaviour. These show serotonin to be an inhibitor of aggression so low levels of serotonin have been linked to violence and suicide in humans. Depomine and norepinephrine are thought to encourage aggression so that high levels do induce violence. These substances, rather like adrenaline, may be produced by aggression rather than cause it, so here again there is a serious problem associated with the nature of the link. In each case it seems that mechanisms in the brain which affect moods or control behaviour may be impaired.

Although scientists have linked all these substances with various sorts of anti-social behaviour the connections are not fully understood: are they linked to particular types of aggression or to all aggression? Dopamine has been linked not just to aggressive behaviour but to risk taking which might be associated more with dangerous sports or risky work (e.g., the stock market) rather than criminology. Levels of these substances in the body, though linked to genetics, can be controlled by drugs but, whether this, in the absence of a change in social circumstances or environment, would have any beneficial effect on criminality or antisocial behaviour is uncertain. At all events, there is some indication that the effect the substance has on the body is affected by the environment. Thus taking more risks when teenagers can desensitise the body to dopamine leading to a need to take more risk as adults to get the same level of effect, and thus affect behaviour. So although genetics may be part of the equation about the level of neurotransmitters a body will produce, the lifestyle and food intake may also affect both this and the effect of the drug on the body.

The main problem is that it is impossible to tell whether environment, food and social factors most affect the levels of these substances or whether genetics is the factor. It is also not possible to say whether the mood causes the production of the neurotransmitters or whether the neurotransmitters cause the mood. It is a classic chicken and egg situation.

7.1.5 An assessment of biochemical factors

Many of the writers in this area accept that these biochemical effects cannot be studied in a void, and note that attention needs to be given to the interaction of behavioural changes, the environment and the psychological characteristics of the individual. But often such links are not clearly defined. The connections between biochemical factors and school problems, or biochemical factors and personality problems, clearly suggest themselves as fruitful areas for future investigation.

What does emerge from this research is that behaviour, including criminal behaviour, is probably linked in some way to biochemical factors. The first problem facing criminologists is to explain that link and to determine whether criminal or antisocial behaviour is caused by biochemical changes or imbalances or *vice versa*; or, indeed, whether both are related to other causes. If, in the future, it should be demonstrated that crime is caused by biochemical imbalances, it would be necessary to consider what response would be appropriate—to try to change the biochemical balance of high-risk individuals through drug therapy; to alter their environment so that the behaviour is not triggered; or to incarcerate offenders for extended periods so as to incapacitate them. But before using any policies based on biochemical theories, we need to understand the causal links, as well as to understand the way in which other factors, such as the environment, may alter that causal relationship.

7.2 Nutritionally induced biochemical imbalances

7.2.1 Introduction

Given the modern obsession with diet and the alleged association of 'bad' diet with many health problems, it is nor surprising that criminality has been linked to diet. In fact the study of diet as a cause of criminality is not new. At the end of the nineteenth century a number of individuals, particularly some of those in charge of institutions, were claiming that diet could affect behaviour as well as health (see Egleston (1893)). Claims of this sort have continued to be made. Some of these were based on scientific observations, others on mere conjecture, but there was little truly scientific study undertaken. Various animal studies (Pottenger (1983) and McCarrison (1981)) have also suggested that nutrition may affect behaviour.

Research on a fully objective basis is complicated in this area because each individual is different. Nutritional needs vary, and so do reactions to different nutrients or combinations of nutrients. For this reason it is hard to assess the effects of food generally on behaviour: in this section an attempt is made to assess the effects of particular food-stuffs.

7.2.2 Blood sugar

It has frequently been suggested that blood sugar levels are connected with antisocial and criminal behaviour. Shoenthaler (1982) describes experiments in which he discovered that by lowering the daily sucrose intake of juveniles who were held in detention it was possible to reduce the level of their antisocial behaviour, especially violence. He later found similar changes in behaviour by altering the ratio of carbohydrates to protein. Basically, he seems to be concluding that no one particular food type is causing the misbehaviour, but rather that it will occur if the whole diet of the individual is unbalanced and not providing proper nourishment. A discussion of the effects of under-nutrition on the central nervous system and thus on aggression can be found in Smart (1981) where the causal connections are discussed in more detail.

The most common claim in this area is that there is a connection between hypoglycaemia (a deficiency of glucose in the bloodstream) and criminality. The main symptoms of hypoglycaemia are emotional instability, nervousness, mental confusion, general physical weakness, delirium and violence. In severe cases, the individual may also be prone to automatic behaviour and to retrograde amnesia (see Clapham (1989)). Although not all these symptoms are evident in any one case or at any one time, they encourage claims that hypoglycaemia affects criminality (see Shah and Roth (1974), pp. 125–6).

Within hypoglycaemia, some claim that there is a particularly strong relationship between violence and reactive hypoglycaemia, that is, a tendency towards very low blood sugar levels as a reaction to being given a large dose of glucose. In a study carried out by Virkkunen (1987), violent, antisocial males were compared both to violent males who did not suffer from similar antisocial personality problems and to normal law-abiding males. Each individual fasted overnight and was then given a set dose of glucose. The blood sugar levels were tested immediately prior to the glucose and then at hourly intervals thereafter for the next five hours. The blood glucose level in the violent and antisocial personality group fell to a very low level and remained at that low level for markedly longer than the smaller drops suffered by either the violent controls or the normal controls. In other studies the same author has linked hypoglycaemia with other activities often defined as anti-social, such as truancy, low verbal IQ, tattooing, stealing from one's own home in childhood, more than two criminal convictions, and violence of the individual's father under the influence of alcohol. The most interesting of these is possibly the connection with alcohol. Hypoglycaemia is often linked with alcohol, and if alco-hol is imbibed regularly and in large quantities, the ethanol can induce hypo-glycaemia and increase aggression. In many studies, habitual violence and alcohol are linked (see 9.5).

Clapham (1989) cites an interesting example of the very excessive effects which may be brought about by hypoglycaemia. A man who had stabbed his wife and caused her death and also slit his own wrists (not fatally) was found not guilty of murder because at the time he was acting as an automaton. The husband had been on a very severe diet for the two months preceding his wife's killing, losing three stones in weight. The diet was basically one of Ryvita, cheese and apple, and he was allowed no sugar, bread, potatoes or fried food. On the morning of the killing he had drunk two whiskies. Immediately after the killing he was found to be suffering from amnesia. He was subjected to some blood sugar tests while in prison. These were administered a few weeks after he had been returned to a normal diet, but they showed that he was still suffering from reactive hypoglycaemia. Medical experts testified that the hypoglycaemia was sufficient to impair normal brain functioning and substantially impair his mental responsibility, perhaps even to render him an automaton. The jury cleared him of all blame. This shows that the effects of reactive hypoglycaemia have been accepted in a court as a defence to murder and therefore as the sole cause of the actions of the individual.

In the above case the reason for the hyperglycaemic condition was fairly obvious —lack of a stable diet. In some cases the explanation is not necessarily directly related to food, and it has been related to the intake of alcohol and even to an allergy to tobacco.

It is possible for some foods and other substances to cause adverse effects on behaviour if the individual is in some way allergic to them. Such behavioural changes and their exact effects will vary from individual to individual, but it may be that some foods, and in particular certain additives, have effects which may lead to criminality or hyperactivity (see Prinz, Robert and Hantman (1980)). Diets high in sugar, which is found in many mass produced sweet foods, produce large amounts of glucose which may increase insulin and so increase dopamine leading, as was seen above, to impaired behavioural control. Similarly diets low in amino acids (found in foods with a high protein content) may not produce enough sero-tonin and, as was seen above, low levels of serotonin have been linked to aggression (see Curran and Renzetti (2001)).

7.2.3 Vitamins and minerals

Another suggested connection is between crime and the levels of vitamins or min-erals in the human body. Generally, the claim is that either deficiencies of certain vitamins or the toxic effects of an excess of certain minerals is the cause of criminality.

Lead—In this category, the toxic effects of lead and its adverse affects on learning are widely accepted. As will become evident later (7.3.3.1), it is often claimed that delinquents are slow learners, but interestingly the connection between lead levels and criminality has only recently been suggested (see for example Bradley (1988)). Modern modes of life have raised the lead levels in the air and other parts of the environment, increasing the levels of lead absorbed by most individuals. There is now a disturbing link made between lead levels and learning abilities, and between levels of lead, intelligence and hyperactivity. High levels of lead have also been linked to low levels of independence, persistence and concentration, and high levels of impulsiveness, daydreaming and frustration (see Bryce-Smith (1983)). The problems caused by high levels of lead absorption may be compounded by a deficiency of vitamin C which reduces the ease with which lead is excreted.

Cobalt (which occurs in vitamin B_{12})—Two studies, Pihl (1982) and Raloff (1983), suggest a link between cobalt and violent behaviour. Each of them found that the lower the level of cobalt, the more violent was the behaviour pattern. Although these studies each claim a close relationship between cobalt and violence, neither explains the role of cobalt in a human body or how its level could be related to violent behaviour.

Vitamin B—A deficiency of the vitamin B complex is common amongst both criminals and hyperactive children. A shortage of vitamin B_1 can give rise to aggression, hostility, sensitivity to criticism and irrational behaviour, all of which are common in many delinquents. Those deficient in B_3 may, it is claimed, become fearful and act immorally because they are less able to discern right from wrong (see Lesser (1980)). Presumably, due to the link with cobalt, B_{12} must also be connected with criminality.

7.2.4 Assessment of nutritional factors

If this is a promising line of research, it is still too early for any proper assessment to be made. A lot of the claims in this area are anecdotal (see, for example, Bradley (1988)), but even the better work (for example, Hippochen (1978)) does not contain systematic proof of the effects of these matters on behaviour or criminality, nor does it explain exactly how these factors work to increase criminality. Much more evidence will be needed to establish: whether there is a link; how the link (if any) works; whether it is causative; and how it relates to other factors.

A particular requirement in this area is for all the research to be double-blind, so that neither the researcher nor the participants know which individuals are receiving treatment, and that information is held by a third party who plays no part in the research. Even if a link is found between diet and criminal behaviour, what should then be the response? Can a change of diet be dictated, particularly prior to offending or after a sentence has already been served?

By using diet to explain criminal behaviour we may be providing criminals with at least a partial excuse for their behaviour, and we may therefore be relieving them of responsibility. If a person is not to be held responsible for his or her actions, it is difficult to insist upon self-restraint or to use the full weight of any punishment system. Before accepting that diet can relieve a criminal of even partial responsibility we need clear proof of the effects of diet and an understanding of how the diet and the behaviour are related. In other words, it is necessary to be sure that there is a causal relationship and of the precise nature of that causal relationship. (For other suggestions for this area of work, see Bradley and Bennett (1987).)

7.3 Criminality and the central nervous system

The central nervous system (CNS) is found in the brain and spinal column and is responsible for conscious thought and voluntary movements. As such it seems reasonable to assume that it controls behaviour of all sorts: learned, unlearned, and behaviour which is partly learned and partly unlearned. Assuming that the brain does control behaviour and that each individual's brain is slightly different both in its structure and the way it operates then it is unsurprising that for many years criminologists have been interested in the CNS and have connected it with criminal behaviour in a number of distinct theories. Some, usually rare, diseases may affect behaviour by affecting brain functioning. Wilson's disease, which can have both physical and psychological effects (see Kaul and McMahon (1993)), is one such problem. These will generally not be discussed here although they may be alluded to in later chapters, especially Chapter Nine.

7.3.1 Electroencephalography

Electroencephalograph (EEG) processes measure brain wave patterns by monitoring the electronchemical processes in the brain. Between 5 per cent and 20 per cent of non-criminals are said to have abnormal wave patterns, but in criminals the abnormality rate rises to between 25 per cent and 50 per cent (see Mednick and Volavka (1980) for a review of the materials). The difference is even more marked if violent recidivist criminals are studied. Williams (1969) studied habitual aggressives and used those who had committed only one aggressive act as controls. He excluded all those with histories of mental retardation, epilepsy and head injuries and discovered that the rate of EEG abnormality was 57 per cent in the persistently violent group but only 12 per cent for the control group.

From Mednick and Volavka's review it is clear that most of the studies have related criminality to an excessive amount of slow brain wave activity. Slow brain wave activity is often found in young children, which has led some researchers to claim that criminality is linked to slow brain development. The other commonly supported explanations are that in a laboratory setting criminals experience a low level of cortical arousal, or that they have suffered head or brain injuries.

Jan Volavka (1987) compares two extensive pieces of research, the first carried out in Denmark and the second in Sweden. Each claimed to have discovered a clear connection between slow brain wave activity (slow alpha frequency) and a specific type of antisocial activity, namely theft. They concluded that those with slow brain waves were more likely to commit theft than were other individuals. They felt that they could not conclude that this meant that thieves had less well developed brain use. In fact, in the Danish study it was argued that the slow brain wave activity was due to low cortical stimulation, but it did not entirely rule out the possibility that this was due to brain or head damage. In the Swedish study, those with head or brain damage were excluded from the research, and this would support the low cortical arousal hypothesis even if it is insufficient to prove such a theory. A low level of arousal has been related to difficulty in learning normative or law-abiding behaviour (see above), and so if alpha slowing is a result of low cortical arousal, this might explain its association with law breaking. This would also be consistent with the claims of Raine (1993) that 'brain imaging' shows abnormalities in the physical structure of the brain in some violent and sex offenders, who may thus be suffering some form of brain dysfunction.

There appears to be some definite link between crime, particularly theft and persistent violence, and EEG ratings. The exact relationship is not yet fully understood, but because testing for EEG ratings generally is taken after crime has been committed, it is always possible that slow EEG activity may be the consequence of criminal activity or a consequence of the operation of the criminal justice system, rather than the cause of crime.

7.3.2 **Cerebral dysfunctions**

There are two schools of thought on this topic, neither of which has a long history. The first research began in the early 1970s and centres on learning disabilities which might predispose an individual to criminality. The second arose towards the end of the 1970s and tries to explain the relationship between crime and brain dysfunctions in a more direct way. It sets out to study neuropsychology, which is the study of the relationship between the brain and the behaviour of an individual.

7.3.2.1 *Learning disabilities*

In this section we are concerned with problems involving thinking, hearing, listening, talking, reading, writing, spelling or arithmetic. The most common problems seem to be dyslexia (reading problems), aphasia (a disorder of language affecting the generation of speech, an inability to express thought in words, or an inability to understand thought expressed in the words of others) and hyperkinesis (a grossly excessive level of activity and a marked impairment of the ability to attend). It has always been accepted that they are probably due to brain damage or dysfunction, but its connection was not understood.

Researchers have suggested that learning disabilities have one of two theoretical effects. First, the poor academic achievement can often be perceived by adults, both teachers and parents, as a disciplinary problem, and the resultant feeling of rejection leads the child to turn for success and acceptance to other young people with similar difficulties. Partly because of the resultant lack of control by adults, and because the youths may encourage each other, there is an increased probability of their turning to crime and being absent from school.

The second theory postulates that learning disabilities create physical and personal problems which in turn create criminal personality defects in children. These children are unable to learn by experience, so that punishments have no lasting effects on behaviour. A child with such disabilities is more likely to be impulsive and unlikely to resist a desire to do something or to have something. The usual learning process of reward and punishment is unable to curb their unacceptable behaviour.

There are problems in this area of research. In particular it does not define learning disability, consequently different writers seem to refer to different learning problems. Secondly, and possibly more important, it does not address the question of what causes the disability. Its usefulness as a means either of explaining criminality or of bringing about any change in criminal behaviour is thus minimal.

7.3.2.2 *Brain dysfunction*

How do differences in the constitution of the brain affect behaviour? Buikhuisen (1987) reviewed all the available literature and research which attempted to answer this question. He noted that almost without exception the researchers discovered that delinquents do not perform as well as control groups. This can be used to uphold the claims that delinquents have a lower IQ than non-delinquents (for a fuller discussion of IQ see Chapter Nine). Buikhuisen's research showed that the delinquents had problems in comprehending, manipulating and using conceptual material (this includes problems with sequencing and with perceptual organisation). They also had problems of recall and with organising visual information, and they consistently performed badly when a task involved sustained concentration.

Many of the learning problems were found to arise in the brain's (pre)frontal lobes. The frontal lobe is important to the regulation of behaviour. It allows people to plan their actions, assess their outcomes and change the actions if necessary. Any damage to this area could therefore seriously affect ability to understand the consequences of actions; seriously impair ability to learn by experience; reduce ability to concentrate; cause a lack of self control and an increase in impulsive actions; induce a lack of understanding of others' feelings; and an inability to feel shame, guilt or remorse. It can also reduce the normal inhibitions which would prevent most people becoming aggressive and/or sexually antisocial. Lastly, it can increase sensitivity to alcohol.

From this it can be deduced that those suffering from this type of brain dysfunction are most likely to commit poorly planned crimes and will often act on impulse. The crimes could be of a relatively serious nature, although they will not involve ingenuity or planning. The fact that they are unlikely to learn from past punishment, are unable to understand the consequences of their actions, and tend to act on impulse, means that they are likely to become recidivists. Another possible association is with what is termed 'mild brain dysfunction', more recently referred to as 'attention deficit disorder', which may appear alone or with hyperactivity. The cause of the problem is not understood but it is diagnosed by the external results which include behavioural, psychological and cognitive responses. In 1988, Loeber assessed a number of studies which measured these difficulties and found that there was a suggestion that the problems were associated with offending behaviour in young males. A more interesting study was completed in 1990 by Farrington, et al. who analysed a longitudinal study of males who were tested at fixed intervals between the ages of 8 and 21. The data included information not only on their attention deficit and hyperactivity but also on conduct problems at home and school, information on home background and official and self-reported delinquency. They concluded that although attention deficit problems and conduct problems are linked to criminality their causal relationships with that behaviour are different and not necessarily wholly biological. There may be a link, but its causal relationship is not understood and it is very heavily affected by social and environmental conditions.

The central nervous system is split into two hemispheres, each of which is responsible for different functions of the brain. Yeudall, Fromm-Auch and Davies (1982) suggested that juvenile recidivists suffered a higher incidence of dysfunction in the nondominant hemisphere. The nondominant hemisphere is usually on the right, and it plays an important role in the understanding of and reaction to negative emotional stimuli such as fear and punishment. Normally, pain or other unpleasant experiences are remembered and connected to the action for which the punishment is used, so that if the individual considers similar action, fear of further punishment will stimulate the pituitary gland to release hormones which will force reconsideration of the action. If the hemisphere regulating this behaviour is damaged, the fear will not be experienced, so sanctions become meaningless and continual criminal behaviour is likely to occur. Interestingly, in these people the dominant hemisphere is usually undamaged. This regulates responses to pleasant stimuli such as joy or praise, and if the right hemisphere is damaged they might be dissuaded from criminality by the rewards for good behaviour rather than punishment for bad or criminal behaviour. Our criminal justice system is unable to cope with this type of approach.

The theorists recognise that these brain dysfunctions alone cannot explain criminality; their effects can only be understood in the social context. The expectations of each culture may vary, but whatever its norms, society expects each individual to learn to live within them. To do this, each child needs all the normal powers of receptive and communication skills as well as the ability to understand and remember external stimuli. A large part of this learning requires the skills which have been shown above to be lacking as a result of certain brain dysfunctions. If the child fails to learn the social or parental norms, the parents may find that they are unable to cope, become frustrated, and begin to reject the child. At school similar problems may arise between the child and teachers, and a similar result of rejection may follow. The child will probably have a negative self-image and may try to look elsewhere for stimulation, acceptance and an enhanced self-image. This they may well find in subcultures, particularly delinquent subcultures, but the place they find this acceptance and enhanced self-image is often a question of chance. If it is in a criminal subculture, then the types of crime they may commit are also a question of chance. Often the chance may be weighted one way or the other, depending on the type of neighbourhood in which they live, their social class, or other matters of that type (for a discussion of such subcultures see Chapter Twelve).

Although this research suffers from problems such as small, unrepresentative samples and unmatched controls, the results are sufficiently convincing to offer fairly strong evidence that brain dysfunction could explain a perceptible amount of criminality. Equally, certain positive methods of coping with criminality could well emerge from this work in the future. Rather than a particular type of medical treatment, this might well lead to proposals which advocate changes in upbringing, both in the home and at school, as well as suggesting alterations which might be made to the criminal justice system in order to encourage law-abiding behaviour.

7.4 Criminality and the autonomic nervous system

The autonomic nervous system (ANS) controls many of the involuntary functions of the body. It will set the bodily functions so as to obtain maximum efficiency. It speeds up and slows down the heart, dilates the pupils of the eyes, controls the rate of breathing and regulates the temperature of the body by means of dilating and contracting blood vessels and by regulating the sweat glands. The most commonly used method of measuring or recording ANS is that used in lie-detectors, i.e., the measurement of the electric activity of the skin (this is generally referred to as GSR or galvanic skin resistance) usually taken from the activity of the sweat glands in the palms of the hands, recorded on a polygraph. In a calm, unemotional state the skin will be dry and disinclined to conduct a current, but if the person to whom the electrical current is applied is emotionally aroused or frightened, then that person's ANS causes the sweat glands in the palms to operate, creating less resistance to the current. Recording the variations in resistance will be indicative of the extent of ANS arousal.

Criminologists are interested in the aspect of this system which depicts emotional moods or feelings. The ANS is one of the best tests of a person's involuntary and therefore natural reaction to external stimuli. If the individual is frightened, then the body takes certain precautions in case it needs to react quickly. This is commonly called the 'fight or flight' situation, and involves increasing the heart rate, re-routeing the blood from the stomach to the muscles, increasing the rate of breathing and stimulating the sweat glands. To do this, the ANS stimulates the production of certain enzymes which tell the body to make ready for action.

The enzyme production can be measured, as can all the above mentioned changes in bodily functioning. These measurements are supposed to decide how well the individual has learnt to live in society, in that they measure condition-ability. The theory is that most children are punished when they act in an anti-social manner, and so they will anticipate punishment when they misbehave. This anticipation brings on the involuntary bodily changes associated with 'fight or flight'. As these body changes are associated with unpleasantness, most children learn to avoid situations where they might arise. The body changes and their associated feelings are often popularly referred to as conscience or guilt. Where the body changes are only affected very slowly or only at a very low level by the use of punishment, or when the return to the normal state is very slow, then the child will be difficult to control and its behaviour is more likely to become criminal.

One of the main proponents of this theory was Hans Eysenck (1977). He argued that personality is central to criminality, but that personality is largely determined by physiological characteristics such as those mentioned above. He pinpoints two key personality traits which are essential to criminality—extroversion or outward-looking personality, and introversion or inward-looking personality. The introvert tends to be quiet, serious, pessimistic, cautious and controlled. The extrovert will tend to be sociable, carefree, optimistic, impulsive and aggressive. The extrovert thus possesses lower inhibitory controls, and so can act without constraint and will possess an enhanced desire for stimulation, all of which renders him more likely to turn to criminality. These traits are seen as being a result of the poor condition-ability of the extrovert which arises due to the different functioning of his ANS.

The research studies into this area are not unanimous about the acceptance of these ideas. In a study in 1970 Hoghughi and Forrest compared a number of persistent property offenders with a control group, and discovered that there was either no difference in the levels of extroversion or that the delinquents were more introverted. In a review of biological tests for comparisons of the operations of the ANS of delinquents/criminals and controls, both Siddle (1977) and Venables (1987) conclude that those with antisocial behaviour portray problems in their ANS such as low levels of electrodermal response and an irregular heart rate acceleration pattern. The tests seem to show a particularly strong connection between antisocial behaviour and slow recovery rates (see S.A. Mednick (1977)). The reason they offer is that when a person can recover from a state of fear quickly, they experience a high degree of relief which greatly strengthens the conditioning. If recovery is low the level of relief is low, and so conditioning is less likely to occur. Slow ANS recovery rates are, in these studies, seen as the answer to the question Mednick's work was designed to explain: why are nearly 50 per cent of all offences committed by just 1 per cent of the population?

The strong relationship between crime and ANS which this suggests has been questioned by a study re-analysing six of the tests. Although the results appeared to support Mednick's conclusion they only did so for those of a low socio-economic status which raised the question why this would be the case (see Yaralian and Raine (2001)). Clearly more work needs to be done in order to understand the relationship and to assess whether it has any causative explanation to offer. Therefore, if the initial research suggests a link between criminality and ANS, the part played by the environment in that relationship, and particularly the effects of different types of upbringing require more attention, as does the issue of whether the relationship is causative.

7.5 Conclusion

In the last chapter some of the worst consequences of biological theories were discussed, e.g., sterilisation. In this chapter the possibility of using other very problematic methods of control are implied, e.g., drug therapy and psychosurgery. The fear of these gross but possible consequences, together with the unlikelihood that purely biological factors are solely responsible for crime, has led intellectuals, researchers and reformers to shy away from supporting biological explanations of criminality in favour of wholly social or environmental factors. These have generally been seen to lend themselves to more acceptable methods of dealing with or treating the problem. Unfortunately, to date attempts to explain criminality and to recondition criminals on this basis have been pitifully unsuccessful.

If the real aim of every criminologist is to seek a clearer understanding of antisocial behaviour in general and crime in particular, then nobody can afford to have a closed mind to any area or any avenue of explanation. Totally to disregard biological explanations because of repugnance of what they might lead to is rendered even more dubious in light of the fact that those who presently research in this area do not usually claim that the individual's biological make-up alone explains criminality. Generally the claim is that biology can possibly explain why some people may be more susceptible to criminality if certain environmental conditions are also met. People may have a propensity for antisocial behaviour, but that does not mean that they automatically become criminal.

If biological explanations are accepted as a partial explanation, there is still a fear that although they may not lead to sterilisation or permanent imprisonment, they may involve other unethical and unacceptable treatments such as psychosurgery or the forcible administration of psychotropic drugs. This is not necessarily the case. For example, providing high-risk adolescents with stable home environments in which to grow up might prove to be an effective way of controlling those young people who are biologically predisposed to criminality. This has been tried on a small scale in some areas by arranging for those who have a stable relationship to foster young delinquents, but as yet it is too early to form any firm conclusion as to its success. Furthermore, although it appears relatively humane, care must be taken to ensure that it does not conceal any prejudice, e.g., it does not lead to the removal of black children from their homes into white homes or areas simply because these white families may be seen as more stable. This type of racial stereotyping, or even of social stereotyping—rich better than poor—needs to be avoided, but otherwise the provision of adults with whom relatively stable relationships could be fostered certainly has potential (see Baker and Mednick (1984)).

Other more acceptable suggestions may come from the effects of diet upon behaviour. If any close relationship is proven to exist between eating habits and criminality or aggression, then it may be possible to devise dietary advice for families, schools and institutions such as prisons which could be used in order to reduce the incidence of antisocial behaviour. As long as such diets were also healthy in other respects, and could be afforded, then their use should remain relatively uncontroversial.

From the above, it can be seen that biological theories do not necessarily involve overly intrusive methods of control but the student of criminology must always be aware that there is work being carried out both on the possible use of drugs and on psychosurgery and other surgery to control crime. These may have a role to play if they do not involve the use of force, if they have no side effects and where their effects are sufficiently localised: but altering nature is rarely so clean and acceptable. From the point of view of civil liberties and humane treatment, the dangers in these methods are self-evident. The use of psychosurgery is slowly losing ground. It has been found to be difficult to control the exact changes which occur and to prevent side effects, whilst obtaining the individual's consent may not be a sufficient safeguard where genuine choice in such cases is often debatable; when an inmate is presented with a choice between psychosurgery or surgery (e.g., castration in sex cases) or very long terms of imprisonment, it is not truly a free choice. Similarly, the agreement to take drugs in these circumstances may not be freely made. Before drugs and surgery become acceptable in this field, there needs to be a clearer understanding of the causative role played by human biology and the effects of the suggested remedy. Even if such incontrovertible proof were to exist, no remedy should be used unless it is clearly beneficial not only to society but also to the individual. No such remedies should ever be used merely because they are cheap.

Furthermore, constant vigilance is needed as scientific boundaries are extended. New biological 'causes' of criminality may arise all the time. In the 1960s and 1970s such research was widely ignored, but it has recently come to the fore again and seems to have been more readily accepted by scientists, politicians and the public. Interestingly, most of the present biological theories are not new, rather they are a reworking and advance of older ideas. They begin from the premise that there is something wrong with the individual criminal—one must look inside criminals to ascertain the reasons for criminal behaviour. Since the late 1970s we have been in a period of political conservatism—even the traditional socialist parties have moved to the right. The strain of conservatism which has been prevalent has stressed individuals' responsibility for their lives and actions, stressed respect for tradition and traditional values, stressed the need for law and order, and has tended to play down or ignore social circumstances or feelings of exclusion from society as being significantly linked to behavioural problems. The fashionable theories, both in explaining crime and in suggesting remedies, have stressed the individual not society—individuals are responsible and therefore must be punished, or there is a biological or mental problem with them which explains their negative behaviour patterns and requires acting on them, not on society. Such individualistic theories also seem more plausible because social theories do not explain why most individuals in unpleasant environments are law-abiding. The political climate thus seems favourable for the acceptance of criminological causes based on biology and for solutions which address or control those biological 'problems'. These theories also lend themselves to simple headlines and make the public receptive to explanations of criminality from which most people are obviously excluded. The *Sunday Times* (15 January 1989) reported that aggression amongst boys in the classroom was simply linked to the production of the male hormone, testosterone. Such reports, by presenting matters in an over-simplified way, may create misleading impressions on the public.

It is important that criminologists do not ignore or try to prevent biological research from taking place and being publicised, as positive and acceptable uses may be found for the work. Nonetheless, it is essential to be aware that it is always possible for such research to be used to justify unacceptable intrusions into civil liberties. Most of the more modern biological theorists recognise that any connection between their research and crime is only a part of the causal relationship which may have led to the perpetration of the crime. They generally recognise the need to work closely with sociologists, social scientists, psychologists and others in order to gain greater insight into the causes of crime.

7.6 Postscript on biology and crime

There are some positive factors which may arise out of the medicalisation of criminality: a sick individual may be blameless. This has very clear knock-on effects for sentencing, because if there is a medical reason for the behaviour it removes the justification for punishment in favour of treatment. Both the individual and society can benefit from improved behaviour, making recidivism less likely. Of course these positive effects are often elusive because, as has been seen above, the link between crime and biology, if it exists, is rarely clean and almost never clearly causative. The negative aspects are many. For example, shifting the explanation of criminality away from the social order on to the individual suggests that certain individuals need to be altered, with all the appalling consequences to which this may give rise. Or, if the individual's biology is deemed to be the cause of the criminality and the condition is untreatable then that individual may be assessed too dangerous to release. This suggests confinement for the good of society and not to punish the individual, but the effect, permanent incarceration, feels the same if not worse. For a fuller discussion see 8.4 below. Another negative aspect arises if there is an acceptance that science does not lie and is morally neutral. This is very debatable because the questions asked will often colour the answers: certainly without full explanations of causative paths the utility and moral neutrality of scientific discovery are debatable. Science also seems to be politically neutral which makes it more difficult to contest: once more the questions asked are crucial and the findings can be politically interpreted. Again without full causative understanding their validity and utility is questionable. The essential point is that science in the modern world is endowed with great authority, partly because of its apparent neutrality and reliance on apparently disinterested experts. The apparent neutrality allows the experts to gain power over the control systems (see Foucault (1980)).

As has been seen above, although some of the biological remedies such as drug therapy and surgery may appear to lead to a lowering of criminal behaviour, we do not fully understand the full effects of what is happening. Should we therefore be 'experimenting' with criminals? As the possibility of genetic manipulation of humans becomes more reality than science fiction, we also need to consider how to deal with these advances. Do we want all humans to be the same? Is some difference, even if rather destructive, not enriching of society in many ways? Even if very strong causative explanations are ever found, which looks dubious, do we really wish to alter human beings irreversibly just to reach certain moral behavioural standards? Are the moral values of today always to exist, or do they portray protection of certain values or particular groups? Even violence is not universally condemned in any society—most societies have warriors to protect them and these warriors may need some biologically violent elements to their characters, if any such thing exists, in order to carry out their function. For these reasons any biological explanation should not lead to irreversible or even permanent (meaning a need for drug therapy for life) intervention. At most, if any biological explanation is found to be causative it may be acceptable to allow transient medical intervention whilst certain socialising elements can be learned or an acceptable environment found for the individual. Permanent intervention, either surgical or genetic, would seem never to be acceptable as its knock-on effects for humanity as well as the individual can never be understood or controlled.

What is important is that no programmes or policies are designed or implemented until more work has been conducted to understand the possible links between biology and criminal behaviour. Fishbein (2001) enumerates four prerequisites for such policy decisions:

1. Clearer assessment of the incidence of various biological states in criminal or antisocial populations. Some of the studies suggested that certain factors were more common in offender groups than in the general population but the extent of these, even if valid, is poorly measured.

2. Is the relationship causative and if so how does the causal mechanism work? This requires clear scientific evidence not only for a link but to prove that the biological state both predates the criminal or anti-social activity and that it causes that activity. There are suggestions of a link but the two latter requirements are almost never satisfied.

3. An assessment of the relationship between biological and social or environmental aspects.

4. Is the biological element capable of being altered to give lower criminal activity? Is there any possible beneficial therapeutic intervention?

Only once science has arrived at the point where they have answers to these questions should policy changes be considered. Even at this point society should visit the moral question of whether intervention is just and justified. That is the scientists may discover a strong causative link and also a therapeutic intervention but the intervention may be unethical, unjust or otherwise unacceptable to society. Just because it might work and solve part of the problem of crime does not mean that we should use it. Killing all convicted criminals would prevent recidivism but that does not make it just. Society, criminologists, politicians and the media often forget this last rung of the process and yet if we are to build a just society it is absolutely essential.

SUGGESTED READING

Curran, D. and Renzetti, C. (2001), *Theories of Crime*, 2nd edn, Boston: Allyn and Bacon.

Fishbein, D. (2001), *Biobehavioural Perspectives in Criminology*, Belmont, CA: Wadsworth.

Mednick, S.A., Moffitt, T.E. and Stack, S.A. (eds) (1987), *The Causes of Crime: New Biological Approaches*, Cambridge: Cambridge University Press.

REVISION BOX

Chapter Seven has seen a linking of criminal behaviour with the substances in the body, mostly those produced by the body itself but a few as the result of diet. Some studies claim to have discovered strong correlations between these substances and behaviour. There are good reasons for treating such claims with care:

- Although some of these studies recognise that the biochemical influences are not the only elements in whether a person becomes a criminal they generally imply that there is a strong pull towards the conclusion that it is an important element and one which should inform policy. Some attention is generally given to such biosocial factors as the role of learning, social status, residential influences and cultural aspects but the clear focus is that the biological can and should be used in setting policy.

- More specifically, most of the work compares those convicted of offending, often those imprisoned for this, with those who are not officially convicted. It fails to take full account of the fact that many on the 'non criminal' control group may in fact be offenders but have not been caught. Possibly the biological aspects are more important to being caught than to criminal behaviour.

- Whilst many find a correlation between biochemical factors (or a particular biochemical factor) and criminal behaviour (they both rise together or whilst one rises the other falls) they fail to ascertain whether this is a causative link. Does the biochemical difference cause the behaviour? Might it be the other way around or do both just happen to occur together? For example the population visiting a doctor's surgery contains a higher (possibly much higher) number of sick people than is found in the general population. Does entering the surgery cause the illness? Correlation should never be enough to base policy decisions on; a causative link should be necessary.

- Even if there is a causative link is this strongly affected by any other factors? For example if we discover that there is a causal connection between dopamine and criminal behaviour is socialisation and education more or equally important to this causative link such that policy should rest on the latter rather than the former?

- Finally, many assume that if they find a link and could by intervention control that element the work is complete. Just because something works it does not mean that it should be used. Ethical questions should always be addressed—is such intervention acceptable? Who should be treated—all those with the trait or only those who have already transgressed?

Basically there are still more questions than answers and as intervention from these scientific findings is intrusive great care needs to be taken.

QUESTIONS FOR REVISIONS

1 Consider the extent to which science should be bounded by ethics both in the area of research into biochemical explanations of criminality and in the design of policies which make use of such research.

2 Is the scientific understanding sufficiently advanced to permit use of these ideas and, if not, what is missing?

3 Where the biological imbalance is introduced into the body from outside do we need to be as rigorous in our testing of theories before they result in policy and could and should the policy be used more broadly than in just the criminal field?

REFERENCES

Baker, R.L. and Mednick, B. (1984), *Influences on Human Development: A Longitudinal Perspective*, Boston: Kluwer Nijhof.

Baldwin, John, D. (1990), 'The Role of Sensory Stimulation in Criminal Behaviour, with Special Attention to the Age Peak in Crime', in Lee Ellis and Harry Hoffman (eds), *Crime in Biological, Social, and Moral Contexts*, New York: Praeger.

Berman, Louis (1921), *The Glands Regulating Personality*, New York: Macmillan.

Bradley, G. and Bennett, P. (1987), 'The Relationship Between Nutrition and Deviant Behaviour', *The Criminologist*, vol. 11, p. 133.

Bradley, Gail (1988), 'If Food be the Cause of Crime', *The Law Magazine*, 22 January 1988.

Bryce-Smith, D. (1983), *Nutrition and Health*, vol. 1, p. 179.

Buikhuisen, W. (1987), 'Cerebral Dysfunctions and Persistent Juvenile Delinquency', in Sarnoff A. Mednick, Terrie E. Moffitt and Susan A. Stack (eds), *The Causes of Crime: New Biological Approaches*, Cambridge: Cambridge University Press.

Clapham, His Honour Brian (1989), 'A Case of Hypoglycaemia', *The Criminologist*, vol. 13, p. 2.

Curran, D. and Ranzetti, C. (2001), *Theories of Crime* (2nd edn.), Boston, MA: Allyn and Bacon.

Egleston, G.W. (1893), Letter to Sterling Morton, 26 May, General Correspondence, US Dept. of Agriculture, Office of Experiment Stations, National Archives, Washington, DC.

Ehrenkranz, J., Bliss, E. and Sheard, M.H. (1974), 'Plasma Testosterone: Correlation with Aggressive Behaviour and Social Dominance in Man', *Psychosomatic Medicine*, vol. 36, p. 469.

Ellis, Lee and Coontz, Phyllis, D. (1990), 'Androgens, Brain Functioning, and Criminality: the Neurohormonal Foundations of Antisociality', in Lee Ellis and Harry Hoffman (eds), *Crime in Biological, Social, and Moral Contexts*, New York: Praeger.

Eysenck, H.J. (1959), *Manual of the Maudsley Personality Inventory*, London: UCL Press.

Eysenck, H.J. (1977), *Crime and Personality*, 3rd edn, London: Routledge & Kegan Paul.

Farrington, D.P., Loeber, R. and Van Kammen, W.B. (1990), 'Long-term Criminal Outcomes of Hyperactivity–Impulsivity–Attention Deficit and Conduct Problems in Childhood', in L. Robins and M. Rutter (eds), *Straight and Devious Pathways from Childhood to Adulthood*, Cambridge: Cambridge University Press.

Fishbein, D.H. (1990), 'Biological Perspectives in Criminology', *Criminology*, vol. 28, p. 27.

Fishbein, D. (2001), *Biobehavioural Perspectives in Criminology*, Belmont, CA: Wadsworth Publishing.

Foucault, Michel (1980), *Power/Knowledge*, ed. and trans. C. Gordon, Brighton: Harvester.

Hare, R.D. (1982), 'Psychopathy and Physiological Activity during Anticipation of an Aversive Stimulus in a Distraction Paradigm', *Psychophysiology*, vol. 19, p. 266.

Hippochen, Leonard J. (ed.) (1978), *Ecologic-Biochemical Approaches to Treatment of Delinquents and Criminals*, New York: Van Nostrand Reinhold.

Hoghughi, M.S. and Forrest, A.R. (1970), 'Eysenck's Theory of Criminality: An Examination with Approved School Boys', *British Journal of Criminology*, vol. 10, p. 240.

Kaul, A. and McMahon, D. (1993), 'Wilson's Disease and Offending Behaviour—a Case Report', *Medicine Science and the Law*, vol. 33, p. 352.

Keverne, E.B., Meller, R.E. and Eberhart, J.A. (1982), 'Social Influences on Behaviour and Neuroendocrine Responsiveness in Talapoin Monkeys', in *Scandinavian Journal of Psychology*, vol. 1, p. 37.

Kreuz, L.E. and Rose, R.M. (1972), 'Assessment of Aggressive Behaviour and Plasma Testosterone in a Young Criminal Population', *Psychosomatic Medicine*, vol. 34, p. 321.

Lesser, M. (1980), *Nutrition and Vitamin Therapy*, New York: Bantam.

Loeber, R. (1988), 'Behavioural Precursors and Accelerators of Delinquency', in W. Buikhuisen and S.A. Mednick (eds), *Explaining Criminal Behaviour: Interdisciplinary Approaches*, Leiden: E.J. Brill.

McCarrison, Sir Robert (1981), *Nutrition and Health*, The McCarrison Society, first published in 1953, London: Faber & Faber.

Mednick, Sarnoff A. (1977), 'A Bio-Social Theory of the Learning of Law Abiding Behaviour', in Sarnoff A. Mednick and Karl O. Christiansen (eds), *Biosocial Basis of Criminal Behavior*, New York: Gardner Press.

Mednick, S.A., Pollock, V., Volavka, J. and Gabrielli, W.F. (1982), 'Biology and Violence', in M.E. Wolfgang and N.A. Weiner (eds), *Criminal Violence*, Beverly Hills, CA: Sage.

Mednick, S.A. and Volavka, J. (1980), 'Biology and crime', in N. Morris and M. Tonry (eds), *Crime and Justice: An Annual Review of Research*, vol. 2, Chicago, IL: University of Chicago Press.

Olwens, Dan (1987), 'Testosterone and Adrenalin: Aggressive and Antisocial Behaviour in Normal Adolescent Males', in S.A. Mednick, T.E. Moffitt and S. Stack (eds), *The Causes of Crime: New Biological Approaches*, Cambridge: Cambridge University Press.

Persky, H., Smith, K.D. and Basu, G.K. (1971), 'Relation of Psychological Measures of Aggression and Hostility to Testosterone Production in Man', *Psychosomatic Medicine*, vol. 33, p. 265.

Pihl, R.O. (1982), 'Hair Element Levels of Violent Criminals', *Canadian Journal of Psychiatry*, vol. 27, p. 533.

Pottenger, F. (1983), *Pottenger's Cats*, Price-Pottenger Nutrition Foundation.

Prinz, R.J., Roberts, W.A. and Hantman, E. (1980), 'Dietary correlates of Hyperactive Behaviour in Children', *Journal of Consulting and Clinical Psychology*, vol. 48, p. 760.

Rada, R.T., Laws, D.R., Kellner, R., Stivastave, L. and Peak, G. (1983), 'Plasma Androgens in Violent and Non-Violent Sex Offenders', *American Academy of Psychiatry and the Law*, vol. 11(2), p. 149.

Raine, A. (1993), *The Psychopathology of Crime*, San Diego, CA: Academic Press.

Raloff, J. (1983), 'Locks—a Key to Violence', *Science News*, vol. 124, p. 122.

Rowe, D.C. and Farrington, D.P. (1997), 'The Familial Transmission of Criminal Convictions', *Criminology*, vol. 35, p. 177.

Rubin, Robert, T. (1987), 'The neuroendocrinology and neurochemistry of antisocial behaviour', in Sarnoff A. Mednick, Terrie E. Moffitt and Susan A. Stack (eds), *The Causes of Crime: New Biological Approaches*, Cambridge: Cambridge University Press.

Scarmella, T.J. and Brown, W.A. (1978), 'Serum Testosterone and Aggressiveness in Hockey Players', *Psychosomatic Medicine*, vol. 40, p. 262.

Schalling, Daisy (1987), 'Personality Correlates of Plasma Testosterone Levels in Young Delinquents: an example of Person-Situation Interaction', in Sarnoff A. Mednick, Terrie E. Moffitt and Susan A. Stack (eds), *The Causes of Crime: New Biological Approaches*, Cambridge: Cambridge University Press.

Schoenthaler, S.J. (1982), 'The effects of blood sugar on the treatment and control of antisocial behaviour: A double-blind study of an incarcerated juvenile population', *International Journal for Biosocial Research*, vol. 3, p. 1.

Shah, Saleem A. and Roth, Loren H. (1974), 'Biological and Psychophysiological Factors in Criminality', in Daniel Glaser (ed.), *Handbook of Criminology*, Chicago, IL: Rand McNally.

Siddle, David A.T. (1977), 'Electrodermal Activity and Psycholopathy', in Sarnoff A. Mednick and Karl O. Christiansen (eds), *Biosocial Basis of Criminal Behavior*, New York: Gardner Press.

Smart, J.L. (1981), 'Undernutrition and Aggression', in P.F. Brain and D. Benton (eds), *Multidisciplinary Approaches to Aggression Research*, Amsterdam: Elsevier/North Holland.

Sunday Times, 15 January 1989.

Venables, Peter, H. (1987), 'Autonomic Nervous System Factors in Criminal Behaviour', in Sarnoff A. Mednick, Terrie E. Moffitt and Susan A. Stack (eds), *The Causes of Crime: New Biological Approaches*, Cambridge: Cambridge University Press.

Virkkunen, Matti (1987), 'Metabolic Dysfunctions Among Habitually Violent Offenders: Reactive Hypoglycaemia and Cholesterol Levels', in Sarnoff A. Mednick, Terrie E. Moffitt and Susan A. Stack (eds), *The Causes of Crime: New Biological Approaches*, Cambridge: Cambridge University Press.

Volavka, Jan (1987), 'Electronencephalogram among Criminals' in Sarnoff A. Mednick, Terrie E. Moffitt and Susan A. Stack (eds), *The Causes of Crime: New Biological Approaches*, Cambridge: Cambridge University Press.

Walker, P.A., Meyer, W.J., Emory, L.E. and Rubin, A.L. (1984), 'Antiandrogenic Treatment in the Paraphilias', in H.C. Stancer et al. (eds), *Guidance for the Use of Psychotropic Drugs*, New York: Spectrum Publications.

Williams, D. (1969), 'Neural Factors Related to Habitual Aggression: Consideration of Differences between those Habitual Aggressives and Others who have Committed Crimes of Violence', *Brain*, vol. 92, p. 503.

Yaralian, P.S. and Raine, A. (2001), 'Biological Approaches to Crime', in R. Paternoster and R. Bachman (eds), *Explaining Criminals and Crime*, Los Angeles, CA: Roxbury.

Yeudall, L.T., Fromm-Auch, D. and Davies, P. (1982), 'Neuropsychological Impairment of Persistent Delinquency', *Journal of Nervous and Mental Disease*, vol. 170, p. 257.

8

Psychological theories of criminality

8.1 Introduction

Psychology is usually used to mean the study of the mind or spirit of people (and sometimes animals) and the application of this knowledge to explain human behaviour and attitudes. More specifically, psychology is the study of individual characteristics or qualities such as personality, reasoning, thought, intelligence, learning, perception, imagination, memory and creativity. Psychology is often separated into two groups of theories or schools of thought: cognitive and behavioural. Cognitive theories place the study of psychology in the mind; they see human action as the result of driving or compelling mental forces or to be the result of mental reasoning and beliefs. These theories take account of internal feelings such as anger, frustration, desire and despair. In fact, all activity is seen as the result of internal mental processes. In contrast, the behavioural theorists, whilst taking account of internal factors, place them in a social context. They see that internal mental processes can be affected and even altered by certain factors in the environment which either reinforce or discourage the behaviour. Clearly there is no strong dividing line between these two. A degree of overlap is likely, whilst some psychological theories may not fit neatly into either school.

There are psychologists who place weight on a biological link in the workings of the mind and link certain types of behaviour and certain thought processes with, for example, genetic or neurological factors (some of this research is sometimes referred to as psychophysiology). Others place so much weight on the environmental factors that they become closer to sociological theories. Either way it is clear that psychological theories should not be studied in a void, but be assessed and balanced in the criminological arena as a whole.

This chapter is concerned with psychological explanations for the behaviour of those who are generally seen as 'normal', in that they are not suffering from a mental defect. Mental abnormality will be considered in Chapter Nine. In both Chapters Eight and Nine there will be some mention of clinical psychology, which is often thought of as the study of those suffering from mental abnormality, but is also concerned with the study of lesser psychological disturbances and, possibly more importantly, with the treatment of all these mental difficulties. For a fuller and more precise account of general psychology, see an introductory text such as those by Gleitman (1999 and 2002), Carlson (2000) and Gross (2001).

As with the biological theories, most of the ideas in this chapter fall into the positivist school of thought. They therefore explain crime as a result of some factor—in this case mental or behavioural constructs—rather than as a result of choice or free will.

8.2 Psychoanalysis and criminality

A number of different ideas are drawn together under psychoanalysis, but the general standpoint is that inner, dynamic forces are used to explain human behaviour. Psychoanalytical theorists perceive criminal behaviour to be the result of some mental conflict of which the criminal may be virtually unaware (i.e., the conflict arises in the subconscious or unconscious mind). Furthermore, they claim that this conflict is always present as an internal conflict between the demands of reason and conscience, and those of instinct. A 'victory' for instinct can lead to thoughts and deeds which will often be socially unacceptable. Every-one experiences this conflict, but some manage to control the instinct better than others. If the conflict is not resolved in a socially acceptable way, it may be expressed in ways which are criminal. Criminality is then seen as one of the outward signs of the disease, or of the problematic resolution of the mental conflict, just as physical deformity may be the manifestation of a physical disease.

Modern psychoanalysis began with the work of Sigmund Freud (1856–1939). He lived most of his life in Vienna and published most of his famous works between 1900 and 1939 (see especially Freud (1935)). His theories have had a profound effect on many aspects of modern life, on philosophy and literature, for example, and have been widely used to explain human behaviour. Freud did not write a great deal specifically about criminality, but it is possible to see how some of his behavioural theories can be used as explanations of criminality, and later theorists have expanded on these to offer slightly different explanations. Psychoanalysis is a complex field, and only a brief introduction to those areas of Freud's writing which are of direct interest to criminology will be offered here. Areas such as those relating to dreams or to the mechanism of transference will be largely excluded, as will suggestions for treatments. There are many detailed texts dealing with Freud's work, e.g., Kline (1984).

8.2.1 The constituents of the personality

Freud split the personality into three parts—the id, the ego and the super-ego. The id is an unconscious area of the mind; it is the most primitive portion of the personality from which the other two are derived. It is made up of all the basic biological urges—to eat, drink, excrete, to be warm and comfortable and to obtain sexual pleasure. It is driven by desire; it is illogical and amoral, and seeks only absolute pleasure at whatever cost. It characterises the unsocialised and unrestrained individual, and its drives need immediate gratification and have no conception of reality. It is the part of the personality with which one is born. It holds all the desires, even those society considers wrong or bad, and to that extent Freud says it needs to be repressed. The repression or control of the id is carried out by the ego and the super-ego.

The ego does not exist at birth, but is something the individual learns. It is largely conscious, although some of it is unconscious. It tempers the desirous longings of the id with the reality of what might happen if it is not controlled, and it also learns the reality of how best to serve the id. A baby learns that it is fed only after crying, and a child learns to say 'please' in order to obtain things. It learns that in some circumstances, giving in to the id leads to punishment or unpleasantness, and so it may not follow its desires in order to avoid these consequences. For example, the child's id may desire a biscuit, but when it takes one, some form of punishment or unpleasantness ensues. The pleasure of having the biscuit is marred by this unpleasantness, and so the child may decide that taking a biscuit is not worth it. The ego has developed and learned to reason with the id about the worth of the action. Slowly, the ego develops and controls or tempers the id.

The super-ego is largely part of the unconscious personality. It may contain conscious elements, for example, moral or ethical codes, but it is basically unconscious in its operation. It is the conscience which exists in the unconscious areas of the mind. The super-ego characterises the fully socialised and conforming member of society.

8.2.2 Formation of the super-ego

Possibly the most important influences on the individual are the precepts and moral attitudes of the parents or those *in loco parentis*. These are the people most loved, most respected and most feared. They are also the people with whom a child has his or her earliest contacts and relationships. These are essential to the child. The super-ego is often seen as the internalised rules and admonitions of the parents and, through them, of society. The super-ego acts on the ego; thus when a child desires a biscuit it may not take one even if it could not be punished because the child starts to reprove itself. The super-ego may therefore praise and punish the child in the same way as the parents do and so the child slowly learns an inner set of rules or values. If the behaviour or thoughts of the child live up to the super-ego, it experiences the pleasant feeling of pride but if they do not the child's own super-ego punishes it by self-reproach and feelings of guilt.

The ego therefore has two masters, each to be obeyed and each pushing in different directions. The id demands pleasure; the super-ego demands control and repression. The result is inner conflict which can never be fully resolved. Freud argued that for the super-ego to develop, the parents scold the child or otherwise show their displeasure, and this leads the child to become anxious that their love will be removed. The next time the child considers a 'bad' deed, he or she will feel anxiety that the parents may leave. The anxiety is unpleasant and leads to repression of the deed. As the child does not understand the difference between thought and action, the mental desire is also repressed in case the parents discover it: thoughts as well as deeds become repressed.

The basis of control or repression is therefore seen as built upon relationships with parents or those *in loco parentis*. This analysis to an extent has been upheld by the work of Aichhorn (1963), who found that environmental factors alone could not account for the delinquency of the children at the institution he supervised. The super-egos of many of the children were underdeveloped, which he maintained rendered them latent delinquents, psychologically prepared for a life of crime. He postulated that the failure to develop a super-ego was the result of the parents being unloving or absent for much of the child's upbringing. Each of these conditions would prevent the child from forming the dependant, trusting and intimate relationships necessary to the development of the super-ego. From this account, the socialising processes had failed to work on these children whose latent delinquency had become dominant; the children were therefore 'dissocial'.

Aichorn treated these youths by attempting to provide a happy and pleasant environment which might foster the type of relationships with adults which would facilitate the formation of the super-ego. He argued that the severe environments offered by most homes for juvenile delinquents merely exacerbate the problem begun by the parents, or by their absence, pushing the youths towards more criminal acts and confirming their 'dissocial' state. Parental neglect was not seen as the only reason for the super-ego to be underdeveloped: over-indulgent parents, allowing the child to do anything, would have a similar effect. It was also possible for children to learn all the lessons of their parents but still end with less than fully developed super-egos because the parents' ability to teach had been impaired by diluted moral standards, often because they were criminals themselves or were not themselves fully socialised. It has to be stated, however, that Aichorn realised that not all delinquents had poorly developed super-egos and that he never claimed that the failure to develop a super-ego explained all criminality.

Other psychoanalysts such as John Bowlby (1946 and 1953), found similar results when he focused on early maternal deprivation as being the cause of criminality. His argument rested on two basic premises: first, that a close, unbroken and loving relationship with the mother (or permanent mother substitute) is essential to the mental health of the child, and secondly, that rejection by the mother or separation from her (or her substitute) accounts for most of the more permanent cases of delinquency. This last sweeping claim has been attacked by both psychologists and sociologists, some of whom reject his methodology while others question his findings and claims. Many do, however, recognise that strong, though not necessarily lasting, damage can be done to a child's mental development if it is rejected by or separated from its mother during the first five years of its development.

A further factor which some argue has a profound effect upon the development of the super-ego, and one of the ideas most commonly associated with Freud, is the Oedipus complex (in boys) and the Electra complex (in girls). These develop during the process of sexual growth. Each is depicted by the child, normally when about 3 years old, being attracted to the parent of the opposite sex whilst feeling general hostility toward the parent of the same sex. In the Oedipus complex (male) the rivalry would be between the father and son. The latter, realising the supremacy of the father, fears castration and this fear forces him to control his desire for his mother. Freud believes that it is from the resolution of this conflict that the male's super-ego, social restraint or conscience, develops, and that all this occurs before the age of about 5 or 6 years. If the conflict is not resolved in this way, then serious personality or behavioural problems may arise. If there is no formation or incomplete formation of the super-ego, then the individual may have little or no conscience and so have no reason to restrain his desires. If the super-ego is overdeveloped then it may lead to guilt feelings or to his developing a neurosis (see below).

The resolution of the equivalent Electra complex in women is more complex and, Freud believes, less complete (see Chapter Sixteen).

Psychologists recognise that other factors such as relationships with individuals outside the family and the general social environment can also affect the formation of the super-ego. Hewitt and Jenkins (1947) categorised a group of 500 juveniles into three types:

(a) inhibited, shy and seclusive (an overdeveloped super-ego);

(b) unsociable and aggressive (underdeveloped super-ego); and

(c) members of a socialised, delinquent gang (having a dual super-ego).

The gang members possess a normal super-ego with respect to the rules of the gang, which therefore they obeyed, but they have inadequate or underdeveloped super-egos with respect to the rules of society. The behaviour of each individual gang member depends on whether or not he is with the gang. If he is, he obeys gang rules. If he is in the outside world, he feels no compulsion to obey the ordinary, everyday rules of society. Such a pattern indicates the strong influence which the environment can exert.

8.2.3 Balancing the id, ego and super-ego

The balance between desire and repression is kept by the ego, and in most people the desires of the id are shaped so that they are acceptable to the super-ego whilst still satisfying the id. This is often done by sublimation or displacement. For example, the desire for aggression may be channelled into sport where it can be usefully dissipated, or destructive instincts might be channelled in childhood away from harming people or animals and towards pulling toys apart and learning how to rebuild them. The balance does not come from total repression of the id, but rather from channelling those desires into more useful activities which are acceptable to the super-ego. In this way both the id and super-ego are satisfied.

Psychoanalysts therefore argue that criminals are those who have not channelled their desires into useful, or at least harmless, pastimes. The id remains uncontrolled, and so the desires are allowed to take over and may give rise to socially unacceptable acts, some of which may be criminal. Occasionally, a criminal may be a person who has over-controlled or repressed these desires. For example, guilt may be felt at the very existence of the desires (especially sexual desires), or at the performing of an act which, though not criminal, is wrong by super-ego standards. The guilt gives rise to a need to be punished as a form of relief or a purging of the guilt. The individual therefore commits a crime, often a very minor crime, and is caught and punished. On this interpretation it is understandable that further crimes are committed: crime brings punishment; punishment brings relief, but only for a time. A vicious circle develops and an habitual criminal comes into existence.

Psychoanalytical explanations are based upon the idea that it is the inner processes and conflicts which determine behaviour. Unresolved inner conflict and lack of emotional stability are seen as the main causes of unacceptable behaviour; environment plays a subsidiary role. Because some of this inner conflict is unconscious the theory is very difficult to test.

8.2.4 'Normal' criminals

So far, most of the criminal tendencies referred to in this section on psychoanalysis have been those of 'abnormal' criminals whose behavioural problems arise from inner conflict (e.g., individuals who suffer from a personality problem, such as neurotics). Psychoanalysis may also be used to explain some 'normal' criminality. The main trait of a 'normal' offender is that the whole personality, including the super-ego, is criminal. As there is no conflict between super-ego and the rest of the personality, there is no personality problem and so they are 'normal' offenders. This means that, presumably because of their environment and upbringing, these people regard crime as normal and acceptable (i.e., as natural) and they suffer no qualms about their criminal conduct. This does not mean that the 'normal' offender is willing to commit any crime, but that upbringing allows certain acts which are condemned by the rest of society, whilst condemning, along with the rest of society, many other activities considered to be criminal. This possibly suggests that society is not homogeneous but is made up of many subcultures (see Chapters Eleven and Twelve).

8.2.5 Extroversion and neuroticism

The idea that extroversion and introversion may play a part in criminality was popularised by Jung (1875–1960), originally a follower, but later a critic, of Freud. In 1947 Jung said that there was a continuance from introversion to extroversion, and that everybody could be placed somewhere along the spectrum. An hysteric condition, fitful or violent emotions, are more likely to be evidence of an extrovert, whereas an anxious condition, apprehensive or obsessive, indicates introversion. These concepts are often used in criminology as an explanation for recidivism—it is said that the introvert, being more careful, is better able to learn societal norms and so easier to condition and less likely to become a recidivist. The flaw in presenting this as a general proposition is that whilst introverts may quickly learn the law-abiding behaviour taught in penal institutions, they will similarly have the capacity to relearn antisocial behaviour after being released. There are both extrovert recidivists and introvert recidivists.

The main work in this area is that of Eysenck (1959), but see also (1977) and (1987), and Eysenck and Gudjonsson (1989), whose work covers a number of disciplines and draws upon psychoanalysis and personality theories as well as learning and control theories. Eysenck's starting-point is that individuals are genetically endowed with certain learning abilities, particularly the ability to be conditioned by environmental stimuli. He also assumes that crime can be a natural and rational choice where people maximise pleasure and minimise pain. An individual learns societal rules through the development of a conscience, which is acquired through learning what happens when one takes part in certain activities: punishment for being naughty and reward for being good. Personality is then based upon a combination of these biological and social factors. Eysenck saw two main dimensions to each personality which affected the individual's learning ability: *extroversion*, which runs from extroversion to introversion and is often referred to as the E scale; and *neuroticism*, which runs from neurotic or unstable to stable and is often referred to as the N scale. These dimensions are continuous and most people fall in the

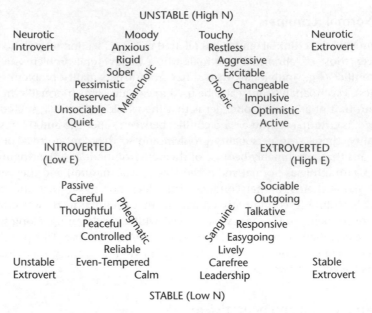

UNSTABLE (High N)

Neurotic Introvert	Moody Anxious Rigid Sober Pessimistic Reserved Unsociable Quiet	Touchy Restless Aggressive Excitable Changeable Impulsive Optimistic Active	Neurotic Extrovert

INTROVERTED (Low E)　　　　　　　　　　EXTROVERTED (High E)

	Passive Careful Thoughtful Peaceful Controlled Reliable	Sociable Outgoing Talkative Responsive Easygoing Lively	
Unstable Extrovert	Even-Tempered Calm	Carefree Leadership	Stable Extrovert

STABLE (Low N)

Figure 8.1: Eysenck's personality dimensions (as modified)

middle range, but with some at the extremes of each. The traits of each are depicted in Figure 8.1 (from p. 685 of Gleitman).

As with Jung's idea, the extroverts are seen as more difficult to condition, but so are the highly unstable or neurotic personalities. Eysenck argues that there is a hierarchy of conditionability:

(a) stable introverts (low N low E) are the easiest to condition;

(b) stable extroverts (low N high E) and neurotic introverts (high N low E) are less malleable but do not encounter great difficulty in social learning;

(c) neurotic extroverts (high N high E) experience most difficulty in social learning.

Later Eysenck introduced a third personality dimension which he called psychoticism, which could well be referred to a psychopathetic dimension since it is generally evidenced by aggressive, cold and impersonal behaviour. The individual, high on this scale, will tend to be solitary, uncaring, cruel, will not fit in with others and will be sensation seeking. It is slightly less well understood than the first two and is associated with the frontal lobe of the cortex. Eysenck associates extremes of this dimension with criminality—the higher the P score, the higher the level of offending. In some studies Eysenck's claims have gained support; see particularly McGurk and McDougall (1981), where they found that neurotic extroverts and neurotic psychotic extroverts were only present in the delinquent group and stable introverts were only found in the non-delinquent group, whereas both neurotic introverts and stable extroverts were found in both groups.

There have, however, been many critics of Eysenck's work. Some attack the very basis of his claims: he has argued for a genetic basis for these traits and drawn his evidence from studies based on twins; thus his theory suffers from the difficulties encountered by such approaches (see 6.3.3). More fundamentally, some scholars assert that his findings are totally discredited. Little (1963) drew upon research at three Borstal training institutions which purported to prove that neither release from these institutions nor recidivism rates connected to them were in any way linked to either extroversion or introversion. His research therefore questioned not only Eysenck's work but all work in this area. On the other hand, others such as McGurk and McDougall (1981) whilst not fully replicating his claims have found that individuals with High E-High N and High P-High E-High N are only found in criminal groups whereas those with Low E-Low N are only found in non-criminal groups. This suggests that there may be some link between these personality traits and criminality, as does a study (Farrington (1994)) which, using this approach, found some link between offending and impulsiveness (see Chapter Seven and 8.3.6.). The overall position is at present unclear and uncertain, but the possible links seem too tenuous to be central to criminological explanation or to policy initiatives.

8.2.6 Criticism of psychoanalytical theories

Psychoanalysts profess, with good reason, that they are scientists. Their central concepts, however, are incapable of being directly observed, making their existence impossible to prove. The id, ego and super-ego are assumed to exist because of particular external manifestations which also exhibit the extent to which each part of the personality has developed. Often these external manifestations alone are not sufficient to diagnose the difficulties. They are supplemented by techniques such as dream analysis, verbal association and hypnosis, but these techniques are subjective since psychoanalysts differ over their interpretation. At the very least, this makes it a very inexact science.

One of the more dubious aspects of psychoanalysis, as applied to this area, is its assumption that because a person commits a crime he/she has some unconscious or subconscious personality conflict. The argument is circular, in that the problem to which a solution is sought is itself used as the proof that the explanation is correct. Moreover, the link between the crime and the alleged psychoanalytical reason for it is often obscure and dependent upon tortuous reasoning. An unknown obsession with a particular type of sexual problem, or with one parent, or with a type of emotion, may give rise to acts involving symbols which represent that problem, e.g., using a gun as a power symbol and therefore as a sexual symbol. In some cases, it is asserted, a certain class of person is injured who represents the real target. For example, a particular criminal might habitually commit a crime against an older, female victim who represents his mother. The implication is that it is really his mother which the offender wishes to harm, perhaps stemming from a feeling that the mother wronged him earlier in his life. The real reason for the crime would not be admitted and may not even be known by the offender, whose motives may be hidden deep in the subconscious or the unconscious.

In such interpretations, the criminality is the outward manifestation of a disease or problem of the mind and personality, which exists in the subconscious or the unconscious. By using subjective methods on information gathered either from anecdote or methods such as dream therapy or hypnosis, the analyst follows the problem into these normally inaccessible areas of the mind and diagnoses the mental or personality problem. When asked to prove the existence of the problem, they point to the criminality. In this way the criminal act becomes both proof of the existence of the problem and the result of the problem. Proof of the worth of these theories is therefore difficult and it seems unlikely that all or even most criminality is associated with psychoanalytical problems. This seems a reasonable judgement despite the current literary fashion to stress psychology in depicting motive and explanation in crime fiction. Nor does psychoanalysis add up to a clear understanding of crime or lead to widespread methods of preventing it—any successes have mainly been at an individual level. This does not mean that crime is not associated with the personality of the offender. It does mean that these theories are unlikely to be central to criminological discourse. The lack of room for social factors and the disregard for rational choice or free will are major deficiencies in any model claiming a general relevance. In any event, psychoanalysis is not the only source of personality theories.

8.3 The normal criminal personality

8.3.1 Introduction

Most theories using a concept of normal criminal personality assume that individuals possess definable and dominant sets of rules which determine how they will behave in virtually any situation. This is often called the central or core personality. Psychologists and psychiatrists believe that criminals tend towards certain well-defined personalities, and that their criminal tendencies can be overcome by controlling or altering those core personalities.

8.3.2 What is normality?

The line between normality and abnormality is impossible to draw exactly. Normality itself is elusive and difficult to define in any positive sense. It is usually negatively described as the state of mind or personality that cannot be classified as having a mental abnormality (i.e., which cannot be classed as mentally defective, psychopathic, neurotic, psychotic or compulsive).

The mere fact that something is numerically common does not make it normal, and similarly the bare fact that something is uncommon does not make it abnormal. An event is not made normal or healthy because it frequently occurs and will certainly re-occur. For example, there will always be murder but this does not make it a normal or socially acceptable activity. Neither does the fact that an activity is socially unacceptable mean that those who take part in it are necessarily psychologically abnormal. If it did, it would follow that all criminals are mentally abnormal, and this is patently not the case.

Although all this is true, the plain fact is that in most of the studies normality is assessed in relation to the average person or the mental standard which is portrayed by most of the population (i.e., a numerical analysis). Furthermore, most of the studies of personality are heavily based on value judgements, such as assuming that because individuals have committed crimes they should portray a different personality from the law-abiding citizen (namely, a criminal personality). The assumption here is that those who participate in socially unacceptable activities must have something which is different from what the researcher, or society generally, considers normal.

This attitude can most clearly be seen in relation to murder, especially when there appears, on the face of it, to be no logical explanation for the killing. In such cases the press and public often refer to the events as motiveless crimes and term the murderer a 'monster' or a 'madman'. The activity is portrayed as something which any 'normal' person would find abhorrent and would not commit (or would like to think that they would not commit). Since most studies are tested against what society considers acceptable and normal, this is in effect the reality of the situation, and it is clear that as values in society change, so too will ideas of normality. For example, at one time homosexuality was a crime and generally considered to be a wholly unacceptable practice. It was considered to be an abnormal activity, and those taking part were deemed to be in need of medical or psychiatric treatment as well as punishment (see the Wolfenden Committee on Homosexual Offences and Prostitution (1957)). Homosexuality (between consenting adults over 16 in private) is now legal (according to the Sexual Offences Act 1967, s. 1 as amended by the Criminal Justice and Public Order Act 1994) and, although such activity is sometimes still considered biologically different or abnormal, it is less generally considered that its participants are in need of medical or psychiatric attention. From this it can be seen that the ordinary man in the street—or even the ordinary reasonable doctor, psychiatrist, psychologist, sociologist or criminologist—does not possess an absolute or constant definition of normality, personality or mental illness.

Any move away from the concept of normality may involve either together or separately at least three aspects: psychological suffering (the affective aspect), judgemental errors (intellectual aspect), and behavioural problems (moral or social aspect). None of these is necessarily a value-free norm and so variations from the 'norm' are laden with subjective assessments. These are particularly strong in the moral or social aspect where society or the expert defines what is to be categorised as 'problem behaviour'; and as seen above, that concept may not be static.

In Britain, in relation to criminology the issue of diagnosing normality and any deviation from normality (or illness) is further complicated by the proximity of the clinical work and the criminal justice system. This renders the diagnosis particularly difficult. In Britain, the psychiatrist, psychologist or probation officer is expected to report at the pre-sentencing stage. To make an assessment of the individual at this stage blurs the role of the diagnosis. Is it meant to determine the level of punishment by assessing the responsibility of the individual for the criminal act of which he or she has been found guilty? Is it to assess whether there is a likelihood of repeat offending of a sort likely to cause much damage to victims (particularly violent or sexual attacks)? Or is it rather to be used to diagnose the individual, mentally and medically, so as to propose methods of treatment or alter the personality and enable the offender to live within the requirements or boundaries set by society? This schism causes problems: it is confusing for the professional concerned; it may provide sentencers with ambiguous information; and it may relieve the offender of any feeling of responsibility. (For a fuller discussion of these aspects see Debuyst (1995).)

Despite these problems in the British tradition, it has been the psychiatric and psychological fields of criminal explanation which have generally carried more weight than the biological; they adapted more readily to the due process system of criminal trial and sentencing which is a feature of the British system. It was generally believed that any necessary treatment could be carried out while the offender was being punished in a prison or elsewhere; and the approach also fits well with a system which is rooted in controlling or altering behaviour so that it conforms to an accepted type. It is also a useful tool because the 'diagnosis' or assessment by the expert is difficult to refute.

It is important to keep these ideas in mind when studying the remainder of this chapter, as well as Chapters Nine and Ten.

8.3.3 Personality tests

Psychologists are still searching for a general explanation of human personality. Over the years almost every aspect of human personality has been studied: the tests include self-administered questionnaires (such as the MMPI, see later), performance tests, free association tests and the Rorschach test (a test designed to show intelligence, personality and mental state, in which the subject interprets ink-blots of standard type). Despite extensive study, the human personality is still an enigma.

Many researchers have tested the difference between criminal and non-criminal personalities. Schuessler and Cressey (1950) carried out a comparison of 113 studies which used 30 different types of personality tests, all of which sought to detect a personality difference between criminals and non-criminals. They found that 42 per cent of the 113 studied showed differences in favour of the non-criminal, while the remainder were indeterminate. These links were too tenuous to conclude that personality traits were consistently and systematically linked to criminality.

Seventeen years later, Waldo and Dinitz carried out a similar comparison of some 94 studies which had been undertaken during the intervening years. In 76 of the studies (81 per cent) they found a difference between criminals and non-criminals. Although these tests seemed to provide evidence of a personality difference between criminals and non-criminals, Waldo and Dinitz felt that the findings were far from conclusive. Thus they too concluded that no personality traits were consistently and systematically linked to criminality. In order to comprehend this conclusion it is necessary to understand one of the main personality tests: the MMPI.

8.3.4 MMPI test

Between the 1950 and 1967 comparative studies a new, and allegedly more reliable, test became more widely operative for assessing the criminal personality. This test was called the Minnesota Multiphasic Personality Inventory, or the MMPI for short. It consists of 550 items which were developed to assist the diagnosis of adults who sought psychiatric help. The subjects decide whether the 550 statements are true or false when applied to themselves. There are a number of checks included in the questionnaire in order to catch untruthful answers. The test is split into ten scales and the subject is given a score on each scale; there is no overall score. The individual's full personality is then constructed from a score profile obtained by entering the scores from each scale onto a graph. The ten scales indicate an assessment of: hypochondria; depression; conversion hysteria or disorder (where unexplained physical symptoms are assumed to be linked to psychological factors); psychopathic personality; masculinity–femininity; paranoia; neurosis; schizophrenia; hypomania (a condition marked by over-excitability); and introversion. As the MMPI is now used for the assessment of the personalities of normal individuals, the scales do not usually bear any names but are usually identified only numerically, e.g., scale 1, scale 2, scale 3 etc. (see Table 8.1).

The items which the study by Waldo and Dinitz had found most often distinguished the criminal from the non-criminal lay in the Psychopathic personality (Pd) scale, or scale 4 of the test. However, they discovered that this part of the test could produce a systematic bias because it included a number of items which were most likely to be answered differently by a criminal. The most obvious was: 'I have never been in trouble with the law'. Other questions which appeared in this scale and to which the delinquent is more likely to answer differently from the non-delinquent were: 'I liked school'; 'My relatives are nearly all in sympathy with me'; 'I often was in trouble in school, although I do not understand for what reasons'. In the studies where personality differences were said to be found, this was based on the different answers given to only four questions out of 50. The small differentiation resulted in a significant difference between criminals and non-criminals in the final statistical analysis. In any event, an explanation could be found in the different environments or situations of the two groups, rather than personality differences.

It is unsurprising that the delinquent scores higher on this Pd scale, as it was designed specifically to differentiate delinquents from other groups, a factor

Table 8.1: MMPI clinical scales

Scale Number	Scale Name	What the Scale Discloses
1	Hs–Hypochondriasis	Tired; inactive; lethargic; feels physically ill.
2	D–Depression	Serious; low in morale; unhappy; self-dissatisfied.
3	Hy–Hysteria	Idealistic; naive; articulate; ill under stress; social.
4	Pd–Psychopathic deviation	Rebellious; cynical; disregards rules; socially aggressive; selfish.
5	Mf-Interest pattern of opposite sex	High score: sensitive. Low score: exaggerated own sex interest pattern. High score in males: gentlemanly; scholarly; feminine. High score in females: rough; ambitious.
6	Pa–Paranoia	Perfectionist; stubborn; hard to know; or, with moderate scores, socially acceptable.
7	Pt–Psychasthenia	Dependent; desires to please; feelings of inferiority; indecisive; anxious.
8	Sc–Schizophrenia	Negative; difficult; odd; pathetic; lacks social grace.
9	Ma–Hypomania	Expansive; optimistic; decisive; not bound by custom.
0	Si–social introversion	Unassertive; self-conscious; shy; or, with low score, socially active.

Source: From Lundman (2001), p. 40.

which Waldo and Dinitz seem to have ignored. The more surprising fact is rather that the score differences on this scale were not greater. But its utility for identifying delinquents is weakened because it has been found to predict characteristics besides delinquency. For example, those who drop out of school have been found to have a higher Pd score than others, as have those who are less shy, particularly if they are more aggressive. The archetypal 'yuppie' or the hardnosed businessman is also likely to score high on this scale. Professional actors also have high Pd scores and so do those who have 'carelessly' shot someone in a hunting accident (see Gleitman (1986) at p. 616). Used as a predictor, one would expect those who scored high on this scale to drop out of school, be outgoing, possibly more aggressive, become professional actors and be involved in hunting accidents. The practical application of such tests in criminology is thus severely limited.

One of the main reasons why these personality tests attracted so much interest was that it was hoped that they would provide predictive information on those most likely to offend in the future, raising the possibility of being able to offer special help before such persons' personalities began to cause criminally defined behavioural problems. Lundman (1993) reports on the utility of the MMPI test as a predictor of criminality. He found that three of the scales were associated with offending: scale 4–Pd Psychopathic deviation; scale 8–Sc Schizophrenia; and scale 9–Ma Hypomania. Of these, scale 8 was the best predictor, with 23.8 per cent of those who obtained a high score on this scale becoming officially delinquent within four years. This still means that 76.2 per cent of those with a high rating on scale 8 did not offend within four years. A slightly better rate of prediction is obtained when high scores on at least two out of three of the above scales are combined: 34.5 per cent of those in this category offended within four years, but this still leaves 65.5 per cent who fall within this category but who did not offend. Crucially, the test was not able effectively to separate out the offenders from the others: it thus gives too many false positives to be a good predictive tool (Farrington (1994)).

8.3.5 Interpersonal maturity tests

A further level of tests which came out with very similar results was based on the social maturity levels of individuals. These are often called 'interpersonal maturity' tests or 'I-Level' tests. In these studies, individuals are tested for their social and interpersonal skills and they are then placed on one of several levels of maturity. These levels are simply given numerical values, but each of the numerical levels is also linked with descriptions of the person's 'core personality'. Both Warren (1970) and Palmer (1974) discovered that most convicted delinquents appeared in Levels 2, 3 and 4 and all were socially immature. Level 2 personalities are asocial, aggressive and power orientated, which is very similar to the descriptions found in the MMPI tests. Individuals on Level 3 are characterised by their conformity to the delinquent group. They claimed that 90 per cent of delinquents fell into one or other of these three levels.

8.3.6 Assessment of personality tests

The MMPI tests and the I-Level studies all suggest that there is a link between criminality and assertiveness, hostility, resentment of authority, dynamic personalities and psychopathy. However, while in the first two of these research studies the findings were statistically significant, their actual sizes were small. This has given rise to doubts about their reliability, and they have been questioned by later researchers. Conceptually, it would be better to begin testing at a very young age and follow the children through to adulthood. Ideally, the tests should cover not only personality and official criminality, but also self-reported criminality. The researcher would then be better able to assess whether their personalities were inherent, learnt from normal socialisation, or were the result of a brush with the criminal justice system. The proposed method of assessment might also show whether these personality types actually commit more crime or whether they are just more likely to be caught. There would still be problems: the perceived personality traits may be the result of earlier conflict with figures of authority such as teachers.

In any event, it seems that the personality trait (sometimes referred to as an antisocial or asocial personality) will not determine the criminal behaviour, but will only predict a certain type of behaviour, of which criminality is but one example. Some even doubt whether there is any real personality trait, claiming instead that the way each individual acts depends rather upon the situation they are in. They point out that a person who is said to have a more aggressive personality will not be generally aggressive; the trait will show only in certain situations. Thus they may be aggressive on the sports field, or whilst driving and at work, but be very gentle in their personal relationships. The argument is that it is the situation, not the individual's personality, which decides their behaviour. For example, if a police car is behind you it would not cause you to stop although it might cause you to drive with more care, but if the blue light on the police car starts flashing, you would stop. The situation of the blue light brought about the behaviour, not any personality attribute of the individual—the same behaviour would probably have occurred whether you were dominant or submissive, sociable or unsociable. But in a different situation you might not stop. If, for example, you had just committed a crime other than a driving offence, you might try to escape. This is not to deny any influence to personality, but rather to say that reactions may depend on a number of factors. For example, the behaviour of a person in a school depends partly on their position—head teacher, teacher, secretary, caretaker, prefect, pupil or parent; partly on the situation—classroom, sports field, parents' evening, disciplinary, social; and partly on the personality of the individual. It might also be affected by the pressures of a peer grouping or by the values of the community (see Chapter Twelve).

The Cambridge study (in which a cohort of young boys was analysed and followed until adulthood) found (Farrington (1994)) that the really significant links were not with personality, but between offending behaviour and impulsivity (acting without stopping to think about consequences). This in turn may be connected with low physiological arousal as discussed in Chapter Seven, especially concerning EEG and the Autonomic Nervous System. Low arousal would lead to overconfidence, sensation seeking and risk taking all of which have been linked to offending behaviour (see Mawson (1987)). In the Cambridge study, low heart rate (one of the measures of low arousal) was linked with violent offending; when a boy appeared to come from a high-risk background, one of the things which appeared most successfully to protect him from turning to offending was being shy, nervous or withdrawn, which Farrington (1994) suggests exhibits high arousal. This may then be one of the important causative links.

8.3.7 Some comments on treatment

The main use to which these so-called personality theories could be put is one of treatment. Some psychologists argue that drug therapy and electroconvulsive treatment is of use in disabusing and re-training delinquents and criminals, but on the whole these methods are avoided or at least do not currently form the central part of any re-training techniques. The better opinion seems to be that greater understanding of personality gives rise to the possibility of controlling actions by behaviour therapy. In this, the psychologist uses the knowledge of the offender's personality, along with general information about other people with similar personality types, in order to choose the learning theory or conditioning which is thought to be most likely to give favourable results (see Chapter Ten for a discussion of cognitive behavioural technique).

Although it would be generally dangerous to use these theories to try to predict who will commit a crime (see 8.4), they may be useful in identifying how best to deal with criminals once they have transgressed. Many writers in this area have suggested that the criminality tends to be committed by those who possess certain personality traits such as not caring what others think, not caring about the consequences of acts when they affect others, weak or no personal ties, irresponsibility, and an outgoing personality. If some of these factors do affect criminality, further criminality might be prevented by helping to alter or manage these personality traits. This may be done by, for example, making these individuals aware of the suffering they cause, making them face responsibilities, and teaching them to live in a social setting. Some of this approach has recently been used in probation work in the UK (Ward et al. (2002)), where probation orders can be accompanied by a range of conditions and are seen as a positive alternative to incarceration. The probation service has worked out strategies which are focused on particular types of offenders. Macdonald et al. (1992), after examining 95 projects, report positive results in at least three-quarters of them. Programmes should enhance the offenders' ability to exercise responsible choices to avoid offending, and should treat them with respect so that they come to value themselves and their rights: it is important that offenders view such programmes as positive and helpful to them rather than just for control and punishment. More recently probation have been required to embrace these working practices under the government's 'what works' strategy. The policies offer a potential as a fruitful means of cutting down on criminal behaviour but such approaches are difficult to sustain when the probation service is generally over-stressed and under-resourced, especially as the introduction of these programmes did not come with large injections of cash (Ward et al. (2002)).

Similar strategies are also tried in some prison establishments, either as part of a group therapy session or in a wider context. Inmates are made to take some responsibility for their living conditions, they are trusted with dangerous implements like scissors and metal cutlery, staff and inmates talk through problems in the units together, and talk through the inmates' difficulties together. These units have taken on some of the most dangerous and uncontrollable inmates, and yet they have reported some quite surprising successes. Possibly their ideas should be used more widely in prison establishments, although this is perhaps unlikely when the prison population is at a record level and still rising.

8.3.8 Criticisms of personality theories

Personality theories are more scientific than those put forward by the psychoanalyst, in the sense that they rely less on assessment and explanation of phenomena and draw more on mainly objective tests. They are more commonly based upon empirical research, which can be more easily assessed.

Most theories assume that each individual has a central or core personality which can explain reactions to most stimuli and will determine the likelihood of becoming criminally involved. However, different theories link different personality types to criminality, whilst the general use of empirical evidence makes it difficult to choose between them. On the other hand, there is much overlap: assertiveness and resentment of authority occur frequently as being linked to criminality.

More fundamental doubts arise from the central concept of the existence of a core personality. It assumes that a small number of characteristics can rule all an individual's actions and relationships. Many clearly believe that this core personality can be altered or controlled, otherwise their suggested treatment techniques would be rendered useless. Others assert that each individual is born with a particular core personality, or at least that it is developed at a very early age (e.g., Eysenck and Trasler): for them very careful and intensive treatment would be required to alter or control that inborn personality. Some researchers have claimed that the core personality can be altered naturally by environmental change, by the passing of time, or the heightened maturity of the person (see Robins (1966)). Such a stance puts the whole concept of a core personality in doubt, as the concept draws its strength from the idea that it is permanent unless it is carefully treated by professionals. However, if the core personality does alter naturally over time, it might help to explain why many people who have a criminal record during their teens grow out of it in their early twenties as they mature and their personality alters. The more basic immediate point is that so wide a range of interpretation of the basic concept must undermine confidence in theories based on personality.

Despite these doubts, common sense suggests that there must be something in the idea of a core personality—we all view Betty as different from Daisy or Freda and would say possibly that one is more reliable than the other, or that one is more friendly, and so on. Similarly, we all have an idea of how a particular person is likely to react to a certain situation, and that somebody else would react differently. If they do not act as expected, we would view it as 'out of character'. So we accept that although our basic idea of a person is that they portray a particular type of personality, we also accept that this can alter in small ways without losing its basic 'core'. We also accept that at certain times a person may not 'feel themselves': a normally cheery person may have an off day, but this does not alter our basic view of them. People are unique, partly because of their personalities.

To go beyond such pragmatic impressions of how criminality and personality might be related needs closer discussion of cause and effect than most of these theories provide. In almost all cases it is assumed that the relationship is direct (i.e., that criminality was a result of the personality attributes) whereas in fact the attributes may have arisen as a result of being arrested, convicted and punished, or both the criminality and the attributes may be the result of some third element. Even if the personality traits are affecting the criminality, it may not be in such a direct way as is implied. The personality traits may, for example, render the making of close relationships very difficult, which would isolate the person, who may then not feel as bound as other people are by societal norms. Alternatively, the traits may just render criminality more likely if certain other factors, for example environmental factors, are favourable to the commission of crime.

The extent to which personality attributes are accepted as a complete and reliable explanation of criminality is probably decreasing. The theories which contain a more sociological element have gained in popularity and acceptance. Despite this, personality must always play some part in the explanation of crime if only to help to understand why it is that not all people from certain social backgrounds and environments end up as criminals. Most sociologists accept this, but they would certainly question the idea of a fixed core personality and rather see personality as a continuing thread which is altered by experience and by relationships, and which of course can be affected by treatment methods.

8.3.9 Offender profiling

As was seen in Chapter Five repeat victimisation is common. There it was considered as a problem for the victim but what this hides is that repeat victimisation also often means that the offender is the same in each case. This is obviously the case in domestic violence; the violence is likely to be repeated at least until the relationship is ended. It is often also true of repeat property victimisation. In these instances victimisation shows a clear pattern, but there can also be a pattern to victimisation and offending in other areas. The British Crime Survey has pinpointed the types of property and persons most likely to be victimised; there are also types of people who are more likely to offend. Since the 1970s detailed analysis of crimes and crime patterns has revealed very useful information concerning offenders and has helped in a number of police investigations. Offender profiling, however, is not new: Rumbelow (1987) refers to a profile of Jack the Ripper provided by Dr Thomas Bond in 1888. In addition much media attention has been given to this use of psychology. It has also led to a whole series of academic books called 'Offender Profiling Series' published by Ashgate. The approach has been used to particular effect in cases of rape, murder and arson and it is these that will be considered here, but a more modern usage is for property offences where the methodology is more statistical and less personal (see Chapter Eleven).

Although no two writers seem to agree on the exact nature of offender profiling, basically it consists of teasing out the characteristics of the offender from a detailed knowledge of the offence and other background information. A profiler will study the scene of the crime; the scene of the discovery of the body (if relevant and different); the surrounding neighbourhood; the last movements of the victim; the type of person the victim is or was; his or her personal appearance; statement by the victim (where it is not a case of murder); and any other information which the investigating team have. From this the profiler constructs a profile, which often covers information concerning the offender's social and physical characteristics, their behaviour and personality. Of course no profile is exact. No profile can tell the police who committed an offence; all it can do is suggest characteristics that the offender is likely to possess. Even in the most accurate profiles, such as Canter's analysis of the railway murderer, Duffy, only 13 of the 17 pointers were correct. As Jackson and Bekerian (1997) point out, the offender profile does not solve the case, it is merely 'one more tool' that the police can use, and it might help to narrow down the pool of suspects. If they have six in the frame and two do not fall within the profile, they might be sensible initially to concentrate on the four who may be closer to the profile. That should not exclude the other two: a profile neither hands the police an offender nor means that any suspect who does not match the profile can be ignored. Besides possibly helping to pin-point an offender, a profile may also suggest ways in which he or she might be most successfully interviewed.

Much offender profiling has been attacked for its lack of scientific basis. Canter and Alison (1999) question the work of both Douglas and Olshaker (1997) and Britton (1997) on this basis. They suggest that Douglas's work (and thereby that of the FBI) is often very general, containing factors which would be common in all such offences and that Britton does not use general psychological principles to build his profiles despite having been trained in these. If these attacks are justified, they would mean that much psychological profiling is little more than intelligent intuition or guesswork. This may be unavoidable. As Smith (1998) points out, in many cases the profiler is only called in once traditional policing methods have failed or are not doing very well. At this point much of the information most important to the profiler, such as the crime scene, will have been destroyed.

The FBI began to use profiling heavily in the 1970s and 1980s. Their method-ology was to work with offenders, interviewing them to discover offender types, which could then be used to aid in building profiles. As Holmes and De Burger (1989) note they classed serial murderers into four types:

1. *Visionary Motive Type*—This serial murderer commits crimes because com-manded to do so by voices or visions, e.g., Peter Sutcliffe, the 'Yorkshire Ripper'. The murder itself is usually spontaneous and disorganised.

2. *Mission-Oriented Motive Type*—This type of killer has a goal, usually to rid the world of a particular type of person. These people are not psychotic but have a strong wish to solve a particular problem, often to eliminate groups they judge 'unworthy', such as prostitutes or tramps. (Terrorists may fall into this category, see Chapter Nineteen.) Such a killer knows the action is wrong and that others con-demn it. They are difficult to spot because they live otherwise normal, and often successful, lives. The victims are usually strangers, chosen because they fit into a particular category. The act is usually well planned, well organised and efficiently committed.

3. *Hedonistic Type*—These killers basically kill for pleasure. According to Holmes and De Burger, there are two main sub-categories of hedonistic serial murderers, each of which derives its pleasure from different sources. The thrill-orientated killer is possibly the most difficult to understand. This type enjoys the excitement of killing and so kills for pleasure. His victims are strangers chosen at random and

with no specific characteristics. They become victims purely because they are in the wrong place at the wrong time. There may be sadistic acts committed against the victims, but for this type of criminal the important thing is the act of killing. The second sub-group is the lust killer. A central part of this crime is sexual. For many of them the sexual pleasure is heightened by the amount of pain and often sexual mutilation they can inflict. They often have normal relationships and live normal lives, except that they have a problem with sexual gratification. For most lust killers the lead-up to the crime is part of the pleasure, so they fantasise about the crime and then take time in the selection of the victim, looking for specific traits, perhaps even following the victim for a period of time before the act. Nonetheless, the victim is usually a stranger who happens to possess the desired characteristics. The act is usually planned and organised and the sexual and killing parts of the crime are often savoured, perhaps even including the disposal of the body.

4. *Power/Control-Oriented Type*—This type of killer is very difficult to distinguish from the lust or thrill-seeking types. Many of the same traits may appear: but this criminal acts out of a desire to show absolute power over another human by taking ultimate control of life or death. In order to prove control he may commit sexual acts, but the sex is only a form of power over the victim. The victim will be a stranger who has specific characteristics, the crime will be organised and planned. The killing is often very sadistic.

Similarly they classify four types of rapist: power-reassurance; power-assertive; anger-retaliatory; and anger-excitement. One of the main aspects in their analysis is the assessment, using a number of variables, of whether the crime was organised or disorganised. Their approach has been used widely in many different countries and probably forms the basis for most offender profiling.

David Canter takes a rather different approach, one that is used alongside the FBI system by the UK Association of Chief Police Officers' Behavioural Science Investigative Support Subcommittee. It has therefore been used in a number of cases in the UK. Rather than trying to fit an offender into a rigid type Canter looks at their behaviour and assesses how this will be reflected in their normal non-offending lives (Canter (1995)). So whilst he and his associates use scientific methods such as the analysis of cases to build up a number of important criteria, they use these to assess aspects of the offender's normal behaviour and lifestyle to come up with more distinctive criteria, than are sometimes contained in the FBI profiles. Yet another system is used by another UK profiler, Britton (1997), who analyses each case from scratch and does not use statistical analysis of previous cases to inform his judgments.

The limitations of the methodology are noted by Ormerod (1996 and 1999); it is useful only in a few cases such as rape, killing or arson; the profile only describes a possible type of person and does not identify an individual; profiles could prove prejudicial, both in the minds of the police in looking for an offender and in the minds of a jury if a case comes to court. The profile can only supplement other investigative methods, both of finding offenders and constructing cases.

Despite its prominence and the belief in offender profiling by both the public and the police its real usefulness has still to be proven. Ainsworth (2000) refers to a study conducted by Copson and Holloway where they note that it was only successful in 16 per cent of the cases in which it was used and only led to the identification in 3 per cent. These low figures may have much to do with the fact that the police prefer to claim to have solved the crimes by more traditional means, but even so they are very low. The criminal justice system must not depend too much on this relatively new investigative device.

8.4 Assessment of dangerousness and criminality

8.4.1 Defining dangerousness

Most Western criminal justice systems include some form of assessing the danger posed by individuals who have been convicted of violent or other serious crimes. Such assessments help to decide how long those people should be removed from society, not as punishment but as protection for other members of the society. In some societies such removal is possible and occurs without any crime having been committed—in the form of civil committal to mental institutions. This is only possible where the individual's mental stability has been questioned, and it is this rather than just the dangerousness which is the deciding factor. In all these instances, someone has to decide what is dangerous and whether a particular individual fits that description. It is therefore essential that there is a definition of 'dangerousness'. On the surface, this may appear to be a very simple task. Almost everyone has an idea of what they consider to be dangerous, and for most it involves at least an element of violence or threat to personal safety. It is on this basis that political groups, 'outsiders' (gypsies, tramps, youths etc.) and writers are often seen as being 'dangers to society' even if they have committed no criminal acts.

Crime, fear, risk and dangerousness now seem to be intertwined in the imagination of the public. As was seen in Chapter Three most reports of criminal activities in the media (fiction and non-fiction) concentrate on two areas: serious interpersonal violence, usually between strangers—the sort most people are most fearful of; and on crimes which undermine feelings of safety within a neighbourhood —groups of drug dealers and users, graffiti and wanton destruction of property (often reported as being widespread and normal in certain parts of society). These depictions both feed public fear, anxiety and insecurity and report on its existence. Usually they also suggest severe methods for dealing with criminality and with these people: generally these methods involve control of individual criminals rather than changes to society. Some very dangerous activities and groups are not represented in this way in the media. For example dangerous drivers cause crashes and deaths, but are not usually portrayed as dangerous people and even when convicted receive relatively light sentences. In contrast, the reporting of certain one off offences as dangerous can have serious consequences both for the law and/or public attitudes. Thus the two children who killed the toddler Jamie Bulger were widely reported as 'evil' and a danger to society. In the mass hysteria which followed many people were ready to impute conscious criminality to very young children. Innocence and lack of understanding would no longer be accepted for this group so the legal rule of *doli incapax* (the rebuttable presumption that children aged between 10 and 13 are not capable of the mental responsibility necessary in most offences) was abolished (Newburn (2002)). Children now face the full power of the law and one factor in this has been the way in which the media raise fears, then report on the existence of these fears and then call for severe measures to still these fears.

In the last 20 or so years dangerousness has become central to our criminal justice system and legal rules. In Britain there have been a number of provisions which have allowed perceived dangerousness of the criminal to play a major role in sentencing. In each case the basic concept is that of the protection of society rather than of dangerousness. The provisions are as follows:

Two interrelated provisions were introduced by the Criminal Justice Act 1991 to allow sentencing to protect the public. These are now contained in the Powers of Criminal Courts (Sentencing) Act 2000 (PCC(S)A 2000). Section 79(2)(b) allows the use of custody for a violent or sexual offence in order to protect the public and s. 80(2)(b) allows use of a longer sentence to protect the public (still within the legal maximum). These provisions should not be used where the person is likely to commit only minor offences. It is important to note that the Act does not say what level of risk is necessary before the provision can be used so that longer sentencing is possible even if the risk is only very slight (s. 81(4)). The court is permitted to consider any information about the offender when it makes its prediction of future conduct, and presumably this could include expert testimony.

Such provisions have freed the courts to use incapacitation in selected cases in which the limiting factors are to be those necessary to protect the public, with no link to proportionality. Dingwall (1998) suggested that the courts had been reluctant to use their extra powers. First he claimed that they had interpreted violent and sexual acts fairly narrowly, secondly that they always wanted some proof that the individual would be a danger to society if released, and finally that they had introduced an element of proportionality into this extra period of incapacitation. Possibly because of this reluctance to use their powers, Parliament has introduced minimum sentences in certain circumstances (see the PCC(S)A 2000, Part V, chapter III, below), while s. 85 of the PCC(S)A 2000 also permits a court to extend the period of licence which a sexual or violent offender must serve. Partly to prepare for this type of extended licence and partly to ensure a better community strategy for dealing with these types of offender the Criminal Justice and Court Services Act 2000 requires the police and probation services to establish arrangements for assessing and managing the risks posed by dangerous sexual and violent offenders. These are intended, together with the use of the sex offenders register, to feed into the powers already available under previously assessed legislation and furnish the courts and enforcement agencies with better and more precise information.

The 2000 Act also led to the setting up of Multi-Agency Public Protection Arrangements (MAPPA) in all areas to develop coordinated systems for dealing with dangerous or risky offenders in the community. One result was the setting up of Multi-Agency Public Protection Panels (MAPPPs) to act as the front line in this work. At the moment the two most important agencies in this work have been the police and probation (though the Criminal Justice Act 2003 adds prison authorities to this and requires other bodies such as health, housing and education to cooperate) and MAPPA has facilitated their partnership work considerably. Basically MAPPA is involved in: the identification of offenders who may pose a risk to society; sharing information on these offenders and in related areas; assessment of the risk posed by these individuals; and management of that risk. It is important to note that they merely manage risk and do not reduce or neutralise it through treatment. Nothing is done to reduce the level of risk, merely to manage it. They are able to intervene and warn individuals where, for example, a known paedophile begins a pattern of activity similar to that which led to his earlier sexual abuse of children. However, probation cannot step in to work on the problems faced by the individuals and try to make it less likely that they will re-offend; this can only happen as part of the original sentence. Assessment and management of risk, tracking offenders, has largely replaced rehabilitation of the offender. Does this make society safer or only appear to be safer?

In addition, life sentences, both mandatory and discretionary, can be used to protect the public from dangerous offenders. Life sentence is, for example, obligatory for those over 18 years of age and those found guilty of murder. The aim is to show that the offence is unacceptable. Risk and dangerousness therefore become an issue in relation to mandatory life sentences only when such prisoners are being considered for release on licence. Under s. 109 of the PCC(S)A 2000, first enacted in the Crime (Sentences) Act 1997, there is now a second category of mandatory life sentence to be applied to persons over 18 convicted of a second serious offence. In England and Wales the Act defines a serious offence to include: an attempt, conspiracy or incitement to murder; soliciting a murder; manslaughter; wounding, or grievous bodily harm, with intent; rape or attempted rape; intercourse with a girl under 13; possession of a firearm with intent to injure; using a firearm to resist arrest; carrying a firearm with criminal intent; robbery while in possession of a firearm or an imitation firearm. In these circumstances, a judge on second conviction must impose a life sentence unless either there are exceptional circumstances relating either to the offence or to the offender which justify not passing such a sentence (these must be stated in open court), or it would be inappropriate, having regard to the circumstances of the offence or the offender. The assumption here is that past behaviour is normally sufficient to prove dangerousness in the future.

In a number of other cases life is a discretionary maximum sentence. It is most commonly used in serious violence and sexual offences. In these cases the court is normally expected to pass a determinate sentence which indicates the severity of the offence. A court is supposed to use the life sentence only when the offence is serious enough to require a very long sentence, when the offender is unstable and likely to repeat such offences, and where if any further offences occurred they would involve serious consequences to others. The Criminal Justice Act 2003 adds it as a possibility in cases where an individual is assessed as dangerous and has committed a violent or sexual offence (even if it was not serious) where the maximum is more than 10 years (in other cases an extended sentence must be used to protect the public).

The element of danger again becomes an issue at the time when a life prisoner is being considered for release or when a possible release date is being set. Such individuals are released on parole licence which will last the rest of their lives.

In the case of discretionary lifers or mandatory lifers under the PCC(S)A 2000, s. 109, the 'tariff' is fixed in strict accordance with the recommendations of the trial judge, and under s. 82A the sentencing court is normally required to calculate what determinate sentence would be necessary to mark the seriousness of the offence. (Part 12, chapter 7 of the Criminal Justice Act 2003 will make this a decision for the judge alone with no intervention by the Home Secretary.) Half the determinate period (less any time already spent in custody or on remand) is then taken as the 'specified period' after which the offender is eligible to have his or her case sent to the Parole Board. If the offence is considered to be too serious, the court may refuse to make this calculation and the offender will not then be eligible for parole. A person must be released on licence as soon as the Parole Board so directs. Where the Board decide against release, the lifer can require reconsideration after a further two years. The prisoner is normally permitted to see reports concerning him or her and can both appear before the tribunal and have representation. He or she is entitled to a decision with reasons within seven days of the hearing. This hearing is to assess the safety of releasing the individual and therefore the assessment of dangerousness is central to its decision. Neither for mandatory nor for discretionary lifers is there a definition of dangerousness or of factors to be considered. In these cases the board is constituted of a judge, a psychiatrist and a lay member. They assess the risk which may be posed if they release the offender and look at factors such as: what the offender did; why they did it; whether anything has altered; how did any change come about; how they have behaved in prison etc. When in doubt in any particular case the 'bottom line . . . has to be the safety of the public' (quote from board member found in Dorby (2003)). The assessment of risk/dangerousness is set to become more central under the Criminal Justice Act 2003.

The Crime (Sentences) Act 1997 introduced minimum sentences for repeat offenders, now contained in the PCC(S)A 2000, part V, chapter III. When dealing with a person over 18 convicted of a class A drugs offence and who has at least two previous class A drugs convictions (at separate times) the court must pass a sentence of at least seven years. When dealing with a person over 18 convicted of a domestic burglary and who has at least two previous convictions (at separate times) for domestic burglary the court must pass a sentence of at least three years. These minimum sentences apply unless there are specific circumstances relating either to the offence or to the offender which would render the minimum unjust (these must be stated in open court). The reason given for these minima is usually that they are necessary to protect the public from a person who has been proven to be a danger to the public in the past. There is no attempt to assess whether there might be any such danger in the future, nor any personal assessment.

There are also the provisions which allow restricted confinement of mentally disordered offenders. In the past the judiciary retained the power to decide when they would be released and did so at the time of sentencing, but in *X v United Kingdom* (1981) 4 EHRR 181 the European Court of Human Rights decided that such offenders should be guaranteed regular access to a tribunal to assess the lawfulness of their detention. This was later enacted and restriction orders are now available if there is a clear mental disorder recognised by the Mental Health Act 1983 and there is a special need to protect the public from serious harm (see s. 41 of that Act). It is generally used to prevent doctors discharging individuals who have committed an offence (which does not have to be serious) and where, having regard to the patient's previous record, there is a risk that further offences may occur which might lead to serious harm. Unless the restrictions are time limited the restriction lasts indefinitely and the patient can be discharged only by the Mental Health Review Tribunal or the Home Secretary. Such reviews must occur regularly. Discharge can either be conditional or unconditional; if conditional the person will be subject to recall. The fact that the authority to release is shared between the Mental Health Review Tribunal and the Home Secretary indicates the ambiguity of the decision: the former should consider mainly the need for, and likelihood of response to, treatment; whereas the latter should be interested in the safety of the public. These will not always coincide.

Finally, in the Home Office and Department of Health (1999 and 2000) consultation document *Managing Dangerous People with Severe Personality Disorder: Proposals for Policy Development* (1999), the Dangerous People with Severe Personality Disorder Bill 2000 (which was not passed), the 2000 White Paper entitled *Reforming the Mental Health Act*, the Criminal Justice Act 2002 (not passed), the Criminal Justice Act 2003, and the Draft Mental Health Bill 2002, the government made clear its intention to give authorities more powers to restrain people who may be classed as dangerous. These new documents are focused on the dangerous person with a severe personality disorder. These are persons who have been thought to cause serious problems for crime control but who, because they do not suffer from any treatable mental health condition fall outside the present normal powers of health care. The intent underlying these documents is to provide a wholly new framework for removing dangerous people for as long as they pose a serious risk and to attempt to deal with the effects of their disorder, even if the disorder itself cannot be cured. Originally it was openly stated that the aim was to provide powers for the indeterminate detention of the dangerous person with a severe personality disorder in both criminal and civil proceedings. Detention would be imposed because of the risk they pose to society and would not rely on convictions. Although this is no longer openly clear in either the 2003 Criminal Justice Act or the Draft Mental Health Bill 2002 neither of which mentions DSPD, the effect is the same. The 2002 Draft Mental Health Bill substantially widens the concept of 'mental disorder' (clause 2) in that it would include those suffering from a personality disorder, even if it is not treatable, and then provides for compulsory detention where the individual, among other things, is deemed to be a substantial risk of serious harm to others (clause 6). This is the detention of DSPD where no offence has occurred.

The intervention is to be available to those incarcerated or in a mental institution. Pilot projects are already underway (see Peay (2003), Bennett (2003) and **http://www.dspdprogramme.gov.uk/default.asp?action=article&ID=28**) and individuals have already been labelled as DSPD. The Criminal Justice Act 2003 will facilitate this by permitting longer sentences for all those deemed to be dangerous and who have committed a violent or sexual offence, these people will then be assessed. In the future there are also intentions to permit MAPPAs (see earlier) to send those they assess as dangerous or posing a particular risk for assessment as DSPD, or under the Draft Mental Health Bill, where although this particular label may not be used the effect would be the same. Pilot projects in community health are thus being designed both for these people and to facilitate and support the release of those who have been in DSPD units whilst incarcerated.

Importantly there is no definition of dangerousness in the proposals nor is there any scientifically accepted idea or clear category of severe personality disorder. Severe personality disorder is often associated with the concept of psychopath, which Cavadino (1999) suggests has no meaning except that these people are either nasty or inadequate. In partial agreement the Fallon report admits that it is not a recognised condition but suggests that it is associated with certain characteristics that can be recognised. Such substantial doubts over the class of person who might be included should perhaps make totally unacceptable the use of these very wide powers. Even with proper definitions of category and dangerousness there might be problems over the moral acceptability of detaining these people, where the detention is on top of any punishment and may even occur without a conviction. Such drastic intervention in the freedom of individuals who may have committed no offence, and may never have shown themselves to be dangerous, is itself dangerous. Even if they have committed an offence can this fact justify detaining them for periods totally outwith those needed to pay for that transgression?

It is thus evident that the contribution of the law of England and Wales to a definition of dangerousness has not been very helpful: apart from the general requirement that there be an offence committed before the assessment of dangerousness could interfere with the liberty of an individual, each of the above categories seems to cover different ideas and the last category might in the future allow intervention even though there is no conviction. The general presumption is that past behaviour alone predicts future behaviour.

Individuals have their own perceptions of danger and of unacceptable danger, often related to their sex, culture, social class etc., and some are deeply personal. To allow a judge unfettered powers to decide what is dangerous and remove someone's liberty on this ground would be unacceptable. Therefore certain frequently accepted boundaries are normally applied. For most people, any assessment of dangerousness such as to justify an individual having his or her liberty restricted would involve the individual in having already committed a serious crime, one they regard as involving danger or the potential for danger. Unfortunately the effect of the Draft Mental Health Bill 2002 would mean that this element would be ignored. Most would agree that crimes involving personal injury are the most serious and the most dangerous, and of these crimes those involving serious injury and/or injury to more than one victim would be the most dangerous. But it is not this simple. It is true that behaviour leading to injury is generally seen as the most dangerous type of conduct, but other factors need to be taken into account in the assessment of danger. There are, for example, many people killed on the roads due to breaches of one or other of the criminal laws—driving without due care and attention; speeding; dangerous driving; driving while under the influence of drink. Despite this fact, speeding, careless and even dangerous driving are often seen as crimes of low culpability and their perpetrators are not normally locked up. Even in the case of drunken drivers, it is rare that the individual is viewed as necessarily dangerous and in need of removal from society. Dangerous or careless use of firearms would, however, generally be viewed as far more unacceptable even if no-one was actually injured, and deprivation of liberty would be far more likely to occur as well as an assessment of the individual as dangerous.

An interesting consideration is that some of the crimes which have the worst consequences in the light of the numbers of lives lost, or levels of serious injuries as well as loss of property, are committed by corporations or those acting for corporations: pollution of the atmosphere; harmful products; breaches of health and safety regulations. The social and economic consequences of this type of crime are probably worse for society than the consequences of traditional street crime. Yet most people fear street crime more than corporate crime, and most would probably view it as more dangerous. Corporate criminals are difficult to locate and convict, but even when this is done they would usually be subject only to a fine, often a fairly small fine. In the rare cases where they are imprisoned, it would only be for as long as was necessary to punish them; they would probably not be removed to protect the public from future dangerous behaviour (for a further discussion of this area see Chapter Three). From this it is clear that neither the law nor the general public seem to have any very clear view of what is dangerous.

Some have taken a very narrow view of dangerousness including only overtly extremely violent and dangerous criminal acts such as murder, grievous bodily harm, or sexual crimes such as rape, child sexual abuse etc. (see Hollin 1989). Many would argue that this was too limiting as it would not permit the law to intervene when a dangerous or potentially dangerous act had been committed but before it had had disastrous consequences. These factors were taken into consideration by Megargee (1976). He defined violent behaviour as: 'acts characterised by the application or overt threat of force which is likely to result in injury to people.' He uses injury to mean personal injury and so excludes all purely property crimes where there is no physical force, either actual or threatened.

Floud and Young (1981) came to a similar conclusion. They defined dangerous offenders as those who have inflicted or attempted to inflict serious bodily harm on other human beings and who are found to be suffering from a severe mental or emotional disorder indicating a propensity towards continuing dangerous criminal activity. Floud also suggested that the reason she so firmly supports longer sentences to protect the public is that it would then allow lower sentences for the run-of-the-mill offences—i.e., a lower tariff which would still mark the seriousness of the offence but exclude extra penalties for dangerousness.

Interestingly the provisions in force in England and Wales incorporate the first part of Floud and Young's definition but largely ignore the second part of the Floud recommendations—that the court should be required to inquire into whether the individual is found to be suffering from a severe mental or emotional disorder indicating a propensity towards continuing dangerous criminal activity. Certainly the category DSPD is not defined anywhere and is not a clinically recognised category. It is unclear what type of behaviour or symptoms will result in a person being labelled as DSPD and yet the white paper estimated that it would apply to between 2,100 and 2,400 individuals.

8.4.2 Attempts to explain and predict violent crime

For many years theorists have been trying to predict who will offend and re-offend. Basically what many of these researchers do is to collect facts about convicted criminals: previous arrests and convictions; social and employment history; and, for juveniles, their school records, particularly truancy rates; drug use; family backgrounds etc. The factors which are statistically most strongly related to recidivism are then singled out as those most likely to predict unacceptable behaviour. These factors are then tested normally in longitudinal studies to see whether the predictors stand up to the rigours of practical application. The studies do suggest a modicum of success—previous criminal records, drug habits and employment histories are the most often quoted predictors, but more recently others, such as family size and the age at which the child starts school, have been included. If these were found to occur in almost all recidivists then they might be used as predictors of dangerousness and so remove the question from the intuition of the judges, but the major problem with this method is that it tends to over-predict. It does very well in picking out groups of people who fit into a high-risk category, but within this group there will be a number of 'false positives'. Many of those with the 'at risk' identifiers will not in fact be dangerous—they will not re-offend. Unfortunately the predictors have been found to be particularly inefficient at discovering those most likely to commit serious crimes, particularly violent offences which is the category we most want to incapacitate. This is partly because of the lack of research material—there are insufficient serious violent offenders around to make a reasonably sized study group from which to glean the prediction characteristics.

More effective might be more personalised psychological predictors. Most of these are related to the idea that it is a disorder of interactions and relationships. Again there are problems with prediction but as they are more an assessment of the individual rather than a group of persons they may be more accurate. Psychoanalysts have, indeed, used a number of different approaches and theories to predict violent behaviour. Several will be briefly discussed here, but for a fuller coverage see Zillman (1979), Siann (1985) or Taylor (1999).

8.4.2.1 *Instinct theories*

Instinct theories assume there is an inner force which desires aggression and violence. Freud called it the death force or Thanatos. The life instinct, Eros, and Thanatos are in conflict and the aggression needs to be allowed to vent itself. Usually this is possible through acceptable means such as sport or competitive business, but if the force is not socially dissipated it will come out in the form of violence, either directed to others or at oneself—suicide. But however interesting, these ideas are impossible either to prove or disprove, which limits their contribution to understanding in the particular area of criminology, and gives them little practical value.

8.4.2.2 *Drive theory*

Drive theories also assume that there is an inner force which desires aggression and violence, but in drive theory the inner force is acquired through experience, and is not innate. The general argument is that each type of behaviour is motivated by a drive, and as the drive increases above its normal levels, the individual takes action to reduce it. In the case of violence the basic assertion is that when individuals are prevented from getting what they want, they become frustrated. This frustration leads to aggressive or violent behaviour, which may be aimed at the obstruction to their desire or may be used on other targets. So-called 'road rage' might-be seen as a manifestation of this. Although these theories are a little easier to verify—for example, by giving people a problem to solve and then moving them onto the next one just before they succeed, or by allowing them to watch all but the last twenty minutes of a film and watching the frustration and violence build up— they are not very useful as predictors of behaviour. It is unclear whether it is being claimed that all aggression is the result of frustration, or that whenever frustration occurs it always leads to aggression. Whichever it is, the interest of the theory is limited because it is not sufficiently precise to be useful as a predictor of dangerousness.

8.4.2.3 *Personality and violence*

There are a number of different ideas under this head. The first claims that people with psychopathic tendencies, sometimes known as sociopaths or antisocial personalities, are more likely than others to commit frequent acts of violence. Sociopaths are generally viewed as those who are unsocialised; they do not hold strong values and are less capable of forming loyal relationships with other individuals or with groups; they are selfish, irresponsible, impulsive, uncaring and do not tend to feel any guilt; they are easily frustrated and tend to blame others for their bad behaviour. As Checkley (1976) points out, the term psychopath or sociopath is fairly wide, and is often used to describe anyone who breaches the law, so that it becomes synonymous with criminal. He argues, however, that the true usage of the term can include businessmen, professionals, sportsmen etc. (see 8.3.4). A brasher idea of sociopathy was expounded by Guze (1976), who said a person was a sociopath if he had been in trouble with the police (other than for traffic offences) and had at least two of the following: a history of excessive fighting; school delinquency; poor job record; a period of wanderlust; and being a runaway. For women, the fact that they had a history of prostitution could also be taken into account. He argued that sociopaths could not be treated, and therefore that they should all be locked up until middle age. This recommendation, if taken seriously, would apply to a large number of people who have never committed serious crimes and may never do so. It also confidently assumes that all sociopaths are readily identifiable without possibility of error. It promotes drastic steps with no sound proof that these would make society any safer. This is reinforced by Rafter's (1997) discussion of the evolution of the term 'psychopath' in criminology. She observes that the term is probably undefinable, being a 'misfit', 'on the borderline' between 'normality and abnormality'. For legal purposes a more precise definition would seem to be in order.

8.4.2.4 *Macho personality and dangerousness*

The final personality difference which in recent years has been closely related to violence, and therefore possibly to dangerousness, is the macho personality as measured by the Hypermasculinity Inventory (see Zaitchick and Moscher (1993)). The macho personality views violence as manly, danger as intrinsically exciting, callous sexual activity aimed at women as acceptable, and interprets being tough as a form of self-control. Zaitchick and Moscher (1993) connected these personality elements with inter-male violence, callousness, violence and sexual attacks on women, gang violence and abuse of children. The utility of this test in predicting dangerousness could therefore be very strong but thus far seems to be largely a matter of definition: more scientific testing of the inventory is necessary before it can be reliably used to remove an individual's freedom.

8.4.2.5 *Risk, mental disorder and dangerousness*

In a 1993 study Steadman et al. (1993) worked in a team of 12 people including those trained in law, psychiatry, psychology and sociology who, after reviewing empirical and clinical research, concluded that there were five central factors to an assessment of risk of dangerousness. The factors are:

(a) the level and type of social support available to the person;

(b) how impulsive the individual is;

(c) reactions, such as anger, to provocation;

(d) the level of ability to empathise with others;

(e) nature of any delusions and hallucinations.

They designed reasonably simple and apparently accurate tests which would assess each of these factors in mentally disordered groups, recognising that these might also be valid for testing other groups. In a pilot study they had some success in these clinically assessed factors, but there were discrepancies and the team felt that these might be the result of not having taken into account the situation or context in which any acts of violence took place.

8.4.2.6 *The Hare Psychopathy Checklist-Revised or PCL-R*

This tries to isolate an antisocial personality disorder, or severe personality disorder, without reference to criminal behaviour. It purports to test for such things as 'absence of guilt or remorse', 'callous/lack of empathy', 'criminal versatility', 'cunning', 'glibness/superficial charm', 'failure to accept responsibility for actions', 'grandiose sense of self-worth', 'impulsivity', 'irresponsibility', 'juvenile delinquency', 'lack of realistic long-term goals', 'manipulative', 'many short-term marital relationships', 'need for stimulation', 'parasitic lifestyle', 'pathological lying', 'poor behavioural control', 'promiscuous'. Hare (1996) suggests that it is now quite a sophisticated measure of severe personality disorder but he also (1998) recognises that there are some problems in administering the test and sets out some troubling examples. The test delivers a numerical score which has an attractive simplicity, which will appeal to government given the current obsessions with league tables for everything. It is one of the main tests used to assess people as DSPD in the new unit at HMP Whitmoor. A major problem is that there is no precise score at which the disorder kicks in. As with all other mental problems the diagnosis is a continuum: those classed as having the disorder are simply those who fall towards one end of the continuum. Clearly there will be clinical disagreement about exactly where the line is crossed. As Taylor (1999) notes, the list of qualities tested comprises things most of us would not want in a friend, and assessments based on these criteria may have as much to do with whether the assessor likes the interviewee as with any scientific analysis. People may have many unappealing characteristics but can still appear, and may be, normal in any scientific or clinical sense. Certainly they often do not feel they have a problem themselves, even if they are causing problems for those around them. What the test may be trying to uncover is in fact nastiness. Reiss et al. (1999) endeavoured to test its utility as a tool for clinical diagnosis on young males in Broadmoor. Its results seemed promising whilst the men were still in the hospital but on their release it failed to predict either the reoffenders or the ability to readjust to society.

8.4.2.7 *The Q-sort and multiple tests*

The Q-sort test was invented by Westin and Shedler (1999) and aimed to get around the subjective problems noted in the previous test. The clinician has to score a person on a scale of 1–7 for each of 200 questions on issues such as 'tendency to act impulsively'. It may prove promising in the future but there are still problems with subjective and uncomplementary assessments.

Broadmoor uses many systems to classify illnesses in general, and severe personality disorder in particular. Assessments are made by nurses and social workers as well as doctors and there are often a number of problems found in one patient. Thus severe personality disorder may be present with other psychotic illnesses. How they interact is unknown.

8.4.3 The dangers of prediction

As can be seen from the preceding section, the psychological prediction of dangerousness is problematic and unreliable. In most countries the penal system is largely based upon an idea of retribution, being intended as a punishment for a crime which has been committed. Where there is some recognition of the possibility of deterrence and rehabilitation, they have generally had to be accommodated with the time period laid down for retribution. Sentences are not generally lengthened simply to enable more time for rehabilitation, and are rarely lengthened for reasons of deterrence. The exception is that most States do considerably lengthen sentences, in certain circumstances, for reason of protecting the public. Clearly, protecting the public is a function of the criminal justice system, but the removal of the liberty of people based on a judgement, difficult to prove, that they may be a danger to others raises acute problems. Can such detention be justified? Of course, in most States confinement to protect others does not take place unless the individual has first committed a crime. Is this a sufficient reason for such action? Does it make it acceptable? Should all rights be removed from an individual merely because of a single, or even a series, of transgressions? Once the individual has paid the debt to society, should they not be again presumed innocent until proven guilty?

It can be argued that such questions ignore the potential harm these individuals may inflict, and abrogates the responsibility to protect the innocent who might be harmed. This argument is most forceful where the lives or the health of others are at risk. An analogy is often made with quarantine—we confine carriers of infectious disease to protect others in society from becoming contaminated and thereby harmed, and so we should be willing to protect the public from dangerous criminals. In the case of disease, we do not protect society from all contagious diseases, only those most likely to have the worst consequences for those who catch them. Similarly, most people would never argue that the public should be protected from the petty criminal. That claim is made only in the case of those whose past conduct suggests they may inflict severe harm on others, usually physical harm to the person.

It has to be noted that the analogy is far from exact. It implies that the danger from a criminal is similar to the danger of catching a disease. There are two differences. First, there is a very high probability, and in most diseases a certainty, that if released the individual will contaminate someone and, secondly, that the contamination will be unintentional. If a supposed dangerous criminal is released, there is no such certainty and, as was seen above, often no strong probability that he or she will re-offend. The criminal has a choice, and that choice may depend upon many factors, including the situations faced on release. For any particular case there is the possibility that the released prisoner may not re-offend, and because there is no sound way of predicting future behaviour he or she has the right to be presumed innocent until the criminal law is actually transgressed.

This is a powerful argument until there is a further victim who may well be killed or suffer serious injury. At that point it will certainly be argued that the rights of the criminal should have been forfeited before anyone else was harmed. Such a reaction has a powerful emotional appeal, but that may not be a sound basis for legal action. If individuals are to have their liberty removed on some judgement of their future behaviour, it is clear that mistakes will be made. Some perfectly safe people will be incarcerated and some very dangerous people may be released. The problem is one of discerning the dangerous from the safe, and as yet the bases for prediction are unreliable. The arguments on both sides have merit; it largely becomes a moral argument of balancing the individual right to freedom against the collective call for safety. Most States allow some use of protective confinement and accept that some will have their liberty wrongly interfered with. Equally, most States allow such protective detention only in certain, usually well-defined, situations and accept that they will thereby release some dangerous people. The secret is to find the right balance of reducing mistakes whilst understanding the justice of confinement to protect others. Even if severe personality disorder can be effectively diagnosed it is still unclear whether the European Convention on Human Rights would be breached where incapacitation is not related to the seriousness of a previous offence, let alone where there is no previous offence.

Floud and Young (1981) argued that the way forward was by taking account of where the burden of risk should lie. Before individuals have committed a serious violent act, even if they fall into the dangerous group, they should retain their liberty and society should bear the risk that they may one day offend and cause some harm. But once people commit serious violent offences and also fall into the potentially dangerous group, then the burden of risk shifts to them and they should be locked up in case they do it again. Floud then argues that any detention above that necessary to mark the seriousness of the past crime should be limited to cases where the harm is severe, such as serious sexual or violent offences.

More recently there has been even more focus on risk as the central element in assessment of dangerousness. In the USA the 1991 Public Health Service report, *Healthy People 2000*, discussed the problems of violence and abusive behaviour from the health, rather than legal, perspective and focused on four main points:

(a) A move away from a legal focus towards one based solely on risk, as assessed by health professionals.

(b) Full realisation that all decisions in this area are on a linear continuum and cannot be split into simple yes/no decisions. Cases rarely clearly fall into one or other category so that decisions whether or not to release should be based on where on the continuum the risk should lie.

(c) The level of risk should never be decided once and for all. A person's potential danger will alter over time and this should be recognised by allowing frequent reconsideration of treatment and release.

(d) In all decisions there needs to be a balance between the seriousness of any possible criminal behaviour and the probability of it occurring. These assessments need to be based on specific risk factors.

Clearly much of the US suggestion accepts the need for protection of the public but allows it to interfere with the liberty of an individual only where this is proved to be necessary and only for as long as is necessary. This highlights a number of problems with our present system. Under ss. 79(2)(b) and 80(2)(b) of the Powers of Criminal Courts (Sentencing) Act 2000 the judge in court will assess the amount of time necessary to punish for a particular offence and, where there is a need to protect the public (in violent or sexual cases), will also set the time necessary for such protection. This type of assessment is being replicated in other Acts (see, e.g., Section 12 Chapter 5 of the Criminal Justice Act 2003). This is a one-off decision which may not be assessed on any objective criteria or advice. With the exception of an immediate appeal it cannot be altered as the person changes and his or her danger to the public is either lessened or increased. In the case of life imprisonment the dangerousness of both mandatory and discretionary lifers will be assessed only once they have served the element necessary to punish for the crime committed. Most of this assessment should be concerned with their dangerousness, but how carefully the seriousness of the possible outcome is weighed against the probability of it occurring is impossible to tell. There are certainly no specific risk factors set out which need to be considered. In relation to mandatory and minimum sentences under part V, chapter III, there is no consideration of individual risk which is assumed if certain past conduct has occurred. This Act applies the first part of Floud and Young's test, but totally ignores the second part relating to individual assent. Finally in relation to restriction orders under s. 41 of the Mental Health Act 1983, these are largely medically assessed on grounds of the need for, and utility of, treatment as well as any consideration of dangerousness. In the method of their review they probably most closely approach the US suggestions, but still no specific risk factors are set out.

One suggestion is that the assessment should take account of both past conduct, particularly very harmful criminal activity, and a personal assessment, often of the offender's mental state or personality type. The second leg of this rather assumes a measurable tendency towards criminality which, as has been indicated above, is very often questionable and thus should never, alone, be used to predict dangerousness. It should be noted that there is no necessary link between mental illness and criminality (no more of those with mental problems commit crimes than do the general population) and that psychiatrists have found it impossible to predict criminal behaviour (see Pitch (1995)). However, it is argued that once the first part (past conduct) of the assessment has been completed then the second (mental state) becomes necessary. For those who have a recognised mental illness, an evaluation of whether, and to what extent, their condition could be treated and whether such treatment could occur in the community is necessary. To safeguard the freedom of the individual, a careful analysis of the mental state might indicate that appropriate care and treatment measures rather than incarceration can reasonably ensure that the offender will not be, or is very unlikely to be, dangerous in the future. In other cases past behaviour may indicate no more danger than is normal, but without some assessment this would be impossible to ascertain. Without professional assessment it will be risky for the judge either to release or to incarcerate someone who has a past history of harmful offences. The tendency would be to refuse such release even where the immediate offence does not call for lengthy incarceration, which may breach basic rights to freedom. Professional assessment does not, of course, remove risk, but it makes possible a more balanced judgment between the need to protect the public and the desirability of maintaining individual rights.

Assessment of dangerousness and imprisonment associated with such assessment are both fraught with problems. Three areas in particular appear to need safeguards: first, procedure; secondly, the factors to be considered in the assessment; and finally, the type of confinement.

The procedure of permitting a judge to assess this aspect at any stage appears to be questionable. This is unlike most other judicial decisions and there are good reasons for allowing the assessment to be made by a panel of persons, possibly including a legally qualified individual but definitely including a psychiatrist or psychologist. In cases where there is an element of dangerousness the judge could still pronounce on the seriousness of the offence committed and then pass the offender over to such a panel to make a preliminary assessment of its extent. There would then need to be a separate tribunal to hear appeals and to reassess the decision at appropriate intervals. This should represent a recognition that the decision being made is different in kind and effect from the judicial decision of punishment.

Secondly, there is a need for guidelines on how to assess dangerousness, what level of proof is necessary and how to balance the possible harm to the public against the probability of occurrence. Some guidelines are necessary as this is a very grave interference with liberty which should not be taken lightly. Open public debate about where the lines should be drawn would be helpful: at present we have almost no criteria and, in some cases, no need for professional advice. The problems are legion but they need to be faced, particularly as the use of longer sentences for the protection of the public seems likely to become more common.

Lastly, there is the question of where to hold such individuals. Clearly some are mentally ill with treatable problems and are held in hospitals; others are in prison either because they are not suffering from a mental condition or because their condition is not treatable. Prisons are generally places we send individuals as punishment: should we be using them for dangerous offenders once they have served the part of their sentence necessary to punish? If they are detained to protect others rather than directly in relation to their behaviour, society should recognise this and place them in different institutions with more rights while retaining the level of security necessary to secure their removal from society. There seems to be little justice in imprisoning them in houses of punishment. However, more recently, a number of researchers have been more positive about the possibility of effective treatment and suggest that this might arise in secure therapeutic surroundings, possibly separate from present mental health provisions (see Lipsey and Wilson (1997); Quinsey et al. (1998)).

As was noted above Taylor (1999) has criticised the diagnosing of severe personality disorder as being too subjective and too closely linked to criminal activity. In fact the close link between diagnosis and crime has been problematic for some time. In effect one type of past behaviour (crime) is being used to prove that the individual has a personality disorder which makes them likely to commit that same behaviour. The results are then used to incapacitate that person, imprison him or her, in order to make society safer. There are clearly problems with this approach. A different approach emerges from the work of Kohnken (1996) and Hodge et al. (1997) suggesting that, for some people, crime can become addictive. Kohnken deduces this from the observation that the best predictor of whether someone would offend was previous offending behaviour. As Hodge et al. note it might be sensible to look at addiction models in order to understand the crime patterns of many who might presently be thought to have a personality disorder or even a severe personality disorder. At least before locking up vast numbers of people for possible future behaviour these avenues should be explored.

8.5 Conclusion

Most people would accept that every individual has a personality which is special to them. What is far more difficult to accept is that certain personalities will always or usually be criminal. It is therefore generally presumed that one cannot predict criminal behaviour by studying personality. Acceptance of these statements does not render personality useless in the study of criminality; it merely limits the ways in which it is, or should be, used. As was seen above in 8.3.7, 8.3.9 and 8.4, personality theories have had practical uses in the treatment of convicted criminals, the detection of certain types of criminals, and in deciding how to deal with certain offenders. These uses are limited, but none the less they are important and should not be ignored in any criminal justice system.

In the 1980s and 1990s there has been a strong tendency to reject any solutions based on reform or on helping offenders in the belief the 'nothing works'. This is based on the assertion that treatment is not effective and therefore should not be tried, even in a prison setting. Supporters of rehabilitative methods are necessarily cautious, but urge that such methods are certainly no worse than other ways of dealing with offenders, and may be better (Palmer (1990) Steadman et al. (1998) and Lees et al. (1999)). In any event, there are indications that there are advantages in recognising the particular problems of individual offenders, even if there is no alteration of criminal conduct, because their incarceration may be made less stressful both for inmates and prison officers (see Genders and Player (1993 and 1994)). What is being suggested is not strictly speaking treatment, but rather measures to encourage such offenders to confront their personality/psychological problems along with the social aspects. The object of such psychosocial interventions is to help individuals to cope without crime. Within this broad framework, as Lösel (1995) reports, different interventions have differing successes depending on the environment within which they are used and the punishment strategy which accompanies them. If the link between crime and addiction proves to be of value (Hodge et al. (1997)), the environment in which the addiction is tackled may be important. One of the major difficulties in improving the success rate arises from the tension between the two aspects of what the professional assessors are expected to do: the criminal justice system expects them to determine the responsibility of the individual so that the court can better decide how to punish; while the system, society and the offender all want the offender's behaviour to alter so as not to include criminality in the future. These functions may conflict and then there is little indication of how best to resolve that conflict (see Debuyst (1995)).

Besides using psychosocial interventions to assess the needs of punishment and/or assistance, it is important not to ignore the rights of offenders, victims and society (Hood (1995)). During the 1990s the uses made of such intervention, especially in assessing dangerousness, have moved towards ignoring the rights of individual offenders in the hope—probably the vain hope—of preventing further victimisation. It is an area in which politicians and judges can be tempted to take the popular line of removing the freedom of the offender to protect society, but there is also a need to ensure the protection of individual offenders. How this is resolved will depend on whether professionals (psychiatrists, other medical practitioners, social workers, lawyers and judges) as well as politicians are willing to reject solutions based purely on social control in favour of solutions which also take account of medical and social solutions. Even in findings of dangerousness, societal responsibilities should not be entirely abrogated.

SUGGESTED READING

Ainsworth, P.B. (2000), *Psychology and Crime: Myths and Realities*, London: Longman.

Hollin, C. (2001) (ed.), *Handbook of Offender Assessment and Treatment*, Chichester: Wiley.

Hollin, C. (2002), 'Criminological Psychology', in M. Maguire, R. Morgan and R. Reiner (eds), *The Oxford Handbook of Criminology*, Oxford: Oxford University Press.

Special issue of *Criminal Justice Matters* entitled 'Dangerous Offenders', Issue No. 51.

QUESTIONS

1 Why do we assess an individual's personality prior to sentencing, what does it have to do with punishment and is it acceptable to carry out such an assessment at this stage?

2 Is it acceptable to confine an individual merely to protect others (once all punishment is over) and what dangers are inherent in such action?

3 Does management of risk necessarily increase safety?

REFERENCES

Aichhorn, August (1936), *Wayward Youth* (first published 1925), New York: Viking Press.

Ainsworth, P.B. (2000), *Psychology and Crime: Myths and Reality*, Harlow: Longman.

Bennett, J. (2003), 'DSPS Units at HMP Whitmoor', *Criminal Justice Matters*, vol. 51, p. 22.

Bowlby, John (1946), *Forty-Four Juvenile Thieves*, London: Ballière, Tindall and Cox.

Bowlby, John (1953), *Child Care and the Growth of Love* (based by permission of the World Health Organisation on the Report: Maternal Care and Mental Health), Harmondsworth: Penguin.

Britton, P. (1997), *The Jigsaw Man*, London: Batman Press.

Canter, D. (1995), 'Psychology of Offender Profiling', in D. Canter and L. Alison (eds), *Criminal Detection and the Psychology of Crime*, Aldershot: Ashgate.

Canter, D. and Alison, L. (eds) (1999), *Profiling in Policy and Practice*, Aldershot: Ashgate.

Carlson, Neil, R. (2000), *Psychology of Behaviour*, 7th edn, Boston, MA: Allyn and Bacon.

Cavadino, M. (1999), 'Editorial', *Journal of Forensic Psychiatry*, p. 254.

Cleckley, Hervey (1976), *The Mask of Sanity*, 5th edn, St Louis, MO: C.V. Mosby.

Debuyst, Ch. (1995), 'Psychological Assessments Before and After Sentencing', in *Psychological Interventions in the Criminal Justice System*, Proceedings from the 20th Criminological Research Conference, 1993, European Committee on Crime Problems, Criminological Research, vol. XXXI, Strasbourg: Council of Europe.

Dingwall, G. (1998), 'Selective Incapacitation after the Criminal Justice Act 1991: A Proportional Response to Protecting the Public?', *Howard Journal of Criminal Justice*, vol. 37, p. 177.

Dorby, J. (2003), 'Dealing with Dangerousness: The Parole Board Perspective', *Criminal Justice Matters*, vol. 51, p. 12.

Douglas, J. and Olshaker, M. (1997), *Mindhunter: Inside the FBI Elite Serial Crime Unit*, London: Mandarin.

Eysenck, H.J. (1959), *Manual of the Maudsley Personality Inventory*, London: UCL Press.

Eysenck, H.J. (1977), *Crime and Personality*, 3rd edn, London: Routledge & Kegan Paul.

Eysenck, H.J. (1987), 'Personality Theory and the Problem of Criminality', in B J McGurk, D.M. Thornton and M. Williams (eds), *Applying Psychology to Imprisonment*, London: HMSO.

Eysenck, H.J. and Gudjonsson, G.H. (1989), *The Causes and Cures of Criminality*, New York: Plenum Press.

Fallon Report (1999), *Report of the Committee of Inquiry into the Personality Disorder Unit at Ashworth Special Hospital*, London: Home Office.

Farrington, David, P. (1994), 'Introduction', in David P. Farrington (ed.), *Psychological Explanations of Crime*, Aldershot: Dartmouth.

Floud, Jean and Young, Warren (1981), *Dangerousness and Criminal Justice*, Heinemann: London.

Freud, Sigmund (1935) *A General Introduction to Psycho-Analysis* (first published in 1920), transl. by Joan Riviere, New York: Liveright.

Genders, Elaine and Player, Elaine (1993), 'Rehabilitation in Prisons: a Study of Grendon Underwood', *Current Legal Problems*, Oxford: Oxford University Press, 235.

Genders, Elaine and Player, Elaine (1994), *Grendon: A Study of a Therapeutic Prison*, Clarendon Studies in Criminology, Oxford: Oxford University Press.

Gleitman, Henry (1999), *Psychology*, 5th edn, New York: W.W. Norton & Company.

Gleitman, H. (2002), *Basic Psychology*, New York: W.W. Norton and Company.

Gross, Richard, D. (2001), *Psychology—The Science of Mind and Behaviour*, 4th edn, London: Hodder and Stoughton.

Guze, Samuel B. (1976), *Criminality and Psychiatric Disorders*, New York: Oxford University Press.

Hare, R.D. (1996), 'Psychopathy: A Clinical Construct whose Time has Come', *Criminal Justice and Behaviour*, vol. 23, p. 25.

Hare, R.D. (1998), 'The Hare PCL-R: Some Issues Concerning its Use and Misuse', *Legal and Criminological Psychology*, vol. 3, p. 99.

Hewitt, Lester E. and Jenkins, R.L. (1947), *Fundamental Patterns of Maladjustment*, Springfield, IL: State of Illinois.

Hodge, J.E., McMurran, M. and Hollin, C.R. (1997), *Addicted to Crime?*, vol. 3, Chichester: Wiley.

Hollin, Clive R. (1989), *Psychology and Crime: an Introduction to Criminological Psychology*, London: Routledge.

Holmes, Ronald M. and De Burger, James (1989), *Serial Murder*, Newbury Park, CA: Sage.

Home Office and Department of Health (1999), *Managing Dangerous People with Severe Personality Disorder: Proposals for Policy Development*, London: HMSO.

Home Office and Department of Health (2000), *Reforming the Mental Health Act* (Cm 5016 (I and II)), London: HMSO.

Hood, R. (1995), 'Introductory Report, General Report of the Conference and Conclusions and Recommendations', in *Psychological Interventions in the Criminal Justice System*, Proceedings from the 20th Criminological Research Conference, 1993, European Committee on Crime Problems, Criminological Research, vol. XXXI, Strasbourg: Council of Europe.

Jackson, J.L. and Bekerian, D.A. (eds) (1997), *Offender Profiling: Theory, Research and Practice*, Chichester: Wiley.

Jung, Carl Gustav (1947), *Modern Man in Search of a Soul*, London: Routledge & Kegan Paul.

Kline, P. (1984), *Psychology and Freudian Theory*, London: Methuen.

Kohnken, G. (1996), 'Social Psychology and the Law', in G.R. Semin and K. Fiedler (ed.), *Applied Social Psychology*, London: Sage.

Lees, J., Manning, N. and Rawlings, B. (1999), *Therapeutic Community Effectiveness. A Systematic International Review of Therapeutic Community Treatment for People with Personality Disorders*. York: University of York.

Lipsey, M.W. and Wilson, D.B. (1997), 'Effective Intervention for Serious Juvenile Offenders: A Synthesis of Research', cited in F.T. Cullen and B.K. Applegate, *Offender Rehabilitation: Effective Correctional Intervention*, Aldershot: Dartmouth.

Little, Alan (1963–64), 'Professor Eysenck's Theory of Crime: An Empirical Test on Adolescent Offenders', *British Journal of Criminology*, vol. 4, p. 152.

Lösel, F. (1995), 'Evaluating Psychosocial Interventions in Prisons and other Penal Contexts', in *Psychological Interventions in the Criminal Justice System* Proceedings from the 20th Criminological Research Conference, 1993, European Committee on Crime Problems, Criminological Research, vol. XXXI, Strasbourg: Council of Europe.

Lundman, Richard, J. (2001), *Prevention and Control of Juvenile Delinquency* 3rd edn, Oxford: Oxford University Press.

Macdonald, G., Sheldon, B. and Gillespie, J. (1992), 'Contemporary Studies of the Effectiveness of Social Work', *British Journal of Social Work* 615.

McGurk, B.J. and McDougall, C. (1981), 'A new Approach to Eysenck's Theory of Criminality', *Personality and Individual Differences*, vol. 2, p. 338.

Mawson, A.R. (1987), *Transient Criminality*, New York: Praeger.

Megargee, E.I. (1976), 'The Prediction of Dangerous Behaviour', *Criminal Justice and Behaviour*, vol. 3, p. 3.

Newburn, T. (2002), 'Young People, Crime and Youth Justice', in M. Maguire, R. Morgan and R. Reiner (eds), *The Oxford Handbook of Criminology*, 3rd edn, Oxford: Oxford University Press.

Ormerod, David (1996), 'The Evidential Implications of Psychological Profiling', *Criminal Law Review*, p. 863.

Ormerod, D. (1999), 'Criminal Profiling: Trial by Judge and Jury, not Criminal Psychologist', in D. Canter and L. Alison (eds), *Profiling in Policy and Practice*, Aldershot: Ashgate.

Palmer, Ted (1974), 'The Youth Authority's Community Treatment Project', *Federal Probation*, vol. 38, p. 3.

Palmer, Ted (1990), 'The Effectivness of Intervention: Recent Trends and Issues', *Crime and Delinquency*, vol. 37, p. 330.

Peay, J. (2003), 'Working with Concepts of 'Dangerousness' in the Context of Mental Health Law', *Criminal Justice Matters*, vol. 51, p. 18.

Pitch, Tamar (1995), *Limited Responsibilities: Social Movements and Criminal Justice*, trans. John Lea, London: Routledge.

Prins, H. (1998), 'Dangerous Offenders: Some Problems of Management', *International Review of Computers and Technology*, vol. 12, p. 299.

Public Health Service (1991), *Healthy People 2000: National Health Promotion and Disease Prevention Objectives*, US Department of Health and Human Services.

Quinsey, V.L., Harris, G.T., Rice, M.E. and Cormier, C.A. (1998), *Violent Offenders: Appraising and Managing Risk*, Washington DC: American Psychological Association.

Rafter, N.H. (1997), 'Psychopathy and the Evolution of Criminological Knowledge', *Theoretical Criminology*, vol. 1(2), p. 235.

Reiss, D., Grubin, D. and Meux, C. (1999), 'Institutional Performance of Male "Psychopaths" in a High-Security Hospital', *The Journal of Forensic Psychiatry*, vol. 10, p. 290.

Robins, L.N. (1966), *Deviant Children Grown Up: A Sociological and Psychiatric Study of Sociopathic Personality*, Baltimore, MD: Williams and Wilkins.

Rumbelow, D. (1987), *The Complete Jack the Ripper*, London: Star Books.

Schuessler, Karl F. and Cressey, Donald R. (1950), 'Personality Characteristics of Criminals', *American Journal of Sociology*, vol. 55, p. 476.

Siann, G. (1985), *Accounting For Aggression: Perspectives on Aggression and Violence*, London: Allen and Unwin.

Steadman, Henry J., Monahan, John, Robbins, Pamela Clark, Appelbaum, Paul, Grisso, Thomas, Klassen, Deidre, Mulvey, Edward, P. and Roth, Loren (1993), 'From Dangerousness to Risk Assessment: Implications for Appropriate Research Strategies', in Sheilagh Hodgins (ed.), *Mental Disorder and Crime*, Newbury Park, CA: Sage Periodicals Press.

Steadman, H J , Mulvey, E.P., Monahan, J., Robbins, P.C., Appelbaum, P.S., Grisso, T., Roth, L.H. and Silver, E. (1998), 'Violence by People Discharged from Acute Psychiatric Inpatient Facilities and by Others in the Same Neighbourhoods', *Archives of General Psychiatry*, vol. 55, p. 393.

Taylor, P. (1999), 'Personality Disorder: Struggles with Definition and Determining its Prevalence', *Criminal Justice Matters*, vol. 37, p. 10.

Waldo, Gordon P. and Dinitz, Simon (1967), 'Personality Attributes of the Criminal: An Analysis of Research Studies', *Journal of Research in Crime and Delinquency*, vol. 4, p. 185.

Ward, D., Scott, J. and Lacey, M. (2002), *Probation: Working for Justice*, 2nd edn, Oxford: Oxford University Press.

Warren, M.Q. (1970), 'The Case for Differential Treatment of Delinquents', in Harwin L. Voss (ed.), *Society, Delinquency and Delinquent Behaviour*, Boston, MA: Little Brown.

Westin, D. and Shedler, J. (1999), 'Revisiting and Assessing Axis II Part I: Developing Clinically, and Empirically Valid Assessment Method; Part II: Toward an Empirically Based and Clinically Useful Classification of Personality Disorders', *American Journal of Psychiatry*, vol. 156, pp. 258 and 273.

White Paper (1990), *Crime, Justice and Protecting the Public*, Cm 965, London: HMSO.

Wolfenden Committee Report (1957), *Report of the Committee on Homosexual Offences and Prostitution*, Cmd 247, London: HMSO.

Zaitchick, Matt C. and Moscher, Donald L. (1993), 'Criminal Justice Implications of the Macho Personality Constellation', *Criminal Justice and Behaviour*, vol. 20, p. 227.

Zillman, D. (1979), *Hostility and Aggression*, Hillsdale, NJ: Lawrence Erlbaum.

9

Mental disorder and criminality

9.1 Introduction

Mental disorder is sometimes referred to as mental abnormality, and many psychologists now refer to it as psychopathology. These three terms are used in the literature, but basically they refer to the same group of people. Where these terms are used, what is being discussed? Essentially, each term refers to states of mind which give rise to some form of problem, usually for the individual. The term 'mental disorder' shows that the mind is in a state of confusion; it is not working properly, i.e., it is suffering from a disease. The term 'mental abnormality' denotes that the state of mind is both uncommon and unpleasant; it shows a negative or bad element. People afflicted with such conditions are referred to as suffering from a psychopathology because it is an illness the symptoms of which are mainly psychological. 'Psycho' indicates the mental element and 'pathology' represents the illness, the overt symptoms produced by an underlying cause or disease. The main object of the psychologist is to treat the underlying pathology or illness. Different schools of psychology have differing ideas about the causes and cures for the various mental illnesses. Some stress physical manifestations—biological or neuroscientific—where the use of chemical therapy and surgery is common. Others look more to cognitive or behavioural understanding and, possibly, alteration. These aspects will not be dealt with in this chapter. Here, we are interested in the connection between mental illness and criminality, and the way in which these diseases are viewed by the law.

Many studies have attempted to discover whether mental disorder or illness is associated with criminality. Most of these studies have been of people in prison, and ascertain how many prisoners are mentally ill. Teplin (1990) notes that recent studies conclude that rates of severe mental illness amongst the prison population range from 4–5 per cent to 12 per cent and that even the most conservative of these is two to three times higher than the comparable rates in the general population. This does not necessarily prove that the crimes committed by these people were induced by their mental problem. It does not even prove that the mental problem existed prior to the criminality. It could have been brought on through traumatic feelings of remorse or guilt, or through their treatment in prison. In order to prove a causative link, rather more is required. A better approach might be to study the criminal behaviour of psychiatric patients. One such study by Rollin (1969) found that 40 per cent of those admitted without recourse to the courts had a criminal record, and 36 per cent were persistent offenders. Of those admitted by the courts, 66 per cent had a criminal record and

44 per cent had previously had a custodial sentence. These figures do suggest some correlation between criminality and mental illness. If there is such a relationship, the way in which it develops depends on the types of mental illness. Before discussing that question, we need first to outline the way the criminal law and the courts have defined mental disorder and the significance of such recognition.

9.2 Legal ideas of mental disorder

There are a number of ways in which the legal rules take mental illness into account. It can be a general defence (see insanity 9.2.1) or a special defence to a particular crime like murder (see 9.2.4 and 9.2.5). Mental illness is also a factor which may be taken into account in sentencing offenders where the individual may obtain treatment instead of punishment (see 9.2.6), but in this case it is only available if there is a form of treatment which it is thought may help the offender. It needs also to be noted that just because someone's behaviour is thought to be unusual does not mean that he or she is mentally ill (see Jaffe (1998) in relation to necrophilia). For a discussion of all the criminal law implications, see the books cited at the beginning of Chapter Two.

9.2.1 Criminal law definition of insanity

Insanity is a defence long recognised in criminal law as being available theoretically in respect of any charge. In the past the accused who successfully pleaded 'not guilty by reason of insanity' was sent to a mental institution for an indefinite period. Often the individual was never released. These severe consequences meant that in the past the defence was restricted to cases of murder, where the alternative was death. Following the abolition of the death penalty and the availability of the defence of diminished responsibility to an accused charged with murder, the defence of insanity became of less practical significance: between 1975 and 1988 there were only 49 findings of 'not guilty by reason of insanity' (see Mackay (1990)). The Criminal Procedure (Insanity and Unfitness to Plead) Act 1991 gives the judge discretion about the appropriate sentence when an individual is found 'not guilty by reason of insanity'. The judge may now order detention in a hospital approved by the Secretary of State (with or without a restriction order); pass a guardianship order under the Mental Health Act 1983; pass a supervision or treatment order; or give an absolute discharge. Despite this the plea is still very rare

In recognising the defence of insanity, the criminal law is acknowledging that people can suffer defects of reason to a degree which makes it impossible for the law to hold them responsible for their actions.

The rules pertaining to this defence were first laid down in 1843 in *McNaghten's Case* 10 Cl & F 200. This was an advice sought by the House of Lords from the judges after the acquittal of McNaghten of the murder of Sir Robert Peel's private secretary, following the finding that he was insane. Their advice, which subsequently has been known simply as the McNaghten Rules, was to the effect that:

every man is to be presumed to be sane and to possess a sufficient degree of reason to be responsible for his crimes, until the contrary be proved (to the satisfaction of the jury); and that to establish a defence on the ground of insanity, it must be clearly proved that, at the time of the committing of the act, the party accused was labouring under such a defect of reason, from disease of the mind, as not to know the nature and quality of the act he was doing; or, if he did know it, that he did not know he was doing what was wrong.

The case determined that it is a defence to any criminal charge for an accused to establish:

(a) that he was suffering from a disease of the mind and as a consequence of this,

(b) he was labouring under a defect of reason, and as a consequence of this,

(c) he did not appreciate the nature or quality of his actions, or if he did appreciate the nature or quality of his actions he did not know that his conduct was wrong.

The judges also determined that if an accused, through a defect of reason arising from a disease of the mind, suffers from an insane delusion, criminal liability should be assessed on the basis that the facts as he or she believes them to be are true. For example, if an accused through an insane delusion had believed another was about to attack and kill him or her, then the killing of that other should be regarded as a possible act of self-defence. If, however, the insane delusion resulted in an accused believing another was stealing his or her wallet, then even if those facts were deemed to be true, the killing of the imagined thief would not be excused (unless the accused did not appreciate his conduct was wrong) since the law does not recognise killing simply to retain the wallet as being justifiable conduct.

The principal characteristic of a disease of the mind within the defence of insanity is that its cause lies internally within the physiology or psychology of the individual concerned, and is not brought about by external sources, e.g., drugs, concussion and so forth. It does, however, include diabetes, which if not treated with insulin may cause a defect of reason (*R* v *Hennessy* [1989] 1 WLR 187 and *R* v *Bingham* [1991] Crim LR 433).

The disease of the mind must produce a defect of reason in an accused. This is more than a temporary bout of forgetfulness or absent-mindedness (*R* v *Clarke* [1972] 1 All ER 219). An individual must be incapable of exercising any semblance of normal reasoning power and thus be unable to accept legal responsibility because:

(a) He or she cannot appreciate the nature or quality of the act. Examples include:

(i) An individual acting as an automaton, i.e., without conscious appreciation of his or her conduct. Such a person has not committed an *actus reus* because the act is not voluntary, this undermines the *mens rea*.

(ii) An individual incapable of realising the consequences of his or her actions, e.g., strangling a small child simply to impose parental punishment without realisation that it will cause death. Here there is *actus reus* but no *mens rea*.

(iii) An individual who is unable to appreciate the circumstances of an act may be unaware of its nature or quality. A rather prosaic example would be the case of an individual firing a shotgun at what is believed, because of a defect of reason, to be a scarecrow but was in fact a next-door neighbour. Here there is both *actus reus* and *mens rea* but no rational understanding and therefore no responsibility.

(b) Although appreciating the nature or quality of the act there may be no realisation that the conduct was 'wrong', in the sense of contrary to law. Again there is both *actus reus* and *mens rea* but no rational understanding and therefore no responsibility.

The narrowness of the concept of defect of reason in the McNaghten rules fails to take into account the greater understanding of the human mind which has been brought about through recent discoveries in psychology and psychiatry. It fails to take into account the possibility of an individual being aware of the nature or quality of an act and knowing that it is in breach of the law and yet feeling compelled to commit it, see *R v Kopsch* (1925) 19 Cr App R 50. In such cases there is both *actus reus* and *mens rea* but no rational understanding and therefore no responsibility. For example, the individual may be acting under a delusion that the victim is planning to kill him or her or that the victim is possessed by the devil and will cause untold harm to others. In these circumstances it is certainly arguable that there is no real responsibility and therefore no criminal culpability. Such an 'irresistible impulse' may well constitute an 'impairment of mental responsibility' within the defence of diminished responsibility (see below).

As mentioned above the defence of insanity is not common and as it does not cover certain types of mental impairment its relevance and utility are now questionable. It is an all-or-nothing defence: if accepted it is a full defence to any crime; if not then, except in certain special instances (see 9.2.2 to 9.2.6 below), the accused is regarded as criminally culpable and will be convicted if the *actus reus* is proven. Thus although the defence is not very common it still shapes the limits of criminal responsibility and so is central to an understanding of the justice of applying sanctions and of the moral indignation to which crime should give rise. The definition is a legal construct and application of the rules leads to absurd distinctions. It can lead to separating mental problems which are clinically assessed as similar or as having similar effects on a person's mental capacity. The defence may cover individuals who suffer from transient problems such as sleepwalking or epilepsy (which are outside the Mental Health Act 1983) and yet does not cover those suffering, for example, from delusions which are clearly covered by that legislation. The failure of the definition to register real differences in responsibility has led to the insanity defence being severely attacked.

It has been argued that without the insanity defence criminal culpability would have no meaning but so sweeping a view does not fit well with modern psychiatric and psychological knowledge. More plausibly the Butler Committee in 1975 suggested a complete redefinition of insanity to reflect the clinical understanding of responsibility: their suggestions formed the basis of the recommendations of the Law Commission in its draft Criminal Code Bill of 1989 (Law Commission No. 177). Similarly, in 1982 Norval Morris attacked the insanity defence stating that the issue was one of free choice and that what should be tested should be the degree of culpability measured on a linear continuum from the entirely rational (fully culpable) to the pathologically determined (no culpability). For Morris the level of culpability would be relevant for both deciding guilt and choosing the appropriate sentence. This approach, requiring an unlikely precision of 'scientific' assessment in each case, presupposes that criminal culpability and mental or psychiatric impairment are linked. Hochstedler Steury (1993) attempted to test this: the finding was that the intersection between the criminal and psychiatrically impaired populations was four times greater than it would have been if the two were entirely independent and she therefore concluded there was a link. The implication is that the definition of criminal culpability needs to take account of reduced or impaired free will in relation to both punishment and condemnation, but before the legal definition is altered there would need to be a very careful consideration of legal culpability in both criminal and civil law. There is a long and very prestigious history of linking justification for punishment, moral blame and criminal responsibility to free will and choice of actions (see, e.g., Hart (1968)), but this literature generally fails to set out what should determine whether a person's free will has been interfered with. It could be that the present defence of diminished responsibility (see below 9.2.4) would indicate how best to formulate such a rule structure which could then be applied to all other crimes, not just restricted to allegations of murder. Any approach would still raise the difficulty of reconciling the need for a legal definition with what is required to make clinical sense. There are (Blau (1998)) no scientific tests to diagnose insanity, which is a legal not a medical concept. Furthermore it is almost impossible to separate people who *cannot* control themselves from those who choose, or do not bother, to control their actions.

9.2.2 Insanity and voluntary intoxication

An accused who, through drink or drugs, has produced a disease of the mind, e.g., delirium tremens, such as to produce a defect of reason, may be able to claim the defence of insanity. (For a discussion of the significance in law of intoxication, see 9.5 below.) A distinction must be made between the temporary impairment of the mental faculties produced by drink and drugs, and the repeated taking of such substances which, over a period of time, produces an impairment of the mental processes which may persist though the individual concerned is sober. Both situations are self-induced, but only the latter can possibly give rise to a defence of insanity (see the House of Lords decision in *Attorney-General for Northern Ireland* v *Gallagher* [1963] AC 349).

9.2.3 Non-insane automatism

To plead automatism one has to prove that movement of the limbs is not voluntary, but wholly unconscious or reflecting impaired consciousness. The mind must not be controlling the body at all (see *Bratty* v *Attorney-General for Northern Ireland* [1963] AC 386, *R* v *Isitt* (1977) 67 Cr App R 44 and *Attorney-General's Reference (No. 2 of 1992)* [1994] QB 91). A finding that the action is involuntary will lead to an acquittal. Where the automatism is the result of a disease of the mind the acquittal will be one of 'not guilty by reason of insanity', in other cases it will just lead to a verdict of not guilty. Any external cause of the automatism is seen as not a matter of insanity (see *R* v *Quick* [1973] QB 910): if the automatism is the result of a blow to the head or the administration of drugs for medication (such as insulin for hypoglycaemia) then a verdict of not guilty should be returned; if it is the result of internal factors such as epilepsy it should be treated as an insanity defence. There have been some interesting cases where automatism has been accepted. In *R* v *T* [1990] Crim LR 256, T, a young woman, was charged with robbery and causing actual bodily harm but acquitted as it was proved that three days earlier she had been raped: the psychologists suggested that at the time of the offence she was suffering from post-traumatic stress disorder which had caused a dissociative state and so she was not acting with a conscious mind. This is interesting as it could have been held that post-traumatic stress disorder was an internal state of mind, but it was held that it was caused by the rape which was external and therefore was simple automatism.

Self-induced automatism is a different issue. It is usually caused by voluntarily consuming drink or drugs, prescribed or otherwise. When the self-induced automatism is due to substances not normally considered to cause problematic behavioural changes, the defence of automatism will be available even if the substance was taken voluntarily as long as the jury do not find that the defendant acted recklessly (see *R* v *Bailey* [1983] 1 WLR 760). The issue is more fully considered under 9.5.2 but generally it is not recognised as a good defence.

9.2.4 **Diminished responsibility**

Since 1957, diminished responsibility has been available as a defence to those charged with murder. If this plea is successful, the individual will be convicted of manslaughter and the judge, in sentencing, can exercise discretion to reflect the degree of responsibility. The prosecution may also choose to charge a person with manslaughter on the basis of diminished responsibility. Under the Homicide Act 1957, s. 2, a plea of diminished responsibility will succeed if: the accused suffers from an abnormality or disease of the mind; that state of mind is caused by arrested or retarded development, some inherent cause, or by injury or disease; and that the abnormality substantially impaired the accused's mental responsibility for the acts and omissions in killing or being a party to the killing. 'Substantial' means that while the impairment need not be total it must be more than trivial in nature (see *R* v *Lloyd* [1967] 1 QB 175). The clearest formulation of the attributes of diminished responsibility are contained in the judgment of Lord Parker in *R* v *Byrne* [1960] 2 QB 396 at 403, where he said:

'Abnormality of mind', which has to be contrasted with the time-honoured expression in the McNaghten Rules 'defect of reason', means a State of mind so different from that of ordinary human beings that the reasonable man would term it abnormal. It appears to be wide enough to cover the mind's activities in all its aspects, not only the perception of physical acts and matters, and the ability to form a rational judgment as to whether an act is right or wrong, but also the ability to exercise will power to control physical acts in accordance with that rational judgment. The expression 'mental responsibility for his acts' points to a consideration of the extent to which the accused's mind is answerable for his physical acts which must include a consideration of the extent of his ability to exercise will power to control his physical acts.

This definition leaves the description of the mental state of an offender and its effects on the responsibility for committing the crime to the professional (i.e., the expert medical or psychiatric witness) to a much greater extent than in the case of insanity. Furthermore, to justify a verdict of manslaughter on the grounds of diminished responsibility the abnormality need not be very marked: *R v Seers* (1984) 79 Cr App R 261, where the accused who suffered from a serious depressive illness was granted the benefit of the defence even though he could not be said to have been partially insane or on the borderline of insanity. Although the expert is charged with assessing the mental state of the accused, it is left to the jury to decide what weight to give that evidence, considered along with all the other evidence in the case; they are then entitled to reject or ignore expert evidence even if this was not contradicted. See the Privy Council decision in *Walter* v *The Queen* [1978] AC 788, which has been upheld in *R* v *Sanders* (1991) 93 Cr App R 245.

Diminished responsibility has been successfully used in a number of cases where one might not have expected s. 2 of the Homicide Act 1957 to have operated, for example, in cases where someone kills due to extreme anxiety, post-natal depression, pre-menstrual syndrome, reactive depression, grief, stress (particularly common in cases of 'mercy-killing'), impossibility or great difficulty in resisting impulses and alcoholism. This shows its flexibility as a defence and this is both its strength and its weakness. There are also cases where one would have expected the defence to be successful but where it failed, for example, the case of Peter Sutcliffe, the 'Yorkshire Ripper', where psychiatrists agreed that he was suffering from paranoid schizophrenia, an abnormality of the mind, which would amount to a lowering of responsibility and yet the jury refused to believe the defence. The discrepancy in decision-making suggests that the jury are making a moral rather than a medical decision. They take into account the offence committed and decide whether the individual deserves to be convicted rather than genuinely assessing the culpability of the offender. On the other hand, in many cases the expert psychiatrists are called on to pass an opinion as to whether the individual's ability to form the relevant mental responsibility was substantially impaired, making it a medical and moral, rather than a legal, issue.

All this contrasts with the position in relation to insanity (see above 9.2.1). There are problems with both positions. The issue for law, society and criminology is to determine for which crimes the various defences should be open. Is there any good reason why diminished responsibility should not be recognised in crimes other than murder? The legal reason for this at the time was that it was only in cases of murder that there was a mandatory sentence. Is this acceptable particularly as judges are now required to pass a life sentence in certain cases? Should we call someone guilty, with the full mental culpability to which that gives rise, when in effect his or her capabilities were affected by state of mind? Legally it would be very difficult to mark a finding in between guilt and innocence, but for a more realistic understanding of criminal culpability such a position may be necessary. The need is reinforced by the consideration that at the sentencing stage the rules of evidence are less clearly drawn which may give the defendant less protection, and by the inherent imprecision of any assessment to capacity or incapacity for intentional action (Pitch (1995)). Resolution of these issues has far-reaching consequences for the legitimacy of the law and for the concept of criminal culpability.

9.2.5 Infanticide

Under the Infanticide Act 1938, s. 1, the offence of infanticide can be charged only against a mother for killing her own child after its birth but before its first birthday.

Alternatively, a woman charged with murder in such an instance may plead infanticide as a defence. In either case, if convicted or if the defence is accepted in relation to the charge of murder, she will be guilty of manslaughter. But note that the mother must adduce evidence that the balance of her mind was disturbed by, and not yet recovered from, childbirth or from lactation consequent on the birth of the child. This offence/defence reflects a belief in our society that the balance of a mother's mind may be disturbed by hormonal changes or imbalance resulting from giving birth to a child (but see also 7.1.1 above and 16.2.3 below). The introduction of this offence/defence into English law in 1922 and its re-enactment in 1938 was significant first from a practical point of view, because at that time the deliberate killing by a mother of her child would otherwise have amounted to murder (the penalty for which was death). Secondly, it was significant from a criminological point of view in that it was an implied recognition that the cause of the crime in question (i.e., the cause of the deliberate killing of her child by a mother) was biological or psychological. The implication was that these were matters that were beyond the mother's control, and that while she should not necessarily be absolved from liability, those 'causes' or 'influences' should possibly be taken into account by way of mitigation in so far as her punishment was concerned. It must be remembered that if a person either then or now was convicted of murder, the penalty or sentence was and is 'fixed by law'. The judge had, and still has, no leeway to consider mitigation. Previously the penalty was death; today it is life imprisonment. The fact that infanticide is rarely charged as an offence or relied on as a defence to murder today can be explained by a combination of factors: prosecutors are now more likely to exercise their discretion and charge a mother in this situation with manslaughter rather than murder, hence removing the need or opportunity to rely on infanticide as a defence; advances in medical treatment and after-care social services may have reduced the number of instances where mothers have become so adversely affected by childbirth or lactation as to kill their children; and there may be no prosecution, as the authorities may try to define the death as accidental in all cases where there is no clear proof to the contrary. Where infanticide is found, the Court of Appeal in *R* v *Sainsbury* (1989) 11 Cr App R (S) 533, observed that in all 59 such cases between 1979 and 1988 the offender had been dealt with by probation, supervision or hospital order. The implication was therefore that although the offence was serious, the mitigating factors were usually overwhelming.

The Butler Committee (1975) argued that infanticide was no different from other mental abnormalities, and suggested that in most cases where a mother killed her young child it had more to do with the stress of caring for a new-born baby than from hormonal imbalance consequent on giving birth. They suggested that infanticide be repealed and that such cases should fall in the defence of diminished responsibility. This ignores the fact that the two defences are different. For infanticide, one only needs to prove the existence of the condition, whereas for diminished responsibility one has to prove that it 'substantially impaired' the responsibility for the act. Cheng (1986) supports this, pointing out that in only six out of thirteen recent cases of infanticide would the disorder have been sufficiently severe to allow a plea of diminished responsibility. It might still be argued that women should have to prove substantial impairment of responsibility, but at present, in law, diminished responsibility and infanticide are different. To resolve these problems the Law Commission in its Draft Criminal Code 1989 (Law Commission No. 177), clause 64(1), suggested that: A woman who, but for this section, would be guilty of murder or manslaughter of her child is not guilty of murder or manslaughter, but is guilty of infanticide, if her act is done when the child is under the age of 12 months and when the balance of her mind is disturbed by reason of the effect of giving birth or of circumstances consequent upon the birth. This has never been enacted and the defence of infanticide is still only available to mothers. If social stresses are in practice an acceptable reason under infanticide laws why is the defence not thrown open to fathers or other carers?

9.2.6 Mental Health Act definition of mental illness

Mental problems may be taken into consideration in sentencing and can lead to the offender being sent to a hospital or psychiatric institution, or being required to seek outpatient help under ss. 36, 37, 41, 43 and 46 of the Mental Health Act 1983. The Act can only be used as an aid to sentencing if the psychologist can offer some hope of a treatment which may alleviate the mental problem. Section 1(2) of the Act defines mental disorder as a:

mental illness, arrested or incomplete development of mind, psychopathic disorder and any other disorder or disability of the mind.

The term mental illness in that definition is not explained, and in practice, therefore, whether a person is to be placed in this category is a matter for clinical judgement. Furthermore, it still seems to have the meaning ascribed to it by Lawton LJ in *W v L* [1974] QB 711. In that case he said, at p. 719, that the words 'mental illness' had no particular medical or legal significance and so should be construed in the way any ordinary sensible person would do. If such a person would have said that to act in that fashion the accused must have been mentally ill, then so be it. This is likely to mean that a criminal act with no apparent motive will be construed as the act of a person who is mentally ill, and therefore as the act of someone who needs to be treated rather than just punished. Foucault would probably view this as the likely interpretation because it would perpetuate what he sees as the modern and dangerous practice of using psychiatric treatment as a form of control (see Kritzman (1988), especially Chapter Eight). The term mental illness was slightly more tightly defined by the then DHSS report (1976), which stated that:

Mental illness means an illness having one or more of the following characteristics:

(i) More than temporary impairment of intellectual functions shown by a failure of memory, orientation, comprehension and learning capacity;

(ii) More than temporary alteration of mood of such a degree as to give rise to the patient having a delusional appraisal of his situation, his past or his future, or that of others or the lack of any appraisal;

(iii) Delusional beliefs, concerning self persecution, jealous or grandiose;

(iv) Abnormal perceptions associated with delusional misinterpretation of events;

(v) Thinking so disordered as to prevent the patient making a reasonable appraisal of his situation or having reasonable communication with others.

In the Draft Mental Health Bill 2002 they talk of mental disorder which is defined as:

. . . any disability or disorder of mind or brain which results in an impairment or disturbance of mental functioning

This is very broad definition and intervention, even compulsory examination, assessment and treatment can take place without there being a criminal act and whether or not treatment is possible (a new departure) when the conditions, including posing a substantial risk of serious harm to others, in clause 6 are met.

These legal and departmental descriptions are painted with broad brush strokes which lose accuracy when faced with the details of different mental conditions and with their possible effect on criminality. Mental illness can include at least all of the problems discussed in 9.3, but its exact meaning will depend upon the professional who is interpreting it. The Mental Health Act is restrictive in the mental disorders that it covers, since hospitalisation as a sentence is available to the court only if the disorder can be treated.

9.3 Medical ideas of mental illness

It is important to consider some of the medical definitions of various illnesses and how they might affect a person's propensity to criminality.

9.3.1 Organic and functional psychoses

Psychoses are a set of related illnesses, but their outward manifestations are often very different. Organic psychoses are caused by some physical illness, either brain dysfunction at birth or by illness such as syphilitic infection. They may also be caused by accidents which have severe traumatic effects; by certain substances such as alcohol (see 9.5 below); by the severe changes in the brain which can be brought about with advancing years, (senile dementia); or by Alzheimer's disease. (One of the best known of the organic psychoses is that of epilepsy: see Chapters Six and Seven.)

Functional psychoses are those which seem to have no organic brain dysfunction as their root cause. It is still possible that they may be the result of severe bio-chemical disorders. It is these that are of most interest to criminologists. The best known of these disorders is schizophrenia; the less well known are referred to as affective disorders. Each of these is also made up of a variety of different illnesses.

9.3.2 Schizophrenia

This is the most frequent and important of the functional psychoses. The common use of the word to describe someone as having 'two minds' or having a split person-ality, where one of the sides to their personality is 'normal' and the other uncontrollable and bad, is inaccurate and incorrect. More properly, the word schizophrenia means that the personality is disintegrated or splintered into very small parts which do not interact with each other in any well-defined manner. The most telling signs are the following:

(a) disorders in thinking, such as an inability to think straight, a tendency to jump from one thing to another with no train of thought;

(b) disorders in fitting, feelings or emotions with thought or, generally, problems with emotions (anxiety, periods of unfeeling or flattened emotions, severe outbursts of rage and opposite reactions to various stimuli, e.g., laughing at something sad);

(c) a general withdrawal from social discourse. This often starts as apathy and slowly involves complete withdrawal, so that the individual lives in a private world (sometimes even refusing to hear or talk);

(d) a break with the real world in the form of delusions—giving real occurrences meanings that they do not hold, and usually related to paranoia or persecution (often a fear that everyone is stealing their thoughts, or that others are trying to drive them mad or ruin them).

Other factors which may appear are:

(a) periods of complete lack of movement which may give way to violence;

(b) hallucinations which are usually in the form of voices. Sometimes the voices command the commission of a crime;

(c) illusions such as believing that an everyday object is something fearful;

(d) defects in judgement, fantasy lives and peculiar mannerisms may also be present.

Not all of these would manifest themselves in one case: schizophrenia is best thought of as a series of disorders rather than a single illness. Basically, the personality is in tatters, and eventually there will be a complete break with reality. The causes of this illness are not fully understood. It is believed to have a lot do with the environment of the individual, although there may be links with genetic or biochemical factors.

Although the psychoses, and particularly the schizophrenias, are severe and can have very marked effects on behaviour, they are not generally closely related to criminality. Lindqvist and Allebeck (1990a) reported on a longitudinal study of 644 schizophrenic patients discharged from Swedish hospitals in 1971 in which their officially recorded level of offending between 1972 and 1986 was noted. They found that 45 of the 330 men (a similar rate as for the general population) and nine of the 314 women (twice the rate for the general population) had committed offences. Although the rate for female schizophrenics looks significant the numbers are too small to draw conclusions. Most of the crimes committed by the schizophrenics were non-violent, mostly property offences, but the rate of violent crime was four times that of the general population. Although this is significant the violence was minor, mostly assault, and no killings were recorded. This trend is noted by Taylor (1993) who states that those with psychosis are more likely to commit property offences and petty assaults rather than serious violent acts. These studies are tentative evidence that there may be a link between crime and schizophrenia but the nature of the link is much harder to ascertain and is certainly not simply causative in nature.

Some specific crimes may, however, be explained by schizophrenia. The most well known are crimes of violence which arise from a delusion or hallucination.

One of the best known of these was Daniel McNaghten, whose case gave rise to the famous McNaghten Rules referred to above (9.2.1). McNaghten suffered from delusions that he should kill the then Prime Minister, Robert Peel. He mistook Mr Drummond, the Prime Minister's secretary, for Robert Peel and killed him instead. He was found 'not guilty by reason of insanity'. These people are particularly dangerous because they may well be classified as mentally normal, and they may also appear 'cured' while still harbouring the paranoia or jealousy. A more modern example is Peter Sutcliffe (the 'Yorkshire Ripper') whose paranoid schizophrenia may have played a role in his crimes (see Prins (1986)). Another type of violent crime committed by schizophrenics may involve severe cruelty, such as mutilation or killing slowly. Such crimes may also involve a sexual element, but it needs to be noted that they are rare. When they do occur, however, they are very newsworthy, and so people may perceive them as being more common. However infrequent, crimes of violence of this type are more prevalent amongst schizophrenics than amongst either other disordered groups or the general population.

Schizophrenics may well be brought before the courts for other, more minor offences, such as minor vandalism (criminal damage) or insulting people (breach of the peace). These and similar petty offences are probably all the result of their withdrawal from normal society. The links between schizophrenia, social problems and criminality are also suggested by Lindqvist and Allebeck's (1990b) finding that in the case of chaotic and socially disabled psychotics who offend there may be a link with substance abuse, alcohol or drugs. In the light of the increase in releases of the mentally disturbed into the community and the lack of sufficient and appropriate community care the effects of this combination of psychosis and social problems is likely to become more prevalent. It will then be dealt with as a criminal justice problem rather than as the social and medical problem which it really is.

9.3.3 Severe affective disorders: severe depression

There are two types of depression: major or psychotic depression and bipolar or manic depression. Major depression is characterised by a profoundly sad mood, strong guilt feelings, lethargy, appetite loss, loss of energy and loss of interest in both the individual and the outside world. These features may also be accompanied by irritability, tension, agitation, inability to sleep normally and sometimes a desire to commit suicide. Manic depression has all these characteristics, but they are alternated with moods of elation and excitement (manic periods). Each of these periods may last a few days or weeks, and they may be interspersed with periods of relative normality.

Like the schizophrenic illnesses, neither psychotic depression nor manic depression can explain all criminality, but they may explain a few particular cases. In the case of psychotic depression, the offence most commonly linked with it is murder followed by suicide. As was mentioned above, sufferers fairly frequently turn to suicide because of the misery they feel and the belief that nothing can be done to improve their position. In certain cases, they see the misery and helplessness also affecting their families, so rather than leave those they love to face 'such awful lives' alone they may kill them as well in order, they believe, to save them from further suffering. Depression may explain a number of murders followed by suicide, as well as some lesser acts of violence against family members. These are difficult to explain as in hospital these patients are not more violent than other mental patients or the general population (see Feldman (1993)). The violence is therefore presumed to be facilitated through social conditions, particularly close personal relationships. In the case of the manic-depressive psychoses, the type of crimes will be characterised by disruptive and often impulsive behaviour, which may be violent and may also be almost obsessive in its persistence: arson is sometimes linked with the manic state.

Of course, it is often difficult to ascertain whether the depression caused the crime. It may be that the individual merely happened to be depressed at the time of the offence without the depression being the cause, or that the depression resulted from the criminality. Whichever of these is correct the National Association of Probation Officers (NAPO) discovered that one in five prisoners, and a higher proportion of those on probation are mentally vulnerable and that 90 per cent of these suffer from depression. They noted that these difficulties were not being addressed, pointing out that only 2 per cent of probation orders included a requirement for psychiatric treatment, and in prison the vast majority of mental disorders are not treated. They also noted that many offenders suffered with mental health problems and of these many had chronic alcohol and drug problems. None of these difficulties was properly addressed by the criminal justice system (NAPO (1994)).

9.3.4 Neuroses

These are similar illnesses to psychoses, but do not involve a complete break with normality and so are not quite so disabling. The experts cannot agree on the precise difference between psychoses and neuroses. Some argue that the latter are merely less severe; others consider that psychotics live in a fantasy world, whereas neurotics simply cannot cope with the strains of the real world. Whichever is correct, the neurotic mostly lives a fairly normal life which is occasionally disrupted by the effects of the neuroses. They are in some respects difficult to diagnose because everyone suffers from similar traits from time to time. Everyone feels some form of 'let-down' or depression, and many feel anxious in certain situations. There is a thin line between these normal feelings and neuroses, which besides feelings of anxiety may also include phobias, obsession, hysteria and mild depression. The neurotic may be suffering from a number of these or may show signs that there is only one main problem.

Most neurotics will have no criminal tendencies (or at least none connected with their illness), but occasionally neuroses may be a cause of criminality. For example, obsessional and compulsive neuroses may be central in explaining a few crimes such as sexual perversions, like exhibitionism (only rarely obsessive) or fetishism (which may or may not be criminal), and pyromania (arson) or kleptomania (theft). In criminology it is the last of these, kleptomania, which is most frequently mentioned. Obsession is a compulsive and genuinely uncontrollable feeling, and often the sufferer realises the feelings are wholly irrational but is still unable to control them because the obsession pervades and overrules everything.

The term kleptomania has been largely devalued by its frequent use to describe otherwise uncharacteristic shop-lifting. The term should not be used simply to mean that the person had a strong desire, which he or she did not control, to take something. To be truly an obsessive thief there must be much more than this.

Obsessional theft is often preceded by certain rituals, or the theft itself is ritualistic; clumsily performed with almost no attempt at concealment (possibly showing an underlying feeling of guilt which drives the thief on in order to obtain punishment); involves the taking of useless objects which may be hoarded, often does not satisfy any desire, and sometimes is even followed by a compensatory act.

9.3.5 The relationship between crime and psychosis

As the discussion so far indicates, the precise relationship between these mental illnesses and crime is uncertain. There is certainly no direct and simple link. There would appear to be some very severe cases where the mental element directly causes the criminality and, as suggested in 9.3.2, there may in some cases be an indirect link. In any event, the uncertainties suggest that the provision of proper support in the community would be the most effective way of using the degree of current understanding.

What is possibly more important to the law is the effect of these illnesses on the mental element necessary for a conviction. It seems illogical that in cases where the offender is recognised to be suffering from a mental illness we convict as if there were full responsibility and then decide that punishment is not justified as the individual was not responsible and should be treated under the Mental Health Act 1983. A more logical stance would be to assess criminal responsibility and culpability at an earlier stage and in a more sophisticated way (for a discussion of this see 9.2.2). It would be desirable for the law to deal with this anomaly but a major impediment arises because there are no hard and fast definitions of mental capacity and impairment nor can there be any precise assessment of whether, and how far, an individual was affected by a state of mind at the time of the offence. Lawyers do not readily embrace such uncertainty which makes a resolution of this issue unlikely in the foreseeable future.

Equally important is the need to recognise the way the criminal justice system is distorted by the policy of care in the community. All organs of the system are affected, from police through the courts to the punishment and treatment providers, and their actions in dealing with these people bear little relation to their intended criminal justice roles. The most affected are the police who often perform a heightened welfare role. These duties distort the functions of the criminal justice system and are performed by those who are ill-equipped to deal with people suffering from mental illness, where the associated problems are often social rather than criminal. That is not to blame the police but rather an argument for a realisation of the problem and a call for a solution. The problem presently appears to be one of crime whereas it may really be one of mental illness.

9.4 Psychopathy

9.4.1 Introduction

Psychopathy is a severe personality disorder, and has been touched upon in Chapter Eight. It is included here because it is mentioned in the Mental Health Act and is often considered to be potentially extremely dangerous. Section 1(2) of the Mental Health Act 1983 defines psychopathic disorder as:

a persistent disorder or disability of mind . . . which results in abnormally aggressive or seriously irresponsible conduct on the part of the person concerned.

What is meant by 'persistent', 'abnormally aggressive' or 'seriously irresponsible' is not specified and will be left to the court to interpret, under the guidance of psychologists. These offenders are dealt with under s. 37 of the Mental Health Act 1983, which allows them to be admitted to a mental hospital rather than sentenced to a punishment. Only three years after the passing of the Mental Health Act 1983, the Department of Health and Social Security (DHSS) and the Home Office produced a consultative document (1986) in which it was suggested that psychopathically disordered offenders would not be treated in the same way as other mental offenders or punished like ordinary offenders. This seems to be a reaction to the perceived increased dangerousness of these offenders and the fear that they might be released by the mental hospitals while still dangerous.

In Chapter Eight recent government proposals for those with severe personality disorder (including psychopaths now often referred to as dangerously severe personality disorder, DSPD) were considered. Basically they would remove dangerous people from society for as long as they are considered to pose a serious risk. This is proposed despite the diagnostic accuracy being questionable and, more importantly, despite there being no sound moral or theoretical basis for this interference with liberty. Should people be detained for periods of time which would be unacceptable for the seriousness of the offence they have committed and in cases where there is no clinical gain to them? These appear to be very politicised decisions, possibly in response to what Howitt (1998) calls an overreaction of the media to such people. Whilst the desire to protect the public is understandable it is difficult to justify these ideas especially as they are not likely to be successful.

9.4.2 What is psychopathy?

It is important to note that psychopathy does not necessarily involve any impairment of the reasoning facilities, and psychopaths may be aware of their actions and have a normal interest in themselves and their surroundings. As Rafter (1997) notes, the term 'psychopathy' virtually defies definition when perceived as a personality defect, although it has more validity when seen as mental incapacity. A psychopath will normally suffer from distortions of, or a perversion of, feelings and affections as well as the possession of strange desires, habits, a strange moral disposition and odd behavioural patterns such as frequent and marked changes in mood and temper, impulsive behaviour and, in particular, violent outbursts. In short, a psychopath is unpredictable, unresponsive to help, and prone to extremely unacceptable behaviour. Hare (1980) names five elements which he says characterise the psychopath:

(a) an inability to develop warm, responsive, and affectionate relationships, a general lack of empathy;

(b) an unstable lifestyle;

(c) an inability to accept responsibility, particularly for their own unacceptable behaviour;

(d) they do not have psychiatric problems nor are they unintelligent;

(e) they have problems in controlling their behaviour.

The 1986 publication from the Department of Health and Social Security and Home Office may also be of assistance in understanding what psychopathy is:

The core problem is impairment in the capacity to relate to others—to take account of their feelings and to act in ways consistent with their safety and convenience.

Psychopaths tend to be loners, and even if they live in or with a family they may have surprisingly separate and private lives. If they do live with their family, it is often the family who suffer most from their mood changes. This is particularly so if the family try to help them, as they are often hostile to those who offer help. Unlike their popular image, they are not constantly intent on harming people or causing pain, suffering and chaos. Instead, they are normally unable to stick to long-term plans, and the pain and suffering caused is often not intended and results rather from the fierce and severe mood changes and impulsive or violent behaviour. This is made worse by the fact that psychopaths seem unable to understand either pain or suffering in others, and this inability may render them unable to comprehend the reactions of others to their behaviour. For a discussion of possible diagnoses see 8.4.2.6 and for further consideration of government proposals for psychopaths see 8.4.1.

9.4.3 The origins of the disease

The outward manifestations of psychopathy may be related to some of the central and autonomic nervous system functions discussed in 7.3 and 7.4. It seems from work carried out by Hare (1970) that psychopaths often have EEG patterns close to those of children, which suggest that they suffer from cortical immaturity. Similar work has suggested that the illness is associated with defective brain functions which are related to emotions. There is also some suggestion that psychopaths suffer from low cortical arousal, related to the ANS, which therefore needs and seeks excessive excitement which might well involve criminal behaviour. Most people, whether psychopathic or not, are right handed, and this means that the left cerebral hemisphere is dominant and contains the speech centres of the brain. Hare and McPherson (1984) point out that in psychopaths part of the speech function is carried out by the right rather than the left cerebral hemisphere. This sharing of the brain functions causes the two sides of the brain to be less well integrated, affecting language and behaviour abilities as well as emotional processes and responses. This might explain why psychopaths can lie without worry and why they can hurt others with seemingly little feeling. Psychopaths have also been found to suffer from a greater lack of autonomic activity than might be found in the general population. This severe lack of autonomic activity also shows markedly lower feelings of guilt, anxiety and emotional tension than would be normal. Merely to list the possible origins of the disease is to illustrate the uncertainty of present knowledge.

Farrington (1994) suggests that the problem is one of impulsive behaviour, while Hollin (1992) also refers to the possibility that cognitive problems may have a causal connection with the psychopathic personality. Interestingly, the lack of learning occurs for physical or social disapproval but not for financial penalties: it may therefore be more sensible, in terms of prevention, to punish psychopaths financially rather than physically or by societal disapproval. These learning problems may explain some of the difficulties which present themselves in the psychopathic personality.

9.4.4 Psychopathy and criminality

What are the connections between psychopathy and criminality? A common view is that the two are synonymous. Foucault suggests that some people are said to have mental problems merely because we are unable to understand their criminality and therefore unable to decide how to punish them. In such cases he argues that psychology is being used to control people whose criminality is perceived as irrational and therefore as more dangerous (see Kritzman (1988), especially Chapters Eight and Eleven). When no other explanation seems possible or likely, they term a criminal a psychopath, particularly if that person's behaviour involves wanton violence. The label 'psychopath' is even more likely to be attached to those who will not respond to punishment or treatment. It is possible that mild personality disorders showing slightly increased psychopathic tendencies may explain a fair amount of both criminality and recidivism (see 8.3), but there is a difference between these and true psychopathic disorders. First, the true psychopathic personality is unlikely to have planned the crime and is less likely to gain from it: in fact they may well lose. The crime may arise out of a wild and inexplicable mood change, and there is often no clear design. If psychopaths indulge in sexual offences or violence, there may be no pattern. The offences are committed at whim and other types of offences may be committed in the interim. The acts of a true psychopath are chaotic and repetitious, the offences often occurring in fairly rapid succession. For further discussion see Chapter Eight and Prins (1998).

Even if it is not as marked as popularly believed, there is clearly a connection between psychopathy and criminality. One possible puzzle is that women are almost never classified as psychopathic. Guze (1976) suggests that women who portray similar traits are classified as hysterics.

9.5 Self-induced mental incapacity

9.5.1 Introduction

This is usually brought about by the intake of drugs (in the broadest sense). Some of these drugs are legal and freely available (e.g., alcohol which is imbibed and glues or lighter fuels which are inhaled); some prescribed (e.g., barbiturates); some are only or normally available on the black market (e.g., amphetamines, LSD and opiates). Alcohol is more significant for criminality than other drugs, partly because its legal and common usage makes it easily available. Self induced incapacity may also be brought about by negligently or carelessly omitting to take the drugs necessary for some illnesses, possibly causing a form of automatism, e.g., not taking the correct medicine or food to prevent onset of a diabetic coma. Clearly, this is only voluntary if the individual is aware of what will result from the omission.

9.5.2 Criminal law, alcohol and drugs

In most instances, the voluntary taking of any drug will not affect the criminality of the individual and cannot be used as a defence. In crimes of negligence and of basic intent, the proof of recklessness is enough to establish the mental element necessary. The exception to this is offences of specific/ulterior intent, where a conviction is only possible on clear proof of the mental intent (e.g., murder). For a fuller discussion of this see *Blackstone's Criminal Practice* (published annually). In the 2003 edition, see A3.8–10.

Clearly, even in cases of specific/ulterior intent an accused who lacks the required mental element at the time of the commission of the *actus reus* through voluntary intoxication or self-induced automatism may still be held criminally responsible for such an offence. This may happen either if there was intent to execute the offence and drink was taken to give 'Dutch courage' to carry out the crime (see *Attorney-General for Northern Ireland* v *Gallagher* [1963] AC 349) or if, despite the intoxication, the court considers the individual was able to form the requisite intention to commit that offence.

An accused who is involuntarily rendered drunk and incapable of forming the *mens rea* of an offence (e.g., by 'spiked' drinks) or is an involuntary automaton (e.g., a person in a state of concussion) may generally have a defence even to an offence of basic intent: see *DPP* v *Majewski* [1977] AC 443. However, where a person, though involuntarily intoxicated, is capable of forming the required *mens rea* with regard to an offence, and the fact of his intoxication merely weakens his ability and will, then he is guilty of any offence he may commit. This remains true whether the offence is one which requires a specific/ulterior intent, a basic intent, or is negligence based (see *Rv Bailey* [1983] 1 WLR 760 and *R* v *Kingston* [1995] 2 AC 355). The fact of his intoxication is then relevant to sentence only.

Alcohol or drug abuse may result in mental impairment. If an accused, through the use of intoxicants or drugs, is rendered insane, the McNaghten Rules apply (see 9.2.1). However, this is not the case if the use of such substances induces a temporary insanity in persons who are mentally unstable but not normally insane (see *Attorney-General for Northern Ireland* v *Gallagher* [1963] AC 349 and 9.2.1 concerning the law relating to insanity). There are also different categories of drugs: those which are known to have effects which may make the taker more aggressive or unpredictable; and those, like Valium, which are not normally associated with problematic changes in behaviour. In the latter case a defence of temporary mental impairment is possible (see above and *R* v *Bailey* [1983] 1 WLR 760 and *R* v *Hardie* [1985] 1 WLR 64).

9.5.3 The effects of alcohol

The social and criminological effects of alcohol are significant. They occur because of the effect alcohol has on our bodies. First, alcohol is a depressant which renders the drinker less able to concentrate, less able to judge situations and less able to control emotions. Because it lowers the ability to control emotions and lessens the ability to judge situations and to act rationally, there is obviously a marked behaviour change brought about by alcohol. Secondly, the change in behaviour may be brought about by the opposite effect: alcohol may stimulate the physical mechanisms involved in violent behaviour. This suggests that it increases the activity of the areas of the brain associated with aggressive behaviour. Lastly, alcohol may just provide a convenient excuse for aggressive behaviour, allowing the individual to attribute to heavy drinking the blame for aggressive behaviour in the expectation that the behaviour will be condoned or treated less seriously. All these effects can lead to what may be termed or considered otherwise uncharacteristic behaviour. For a full consideration of how these may operate see Pihl and Peterson (1993). More recently the chemical link between alcohol and aggressive behaviour or alcohol and crime has been challenged and the suggestion is that it is linked to social and cognitive elements which may be affected by the alcohol consumption (see Deehan (1999)).

Despite these fairly drastic effects, alcohol is both freely available and socially acceptable. Most adults in this country use alcohol, but the quantity depends on their lifestyle and habits. Alcohol is used at most social occasions such as weddings, deaths, parties, presentations. Used in moderation, its effects can be beneficial in breaking down some inhibitions and so helping the socialising process. However, even the moderate use of alcohol may break down inhibitions sufficiently to release individuals to do uncharacteristic things. The danger is obviously most likely to arise when alcohol is consumed to excess, either on one occasion or habitually.

There are recognised to be a number of different types of drinker. One classification might be:

1. the light social drinker,
2. the occasional intoxicant,
3. the heavy social drinker (i.e., one who engages in regular excessive use of alcohol),
4. the alcoholic, and
5. the chronic alcoholic (i.e., one who is totally dependent on alcohol).

The demarcation between each is blurred: the point at which drinking moves from light and generally acceptable social drinking to heavy social drinking cannot be assessed in terms of amount, but rather by attitude. The heavy drinker is likely to attend social occasions for the alcohol, or while there, to be preoccupied in obtaining as much alcohol as possible. For such people, drinking tends to become more important and to occur at all times of the day, affecting efficiency in other aspects of life, such as work. There will be lapses of memory and deterioration in relationships, particularly within a family. At this point other physical effects may occur, such as loss of appetite, hand tremors and reduction in sexual urges and vitality and sometimes suicide attempts or suicidal thoughts and feelings. Exactly how one defines an alcoholic or alcohol-dependent is difficult, but its essential element seems to be an inability to refrain from the use of alcohol.

9.5.4 Crime and alcohol

Alcohol has long been connected with antisocial activity, crime and criminality. As far back as the seventeenth century there was legislation against intoxication because it was perceived as the:

. . . Root and Foundation of many other enormous Sins, as Bloodshed, Stabbing, Murder, Swearing, Fornication, Adultery, and such like, . . . to the Overthrow of many good Arts and manual Trades, the Disabling of divers Workmen, and the general Impoverishing of many good Subjects (An Act for Repressing the Odious and Loathsome Sin of Drunkenness, 1606; 4 James I, c. 5).

In more modern times, a similar root and branch belief in its evils led to its prohibition in the United States for 13 years from 16 January 1920. Ironically, prohibition was one of the most crime-ridden periods in American history. But whatever the verdict on that large social experiment, there is a deep-seated belief that, whatever its benefits, drink causes criminality. Is this reputation deserved?

Alcohol is related to criminality in a number of different ways. First, there are some offences which have the drinking of alcohol as an essential component. These include simple drunkenness, being drunk and disorderly (in a public place) and driving whilst under the influence of drink in contravention of road safety regulations, which account for about 40 to 50 thousand prosecutions a year. Of greater interest is how significant is alcohol in the commission of other offences. Assessments of this are more difficult, partly because the alcohol consumption of offenders is not recorded in the official statistics. Most information in this area is either an intelligent guess or calculated after studying a sample of arrested persons. However, a number of studies do suggest a link between alcohol and general levels of criminal violence (see Collins (1988 and 1989); and Fagan (1990)). Murdoch et al. (1990) compared 26 studies from 11 countries and discovered that overall 62 per cent of violent offenders were drinking at the time of their offence (the range was 24 to 85 per cent in violent crime against 12 to 38 per cent in non-violent crimes). Also interesting was that 45 per cent of victims of violence had been drinking at the time they were victimised. The studies suggest that alcohol may be very closely related to violent criminality, but cannot establish that it was the cause of such criminality. Abram (1989) has suggested that both the alcohol use and the criminality may be the result of a third factor such as antisocial personality disorder.

The evidence does, however, suggest that some crimes, particularly of violence or criminal damage, are clearly related to alcohol and probably only take place because the normal inhibitory factors have been broken down by drink. Alcohol may not cause the criminality, but it does break down the normal inhibitions. The violence may have arisen out of an argument; or drinking and violence may both arise out of other problems, such as family difficulties. In some cases the crime may well have been planned before the alcohol was consumed, and it was only drunk either to pass the time or to build up 'Dutch courage'. Clearly, alcohol use and criminality may both be caused by a third, common factor such as peer group pressure, broken homes and parental disharmony. Some writers have also suggested a connection between alcohol dependence, crime and physical attributes (for a discussion of this, see Chapter Seven). However, Teplin et al. (1993) found that alcohol use disorders such as alcoholism did not predict violence. This finding is backed up by Pihl and Peterson (1993) who found that in some circumstances alcoholics were less aggressive. However, in non-alcoholics they discovered a more complex relationship between alcohol and crime: in low doses alcohol seemed to increase sensitivity and probably reduced criminality; in high doses sensitivity was reduced and this sometimes led to violent criminality. If this constituted one explanation of the relationship between alcohol and violence they also acknowledged that the effects of the drug may be affected by the state of mind with which the user approaches the alcohol and the surroundings in which this occurs. In a 1994 study, the National Association of Probation Officers (NAPO) asserted that almost half of all property crime was committed to sustain drug and alcohol addictions and that almost three-quarters of all those on probation committed their last offence to maintain such a habit. Mott (1990) suggests that the forceful link with criminality may not be the chemical effect of alcohol but rather the social context and wider culture involved in the consumption of alcohol.

It is obvious that crime and alcohol appear together in many different situations. It is difficult to assess whether the crime was the reason for the drink—to get Dutch courage or through guilt after the crime is committed; or drink was the reason for the crime—a breakdown of the inhibitory factors releasing the individual to transgress; or whether both crime and drinking are connected by other, often situational factors—both are encouraged by the peer group, or both can result out of depressing factors in home life.

9.5.5 Drugs

Drug taking does not have as long a connection with criminality as does alcohol. It was only at the beginning of this century that drugs were labelled as a major social problem and became regulated. Prior to that, many now prohibited drugs, especially the opiates, were used to treat even fairly minor ailments and could be purchased at the local pharmacy. In Britain the first attempt to regulate drugs appeared in the Pharmacy and Poisons Act 1868, but these controls were only very minor and piecemeal. Early in the twentieth century, there were strong international calls for the control of drugs which culminated in the passing of the Hague Convention of Private International Law 1912. Article 20 of this Convention called for:

contracting powers to examine the possibility of enacting laws or regulations making it an offence to be in illegal possession of raw opium, prepared opium, morphine, cocaine and their respective salts . . .

Eight years later Britain passed its first full drug control legislation, the Dangerous Drugs Act 1920, which regulated the import, export and possession of the drugs referred to in the Convention. Some claim that outlawing the possession and sale/purchase of drugs led to an increase in addiction. Toch (1966) quotes an estimate that there was a 1,500 per cent increase in drug addiction in the opiates in the States between 1914 (the year they were outlawed by the Narcotic Act in that country) and 1918.

Despite its fairly short connection with the criminal law, many people now connect drug taking with criminality. Some of the difficulties with alcohol also pertain to drug taking. Clearly drugs can alter perceptions, break down inhibitions and generally alter behaviour, and so may be connected with crime in many of the same ways as alcohol. The same problems in calculating the significance of drugs as a cause of crime exist as in the case of alcohol.

Many drugs are illegal and so their possession, sale or consumption is an offence in itself. This leads to vast networks of organised crime which are built up on the proceeds from the sale of controlled substances. It also means that anyone wishing to use any of these substances is immediately criminalised, and this has brought many otherwise law-abiding citizens into contact with the criminal justice system, which can devalue the criminal law and possibly lead to more people having a disrespect for the system and so being willing to commit other crimes. There are at least five ways in which drugs are connected with crime.

First, users may commit crimes, including violent crimes, to get hold of the substances they want. Because of their illegality they are sold on the black market, often at high prices, encouraging addicts to commit property offences (theft, burglary, robbery etc.). Chaiken and Chaiken (1991) suggest that most drug-related crime falls into this category of non-violent property offences or, as Plant (1990) says, prostitution. Jarvis and Parker (1989) suggest that crime is causally linked to heroin use because of the need for recurrent supplies to feed the habit. Some users may be willing to use violence to secure the property or to obtain drugs from another who has them.

Secondly, drug use and criminal behaviour just happen to occur together because third factors may predispose individuals to both activities (such as an antisocial personality disorder), whilst there is strong evidence to suggest that crime leads to drug use rather than vice versa (see McBride and McCoy (1982); Auld et al. (1986)). In Scotland, Hammersley et al. (1989), carried out extensive research which suggested that criminal activity before drug use is much more important and reliable a predictor of later criminal activity than is the drug use itself. Furthermore they undermined the link between heroin and crime, finding a similar link with other drugs and, in particular, noting that moderate use of heroin seemed to have no greater connection with criminality than did cannabis or alcohol. It seems not to be possible to resolve whether crime results from drug use or drug use begins as further proof of the deviant behaviour of an individual which may have a different cause. It is probable that each can be true in different cases.

Thirdly, dealers and others involved in the trade in drugs will tend to protect their 'business' interests by violent means, especially as they cannot call on legitimate forms of protection. The resultant level of violence and protection is difficult to estimate. It has been suggested (see Ruggerio and South (1995)) that in Britain the market is not controlled by large, organised criminal syndicates so methods of protection will vary from area to area. Even if much of the drug market is not fully controlled in a 'mafia' type operation there are elements which involve highly organised international criminal cartels. In any event, whether organised or not there is an increasing use of violence, particularly gun violence, in the protection of interests within the market. The media reports this as a black criminal problem, especially through their focus on Yardies yet this seems to be a misplaced and distorted image of the situation (see Murji (2002)). Of the drug hauls of HM Customs even in cocaine (especially crack cocaine) normally stated to be a Caribbean problem, only 7 per cent originates from Jamaica and the majority of users of the drug are white (see Gray (2002)). This complex makeup of the UK drugs market requires flexible and inventive methods on the part of the control authorities in order to deal with all aspects.

Fourthly, drugs are chemicals and their ingestion alters the chemical balance of the body and the brain, and this can affect behaviour. The way in which behaviour is altered varies from drug to drug and, as with alcohol, sometimes varies with the intensity of the drug taken and the frequency of use (for a fuller discussion see Pihl and Peterson (1993) and Fishbein and Pease (1990)). Interestingly the biological effects of opiates such as heroin, which are most commonly associated with criminality, tend to reduce aggressive and hostile tendencies. On the other hand the immediate biological effects of cocaine and its derivative crack are more closely associated with violence. Their immediate effects may be positive, feeling elated, assertive and alert; but later this may turn to feelings of suspicion and paranoia, irritability, vigilance, nervousness, feelings associated with some psychotics and the effects may be violent criminal activity (Fishbein and Pease (1990)). As with alcohol, the genetic make-up of the individual and the social and environmental context may be as important as the chemical effects of the drugs. The media (and often the police) claim a very strong link between crack cocaine and violence but this is not proven and as with alcohol there is no necessary link between the drug and violence (Gray (2002)). The level of criminal activity due to these chemical changes is probably relatively small as the level of frequent use in Britain seems still to be quite low.

Lastly, there is State involvement in the narcotics trade. Dorn and South (1990) have suggested that in the US there is some State-sponsored trading in drugs, notably by the CIA. The extent of these activities is impossible to assess but their use of normally legitimate services, such as banks, is especially threatening for the fabric of society.

9.5.6 Treatment

In discussing the connection of drugs and alcohol with crime, one needs to be aware of an important and unresolved conflict of approach. Some see both these activities as intrinsically wrong and *per se* in need of punishment; others see them as social and personal problems to be understood and treated as any other illness; more recently a third view has emerged, that they are or cause a danger or risk to non-users in society and this risk needs to be managed in order to protect 'us'. The first solution has generally won out in the case of drugs where a firm law and order policy has been taken; the second has been more accepted in the case of alcohol and in the 1980s and 1990s was becoming accepted even in the drugs area; there has now been a move towards the third particularly in the case of drugs.

In the nineteenth century a number of attempts were made to 'help' or 'cure' habitual drinkers. In 1879 the Habitual Drunkards Act allowed justices to send these people to retreats, and in 1898, under the Inebriates Act of that year, they were given power to send them to certified Institutes for Reformation for up to three years. Very few retreats were ever established, and by 1921 they had all closed. More recently, similar provisions have re-appeared in s. 34 of the Criminal Justice Act 1972, as amended by sch. 6, para. 21 of the Police and Criminal Evidence Act 1984, which empowers the police to take drunkards to a medical treatment centre rather than arresting and charging them. This can only be done if they are arrested for an offence under s. 12 of the Licensing Act 1879 or s. 91(1) of the Criminal Justice Act 1967. Unfortunately, very few such centres have been made available. Similarly, although probation orders (now called community rehabilitation orders) can have treatment requirements attached to them and treatment can be made available within prisons, such measures are insufficiently used (NAPO, 1994). In the case of drugs there has always been a strong element of strict law enforcement in trying to prosecute users and, especially, producers, importers and dealers. This was intended to increase associated costs and so act as a deterrent. The policy does not really work to reduce drug availability or use. As drug use and experimentation with drugs has increased (see Boys et al. (2001) and Sharp et al. (2001)) so the police time spent on its detection has gone up exponentially. A recent report (May et al. (2001)) claims that 7 out of every 10 known offenders in England and Wales were arrested for the possession of cannabis and that the financial costs of policing etc. cannabis was at least £50 million and took up the time of 500 full-time police officers. It is obvious that substantial savings in police time and money might be saved were they not required to police the use of cannabis quite so vigorously, whilst there might also be a very real reduction in the animosity between police officers and some communities. For this reason there was a recommendation that cannabis be reclassified as a Class C drug, a less serious infraction. This is now part of government policy but they wish to preserve the possibility that police could arrest for possession of cannabis and therefore s. of the Criminal Justice Act 2003 would make possession of a Class C drug an arrestable offence. Logically from a scientific and medical viewpoint the decriminalization of cannabis should be accompanied with similar action in relation to magic mushrooms and even cocaine (Shiner (2003)).

Added to the law and order approach there has also been a strand of policy involved with the treatment of drug users. Traditionally this was aimed at helping the user. In the 1980s and 1990s the treatment element started to move more towards a safe and controlled use of drugs even if not complete abstinence. This came to the fore partly in order to stem the spread of HIV/AIDS and took the form of needle exchange programmes and safe environments in which to inject. On top of these there have always been counselling programmes and treatments centres to help people to control or kick the use of drugs. Many of these are run by private or charitable bodies some of which have received substantial financial support from government. In the past any financial backing or strategic planning concerning drug treatment has been run by the Department of Health. In the last few years this landscape has altered almost completely. The focus of government concern has turned from concerns about dangers to the health of the user towards the control and management of risks or dangers posed by these users to other people. This approach arises partly because many of those who offended were found to be or believed to be drug users; partly because drug taking amongst young people was on the rise, and partly due to a popular perception that drug taking and the attendant paraphernalia was causing feelings of fear and insecurity in some communities.

A similar attempt to tighten control was introduced in prisons from the mid-1990s through the mandatory testing of their inmates with the intention of controlling drug use in the criminal population and improving the health of individuals. The policy raises ethical problems; it seems, for example, to violate Article 8 of the European Convention on Human Rights (the right to privacy). Prisoners who test positive face extra imprisonment. There is a worrying concern noted by Stevens (1996) that, because cannabis remains in the blood for 28 days whereas many hard drugs are gone after a few days, prisoners are turning to harder drugs. Prisoners are also using very dangerous products such as bleach to hide the drugs in their bloodstream. Despite these problems mandatory drug testing is being used in some pre-sentence tests. Furthermore under ss. 42, 48 and 58A of the Powers of Criminal Courts (Sentencing) Act 2000 there are now stringent drug abstinence orders which can be used both as separate punishments and as a requirement in other community sentences. The measures include mandatory drug testing and severe punishments for breach. These powers are only available for those over 18 where the drugs were connected with the offence or where they are being punished for a 'trigger offence' (largely serious property crimes and drug offences). There is no treatment requirement in these orders and offenders do not have to consent to them. Section 52 of the Powers of Criminal Courts (Sentencing) Act 2000 provides for a treatment and testing order where the offender is dependent on or may have a propensity to misuse drugs. Although an offender would have to accept this order, the reality of the consent is questionable as the alternative would probably be custody. With both these orders there are problems of human rights and ethics.

As part of the change in emphasis and direction the whole drugs strategy seems now to be moving. Most of the money associated with drugs treatment is not now handled by the Department of Health but rather by the Drugs Prevention Advisory Service which is part of the Home Office. One likely result is that most of the money to deal with drug problems and treatment will be attached to criminal justice policy on crime reduction. More offenders will probably be passed to the system but probably fewer individuals will choose to ask for help. This is because there will to be a growing tendency to equate drugs and crime, so anyone having treatment will be seen as criminal. The ethos of treatment within a criminal justice model (to prioritise abstinence) will be very different from that in a health model (to aim for controlled use). The confidentiality of drug treatment centres and counsellors is likely to be eroded as they become subsumed into the criminal justice model; and as more are directed to treatments by the criminal justice system there will be fewer places for others—there is soon likely to be an even greater dearth of treatment places for non-offenders so the paradox may be that if you want treatment you will have to offend.

The problem of both drug and alcohol abuse has therefore largely been left to the criminal law to solve. In each case, due to pressure on police work, the problem is often ignored until a further crime is committed. Possibly these further offences could be prevented by an effective system of treatment provisions.

9.6 Conclusion

The central discussion in this chapter has been concerned with the mental state of the offender at the time of committing the offence. In some instances, the law recognises that the mental element affects the individual's culpability, and therefore allows it to be used in his or her defence. For example, insanity and automatism are full defences and diminished responsibility and infanticide are partial defences. In practice, insanity is used only in cases where the charge is murder, and in law diminished responsibility and infanticide can be used only when the charge is murder, and can be used only to reduce the conviction. Therefore, in most cases the full mental state of the defendant is not medically questioned or tested until after he or she is convicted. The defendant's mental capacity or understanding, which may reduce or interfere with the *mens rea* (mental intent) of the offender, are therefore often ignored until after there is a finding of guilt. At that point, the court may ask why the offender committed the offence and may well consider his or her mental capacity under the Mental Health Act 1983. If a psychologist then suggests that the offender is suffering from a mental illness which falls under that statute, the court may decide that the offender should be helped in a hospital and sentence him or her accordingly. If the mental element is seen to be sufficiently important to become an issue at the sentencing stage there may, in some cases, be an argument for its consideration at an earlier stage, before conviction. Some (such as Samuels (1988)) have even argued that mental disorder should be allowed as a full defence to criminality. Samuels suggests that if this was accepted the court could use the civil powers of the Mental Health Act 1983, and the local authority could then oversee the treatment received by such people. If this seems excessive there may be an argument for the introduction of a partial defence of mental incapacity to all crimes which would result in a finding of guilt, but with diminished culpability, similar to the diminished responsibility defence which is available in cases of murder (see Cranston Law (1983)). This would give the mental element further recognition, and also allow the medical evidence to be more carefully scrutinised than is the case when it is brought up at the sentencing stage. Of course, such a verdict would not be a full acquittal, but the disposals available to the court on such a finding would be limited to treatment or public safety measures rather than punishment.

Interestingly, the judges and legal system, helped by the medical and social professionals, seem to be moving the other way. As the medical profession turns away from being willing to define an offender as irresponsible, so the number of prisoners in ordinary prisons who suffer from psychological disorders or imbalances rises. This is causing immense problems for staff and inmates of these institutions. Although there are proposals to deal differently with those suffering from Dangerous Severe Personality Disorders (DSPD) these are fairly punitive in effect and seem to revolve more around the protection of the public, even where no offence has been committed rather than the treatment of the individual. It may be that the new What Works? approach to probation will help those on community orders to address mild antisocial personality disorders but this still leaves a gap of those incarcerated but not DSPD. As suggested in the last chapter, it may be time for a rethink to address the responsibility and needs of offenders and to examine how the rights of offenders, victims and the public can be respected.

SUGGESTING READING

Hollin, C.R. (1992), *Criminal Behaviour*, London: The Falmer Press.

Hollin, C. (ed.) (2001), *Handbook of Offender Assessment and Treatment*, Chichester: Wiley.

South, N. (2002), 'Drugs, Alcohol and Crime', in M. Maguire, R. Morgan and R. Reiner (eds), *The Oxford Handbook of Criminology*, Oxford: Oxford University Press.

Special issue of *Criminal Justice Matters* entitled 'Drugs', Issue No. 47.

QUESTIONS FOR REVISIONS

1   Should people be detained for periods of time which would be unacceptable only on the
    basis of the seriousness of the offence they have committed (or even in cases where they have

committed no offence)? Is detention justifiable where there may be no clinical gain to the person but merely because they are believed to pose a future risk to others?

2   Should people be forced to undergo drugs testing and treatment? Is such forced treatment likely to be effective?

3   Is there really a drug 'problem'? Does linking drugs and crime solve or cause problems? How should society approach the issue of drugs?

REFERENCES

Abram, K.M. (1989), 'The Effect of Co-occurring Disorders on Criminal Careers: Interaction of Antisocial Personality, Alcoholism, and Drug Disorders', *International Journal of Law and Psychiatry*, vol. 12, p. 133.

Alcohol Concern (2001), **http://www.alcoholconcern.org.uk**.

Allen, Michael J. (1997), *Textbook on Criminal Law*, 4th edn, London: Blackstone.

Auld, J., Dorn, N. and South, N. (1986), 'Irregular Work, Irregular Pleasures: Heroin in the 1980s', in Roger Matthews and J. Young (eds), *Confronting Crime*, London: Sage.

Blackstone's Criminal Practice, published annually, Peter Murphy (ed.), London: Blackstone.

Blau, T.H. (1998), *The Psychologist as Expert Witness*, 2nd edn, New York: Wiley.

Boys, A., Dobson, J., Marsden, J. and Strang, J. (2001), *Cocaine Trends: A Quantitative Study of Young People and Cocaine Use*, London: National Addiction Centre.

Butler Committee (1975), *Report of the Committee on Mentally Abnormal Offenders*, Cmnd 6244, London: HMSO.

Chaiken, J. and Chaiken, M. (1991), 'Drugs and Predatory Crime', in M. Tonry and J. Wilson (eds), *Crime and Justice: a Review of Research*, vol. 13, Chicago, IL: University of Chicago Press.

Cheng, P.T.K. (1986), 'Maternal Filicide in Hong Kong, 1971–85', *Medicine, Science and the Law*, vol. 26(3), p. 185.

Collins, J.J. (1988), 'Suggested Explanatory Frameworks to Clarify the Alcohol Use/Violence Relationship', *Contemporary Drug Problems*, Spring, p. 107.

Collins, J.J. (1989), 'Alcohol and Interpersonal Violence: Less than Meets the Eye', in A. Weiner and M.E. Wolfgang (eds), *Pathways to Criminal Violence*, Newbury Park, CA: Sage Periodicals Press.

Cranston Law, N. (1983), 'Neither Guilty Nor Insane', *Medicine, Science and the Law*, vol. 23(4), p. 275.

Cross, Sir Rupert, Jones, Phillip Asterley and Card, Richard (1995), *Introduction to Criminal Law*, 13th edn, London: Butterworths.

Deehan, A. (1999), *Alcohol and Crime: Taking Stock*, Policing and Crime Reduction Unit, London: Home Office.

Department of Health and Social Security (1976), *A Review of the Mental Health Act, 1959*, DHSS Report, London: HMSO.

Department of Health and Social Security and Home Office (1986), *Offenders Suffering from Psychopathic Disorder*, London: DHSS and Home Office.

Dorn, N. and South, N. (1990), 'Drug Markets and Law Enforcement', *British Journal of Criminology*, vol. 30, p. 171.

Draft Mental Health Bill 2002 Cm 5538-I. See **http://www.doh.gov.uk/mentalhealth/draft bill2002/index.htm**.

Fagan, J. (1990), 'Intoxication and Aggression', in M. Tonry and J.Q. Wilson (eds), *Crime and Justice: a Review of Research*, vol. 13, Chicago, IL: University of Chicago Press.

Farrington, D.P. (1994), 'Introduction', in D.P. Farrington (ed.), *Psychological Explanations of Crime*, Aldershot: Dartmouth.

Feldman, Philip (1993), *The Psychology of Crime*, Cambridge: Cambridge University Press.

Fishbein, Diana, H. and Pease, Susan, E. (1990), 'Neurological Links between Substance Abuse and Crime', in Lee Ellis and Harry Hoffman (eds), *Crime in Biological, Social, and Moral Contexts*, New York: Praeger.

Frost, C. (1986), 'Drug Trafficking, Organised Crime and Terrorism: the International Cash Connection', in V. Raanan, R. Pfaltzgraff and R. Shultz (eds), *Hydra of Carnage*, Lexington, MA: Lexington Books.

Gray, A. (2002), 'Crack in the System: Examining the myths', *Criminal Justice Matters*, vol. 47, p. 36.

Guze, S.B. (1976), *Criminality and Psychiatric Disorders*, Oxford: Oxford University Press.

Hammersley, R., Forsyth, A., Morrison, V. and Davies, J. (1989), 'The Relationship between Crime and Opoid Use', *British Journal of Addiction*, vol. 84, p. 1029.

Hare, R.D. (1970), *Psychopathy: Theory and Research*, London: Wiley.

Hare, R.D. (1980), 'A Research Scale for the Assessment of Psychopathy in Criminal Populations', *Personality and Individual Differences*, vol. 1, p. 111.

Hare, R.D. and McPherson, L.M. (1984), *Journal of Abnormal Psychology*, vol. 93(II), p. 141.

Hart, H.L.A. (1968), *Punishment and Responsibility*, Oxford: Clarendon Press.

Hochstedler Steury, Ellen (1993), 'Criminal Defendants with Psychiatric Impairment: Prevalence, Probabilities and Rates', *Journal of Criminal Law and Criminology*, vol. 84, p. 352.

Hollin, Clive, R. (1992), *Criminal Behaviour*, London: The Falmer Press.

Hough, M. (1996), 'Drugs Misuse and the Criminal Justice System: A Review of the Literature', London: Home Office, Drugs Prevention Initiative.

Hough, M. (1996a), 'Drug Misuse and the Criminal Justice System', *Criminal Justice Matters*, vol. 24, p. 4.

Howitt, D. (1998), *Crime, the Media and the Law*, Chichester: Wiley.

Jaffe, P.D. (1998), 'Necrophilia: Love at Last Sight', in J. Baros, I. Munnich and M. Szegedi (eds) *Psychology and Criminal Justice: International Review of Theory and Practice*, Berlin: Walter de Gruyter.

Jarvis, G. and Parker, H. (1989), 'Young Heroin Users and Crime', *British Journal of Criminology*, vol. 29, p. 175.

Kritzman, Lawrence D. (ed.) (1988), *Michel Foucault: Politics, Philosophy, Culture: Interviews and other Writings 1977–1984*, New York and London: Routledge.

Lindqvist, P. and Allebeck, P. (1990a), 'Schizophrenia and Crime: a Longitudinal Follow-up of 644 Schizophrenics in Stockholm', *British Journal of Psychiatry*, vol. 157, p. 345

Lindqvist, P. and Allebeck, P. (1990b), 'Schizophrenia and Assaultative Behaviour: the Role of Alcohol and Drugs', *Acta Psychiatrica Scandinavica*, vol. 82, p. 191.

McBride, D. and McCoy, C. (1982), 'Crime and Drugs: the Issues and Literature', *Journal of Drug Issues*, Spring, p. 137.

Mackay, R.D. (1990), 'Fact and Fiction about the Insanity Defence', *Criminal Law Review*, p. 247.

May, T., Warburton, H., Turnbull, P.J. and Hough, M. (2001), *Times they are A-Changing: Policing of Cannabis*, London: YPS in conjunction with the Joseph Rowntree Foundation. See **http://www.jrf.org.uk/bookshop/details.asp?pubID=421**.

Morris, Norval (1982), *Madness and the Criminal Law*, Chicago, IL: University of Chicago Press.

Mott, J. (1990), 'Young People, Alcohol and Crime', *Home Office Research Bulletin*, vol. 28.

Murdock, D., Pihl, R.O., and Ross, D. (1990) 'Alcohol and Crimes of Violence: Present Issues', *The International Journal of Addictions*, vol. 25, p. 1065.

Murji (2002), 'It's Not a Black Thing', *Criminal Justice Matters*, vol. 47, p. 32.

National Association of Probation Officers, (1994), *Substance Abuse, Mental Vulnerability and the Criminal Justice System: A Briefing Paper From the National Association of Probation Officers*, London: NAPO.

Packer, Herbert (1968), *The Limits of the Criminal Sanction*, Stanford, CA: Stanford University Press.

Pihl, Robert O. and Peterson, Jordan B. (1993), 'Alcohol/Drug Use and Aggressive Behaviour', in Sheilagh Hodgins (ed.), *Mental Disorder and Crime*, Newbury Park, CA: Sage Periodicals Press.

Pitch, T. (1995), *Limited Responsibilities: Social Movements and Criminal Justice*, trans. John Lea, London: Routledge.

Plant, M. (1990), *AIDS, Drugs and Prostitution*, London: Routledge.

Prins, H. (1980), *Offenders, Deviants, or Patients? An Introduction to the Study of Socio-Forensic Problems*, London: Tavistock.

Prins, H. (1998), 'Dangerous Offenders: Some Problems of Management', *International Review of Computers and Technology*, vol. 12, p. 299.

Rafter, N. (1997), 'Psychopathy and the Evolution of Criminological Knowledge', *Theoretical Criminology*, vol. 1(2), p. 235.

Raistrick, D., Hodgson, R. and Ritson, B. (eds) (1999), *Tackling Alcohol Together: The Evidence Base for a UK Alcohol Policy*, London: Free Association Books.

Rollin, H. (1969), *The Mentally Abnormal Offender and the Law: an Inquiry into the Working of the Relevant Parts of the Mental Health Act 1959*, Oxford: Pergamon.

Ruggiero, V. and South, N. (1995), *Eurodrugs: Drug Use, Marketing and Trafficking in Europe*, London: University College London.

Ryan, Christopher and Scanlan, Gary (1991), *Swot: Criminal Law*, 3rd edn, London: Blackstone.

Samuels, A. (1988), 'Mental Condition as a Defence in Criminal Law: A Lawyer Addresses Medical Men', *Medicine, Science and the Law*, vol. 28(1), p. 21.

Sharp, C., Baker, P., Goulden, C., Ramsey, M. and Sondhi, A. (2001), *Drug Misuse Declared in 2000: Key Results from the British Crime Survey*. Findings 149, Research, Development and Statistics Directorate, London: Home Office. **http://www.homeoffice.gov.uk/rds/pdfs/r149.pdf**.

Shiner, M. (2003), 'Out of Harm's Way?: Illicit Drug Use, Medicalisation and the Law', *Brit. J. Criminol.*, vol. 43, p. 772.

Smith, John Cyril and Hogan, Brian (1996), *Criminal Law*, 8th edn, London: Butterworths.

Stevens, A. (1996), 'The Mandatory Drug Testing Programme in Prisons', *Criminal Justice Matters*, vol. 24, p. 20.

Taylor, David (1981), *Alcohol: Reducing the Harm*, London: Office of Health Economics.

Taylor, Pamela, J. (1993), 'Schizophrenia and Crime: Distinctive Patterns of Association', in Sheilagh Hodgins (ed.), *Mental Disorder and Crime*, Newbury Park, CA: Sage Periodicals Press.

Teplin, Linda, A. (1990), 'The Prevalence of Severe Mental Disorder among Male Urban Jail Detainees: Comparison with the Epidemiologic Catchment Area Program', *American Journal of Public Health*, vol. 80, p. 663.

Teplin, Linda A., McClelland, Gary M. and Abram, Karen M. (1993), 'The Role of Mental Disorder and Substance Abuse in Predicting Violent Crime among Released Offenders', in Sheilagh Hodgins (ed.), *Mental Disorder and Crime*, Newbury Park, CA: Sage Periodicals Press.

Toch, Hans (ed.) (1966), *Legal and Criminal Psychology*, New York: Holt, Rinehart and Winston.

10

Intelligence and learning

10.1 Intelligence and crime

10.1.1 Introduction

There are several links between IQ and the law. Some have little or no connection with the criminal law and will be dealt with only in passing; others have sometimes been very closely linked to criminality and form the basis of this section. There is very little discussion of high intelligence and criminality, and this will not be considered.

10.1.2 Legal definition of low intelligence

There are two distinct types of mental defect, amentia and dementia. Amentia literally means 'lack of mind', and describes a person who is born with a reduced intellect. These people are often known as subnormal. Dementia describes someone who once had a normal intelligence but later lost it through disease, decay or accident.

Under the Mental Health Act 1959, these conditions were referred to as subnormality and severe subnormality, and included people with low intelligence who were considered unable to live an independent life and unable to guard themselves against exploitation which might exist outside a State institution. Since the enacting of s. 1 of the Mental Health Act 1983, these problems have been referred to as mental impairment and severe mental impairment. They include a state of arrested or incomplete development of the mind which includes (severe) impairment of intelligence and social functioning, associated with abnormally aggressive or seriously irresponsible conduct on the part of the person concerned.

There are two important differences between these definitions. First, there is a move away from the term subnormality towards mental impairment. This change has been severely criticised, both by individual experts and by bodies such as MIND, because it might be used to catch more individuals and therefore prejudice those of reduced intellect. Secondly, although both these definitions admit that assessment of mental inability cannot be tested on IQ ratings alone, they differ on the extra element required. The 1959 version included the ability of individuals to care for themselves; the 1983 version looks at their danger to themselves and, importantly, to others. It talks about abnormally aggressive or seriously irresponsible conduct. The 1983 version seems to move closer to a connection with criminality or criminal tendencies, something which has worried many professionals, as it may suggest that such tendencies accompany low intelligence. They find the wording to be particularly distressing because it is similar to that used to describe psychopathy in the 1959 Act. The Draft Mental Heath Bill 2002 continues this move towards the connection between danger to others and mental impairment.

These definitions are used to decide which individuals need treatment or help. They are used on both criminals, who may be forcibly treated if they fit into these categories, and non-criminals who may receive voluntary treatment. They indicate the way in which the law deals with severe problems in this area, and may reflect the changes taking place in the view taken of the connection between intelligence and criminality.

Table 10.1 might give a better idea of the medical assessment of mental retardation.

The percentage of the population which is sufficiently mentally retarded to fall under this legal definition is generally regarded as being very small, and of these over 90 per cent would be only mildly or moderately retarded. Thus only a very small group is involved, and even then only part of this group would have criminal tendencies. The interest of criminology is thus not centred on these but on the wider group with reduced intellect.

Table 10.1 Medical assessment of mental retardation

CHARACTERISTICS OF THE MENTALLY RETARDED

Degree of retardation	IQ range	Level of functioning at school age (6–20 years)	Level of functioning in adulthood (21 years and over)
Mild	50–5 to approx. 70	Can learn academic skills up to approximately sixth-grade level by late teens; can be guided toward social conformity.	Can usually achieve social and vocational skills adequate to maintain self support, but may need guidance and assistance when under unusual social or economic stress.
Moderate	35–40 to 50–55	Can profit from training in social and occupational skills; unlikely to progress beyond second-grade level in academic subjects; may learn to travel alone in familiar places.	May achieve self-maintenance in unskilled or semiskilled work under sheltered conditions; needs supervision and guidance when under mild social or economic stress.
Severe	20–35 to 35–40	Can talk or learn to communicate; can be trained in elemental health habits; profits from systematic habit training.	May contribute partially to self-maintenance under complete supervision; can develop self-protection skills at a minimum useful level in controlled environment.
Profound	below 20–25	Some motor development present; may respond to minimal or limited training in self-help.	Some motor and speech development; may achieve very limited self-care; needs nursing care.

Source: Gleitman (1999), p. 638

10.1.3 How to measure intelligence

The link between reduced intellect and crime was made because it was assumed that intelligence was linked to the ability to learn and understand complex societal norms and rules. Furthermore, it was considered that those of low intellect were less able to control their emotions and their behaviour. It was not until around 1900 that reasonably reliable tests to assess intelligence were produced. The first generally accepted test was constructed by Binet and Simon, and was called the 'Scale of Intelligence'. By 1908 they had assigned each test to a mental age. For example, an average 7-year-old could do certain tasks which would be too difficult for an average 6-year-old. The level of the hardest tasks performed represented the mental age of the individual. These form the basis for the intelligence tests which are still used today. The validity of these tests has, for some time, been controversial and although we are not centrally concerned with this point, it should be borne in mind.

Binet devised the test so that he could pin-point children who had learning difficulties and give them special help. He set up special classes for these children in Paris, and discovered that with special teaching techniques they became both more intelligent (in this sense) and more able to learn. He claimed that this proved that intelligence was not inborn and unchangeable.

Intelligence tests were also used to discover whether there was a link between criminality and intelligence: some authorities who claimed to have discovered such a link argued for the limitation of the right of these people to have children (see 10.1.7).

10.1.4 Link between crime and intellect

The earliest reputable studies into the link between criminality and intelligence were perhaps those conducted by Goddard (1912), starting with an unscientific study of the Kalikak family; by using a subjective assessment of 'feeble-mindedness' it largely begged the question it claimed to prove. Goddard's later studies were more acceptable 'scientifically', as they used the objective IQ tests to measure for 'feeble-mindedness'. He studied the inmates of 16 reformatories, and found that the proportion of feeble-minded inmates ranged from 28 per cent to 89 per cent, the average being about 50 per cent. His results, which were published in 1914, led him to conclude that criminals were 'feeble-minded'. He went further and suggested that all 'feeble-minded' individuals were potential criminals. Since he argued that this condition was basically inherited, he recommended their institutionalisation or sterilisation to prevent them breeding.

Most research carried out at the time arrived at similar conclusions until, during the First World War, the United States army began to test the IQ of their draftees, with the intention of declaring all the 'feeble-minded' as being unfit for military service. The unpalatable outcome was that about 50 per cent were 'feeble-minded'. The army could not accept this, and revised the level of 'feeble-mindedness' so as to catch fewer individuals. Following the war, theorists adopted the army's arbitrary revision. Goddard himself admitted that his previous findings were inaccurate, and even accepted that intellect was not purely hereditary but could be, at least partially, corrected by careful educational practices.

Investigations in the 50 years after 1920 largely failed to discover a connection between criminality and 'feeble-mindedness'. For example, the representative work of Mary Woodward (1955) concluded that 'low intelligence plays little or no part in delinquency'.

More recently, the possibility of a link has been revived and has had some support. The modern proponents of a link between intelligence and criminality have had a more scientific approach than their predecessors. Hirschi and Hindling (1977) found that low IQ was as good a predictor of delinquency as the more commonly accepted factors such as social class and upbringing. They argued that delinquency within a racial or social grouping is likely to be connected to IQ, so that low IQ blacks are more likely to be delinquent than high IQ blacks, and low IQ whites are more likely to be delinquent than high IQ whites. Similarly, lower-class delinquents will have lower IQs than lower-class non-delinquents. They discovered that delinquents on average had an IQ eight points lower than non-delinquents, and asserted that this difference was too significant to be ignored. They do not accept the idea that IQ is wholly related to hereditary factors, but argue that an individual's IQ potential may be affected by environmental factors. Finally, they do not claim that IQ has any direct effect on criminality. They speculate instead that the inability (or reduced ability) of low IQ juveniles to compete in certain fields leads them to look elsewhere for recognition (see, for example, the theories relating to school and criminality (13.6.2) and youth deviance (12.3)). Against this Wilson and Herrnstein (1985) link low intelligence with lack of moral reasoning leading to criminality.

In Britain, one of the foremost pieces of research in this area is the Cambridge Study in Delinquent Development carried out by Cambridge University Institute of Criminology, directed by West. It was a longitudinal study (i.e., followed the subjects over a period of time) on boys from north-east London, who were under scrutiny from the age of 8 until the age of 25. The results of this study have been the material for a number of books dating from 1969. One written by West (1982) draws together all the findings. The survey included a number of factors which are commonly related to criminality, such as parental conflict, separation or instability, unsatisfactory child-rearing (such as neglect, cruelty, incorrect discipline or supervision), pupils who are 'troublesome' at primary school, low income families, large family size (which was found to be a particularly important predictor for those with a number of older siblings), and one or more criminal parents.

All those associated with the study were surprised to find that low IQ seemed as closely related to criminality as these other, more widely accepted, factors. The average IQ of future juvenile delinquents was 95 and that of future non-delinquents 101. This sounds a very small difference, but its significance is masked because it reflects averages. Close examination showed a distinct deficit of delinquent boys in the high IQ group, over 110, and a substantial excess of delinquent boys in the low IQ group, under 90. The far more frequent (almost twice as frequent) appearance of delinquent boys amongst the low scorers was sufficient to allow West to include this as one of the most important predictors of criminality. Even more interestingly, he discovered that low intelligence was particularly closely related to young convictions and recidivism.

Farrington (1992), again working with the Cambridge data, found that a third of those scoring below 90 on a non-verbal intelligence test at ages 8–10 later became convicted juvenile offenders. This is twice as many as those who scored over 90. This may suggest that those with low intelligence are less able to avoid conviction but it was also very closely related to high levels of self-reported delinquency. Low non-verbal ability was linked to low verbal ability and to low school attainment at the age of 11, both of which were linked to juvenile convictions. All of these were also connected to high truancy rates and early school leaving, though they were independent of other social links, such as large family size and low income (Lynam et al. (1993)).

If there seems to be a relationship between criminality and intelligence the nature of that relationship is both interesting and unclear. Apparently these individuals have difficulty in dealing with abstract concepts and reasoning, which reduces their ability to foresee the consequences of any actions either to themselves or to others. They may thus be less likely to be deterred by the possibility of detection, conviction and punishment, or by compassion or empathy for their victims. This lack of intellectual capacity may be linked to a number of factors. First, it could be the result of different or reduced brain functioning. The frontal lobes of the brain control abilities such as abstract reasoning, comprehension of abstract concepts, forward planning and anticipation of problems, self-control—particularly of impulsive and socially unacceptable behaviour—and interest or concentration span. Moffitt and Henry (1989) have suggested that these functions are linked to low intelligence, offending and general antisocial activity, suggesting a causal link with brain dysfunctions (see 7.3.3). Secondly, the abilities set out above are those found to be problematic in cognitive learning (see 10.2.6) and Farrington (1994) suggests that some families are less likely to develop abstract reasoning in their children. He argues that lower class, poorer parents tend to live more for the moment and talk mostly in concrete terms, making them less likely to help a child's abstract reasoning and possibly over-developing a child's impulsive behaviour. A third suggestion (Kohlberg (1976), Kohlberg and Candee (1984) and Smetana (1990)) links lack of intellectual capacity to failure to go beyond the first stage of moral development. In Kohlberg's scheme this is the preconventional stage which he says typifies many criminals (here people put their own desires first, only obeying law because of fear of punishment; it is associated with concrete, one-dimensional thinking). Beyond this are the conventional stage (people learn the law, accept it and obey it because it is law and ought to be followed) and the postconventional stage of a fully developed moral character (the individual can test the law against abstract concepts such as justice, fairness and respect for human beings and their rights).

It is important to note that the link between genetics and intelligence, although not wholly rejected by these studies, is certainly relegated to a less important role than the effects of the environment and of learning on the development of the intellect. This conclusion is very different from that of researchers at the beginning of this century when faced with similar results.

10.1.5 **Race, crime and intellect**

In the United States, this type of research took on a disturbing form, in that it related low intellect to racial differences and then to criminality. This arose from the claim that, on average, blacks scored about 15 points lower than whites in IQ tests. An article by Jensen (1969) claimed to prove that at least 80 per cent of these differences were determined by hereditary rather than environmental factors. This research was drawn on by Robert Gordon (1976). In his study on delinquency prevalence rates (the proportion of a given age cohort that have committed delinquent acts by a specific age) he argued that the prevalence of low IQ for white youths was the same as, or very similar to, the delinquency prevalence rates for that group. He further asserted that the differences in the prevalence for low IQ between blacks and whites equalled the differences in the delinquency prevalence rates for blacks and whites. The rates of delinquency could, he argued, be substantially explained by assuming that all individuals with an IQ below a particular level were criminal. He went on to claim that some minority races such as the Chinese and Jews have similar low economic status to the blacks but have a very low crime rate, often a lower crime rate than the more affluent whites, and that therefore crime rate could not be related to poverty and environment. The conclusions he drew were: that IQ cannot be environmental; it must be hereditary; and low IQ must be related to criminality. His claim is that IQ causes delinquency, not only because it inhibits the ability to learn the socialising element of life but also because, as it is inherited, those with low IQs are going to be reared by parents with low IQ, who are therefore going to be less able to teach the socialising process.

This seems highly plausible, but it needs to be stressed that a large edifice has been built on weak foundations. The little evidence shown is practically untested, and very few control groups are studied. There is, for example, no proof that low IQ delinquents have low IQ parents nor any examination of the possibility that those with high IQ may be delinquent but evade detection or conviction.

A further problem with Gordon's research is the assumption that intelligence is inherited. Many researchers in this area have argued that it is the result of massively inferior environmental conditions of blacks; wide and systematic discrimination, poorer living conditions, lower life expectancies, inadequate diets, bad housing and inferior schooling. To test the veracity of these conflicting claims, Loehlin, Lindzey and Spuhler (1975) tested the IQ of two matched groups—white children in deprived areas and black children in similarly deprived areas. They found that, although the IQ differences were not wholly eradicated, they were substantially reduced. They explained the remaining discrepancy as a result of the discrimination suffered by the black children, whereas Gordon and his followers claim it proves at least some hereditary basis for intellect. Another study looked at black children who, at an early age, had been adopted into white middle-class families (Scarr and Weinberg (1976)). They discovered the mean IQ of these children was 110, which is at least 20 points above the national average for black children. Such studies suggest a strong correlation between environment and IQ: if criminality is related to low IQ it may well be that the environmental factors caused both the low IQ and the criminality.

Caution is still needed. It is easy to leap to strong causal connections from the observation (Jones (1993)) that black people tend to live in areas of social stress with high crime rates, and also tend to be disadvantaged in terms of higher unemployment, lower living standards and greater poverty than whites. But against this is the equally valid observation that Asians suffer on all these counts but have a markedly lower crime rate, lower than for whites. The difference may be explained by a variety of factors: Asians experience greater socialisation within their own community (a powerful control mechanism—see Chapter Thirteen); they have not suffered discrimination as openly and frequently as Afro-Caribbeans; they have been more insular, relying on their own communities for jobs and housing; and they are not as stigmatised by the criminal justice agencies (especially the police) which deal with them in a less biased manner. Though some of these elements have altered in the past few years, degrees of discrimination and bias are significant because they feed feelings of exclusion, anger and resentment (see Smith (1994)). Many of these factors will be considered at points later in this book; what is important here is to understand that the reasons for the higher crime rates of Afro-Caribbeans are very complex. To try to pin it on one factor such as lower IQ is both dangerous and misleading. Besides the points already made, such an approach fails to explain the low crime rates amongst this group earlier in their immigration and the current low crime rates of the older populations of Afro-Caribbeans. In any event, the assertions about lower IQs look less secure against the marked rise in the numbers of Afro-Caribbeans now attending higher education establishments; perhaps all that was needed was reduced discrimination and enhanced encouragement for youngsters in these communities. Such considerations reduce the plausibility of citing low IQ as a cause of criminality or as an explanation for differing crime rates in different communities. More likely are the social conditions and treatment of these groups since their arrival in Britain (for a further discussion see the later chapters in this volume, and see also Gelsthorpe and McWilliam (1993)).

10.1.6 Criticisms on intelligence and criminality

First, it is reasonable to expect that those with a lower IQ are less able to avoid detection. Also, once detected they will be less able to give a good account of their activities, so they are more likely to end up in court and to receive a harsher sentence. It is also worth noting that criminal activity (such as embezzlement and white-collar crimes) which are likely to be mostly committed by individuals with high intelligence are generally less likely either to be discovered, or to form the basis of a prosecution. All these factors may lead to the over-representation of those with low IQs in the official statistics, but cannot explain the similar findings in such self-report studies as the Cambridge Study in Delinquent Development.

Another criticism which has often been made of the IQ theory is that, far from testing innate intelligence or intellect, it assesses the individual's school level, i.e., measures levels of comprehension and vocabulary. The scores would therefore reflect educational attainment or cultural background rather than potential intelligence. If studies test educational attainment, then clearly those will suffer whose education is not as thorough. Some claim that non-verbal studies are therefore better indicators of ability than verbal tests, and some studies have found that delinquents perform better on these tests than on verbal ones. This was not borne out by the Cambridge Study in Delinquent Development, where they obtained the same results from both verbal and non-verbal tests. They also claimed to refute another criticism, namely that delinquents are less motivated in school generally and so would be less motivated to perform well in IQ tests; in their study the boys were generally equally motivated to succeed.

Others allege that IQ tests simply measure class bias. The types of skills which are measured are not objective, but rather represent a cultural skill which is most likely to be held by, and be useful to, a middle-class urban dweller. When Jane Mercier (1972) constructed simple behavioural and practical tasks, such as the ability to tie a shoe lace, to test intelligence, she claimed that the results were different. Those who under the usual IQ tests would be labelled 'low intelligence', often performed better than the normal high performers, and the low IQ lower-class individuals performed better on these tasks than did low IQ middle-class individuals.

There are therefore some inherent problems in making a link between criminality, delinquency and intelligence. The Cambridge study certainly suggests that there may be some link, but it is impossible to assess how direct it is. In any event, it is still possible that both low intellect and criminality are caused by some third factor.

10.1.7 The danger of linking criminality and IQ

The reason for mental deficiency or lower intellectual ability is still not fully understood. Years ago, the reason given was the Devil; a later explanation was heredity, and the modern reason is part heredity and part environmental or social. The move towards hereditary explanations derived from the acceptance of Darwin's theories of evolution. Proof of a link with hereditary factors was said to be obtained from studies such as that of Dugdale (1877) and Goddard (1912), where whole families were studied to discover their hereditary tendencies. All this led to apparent scientific justification for arguments that charitable works for these people were mistaken, since they encouraged them to reproduce and thereby cause a general deterioration of the human race. It was asserted that natural selection should at least be allowed to take its course, and so reduce the number of feeble-minded. Some wanted natural selection to be helped along by placing these inferior people in institutions, segregating them from normal people and not allowing them to breed.

A basis was thus provided for a strong opposition to any form of social welfare, as this would merely perpetuate the survival of lazy, immoral, devious and less intelligent people, slowing down the development of the nation. Only citizens who were hard working, careful and moral should be nurtured. Most countries bowed to this type of argument to a varying extent. The previous chapter referred to various measures which were used to punish and prevent crime. The method most specifically connected with low intelligence was sterilisation.

In America between 1911 and 1930 most states passed laws either permitting, or in certain instances requiring, sterilisation for behavioural traits thought to be hereditary. These laws were used particularly frequently against the feeble-minded and criminal, although they were also used to control alcoholism and certain sexual perversions (see Beckwith (1985)). Under these laws, at least 64,000 people were sterilised, and these sterilisations continued into the 1970s. In Virginia alone between 1927 and 1972 8,000 individuals were sterilised because they were feeble-minded (see Lilly, Cullen and Ball (1989)). Those sterilised in this way were without any means of support or anyone who would provide support. Therefore, it was generally only the feeble-minded poor who were so sterilised. The words of Justice Holmes in the Supreme Court of America when deciding the case of *Buck* v *Bell* (1926) 274 US 200, at 207, are indicative of this train of thought:

We have seen more than once that the public welfare may call upon the best citizens for their lives. It would be strange if it could not call upon those who already sap the strength of the State for these lesser sacrifices, often not felt to be such by those concerned, in order to prevent our being swamped with incompetence. It is better for all the world, if instead of waiting to execute degenerate offspring for crime, or to let them starve for their imbecility, society can prevent those who are manifestly unfit from continuing their kind. The principle that sustains compulsory vaccination is broad enough to cover cutting the fallopian tubes.

In Britain, some sterilisation took place, usually of those in institutions. Some might even say there was a eugenics policy in operation in Britain between 1900 and 1930, but policies as far-reaching as those enunciated in *Buck* v *Bell* (above) were probably never explicitly adopted. It is, however, difficult to ascertain just how many people were sterilized in the early part of this century in Britain, as the official documents recording the numbers and the reasons for sterilisations are contained in a document which will not be available to the public until 2030 (see Robertson (1989), p. 164). It is probably true to say that sterilisation of criminals in this country tended to take place on what the officials like to refer to as a voluntary basis. In this vein, it has sometimes been offered to sex offenders and, in such cases, is not directly connected with IQ.

Although a full eugenics policy was never introduced into Britain, the ideas and arguments which eugenists encompass were well received in theories of penology. Segregation of the unfit, through imprisonment, had the same effect as sterilisation. At the turn of the century there were therefore many calls for long sentences, even of petty offenders. For example, Darwin (1914/15) wrote of persistent petty offenders:

increased periods of detention of habitual criminals would produce both immediate social advantages and ultimate improvements in the racial qualities of future generations, and, if this be the case, the social reformer and the eugenist ought to be able to march together on this path of criminal reform. (p. 212)

This type of attitude led to longer sentences being more readily accepted, possibly more so in the case of the lower IQ criminal. Long sentences have lasted up until the present day in our penal system, although their survival may have a different basis.

In Germany there was a complete and very strong eugenics policy which involved either executing, or at least sterilising anyone who was feeble-minded, criminal or otherwise 'inferior'. Nazi Germany illuminates the very dangerous possibilities of a complete acceptance of theories of the sort outlined above.

Towards the middle of the last century, the reason for lower mental ability moved on again. It became understood that although some severe forms can be inherited (e.g., mongolism or Down's syndrome), most were caused by disease, exposure to certain drugs, brain damage, lack of mental stimulation, malnutrition or other environmental factors. This moved the ideas of sterilisation out of vogue and encouraged concentration on the environmental causes. Acceptance of this might have beneficial consequences, such as both improved living conditions and educational opportunities for those worst off in our society.

However, in the work of Gordon discussed above (10.1.5), with its assumption that intelligence is inherited and that the lower intelligence of blacks explains their higher rates of criminality, there is a tendency to return to the views held earlier this century. If such a shift is associated with a move away from a social welfare policy and towards more stress being placed on self-determination, self-betterment and success, it may indicate some reinstatement of a system of natural selection.

Many liberal commentators detect ominous signs in some recent British cases in this area. In *Re F (Mental Patient: Sterilisation)* [1990] 2 AC 1, the sterilisation of an adult female was considered. The woman had a mental age of about 4, and if she had become pregnant would have been unable to understand what was happening. It was felt that this would be bad for her health and well-being. The case was finally decided upon what were deemed to be the woman's best interests, but certain of the judges made comments which seemed to suggest that the sterilisation should be allowed if it were in the public interest. Some see the inclusion of public interest in such an area as a portent allowing for a return to earlier, insidious types of policies.

Gordon's work raises particular dangers, as it emphasises racial differences in IQs. He asserted that the blacks were less intelligent and committed more crime than the whites. But if one looks back at earlier American studies it was the Italians and other Southern and Eastern European peoples who were seen as the inferior, criminal races. It was then found that these people had an IQ 16 points below the general American population (see Pinter (1923)). These findings were instrumental to the passing of the Immigration Restriction Act of 1924, which controlled the immigration of Eastern Europeans into America partly because these people were thought of as biologically inferior. One of the rationalisations behind the immigration controls was this desire to keep the racial standards high, but there was already substantial evidence that the IQ differences were due to language problems and disappeared after about 20 years in America. This information seems to have been ignored, possibly because the majority wished to protect the economic *status quo* against a large influx of cheap labour.

Even earlier, the Irish had been seen as the criminal and inferior section of American and British society; now it is the blacks. There seems to be a tendency to 'prove' that the poorest groups in a society, especially if they are easily identified by ethnicity or colour, are the most criminal and, according to some studies, the least intelligent. This might more plausibly suggest that criminality and intelligence have similar, environmental causes (see 10.1.5).

Such a claim is borne out by the work of Offord, Poushinsky and Sullivan (1978). Their study suggests that criminality and delinquency are both caused by external factors such as adverse family influences, and that the educational retardation itself is not causally related to criminality. The fact of an environmental cause of low intelligence is lent support by the work of Simons (1978) who discovered that when low IQ, lower-class children were placed in special educational classes they made gains of about 15 points, which would equal out even the worst predicted differences. Simons also claimed that if the IQ tests were carried out on very young children, before school had time to affect them, then the scores of lower-class and middle-class children would be similar. A few years later, once school had affected their relative rates of progression, the lower-class children would appear less intelligent.

From this it can be seen that there are very real dangers in the full acceptance of some of the above theories. These have not deterred Murray and Herrnstein (1994) from suggesting significant links between crime, IQ and race, even arguing that the basis of differences in modern societies is, and should be, intelligence. Of course, it is not the theories themselves which are dangerous, but the use to which they are put. For this reason, particular care is necessary in carrying out and analysing such research, as well as in basing decisions upon it.

10.2 Learning

10.2.1 Introduction

Very few behaviours and actions are actually natural or instinctive; most must be learned. If an opportunity for advancement by criminality were to arise, an individual might well not recognise it, or not know how to take advantage of it, unless they had learned certain behaviours or ways of taking advantage of illegitimate opportunities. Basically, these theories see criminality as normal learned behaviour. Some behaviour is instinctive and is possessed by an individual at birth; the possession of this is determined by biological factors. Learned behaviour depends upon knowledge, skills, habits and responses that have been developed as a result of experience, or of the need to adjust to the environment.

Learning theories and their effects on individual behaviour are not new—one of the first proponents of a learning theory was Aristotle (384–322 BC). His ideas were based upon learning by association. For Aristotle, this meant the association between sensory experiences which were internal to the individual and upon which the outside world worked. The theory of association is still strong, but rather than the association being with internal sensations, it is now argued that it is a response to external stimuli or the association between stimuli.

It is important to note that learning theories are not closely connected with intelligence. Of course, the level of intelligence may affect the ability of a particular individual to learn complex types of behaviour, just as their physical make-up may affect their ability to perform certain activities. Learning theories are not concerned with either of these problems, but with the way in which learning takes place, and what affects the type of behaviour that might be learnt. The main learning theory to be connected with explanations of criminal behaviour is 'differential association', which was expounded by a social learning theorist called Sutherland (1939). This theory will be discussed later. First, it is important to understand some of the basic psychological theories on learning.

10.2.2 Learning structures

The old school of learning, sometimes referred to as the *classical conditioning* or *classical learning* theory, can be characterised by the work of Pavlov (1927). Pavlov noticed that certain external stimuli always produced certain responses, and that these responses seemed to be natural. The example usually chosen is that a dog always salivates when it is given meat, but it does not salivate when presented with most other stimuli, e.g., a bell ringing. Pavlov tried to alter this. He persistently rang a bell when giving the dogs meat and after a time he stopped presenting them with meat and discovered that they still salivated when they heard the bell. By this experiment Pavlov showed that behaviours could be learned by association—the dogs had come to associate the bell with meat, and so the ringing of the bell triggered off a response to the expected stimuli of being fed.

A certain amount of human behaviour may be explained in this way. For example, fear is a natural response in that it is a largely uncontrolled response to certain stimuli which can be quite varied. What an adult learns to fear may be the result of what was associated with that feeling in childhood. If a child fell and hurt himself he may come to fear heights; similarly, if he was punished he may come to fear whatever he was punished for. This might help to explain the use of punishment as a deterrent to certain activity. If a certain activity gives rise to punishment and/or unpleasantness, and so to fear, then the mere thought of the activity might later result in the fear, making it unlikely that the individual will take part in that activity. In the area of crime deterrence a fear response might follow if there was an increased likelihood of detection and/or severe punishment. Alternative strategies might include reducing the opportunities for criminal activity or for criminal activity which would not attract detection.

This type of learning is useful to our understanding of some behaviour, but it is of limited use because the individual is passive. The subject learns or is conditioned to correct its behaviours in response to the environment, and its learning can only take place because of the existence of certain innate reflexes which trigger off some responses, which could then later be triggered off by an associated different stimulus. Of much more interest is operant conditioning, which has also been referred to as instrumental conditioning.

In *operant conditioning* the individual interacts with the environment and thereby learns what behaviour will bring about the desired end. Skinner is probably the best known, though not the first, proponent of this type of theory, which is probably one of the most prominent learning theories in psychology today (Skinner (1938) but for a modern discussion see O'Donohue and Kitchener (1999)). Its basis is that behaviour is learnt through the use of rewards and punishments. Behaviour which is rewarded will be reinforced and become more frequent in order to maximise the rewards, and behaviour which is punished or which meets with aversive consequences will be discouraged. Behaviour changes to secure more of what is liked, and less of what is disliked. Thus far, classical and operant learning are very similar, but in operant learning behaviour is not just affected by the environment, but operates on the environment to attain various ends. So, although people may learn that certain behaviour has unpleasant connotations, they may learn to avoid the unpleasant consequences whilst still enjoying the initial behaviour. A child might learn that stealing biscuits brings an unpleasant result, and so possibly stops the theft. The child may discover that by stealing in a different way, when everyone is out, it is not likely to be caught. The child thus learns that it might be able to gain the desired end and also avoid the unpleasantness by altering its behaviour to make the desired result most likely and the punishment least likely. If the risk seems worth it, the child may continue with the unacceptable activity. This theory is based on what the individual finds rewarding or unpleasant, and assumes that everybody seeks to maximise rewards and minimise punishment. Note that what is considered to be pleasant or unpleasant differs from person to person, but neither of these theories seems to assume that the individual has any clear understanding of what is learnt and why. Even from this brief discussion there are clearly two factors which limit its usefulness in tackling crime: first, there is little cognitive thought attributed to the subjects so free will is almost entirely absent from the theory; secondly, and far more important, is the lack of understanding about how this conditioning works, which makes it more difficult to alter unacceptable behaviour on the part of an individual.

Cognitive learning is rather different from either of the above, each of which was based on responses. Cognitive learning considers the ability to understand. It might explain how people understand concepts and solve problems, and also how they arrange the information they obtain from response theories so as to give their behaviour meaning. It includes an understanding of the physical world as well as learning and shaping attitudes and beliefs about that world. In particular, it involves learning about other people, their behaviour and how we interact with them. It thus includes learning respect for the feelings of others, learning to take responsibility, learning to make rational choices about behaviour, learning to control impulsive desires and behaviours, learning to develop powers of moral reasoning, and learning how to solve interpersonal problems.

Programmes intended to produce behavioural changes using cognitive ideas usually need to deal with or focus on a number of aspects of behaviour and are referred to as *multimodal programmes*. They work on areas such as information processing, problem solving, skills training, social skills training, emotional control training and moral reasoning. If only one of these areas is worked on, any new behaviours are unlikely to be sustained outside the programme environment. Very often programmes are built up to act on or help to deal with particular issues in criminal behaviour, e.g., Aggression Replacement Training (Goldstein et al. (1998)) but these will normally use *multimodal programmes* to address the issue. This type of programme or aspects of it are central to the new What Works strategy of the probation service. There are indications that they may be fairly effective but they need to be operated by trained professionals and, the recipient needs to be freely compliant. Where there is coercion they are less likely to be effective and therefore their use in the criminal justice system, particularly with any incarcerated groups may be less likely to succeed.

These learning processes can take place through a number of different modes. In the above techniques, the learning was portrayed as taking place through direct experiences, but learning can also be observational or based on models. That is, learning can take place by watching the behaviour of others and seeing whether it is rewarded or punished. This type of learning is thought to be most powerful for children, who may model their behaviour on family, teachers or peer groups. In adolescence, the peer group is probably the strongest model, and the effects of this are discussed in Chapter Twelve.

Generally, for a particular type of behaviour to become part of a pattern it needs to fit in with the attitudes of the individual or the attitudes which fit the behaviour which needs to be learnt. Such attitudes are learnt from interactions with others. Most people act within what they consider to be acceptable: a strong negative attitude to crime is thus less likely to lead to violations than an ambivalent or positive attitude.

The effects of behavioural learning are often thought to be related to the environment in which individuals live, and to their social groupings, and it is at this point that Sutherland's theory becomes important.

10.2.3 Differential association

This term is inextricably linked with the name of Edwin H. Sutherland (1939). It is also clearly set out in Sutherland and Cressey (1978), which retains the basic theory but makes certain clarifying alterations. Sutherland was concerned with white-collar crime (for that part of his work, see Chapter Three). He attempted to explain why and how the upper classes turn to criminality, and to show that the same factors acted upon them as upon most other criminals. It was therefore an explanation which both he and others have used to explain criminality generally. In fact, some supporters of the theory believe it explains all criminal behaviour. This claim and others will be discussed in the consideration and evaluation of the theory.

Differential association is a theory of learning. Fundamentally, it asserts that crime is learnt by association with others. It has been said to have been conceived out of a refinement of the work of G. Tarde (1843–1904). Tarde's theory was one of imitation, stating first, that all men imitate each other.

Although Sutherland never gave much acknowledgement to Tarde, it seems he probably used this theory of imitation, expanded it, refined it and made it more popular. Instead of imitation, his theory was based upon a wider idea involving all the normal mechanisms involved in the learning process. He argued that all behaviour was learnt, and to decide whether someone would be criminal you needed to split criminal behaviour from non-criminal behaviour. The central hypothesis is that crime is not unique or invented by each criminal separately but, like all other forms of human behaviour, it is learnt from direct contact with other people. This leads into the second hypothesis: that behavioural learning takes place through personal contacts with other people. He does not rule out the possible influences of media, but claims that these are very much secondary to the direct personal interactions.

The learning takes place in small informal group settings, and develops from the collective experience and personal interaction as well as from particular situations. A third assertion is that the learning involves both the techniques for committing the offences and the motives, drives, rationalisations, values and attitudes for its committal, i.e., why it is committed. Finally, whether a person takes part in criminal activities depends on the amount of contact they have with criminal activities or with those who support or are sympathetic towards criminal activities. Non-criminal input or definitions generally come from law-abiding citizens and those who reinforce such behaviour, both by their actions and their words. Criminal input or definitions come from criminal offenders and those who may verbally approve of such behaviour, or those who may verbally disapprove of crime but who are nevertheless willing to participate in certain types of criminal activity. The attitudes and definitions are not as clear-cut as this, and there are often mixed emotions. For example, parents and others close to an individual may approve of, or at least not disapprove of, certain types of theft; to feed the hungry, to clothe children, or from certain types of victims like large stores or large employers. They might teach sympathy to these whilst still teaching that theft is generally wrong.

All of these differing and sometimes conflicting definitions are experienced, and will lead to criminality if the individual is more exposed to views which are supportive of crime than to views which are against it. This is the central idea of the theory, and basically the idea can be summed up in the following words:

A person becomes criminal if there is an excess of definitions favourable to the violation of the law over definitions unfavourable to violation of the law.

The criminal activity may also be affected by the frequency, duration, priority and intensity of the definitions either for law-abiding or law-breaking behaviour. The longer and more frequently one is exposed to a particular type of behaviour or attitude, the more effect it is likely to have. The stress on priority is intended to denote that the earlier the attitude is experienced, the more forcefully it is likely to affect later behaviour. Finally, intensity has to do with the prestige of the person portraying a particular type of behaviour and the emotional reactions related both to the source and the content of the information. To an extent, this may explain why policemen and prison officers do not generally become criminal despite being in constant and close contact with criminals—they hold them in very low regard, and therefore only wish to learn from them how to remain as little like them as possible. Similarly, if a particular input brought with it great sorrow or great joy, this might affect the way in which it effects the learning process.

It is important to note that Sutherland does not consider that offenders are driven by different goals and desires from non-criminals, but rather that they choose different means of achieving those ends. Criminality may be entered into for financial gain or happiness, but most people manage to pursue financial gain and possibly even happiness in law-abiding jobs. To explain criminal behaviour by reference to its ends is therefore futile, as most non-criminal behaviour is driven by the same desires or ends. It was the reason for choosing the particular method of reaching the end that was important.

Since its inception, the theory of differential association has been modified and changed in order to widen or to narrow its scope, depending on the intentions of the writer. For example, Glaser (1956) suggested that criminal learning was not only, or even primarily, based on associations between individuals, but involved identification with criminal roles and therefore a desire to emulate them.

10.2.4 Evaluation

Criticisms concerning this theory abound, and only the most important will be dealt with here. The first few are intended to refute claims that it can be used to explain all criminality. Thus, it has been argued that it is impossible for this theory to explain the origins of criminality, because if the behaviour does not already exist, it cannot be learned by a second person (see Jeffery (1959)). Secondly, there are new and very inventive crimes which occasionally appear; certainly the mechanics for these could not have been learnt by differential association, although of course the desires and motives behind such crimes may have been learnt (see Parker (1976)). Thirdly, it does not explain the criminality of those who have never been subjected to criminals or to people who would hold criminal ideas. Such people could not have learnt criminality by interpersonal contact; if it was learnt at all, it would probably have been from the media, which Sutherland relegates to a relatively unimportant position in the learning process. One answer to the last point is that criminality may arise from having observed parents, or others close to the child. These, despite perhaps strongly teaching the child that, say, theft is wrong, none the less commit some dishonest acts, such as not telling a shop assistant that they have been given the wrong change; or while renouncing violence they take part either in domestic violence, or use overtly violent methods of punishment. In any event, as Wilson and Herrnstein (1985) note, the theory cannot explain why some individuals might learn criminal behaviour from a peer group while failing to learn non-criminal behaviour from a family (or *vice versa*).

A further criticism is that this approach cannot explain irrational, impulsive, opportunist or passionate criminals, who would then be acting due to one of those factors rather than as a result of anything they have learnt. The implication is that there are probably some crimes which could never be explained by differential association, which cannot therefore, constitute an all-consuming theory. Most of the criticisms have not been verified, and of course they do not necessarily bring the theory as a whole into question.

It is virtually impossible to measure the impact of differential association as an explanation of criminal behaviour, as the key concepts cannot be reduced to quantitative elements. It is, for example, impossible to make any objective measurement of whether there has been an 'excess' of definitions favourable to law-breaking of any particular type and for any particular person. It is hard enough, after the event, to try to reconstruct a person's thoughts and intentions immediately before they commit a crime, but impossible to go through their whole life and assess the effects on their actions of each input, both for and against crime committal. The difficulties are compounded when Sutherland attributes different weighting to certain material, and to factors such as intensity and priority. Most importantly, it is sometimes difficult to tell whether certain feelings and motives existed before a particular relationship was begun or only arose afterwards, e.g., did membership of a gang or group come about because of like thinking at the time, or has membership of the group given rise to that type of behaviour being learnt. Possibly even more telling is the fact that one can never be sure exactly what is a 'definition favourable to law-breaking', nor what is an 'excess' of such definitions. How much more of one than the other does it take for that activity to take over? Why, even if it could safely be asserted that an individual has an excess of definitions favourable to law-breaking, are most of that person's activities lawful?

Despite these great drawbacks, there have been various studies which go some way towards supporting a causal link between differential association and criminality (e.g., Jensen (1972) and McCarthy (1996)). In most of these studies the main idea was supported in a fairly basic sense, but the research generally showed that differential association was only one of several causes of criminality. Factors such as the effects of a broken home, or of lax supervision within the family, or general emotional insecurity, were also present. Sutherland claims that what differential association helps to explain is why some people who suffer these other factors are not criminal whilst others are.

A further criticism is that differential association fails to account for the individual in the calculation. It seems to assume that these people are vessels into which is poured the definitions for and against law violation: their eventual behaviour is then decided by the balance. This allows very little room for the individual to assess these influences. Differential association does recognise some sifting, especially in the 'intensity', but it allows no room for free will, the personality of the individual, or for differences in types of response. Sutherland claimed that the response of each individual to a particular set of circumstances would depend upon the learning process already encountered. In some situations it is unclear whether it is a law-abiding or law-breaking situation, and it may depend upon the response of the individual. For example, finding a purse full of money might receive the response of an opportunity to better one's position, or could provoke the response of an opportunity to do someone a good deed. The way the person responds may affect the lesson learnt in that instance. Sutherland says that such responses depend upon earlier learning and would trace this all the way back to birth, to zero learning. Others would argue that there may be other factors concerned in this response.

Lastly, the theory is criticised because it does not explain why one person has one set of associations and another person has a different set, although the two may come from similar backgrounds. Sutherland considered this to be a red herring, and asserted that the important point was what was learnt from the associations, not why those associations occur. However, a secondary theory which he expounded, differential social organisations, may help to explain these differences. The theory of *differential social organisations* argues that every social setting, whether criminal or not, is organised. The likelihood of criminality is influenced by the social organisation of things like norms, values and acceptable behaviour. Such social organisation makes it more or less likely for inhabitants of a particular area to come into contact with definitions favourable to law-breaking. In this way it affects the individual's associations.

The numerous criticisms seem to suggest that the theory is of little value. The inability to test it, and the difficulty in applying it to particular circumstances, do reduce its utility. None the less, there are areas where it might be particularly pertinent. The most important is in the area in which Sutherland first expounded the theory—white-collar or corporate crime. As Steven Box (1983) has suggested, many businessmen may learn to, and be willing to, commit crimes to enhance the company where they would never consider other forms of criminality. It would seem absurd that a hitherto law-abiding individual arrives in a corporation and suddenly, for no reason, begins committing crimes. Far more likely is the idea that the individual slowly learns the 'realities of business', one of which may be that certain laws can be broken for the well-being of the firm. Furthermore, promotion procedures may reinforce such learning by rewarding those who internalise these 'realities'. There is little deterrent for such behaviour when neither the individual's peer group nor the wider society are likely to condemn it, or even hear of it or of similar activities (see Slapper and Tombs (1999) and Croall (2001)). For a fuller discussion of this, see Conklin (1989) and Box (1987).

Braithwaite (1988) and Fisse and Braithwaite (1993) proposed a system—reintegrative shaming—of crime control and punishment which seems to be at least partially built on Sutherland's ideas of differential association. In reintegrative shaming the key to altering future behaviour is to shame offenders, but to ensure that they are also provided with the means and the commitment to be accepted back into society as law-abiding persons. Basically the offender should be made aware of the effects of his or her actions, be held accountable and, possibly through restitution, be able to undo or make good the problem. This is usually mooted to occur in victim–offender mediation/conferencing schemes, which (see Chapter Two) have received considerable backing and have proved to be supportive of victims in some cases, especially as restitution payments have tended to be fairly reliably paid. They have arguably (Snare (1995)) been less useful for offenders since they seem not to have had an impact on rates of recidivism.

10.2.5 Differential reinforcement theory

This builds on differential association but includes all the elements of reinforcement and punishment which are central to operant learning, which argues that most behaviour is learnt. Behaviour will be repeated when the positive reinforcers outweigh the negative reinforcers and the frequency will depend on the differential between these two. Clearly this includes taking account of all the positive aspects to which crime may give rise. These include the external gains such as the obvious financial and material gain as well as the less obvious reinforcement from peer groups either because they reward crime *per se* or because the gains to which the crime gives rise enhance the status of the individual. They also include internal gains such as the feelings of power, autonomy, etc.: there is some evidence to suggest that in many people there is a physiological process which occurs in the brain when a risky and often difficult task is undertaken and which acts as a positive reinforcer of that behaviour (Gove and Wilmoth (1990)). The suggestion is that there is an '. . . internal biological system that rewards operant behaviours, and that this system does *not* simply reflect external reinforcement processes' (Gove and Wilmoth (1990), p. 263). The neurological 'high' produced by risky and difficult tasks is thought to be associated with the dopamine synapse (the same brain functioning associated with amphetamine, cocaine and heroin use) which when activated gives a good feeling. The strength of this effect varies between people, which would partly explain why an external positive reinforcer is enough for one person to commit an offence but not for another: the stronger this neurological effect the more likely one is to commit crimes to experience the rush. Negative reinforcers are also important. Examples of external negative reinforcers may be the possibility of arrest, loss of liberty, fear of injuring someone or oneself, fear of being ostracised by family and friends. Unfortunately such effects are often blunted when such crimes are rarely reported (Tombs and Whyte (2000)). Where there are media reports the stress is, they argue, often to attack the State for making it more difficult for legitimate businesses to function. For example, they quote headlines in tabloids following the e-coli outbreaks in Lanarkshire in 1997 (which had resulted in deaths) saying 'Butchers Could Go Bust in Food Safety Clampdown' (*Sun*, 9 April 1997) and 'Butchers Face Closedown Under New Rules' (*Daily Telegraph*, 9 April 1997). Although Levi (2001) notes that some such crimes are not so generously reported, the overall impression is that negative reinforcers would be less likely to influence such potential offenders. In addition there is the possibility of internal negative reinforcers, examples of which may be the production of adrenalin and other chemicals referred to in Chapter Seven. Clearly in any one individual the ways in which these elements may interact are very complex. For an example see Hollin (1992), p. 56.

This theory suffers from at least one very basic problem: it is tautological. The argument is that behaviour is repeated only if there is strong positive reinforcement for it; but the strong positive reinforcement is recognised only because of the repetition. In any event, behaviour and learning are complex concepts and it is difficult to pinpoint which events are links to, or 'cause', what behaviour. It seems almost impossible to break out of this circle: that does not necessarily undermine the claim that it has an effect on the cause of crime, but it does question the proof of that connection. As will be seen later this may be dealt with if rehabilitative techniques are successful.

10.2.6 Social learning theory and cognitive social learning theories

Social learning theory is an extension of differential reinforcement theory in that it builds on the operant learning experience and adds cognitive experiences and learning to the equation. Its most well known proponent is Albert Bandura (see especially 1973, 1977 and 1986). There are many facets to this theory, which is one of the most complex criminological theories. The motivation associated with the theory includes the reinforcements connected with the operant learning theory as well as reinforcement gained from watching others (vicarious), and the sense of pride and achievement in what we do (self-reinforcement). The basis of the theory is that the learned behaviour is a combination of the physical acts and how to perform them (skills) and the attitudes and mental understanding necessary to the behaviour (including social skills, moral considerations and choice). Criminal behaviour can be learnt through practice, as in operant learning, or through watching the environment in which one lives, the activities of friends, family, neighbours, teachers etc., as well as in socially constructed environments such as books, magazines, television and films. In an interesting piece of research involving interviews with convicted female offenders, Giordano and Rockwell (2000) build up a picture of how exposure to antisocial activities or definitions affects chronic delinquent behaviour among females. There is no reason why these findings should not be equally relevant to males. A few of the elements of the theories mentioned above will be considered here.

In order to perform a crime one must have the physical skill for the necessary tasks. These motor skills tend to be learnt from watching, or being taught by, others. Their presence or absence often dictates the type of crime to be entered into rather than whether a crime will occur. Bandura (1973 and 1977) bases much discussion on this idea of modelling and notes that whether it leads to criminal activity will depend on the message behind the behaviour as well as the behaviour itself. The physical attributes of the offender are also significant: constant aggressive models will not transform the behaviour of a physically weak person unless they are also given a way of carrying out the violence, such as a gun.

The level of social skills which individuals have learnt may be connected with the amount of crime they perform. Each person needs to learn how to understand both linguistic and symbolic communication, but some are never, or are insufficiently, taught by their parents or peers, or have been slow to acquire such skills. Whatever the reason, this situation has been linked to criminality, but whether that link is causal or not is still unclear (see Gaffney and McFall (1981)). Much of the research has been carried out on young offenders but is generally inconclusive: there seem to be stronger, though still not conclusive, links between lack of social skills and rape; but the strongest and almost irrefutable links are found between lack of social skills and child sexual abuse (see Hollin (1992)). Linked to this is the ability to assess and resolve social problems in socially acceptable ways. Slabby and Guerra (1988) suggest that criminals learn fewer solutions to interpersonal problems and often fall back on verbal or physical aggression to resolve difficulties.

Offenders usually need to be in a particular frame of mind for criminal behaviour to take place—this involves elements such as attitude, moral standards, feelings for and about other people, and ideas of responsibility, blame or control. Attitude is learnt from others; the esteem with which the messenger is regarded will affect whether the message is believed and learnt. Some have associated a low level of ability for moral reasoning with criminal activity, but this is not necessarily so (see Hollin (1992)). Thus, although most people would consider theft unacceptable, they may have fewer inhibitions about stealing small items from work; although killing is unacceptable, soldiers can be trained to kill in defined situations. Similarly, people label something differently in order to absolve them of the need to feel moral guilt: a terrorist is punishing the enemy, a burglar is carrying out a job. These euphemisms remove the problems to which full moral reasoning capabilities might otherwise give rise (Bandura (1986)).

There is also comparative moral reasoning: people may excuse their own lapses of conduct if they are aware of more heinous acts by others which have not been punished or not severely punished. They may see white-collar criminals go very lightly punished for stealing large amounts of money and therefore consider the small amounts they have taken as unimportant. Attached to this is a desire to believe that their acts are not very harmful by saying that the victim can well do without it, particularly easy if it is a large corporation or a rich individual, or someone covered by insurance. Offenders may also need not to empathise with their victims. This may involve putting the victims into a group with a derogatory label, often racial, or belittling them personally, e.g., 'He's an idiot' or 'She does not deserve x' (see Bandura (1977) and Kaplan and Arbuthnot (1985)). In other cases offenders see their actions as controlled by forces outside their control (Hollin (1992)). They often blame the victim: for example, in a personal attack, 'He should have given me what I wanted', or in rape cases, 'She was asking for it' and 'She led me on', and in property offences 'He should have been more careful where he left the car'.

Lastly, there is the question of rational choice, which some view as a separate theory (Cornish and Clarke (1987)) and others as part of the cognitive social learning theory (Akers (1990)). Rational choice assumes that there is a possibility of committing a crime, an opportunity, and then postulates that the offender weighs up the benefits and the dangers and makes a rational decision whether to commit the crime. Those who see rational choice as a distinct theory argue that social learning theory is largely deterministic: that is, the individual learns and the resultant behaviour is largely determined by that learning. Others argue that the learning processes outlined above merely provide tools and that it is then up to the individual how and when to apply these tools.

Learning theories have problems; there is always an element of tautology as well as many unproven and possibly unprovable relationships. Nonetheless, as will be seen in 10.2.8, the ideas set out here may be useful in designing certain strategies for preventing criminal behaviour.

10.2.7 Media and crime

In any discussion of learnt behaviour the effects of media images need to be considered, especially television and films (here this area will be referred to as TV). The effects seem particularly obvious in relation to learning concerned with observation or modelling but can also be apparent in moral and other aspects of cognitive learning. The assertion is that humans learn from the screen in the same way that they learn from face-to-face interactions. Where a link is said to exist between criminality and the media it is usually perceived as influencing violent behaviour, particularly in the young, or sexual offences where the claim is that pornographic literature and movies reinforce both the normality of the feelings and the acceptability of the activity. Here we will be concerned mainly with its effects on violence.

The claim is that TV teaches methods and tactics of violence, and shows how aggressive behaviour can be rewarding. People may imitate the behaviour they see on the screen or, by seeing a lot of screen violence, become desensitised and thus less inhibited, about using violence in their own lives. In evidence to the Broadcasting Group of the House of Lords, Sims and Gray (1993) listed more than 1,000 studies which had linked exposure to media violence with aggressive behaviour. More recently Petley and Barker (1997) came to a similar conclusion after analysing much of the available literature. In April 1994, 25 leading psychologists, psychiatrists and child care experts supported a paper written by Professor Elizabeth Newson which posited a connection between criminal violence and media violence and called for a restriction on the availability of 'video nasties', although no new data were provided (Newson (1994)). She makes a further interesting point: the amount spent on advertising shows that most corporations believe images to be effective in persuading people to behave differently but misses the fact that these images may impact differently on people's minds. A common weakness is that none of these studies explains how the learning is taken in nor the fact that 99 per cent of those who watch screen violence do not become violent. It may be that those who are already aggressive get their activities reinforced and learn new methods of carrying out violence. But Howitt (1998) questions even this copycat activity in his very full consideration of the link between crime and the media.

In any event, others have denied such a link, or say that the correlation is much more complex than the above suggest. Messner (1986), much to his own surprise, discovered that exposure to TV was inversely related to rates of violent crime. Hagell and Newbury (1993) questioned the suggestion of a link between violent media images and criminality, after finding that persistent offenders do not watch more violence either in films or on the television than their non-criminal counterparts. However, the utility of this research for the immediate issue is diminished because they did not look specifically at very violent acts. Bailey (1990) studied the effects of media presentation of capital punishment in USA and discovered that it acted neither as a deterrent nor as a brutalising agent. The German Society for Media Research (VFM) (1994) exposed 500 individuals to violence in both newsreels and drama, and interim results suggest: that increased media violence led to reductions in aggressive behaviour but to increased fear of aggression and to an increased likelihood that people would sympathise with the victim; that social tolerance towards friends was marginally increased; that there was an adverse effect on stress management; and lastly that the effects differed with age, older people being more horrified by the violence, whereas younger viewers were more affected by the situation and whether there was a negative value placed on the violence they were watching (see Lewis and Von Gamm (1994)). If the value placed on violence and other criminality is more important than the fact of the violence or criminality itself then the trend towards more complex moral and social forms in which it is depicted, as noted in Reiner et al. (2001), may in part cause the problem. This suggests that the context of the violence is essential to the effect (see also 10.2.6).

Whatever the evidence, there is clearly a willingness on the part of the public, the press and even professionals to accept a link between screen violence and criminality. In the Bulger trial when two very young boys killed a toddler, Morland J, without any evidence to support his assertion, stated that 'It is not for me to pass judgment on the boys' upbringings, but I suspect that exposure to violent video films may in part be an explanation.' This was seized on by the press, anxious for something to blame, as more or less positive proof, though none has ever been provided in this case. Press presentations implying clear links between screen violence and criminal behaviour, especially violent behaviour, are not uncommon: the press linked at least ten murders to Oliver Stone's film *Natural Born Killers*, with reports such as: 'Two young men have murdered four people—including three pensioners—in a real-life imitation of a brutal new Hollywood blockbuster' (*Sunday Mirror*, 11 September 1994). Again, these assertions, although making good stories, were unfounded. As was reported by the British Board of Film Censors in 1994, in all bar one of the cases the leader in the activities had already served a prison sentence for serious acts of violence, including, in three cases, murder (one had also been in a mental institution). In the other case the intention to kill had been stated to a friend many months earlier and the murderer had already sourced guns. No links to that film or any other have ever been proven (see Howitt (1998), ch. 6).

From these brief and very selected reports it is clear that there is much disagreement about the effects of violence in the media. There are even stronger doubts (Wilson and Herrnstein (1985)) about any causal links. If the German research is to be believed media violence does not increase violence; indeed, it may actually have a therapeutic effect. It has similarly been argued (Sparks (1983, 1992 and 2001) and Reines et al. (2001)) that violent crime fiction actually reassures most audiences by portraying the victory of the good detective or the police over evil. It has tended to reinforce moral order and send the (mostly) misleading message that punishment will follow criminality. Harbord (1996) argues that the problem may not be the level of violence in the newer Hollywood output, but rather the lack of a clear moral message—everyone seems (relatively) bad and there is no-one to restore order and ensure justice is done (see also Reiner et al. (2001)). Altogether it could be that TV teaches methods of violence to those who are already susceptible to it and reinforces attitudes supportive of violence, but it may not go further than that. It is a fiercely disputed area amongst behavioural theorists.

These discussions almost always take place in the context of whether to censor such material. Because any benefits which may accrue from censorship have to be balanced against the loss of liberty which censorship involves, it is necessary to consider the size of the problem. Even if we assume some causative effect between violent crime and violence in the media, the level of increase is likely to be very low. Most studies, even if they found increased aggression, did not discover increased criminal violence: individuals may stop short of translating increased feelings of aggression into criminal violence. It seems that the number likely to commit criminal violence is likely to be very low and, if the German research is correct, restricted to those less capable of cognitive reasoning. The effects of the actions of this small number may still be appalling but they have to be weighed against the interference with liberty involved in preventing access to materials. Given the unlikelihood of decisive proof, the decision will come down to balancing benefits against harm or, more realistically, the political expediency of the situation. The views of those who may influence the direction of political expediency may themselves be fed by the news-media presentation of the arguments and issues, in particular very isolated cases like that of James Bulger where a wholly unproven link was suggested and planted in the minds of the public as the explanation for this otherwise seemingly inexplicable behaviour. Under this pressure political expediency led the government to pass s. 89 of the Criminal Justice and Public Order Act 1994, requiring the British Board of Film Classification to take account (amongst other aspects) of the psychological impact of videos on viewers, especially children, and to consider the possibility that they might lead them to behave in a manner harmful to society. This gives Britain the most powerful film censorship in Europe in formal terms, although its application is more ambiguous. Whether this is judged as acceptable and to be welcomed largely depends on subjective value judgments which may have little connection with the evidence of 'scientific' studies. A more fundamental problem arises if, as many consider (Harbord (1996)), the new violence in films (and other art forms) largely reflects the reality of contemporary society: censoring the arts will not on its own alter social realities.

10.2.8 Practical implications for learning theories

The techniques and methods of learning theories can be used to re-train criminals in a more acceptable behavioural pattern. This may include teaching them some or all of the following: law-abiding attitudes and emotions; greater interactive or social skills; acceptable types of behaviour; acceptable reactions to certain stimuli which they may encounter; and life skills so they are more able to cope with everyday problems such as finding and keeping a job. The effectiveness of such learning depends on a number of factors, including the skill of the teacher and the willingness of the criminal to learn, but also including: the need to classify offenders by the risk posed in order to focus intensive programmes on high-risk offenders; highly structured programmes to address a distinct problem, e.g., anger management; to target the factors which directly affect the behaviour (antisocial attitudes, drug dependency, cognitive or social deficit); to respond to the learning needs of the offenders; to ensure that staff are motivated and supported; the use of skills-based approaches to address problem-solving and social interaction while also challenging belief structures and attitudes; and the programme should be based in the community. For a full discussion of these see Vennard and Hedderman (1998) and Hollin (1995).

A qualification of this method of countering criminality is that when the learning is only partially successful, it may lead to a hightened ability to avoid detection rather than a true change in behaviour. The individual may appear to learn by giving acceptable responses and the absence of further convictions might suggest success, but as the crimes would still occur, there is no real benefit to society. For real success, the individual has to internalise all aspects of the training, and be able to use a trained response when the stimulus is different from the training environment. This indicates understanding and a change of attitude. The implication is that for success, learning theories have to be applied by skilled staff to a willing individual over an extended period of time (Roberts (1995)).

Success also depends on whether the programme for treatment is designed for an individual, or a small group with very similar problems, rather than used very generally. Applied especially to high-risk offenders, such programmes could provide a positive and structured removal from society. Even so, such programmes would need to alter not only the outward behaviour but also the cognitive learning of factors such as attitude, values, self-control, social problem-solving, and moral reasoning. Hollin (1992, 1995 and 2002) considers that such treatment is more likely to succeed if it is given in the community rather than in institutions. In this class he includes ideas such as probation, diversionary projects including intermediate treatment and reparation, more positive encouragement at school, and parent management training at the important level of the family. This has a difficult message in relation to offenders that some might class as dangerous: the public may want dangerous offenders removed from society in order to protect others, whilst the treatment most likely to succeed and render these individuals safe needs to be given in the community. One possible compromise is to require criminals to spend sufficient time in prison to mark the damage caused by their criminality, and then for them to be considered for therapy in the community. With care in the choice of persons it might prove to be a positive way forward, especially since most of these people are eventually released into the community: if there is a real possibility of changing their behaviour this would render them safer once this time arises. Such possibilities seemed to open up with the setting up of Multi-Agency Public Protection Arrangements (MAPPA) in 2000 to deal with danger faced by the public, and the establishment of Multi-Agency Public Protection Panels (MAPPPs). The latter were to identify the most risky or dangerous offenders and manage their safe existence in the community. However, any expectations that they might work with the individual to alter their behaviour is ill founded: their function is to manage the risk. A real opportunity to reduce danger seems to be being missed (for further discussion see Chapter 8).

A specific example might indicate the possibilities. Anger management or reduction programmes often work best in groups but can be applied one to one. They begin with cognitive preparation or opening the individual to the problem area, encouraging them to analyse their own anger, identify what triggers it off, and to recognise these situations. They are then introduced to skills to deal with the problem situations they have identified. The skills taught will depend on the offender but may include relaxation, better communication or problem-solving. Finally the idea is to allow them to apply these skills in practice, in controlled situations— usually through role-play. In these the trigger situations are simple to begin with but get progressively more provocative as the training progresses. This type of approach has been very successful and can be altered for different situations. For example, in tackling domestic violence—male aggression focused on a partner— the most successful approaches have been found to be those which force the men to recognise and deal with their feelings of power and control over women. These new cognitive behavioural approaches have been found to be more successful than previous psychodynamic approaches to childhood problems (Dobash and Dobash (1999)). The greater success emerges especially strongly when information from the women who have been victims of this violence is taken into account, rather than only measuring by reconviction rates (see Dobash et al. (1999)). The government document written by the Women's Unit, *Living without Fear—An Integrated Approach to Tackling Violence against Women*, included this as one of the measures to make women safer from male violence.

In fact much of the work being done and planned in the new community rehabilitation orders and the mixed community punishment and rehabilitation order is intended to use these programmes. It is still early in their operation but a number of factors can be noted. The schemes are generally soundly based on proven successful research techniques which use broadly cognitive-behavioural methods to provide opportunities to reflect on past acts and to learn new thinking and behaviour patterns. They focus on aspects which contributed to offending, are structured and require active input from the offender who is not permitted to remain passive. In most areas the staff delivering the courses are fully trained. There are a few issues which may cause them to be less successful than might otherwise have been the case. The Home Office insistence on centrally accredited schemes may be a limitation: standardisation may not be the best way to deliver success in all areas or for all offenders. Such rigidity might cause particular difficulties in rural areas where group programmes might be unable to fill places, nor is such an approach likely to suit all ethnic groups. Besides the prescriptive and managerial tendencies, the increased punitive nature of the new community orders may also reduce the necessary willing participation and so reduce their effectiveness. In line with the recommendations of the Halliday Report 2001 The Criminal Justice Act 2003 (ss. 181 and 182 for custodial sentences of under 12 months and Part 12 chapter 5 deals with dangerous offenders) will make similar programmes a requirement for those who have just been released from prison in an attempt to help them to address their criminalogenic behaviour patterns.

10.3 **Conclusion**

Sutherland's theory is based on the idea that criminality is the normal result of normal learned behaviour. Just as some people learn non-criminal behaviour, so others learn criminal behaviour. In the learning process he says that the individual learns ideas, desires, motives, morality, goals, and whether types of behaviour are acceptable in particular social settings, as well as learning methods of carrying out those ideas or obtaining the goals. This is a wide-ranging theory of criminology, and although it cannot explain all crime, the learning process must play some part in almost all activity.

By making learning so central to the process such writers have claimed that those with low learning capacity are unable to grasp the moral and other elements which are so essential to law-abiding behaviour. This allows them to conclude that those of low intelligence are more likely to be criminal. Against this it can be said that social learning is not simply dependent on innate intellectual ability: behavioural learning is affected to a far greater extent by the social setting, social interactions, personal associations and the environment, than it is by innate intelligence.

The learning theories can thus have a powerful input to rehabilitation and make a positive contribution to the problem of criminality. To be effective, practitioners of this approach need to be able to interact with others concerned in the criminal justice process: the judiciary and the probation and prison services might consult with them more openly and more frequently. Any system which might result in a diminution in criminality needs to be cultivated. Nonetheless it must be emphasised that the approach is not a panacea: its use needs to be confined to those situations and individuals where it seems most likely to give positive results, which might include some of those classed as dangerous in the discussion in Chapter Nine as seems set to occur under the Criminal Justice Act 2003.

Although learning theories may have this positive aspect to offer the criminal justice system, they may also cause restrictive practices to be forced even on the law-abiding, e.g., censorship of the media, which as shown above, is difficult to justify on the basis of harm. This renders such censorship questionable. If one accepts the operant learning theories as paramount, such censorship may be acceptable to avoid a form of copycat behaviour. If the cognitive learning theories are embraced, the learning process is seen to be more complex and takes account not only of the skills but also of the moral standards, feelings of responsibility and respect for others which are portrayed in the media. Merely censoring violent media images is then less acceptable, being too simplistic. There is a need to take account of the whole media presentation, not just the fact of violence but the social and moral setting of that image. On this basis, simple censorship becomes less valid or, at least, questionable. This is not to claim that the media do not play a part in the learning process, but rather to recognise the complexity of their role and to question the validity and justification of censorship.

The utility of learning theories may be greater than these uncertainties suggest. They could provide a fruitful method of altering the behaviour of offenders. They do not indicate that most offenders are in need of treatment, but rather that they have not been effectively taught to live within the rules which happen to exist within their society. The technique is therefore designed to reflect and encourage officially accepted forms of behaviour, values and responses to situations; the aim is not a 'cure' but to alter future behaviour. It is not implied that offenders were not responsible for their actions; the aim is to induce them to make more socially constructive choices in the future. These techniques could, moreover, be applied along with more traditional treatments, such as biological or drug therapies and/or working on the personality of the offender (Elchardus (1995)). It is, however, usually considered that cognitive learning techniques will be more likely to succeed if utilised in the community than in an institution (Hood (1995)). In the community offenders are in daily contact with the pressures which they are being taught to deal with, making it simpler to transpose the learnt behaviour into different situations, and perhaps ensuring that the new behaviour is better internalised.

Lastly, there is the notion that criminality is a normal and learned behaviour. How the learning process is seen to occur is of less importance. The fact that criminal behaviour is learned puts into question some of the theories of an innate criminal trait or criminal propensity. The fact that it is normal would suggest that there is nothing inherently bad about criminal behaviour. In so far as it is accepted, the theory implies that part of criminological study should be about why certain normal learned behaviours are criminalised and others are not. This is a theme which Sutherland studied in his discussion of white-collar crime, and is a subject which was discussed in Chapter Three and also in Chapters One and Fifteen.

SUGGESTED READING

Goldstein, A.P., Glick, B. and Gibbs, J.C. (1998), *Aggression Replacement Training: A Comprehensive Intervention for Aggressive Youth*, 2nd edn, Champaign, IL.: Research Press.

Hollin, C. (1995), *Psychology and Crime: An Introduction to Criminological Psychology*, London: Routledge.

Sutherland, E.H. and Cressey, D.R. (1974), *Principles of Criminology*, 9th edn, Philadelphia, PA: Lippincott.

QUESTIONS

1   Are the new 'What Works' programmes operated by the probation service doomed to failure on the basis that you can make someone attend but cannot force them to learn?

2   Is there any useful purpose in pursuing the claim that crime is related to low intelligence? Does it have any useful links with the utility of learning theories and how to deliver them?

REFERENCES

Bailey, S.M. (1993), 'Media and Violence', *Criminal Justice Matters*, vol. 6.

Bailey, William, C. (1990), 'Murder, Capital Punishment, and Television: Execution Publicity and Homicide Rates', *American Sociological Review*, vol. 55, p. 628.

Bandura, Albert (1977), *Social Learning Theory*, Englewood Cliffs, NJ: Prentice Hall.

Bandura, Albert (1986), *Social Foundations of Thought and Action*, Englewood Cliffs, NJ: Prentice Hall.

Beckwith, Jan (1985), 'Social and Political Uses of Genetics in the United States: Past and Present', in Frank H. Marsh and Janet Katz (eds), *Biology, Crime and Ethics: A Study of Biological Explanations for Criminal Behaviour*, Cincinnati, OH: Anderson.

Binet, Alfred and Simon, Theodore. See Gleitman, Henry (1986), *Psychology*, 2nd edn, New York: W.W. Norton and Company.

Box, Steven (1983), *Power, Crime and Mystification*, London: Tavistock.

Box, Steven (1987), *Recession, Crime and Punishment*, London: Macmillan Education.

Braithwaite, John (1988), *Crime Shame and Reintegration*, Cambridge: Cambridge University Press.

Conklin, John Evan (1989), *Criminology*, 3rd edn, London: Collier Macmillan.

Cornish, D.B. and Clarke, R.V. (1987), 'Understanding Crime Displacement: the Application of Rational Choice Theory', *Criminology*, vol. 25, p. 933.

Croall, H. (2001), *Understanding White Collar Crime*, Buckingham: Open University Press.

Darwin, Leonard (1914/15), 'The Habitual Criminal', *Eugenics Review*, No. 6.

Dobash, R.E. and Dobash, R.P. (1999), 'Criminal Justice Programmes for Men Who Assault Their Partners', in C.R. Hollin (ed.), *Handbook of Offender Assessment and Treatment*, Chichester: Wiley.

Dobash, R.P., Dobash, R.E., Cavanagh, K. and Lewis, R. (1999), 'A Research Evaluation of British Programmes for Violent Men', *Journal of Social Policy*, vol. 28, p. 78.

Dugdale, Richard (1877), *The Jukes in Crime, Pauperism and Heredity*, New York: Putnam.

Elchardus, J.M. (1995), 'Problems of Therapeutic Interventions Regarding Certain Categories of Offenders, for Example in the Fields of Sexual Offences, Violence in the Family and Drug Addiction', in *Psychological Interventions in the Criminal Justice System*, Proceedings from the 20th Criminological Research Conference, 1993, European Committee on Crime Problems, Criminological Research, vol. XXXI, Strasbourg: Council of Europe.

Farrington, D.P. (1992), 'Juvenile Delinquency', in J.C. Coleman (ed.), *The School Years*, 2nd edn, London: Routledge.

Farrington, David, P. (1994), *Psychological Explanations of Crime*, Aldershot: Dartmouth.

Fisse, Brent and Braithwaite, John (1993), *Corporations, Crime and Accountability*, Cambridge: Cambridge University Press.

Gaffney, L.R. and McFall, R.M. (1981), 'A Comparison of Social Skills in Delinquent and Non-Delinquent Adolescent Girls Using a Behavioural Role-Playing Inventory', *Journal of Consulting and Clinical Psychology*, vol. 49, p. 959.

Gelsthorpe, L. and McWilliam, W. (eds) (1993), *Minority Ethnic Groups and the Criminal Justice System*, Cambridge: Cambridge University Press.

Gillan, Patricia (1978), 'Therapeutic Uses of Obscenity', in Rajeev Dhavan and Christine Davies (eds), *Censorship and Obscenity*, London: Martin Robertson.

Giordano, P.C. and Rockwell, S.M. (2000), 'Differential Association Theory and Female Crime', in S.S. Simpson (ed.), *Of Crime and Criminality*, Thousand Oaks, CA: Pine Forge.

Glaser, D. (1956), 'Criminality Theories and Behavioural Images', *American Journal of Sociology*, vol. 61, p. 433.

Gleitman, Henry (1999), *Psychology*, 5th edn, New York: W.W. Norton & Company.

Goddard, H.H. (1912), *The Kallikak Family, A Study in the Heredity of Feeble-Mindedness*, New York: Macmillan.

Goddard, H.H. (1914), *Feeble-Mindedness: Its Causes and Consequences*, New York: Macmillan.

Goldstein, A.P., Glick, B. and Gibbs, J.C. (1998), *Aggression Replacement Training: A Comprehensive Intervention for Aggressive Youth*, 2nd edn, Champaign, IL.: Research Press.

Gordon, Robert (1976), 'Prevalence: The Rare Datum in Delinquency Measurement and Its Implications for the Theory of Delinquency', in Malcolm W. Klein (ed.), *The Juvenile Justice System*, Beverly Hills, CA: Sage.

Gove, Walter, R. and Wilmoth, Charles (1990), 'Risk, Crime, and Neurophysiologic Highs: a Consideration of Brain Processes that May Reinforce Delinquent and Criminal Behaviour', in Lee Ellis and Harry Hoffman (eds), *Crime in Biological, Social, and Moral Contexts*, New York: Praeger.

Hagell, Ann and Newbury, Tim (1994), *Young Offenders and the Media*, London: Policy Studies Institute.

Halliday Report (2001), *Making Punishments Work: Report of a Review of the Sentencing Framework for England and Wales*, Home Office Communications Directorate, London: Home Office **http://www.homeoffice.gov.uk/docs/halliday.html**.

Hirschi, T. and Hindling, M. (1977), 'Intelligence and Delinquency: A Revisionist Review', *American Sociological Review*, vol. 42, p. 571.

Hollin, Clive (1992), *Criminal Behaviour: A Psychological Approach to Explanation and Prevention*, London: Falmer Press.

Hollin, C.R. (1995), *Psychology and Crime: An Introduction to Criminological Psychology*, London: Routledge.

Hood, R. (1995), 'Introductory Report, General Report of the Conference and Conclusions and Recommendations', in *Psychological Interventions in the Criminal Justice System*, Proceedings from the 20th Criminological Research Conference, 1993, European Committee on Crime Problems, Criminological Research, vol. XXXI, Strasbourg: Council of Europe.

Howitt, D. (1998), *Crime, the Media and the Law*, Chichester: Wiley.

Jeffery, Clarence Ray (1959), 'An Integrated Theory of Crime and Criminal Behaviour', *Journal of Criminal Law, Criminology and Police Science*, vol. 49, p. 537.

Jensen, A.R. (1969), 'How Much Can We Boost IQ and Scholastic Achievement?', *Harvard Educational Review*, vol. 39, p. 1.

Jensen, Gary F. (1972), 'Parents, Peers and Delinquent Action: A Test of the Differential Association Perspective', *American Journal of Sociology*, vol. 78, p. 562.

Jones, T. (1993), *Britain's Ethnic Minorities*, London: Policy Studies Institute.

Kaplan, P.J. and Arbuthnot, J. (1985), 'Affective Empathy and Cognitive Role-Taking in Delinquent and Non-Delinquent Youth', *Adolescence*, vol. 20, p. 323.

Kohlberg, L. (1976), 'Moral Stages and Moralisation: The Cognitive-Development Approach' in T. Lickona (ed.), *Moral Development and Behaviour*, New York: Holt, Rinehart and Winston.

Kohlberg, L. and Candee, D. (1984), 'The Relationship of Moral Judgement to Moral Action' in L. Kohlberg (ed.), *The Psychology of Moral Development*, San Francisco: Harper & Row.

Levi, M. (2001), 'White-Collar Crime in the News', *Criminal Justice Matters*, vol. 34, p. 24.

Lewis, John and Van Gamm, Andrew (1994), 'Alton Turns Attention to Violence on 'Television', *Broadcast*, 15 April, p. 3.

Lilly, J. Robert, Cullen, Francis T. and Ball, Richard A. (1989), *Criminological Theory: Context and Consequences*, Newbury Park, CA: Sage Periodicals Press.

Loehlin, J.C., Lindzey, G. and Spuhler, J.N. (1975), *Race Difference in Intelligence*, San Francisco: Freedman.

Lynam, D., Moffitt, T. and Stonthame-Loeber, M. (1993), 'Explaining the Relation Between IQ and Delinquency: Class, Race, Test Motivation, School Failure or Self-control?', *Journal of Abnormal Psychology*, vol. 102, p. 187.

McCarthy, Bill (1996), 'The Attitudes and Actions of Others: Tutelage and Sutherland's Theory of Differential Association', *British Journal of Criminology*, vol. 36, p. 135.

Matsueda, R. and Heiner, K. (1987), 'Race, Family Structure and Delinquency: a Test of Differential Association and Social Control Theories', *American Sociological Review*, vol. 52, p. 826.

Mercier, Jane (1972), 'IQ: The Lethal Label', *Psychology Today*, p. 44.

Messner, S.R. (1986), 'Television Violence and Violent Crime: an Aggregate Analysis', *Social Problems*, vol. 33, p. 218.

Moffitt, T.E. and Henry, B. (1989), 'Neuropsychological Assessment of Effective Functions in Self-Reported Delinquents', *Development and Psychopathology*, vol. 1, p. 105.

Mulvey, E. and Arthur, M. (1993), 'The Prevention and Treatment of Juvenile Delinquency: a Review of the Research', *Clinical Psychology Review*, vol. 13, p. 133.

Murray, C. and Herrnstein, R. (1994), *The Bell Curve: Intelligence and Class Structure of American Life*, New York: Free Press.

Newson, Elizabeth (1994), *Video Violence and the Protection of Children*, Child Development Research Unit, University of Nottingham.

O'Donohue, W. and Kitchener, R. (eds) (1999), *Handbook of Behaviorism*, San Diego, CA: Academic Press.

Offord, D.R., Poushinsky, M.F. and Sullivan, K. (1978), 'School Performance, IQ and Delinquency', *British Journal of Criminology*, vol. 18, p. 110.

Parker, Donn, B. (1976), *Crime by Computer*, New York: Scribner.

Pavlov, Ivan Petrovich (1927), *Conditioned Reflexes*, Oxford: Oxford University Press.

Petley, J. and Barker, M. (1997), *Ill Effects: The Media/Violence Debate*, London: Routledge.

Phillips, D.P. (1983), 'The Impact of Mass Media Violence on US Homicides', *American Sociological Review*, vol. 48, p. 560.

Pinter, I. (1923), *Intelligence Testing: Methods and Results*, New York: Barnes & Noble.

Reiner, R., Livingstone, S. and Allen, J. (2001), 'Casino Culture: Media, and Crime in a Winner-Loser Society', in K. Stenson and R.R. Sullivan (eds), *Crime, Risk and Justice*, Cullompton: Willan Publishing.

Roberts, J. (1995), 'Implementing Psychosocial Interventions Linked to Community Sanctions', in *Psychological Interventions in the Criminal Justice System*, Proceedings from the 20th Criminological Research Conference, 1993, European Committee on Crime Problems, Criminological Research, vol. XXXI, Strasbourg: Council of Europe.

Robertson, Geoffrey (1989), *Freedom, The Individual and the Law*, Middlesex: Penguin Books.

Scarr, S. and Weinberg, R.A. (1976), 'IQ Test Performance of Black Children Adopted by White Families', *American Psychologist*, vol. 31, p. 726.

Simons, Ronald, L. (1978), 'The Meaning of the IQ-Delinquency Relationship', *American Sociological Review*, vol. 43, p. 268.

Sims, A.C.P. and Gray, P. (1993), 'The Media, Violence and Vulnerable Viewers', Evidence presented to the Broadcasting Group, House of Lords.

Skinner, B.F. (1938), *The Behaviour of Organisms*, New York: Appleton-Century-Crofts.

Slabby, R.G. and Guerra, N.G. (1988), 'Cognitive Mediators of Aggression in Adolescent Offenders: 1. Assessment', *Developmental Psychology*, vol. 24, p. 580.

Slapper, G. and Tombs, S. (1999), *Corporate Crime*, London: Longman.

Smetana, J.G. (1990), 'Morality and Conduct Disorders', in M. Lewis and S.M. Miller (eds), *Handbook of Developmental Psychology*, New York: Plenum.

Smith, David, J. (1994), 'Race Crime and Criminal Justice', in Mike Maguire, Rod Morgan and Robert Reiner (eds), *The Oxford Handbook of Criminology*, Oxford: Oxford University Press.

Snare, A. (1995), 'Psychological Interventions Aimed at Resolving the Conflict Between the Perpetrator and the Victim, for Example Within the Framework of Mediation and Compensation Programmes', in *Psychological Interventions in the Criminal Justice System*, Proceedings from the 20th Criminological Research Conference, 1993, European Committee on Crime Problems, Criminological Research, vol. XXXI, Strasbourg: Council of Europe.

Snare, J. (1995), 'Implementing Psychosocial Interventions Linked to Community Sanctions', in *Psychological Interventions in the Criminal Justice System*, Proceedings from the 20th Criminological Research Conference, 1993, European Committee on Crime Problems, Criminological Research, vol. XXXI, Strasbourg: Council of Europe.

Sparks, Richard (1983), *Fictional Representations of Crime and Law Enforcement on British Television*, Cambridge: Institute of Criminology.

Sparks, Richard (1992), *Television and the Drama of Crime: Moral Tales and the Place of Crime in Public Life*, Buckingham: Open University Press.

Sparks, R. (2001), 'Bringin' it all back home': populism, media coverage and the dynamics of locality and globality in the politics of crime control', in K. Steneon and R. R. Sullivan (eds), *Crime, Risk and Justice: the Politics of Crime Control in Liberal Democracies*, Cullompton: Willan Publishing.

Sutherland, Edwin, H. (1939), *Principles of Criminology*, 3rd edn, Philadelphia, PA: Lippincott.

Sutherland, Edwin, H. and Cressey, Donald, R. (1978), *Principles of Criminology*, 10th edn, Philadelphia: Lippincott.

Tombs, S. and Whyte, D. (2001), 'Reporting Corporate Crime out of Existence', *Criminal Justice Matters*, vol. 34, p. 22.

Vennard, J. and Hedderman, C. (1998), 'Effective Treatment with Offenders', in P. Goldblatt and C. Lewis (eds), *Reducing Offending: An Assessment of Research Evidence on Ways of Dealing with Offending Behaviour*, Home Office Research Study 187, London: Home Office Research and Statistics Directorate.

West, D.J. (1982), *Delinquency: Its Roots, Careers and Prospects*, London: Heinemann.

Wilson, James Q. and Herrnstein, Richard J. (1985), *Crime and Human Nature: The Definitive Study of the Causes of Crime*, New York: Simon & Schuster.

Women's Unit (1999), *Living without Fear—An Integrated Approach to Tackling Violence against Women*, London: Cabinet Office.

Woodward, Mary (1955), 'Low Intelligence and Delinquency', *British Journal of Delinquency*, vol. 5, p. 281.

11

The sociology of criminality

11.1 Introduction

Most of the explanations for crime so far discussed have focused on biological or psychological characteristics as causes of criminality. Claiming to be neutral and scientifically based, they mostly situate the causes of crime in the individual offender and so divert attention away from social or societal problems. In contrast, the theories which follow minimise these factors and instead concentrate on extraneous influences such as the environment, poverty and unemployment. The numerous theories linking criminality with these social factors focus on the problems related to vagrancy, unemployment, social controls, cultural values, and general poverty and despair. Their history stretches back over many centuries, but the accurate collection and keeping of data on criminality and other arguably related social factors only dates from the nineteenth century. In consequence, only this recent period is of interest to our study. Much of the early work in this area was published by social and political reformers, often as a small part of much wider treatises. In this country their views really began to be publicised after industrialisation had made drastic changes to population distribution, changing society irrevocably from an essentially rural culture. One aspect of this change was a shift from small, close-knit communities. The changes produced a largely urbanised community having wide and diverse aims. Many, both at the time and since, have felt that the altered living style brought with it a marked change in criminal practices, leading to new problems of lawlessness. Crime in pre-industrial society was more dispersed and therefore tends now, though not necessarily then, to be perceived as being less acute. The concentration of population in urban areas was the start of our modern society and of the modern sociological explanations of crime.

Major problems were created by the fact that the system of control had not really changed, despite the transition from an agrarian society to an industrial one. The old controls were proving to be largely ineffectual in the new social situation. The difficulty in policing led many writers, including Chadwick (1839) to argue for a professional police force, particularly in the larger and fastest growing conurbations such as Manchester. Migration, population growth, rapid urbanisation and the emergence of extensive slum dwellings led many nineteenth-century commentators to fear the formation of a dangerous sub-group, commonly referred to as the 'Residuum' (see Phillips (1977); Tobias (1972); and Jones (1982)).

The size of the problem is difficult to ascertain with any certainty. There were (and are) many deficiencies in the statistics. Despite this, attempts were made both to assess the scale of criminal activity and to explain the reasons for it. An early work which contained a significant discussion of criminality and society was published by Fredrick Engels in 1844. Engels, a German-born industrialist whose family partly owned a textile mill in Manchester, spent most of his adult working life in England and, with Karl Marx, is the founder of the communist ideology. Their concept of dialectical materialism became the underlying philosophy of Communism. Engels used some telling figures from the official statistics for England and Wales to show that the number of arrests for criminal offences rose steadily in the first part of the century from 4,605 in 1805 to 31,309 in 1842, a sevenfold increase in 37 years. Most of that increase occurred in the fast growing urban industrial areas of the North. Liverpool and Manchester alone accounted for 14 per cent of the whole. London, whose mid-century population was probably greater than all the other main towns put together, accounted for 13 per cent of the total number of arrests. The industrial areas of Scotland showed the same trend. In Lanarkshire, the population doubled once every 30 years whereas the crime rate doubled once every five-and-a-half years (i.e., almost six times as fast).

Engels (1971) found this neither surprising nor difficult to explain. He documented the widening of class differences and the increased exploitation of the working class by the bourgeoisie, who were prospering under free competition. In his view, the workers became more brutalised, exploited and demoralised; as they lost any real control over their own lives, their resentment grew. He claimed that the growth of underlying class conflict was powerful and inevitable, and that criminality was an obvious result. He said:

If the demoralisation of the worker passes beyond a certain point, then it is just as natural that he will turn into a criminal—as inevitably as water turns into steam at boiling point. (Engels (1844), from 1971 translation, p. 145)

He predicted that this class conflict would erupt into warfare (i.e., civil war) because the bourgeoisie had failed to understand its significance. This never happened in Britain. Although there were many bitter industrial conflicts, the last armed 'rising' against the State, the Chartist march on Newport in 1839, had already taken place before Engels was writing.

The idea of social conflict as an explanation of criminality was, however, taken up and refined by proponents of 'The New Criminology' into a full conflict theory (see Chapter Fifteen). Engels thought the answer to the problem of crime lay in idealistic political change, particularly in a breakdown of the system of exploitation. This would involve changing the whole of society, altering both its economic and social structures. Until recently, such a whole-hearted allocation of blame and such a drastic solution was generally uncommon amongst British criminological writers. Even those who saw societal reasons for criminality generally tended to suggest that it was caused by more specific elements, and proposed more limited 'cures' than those expounded by Engels.

One of the most common crimes in the nineteenth century was vagrancy. At times it became almost synonymous with the term 'dangerous class'. Vagrancy caused most alarm in the periods 1815–19, the late 1840s, the late 1860s and the mid-1890s. It was seen as a threat to the very fibre of society, as the vagrant's lifestyle did not espouse the Protestant work ethic, and was perceived to be a violation of respectability and religion. Vagrants were thought of as carriers of disease, and as criminals who often victimised respectable traders. Lastly, but significantly, in the acute economic distress of the late 1830s and early 1840s, they were thought to constitute a potential danger to stability in times of political tension. The Chadwick Reports (1839) are full of the iniquities of vagrants. It is important for us to remember, even though it was often lost sight of at the time, that not all vagrants were criminals; some were migrant workers following seasonal jobs; or they were navvies who moved with their jobs; or showmen and hawkers; or, as was the case with most female vagrants, they had lost their jobs and travelled to find work; or they were too poor to find homes or too old to work. Despite this more acceptable face of vagrancy, the vagrant was generally the first to be suspected of any crime which took place in a locality: they were believed to be the criminal class and were treated as such.

This view of the vagrant persisted despite the fact that they were rarely convicted of any really serious crimes—mostly drunk and disorderly, begging, sleeping out and stealing essentials such as clothes and food. Because vagrants were viewed as a social menace they were closely controlled, largely by means of the Vagrancy Acts of 1824 and 1838, which were given a wide interpretation in order to criminalise large areas of their lifestyle. The vagrant was thereby restrained before any real crime, apart from sleeping rough etc., had been committed. In this way, the British sought to control vagrancy which was seen as contributing to the crime problem, rather than seeking ways of solving that problem. This pragmatic approach epitomises many of the legal changes of this time: the heightened concern for the rights of property enacted or enforced laws against many activities of the poor, such as collecting fire wood, collecting coal, and using common pasture land. The intention was to control those who were seen as most likely to cause real problems, especially trouble related to crime, before they became too difficult.

In this way, British criminology was more practical than theoretical, and even slightly before Lombroso (see 6.2), but certainly after him, it adopted the positivists' view that certain factors, largely outside the control of the individual, determine behaviour (i.e., that there were large constraints upon the operation of free will). It is possibly partly because of this pragmatic approach that Lombroso's work did not have such a marked effect on British criminology as it had on the Continent. In Britain the pragmatic approach already existed, and people were already being punished both for their own and the collective good. The British criminological tradition has largely been to study and sometimes explain the *status quo* rather than to question it (for a criticism of the position, see Chapter Fifteen).

An example of this early pragmatic approach can be seen in Henry Mayhew's mid-century studies of London. Mayhew (1861–2) tended to see crime as an ecological phenomenon, but one which was tied in with the working classes and with social problems. He did not see criminals as a separate, dangerous class distinct from the working class. Rather, he recognised that many people were driven into poverty: some because they were unable but willing to get work, others because they became ill or otherwise incapacitated. Any of these positions might lead to criminality through need. In recognising social factors as the cause of criminality, he was not blaming the social structure in the same way as Engels. He did not argue for dramatic social upheaval. He saw that certain broad social changes, such as the move from rural to urban living, were necessarily latent causes of criminality. From this perspective, no blame could be placed either on the propertied classes or on the criminals themselves. They were seen as acting in a largely deterministic way which reduced the operation of free will. If the blame did not fall on urbanisation, then it might well fall on some other 'cause' such as immigration. In the mid-nineteenth century, it was the Irish immigrants arriving in the 20 or so years after the potato famine of 1846 that were seen as the cause of the problem (see Pike (1876)).

The significance of the essentially deterministic approach cannot be stressed enough. It is prevalent in the theories of most British and American criminologists up until about 1970, and can still be found in many theories today. It can be seen as a trend in most of the sociological explanations for crime. This is starkly illustrated by Hermann Mannheim's assertion that 'every society possesses the type of crime and criminals which fit into its cultural, moral, social, religious and economic conditions' (Mannheim (1965), p. 422). Similarly, the inertia which such a stance can produce can be demonstrated by the attitude behind the 1959 Home Office White Paper, which did not propose to deal with the 'deep-seated' causes of criminality, but rather set out the facts and the way government should deal with them or respond to them. In effect, it elected to accept the crime problem and merely to try to minimise its effects. This idea that a response might be made to crime without understanding it is one which has pervaded British criminology for a long time.

Despite this, some criminologists have attempted sociological explanations of criminality, albeit in a continuing deterministic fashion and with the clear aim of maintaining a pragmatic approach to the resolution of the problem.

11.2 **The ecology of crime**

11.2.1 **Introduction**

In this context, ecology is the study of peoples and institutions in relation to environment. The ecological school of criminology has a long history. Much of the work carried out in the last century studied the correlation between criminality, poverty and population density or type. It often used maps and charts to display the quantitative distribution of criminality: Henry Mayhew essentially studied the ecology of crime in London in the mid-nineteenth century (Mayhew (1862)). Perhaps because these early studies lacked any clear theoretical explanation for the distribution they discovered, they became overshadowed by more individualistic explanations. In the twentieth century, however, there has, from time to time, been a revival of interest in ecological theories, influenced by a general tendency to tie criminality with high population density and hence with cities. This popular belief is borne out by Ingram (1993) who concludes that urbanism is a significant predictor of criminality, whilst others (Campbell (1993)) have demonstrated that particular areas may be especially prone to criminal activity. In a broad sense studies in this area can be divided into two groups: the first draws on research in Chicago early in the century and is centred around the study of the areas in which delinquents reside (high offender rate areas); the second, more recent, studies the areas where crimes are committed (high offence rate areas). These two schools will be considered separately below.

Before doing so, however, it seems prudent to consider the popular conception that criminality is attached more to urban than rural areas. This is not straightforward: definitions of 'rural' and 'urban' are neither clear nor self-evident. Nor would the mere establishment of such a connection be sufficient: to be useful there must also be an explanation for the connection. If one goes back to the eighteenth century the popular conception of crime and many of the figures which are available for that time would suggest a greater concentration of criminal activities in rural rather than urban areas. By the middle of the nineteenth century, as mentioned above, Mayhew was implying that this had altered. Part of the reason could have been the changing construct of social organisation, including the way in which the criminal law was defined and enforced. Part of the apparent change in ecological factors associated with criminality may thus be due to such factors, and especially in the new methods of enforcement centred around a police force which concentrated both its manpower and its efforts in urban areas. When analysing the modern information it is important to keep in mind that some of the apparent differences may be explicable by reference to these social constructs and their operation rather than to actual differences in criminality or behaviour (for a fuller discussion see Chapter Fourteen).

Lastly, it is necessary to register the fact that—despite the strong popular association of crime with towns, and the support given to this view by police data and victim studies—this is an area which has been very little researched. Most criminological study of the effects of the environment have concentrated on urban areas, ignoring rural areas. Indeed, any explanations of rural criminality have been constructed by contrast with theories tested in the urban environment, for example, that in urban areas there are less strong social bonds holding the society together (this is discussed under the control theories considered in Chapter Thirteen), and that there are fewer opportunities for criminality in rural areas (a factor considered below in 11.2.3). With these factors in mind it is now necessary to assess the way in which crime and environment may be linked and, hopefully, to consider why such links operate.

11.2.2 Environment and high offender rate areas

This area of study is closely associated with the Chicago School of Human Ecology (also referred to as The Chicago School). It had its roots in the department of sociology at the University of Chicago, and was most influential in the 1920s and 1930s. Chicago grew from a town of 10,000 inhabitants in 1860 to a large city with over two million inhabitants by 1910. Most of the increase was due to immigrants, many of whom came from Europe. The city was therefore a fruitful place for sociological work and the Chicago School studied every aspect of its life. All the information was recorded in meticulous detail, and used to test and formulate sociological theories. Much of this work was criminological, but before turning to those aspects, it is important to set the scene by introducing some of the basic sociological ideas upon which much of this explanation of crime is based.

The Chicago School was primarily the brainchild of Robert Park, who saw the city not just as a set of buildings in a particular geographic location, nor as formed by its institutions, but as a living ecological environment or as a kind of social organism. By this, he meant that the people and the institutions were so intimately bound together that they tended to interact as a whole. As with any ecological community, there were areas where the inhabitants were mainly of a particular type or types: racial or ethnic communities; immigrant communities; similar income and occupational groupings etc. Within each community there were symbiotic relationships: the grocer needed customers and vice versa, whilst the inhabitants of different geographical areas needed each other to demand and supply work etc. There were particular physical features of the city which were important to its inhabitants, the most obvious of which was Lake Michigan. The city was seen as an ever-evolving organism which was altering as people moved within it (Park (1952)).

Another member of the Chicago School, Burgess, elaborated on this model. He saw the city as an organism which grew largely from the centre in a series of concentric circles. The central area he named Zone I or the 'Loop'. It housed the business area with the major banks, large department stores, expensive shops, and the main administrative buildings of the city. It was an area in which few people lived. Zone II was what Burgess called the transitional zone. This was the oldest part of the city and was largely residential, but its housing was dilapidated and unlikely to be renovated as it was constantly in danger of being taken over or pulled down to make way for businesses, which in turn altered the character of the area. The worst housing in the city was in this sector, a lot of it split into rooms for rent. It comprised the ghetto area of the city and the poorest citizens lived there. Very often, the poorest ghetto dwellers were the newest immigrants. Zone III contained the workers' houses, the homes of the skilled and semi-skilled workers. Many of these inhabitants had originated in Zone II but had since progressed to the slightly better housing of Zone III; it was the next place to which the successful immigrants would graduate. Zone IV had more desirable and expensive houses, and Zone V was the commuter zone or suburbia. In Chicago each zone was calculated at that time to be approximately two miles in width (Burgess (1928)).

Obviously, no city can be precisely categorised in this way. There are always pockets of less desirable housing near industrial areas and railways, but Burgess claimed that the general pattern was discernible. None of this was directly to do with criminology, but it laid the foundations for a particular criminological theory.

11.2.2.1 Shaw and McKay

In the early part of this century Chicago suffered an ever-increasing crime problem, and the search for an explanation to this became the major preoccupation of the Chicago School. Shaw began work in this area, but his most famous work was done in conjunction with McKay when they studied juvenile crime rates in Chicago (Shaw and McKay (1942) and (1969)). They measured official levels of juvenile crime (boys aged 10 to 16) recording the area where the delinquent lived, not the area where the crime was committed, and then calculated the areas with the highest juvenile delinquency rate. By this measurement, the neighbourhoods with the highest crime rates were those in the centre of the city, closest to concentrations of industry. These were sparsely populated and population was further decreasing as the land was being taken over by industry. Crime rates decreased as the neighbourhoods got further from the centre: on the zonal maps, Zone I or the 'Loop' had the highest crime rate, and the rate decreased as the zones moved outwards away from the centre.

They also claimed that the crime rate of a particular area over time remained constant, despite vast changes in the inhabitants of that area. The central zones retained their high crime rate even when the ethnic origins of the inhabitants completely altered. The implication seemed to be that individuals who once lived in the high crime rate zone became more law-abiding as they moved away from the centre. From all this they concluded that the delinquency rate was more a result of economic position and living environment than of racial or ethnic characteristics. More generally, Shaw and McKay claimed that official rates of delinquency and crime are highest in the centre of cities; decline with movement away from the centre; and do not depend upon the people who inhabit those regions. Their theory is positivist, in that the individuals are seen as inert and their behaviour is largely determined by their environment or the level of social disorganisation.

The latter factor arose from their observation that the crime problem of a particular area was, first, related to such social problems as: high rates of suicide and truancy; a declining population concentrated into a small living space; infant mortality, tuberculosis and mental disorders. And secondly, to such economic factors as: number of families living on State relief or who are dependent on charity; low rates of home ownership; and low rental values of properties. They did not connect criminality with poverty, on the grounds that rates of criminality did not significantly increase during the depression when poverty was at its peak. They point instead to social disorganisation, or what is sometimes termed differential social organisation (see also Sutherland's theory of differential association (10.2.3, and 10.2.4), and control theories in Chapter Thirteen). In the central areas of the city, or those around industry or business, there is a very rapid shift in population, which means that the residents see themselves as transients and do not take an interest in their surroundings. The social disorganisation means that the normal social controls of school, Church and family may also be less forceful (see also Chapter Thirteen). As criminal behaviour is more common in these areas, so criminal values are likely to be more common and more tolerated, and so each individual is more likely to come into contact with them and more likely to learn advancement by illegitimate rather than legitimate methods (Shaw and McKay (1969)).

Shaw and McKay claimed that all these factors led to an increased rate of criminality in certain areas of the city, those in the centre or near the industrial centres being the worst.

11.2.2.2 *Evaluation and updating*

The reliance on officially recorded criminality exposed their findings to all the deficiencies of bias and imprecision which, as Chapter Four showed, the official statistics incorporate. Self-report studies (see 4.3.1) suggest crime is fairly evenly distributed across classes: the crimes of the poor are simply more often detected and punished and so loom larger in official records. Shaw and McKay could deflect some of the criticism by pointing out that their research mostly concentrated on street crimes where the lower classes do figure more prominently. But that is to define the problem (crime) as one which necessarily points to their conclusion.

The Chicago School theory, based on the idea of concentric circles, has also faced severe criticism, especially in Britain and the rest of Europe, where cities tend to be a lot older than in America. Morris (1957), in one of the fullest accounts of ecological or area studies, attacks not only the concentric circle theory but the central idea that areas generate high levels of crime even if the make-up of its inhabitants changes. Although he found that certain areas did contain more delinquents, he argued that this situation was artificially constructed by the authorities, who tended to house all 'problem families' in the same locality. In his interpretation it was the socio-economic position of these families, the administrative procedures, and the class differences, and not simply the area, which led to the high criminality. Such simple linking of offender areas with social deprivation has been questioned by the work of Wikström (1991). Using housing tenure variables (owner-occupier, private rented etc.) as an indicator he found no simple causative link between social status/class and criminality. This suggests that the study of high offender areas is not merely the study of social class. A number of these factors will be discussed in this and later chapters.

The connection with both social class and social disorganisation can be assessed by making smaller and closer studies of particular areas. One such is mentioned in Bottoms et al. (1989) and (1992) which compares three pairs of estates to discover why estates with seemingly similar housing facilities and very similar social variables (such as age, sex, social class, ethnic origin, size of household, rate of male unemployment, age of leaving full-time education and length of residence in present dwelling) might have very different offender rates (and notably differing offence rates). Thus comparing two low-rise housing estates they discovered a large, persistent difference in offender rates despite the fact that both estates had a very similar socio-economic status and both had a similar turnover of residents ruling out differences in social disorganisation as suggested by Shaw and McKay (above). (However, in the other two pairs of housing areas the high offender area did have higher rates of social disorganisation.) One clear difference was that the local authority in allocating housing placed those with the most acute housing need in the high crime rate area and also placed there families who had prior links with other residents in the area. Although both of these housing choices would seem to perpetuate the high offender rate, such a direct link between housing allocation and criminality was not accepted. It was instead argued that the allocation had its effect by influencing both the way in which the residents interacted, and the way in which outsiders perceived the area and its inhabitants. The first of these might affect the level of opportunity for criminal activity as well as driving some residents to apply for a move away from the area. The second might affect the attraction of the estate to housing applicants and also the way in which it was viewed by officials such as social workers, health workers and control agencies. The high offender rate area also had certain characteristics or area contextual effects which others have associated with high-crime areas, including: the effect on residents and potential residents of the labelling of the high rate area in a negative way; differences in the schools to which the children from each area would be sent; differences in peer groupings and the presence of a criminal subculture in the high-rate area; differing relationships with parents. (For further discussion see Bottoms and Wiles (2002).) It could be argued that these represent more individual explanations of the criminality, but there is also a place for the environmental and wider social contextual elements in offender activity. For example, a follow-up study showed that the gap in offending rates had narrowed. The only large change (Bottoms et al. (1992)) was that the council now allocated homeless persons to both estates, which may have altered perceptions of the area and so altered other social factors such as crime. In effect, this whole study simply emphasises the complexity of the links between offending rates and environment.

For example, a study by Wikström and Loeber (2000) suggested that neighbour-hoods could have very large effects on the behaviour of individuals, perhaps being more significant than any individual characteristics. It may be that an individual's choice to commit a crime may be encouraged by others and/or that the whole way they think, process information, make choices, act on a daily basis may be shaped by the social links within the area. On this basis neighbourhood socialisation would shape many aspects of personality. Clearly the links with environment are far more complex than suggested by early work in this area but the area of study is still relevant and fruitful today.

At a more specific level, the link between crime and areas of social disorganisa-tion is now fairly well accepted (see Bottoms et al. (1992) Hancock (2001) and results from British Crime Surveys). The broad signs of disintegration are: a move towards rented and multiple occupancy dwellings; an increase in the number of households creating communities of individuals who are unrelated and little known to each other; an increase in the turnover of residents; increase in empty (often boarded-up) properties; more unskilled or unemployed occupants; and sometimes a more diverse or less native ethnic base. These have also been linked with visual signs of disorder such as broken windows, graffiti, litter, visible signs of drug use, soliciting etc. suggested by Wilson and Kelling (1982) to be firmly linked with criminality (see discussion in Chapter Sixteen). Although the structural and social changes and the feelings of insecurity seem all to be linked to criminality this does not mean that the mechanism through which this works is fully understood (Taylor (2001)).

A rather different strand of enquiry (Sampson et al. (1997)) linked to social dis-organisation claims the causal connection to be the inability of a neighbourhood collectively to express and enforce non-criminal values (even if most individuals have non-criminal views). The suggestion is that the lack of cohesion in the com-munity leads to a collapse in community control structures thus offering greater opportunities for criminality. The control vacuum can lead to strange results. Thus Walklate and Evans (1999) document a case where a criminal gang known as the 'Salford Firm' took over an area by means of rough street 'justice', punishments, and by dissuading locals to use the police though a campaign of fear and used the control to keep more random crime out of the area. The result was insecurity and fear in locals and dread about the effects on their children but also a relief in the fall in general crime and the absence of drugs in their area. The wider non-criminal efficacy had been enforced through criminal structures. Is this an organised or disorganised community?

11.2.3 Environment and high offence rate areas

In the 1970s there was a move towards studying offence areas rather than offender areas. One of the earliest British studies of this kind was carried out for the Home Office by Mayhew et al. (1976) and covered one of the theories concerned with this area—opportunity and crime. Bottoms and Wiles (1997) refers to many studies which consider the differential offence rates between areas and concludes that there are marked geographical differences in offence rates, and that these can vary for different types of offences: one area may be high for burglary while another has a high rate of family violence etc. Moreover, even within high offence rate areas there will be some smaller locations which have still higher rates or greater concentrations of particular offences.

A related feature is multiple victimisation. One of the most interesting and useful pieces of information to come out of crime surveys is the rate at which repeat victimisation occurs. Recent British Crime Surveys (now published annually as part of *Crime in England and Wales*) note that in about 35 per cent of cases of violence the victim suffered two or more victimisations (domestic violence recorded the highest levels) and about 20 per cent of victims of burglary had suffered two or more incidents. The same holds true for victimisation of businesses (see Mirrlees-Black and Ross (1995) and Wood et al. (1997)). Repeat victimisation has become so common that it is considered a very reliable predictor of future criminal activity, as Ken Pease (one of the main researchers in this area) has stated:

It is arguably the best single predictor routinely available to the police in the absence of specific intelligence. Even if sophisticated analysis of more extensive demographic and other information is available, prior victimisation has so far been found to survive as the best predictor. (1996, p. 3.)

Here we will concentrate on repeat burglaries. These may occur because the first offender found it an easy and lucrative target, and may return either to remove the goods that he or she could not manage the first time or to take the items which have been replaced on the insurance (see Ashton et al. (1998)). The returning burglar knows the way in and the layout of the house and got away with it once so feels safer. The first burglar may talk about his offence and other offenders may then hit the same target. The same aspects about the property, its lack of security and being left empty, easy getaway etc. may suggest it as a good target for a number of unconnected offenders. Although Pease (1998) cannot say precisely which of these explains repeat victimisation, he has estimated that about half of repeat victimisations involve the same offender. Townsley et al. (2001) note that near repeat burglary (involving houses near the original crime) is also very common. This does not need to be as bleak as it appears. First, burglary victims can make their premises more secure both physically and by occupying them for longer periods (Pease (1998)). For crime control agencies it is a very good predictor of future offending and therefore may allow them to prioritise resources both to solve offences and to prevent them. G. Taylor (1999) found this effective for commercial premises. Furthermore, as it has been found that repeat offenders tend to be career criminals (Gill and Pease (1998) and Ashton et al. (1998)), there is an extra bonus in catching and convicting these offenders.

Crime prevention may be able to make other uses of crime mapping. Just plotting crime scenes on a map is too crude: it shows crime hot spots that might be targeted for greater police presence but on its own is not sufficiently precise. However, sophisticated technology allows the placing of other physical features (footpaths, high hedges or fences, presence of attractive and/or easy targets, escape routes, bus routes and security cameras) as well as recording when the crimes occur. This geographical mapping is extensively used by some US police forces (see Goldsmith et al. (2000)). The US system uses various analytical tools as well as geographic and social factors and has been used by some police forces in the UK where Murray et al. (2001) found its potential was enhanced when such physical features as bus stops were added. The technique can also be helpful in correcting wrong police perceptions about crime high spots (Ratcliffe and McCullagh (2001)). This also helps to ensure efficient deployment of police officers and crime prevention schemes (Shapland (2000)). However, more research is needed to analyse exactly how spatial patterns interact and how each type of design works in specific circumstances (Hillier and Shu (2000)). The government has recognised both the power and limits of geographical analysis by permitting and encouraging its use by the police whilst also accepting other links, so in its Burglary Reduction Programme it allows bids based on geographical space but will also look at bids based on other grounds, e.g., groups of people which suffer disproportionately.

There are other sides to this, such as the use of psychological analysis either instead of or as well as geographical and social factors (some of these were discussed in profiling above). Canter (1995), for example, believes that rapists tend to attack within a two-mile radius of their home and that few such offenders travel long distances to offend. Those that do are the hardest to catch. Barker (2000) builds on this to suggest that the same is true for property offenders where their home forms the focus and their crimes are committed within their home range. It is likely to be a facet of most other offences as well, and therefore tagging offenders may help in solving crimes. Furthermore, the authors in Canter and Alison (2000) have successfully used offender profiling to throw light on property offending. Within an offence category there are often different psychological and geographic patterns to the offending. There are different ways of carrying out the offences (in burglary, the house may be searched with care or ransacked, there may be destruction etc.). Finally, there may even be particular elements peculiar to that offender (offence signatures). Where information is carefully collected and analysed, all of these may help in solving crimes. They may also help in deciding where to focus crime control resources.

11.2.3.1 *Opportunity and routine activity explanations of high offence rate areas*

In the UK the first modern analysis of these variables was begun in the research and planning unit of the Home Office. In 1976 Mayhew et al. produced a short report in which opportunity became the central focus of research and suggested that levels of offending could be reduced by taking account of the situation in which the offence occurred. This was the start of a serious consideration of opportunity analysis which is related to a number of factors. One such is referred to as target attractiveness which considers the likely gains from criminal activity and the ease of performing the crime undetected (the level of surveillance). For example, Clarke (1983) reported that public telephones were much more likely to be attacked if they were located on the street rather than in pubs, launderettes and other buildings regularly frequented by the public. In earlier research Clarke (1978) noted that vandalism on double-decker buses was more likely to arise on the upper deck, and especially in the back rows. This area was the least likely to be supervised, particularly in driver-only buses. Introducing conductors produced interesting results: the levels of vandalism dropped but attacks against the conductors rose. Thus the criminality was related to other factors besides opportunity. This also shows that altering the environment will not necessarily prevent offending, although some target hardening can be very effective: Painter and Farrington (1999) report that increasing street lighting decreased criminality and paid for itself within a year. The findings were corroborated by a later self-report study (Painter and Farrington (2001)).

The other most important element in opportunity theories is the availability of the means to commit the offence so that a shooting will not occur unless there is a gun whilst on the other hand, the absence of a helmet makes motor bike theft less likely as the possibility of detection is high.

The routine activity theory is, in part, an extension of opportunity theory (Felson (1997)). It arose partly because the opportunity theory could not explain why some areas with attractive targets (lucrative pickings for offenders) suffered high victimisation whereas others did not and why the highest victimisation rates are suffered in poor areas where attractive targets are largely absent. It includes three basic dimensions: an attractive target, how well that target is guarded or surveilled; and the availability of an offender. The focus is mostly on the second of these. Thus it considers the day-today activities of victims and of those, such as neighbours, who might be able to offer surveillance. In an environment where most of the inhabitants are predictably absent for large parts of the day either because of work or other recreational activities there is greater opportunity for crime, especially if the targets have more portable and desirable goods. This links crime with differences in lifestyle and with economic changes, both of which are recognised to alter over time and space. It is believed that rural communities have lower crime rates partly because of higher surveillance by neighbours etc. than in either urban areas or old rural areas which have now become commuter belts. Routine activity theory is therefore wider-ranging than opportunity theory though they are both directed at similar aspects of offending.

Unfortunately, although initially including the need for an offender, routine activity theory rather ignores the fact that the routines, choices and modes of operation of offenders may have profound effects on the process. Clearly the factors of opportunity and routine activity have a part to play in assessing whether a crime will occur but these are not the only important factors and the environmental aspects need to be seen in their wider social and other contexts.

11.2.3.2 Use of space and high offence rate areas

Studies have been made on where an offence occurs in relation to the offender's use of space on the hypothesis that offenders will commit offences in areas with which they are familiar, close to home, to work, to places of entertainment and so on. This theory has been most strongly postulated by Patricia and Paul Brantingham (1989, 1991 and 1993). Wiles and Costello (2000) support this by finding that offenders normally travel under two miles from their homes. These journeys were not generally made specifically to commit the crime, rather the crime was committed whilst they were engaged in their routine activities. However, most offenders in their study had no job and a number were excluded from areas of shopping or entertainment outside their home neighbourhood. Thus in this study home was the only connector. Such findings could be useful in suggesting ways to reduce offending.

11.2.4 **Practical applications of the ecological theory**

Shaw and McKay's research essentially pointed to social disorganisation as the main reason for criminality. It led them to believe that treating or severely punishing individual delinquents would do little to alleviate the problem. For them, the solution is to be found in social organisation and stability. In an attempt to counteract the problems faced in these areas, Shaw established what he called the Chicago Area Project (1932). He set up 22 neighbourhood centres which were basically run and staffed by local residents, and encouraged and aided other organisations within the community. The intention was to reduce criminality by increasing social organisation and community feeling: youths were attracted into acceptable recreational activities; staff would help juveniles who got into trouble and watch out for difficulties which might be starting on the street; and residents were encouraged to take a pride in their community by improving their environment. Some of the projects ran for over 50 years and seemed to help the residents in many ways, but their effects on juvenile delinquency are difficult to assess and have been inconclusive (see Schlossman et al. (1984)). The Chicago Area Project facilitated the community to help itself and set up support and other structures of its own. It did not attempt to alter the political *status quo*, nor did it attack the distribution of power. This type of approach would now be labelled 'community crime prevention'; the model they introduced was very much a bottom up system—to get the community, ordinary citizens, involved and take control. This approach is seen by some to be flawed (Hope (1995) and Heindensohn (1998)): it helps people to cope with existing circumstances, but there is little attempt to deal with the structural or political problems faced within the communities.

In Britain ecological data have been used rather differently. For example, Alice Coleman (1990) took a solely ecological approach in studying design problems in public sector housing. Coleman argues that the design of the area can induce bad behaviour which might well include criminality. Thus, to a far greater extent than Shaw and McKay, she argues that environment determines criminality, and her ideas are strongly positivist. She accepted three design factors which facilitated criminality—anonymity; lack of surveillance; and easy escape (which had been put forward by Newman (1982)). She argued that designs, particularly of public sector houses and housing estates, should be concerned to give the area character and allow easy surveillance. She and her research team from King's College London made certain more specific recommendations about public sector housing:

(a) No more flats should be built. This was seen as necessary because the study had related many unpleasant factors, including bad behaviour and certain acts of criminality, with the number of dwellings per entrance, the number of dwellings per block, and the number of storeys.

(b) Designs should have greater stabilising features. This was suggested because items such as overhead walk-ways and thoughtless use of space were found to be connected with bad behaviour and acts of criminality. Each dwelling or each block of flats should have its own enclosed garden rather than leaving the space completely open.

(c) Any existing flats and housing estates should be altered so as to remove the worst of the design features and so cut down their adverse effects.

Coleman drew particular attention to the strong effects of these design factors when there are children living in the area. Her work has been widely accepted, and she has worked with a number of London boroughs and with the Metropolitan Police, designing new housing areas and redesigning blocks of flats so as to reduce their effects on criminality. She has had very marked success in a number of her projects. In the Lisson Green estate, the removal of walkways was followed by a 50 per cent fall in the crime rate, and the fall was maintained for at least a year (Coleman (1988)). Her most marked success has been in the Lea View estate, where the crime rate fell from a very high level to near zero when her design suggestions were implemented. The estate remained virtually crime-free for four years. In a similar Wigan House estate, where these improvements were not made, there has been no such drop in the crime rate (Coleman (1988 and 1990)). Coleman's urban designs are largely based on the idea that a 'defensible space' will limit criminal activity. The logic of this depends on people bothering to defend the space: the design presumes a reasonably strong community feeling and involvement. This presumption is implicit and hence never really discussed. Furthermore, it is possible to have bad design with little defensible space and yet still have a low crime rate. Some progress towards a greater understanding has arisen from the setting out of more general crime prevention standards in Secured by Design (SBD) housing (see **http://www.securedbydesign.com**). An evaluation of this standard claimed it gave rise to up to 30 per cent less crime than equivalent housing which was not SBD (Armitage (2000)).

Much of what Coleman did might be termed target hardening. This became a useful tool of government in the 1980s—they could claim to be doing something about crime control and prevention. Target hardening in the UK largely grew out of work by Ron Clarke, former head of the Home Office Research and Planning Unit (Clarke (1980, 1992 and 1995)); see also Clarke and Cornish (1983) and Clarke and Felson (1993)). He believed that a criminal act required the combination of opportunity with the presence of a person disposed to criminality. For Clarke both factors needed to be present. The criminality side of the equation is centred on the person—why he or she chooses the criminal avenue. For the person the choice is rational and may be based on economic factors, excitement, impulse or limited information. The stress on the individual was typical of 1980s attitudes. It is, however, the first part of the equation which has been most seized on by policy makers—the need for the opportunity to arise. This notion also fitted well with thinking in the 1980s by aiming to make crime more difficult, reduce opportunities—target hardening. This gave government a fairly simple and often cheap initiative to make crime more difficult: it did nothing about any underlying causes of crime. Ekblom and Tilley (2000) suggest it has concentrated on opportunities to the exclusion of considering the resources of the offender. To take advantage of an opportunity an offender may need certain resources physically to carry out the crime. Similarly changes in technology can swiftly alter the opportunity structures requiring manufacturers and society in general to build in crime-reduction attributes at the design stage of all items (see Laycock and Webb (2000)). The almost total disregard of these factors significantly lessens the utility of the theory which, in any event as already noted, does not address the causes of crime and can only help to prevent rather than to solve the problem.

Three studies serve as examples. First, Painter (1988) studied people's experience of crime in a small area six weeks before and six weeks after street lighting was installed. Crimes fell from 21 before to three after. Initially this was attributed simply to better lighting enabling more surveillance, but more recently the link has been recognised to be more complex. The installation of lighting increases community pride in their environment encouraging more social cohesion and informal control. It was this complex web which was said to deter criminals and criminality (Painter and Farington (1999)). Secondly, Laycock (1985) tried property marking and discovered that in three villages in a Welsh valley burglaries were reduced, in one by 40 per cent, over a 12-month period. However, the area chosen was small and sufficiently cohesive that the prospective burglars were as aware of the property marking as were the prospective victims. The results from this close community might not occur in a large urban centre. Thirdly, Mayhew et al. (1992) show some of the limitations of this process. They compared the effect of the introduction of steering locks in both Britain and West Germany. In Britain these were introduced for all new cars and resulted in a reduction of the theft of such vehicles and an increase in theft of older cars without the locks. The effect was to displace crime from one target to another rather than to reduce the number of crimes. The West Germans required all cars, new and old, to have steering locks fitted by a particular date. This produced a clear reduction in the absolute number of car thefts of all kinds and the reduction remained significant for a number of years. The lessons, if any, of these three examples are far from uniform. Only the first involved actual State action; the second suggests that target hardening involves potential victims in protecting themselves; and the third indicates that other sectors of society, such as commercial corporations, may be expected to consider crime reduction in the design of their products. Thus in general this approach was attractive for governments since it allowed them to pass much of the responsibiity for crime control to others, including individuals, though policies such as 'Crime: Together We'll Crack It' (see Garland (1996)).

Where target hardening or other environmental measures are taken by the State, they often help to enhance surveillance—the design of estates or the installing of street lights seen above. A more clearly surveillance-led initiative which has been gathering support in the 1990s is closed circuit television (CCTV). There is now an enormous literature building up on this subject (see, for example, Fyfe and Bannister (1996); Fyfe (1997); Taylor (1997); Norris and Armstrong (1997); Norris and Armstrong (1999); Williams et al. (2000); Williams and Johnstone (2000); Von Hirsch and Shearing (2000); Shapland (2000); together with writings concerning the control of public space (Davis (1990) and Fyfe (1997a)) and semi-public space (Wakefield (2000)). CCTV is perceived as a measure which can deliver control and deterrent effects because it relies on intensive surveillance. The hope here is that possible or prospective criminals (people who in the right situation might choose a criminal avenue) will worry about being watched; about the possibility of rapid intervention by the police; and about the clear evidence which the cameras will provide in any future court case. CCTV is a fairly expensive system to install and monitor; most early schemes were initiated and paid for in partnership between local authorities and the private sector. CCTV soon gained strong governmental backing. It is estimated (Koch (1998)) that by 1995, 78 per cent of the government budget for crime prevention was spent on CCTV and (Williams et al. (2000)) that between 1994 and 1998 £120 million was spent on the hardware alone. Initially most of the schemes were to protect shopping centres and tourist resorts, but the later money is largely meant to assist in the regeneration of socially marginalised, crime-ridden public-sector housing estates. All of this shows strong political support for CCTV spanning at least a decade and is embraced by both Conservative and Labour administrations. The faith in these systems is particularly interesting when their success is questionable. The most extensive long-term study concluded that any reduction in crime was so minimal as not to be worthy of note (Ditton et al. (1999)), whilst some of this reduction may simply have been by the displacement of crime to areas not protected. The system might, of course, have other more positive effects, increasing the feelings of safety of the law-abiding community and aiding in crime control (in a brawl CCTV can help decide who to arrest) and as evidence in court. Nonetheless most of the enthusiasm for CCTV arises, it is suggested (Williams et al. (2000)), from factors other than its success in controlling crime. Four such factors are mentioned: the police support it as it is an aid to their work, which is paid for by others; the State can claim to be tackling crime without direct involvement; commercial competition between town centres making claims on safety; and the legitimacy derived from general popular support which results from press and political presentation implying the effectiveness of CCTV. Even so there is evidence that for the public at large CCTV is not the most sought-after method of crime control or prevention (Williams and Johnston (2000)). Because bids are made by local areas for central funds to install CCTV this is often presented as a 'community crime prevention' initiative, but it is usually a top down initiative from official local bodies rather than from the community itself.

The public preference might be for more police on the streets, but it also sees that the cameras mostly survey and protect the fairly affluent shops in town centres. There are also more general disadvantages. First, some claim that crime is displaced to surrounding areas and to other types of criminal behaviour: in Clarke's theory, one needed both a propensity to commit crime and an opportunity; these initiatives address only the second of these and do so only in a small area of the city/ town. Secondly, CCTV may increase public indifference—people may be less inclined to report incidents if they believe the cameras should pick them up. Here the cameras are perceived not in a negative way—not as 'big brother' watching them—but rather as 'big father', solving all their problems for them. Lastly, such surveillance techniques raise problems concerning civil liberties issues: there are problems of privacy (although a CCTV Code of Practice was issued in 2000 by the Data Protection Commissioner); they allow the State to regulate more intrusively the activities of a civil society; importantly, they may be used to control order rather than crime, being used to move on undesirable elements who are not necessarily committing any offences, and it is an approach which may erode the quality of life with its encouragement of a fortress existence.

This last element is the most worrying. Norris and Armstrong (1999) have discovered that black males were regularly targeted for surveillance and that this had as much to do with appearance as with behaviour. Similarly, Williams et al. (2000) found that the cameras were sometimes used in the policing of order rather than crime and Williams and Johnstone (2000) found that they were used to move people on, particularly the young and unprepossessing, not because they had committed a crime but because they appeared not to have a respectable reason for being in that area at that particular time, or were involved in some low-level public order activities (see also Von Hirsch and Shearing (2000) and Wakefield (2000)). This type of use may become more worrying when cameras are more widely used in residential areas where people not committing offences may be prevented from legitimate use of the public spaces. The danger is that such a practice would, in this context, have everything to do with the policing of order and dealing with appearances rather than with crime (see 16.2).

A more broadly supported method of increasing surveillance might be a system of community policing, the impetus for which has come from this ecological approach to crime. Extra, or more obvious, surveillance is generally seen as a positive deterrence: when Neighbourhood Watch is properly focused it is seen to have a similar effect (Pease (1992)). The possible secondary effects of community policing could also lend support to the ecological approach: if crime is reduced and safety increased more people are encouraged to use the streets which further raises the levels of surveillance.

Policing methods are also important in reducing criminality. Crime prevention has always been a police ideal and one which is said to be central to the policing role. Until recently it has not been given priority either in training or in financing the police. However, some positive policing initiatives were set up under the Police and Criminal Evidence Act 1984 and its requirement for consultative committees. More recently ss. 5 and 6 of the Crime and Disorder Act 1998 require local authorities and the police to cooperate in an audit of levels of crime and disorder in their area and over the formulation and implementation of crime reduction strategies. The strategy has to contain long and short-term objectives that can be measured to ensure success. The idea is to enforce partnership in crime reduction and to bring the issue of crime and its resolution down to a local level so that strategies that best suit that area can be enforced. All this fits within the government's overarching crime reduction strategy (see **http://www.crimereduction.gov.uk**) and each of the authorities must report to the Home Secretary. However, as pointed out by both Wiles and Pease (2000) and Laycock and Webb (2000), s. 17 of the Crime and Disorder Act 1998 may be equally, if not more, important in delivering community safety since it aims to ensure that community safety is considered in all local authority provision of services. Ballintyne and Fraser (2000) argue that this community responsibility and consultation hold the key to successful delivery of community safety. They note that if this section is properly implemented then it should ensure that community safety and full consultation are delivered in local authority services, policing by consent and tackling social exclusion. The success of the schemes is thus based on the consultative committees being genuinely representative and on police willingness to internalise some of their views.

Properly applied, community safety enters all decision making at a local authority level; they should consider crime reduction and community safety when making decisions in the areas of: planning; public transport routes and timetables; licensing; schools; social housing. Crime prevention is thus intended to enter the fabric of all local authority decisions. Failure to do so may mean that they are held to account through judicial review or in claims for damages. Interestingly central government and devolved authorities are not bound to consider crime reduction in their decision making.

More recently language has altered—the talk is not now about 'community crime prevention' but rather about 'community safety'. The ethos is of crime being tackled through a multi-agency approach so that the responsibility rests not just with the police or central government, but is more diffuse. This is part of the move towards governance discussed in detail in Chapter Twenty. It involves individuals and communities taking responsibility for crime and its prevention, blaming fellow citizens not the wider society for any criminal activity. The way in which it has been introduced within the Crime and Disorder Act 1998 does rather less than this. First, there is an assumption that community safety is synonymous with crime: if the crime problem is solved communities will be safe. This is a very simplistic view; many things make a community unsafe, traffic regulations and flow, health risks through dangerous emissions from factories vehicles etc., food safety, lack of resources for nutritious foods, unsafe or inadequate housing, employment hazards etc. The list is endless yet the Crime and Disorder Act 1998 assumes that the link is with crime which thus takes priority both in terms of public fear and in actions by authorities. To be worthy of public attention there has to be a crime angle. This can be seen in the way drug policy is moving where in order to get treatment it may, in the future, be necessary to offend first. This makes a nonsense of dealing with individual interests and of making life safer for all. The Act also assumes that in a community all suffer the same problems of crime: in reality, dealing with the safety of some may ignore the problems of others or may actually increase their risks. Thus small pockets of high crime rates may be tolerated or actually encouraged in order to deliver relative safety in other areas of the community. One consequence of placing the resolution of crime problems in the local arena is that power and responsibility are moved from the State to other, more localised agencies and in taking a multi-agency approach accountability is made more difficult (for further discussion of how this fits into the changing role of the State in crime control see Chapter Twenty).

Lastly, an important role which police could play was suggested by Goldstein (1990) and entitled 'problem-oriented policing'. It requires police to identify particular crime problems and then carry out research to discover how best to prevent them. In this way police attention would be focused and might lead to crime reduction. The identification of problems can now, with computerised information, be carried out for very small crime areas. However, it has been recognised by Kevin Heal (1992) that purely physical changes suggested by the environmental approach are likely to be of only limited success. Any wider success would need to include psychological, and social measures as a recognition that environmental factors may not cause crime but rather offer the oportunity for it to occur. This seemingly innocuous conclusion has been questioned by Smith (2000) and Painter and Farington (1999), who claims that some situational crime prevention strategies produce unintended results because their impact on the psychology of those who live in the area greatly changes their behaviour and use of the space.

11.2.5 Weighing the ecological approach

The ecological approach seems to have a popular appeal. The people living in each city usually associate particular areas with criminality. Those living in these high crime rate areas, especially the vulnerable or those who feel most vulnerable (often the elderly and women), perceive crime as a major factor affecting their lives and governing their activities. Almost all autobiographical accounts written by male criminals include a section about the area in which they were reared, and tend to associate that with their own criminality. Ecological ideas have also been given official recognition. Lord Scarman included environment, housing and inner city location as part of the reasons for the Brixton riots of 1981 and successive BCSs

since then have found similar links. These facts, together with some of the statistical evidence, strongly suggest that there is knowledge to be gained by studying
the areas with high crime rates to see if factors can be identified which influence the
level of criminality.

This is not necessarily to accept that the studies of the ecologists are correct in
their approach or in their results. The limits of the usefulness of this research must
always be recognised. It only really studies street crime or public crime, and never
addresses the more secret and private crimes of child abuse or domestic violence.
Nor does it address the crimes (apart from burglary) committed by or against the
commercial businesses within these areas. It also almost exclusively studies male
criminality and youthful criminality. Many of these studies show little awareness of
these limitations: they might accept that they are mostly concerned with juvenile
crime, but few recognise that they are studying male criminality. Thus gender
issues or the power basis which may be involved are not addressed. Some of the
differences may be seen when looking at autobiographies of female criminals
which, instead of or as well as having accounts of the neighbourhood and its effects
on their activities, generally include reference to the family.

Ecological studies, particularly the older ones, are further constrained by being
based almost exclusively on official statistics. Again, the consequences of this are
rarely given explicit recognition. In the absence of any attempt to assess the true
rates of criminality, these studies are therefore open to the charge that they only
measure official perceptions and reactions to activities in certain areas: they do not
necessarily measure or relate to the criminal activities themselves (see labelling in
Chapter Fourteen).

If we are trying to weigh the contribution to criminological understanding made
by this approach, these limits must be recognised. And so must the possibility of
change in the broad conditions on which much of the work has been based. For
example, the close ties with youth in many of these studies may make them less
and less important as the mean age of the population increases, but this can be said
of many of the theories in this book. Also, as inner city regeneration occurs, such as
in Cardiff, Liverpool and London dock-land areas, there may well be a change in
the location of the high crime rate areas, although the reasons for their existence
may remain the same. New technologies, changing the methods of industrial production, may reduce the concentration of population in cities. Such demographic
changes have already begun, e.g., London's population has declined since the
inter-war years, and the population of most rural areas in England and Wales has
been increasing, often reversing a trend which has lasted for over a century. However, cities are likely to remain the areas of social conflicts of all sorts—riots, crimes
and racial problems, as well as most labour disputes and demonstrations. Research
into the crime rates of the city areas is thus likely to remain an important sphere of
study in the future. None the less, it needs to be complemented by ecological
studies into crime in rural areas.

The ideas expounded in the ecological studies have, as already indicated, led to
many practical changes. Despite some success in the way such schemes or design
changes have, in certain cases, cut down on levels of criminality, too much
emphasis on this type of factor may have some unfavourable features. This is particularly so in cases where it leads to a form of victim blaming—saying crime is
committed because victims are careless (see 5.6 and also Duff and Marshall (2000)

and Kleinig (2000)). With this reservation, some of the reforms have been fairly successful.

Possibly the most important implications of the work of Shaw and McKay lie not so much in the pure ecological area, but rather in the fact that they introduced or strengthened two ideas in accepted criminological knowledge: that which connects social control and criminality; and that of cultural support for behaviour. The first of these ideas was partially introduced by Durkheim, whose work will be considered in the next chapter, but was fully elaborated by the control theorists whose work will be considered in Chapter Thirteen. The second idea is a mixture of social learning theories, which were considered in Chapter Ten, and cultural and sub-cultural theories, which will be discussed in the next section and Chapter Twelve. All these approaches are mostly concerned with limiting or controlling observable behaviour and are less directed at motivation, intent and social pressure. The focus is on practical crime prevention and altering behaviour through reducing opportunity and increasing surveillance. One complication is that situational crime prevention strategies have different uses: some aiming to support the most vulnerable, repeat victims and ethnic minorities; others to protect business and the more affluent (much of CCTV and private policing). This diversity of use makes evaluation of the benefits and problems of situational crime prevention more complex (see for a discussion of these issues Von Hirsch et al. (2000)).

11.3 Poverty and unemployment

11.3.1 Poverty and economic or income inequality

The theorists considered in the last section connected criminality with social disorganisation. In general, however, they found that the areas of greatest social disorganisation were also the poorest, but they failed to prove conclusively that it was disorganisation rather than poverty which caused the criminality. As was mentioned above, when Sainsbury (1955) did separate these elements he found crime was connected more closely to poverty than to social disorganisation, while others (e.g., Bottoms et al. (1992)) would also wish to include a link with ecological aspects.

In any event, the link between poverty and criminality is not as simple as Sainsbury's findings might suggest. Clearly, poverty *per se* does not cause criminality, as there are many tribes and peoples who are materially very poor but do not have a high crime rate. One possible hypothesis is that poverty is only a major factor in criminality if wealth is given great status in the society, and/or if it leads to some groups or individuals being deprived of the necessities of life. Bound up with this there are two related factors—economic or income inequality, and relative deprivation. Economic or income inequality exists where there is a substantial difference between the material or income level of those who have least in a society and that of other groups. It is the gap between rich and poor which is important: it is not necessary for there to be absolute poverty (if we could define such a term) in the society. The implication is that in a society with a relatively equal distribution, even if every member were poorer, the crime rate would be lower. Many writers (such as Stack (1984)) try to define the connection even more closely by suggesting that it is not just the inequality itself which affects the crime rate, but the feeling that such inequality is unfair (i.e., relative deprivation). This is especially likely to arise in societies where material success is put forward as an acceptable goal and citizens are officially told that individuals are equal. Confusion arises where the notion of poverty is discussed without consideration of such aspects as income inequality and relative deprivation.

Most of the theories which consider a simple link between crime and poverty are older and have been largely discredited. Today the viable theory is the possible link between crime and economic or income inequality. Box (1987) concluded that for crimes other than homicide there seemed to be a very strong relationship, which may even be causal, with equality. Even the exception of homicide has been questioned. Vold, Bernard and Sniper (2002) refer to six studies which show a clear link between social inequality and homicide, but a much weaker link in the case of property offences. The issue will be revisited through a discussion of relative deprivation in 12.2.

As shown earlier (Chapter Four) what cannot be denied is that more offenders are poor and that most offences are committed against the poor. Hence poverty has come to be recognised as a factor in a number of countries. The Australian National Crime Prevention (1999), for example, sees poverty as being closely related to high crime rates and thus accepting that there is a higher risk of criminality by and against the poor, while recognising that many of the poor were not affected. The intention is to address the problem through such means as building ties within the community. Such an approach is supported by many academics (see, e.g., Tolley and Tregeagle (1998)). The Crime Prevention Council of Canada, which also recognised the link between crime and poverty, suggested the need for structural and economic support as well as building community cohesion. An American study Lee (2000) has suggested a more specific link between crime, particularly violence, and concentrated poverty, (i.e., where the poor live in ghettos rather than being more dispersed). This might be seen to be a link between social exclusion and criminality. Since 1997 the UK has taken a middle ground. Recognising the problems caused by poverty, crime being one, the government chose to tackle some of these but largely for those who were willing to help themselves—policies such as the national minimum wage, abolishing national insurance for the low paid and working families' tax credits have all taken many families out of poverty. However, these are only for those who work. State benefits have been very slow to rise. Many of the social cohesion policies involve pressures on individuals through orders such as those on antisocial behaviour, parenting and child safety. There are also the strategic plans set by local authorities and police. Thus although the link between crime and poverty is back on the agenda, many of the ways of coping with it address individual issues and community structures but not the underlying poverty.

11.3.2 Unemployment

Unemployment is also associated with wealth or the lack of it. Unemployment is both an indicator of the general economic well-being in a State, and of the equality of distribution of that wealth. Unemployment generally increases in times of depression, and decreases in times of prosperity and growth. If crime increases with unemployment, this might indicate a feeling of unfair treatment ('why should I lose my job?'), but it might also show that the resultant inequality in economic position, the pure fact of poverty, or boredom and free time might be factors in the equation. Is there a relationship between crime and unemployment?

Not surprisingly, there is no simple answer to this question. Studies are inconclusive. Some, such as Danziger and Wheeler (1975), discovered that crime (they studied in particular aggravated assault, burglary and robbery) was not related to unemployment. Others, such as the British researcher Brenner (1978), reported a significant relationship between crime and unemployment. However, in analysing these studies, Crow et al. (1989), Box (1987), Vold, Bernard and Snipe (2002) and Long and Witte (1981) all conclude that on balance crime and unemployment are related; that this relationship is not consistently strong; that it is seen at a localised rather than a national level; and that it is probably strongest and most consistent in the case of young males. The last aspect is supported by Allan and Steffensmeier (1989), who found that unemployment was most clearly associated with the arrest rates of 14–17-year-old males (juveniles) for property crimes. Their use of arrest rates rather than criminality prompts caution, but nonetheless it is probably indicative of a connection between employment status and crime.

In Britain there has been a continuing heated debate concerning links between unemployment and crime. In 1994, the Home Office proposed including rates of unemployment and of long-term unemployment as two of the predictors of high levels of crime in an area (others included rates of lone parent families and the number of council estates). The intention was to base police funding on these aspects. The then government were ideologically unconvinced of such links and quickly funded further research. Orme (1994) found no such links and so these predictors were withdrawn for funding purposes. Orme's report was heavily criticised: it took recorded notifiable offences as the indicator of criminality (as was seen in Chapter Four, this is a very imprecise base); it looked at large police force areas, which may have missed smaller problem communities; and it took the number claiming unemployment and related benefits as the indicator of unemployment, but this measure excludes most of those under 18, the largest criminal group and the one which has a particularly high rate of unemployment. A number of other studies (see, e.g., Dickenson (1994) and Wells (1995)) have found definite, but not overwhelming, links with unemployment.

The balance of the evidence suggests that, despite government assertions to the contrary in the 1980s and early 1990s, there is some link between crime rates and rates of unemployment. This view is firmly supported by Pyle (1998) who analysed the extensive literature in this area and concluded that there is a link between the economy and the rate of recorded crime. Considerable empirical evidence existed to show that in a period of economic recession (which includes unemployment) the level of recorded crime, especially against property, increases; and when there is a boom it falls. What is less clear is the nature of the link. The issue acquired particular relevance in the 1980s and 1990s when the level of unemployment was consistently high. We shall look briefly at two contrasting interpretations of the link between this experience and crime. Petras and Davenport (1992) pointed out that the high levels of unemployment have had far-reaching destructive effects on individuals and communities. They link these destructive effects with the effects of the free-market economy, which they view as a form of social engineering which has further destructive effects on poor communities. Amongst the negative effects they identify: the exclusion of those most affected from the benefits of a consumer society, and their experience of poor health, high levels of suicide and early death. They also point to a substantial increase in criminal activity; very high levels of property offences, both acquisitive and destructive; and a rise in interpersonal violence. These have certainly occurred during this period, making the causative link at least highly plausible. In particular, the link between the unemployment of the 1980s and high rates of criminality amongst the young are forcefully suggested.

In a very different study of unemployment in parts of London, Hagan (1993) offers a quite different reading. He accepts an association between the overall rising trends in unemployment and crime, but argues that at a micro level it was early criminal behaviour and its continuation over time which tended to lead to adult unemployment. Criminal activity may remove individuals from the legitimate culture making it more likely that they would remain unemployed. Reinforced by peer-group pressures and parental criminal activity, criminality in youths would in turn lead to unemployment of youths: the stronger the criminal embedment, he claimed, the more likely that adult unemployment would follow. On this view, the individual's criminal behaviour is used to explain their unemployment whilst structural problems linked to unemployment are ignored.

These two approaches show very different aspects of the possible link between crime and unemployment. They may each be of some validity. The first suggests that, in areas of high and continuing unemployment, youths, especially, may be driven to crime; the latter suggests that those with a criminal record may find it difficult to break out of unemployment. These are arguments about the *direction* of causation: from unemployment to criminality or vice versa. Others question whether there is a causative relationship at all. For example, Wilson and Herrnstein (1985) suggest that differences between individuals may precede, and be associated with, unemployment and criminality. This would make it possible for there to be correlation between the two without any necessary causation. Unemployment may not be a causative factor in criminality, but to suggest that unemployment, particularly at the levels suffered in Britain through the 1980s and early 1990s, stemmed only from elements internal to the individual seems unlikely. It is far more probable that the demise of the larger manufacturing industries and the major restructuring of the economy in line with a free-market enterprise-led economy would have had some influence. Through the 1980s and 1990s there was a widening gap between rich and poor. In 1979 there were 5 million (5 per cent of all households) living on less than half the average national household income (the basic measure of poverty in Britain); by 1991 this figure had risen to 13.5 million (12 per cent of households). Although there was then a drop in the mid-1990s they rose again to about 10 per cent of households from 1996 to 2000 (*Social Trends*, 2002). Moreover, many unofficial estimates put the figure much higher so that Opportunity for All (1999) gave comparable figures for these dates of 10, 24 and 22 per cent. Official crime rates doubled over the same period. Much of the poverty is suffered by the unemployed, whose unemployment benefit has dropped by 20 per cent in real terms since 1979. The young have been hardest hit, being largely excluded from full benefit. The young are also the group most affected by State reduction in public housing (another result of a free-market economy) which Shelter estimates leads to about 150,000 young people becoming homeless every year. Since these trends particularly affect the young, and since all criminologists agree that delinquency is most prevalent among the young, particularly teenagers, it would be surprising if there were no link between unemployment, poverty, homelessness and crime. Such factors may not be causative—and, as we have seen, establishing causal connections in this area with so many variables is very tricky— but to suggest that they could be explained away on purely individualistic reasons is intuitively untenable, especially when all these factors have obvious connections with society. They are largely socially constructed problems, which in the case of unemployment, poverty and homelessness have been directly related to market society. One influential writer (Currie (1997)) has also argued for a causal connection between the free market and violent crime, both because of the greed and selfishness engendered by unregulated markets and because of the dehumanising effects of unemployment and poverty. Currie has further suggested that there may also be a tangential link—unemployment causes poverty and both of these lead some to feel disruption, hopelessness and depression encouraging drug use (and rates of opium use have been correlated with unemployment); in order to finance the drug use, they then turn to crime. Similarly Jock Young (1999) draws clear links between these factors and young male criminality where crime may be one of the few roles open to them in a modern era where there is unemployment and where women are frequently choosing not to pair up with men on a permanent basis. In the male-dominated power of crime they seek and find macho images and sub-cultural respect. These feelings are often directed against other groups—from other areas, other races or other football teams. Much of this is violent but it may include property offences. Similarly Taylor (1999) relates youth crime directly to the declining fortunes experienced by this group. He is not suggesting that unemployment or poverty cause crime but rather that the enormous economic changes over the past 30 years have so altered social interactions that the nature of crime has both shifted and increased.

11.3.3 Evaluation of theories of poverty and unemployment

There is now widespread, though not total, acceptance that there is a strong relationship between criminality and economic or income inequality; that there is probably a relationship between crime and unemployment; and that this relationship is strongest in the case of young males. All of this may go some way towards explaining why the community project carried out by Shaw and McKay in Chicago did not succeed in reducing crime (see 11.2.4)—it did not attempt to alter the social and economic conditions, but instead tried to teach the people to come to terms with these problems.

11.4 Lower-class culture

11.4.1 Early class theories

The previous sociological theories in this chapter examined some views on the connection between crime and two broad social factors—ecology (particularly social disorganisation), and wealth distribution. This section examines some theories on the way crime is related to the people in society, not as individuals but as collective groups, and to the way of life of certain classes, particularly the lower or working classes. In such an approach, it is the lower-class culture *per se* which causes criminality. The argument is that, by conforming to lower-class values, the individual will break the law. The work of three criminologists, one American and two British, will be briefly discussed. They were all writing at a time and in a context when class differences and distinctions were more marked than they now are. Nonetheless they are included because they express in a purer and starker form views and attitudes which are still held.

11.4.1.1 *Miller*

Walter Miller, an American writer, presents the idea that working-class values include a delinquent subculture. He argues that there are distinctive working or lower-class values, many of which are quite different from the middle-class values upon which our legal system is based. Adherence to the lower-class values in some instances more or less automatically leads to breaking the law. Those whose upbringing and behaviour falls within the lower-class norms are highly likely to be led to violate some aspects of the law (Miller (1958)).

Miller offers no explanation for the origins of these social values. All he does is to mark their existence and explain that conforming to them will lead to criminality adding that it is common in lower-class households for the father to be absent, often because he has breached the criminal laws. The home life is a female-dominated environment which, he says, leads lowerclass boys to look for male role models outside the home. They often find them in street gangs which Miller calls 'one sex peer units'. These gangs take part in activities which uphold the lower-class 'focal concerns' and give the youths a sense of belonging and status.

11.4.1.2 *Mays*

From a similar standpoint, Mays (1954, 1968 and 1975), a British analyst in this field, argues that in certain areas, particularly older urban areas, the residents share a number of attitudes and ways of behaving which predispose them to criminality. These attitudes have existed for years and are passed on to newcomers. Lower-class culture is not therefore intentionally criminal; it is just a different socialisation which, at times, happens to be contrary to the legal rules. He sees it not as a symptom of maladjustment but rather as a very well-adjusted subculture. The problem arises because the subculture is in conflict with aspects of the culture of the country as a whole, especially that which is enshrined in our legal system. Criminality, particularly juvenile criminality, is not therefore seen as a conscious rebellion against middle-class values. It arises from an alternative working-class subculture which has been adopted and altered over the years in a haphazard sort of way. The driving force may never have been to breach the criminal rules, but the result was sometimes to do so. He says:

it seemed to me that excessive leisure time, the absence of adequate parental models and care, the presence of known adult offenders in the locality together with the boys' own natural desire to test themselves in acts of daring, bravado and danger, were a sufficient explanation for delinquent behaviour which invariably tapered off after leaving school and was almost certainly phasic in character. (Mays (1975), p. 63; see also Mays (1968) and (1975))

Like Miller, Mays does not discuss the origins of the social values, except in the negative sense of saying that it is not a hostile reaction against middle-class values. Or, more positively, that it is the set of values which best meets the social needs of that sector of society.

11.4.1.3 *Morris*

The third theorist is Terence Morris (1957), who is basically an ecologist. He argues that social delinquents abound in the lower classes, and that it is the class characteristics which have caused the criminality. Antisocial behaviour exists throughout society and in all classes, but the way in which it is expressed differs and depends upon membership of a particular class. Criminality he sees as largely a lower-class expression (Morris (1957)).

This is because the whole socialisation process in the lower class is more likely to produce criminality than the same process in the middle classes. The upbringing in the middle-class home is controlled by the family, is very ordered, and almost all activities are centred around the home and family. In the lower classes, the child's upbringing from a young age, about three or four, was split between family and home on the one hand, and peer group and street acquaintances on the other. The working-class child is likely to have a less ordered and regulated upbringing and to be sent out to play in the street. The peer group is therefore a much stronger influence from a much earlier age. Like Miller and Mays he depicts the lower-class culture as driven by a desire for immediate gratification of both material and physical needs: self-control and deferred goals are much less common. Controls of these youths within their own community are negligible: they only come to be controlled when they commit a crime and the official systems of control step in. The essential message of Morris is that the whole ethos of the working class is more oriented towards criminality and antisocial behaviour.

11.4.1.4 *Evaluation*

Each of these three theories suffers from a common defect. They predict too much criminality, and cannot account for law-abiding behaviour within the lower classes. There is also an implicit prediction that individuals would continue in their criminal activity, or at least their support of such activity, throughout their lives. This conflicts with a widespread finding that most people's delinquency reduces considerably at about the age of 20. This approach carries the implicit assumption that man is rigidly socialised and virtually unable to think outside the social constraints: if the social group accepts crime as normal and natural, the individual passively participates. Critics resist this argument and say that the individual usually needs a reason or a motive to act.

Mays attempted to answer criticism by asserting that people living in the lower classes who are non-criminal, or those who wish to protect their children from criminality, do not subject their children to the full lower-class values or, at least, not the more criminalogenic ones. It is a concession which leaves much of the original explanation in tatters. Mays goes on to assert that of those who embrace the full lower-class values, probably most do at some time commit a criminal act, but only a small number get caught. He seems to be saying that certain types of offences are thought of as normal, and although they might be easy to detect, they do not attract attention from the rest of the community and so are less likely to be either reported or solved.

All these approaches suffer from at least two major confusions. First, there is the confusion between area and class, which are often used as more or less inter-changeable terms. Secondly, and more fundamentally, there are the confusions arising out of an implicit treatment of the 'working class' as constituting a more or less homogeneous group. Even in the nineteenth century historians had recognised the existence of, for example, a 'labour aristocracy', where a strong desire was for 'respectability'. More recently, the whole notion of 'the working class' is often questioned. But for our purposes we only need to note that the dangers of sliding into an imputed homogenicity are quite general. To put it another way:

... not everyone in a 'Catholic country' is devout, nor are even the devout always at mass or confession. (Heidensohn (1989), p. 21)

Certainly, in a criminal class (if there be such a thing) not everyone need be criminal, nor are criminals constantly involved in crime.

Furthermore, many of the definitions of class are based on concepts of the occupation of the traditional adult male breadwinner, which is not so relevant today. In many households both parents work, whilst there are also many single-parent households: neither of these groups necessarily falls neatly into the older definitions of class. The whole concept of class as used by the above researchers has become more problematic and some now argue that there is no relationship between class and crime (see Dunaway et al. (2000)).

Nonetheless several recent studies suggest that it would be premature to declare the total demise of a correlation between lower class and offending. After observing 1,000 Toronto school and street youths, Hagan and McCarthy (1992) concluded that class conditions still caused offending and delinquency (in its wider socio-logical concept). They considered that an important causative element in the correlation was something which they termed 'streetlife'. The clear correlation found between class and 'streetlife' and criminality was also identified by Foster (1990) and Farnworth et al. (1994). Foster discovered that in certain high crime rate areas, juvenile street crime was the norm and progressed on to crimes in the black economy as offenders got older. She found that although deviance was not supported by the community, particularly the older community, it was not really condemned either; there was a sort of ambivalence—it is wrong but not very harmful. This tolerance of minor criminality did not cross over into severe violence which was condemned. But mostly Foster was struck by the normality of the whole process. Although some studies (Benoit et al. (2003)) indicate that the link between streetlife and lower-class offending was neither simple nor linear, there is wide acceptance of some connection. Farnworth et al. (1994) tried to explain the link, finding correlations when using measures of class; but strong correlations between serious street crime, delinquency and the concept of 'underclass'. The last is seen as long-term material deprivation with little possibility of being legally altered: it can be measured by such factors as persistent parental unemployment and long-term receipt of benefit. In any event, there is still some vigour in class theories as long as they consider other aspects of the equation, define class more clearly, and/or look for causative links rather than just assuming that a correlation automatically implies a causation.

11.4.2 Socio-economic status (SES)

Closely related to class are the numerous reports (e.g., West (1982) and Farrington (1992)) concerned with SES. They found that, even on their own, such factors as family income, housing, employment instability and family size related to criminality: large family size was seen as a particularly strong predictor. In these Cambridge studies a low SES was consistently associated with higher self-reported and official offending, although there was no such consistent link between parental occupational groups and crime. Again, the implication is that SES seems now to be associated with criminality, whereas old concepts and measures of class are less reliable predictors. But the reasons are uncertain: SES may be associated with deprivation or with unemployment, both of which were considered above. For example, Farrington (1986), reported that an erratic work record of the father is a good predictor of youth offending and an unstable or bad employment record for a young man is a firm predictor of criminality in early adulthood.

11.4.3 Modern associations of an underclass with criminality

In the introduction to this chapter there was mention of a connection between offending and an underclass in the nineteenth century. More recently very similar arguments have arisen. Much of the discussion in connection with criminality has emanated from an American writer, Murray (1990 and 1994), who has used both US and British examples to make his point. He is not alone in writing about what he consciously stigmatises as a new underclass and in considering welfare dependency as a social problem which causes many social ills. Much of the new right ideology which has had political prevalence in the past 20 years or so also centres around some of this debate, although not everyone has associated the problems of offending directly with welfare dependency. Murray suggests that the welfare provision has permitted some to survive outside the legitimate job market for too long. He directly echoes the early nineteenth-century arguments about pauperism in claiming that: those on welfare become dependent and take no responsibility for their own situation; that some young women have deliberately become pregnant to increase their welfare provision or to obtain housing. The final element Murray adds is criminality: men without families use crime to prove their masculinity. He makes the undemonstrated assertion that this can explain most of the officially recorded 60 per cent increase in violent offences which arose in Britain between 1980 and 1988. Murray should not be read without understanding his political subtext: the removal of benefits to force individuals to support themselves which, in his subjective judgement, would restore their enterprise. Liberal welfare writers such as Frank Field (1990) attack Murray for having invented a Victorian-style undeserving poor, to be distinguished from the deserving poor who are trying to support themselves but may occasionally need a little help. In Field's view at that time (it was much modified later) any dependent class has been politically and socially constructed by such new right policies as mass unemployment and regressive taxation. In the face of increasing inequalities the unsocial activities of some in this group, while still condemned, can be seen as understandable. In particular, as mentioned above (11.3.2), the massive structural unemployment can have far-reaching destructive effects, including poverty, homelessness, illnesses, drug abuse and an undermining of social controls and constructs, all of which may then lead to increased criminality. On this analysis it is not the underclass, if any such group exists, that is the problem but the society which has excluded certain groups from the benefits of a free-market economy. The difficult question is whether membership of the underclass arises because of the attitudes, or whether the attitudes and criminal activity arise as a result of the structure of the society. It may only mean that the organisation of society has so reduced the options of these people that offending becomes a rational choice. An historical study of social deprivation (Kennedy (1997)) finds similar fears of social disorder and dangerous classes, requiring changes in society and in methods of social control. The underclass is not of itself more criminal, but criminality is generated when other social choices are closed (see Young (2000) and Taylor (1999)).

In England the problems of an underclass were taken seriously by the Labour administration of 1997. They set up the Social Exclusion Unit with a brief to work towards reintegrating even the most socially deprived individuals and communities. The unit has worked mostly at the re-inclusion of communities which are distinguished by membership of the most socially deprived and crime-ridden housing estates. It has taken time to set in place its strategy entitled *A New Commitment to Neighbourhood Renewal: National Strategy Action Plan* (referred to as the 'National Strategy Action Plan') which was launched in January 2001. Their main initiatives include the following:

- *Jobs*: Increase employment rates in the areas worst hit by unemployment.
- *Skills*: Set levels of achievement for all LEAs and ensure that the lowest do not fall below a predetermined threshold.
- *Crime*: Reduce domestic burglary by 25 per cent, with no area having a rate more than three times the national average.
- *Health*: To reduce health inequalities, by at least 10 per cent between those areas (one in five) with the lowest life expectancy at birth and the population as a whole.
- *Housing*: Reduce by 33 per cent the number of households living in non-decent social housing, with most improvement in the most deprived local authority areas.

These are designed to address some of the aspects that mark out the underclass, in order to alter attitudes, reduce criminality, and make the term 'underclass' irrelevant. It is an ambitious target. There has been some progress (see *Preventing Social Exclusion* (2001)) and it is necessarily a slow process, but whether its delivery will be effected, or possible, remains to be seen. Similar units have been set up by each of the devolved powers: Scottish Social Exclusion Strategy; Building on Inclusion Wales; and New Targeting Social Initiation for Northern Ireland.

11.5 Conclusion

The first two theories in this chapter (ecology and poverty and unemployment) relate criminality to 'objective' social and economic facts. They claim to prove that crime is statistically related to poverty or wealth distribution, or to social disorganisation. The incidence of a statistical link is, of course, highly important, but it does not necessarily mean that there is a direct causal connection. One objection arises from the frailty of the statistical base, especially the shortcomings (already rehearsed) of official statistics of crime. Another is that the statistical connection is inadequate to establish whether the real causal connection is with poverty, with relative inequality, or with some other factor. Part of the causal relationship may be tied up with feelings of unfairness which may put the individual into a stressful position. Strain will be discussed in the next chapter (12.2). More generally, the aspects examined in this chapter have been more concerned with practical crime prevention rather than causes. In the absence of any firm underpinning, however, this narrow approach is likely to fail as often as it succeeds, or to have substantial drawbacks. For example, the use of CCTV involves a great deal of surveillance of the law-abiding (the majority) in the hope of catching or deterring a few.

There were similar objections to any general acceptance of the Chicago School's claim that there was a close relation between social disorganisation and criminality. The final set of theories posited a connection between criminality and lower-class values. The claim made in some of the earlier studies was that different sectors of society live by slightly different rules, and some of the values of some sectors are criminal. Nowhere are these rules closely defined or proven to exist.

In more recent research there is consideration of the links between offending and class which gives some insight to how the situations may be linked. In later claims there is either an amalgamation of factors, some of which would have been considered separately under poverty or unemployment, or a very politicised claim about what causes the particular correlation between offending and class/SES/underclass which is claimed to exist.

This chapter has examined various approaches to the possible connection of crime to a variety of social aspects (ecology, poverty, unemployment and lower-class values). The results are often illuminating but, even where there is a strong statistical connection, it is not possible to prove a causal connection. In particular, none of the studies can explain why men seem to be so badly affected and women so little affected. These theories are largely building blocks from which more elaborate structures may be constructed.

SUGGESTED READING

Felson, M. (1997), *Crime and Everyday Life*, 2nd edn, Thousand Oaks, CA: Pine Forge.

Hope, T. (1995), 'Community Crime Prevention', in M. Tonry and D. Farrington (eds), *Building a Safer Society: Strategic Approaches to Crime*, Chicago, IL: University of Chicago Press.

Painter, K. and Farington, D. (1999), 'Street Lighting and Crime: Diffusion of Benefits in the Stoke-on-Trent Project', in K. Painter and N. Tilley (eds), *Surveillance of Public Space: CCTV, Street Lighting and Crime Prevention*, Monsy, NY: Criminal Justice Press.

Wikström, P-O. and Loeber, R. (2000), 'Do Disadvantaged Neighbourhoods Cause Well-Adjusted Children to Become Adolescent Delinquents?: A Study of Male Serious Juvenile Offending, Individual Risk and Protective Factors, and Neighbourhood Context', *Criminology* 38: 1109.

REVISION BOX

Most of the themes in this chapter although dealing with social factors are still basically deterministic; they largely view the factors as antecedents to criminal activity with little room for the free will. The behaviour is explained by or a result of the antecedent situations arising. If they are seen as the main or only explanations they represent a real challenge to the idea that criminals are responsible for their behaviour and therefore should face the consequences when caught. For this reason theories based strongly on these aspects are not fully supported by politicians and society where the desire to hold individuals to account and to inflict severe punishments for transgressions is strong, at least in the rhetoric. However, it does fall in with the modern desire to remove from society those people who are dangerous whether that danger arises because of something within or outside the individual or a combination of these.

   So if one looks at ideas relating to social disorganisation and some of the class theories, the claims are largely that due to this social situation or pathology individuals are likely to commit criminal activities. Many find this difficult to accept as it largely removes or denies the human decision-making from the process and thus they would argue removed the true meaning or understanding from it. Furthermore it assumes that law abiding behaviour is necessarily accepted by most whereas most are unaware of what the law provides and might not support much of it (see Chapters Two and Three). More importantly these theorists assume that there is a 'normal' society and that different forms of socialisation and social organisation are therefore pathological and so necessarily equated with negative behaviours, such as criminality. There are therefore all kinds of value judgements underlying the theories which are ignored in their description and in many of the discussions concerning their veracity or their utility as causative factors.

   The one discussion within this chapter where some free will was seen to shine through was opportunity and crime and routine activity theory. This is part of what is referred to as rational choice theory. Rational choice theory postulates that offenders act in order to gain an advantage and whilst some of rational choice theory deals with the early sections of this choice process within this chapter it has merely been looking at the final decision of whether to commit this offence in this place at this time. Here the idea is that a particular crime is the rational choice of a particular individual at a particular time. The aspect of rational choice theory used in this chapter has nothing to do with why the individual may be willing to offend but rather looks at trying to make particular crimes less attractive or less rational a choice. Here free will does enter the equation but only in so far as it might impinge on an immediate decision to commit this crime or not at this time and in this place. As was seen earlier the claim is that crime occurs when one gets a motivated offender, an attractive target and lack of security or surveillance of that target. The theory is really built on a practical means of fighting crime—situational prevention. Therefore practical changes are made to the environment which it is hoped might reduce criminal behaviour, design changes to products, alteration to the distribution, maintenance and delivery of services and products, greater security and surveillance etc. The essence is that it limits vulnerability to crime. Whilst these have proved to be successful in reducing crime one should not really see them as addressing the causes of crime. Leaving money accessible in an open case does not cause an individual to take it; it merely facilitates this activity if the individual is anyway willing to perform such acts. Removing the attractive targets or making it more difficult to perform the criminal act in that place at that time does not alter or influence whether an individual is willing to commit crime, it merely impinges on whether they are willing to perform that crime at that time. If they are really intent on criminality they will find other targets, will take greater risks or find other ways of committing the crime. It does not therefore address the underlying issue though, as many offenders may not be bothered to go out of their way to offend, it may well solve a number of the problems society feels it is suffering from. In doing so it may however reduce enjoyment of others or intrude into their privacy to an unacceptable degree and therefore although it may have some success the price in the change to our society and the lack of trust engendered may be too high.

QUESTIONS FOR REVISIONS

1 In governmental policy community safety has become synonymous with crime reduction. Consider what advantages and problems may flow from this political fact. In consideration of this you might use material both from this chapter and Chapter Ten.

2 Consider the situational preventative methods discussed in this chapter and consider whether policies should be led by pragmatism or justice.

3 Is governmental willingness to address social exclusion politically innovative and how does it relate to the crime problem? Should reduction in criminal activity have been included in the targets to be met for tackling social exclusion and if so is an across the board reduction in domestic burglary the correct goal to aim for?

REFERENCES

Anderson, E. (1999), *Code of the Street: Decency, Violence and the Moral Life of the Inner City*, New York: W.W. Norton & Company.

Armitage, R. (2000), *An Evalution of Secured by Design Housing in West Yorkshire* Briefing note 7/00. London: Home Office. **http://www.homeoffice.gov.uk/rds/prgpdfs/brf700.pdf**.

Ashton, J., Brown, I., Senior, B. and Pease, K. (1998), 'Repeat Victimisation: Offender Accounts', *International Journal of Risk Security and Crime Prevention*, vol. 3, p. 201.

Australian National Crime Prevention (1999), *Pathways to Prevention: Developmental and Early Intervention Approaches to Crime in Australia*, Canberra: Commonwealth Attorney-General's Department.

Ballintyne, S. and Fraser, P. (2000), 'It's Good to Talk, but It's Not Good Enough', in S. Ballintyne, K. Pease and V. McLaren (eds) *Secure Foundations: Key Issues in Crime Prevention, Crime Reduction and Community Safety*, Southampton: Institute for Public Policy Research.

Barker, M. (2000), 'The Criminal Range of Small-Town Burglars', in D. Canter and L.J. Alison, *Profiling Property Crimes*, Aldershot: Dartmouth.

Benoit, E., Randolph, D., Dunlap, D. and Johnson, B. (2003), 'Code Switching and Inverse Imitation among Marijuana-Using Crack Sellers' *British Journal of Criminology*, vol. 43, p. 506.

Bottoms, A.E., Claytor, A. and Wiles, P. (1992), 'Housing Markets and Residential Community Crime Careers: a Case Study from Sheffield', in David J. Evans, Nicholas R. Fyfe and David T. Herbert (eds), *Crime, Policing and Place: Essays in Environmental Criminology*, London: Routledge.

Bottoms, A.E., Mawby, R.E. and Zanthos, P. (1989), 'A Tale of Two Estates', in David Downes, *Crime and the City*, London: Macmillan.

Bottoms, A.E. and Wiles, P. (2002), 'Environmental Criminology', in Mike Maguire, Rod Morgan and Robert Reiner (eds), *The Oxford Handbook of Criminology*, Oxford: Oxford University Press.

Box, Steven (1987), *Recession, Crime and Punishment*, London: Macmillan Education.

Brantingham, P.J. and Brantingham, P.L. (eds) (1989), *Patterns in Crime*, New York: Macmillan.

Brantingham, P.J. and Brantingham, P.L. (1991), *Environmental Criminology*, 2nd edn, Prospect Heights, IL: Waveland Press.

Brantingham, P.J. and Brantingham, P.L. (1993), 'Environment, Routine and Situation: Towards a Pattern Theory of Crime', in R. Clark and M. Felson (eds), *Routine Activity and Rational Choice*, New Brunswick, NJ: Transaction.

Brenner, H. (1978), 'Review of Fox's "Forecasting Crime" ', *Journal of Criminal Law and Criminology*, vol. 70, p. 273.

Burgess, Ernest, W. (1928), 'The Growth of the City', in Robert E. Park, Ernest W. Burgess and Roderick D. McKenzie (eds), *The City*, Chicago, IL: University of Chicago Press.

Bursik, R.J. (1986), 'Ecological Stability and the Dynamics of Delinquency', in A.J. Reis and M. Tonry (eds), *Communities and Crime*, Chicago, IL: University of Chicago Press.

Campbell, B. (1993), *Goliath: Britain's Dangerous Places*, London: Methuen.

Canter, D. (1995), 'Psychology of Offender Profiling', in D. Canter and L.J. Alison (eds), *Criminal Detection and the Psychology of Crime*, London: Ashgate.

Canter, D. and Alison, L.J. (2000), *Profiling Property Crimes*, Aldershot: Dartmouth.

Chadwick Reports (1839), Royal Commissions on the Rural Constabulary Force, 'First Report of the Commissioners Appointed to Inquire as to the Best Means of Establishing an Efficient Constabulary Force in the Counties of England and Wales', 169 *Parliamentary Papers*, Reports, vol. 19, p. 1.

Clarke, Ronald (1978), *Tackling Vandalism*. London: HMSO.

Clarke, Ronald (1980), 'Situational Crime Prevention: Theory and Practice', *British Journal of Criminology*, vol. 20, p. 136.

Clarke, Ronald (1983), 'Situational Crime Prevention: Its Theoretical Basis and Practical Scope', in M. Tonry and N. Morris (eds), *Crime and Justice: an Annual Review of Research*, vol. 4, Chicago, IL: University of Chicago Press.

Clarke, Ronald (1992), *Situational Crime Prevention: Successful Case Studies*, New York: Harrow & Heston.

Clarke, Ronald (1995), 'Situational Crime Prevention', in M. Tonry and D.P. Farrington (eds), *Building a Safer Society*, Chicago, IL: University of Chicago Press.

Clarke, Ronald and Cornish, D. (eds) (1983), *Crime Control in Britain a Review of Policy Research*, Albany, NY: State University of New York Press.

Clarke, R. and Felson, M. (eds) (1993), *Routine Activity and Rational Choice*, New Brunswick, NJ: Transaction.

Coleman, Alice (1988), 'Design Disadvantage and Design Improvement', *The Criminologist*, vol. 12, p. 20.

Coleman, Alice (1990), *Utopia on Trial*, 2nd edn, London: Hilary Shipman.

Crime in England and Wales (annual publication), London: Home Office **http://www.homeoffice.gove.uk/rds/hosbarchive.html**.

Crime Prevention Council of Canada (1997), *Preventing Crime by Investing in Families*, Ottowa: National Crime Prevention Council.

Croall, H. (1998), 'Business Crime and the Community', *International Journal of Risk Security and Crime Prevention*, vol. 3, p. 281.

Crow, Iain, Richardson, Paul, Riddington, Carol and Simon, Frances (1989), *Unemployment, Crime and Offenders*, a NACRO publication, London: Routledge.

Currie, Elliot (1997), 'Market, Crime and Community: Toward a Mid-range Theory of Post-industiral Violence' *Theoretical Criminology*, vol. 1, p. 147.

Danziger, S. and Wheeler, D. (1975), 'The Economics of Crime: Punishment or Income Redistribution?', *Review of Social Economy*, vol. 33, p. 113.

Davis, Mike (1990), *City of Quartz*, London: Verso.

Dickinson, D. (1994), *Crime and Unemployment*, Department of Applied Economics: University of Cambridge.

Ditton, J., Short, E., Phillips, S., Norris, C. and Armstrong, G. (1999), *The Effect of Closed Circuit Television Cameras on Recorded Crime Rates and Public Concern about Crime in Glasgow*, Edinburgh: Scottish Office Central Research Unit.

Duff, R. and Marshall, S. (2000), 'Benefits, Burdens and Responsibilities: Some Ethical Dimensions of Situational Crime Prevention', in Von Hirsch et al. (2000).

Dunaway, R.G., Cullen, F.T., Burton, V.F. (Jr) and Evans, T.D. (2000), 'The Myth of Social Class and Crime Revisited', *Criminology*, vol. 38, p. 589.

Ekblom, P. and Tilley, N. (2000), 'Going Equipped: Criminology, Situational Crime Prevention and the Resourceful Offender', *British Journal of Criminology*, vol. 40, p. 376.

Empey, Lamar T. (1982), *American Delinquency*, Homewood, IL: Dorsey.

Engels, Fredrick (1971), original 1844, *The Condition of the Working Class in England*, trans. W.O. Henderson and W.H. Chalenor (eds), Oxford: Basil Blackwell.

Farnworth, Margaret, Thornberry, Terrence P., Krohn, Marvin D. and Lizotte, Alan J. (1994), 'Measurement in the Study of Class and Delinquency: Integrating Theory and Research', *Journal of Research in Crime and Delinquency*, vol. 31, p. 32.

Farrington, D.P. (1986), 'Stepping Stones to Adult Criminal Careers', in Dan Olwens, J. Block and M.R. Yarrow (eds), *Development of Antisocial and Prosocial Behaviour*, New York: Academic Press.

Farrington, D.P. (1992), 'Juvenile Delinquency', in J.C. Coleman (ed.), *The School Years*, 2nd edn, London: Routledge.

Felson, Marcus (1997), *Crime and Everyday Life*, 2nd edition Thousand Oaks, CA: Pine Forge.

Field, Frank (1990), 'Response to Murray', in Charles Murray, *The Emerging British Underclass*, London: IEA Health and Welfare Unit.

Field, S. (1990), *Trends in Crime and their Interpretation*, London: HMSO.

Foster, J. (1990), *Villains: Crime and Community in the Inner City*, London: Routledge & Kegan Paul.

Fyfe, Nicholas R. (1997), 'The "Eyes on the Street": Closed Circuit Television Surveillance and the City', in N.R. Fyfe (ed.), *Images of The Street: Representation, Experience and Control in Public Spaces*, London: Routledge & Kegan Paul.

Fyfe, Nicholas R. (ed.) (1997a), *Images of The Street: Representation, Experience and Control in Public Spaces*, London: Routledge & Kegan Paul.

Fyfe, Nicholas R. and Bannister, Jon (1996), 'City Watching: Closed Circuit Television Surveillance in Public Spaces', *Area*, vol. 28(1), p. 37.

Garland, D. (1996), 'The Limits of the Sovereign State: Strategies of Crime Control in Contemporary Society', *British Journal of Criminology*, vol. 36, pp. 445–71.

Gill, M. and Pease, K. (1998), 'Repeat Robbers: How are they Different?', in M. Gill (ed.), *Crime at Work: Studies in Security and Crime Prevention*, Leicester: Perpetuity Press.

Goldsmith, V., McGuire, P.G., Mollenkopf, J.H. and Ross, T.A. (2000), *Analyzing Crime Patterns: Frontiers of Practice*, Thousand Oaks, CA: Sage.

Goldstein, Herman (1990), *Problem Oriented Policing*, New York: McGraw-Hill.

Hagan, John (1993), 'The Social Embeddedness of Crime and Unemployment', *Criminology*, vol. 31, p. 465.

Hagan, John and McCarthy, Bill (1992), 'Streetlife and Delinquency', *British Journal of Sociology*, vol. 43, p. 533.

Heal, Kevin (1992), 'Changing Perspectives on Crime Prevention: the Role of Information and Structure', in David J. Evans, Nicholas R. Fyfe and David T. Herbert (eds), *Crime, Policing and Place: Essays in Environmental Criminology*, London: Routledge.

Heidensohn, Frances (1989), *Crime and Society*, London: Macmillan Education.

Hillier, B. and Shu, S. (2000), 'Crime and Urban Layout: The Need for Evidence', in S. Ballintyne, K. Pease and V. McLaren (eds), *Secure Foundations: Key Issues in Crime Prevention, Crime Reduction and Community Safety*, Southampton: Institute for Public Policy Research.

Home Office White Paper (1959), *Penal Practice in a Changing Society*, Cmnd 645, London: HMSO.

Hope, T. (1995), 'Community Crime Prevention', in M. Tonry and D. Farrington (eds), *Building a Safer Society: Strategic Approaches to Crime*, Chicago, IL: University of Chicago Press.

Husain, S. (1988), *Neighbourhood Watch in England and Wales: a Longitudinal Analysis*, Crime Prevention Unit Paper 12, London: HMSO.

Ingram, A. Leigh (1993), 'Type of Place, Urbanism, and Delinquency: Further Testing the Determinist Theory', *Journal of Research in Crime and Delinquency*, vol. 30, p. 192.

Jones, David (1982), *Crime, Protest, Community and Police in Nineteenth Century Britain*, London: Routledge & Kegan Paul.

Kennedy, D. (1997), 'Crime Waves, Culture Wars and Societal Transformations', *Crime, Law and Social Change*, vol. 26, p. 101.

Kleinig, J. (2000), 'The Burdens of Situational Crime Prevention: an Ethical Commentary', in Von Hirsch et al. (2000).

Koch, B. (1998), *The Politics of Crime Prevention*, Aldershot: Ashgate.

Laycock, G. (1985), Property Marking: *A Deterrent to Domestic Burglary?*, Crime Prevention Unit Paper 3, London: HMSO.

Laycock, G. and Webb, B. (2000), 'Making it Happen', in S. Ballintyne, K. Pease and V. McLaren (eds), *Secure Foundations: Key Issues in Crime Prevention, Crime Reduction and Community Safety*, Southampton: Institute for Public Policy Research.

Long, S.K. and Witte, A. (1981), 'Current Economic Trends: Implications for Crime and Criminal Justice', in K.N. Wright (ed.), *Crime and Criminal Justice in a Declining Economy*, Cambridge, MA: Oelgeschlager, Gunn & Hain.

Mannheim, Hermann (1965), *Comparative Criminology*, London: Routledge & Kegan Paul.

Mayhew, Henry (1861–2), *London Labour and the London Poor*, vols. I–IV, London: Griffin, Bohn and Co.

Mayhew, Pat, Clarke, Ronald V., Sturman, A. and Hough, Mike (1976), *Crime as Opportunity*, Home Office Research Unit Study No. 34, London: HMSO.

Mayhew, Pat, Clarke, Ronald V. and Hough, Mike (1992), 'Steering Column Locks and Car Theft', in Ronald V. Clarke (ed.), *Situational Crime Prevention: Successful Cure Studies*, New York: Harrow & Heston.

Mays, John Barron (1954), *Growing Up in the City*, Liverpool: University of Liverpool Press.

Mays, John Barron (1968), 'Crime and the Urban Pattern', *Social Review*, vol. 16, p. 241.

Mays, John Barron (1975), *Crime and its Treatment*, 2nd edn, London: Longman.

Miller, Walter B. (1958), 'Lower Class Culture as a Generating Milieu of Gang Delinquency', *Journal of Social Issues*, vol. 14, p. 5.

Mirrlees-Black, C. and Ross, A. (1995), *Crime Prevention against Retail and Manufacturing Premises: Findings from the 1994 Commercial Victimisation Survey*, Research Study 146, London: Home Office Research and Statistical Directorate.

Mitchell, David (1992), 'Initiatives in Policing London's Brixton since the 1981 Riots', in David J. Evans, Nicholas R. Fyfe and David T. Herbert (eds), *Crime, Policing and Place: Essays in Environmental Criminology*, London: Routledge.

Morris, Terence, P. (1957), *The Criminal Area: A Study in Social Ecology*, London: Routledge & Kegan Paul.

Murray, A.T., McGuffog, I., Western, J.S. and Mullins, P. (2001), 'Exploratory Spatial Data Analysis: Techniques for Examining Urban Crime', *British Journal of Criminology*, vol. 41, p. 309.

Murray, Charles (1990), *The Emerging British Underclass*, London: IEA Health and Welfare Unit. The book includes a number of responses to Murray's thesis.

Newman, O. (1982), *Defensible Space: People and Design in the Violent City*, London: Architectural Press.

Nilsson, A. and Estrada, F. (2003), 'Victimisation, Inequality and Welfare During an Economic Recession', *British Journal of Criminology*, vol. 43, p. 655.

Norris, C. and Armstrong, G. (1997), *The Unforgiving Eye: CCTV Surveillance in Public Spaces*, University of Hull: Centre for Criminology.

Norris, C. and Armstrong, G. (1999), *The Maximum Surveillance Society*, London: Berg.

Orme, J. (1994), *A Study of the Relationship Between Unemployment and Recorded Crime*, London: HMSO.

Painter, Kate (1988), *Lighting and Crime Prevention: the Edmonton Project*, London: Centre for Criminology and Police Studies, Middlesex Polytechnic.

Painter, K. and Farrington, D. (2001), 'Evaluating Situational Crime Prevention using a Young People's Survey', *British Journal of Criminology*, vol. 41, p. 266.

Painter, K. and Farington, D. (1999), 'Street Lighting and Crime Diffusion of Benefits in the Stoke-on-Trent Project', in K. Painter and N. Tilley (eds), *Surveillance of Publc Space: CCTV, Street Lighting and Crime Prevention*, Monsy, NY: Criminal Justice Press.

Park, Robert E. (1952), *Human Communities*, Glencoe: The Free Press.

Pease, Ken (1992), 'Preventing Burglary on a British Public Housing Estate', in Ronald Clarke (ed.), *Situational Crime Prevention: Successful Case Studies*, New York: Harrow & Heston.

Pease, Ken (1994), 'Crime Prevention', in Mike Maguire, Rod Morgan and Robert Reiner (eds), *The Oxford Handbook of Criminology*, Oxford: Oxford University Press.

Pease, K. (1996), *Repeat Victimisation and Policing*, unpublished manuscript: University of Huddersfield, quoted in Ainsworth, P.B. (2000), *Psychology and Crime*, Harlow: Longman.

Pease, K. (1998), *Repeat Victimisation: Taking Stock*, Crime Prevention and Detection Series Paper 90, London: Home Office Policy Research Group.

Petras, J. and Davenport, C. (1992), 'Crime and the Development of Capitalism', *Crime, Law and Social Change*, vol. 16, p. 155.

Philips, David (1977), *Crime and Authority in Victorian England*, London: Croom Helm.

Pike, Luke Owen (1876), *A History of Crime in England*, London: Smith Elder & Co.

Preventing Social Exclusion (2001), Report by the Social Exclusion Unit, London: HMSO. **http://www.socialexclusionunit.gov.uk/publications/reports/html/pse/pse_html/05.htm**.

Pyle, D. (1998), 'Crime and Unemployment: What Do Empirical Studies Show?', *International Journal of Risk Security and Crime Prevention*, vol. 3, p. 169.

Ratcliffe, J.H. and McCullagh, M.J. (2001), 'Chasing Ghosts?: Police Perceptions of High Crime Areas', *British Journal of Criminology*, vol. 41, p. 330.

Sainsbury, Peter (1955), 'Suicide, Delinquency and the Ecology of London'. From *Suicide in London*, Institute of Psychiatry, reprinted in W.G. Carson and Paul Wiles (eds), *The Sociology of Crime and Delinquency in Britain*, vol. 1, Oxford: Martin Robertson.

Sampson, R.J., Raudenbush, S.W. and Earls, F. (1997), 'Neighbourhoods and Violent Crime: Multi-Level Study of Collective Efficacy', *Science*, vol. 277, p. 918.

Scarman, Lord (1981), *The Brixton Disorders, 10–12 April 1981* (Scarman Report, 1981), Cmnd 8427, London: HMSO.

Schlossman, S., Zellman, G. and Shavelson, R., with Sedlak, M. and Cobb, J. (1984), *Delinquency Prevention in South Chicago: A Fifty Year Assessment of the Chicago Area Project*, Santa Monica, CA: Rand.

Shapland, J. (2000), 'Situational Prevention: Social Values and Social Viewpoints', in Von Hirsch et al. (2000).

Shaw, Clifford R. and McKay, H.D. (1942), *Juvenile Delinquency and Urban Areas*, Chicago, IL: University of Chicago Press.

Shaw, Clifford R. and McKay, H.D. (1969), *Juvenile Delinquency and Urban Areas*, revised edn, Chicago, IL: University of Chicago Press.

Smith, D. (2000), 'Changing Situations and Changing People', in Von Hirsch et al. (2000).

Social Trends (2002), edited by Matheson, J. and Babb, P., *Social Trends No. 32* National Statistics Publication, London: HMSO. **http://www.statistics.gov.uk/downloads/theme_ social/ Social_Trends32/5.17.xls**.

Stack, S. (1984), 'Income Inequality and Property Crime', *Criminology*, vol. 22, p. 229.

Taylor, G. (1999), 'Using Repeat Victimisation to Counter Commercial Burglary: The Leicester Experience', *Security Journal*, vol. 12(1), p. 41.

Taylor, Ian (1997), 'Crime Anxiety and Locality: Responding to the "Condition of England" at the End of the Century', *Theoretical Criminology*, vol. 1, p. 53.

Taylor, I. (1999), *Crime in Context: A Critical Criminology of Market Societies*, Cambridge: Polity Press.

Tobias, J.J. (1972), *Crime and Industrial Society in the Nineteenth Century*, Harmondsworth, Penguin.

Tolley, S. and Tregeagle, S. (1998), *Children's Family Centres: Integrated Support Services to Prevent Abuse and Neglect of Children*, Sydney: Bernardo's Australia, Monograph 34.

Townsley, M., Homel, R. and Chaseling, J. (2003), 'Infectious Burglaries. A Test for the Near repeat Hypothesis', *British Journal of Criminology*, vol. 43, p. 615.

Vold, George B., Bernard, Thomas, J. and Snipes, Jeffery, (2002), *Theoretical Criminology*, 5th edn, Oxford: Oxford University Press.

Von Hirsch, A. (2000), 'The Ethics of Public Television Surveillance', in Von Hirsch et al. (2000).

Von Hirsch, A., Garland, D. and Wakefield, A. (eds) (2000), *Ethical and Social Perspectives on Situational Crime Prevention*, Oxford and Portland, Oregon: Hart Publishing.

Von Hirsch, A. and Shearing, C. (2000), 'Exclusion from public space', in Von Hirsch et al. (2000).

Wakefield, A. (2000), 'Situational Crime Prevention in Mass Private Property', in Von Hirsch et al. (2000).

Wells, J. (1995), *Employment Policy Institute, Economic Report*, vol. 9, No. 1.

West, D.J. (1982), *Delinquency: Its Roots, Careers and Prospects*, London: Heinemann.

Wikström, P-O. and Loeber, R. (2000), 'Do Disadvantaged Neighbourhoods Cause Well-Adjusted Children to Become Adolescent Delinquents?: A Study of Male Serious Juvenile Offending, Individual Risk and Protective Factors, and Neighbourhood Context', *Criminology*, vol. 38, p. 1109.

Wiles, P. and Pease, K. (2000), 'Crime Prevention and Community Safety: Tweedledum and Tweedledee?', in S. Ballintyne, K. Pease and V. McLaren (eds), *Secure Foundations: Key Issues in Crime Prevention, Crime Reduction and Community Safety*, Southampton: Institute for Public Policy Research.

Williams, K.S., Goodwin, M. and Johnstone, C. (2000), 'Closed Circuit Television (CCTV) Surveillance in Urban Britain: Beyond the Rhetoric of Crime Prevention', in J.R. Gold and G. Revill, *Landscapes of Defence*, Harlow: Prentice Hall.

Williams, K.S. and Johnstone, C. (2000), 'The Politics of the Selective Gaze: Closed Circuit Television and the Policing of Public Space', *Crime, Law and Social Change*, vol. 34, p. 183.

Willmott, Peter (1963), *Adolescent Boys of East London*, London: Routledge & Kegan Paul.

Wilson, J.Q. and Herrnstein, R.J. (1985), *Crime and Human Nature*, New York: Simon & Schuster.

Wood, J., Wheelright, G. and Burrows, J. (1997), *Crime against Small Businesses: Facing the Challenge*, Swindon: Crime Concern.

Young, J. (1999), *The Exclusive Society: Social Exclusion, Crime and Difference in Late Modernity*, London: Sage.

12

Anomie, strain and juvenile subculture

12.1 Anomie and criminality

Chambers 21st Century Dictionary defines 'anomie' as: '1. a lack of regard for the generally accepted social or moral standards either in an individual or in a social group. 2. the state or condition of having no regard for the generally accepted social or moral standards.' In criminological terms it is normally used to depict a state of lawlessness or normlessness.

12.1.1 Durkheim

In common with the other approaches used in this chapter, the concept of anomie has a long history. The term was first used in the nineteenth century as an explanation of human behaviour by the French sociologist and criminologist Émile Durkheim (see the 1933 and 1970 editions of his works). Much of his theory is derived from his work on suicide, rather than on general criminality, but his published ideas have had a lasting effect upon criminological writing. Durkheim describes how societies begin in simple forms of interaction and are held together by solidarity and likenesses. In such societies, the members have similar aims and roles. These generally homogeneous societies he called 'mechanical'. The growth of societies, together with technical and economic advances, make the interrelationships more complicated and diverse. When this happens the functions and positions of individuals in societies will vary and each person's work becomes more specialised. Members of society also become more interdependent. Durkheim called these 'organic societies'. He viewed these changes in society as being natural and unavoidable, leading to greater happiness for individuals because they would be released to enjoy goods produced by others. This transformation in most societies is a gradual occurrence leading to a healthy society. No one society is wholly mechanical or wholly organic. In even the most primitive societies there is some division of labour, and in the most complex there is some uniformity. Every society therefore exhibits elements from each of his categories.

In both types of society law plays an important role. In mechanical societies, its main function is to enforce the uniformity and the *status quo*. In organic societies, its main function is to integrate the diverse parts of the society and ensure that they co-exist without problems. Partly due to the different functions of law in the different societies, crime also plays a different part.

Durkheim saw crime as a normal occurrence, and said that it is impossible to have a society totally devoid of crime. All societies generate some rules and provide sanctions in case these are broken. This would clearly not be necessary unless the activities so prohibited were 'natural' and likely to occur. Therefore, crime is a necessary feature of every society and, provided it does not exceed certain levels, the society is healthy. Durkheim argues that crime originates in society and is a fundamental condition of social organisation (this area of his discussion was picked up by the 'New Criminologists' and will be discussed in Chapters Fourteen and Fifteen). He claimed that the best examples of healthy levels of criminality were to be found in simple, mechanical societies.

An unhealthy level of criminality is more likely to arise in an organic society, and to be the result of the law being inadequate to regulate the interactions of the various parts of that society. The incomplete integration gives rise to anomie, one of the results of which is excessive or unhealthy levels of criminality. He used a number of examples, most of which arise from an unbalanced division of labour. These can largely be fitted into three categories. The first was a combination of financial crisis and industrial conflict. The second was rigid and unnatural class divisions, such that the oppressed may rebel. The third and final situation he mentions is where there is an abnormal division of labour, such that workers become alienated from their jobs and become disinterested in them.

In each of these three examples, before anomie can be said to exist the major factor which needs to be present is a financial or industrial crisis—this may be a depression as experienced in the 1930s, or it may arise from a time of unrealistic and precarious prosperity, or from an overly fast industrial growth. For later writers, anomie could exist without the prior need for such an upheaval. But for Durkheim upheavals were necessary. For him anomie was the result of a lack of societal norms or regulations over people's desires and aspirations. 'No living being can be happy or even exist unless his needs are sufficiently proportioned to his means' (*Suicide*, original 1897, reprinted 1970, at p. 246). The only way he saw of regulating or controlling the insatiable desires of humans was by public opinion or morality persuading individuals that what they have is all they morally deserve. A healthy society is therefore one in which the upper and lower limits of the acceptable and reasonable expectations of workers or members of each social class are carefully defined and enforced. He recognised that these societal rules and norms would change over time as economic standards changed. A slow and progressive shift would ease such adjustments, but abrupt or violent economic disasters, or sudden growth of power and wealth, disturb the factors of control and produce anomie. When societal norms are overthrown, there may be resistance to new limitations, and so new norms take a long time to develop. It is at such times that suicide and homicide rates rise. (Later criminologists have attributed growth in crime generally to such changes; see Merton below.) To sum up: Durkheim viewed anomie as a state of lawlessness existing at times of abrupt social change, and affecting in particular the state of 'normlessness' which exists when the insatiable desires of humans are no longer controlled by society.

If this explained the social changes which accompanied modernity and its loosening of old normative social structures, it offered little concerning the way new normative structures might be developed beyond a rejection of violence in this process (not a rejection shared by later totalitarian regimes, see Chapter Nineteen). What Durkheim did suggest was that once society had worked out that its well being and that of all its members relied on each member having regard for every other it would enjoy a healthy society. In postmodernity this seems more elusive than ever. Through enormous upheavals in industrialisation, technology and globalisation individuals' aspirations and empathies may be closer to those of someone on the other side of the world rather than someone in their own State. These tendencies, together with the effects of greater materialism have resulted in people becoming more separated rather than unified, (Bauman (2001)). Within this terrain a healthy society in Durkheimian terms becomes less realistic and helpful as a means of tackling crime.

Durkheim's ideas have, to an extent, been attacked by some writers who claim that crime rates did not increase over the period of the French revolution or during the industrial revolution, periods depicted by Durkheim as being in a state of upheaval and anomie (see McDonald (1982)). The discrepancy in the figures arose because Durkheim based his theories on rates of suicide, which he found to be increasing, and assumed that crime rates were similarly affected. However, Durkheim's main thesis was that crime is associated with breakdown of social norms and rules giving rise to an absence of social control. There are two elements to this: the first is the breakdown of regulations, rules and informal limits, undermining confidence in the social structure; the second is that this structural problem leads to psychological feelings of isolation. The overall disorder and disorganisation, social and personal, shifts behaviour in the direction of crime. There may still be substance in this. Historically Durkheim's most important contribution has been to provide an analysis of the effect of social forces on individual behaviour. At a time when blaming individuals for all their actions is so powerful, this may be a most useful perspective.

12.1.2 **Merton and after**

12.1.2.1 *Merton*

After Durkheim, the most famous criminological writer on anomie is the American Robert K. Merton. He drew on Durkheim's ideas to try to explain the crime problem in the United States of America. Instead of centring problems of anomie on the insatiable desires of human beings, he explains them as something which may exist when desires and needs, though limited, still go beyond what could be satisfied in socially acceptable ways. This is very close to Durkheim's idea of anomie in that it would suggest that to prevent an anomic situation arising, carefully structured norms must be enforced. The difference is that, for Durkheim, the moral norms to be upheld or enforced regulate the individual's desires, whereas for Merton, they would regulate and control the individual's willingness to use unacceptable ways to achieve those desires. Merton therefore argues that society will not be anomic if its members only use legitimate means of advancement, even if their desires are totally unrestricted; it is the relationship between desires and the means of achieving those desires which is fundamental (Merton (1949)). This link between desires and means has led to his theory being called a strain theory; one in which everyone is pressured to succeed, but those who are unable or least likely to succeed by legitimate means are under most strain to use illegitimate or illegal opportunities.

Durkheim said the individual's desires are derived from within the person; in Merton's view the desires of individuals are largely defined by society. Each culture and society has different elements which it considers worth striving for. In America and much of the Western world, this is wealth and, through wealth, material possessions. Merton argues that Western cultures, and the American culture in particular, far from limiting desires actually encourages everyone to seek absolute wealth. Everyone is told that further enrichment is possible and that they should all strive towards it. If they do not, they are considered lazy and of less worth (Durkheim would have considered that this alone renders the culture anomic).

Merton maintains that the healthy society lays down accepted means of achieving the ends or goals: his work is, indeed, often described as a means-end theory. In Western cultures, the means of achieving those ends are supposed to be through hard and honest toil, not through theft and fraud. However, the latter means may well be more efficient. If society is to remain healthy, therefore, it is important that participating in the accepted means carries some reward. Merton argued that if society laid sufficient emphasis on conformity (e.g., via systems of reward for conformity or acknowledging any sacrifices made) then it would remain healthy. The philosophy behind this thesis might well be: 'It's not whether you win that matters, it's how you play the game.' However, if the emphasis is on reaching certain goals with no control of the way in which that is achieved, then society would be anomic. He accepted that this unhealthy attitude is prevalent in America, and embodied in commonplace attitudes such as: 'It's winning that matters, not how you play the game.' The 'American Dream' centres on wealth. How that goal is reached has become unimportant, so that the person who achieves wealth through unacceptable or dubious means is still rewarded with prestige, power and social status.

Merton only intended to explain street crime and to provide an explanation of the pattern of crime as revealed by the official US statistics. This led him to accept that there was more crime committed by the lower classes than any other sector of society. It was this discrepancy that he sought to explain. The basic theory was constructed to fit the statistics and the distribution of crime. Consequently, he argued that only part of American society was anomic, or at least that the anomic nature of that society only caused criminality to arise in one well-defined stratum, namely the lower class (for criticism of this, see Box (1981)). Criminality arose, not necessarily because of discrepancies between the goals and the approved means of achieving those goals, but because all the members of that society were led to believe that there was equality of opportunity. In practice, there were sharp constraints on such purported equality. The consequent feelings of unfairness could lead to criminality. Since the lower classes suffered most from educational and occupational discrimination, they were least likely to attain the 'American Dream' through the legitimate opportunity structures. It was these people who were most likely to escape from low paid and boring jobs by engaging in criminal activities. He argues that anomie becomes the differential application of opportunity rather than an application of social controls or norms; it is a strain theory. Frustration with the system, or possibly economic necessity, gives rise to strain and drives these people to resort to criminality.

Merton describes five types of social activity or reaction by individuals to the society in which they live. The first is conformity. In this reactive state, individuals accept both societal goals and society's means of achieving those goals, even when they cannot or clearly will not achieve them. In Merton's view it is because most people fall into this category that society remains basically stable and, according to official statistics, most people are not criminal. However, as was seen in Chapter Four, criminality is committed by a much wider population base than officially recorded. The 'conformity' category is much smaller than envisaged by Merton and, even in stable communities, it may actually be a minority. Nonetheless conformity to goals and means, even if it places individuals in a very unpleasant and undesirable position in society, is very common behaviour.

The other four types of behaviour are all categorised by Merton as deviant, although each covers a very different type of reaction. Of these, the first is called 'innovation', and comprises the individuals who accept social goals but reject the legitimate means of achieving them in favour of more effective but officially pro-scribed means. It is into this category that he fits most of the individuals who are included in the criminal statistics. Therefore, he sees innovation as most common among the lower class Americans because they are stigmatised because of their low skill, low pay and greater vulnerability to unemployment. Their reaction would be most likely to give rise to crimes against property, such as theft and burglary, or possibly to organised crime where the sole end is financial gain.

The second of Merton's deviant reactions, he calls 'ritualism'. In this category the goals are abandoned but the means are almost compulsively adhered to. This encompasses many lower-middle-class Americans who abandoned any dreams of bettering their lot in life but still stick rigidly to the rules of society. It is question-able whether this is actually a deviant state; it certainly does not involve any crim-inality. Merton suggested that, because the society sets the goals, lack of desire to fulfil those is itself deviant because it denies part of the culture.

The third deviant reaction he labels 'retreatism', whereby an individual rejects both goals and the means of achieving them. Merton felt that these people did not really belong to the society in which they lived. In this category he included the vagrant or tramp, alcoholics and drug addicts. It might also include racial or religious minorities, particularly if they are severely disadvantaged. All these people might well reject society's goals and the means of achieving them but feel no desire to fight for new ones. Their deviance is negative. The vagrant might well commit public nuisance offences. Alcoholics and drug addicts may commit offences while under the influences of such substances, and might also be driven to commit offences (usually property offences) in order to obtain those substances. The mem-bers of minority racial and religious backgrounds might also simply retreat and become introspective, committing no crime in so doing, but not really contribut-ing to society. This behaviour might be viewed as unsociable but clearly cannot be considered deviant in a criminal sense.

Merton then includes 'rebellion' as the last of the reactions resulting in anomie. In this category again both goals and means of achieving them are rejected, but rebellion also includes a desire to substitute new goals in place of the conventional ones. What is involved is a conscious rejection of accepted goals, often combined with a cause or an ideal for which to fight. Their deviance has a positive end which is often pursued by negative means. In this category are the street gang members, the terrorist and/or freedom fighter (see Chapter Nineteen). The rebellious reaction often involves destructive crimes, such as wilful damage to property and crimes of public disorder. It may even include murder, terrorist offences and any crime designed to attack the basis of the culture.

These five possible reactions of individuals to their society are not mutually exclusive. People may react differently at different times in their lives or in different spheres of their lives. For example, a person at work may be a true achiever and hard and dedicated worker who fits into the non-deviant and non-criminal role of conformity. In private, that same individual may use drugs, fitting into a retreatist and necessarily criminal response; and in the public sphere he or she may fight for a political ideal different from that presently existing, and involving a rebellious response which may or may not include criminality, depending on the behaviour chosen to express this political ideal.

12.1.2.2 *Messner and Rosenfeld*

Merton claims that American society, with its concentration on personal wealth and achievement at any cost, generates crime because citizens are encouraged to want and expect a lot but the societal structures necessary to deliver it do not exist. Recently a large part of this thesis has been given renewed attention in the work of Messner and Rosenfeld (2001), who argue that crime (in America) results from the culture of prioritising wealth, which is heavily supported by State institutions which give power to the economy. The cultural pull is the same as that marked out by Merton, but the structural analysis is rather different. For Messner and Rosenfeld the State structure and social institutions (family, work, polity, education) are designed to give strength to the economy. The American people are socialised to back these structures as supports for the economy—so education is not prized as an end in itself, for learning or personal development, but merely as a means to better paid employment. The culture and institutions centre on money and set values which support the free market. This encourages people to use the most efficient means available to them to attain the desired goals: the opportunities offered in the market economy are accepted by most as the approved and legal way of achieving this; but for some the most efficient means may be criminal. They argue that this preoccupation with financial success and economy interferes with the ability of institutions in America to properly socialise individuals into law abiding and healthy roles. It can also be used to sanction some breaches of the criminal law, if their object is seen to be the pursuit of the American Dream. They argue that if other aspirations were to come to the fore society would exhibit less crime and be healthier. They suggest that the family should be more valued and strengthened by altering working practices; that education should not turn so closely around training for work and more around learning for the sake of education; and that people should be given a sense of community through a national service corps. They want goals to be altered away from the American Dream to include more caring facets. Messner and Rosenfeld argue that other societies which are less focused on purely monetary values suffer less crime. However, Britain in the 1980s and 1990s moved towards a similar priority for market values: it is unclear whether the rising crime rates of that period validate the theory.

12.1.2.3 *Policy implications*

The policy implications of these approaches are largely outside the purview of the criminal justice system. They require wider political objectives—to provide greater educational and job training opportunities; to build up the possibilities for people to obtain jobs with good wages and reasonable hours; to encourage cultural ideals which focus on community and respect for humanity; to encourage other aspirations besides the pursuit of wealth; and to ensure that more weight is given to the obligations of citizenship (so far as this involves respect for others)—being considered alongside individual freedom and rights.

12.1.3 Durkheim and Merton: a comparison

Durkheim and Merton did not see things in entirely the same light. The former places heavy emphasis upon a condition of 'normlessness' arising out of abrupt change; the latter sees anomie as an endemic condition. Merton says this can exist at any time in any society, as long as the factors mentioned above exist. A society can be basically stable while part, even a large part, of it is anomic.

Durkheim and Merton each document a slightly different idea of anomie. There are two main differences. The first is the more fundamental. Durkheim states that the desires of individuals are natural and fixed, the level of criminal behaviour and of anomie is decided by the efficiency with which these desires are restrained, and that they are most likely to crumble and generate crime in periods of rapid change. Merton, on the other hand, says that society, not the individual, sets the desires and goals, and that same society also sets the acceptable means of achieving the ends. If rewards are only bestowed for obtaining the ends, the restraining means become weakened, encouraging the use of unacceptable and illegal means.

The second, and more practical difference, is that Durkheim talks about a whole society being anomic. Merton would consider that the condition only affects certain parts of the society (i.e., those parts which appear in the official crime statistics), and generally speaking those parts are drawn from the lower classes. Merton in effect focuses on the availability of legitimate opportunities to achieve wealth. These opportunities exist for the higher classes, but not for the lower classes.

Some now refer to Merton's theory as a strain theory rather than anomie. This is because of his assertion that the motivation to commit crime arises when the legitimate means of achieving success are unavailable. The pressure to succeed exists, but the means are absent. The conflict or strain drives the individual towards a criminal way of achieving the success. This type of pressure is depicted again in subcultural theories (see 11.3). It can be seen as similar to, or closely related to, ideas of relative deprivation (see 12.2).

Most recently, anomie has been used as an explanation for the increase in crime during times of unemployment and recession. This last possibility fulfils Durkheim's need for a major upheaval before anomie can exist. Its effects are reinforced if the moral norms promoting acceptance of the rules of society appear to be missing. Some see this absence in the way the mass media, particularly TV, churn out the ideal of a materialistic existence as the norm to which all right-thinking members of society should aspire, even though few will ever achieve such a financial 'nirvana' through legitimate means. For Durkheim, these two factors would make the society anomic and so cause criminality to increase.

Merton concentrates more on the opportunity structures. He argues that even in a recession, people are told that there are opportunities and that they are fairly administered. These messages clash with the experience of many, especially the unemployed who have little realistic chance of achieving financial or occupational success. Many will accept their lot, or simply give up any dreams of attaining more than they already have; but there will be others who become sufficiently disillusioned and frustrated for criminality to provide both a release and an achievement. This is especially likely if they view their failure as a fault of the unfair operation of the system, rather than a reflection of their own ability. Although Merton saw this phenomenon as confined to the lower classes, there is no compelling reason why this should be the case. See, for example, the discussion of corporate crime in relation to this theory in Chapter Three. Each corporate body has a goal, usually financial, to achieve (i.e., high and ever-increasing profit). In times of recession, it is more difficult to achieve these goals, and the pressure to use unacceptable and criminal means is much stronger. The large-scale fraudulent accounting practices of such major companies as Enron which were revealed by the collapse of the dot.com boom at the start of the twenty-first century demonstrated that corporate temptation went well beyond marginal tax evasion or avoiding health and safety regulations to cut cost.

Recently, themes such as those found in anomie have been appearing in the theories of Left Realists (see Chapter Sixteen) and in links between crime and modernisation. For a full discussion of these see Downes and Rock (1995), but the core is that there is a problem with the interplay between civilisation and modernity. The assumption is that as civilisation develops the external controls on people's actions become more sophisticated and diverse. Alongside this, people develop internal psychological controls or inhibitions to take into account the more complex standards of acceptable behaviour. Personal conduct as it affects others is thus presumed to have generally improved as civilisation progresses. This supposedly is seen in a general reduction in violence between about 1500 (the late medieval period) and the mid-twentieth century. It is then asserted that, unfortunately, that trend has regressed since the mid-twentieth century, as exemplified both in wars and such brutality as experienced in Germany in the 1930s, or in the former Yugoslavia in the 1980s and 1990s. Ideas of modernity, on the other hand, centre on disruption caused by industry, social and economic upheavals to explain how controls, both internal and external, designed to prevent criminal activities may break down. The result is the increase in criminality, especially property crimes, in more modern cultures. Both the assumptions and the empirical basis for these sweeping assertions are questionable: they are presented here as one of the ways in which anomie might be used by present theorists to explain crime trends.

Anomie, however defined, helps to explain why some people may be motivated to commit a crime. Mertonian anomie offered a means of countering rising crime through improvement of legitimate life chances; this might be partially what underpins the policies to address exclusion. In an age of managerialism and administrative criminology it would be difficult to assess whether these changes had succeeded. How can you measure levels of strain? For this reason the goals within social exclusion are made precise and measurable—reduce burglary by 25 per cent etc. Here tackling particular targets is the element of success not whether it prevents social exclusion or improves life chances. In our more globalised and transient society where goals are more diffuse solving crime through a means–ends approach is probably less tenable.

Messner and Rosenfeld would claim that even were it possible to alter the means and to make them fairer there would still be those who would win and those who would lose in the pursuit of wealth. If the means were fair and just failure would mean that the individual was not good enough which would be even more corrosive and stressful, and might thus strengthen the impetus for criminality. The implication of their theory is to alter the goals: to move away from success and worth being measured by wealth alone, and to focus societal approval on caring facets of personality and on encouraging other goods, such as education, for their own worth rather than merely a means to a financial end.

REVISION BOX

	Main theories on nature of Anonie	The Problem	Policy Implications
Durkheim	Anomie is a State of normlessness which arises at times of major societal upheaval, particularly financial or industrial crisis.	A healthy society has strong normative regulation and ethical guidance. It encourages or requires each member to aspire to expectations or ends that they might reasonably achieve, taking account of their position in life.	Society must encourage each individual to recognise their interdependency with others, and to accept his/her station within this society. Basically a strengthening of social controls.
Merton	Anomie arises when there is a discrepancy between the cultural goals and the legitimate means of achieving them. It is a form of strain, achieving the goal is powerfully sold but impossible for most, or for sections of a community.	In America the main, almost sole, goal is the acquisition of wealth. Everyone is made to believe they can achieve great wealth (power, prestige and self-worth are measured by it) but for most this is a pipedream, their situation and opportunities would never lead to great wealth.	Provision of fairer more open and effective means of achieving society goals. This might well necessitate dealing with poverty, with social exclusion and ensuring high educational standards to give everyone in a society a similar chance of achieving the goals. The need for an open, just and non-discriminatory process in awarding of such goods as jobs etc.
Messner and Rosenfeld	Institutional anomie— support for the goal of wealth in the societal structures which are designed to use their social control mechanisms to give strength to the economy and to the promotion of the goal.	Preoccupation with financial success and economy interferes with the ability of institutions in America to socialise individuals into law abiding and healthy roles. Everything is secondary to financial success.	Institutions should be strengthened in relation to the economy and the impact of the economy on them should be lessened; Goals other than wealth should be encouraged: education, parenting, caring, teaching and serving the community.

12.2 **Strain and relative deprivation**

In the previous chapter, the relationship between crime and both poverty and economic inequality was studied. It seemed that, whereas lack of wealth in itself was unlikely to be linked with criminality, there was a link with the unequal distribution of wealth. The possibility thus arises that it is the feeling of unfairness arising from that inequality that causes crime. The relative deprivation theory considers this point.

The idea is straightforward. Some individuals see their present position as comparing unfavourably with others; they desire more; they often feel they deserve more; but if there seems to be no legitimate chance of acquiring more, they may use illegitimate means. Thus if relative deprivation is present, feelings of envy and injustice will be present and might influence behaviour.

Some radical criminologists such as Stack (1984), have used this in explanations of criminality. In Stack's view, the problems caused by relative deprivation grow as more people fall into the category and as the gaps between these people and others grow. He argues that relative deprivation alone will not cause criminality. An individual might fulfil his desire by legitimate means, in this case generally through political struggle to rectify these imbalances. If there is a party which will fight for redistribution of income, or a union which will do the same, criminality is less likely to result. But those who believe that their plight is not addressed by these political means, or consider them irrelevant, may turn to other forms of redress, such as criminality. The criminality here is not a politicised act of trying to redress an unfair imbalance, but rather involves a person acting to try to better his position, often at the expense of others who may well be no better off, or only marginally so.

Relative deprivation as a theory of criminality carries with it the implication that the problem will not be fully redressed until there is a redistribution of income through policies such as full employment, high minimum wages and more equal wealth distribution. It is argued that the problem might be alleviated if fewer people felt politically marginalised and more believed that something might be done. From this standpoint, the criminality arises out of the unfair distribution of wealth which our system upholds.

A dramatic redistribution of wealth such as that envisaged in the previous paragraph would not necessarily stop the crime problem. Indeed, the same theory might well be used as an explanation of the new criminality. In relative deprivation, the feeling of deprivation may arise when an individual compares his situation with that of others or with that of himself at an earlier time. Those made worse off by the redistribution of wealth may feel unjustly treated, and be tempted to turn to criminality in order to regain their former position. The main difference is that the number in this group is likely to be smaller than the number who currently feel relatively deprived.

Box (1987) argues that the explanations provided by theories of relative deprivation are useful to explain higher crime rates in recessions. At such time, he argues, the strain to turn to criminality is stronger because the possibility of serious alterations in wealth distribution seem to be receding. In a society where wealth and possessions are important, and where the media stress this and strengthen people's desires, the feelings of envy and unfairness can only grow in a recession.

The resultant strain is particularly strong in certain groups—the young; ethnic minorities; and women, all of whom feel politically marginalised because the solutions which might best address their situations are the least likely to be supported at these times. Criminologists who see this as an important element in criminality tend to advocate socialist solutions of greater equality of position and wealth as the only real solutions to the crime problem.

Currie (1985, 1995 and 1997) has noted that the result of the market economy has been deprivation, a widening of the gap between the rich and the poor. These trends in the 1980s and 1990s were accompanied by a withdrawal of public support (financial and social) and an undermining of less formal support mechanisms and control structures such as family and community. He claims that the deprivations, exacerbated by the consumerism so central to a market economy, have fostered crime. To counter this and so address both the social and crime problems, he argues for a move towards full employment at good wages with reasonable hours by:

... substantially expanding employment in public and non-profit making sectors of the economy, and developing policies for worksharing and reduction of work time. (Currie (1997), at p. 168)

This is expected both to provide more people with work and an income, and also to finance the staff for State agencies to support the less fortunate. In the current political climate of extending public–private partnerships the claim that such a programme would reduce strain, and with it crime, is unlikely to be tested.

Most of the above strain theorists centred on economic deprivation or relative deprivation, but other, more general strain theorists have different suggestions. So Agnew (1992 and 1997) has taken a wider view and come up with what he terms a 'general strain theory' which includes three distinct types of strain:

(a) Strain resulting from failure to achieve positively valued goals or goods, which could be seen as the most common form of strain theory used by criminologists in the past. This he once more split into three. The first subgroup arises when aspirations are not achieved and is the form which arises in the strain theories of Merton (see above 12.1.2), Cohen (see below 12.3.2) and Cloward and Ohlin (see below 12.3.3). The goals envisaged in this form have generally been middle-class aspirations. The second subgroup includes those who feel strain as a result of expectations not materialising into desired ends or goals. The expectation arises when people see others similarly placed achieving the desired goals: as their expectation is based on a realistic assessment, and not just on a vain hope or aspiration, the feeling of strain induced by failure is all the stronger. In the final subgroup strain arises when the outcomes are not seen to be based on just decisions. This type of strain involves comparisons with other similar cases. Each of these assumes that the actors are pursuing some sort of goal. The first subgroup has been most studied by criminologists and yet Agnew notes that it is the other two which are most likely to give rise to anger and frustration: Agnew calls on researchers to include all three in testing strain theory.

(b) Strain resulting from the removal of positively valued stimuli. Stack (above) had considered this but was interested mainly in money and employment/

unemployment whereas Agnew widens the scope to losing a person through death, divorce, moving away or through argument. All these could be equally traumatic experiences.

(c) Strain resulting from negative stimuli. Strain may arise when a person is faced with an unpleasant consequence or likely consequence such as psychological and other effects of child abuse or family break-up, threats, physical pain or attack, detection, criminal prosecution, punishment or even just embarrassment. This type of strain may give rise to criminality to escape (driving at speed, drug taking), to seek revenge, or to stop the unpleasant experience. Agnew, in earlier research projects, reports that he has found some correlation between crime and this type of strain.

The suggestion is that each of these types of strain is likely to give rise to negative emotions such as disappointment, depression, fear and, most importantly, anger. Agnew associates each of these with offending but the relationship with anger is the strongest. The effects will depend on the magnitude of the strain on the individual (a subjective test), how recent it was, how long it continued and whether incidents were clustered into a short period. Of course there is nothing fatalistic about the relationship and Agnew recognises that even very acute feelings of strain may not result in offending. Much will depend on cognitive abilities to reason the problem through and to place it in perspective, the availability of legal behavioural coping strategies which may work out anger, and emotional coping strategies such as throwing the anger into positive use by digging the garden or by calming the emotion with breathing exercises. Agnew suggests that strain is more likely to lead to criminality; if it arises from the deliberate actions of others; if the individual is disposed to crime (impulsive, irritable etc.); if they have low levels of social control acting on them; if they have experience of criminality or have been taught to participate in crime.

As can be seen from the above, Agnew in his general strain theory recognises that there are many non-criminal ways of dealing with strain. Thus whereas Joe and Chesney-Lind (1998) show young males often used peer groupings for criminality (both property and violent crime), they found that young females normally used such groupings (or gangs) to build largely non-criminal strategies for coping with problems (often strain). Perhaps this explains why many researchers had found only a very weak link between strain and crime. It thus becomes necessary to discover how criminal behaviour might be chosen. Agnew suggests the choice will be influenced by such features as: the importance of the goal to the individual and the presence or absence of other important goals; the differing abilities of the individual to cope through cognitive or problem-solving skills; social support; constraints to criminal activity such as social control (see Chapter Thirteen); fear of getting caught; and whether the wider social environment provides other opportunities or affects choices in other ways. Some of these clearly depend on the temperament of the individual, as well as learning abilities, peer groups and social control. He explains these within a school environment in an article on the links between crime and strain in American schools (Agnew (2000)).

This is a far more rounded concept of strain and answers many of the problems associated with earlier theories. Despite this there are still problems: it is unclear why individuals respond negatively to some forms of strain more than others; and it is unclear how strain interacts with other factors to give rise to crime.

12.3 Subcultural theories of juvenile deviance

12.3.1 Introduction

The theory of anomie undoubtedly has had a profound effect upon criminology, but its explanations are more pertinent for some aspects of crime than for others. The concept of anomie may be useful as an explanation of property offences, or those offences designed to enhance a person's social or economic standards. These are the crimes which aim to transport people closer to the glossy 'dream', the ideal of today's advertising agencies. The anomie theory is not nearly so useful as an explanation of the negative and damaging offences which are especially frequent in the officially recorded criminality of young persons, while the approaches of strain and relative deprivation only partially fill this gap. This section will thus concentrate on delinquency rather than criminality (see 12.3.2, 12.3.3 and 12.4).

There are two strong reason for concentrating on delinquency. As long ago as 1895 the Gladstone Committee in the UK recognised that the juvenile delinquent of today is the hardened and persistent adult criminal of tomorrow. By this hypothesis, if juvenile delinquency could be understood and possibly prevented, a large amount of adult criminality could be pre-empted and prevented.

The second reason for the preoccupation with juvenile crime is simply its scale. The fastest rising criminal statistics since the Second World War have been for this group, which now accounts for over one third of all officially recorded crimes. It has thus naturally been perceived as an increasing social problem, which has led to public concern and growing embarrassment for politicians and policy-makers. This perception is sharpened because the crimes with which youths are most often associated are those of wanton violence and destruction where a motive is often difficult to discover. The exact types of menacing behaviour have changed over time, but in Britain have been personified by such groups as Teddy Boys in the 1950s, muggers, and football hooligans in the 1970s and 1980s and carjacking drug taking and selling in the 1999s. It was also largely youths who were involved with the riots of the early 1980s (see the Scarman Report (1981)). Thus, amongst the criminality which engenders most fear in the community are some forms of youth crime, putting it at the forefront of many recent sociological discussions. For a critical survey of the stress, past and present, on youth crime see Brown (1998). With the demographic decline in the proportion of youths in our society, this factor may become less prevalent.

Most of the literature on this topic has centred on gang delinquency and the notion that the gang is a delinquent subculture or part of a lower-class male subculture. The assumption was that most juvenile delinquency took place in gangs or groups, or that it was committed because of pressure from peer groupings. Likewise, it was assumed that the delinquent problem was largely confined to males from the lower or working classes. In part, these assumptions arose because the work was heavily dependent on the official statistics, which in itself leaves it open to criticism.

Two early American works (Cohen (1955); Cloward and Ohlin (1960)) were influential in directing attention to the notion of the deviant subculture of young boys as a source of criminal activity. Their views also set part of the agenda for British criminology in the succeeding decades. They will be briefly examined here with the necessary cautionary comment that they were only interested in explaining certain types of criminality, largely street crimes—brawls, physical attacks which occur in a public place, theft and burglary, criminal damage or similar offences. They are thus limited in their explanation of criminality, although some could have been included in discussions of class theories (11.4) or strain theories (12.2), giving them a degree of validity outside peer culture.

12.3.2 Cohen

Cohen's major work, *Delinquent Boys*, was published in 1955. In it he claimed that crimes committed by the young could be explained by the subcultural values of the peer grouping. In other words, for the youths concerned, certain activities were correct by the standard of the subculture simply because they were wrong by the norms of the general culture (i.e., the culture of the middle class). He assumed that middle-class values placed more weight on qualities such as drive and ambition; individual responsibility; personal achievement; rational planning and the ability to postpone the gratification of immediate desires for the expectation of future gain; the control of aggression and violence whether verbal or physical; constructive and healthy use of leisure time; and last, but certainly not least, the respect for property, particularly that belonging to other persons. Lower-class values often conflicted with those of the middle class, and included toughness, excitement and immediate gratification.

Cohen argued that, for the working-class boy, the socialisation at home often clashed with that at school leading to inner conflicts and confusion. He maintains that there are three possible solutions to the dilemma faced by the working-class boy. The first two he drew from W.F. Whyte's classic categories of college boy and corner boy (see Whyte (1955)). In the college boy solution, youths wholly internalise the values of the middle class and compete for success wholly on those terms—they must try to beat or match the middle class at their own game. Much more common was the corner boy solution, which involved youths accepting their limitations and living within them, making the most of what legitimately comes their way. Both the college boy and the corner boy reactions were essentially conformist and are similar to Merton's conformity referred to above (12.1.2).

The problem solution is the third response, which creates what Cohen described as the delinquent corner boy who engages in negative and malicious behaviour as a reaction against school and middle-class standards and values. Basically, this conduct epitomises the actions of someone who desires but is denied success in the middle-class sense. Even during reaction formation and the negative behaviour performed to show contempt for middle-class values, it is implied that the working-class boys secretly still desire the all-pervasive middle-class success values. Such secret desires may lead to psychological, and sometimes psycho-pathic, problems.

12.3.3 Cloward and Ohlin

Cloward and Ohlin (1960) also concentrated their efforts upon lower- or working-class youths. They accepted that delinquent acts do occur amongst adolescents from all classes of society, but that for middle-class youths it was far more of an individual struggle. Cloward and Ohlin attached more importance to the criminal-ity of the lower-class juvenile because it illustrates the existence of gangs or sub-cultures which support and approve of the actions of the delinquent. Furthermore, the lower-class delinquent is more likely to receive the support and approval, or at least will not suffer the disapproval, of the non-delinquent and adult members of their class.

They point out some of the problems with Cohen's arguments by showing that he relies too heavily on the idea that the working-class boy desires middle-class success. They say that this may be true of the college boy if he fails, but it does not apply to most lower or working-class boys. They argued that, although these boys might have dreams and aspirations far beyond their expectations, they did not necessarily covet status in terms of middle-class values. Like Merton, they saw most lower- or working-class boys as goal oriented, and saw their problem as a discrep-ancy between the available means and the desired ends. They called their theory 'Differential Opportunity Structure'.

In formulating their theory they draw extensively on the ideas of Merton (see above 12.1.2), who argued that crime results from exclusion from legitimate means of achieving success, and of Sutherland's Differential Association (see above 10.2.4), which argues that criminal behaviour is learned from group relationships. Crime occurs because of blocked legitimate opportunities: the type of criminal behaviour which will arise depends on the area and peer grouping or gang with which the individual is connected.

They argue that adherence to the conventional and legal behaviour patterns becomes unnecessary when legitimate means are seen to be unfairly applied, i.e., if they feel that the system has caused them to fail. The society professes equal opportunities for all, but the reality is very different. Basically, there are too many people with the natural and necessary ability for the best positions and the high-est paid jobs, so selection may be based on subjective criteria such as accent, class, ethnic origin, religion and 'who you know'. The lower-class boys see their legit-imate opportunities of success being unfairly blocked by the conventional institu-tions in society, such as the school and employers. The resultant strain leaves the lower-class youth free to join with others in a similar predicament to form gangs, and possibly to take part in criminal acts without feeling guilty about the morality of his actions. Unlike Cohen's explanation, no psychological problems need arise.

Cloward and Ohlin list three types of illegal opportunity which may be available to the lower-class juvenile: criminal; conflict; and retreatist (the latter is sometimes also known as 'drug-oriented'). It is for this classification that Cloward and Ohlin are probably best known, as it draws together Merton's anomie and Sutherland's differential association theories.

The 'criminal gang' is a juvenile gang whose most important activity is the illegal taking of property. It will only develop in an area where there are opportunities for such offences as stealing and for the receiving and handling of stolen goods. Cloward and Ohlin argue that this environment is most likely to exist if there is some tolerated adult criminal activity within the neighbourhood so that the neighbourhood gives certain limited criminal activities an air of respectability and apparent legitimacy. The area is relatively stable, but is applying norms different from those present in the rest of society. In such areas the juvenile gangs are most likely to be driven to relatively orderly criminal activity for financial goals. Unpredictable individuals will not be accepted as members; they will therefore be driven to one of the other two types of behaviour.

One of these is the 'conflict gang'. The areas most likely to spawn conflict gangs are usually transient or unstable, often because of shifts in population or because of lack of pride in the community. In such environments, neither criminal nor legitimate role models readily exist for young boys. As a result, they may lack purpose in life, become negative and violent, and form a conflict gang. Lacking social control, whether criminal or legitimate, the result is often a feeling of anger and a desire to prove their worth and status. It is this that turns them to violence.

Cloward and Ohlin's third type of gang—the retreatist or drug-oriented gang— may exist in any neighbourhood where drugs can be obtained. The members of these gangs are 'neither fish nor fowl'; they have failed both in the legitimate and the criminal spheres. Some of these 'failures' may become the stable corner boys referred to by Cohen, but some become members of these retreatist gangs. Which way an individual turns will depend upon their own personalities as well as on their associations and the availability of drugs. Cloward and Ohlin recognise that many gangs probably partake in some drug use, but in most this will only be a peripheral activity.

Cloward and Ohlin predicted a growth of conflict-type violent and aggressive behaviour. They saw this as a response to the collapse of community spirit in lower-class areas, possibly due to the political changes in slum organisation or clearance.

12.3.4 Evaluation

Some critics have argued (see Box (1981)) that these theories suffer from a basic implausibility. They require lower-class youths to experience strong disappointment with the dominant culture when it does not deliver them to success, whereas, it is argued that most working- or lower-class boys never expect or aspire to any great success under those values. Such an approach might suggest that it is the lower-stream grammar school boys and mid to upper-range comprehensive boys (or as Cohen calls them, the 'college boys') who are most likely to suffer disappointment because of their relative lack of success. It is an hypothesis which raises its own set of possibilities and problems. As will be seen from the sections concerning school and control theories (see Chapter Thirteen), there is much evidence that school itself does not cause rebellion against middle-class norms, but boredom may lead to outbursts of energy which may be of unacceptable and possibly even criminal behaviour.

In addition, the explanations described in this section provide no convincing basis to account for the fact that many of the youths tend to reform or stop committing criminal acts at the end of their teens and the onset of adulthood. They mostly remain members of the same social class, and there is no obvious reason to believe that they all find their lot improving and enjoy sudden success at the age of about 20. If the initial juvenile criminality is due to a reaction against the middle-class norms, or at least influenced by them, why does this behaviour change although there is little or no change in those values? Of course, it may simply be that the young feel more outrage at what they may see as unfair workings of society, and as they mature they slowly come to accept the *status quo* or limit their opposition to passive resistance. It may also be that as they grow older they become more domesticated, and acquire responsibilities which leave them less free to participate in criminality. Perhaps adult frustration comes out in different ways, such as in domestic violence (crime), or in antisocial rather than criminal ways.

Both Cohen and Cloward and Ohlin draw to a large extent on the strain or anomic theories of Merton. They usefully show how that theory might be adapted to explain crimes which do not appear to be motivated by greed. They draw on Merton to explain how the strain might result in crimes of protest as much as in crimes of purpose.

12.3.5 The British situation

It was initially indicated that most of these theories originate in the US: the irrelevance to British criminality must be considered. One consistent theme was that of the delinquent subculture, peer group or gang. Do such gangs exist in Britain? British studies of the 1960s and 1970s generally found that strong, structured juvenile gangs, particularly gangs whose central intention was to commit delinquent acts, were largely absent.

More recently perceptions have changed. Thus Young (1999) claims that young men who are excluded from any 'normal' social position tend to come together to form gangs to regain a place and some self-respect. It is also suggested that this subculture is often premised on physical strength, is sexist and racist, forms around ethnic or geographic lines and may also connect with football teams. Similarly, Campbell (1993) perceives young men, excluded from mainstream social activities, as turning to a form of militaristic culture of group violence as a means to get what they want and to give them a legitimate masculine status. She identifies the most prevalent activities of these groups as joyriding, drugs, ram-raiding, burglary and rioting. However, both she and Walklate (1995) see this type of public portrayal of masculinity as present through much of society: amongst young males it is simply more zealously exercised and less culturally accepted than in other manifestations. Campbell also observed that young women form subcultures but argues that these are largely constructive and based on self-help, and thus their effect is more to help than to destroy communities. An essentially similar conclusion is reached by McRobbie (1991), who sees the typical female subculture as using a style of dress and behaviour embodying femininity as a way of opposing established norms, especially in schools. All this was some way removed from American experiences where young excluded women found refuge in gangs where crime, violence toughness and independence were pursued (Campbell (1981) and (1984)). Of course it may be that the criminal behaviour manifests because of the sheer pleasure in doing it which may be enhanced by performance in a group (Katz (1988)). The suggestion is that crime allows the individual to escape the mundane nature of modern living and may also be a way of self-expression. Thus the tendency of girl gangs to assert their identity through aspects of fashion may indicate that the link may not be with strain. Or the strain may be the uniting feature but the criminality may be born of other things.

A rather different example of British criminal groupings is given by Donald and Wilson (2000) who discuss the activities of groups of males who come together to carry out criminal activities, in this case ram-raiders. They report these as clear groups with leaders and apprentices and containing specialists in areas such as driving or violence. These groups are said to work together in much the same way as legitimate work groups might but their connection outside this activity is less clear, so that it is uncertain whether this is really a subculture rather than just a gang structure for the job. In this sense clearer examples can be gained from football hooligans. Van Limbergen, et al. (1989) saw these as very structured and fairly long-lasting units. He noted three layers: the close-knit 'core' who organised, planned and took part in all the violence; the 'stagiaries', more loosely linked to the core and participating in violence but not yet members; and the peripheral adolescents who were numerous, vociferous but only loosely connected and not involved in real acts of violence. Johnston (2000) has tentatively replicated this type of grouping in her analysis of seven football hooligan groups. Her study showed that the age membership of these gangs went from 19 to 44 with 70 per cent being between 20 and 30. They often had long criminal careers, especially the core members. But an additional finding of some significance is that members are not necessarily disaffected youths; many have jobs, sometimes highly paid and high-powered posts. This raises further questions but these groups are perhaps the closest the British seem to come to the highly structured gangs.

It is thus not obvious that any easy translation can be made into a British context of Cloward and Ohlin's notion of dividing delinquency into three types: criminal; conflict; and retreatist. In the US they found that the criminal type prevailed in districts where there were strong opportunities, often arising out of the existence of Mafia-type organisations. This structure is less pervasive in Britain, although there is of course organised crime in drugs, prostitution, gambling and 'protection'. Conflict delinquency in the US is closely related to Cohen's notions of gang fights and protection of 'turf'. Again this seems to have been less widespread in Britain, although drugs and football hooliganism might be changing this. Acts of destruction, which Cloward and Ohlin also mention in this connection, are, however, a much more general and visible part of British juvenile crime and behaviour. Their third category of retreatism has perhaps become more important in recent years as British youths turn more to alcohol and drug abuse, though this is activity which is less structured.

The perhaps surprising conclusion, given the pervasive nature of the British class system is that the strong class-based and subcultural theories of both Cohen and of Cloward and Ohlin seem to be of only limited relevance in Britain. Nonetheless, when allowances are made for cultural differences the American findings may be of substantial relevance to juvenile crime in Britain. Thus workers from both countries (Young (1999), Campbell (1993) and Joe and Chesney-Lind (1998)) see relevance in Cohen's notion that gang members draw self-esteem from association with other members. In any event, even ruling out highly structured concepts of peer influence does not remove the possibility that youths are encouraged to offend partly due to the influence of the peers, using the word in a looser sense than that of gangs. This is reflected in the work of West and Farrington (1973) and that of Agnew (1991) who found the strongest correlation between offending and peers emerged when an individual felt more attached to his or her peers, was in frequent contact with them, and the peer group was involved in serious offences. Some support for this comes from the finding of the Youth Life-style Survey (Flood-Page et al. (2000), p. 34) that people who had friends or relatives 'who had been in trouble with the police were over three times as likely to be offenders themselves'.

Much of the British literature on youth gangs and subcultures is drawn together in an interesting survey by Muncie (1999) who critically examines developments since the 1950s. He identifies two broad periods in this subculture. The earlier phase he dubs as a time of resistance, one in which through both their styles and behaviour youths were resisting dominant culture. He sees two broad aspects to this: the white working-class youth culture as portrayed in the Teddy boys, mods, skinheads and punks; and the black youth cultures—rude boys and the very different Rastafarians. Each of these is a very male cultural type; if women are included at all it is only on the peripheries. The other phase he sees as one of counter-culture in which many middle-class youths noted their disillusionment with society, often including political movements and alternative lifestyles. Here he includes: the beats, CND and the New Left; hippies; political anarchists and anarchism; DIY culture—New Age, sabs and eco-warriors. In this last grouping activists are often drawn together on single-issue politics rather than being a group or subculture with similar values and these ad hoc groupings are now usually addressed and organised via the Internet. Interestingly in the 1990s many of the activities of these groups were criminalised in the Criminal Justice and Public Order Act 1994. This and the fascination of the dominant culture with demonising these groupings (see Hall et al. (1978) and Hall (1980)) give them a unifying force and political weight that they might otherwise not enjoy. In all these subcultures although the main linking element may be non-criminal, many criminal problems and crime waves have been linked with them (see Hall et al. (1978)). Even where this has not been the case their otherwise law-abiding activities have been criminalised as they do not fit the mainstream accepted behaviours.

Amidst all these various complications it does at least emerge clearly that interpretation of the information is difficult, especially, and crucially, in terms of causation. Does it mean that offenders forge close friendships because they are isolated and rejected by non-offenders or because they seek out those who indulge in similar activities or is the criminal activity committed only because of encouragement from friends? Since many young males commit offences in pairs or other groupings does this mean that the dynamics of these friendships influence the criminality, or simply that the offenders are out together when they decide to offend when they might have decided to do something else, such as catch a bus? Is peer-group influence only a factor because the shared experience makes it more pleasurable and, if so, why is it more pleasurable? Is there a causal relationship, a link, a chance incidence or some combination of these?

12.4 **Matza and Sykes**

In 1957, David Matza and Gresham Sykes produced a theory of delinquency which, because he later extended it, has come to be generally attributed to Matza alone (Sykes and Matza (1957); Matza (1964) and (1969)). Although it was designed to explain juvenile crimes, and most of this section will be devoted to that area, the central thesis may be extended to cover some adult crime, and some of the examples in this section are designed to show how this might be possible. Matza's main theme concerned what he called drift. In contrast to the theories so far covered Matza's theory of drift involves an element of free will, individual choice and judgement on behaviour. This admission of free will into his doctrine is, to a certain extent, a return to the classical school of criminology which existed before positivism became popular.

The analyses of the positivists seem to imply that there should be much more criminality: they cannot explain why those we think of as criminals are law-abiding in most respects; nor can they explain why most criminals reform in their early 20s; and they cannot account for the fact that in areas where the social forces militate towards criminality most people are in fact law-abiding. Sykes and Matza argued that individuals are not committed to criminality. The concept of drift basically situates the individual as drifting at will between law-abiding and delinquent or criminal behaviour, being never committed to either type of behaviour. The state of drift is reached because of what Matza terms 'neutralisation'. Neutralisation arises from the fact that every criminal law has its limits, usually denoted by official defences to the activity, and therefore every law is qualified. Matza suggests that the juvenile uses these limits, extending their interpretation in ways which allow the action without guilt or remorse: it can be justified both to self and others by pleading, say, self defence, duress or even insanity. Part of this process also involves a distortion of other areas of the dominant value system. A minor element of the dominant value system encourages individuals to seek excitement and adventure. These objects are normally made subordinate to more dominant ideals such as hard work. Matza argues that delinquents take these subordinate values, extend them, and use them in inappropriate ways and times. Thus violence may be acceptable in boxing or possibly other sports, but the delinquent, without generally approving of violence, may extend the times and places where it is acceptable, for example by using it in gang fights or pub brawls. Similarly, no action is absolutely condemned; even killing is permitted as self defence or by accident, and it may be positively required at times of war or for the purposes of judicial execution. In those who take part in criminal activities, such reasons are given a wider interpretation than those accepted by the conforming members of society. The justifications for the criminality are therefore in a perverse way derived from the norms of the dominant culture. In Matza's theory, the individual does not fully accept or internalise any set of rules or norms, but has rather learnt a set of 'definitions favourable to violation', while still tacitly subscribing to many of the middle-class rules.

Matza and Sykes (1957) list five justifications (before the act) or excuses (after the act) which delinquents (and others) may use to explain or neutralise criminal acts:

1. Deny responsibility, usually by claiming that the act was a result of uncontrollable factors: an accident, parental neglect, poverty, broken home, being led astray by friends. This type of excuse is not restricted to juveniles and is often seen in offences committed by white-collar and, especially, corporate criminals. Such offenders frequently claim that they were forced to act by their superiors; or acted only out of a sense of responsibility to some larger entity; or that it was the fault of subordinates who had been negligent.

2. The criminal may claim that no one was actually harmed, either physically or financially. If items are stolen from wealthy individuals, or from employers or large shops, it may be said that they can afford the loss or that the insurance company will pay. The same person might well perceive theft from an identifiable fellow individual as immoral. Again, this may be used to explain a lot of white-collar and corporate crime. A quite different set of activities, gang fights, pub brawls or domestic violence, are often seen by their perpetrators as private and therefore not criminal. In all these cases the perpetrators may be basically law-abiding but have an extended view of acceptable behaviour.

3. The claim that the victim deserved the harm caused and so is not a true victim (e.g., the victim is also criminal and so should not complain; or the victim started the trouble and so 'only got what was coming'). Similarly, in the case of sex crime: 'she was asking for it because of the way she was dressed'; and in domestic violence, that the victim deserved the violence as he or she had 'misbehaved'.

4. An offender might claim that since everyone has at some time committed a criminal act, no one is in a position to condemn him.

5. The approval of the group or gang (or the corporation) may be said to be more important than those of the family or of society. Thus, where the group calls for delinquency it is justified.

In part, these justifications underline Matza's main point that the individual has in a particular instance chosen delinquent behaviour. The way in which free will is exercised is influenced by a variety of factors, but the youth is not bound by the constraints of a group. A person can react and respond to opportunities to commit crimes, or can decide whether a particular time, place and environment is well suited to breaking the rules. The group, subculture or gang may make such activity more likely by promoting it, but it does not make the behaviour mandatory. For Matza, there is a major flaw in the works of both Cohen and of Cloward and Ohlin: in each case the individual who turns to the peer group gives up or escapes the constraints of conforming to official behaviour for the equally demanding and constraining requirement of conforming to the subcultural values. Matza rejects this idea, and gives the individual greater freedom to choose whether to commit a criminal act and to do so for a personal reason, rather than merely as a requirement of a group.

12.4.1 Evaluation

Matza's ideas became widely accepted. This can be partially explained by the time in which they were posited. The end of the 1950s and the early 1960s were seen as a period in which society began to change. In both America and Europe there had been a very conventional acceptance of family life and legality. This began to be questioned by such movements as the Southern Christian Leadership Conference (SCLC) led by Martin Luther King, and the civil rights movement. This was also reflected in the arts, which were exploding with radical and rebellious ideas, evidenced in literature by the 'angry young men' and in music by 'rock and roll'. The cultural change extended the acceptable areas of behaviour. Convention, for example, had made alcohol the only acceptable social drug, whereas acceptability began to be extended, in certain sectors of society, to marijuana and in some cases the more psychedelic drugs.

Matza asserts that neither the individual nor the peer group is totally opposed to the norms of the dominant social order. He suggests that it would be impossible for a juvenile subculture to evolve in which the members' views were diametrically opposed to adult (or middle-class) values, as the latter are too closely connected with the juveniles to allow such a wholesale breach with dominant culture. His central starting point is rather the significance of individual 'drift', to which is added the importance of peer group setting, particularly during adolescence. Although the members of the peer group may not be individually opposed to adult values, the desire to feel 'strong','virile' or 'masculine', or to prove loyalty to the group, may lead them outwardly to express opinions or partake in activities contrary to the adult values.

Matza's is not a pure subcultural theory because, despite its close connection with a delinquent group, the delinquency arises out of the state of drift which is an individual feeling. Juveniles are subject to both conventional values, as promoted by adults, and delinquent influences, as arise in the peer group or subculture. They respond to both these pressures; some of their activities mostly derive from one and some mostly from the other. Unlike Cohen, or Cloward and Ohlin, where the delinquency was a direct result of the peer group, in Matza's theory it can exist apart from it. For him, the subculture permits delinquency but it does not demand it.

The negative element of some juvenile delinquency can also be explained by Matza's theory. An individual in a state of drift and wishing to prove his ability to control his life might perform an action merely because it is criminal. No prediction is attached to this: there is simply the possibility that an individual might decide to perform a criminal act and might also be able to exercise some choice over the type of criminality.

However, the distinctive feature to emphasize is that Matza sees most delinquents as being neither committed to criminality, nor to law-abiding behaviour: they have some area of choice as to whether they will perform criminal acts when both the opportunity and the temptation arise.

12.5 Conclusion

This chapter has sought to introduce a variety of long-established sociological and pseudo-sociological explanations of crime. Recent developments which stand somewhat apart from the others are Agnew's general strain theory (see 12.2), which allows a subjective assessment both of what is important and of differing personal ways and abilities of coping with strain, and Currie's explanation of how relative deprivation can create tensions leading to criminality. The increased emphasis on personal, as against social and cultural, factors represents an exciting new facet to strain theory and one which needs rigorous empirical testing. The other writers surveyed in this chapter all stress various aspects of the relationship between individuals and society, emphasising the greater likelihood of criminal activity arising whenever this relationship is seriously lacking in harmony. Several manifestations of possible antagonism or conflict between individuals (or specific groups) and the dominant values and behaviours of society have been explored. The explanations have been broadly categorised under three main concepts: anomie; strain; and subculture. To a large extent, these explanations have in common a strong tendency to situate these disjunctures primarily—but not exclusively—in the lower orders of society, and to find them to be especially potent amongst young males in those groups. They fail to address the reasons why women, who suffer from the same social conditions, are not similarly affected and do not also turn to crime in large numbers. This failure reduces the explanatory power of these theories (see also Chapter Eleven). Consequently, the contribution these explanations make to understanding criminal behaviour is greatest when working-class, youth crime and delinquency is being considered.

The policy implications are various. In the criminal justice sphere they mainly seem to be aimed at preventing the problem manifesting itself as criminal activity. The implication seems to be that offenders, following one or a few violations, should be removed from society for a period of time. This is both an expensive option and one which is invasive of personal freedom, but many see it as a necessary preventative measure. Other possible policies might be to require proof of acceptable lifestyles and conduct before any access to welfare, and/or a type of fortress existence whereby the 'worthy' are protected from the activities of the 'underclass' who are left to prey on each other. The latter proposal assumes that the population can be clearly and fairly divided up into moral groups: this seems unlikely on any proper study of society and criminality, including white-collar, corporate and domestic crimes. Other policy implications largely lie outside the criminal justice system: provision of greater educational and job training opportunities; increased job opportunities involving good wages and reasonable hours; an expansion of the public sector to provide services to the less well off; promoting feelings of inclusion of all citizens; and encouraging cultural ideals which focus on community and respect for others.

SUGGESTED READING

Agnew, R. (1992), 'Foundations for a General Strain Theory of Crime and Delinquency', *Criminology*, vol. 30, p. 47.

Agnew, R. (1994), 'The Techniques of Neutralisation and Violence', *Criminology* 32: 555.

Messner, S. and Rosenfeld, R. (2001), *Crime and the American Dream*, 3rd edn, Belmont, CA: Wadsworth.

Muncie, J. (1999), *Youth and Crime: A Critical Introduction*, London: Sage.

QUESTIONS FOR REVISIONS

1   Merton's theory emphasises wealth as the primary goal in American society. In so doing does it suggest that poverty, in and of itself, causes crime? Messner and Rosenfeld suggest that the American Dream is structurally undermining society, how do they see this happening? Is the pursuit of wealth the primary goal in the UK today?

2   Consider your own life experience. In school and university (and work if you have that experience) what are/were the 'cultural goals' and are the 'institutional means' sufficient to attain these, are they fair and equally applied? Are the goals focused on financial success?

3   What does Agnew consider to be the three main types of strain? Could there be measures to test the theory? Agnew argues that individual aspects are also important, what are they and how do they interact with strain? Could one build policies on either tackling strain or dealing with the individual aspects? Which would be most likely to give results?

4   Is the formation of gangs linked to the strains set out by Cohen and Cloward and Ohlin? Is the criminality a result of the same factors? Might other explanations better explain these phenomenon?

5   How does neutralisation work? Is it really necessary? Does it arise before the event and act as a causative factor in allowing the individual to feel released to commit the offence or is it merely a rationalisation, a strategy used to explain the offence to the authorities (and possibly others) after the event in order to avoid punishment or blame?

REFERENCES

Agnew, R. (1991), 'The Interactive Effects of Peer Variables on Delinquency', *Criminology*, vol. 29, p. 47.

Agnew, Robert (1992), 'Foundation for a General Strain Theory of Crime and Delinquency', *Criminology*, vol. 30, p. 47.

Agnew, R. (1997), 'An Overview of General Strain Theory', in R. Peternoster (ed.), *Essays in Criminological Theories*, Los Angeles: Roxbury Park.

Agnew, R. (2000), 'Strain Theory and School Crime', in S.S. Simpson (ed.), *Of Crime and Criminality*, Thousand Oaks, CA: Pine Forge.

Agnew, Robert and White, Helen Raskin (1992), 'An Empirical Test of General Strain Theory', *Criminology*, vol. 30, p. 47.

Bauman, Z. (2001), *The Individualized Society*, Cambridge: Polity Press.

Box, Steven (1981), *'Deviance Reality and Society'*, 2nd edn, London: Holt, Rinehart and Winston.

Brown, S. (1998), *Understanding Youth and Crime*, Buckingham: Open University Press.

Campbell, A. (1981), *Girl Delinquents*, Oxford: Basil Blackwell.

Campbell, A. (1984), *The Girls in the Gang*, Oxford: Basil Blackwell.

Campbell, B. (1993), *Goliath: Britain's Dangerous Places*, London: Methuen.

Cloward, Richard and Ohlin, Lloyd (1960), *Delinquency and Opportunity*, London: Collier-Macmillan.

Cohen, Albert (1955), *Delinquent Boys: The Culture of the Gang*, New York: The Free Press.

Currie, Elliot (1985), *Confronting Crime: An American Challenge*, New York: Pantheon Books.

Currie, Elliot (1995), 'The End of Work: Public and Private Livelihood in Post-employment Capitalism', in Stephen Edgell, Sandra Walklate and Gareth Williams (eds), *Debating the Future of the Public Sphere*, Aldershot: Avebury.

Currie, Elliot (1997), 'Market, Crime and Community: Toward a Mid-range Theory of Post-industrial Violence', *Theoretical Criminology*, vol. 1, p. 147.

Donald, I. and Wilson, A. (2000), 'Ram Raiding: Criminals Working in Groups', in D. Canter and L. Alison (eds), *The Social Psychology of Crime: Groups, Teams and Networks*, Aldershot: Ashgate.

Downes, David and Rock, Paul (1995), *Understanding Deviance: A Guide to the Sociology of Crime and Rule Breaking*, 2nd edn, Oxford: Clarendon Press.

Durkheim, Émile (1933) (original 1893), *The Division of Labour in Society*, Glencoe, IL: The Free Press.

Durkheim, Émile (1970) (original 1897), *Suicide*, London: Routledge & Kegan Paul.

Flood-Page, C., Campbell, S., Harrington, V. and Miller, J. (2000), *Youth Crime: Findings From the 1998/9 Youth Lifestyles Survey*, Home Office Research Study 209, London: HMSO.

Hall, S. (1980), *Drifting into a Law and Order Society*, London: Cobden Trust.

Hall, S., Cutcher, C., Jefferson, T. and Roberts, B. (1978), *Policing the Crisis*, London: Macmillan.

Hirschi, T. (1969), *Causes of Delinquency*, Berkeley, CA: University of California Press.

Joe, K.A. and Chesney-Lind, M. (1998), ' "Just Every Mother's Angel": An Analysis of Gender and Ethnic Variations in Youth Gang Membership', in K. Daly and L. Maher (eds), *Criminology at the Crossroads: Feminist Readings in Crime and Justice*, Oxford: Oxford University Press. First published in 1995 in *Gender and Society*, vol. 9, p. 408.

Johnston, L. (2000), 'Riot by Appointment: An Examination of the Nature and Structure of Seven Hard-Core Football Hooligan Groups', in D. Canter and L. Alison (eds), *The Social Psychology of Crime: Groups, Teams and Networks*, Aldershot: Ashgate.

Katz, J. (1988), *The Seductions of Crime*, New York: Basic Books.

Katz, J. (2000), 'The Gang Myth', in S. Karstedt and K-D. Bussmann (eds), *Social Dynamics of Crime and Control: New Theories for a World in Transition*, Oxford and Oregon: Hart Publishing.

Matza, David (1964), *Delinquency and Drift*, London: Wiley.

Matza, David (1969), *Becoming Deviant*, New Jersey: Prentice Hall.

McDonald, Lynn (1982), 'Theory and Evidence of Rising Crime in the Nineteenth Century', *British Journal of Sociology*, vol. 33, p. 404.

McRobbie, A. (1991), *Feminism and Youth Culture*, London: Macmillan.

Merton, Robert K. (1949), *Social Theory and Social Structure*, New York: The Free Press.

Messner, S.F. and Rosenfeld, R.R. (2001), *Crime and the American Dream*, 3rd edn, Belmont, CA: Wadsworth Publishing.

Muncie, J. (1999), *Youth and Crime: A Critical Introduction*, London: Sage.

Scarman, Lord (1981), *The Brixton Disorders, 10–12 April 1981* (Scarman Report, 1981), Cmnd 8427, London: HMSO.

Stack, S. (1984), 'Income Inequality and Property Crime', *Criminology*, vol. 22, p. 229.

Sykes, Gresham M. and Matza, David (1957), 'Techniques of Neutralization: A Theory of Delinquency', *American Sociological Review*, vol. 22, p. 664.

Van Limbergen, K., Colears, C. and Walgrave, L. (1989), 'The Societal and Psychological Background of Football Hooliganism', *Current Psychology Research and Reviews*, vol. 8(1), p. 4.

Walklate, S. (1995), *Gender and Crime: An Introduction*, Hemel Hempstead: Prentice-Hall Harvester.

West, D.J. and Farrington, D.P. (1973), *Who Becomes Delinquent?*, London: Heinemann.

West, D.J. and Farrington, D.P. (1977), *The Delinquent Way of Life*, London: Heinemann.

Whyte, William Foote (1955), *Street Corner Society: The Social Structure of an Italian Slum*, 2nd edn, Chicago, IL: University of Chicago Press.

Willis, P. (1977), *Learning to Labour*, Aldershot: Gower.

Wilson, J.Q. and Herrnstein, R.J. (1985), *Crime and Human Nature*, New York: Simon & Schuster.

Young, J. (1999), *The Exclusive Society: Social Exclusion, Crime and Difference in Late Modernity*, London: Sage.

13

Control theories

13.1 Introduction

The term control, and particularly social control, can be taken to have all sorts of meanings. To most politicians or political theorists it would mean the control of political opposition, or possibly its suppression. To most sociologists it includes all the social processes which militate for conformity, from infant socialisation, through school and job to the public and State control systems such as the police, the courts and the punishment systems.

Most of the theorists discussed in earlier chapters have assumed that conformity is normal or natural, and criminality is abnormal. It is then often argued that there is no justification for individuals to break the law unless something abnormal is present. Some base that abnormality in the individual, such as biological abnormalities or personality defects. Others see criminality as a social problem, arising out of social disorganisation, unemployment, culture conflicts or strain. At least one such factor is seen as being necessary before the natural order of conformity can be broken.

The control theorists largely attack that central assumption. Their basis is that every individual is born free to break the law. It is criminality which is natural, and conformity needs explanation. The main question here is therefore: why don't we all break the law? Conformity is seen as the result of special circumstances, and criminality is to be expected if these special circumstances break down. For example, there is nothing natural about driving on one side of the road, and yet motorists do keep to the required side. It is not natural to buy rather than take food when one sees it, and yet in our society most people buy rather than take. There is clearly nothing natural about conformity, as most of our formative years are spent learning what is permitted behaviour and what is not, and often why the difference exists. Parents at home, teachers at school and other individuals in the community, particularly the social control agencies such as formal religious bodies, the police and the courts, spend a lot of time and effort in controlling each of us.

Each society makes rules and tries to restrict its members to partake only in activities which are acceptable to the social order. Control theories explain how societies persuade people to live within these rules. It is important to note that conformity is always seen as fragile, as something which might be broken at any time if the reason for conformity is weakened, lost or momentarily broken. Criminality is therefore the breakdown of the socialisation process.

All this is open to a variety of interpretations, but this chapter will concentrate on the more influential. To illustrate some of the diversity the work of Reiss and

Reckless will be mentioned, but the main thrust will be on Hirschi and others who have drawn on his work. Most of these worked with juveniles, but unlike the sub-cultural theories in Chapter Twelve, many of these can also be used as explanations of adult crime.

13.2 **Early control theories**

Control theories draw on both psychological and social factors to explain criminality. The psychological aspects can be seen most clearly in the earlier work of writers like Reiss and Reckless.

Reiss (1951) discussed the effects of 'personal control' and 'social control' on delinquency. Here, 'personal control' denotes how well the juvenile manages to resist using socially unacceptable methods to reach his goals. This assessment of the individual control is based in the psychological diagnosis of the development of the super-ego, and therefore indicates a Freudian basis. In this case conformity meant that the individual accepted the rules and norms as his or her own, or submitted to them as a rational control of behaviour in a social setting—a healthy super-ego. Delinquency denoted the opposite of this.

'Social control' is the ability of social groups or institutions to make norms or rules effective. Conformity resulting from social controls tends to involve submission to the rules and norms of society. Reiss's work was concerned with predicting juvenile crime. He tried to base predictions on the willingness of the individual to submit to social controls, particularly in school, but found this to be an invalid predictor. A much better predictor he found in the psychiatrists' analyses of the individual's super-ego or internal controls (see 8.2).

Reckless (1967) and (1973), posited a containment theory in which the main thread is that there are pushes (drives) and pulls which tend to tempt a person towards delinquency. Prevention requires the exercise of control by factors which insulate the individual against such temptations. Drives, pulls and insulation could all arise either within the individual or outside him.

Psychological desires or propensities, such as restlessness and aggression, might be the internal elements which push the individual towards criminality. External factors which may push towards criminality could be social pressures such as poverty, family conflicts and lack of opportunities. Pull factors are generally external and might include the availability of illegitimate opportunities, criminal peer groups and, he claims, some mass media images (but see 10.2.2).

Similarly, insulators or containments against criminality might be both internal or external. Internal insulators could include the psychological position of the individual such as the development of the super-ego; a sense of direction; the ability to find alternative legitimate fulfilment; and a commitment to values or laws and feelings of responsibility. External insulators may be illustrated by having a meaningful role to play in society, reasonable expectations, a sense of belonging and identity, supportive relationships, especially in the family, and adequate discipline.

The most distinctive element in the writings of Reckless is that of the self-concept. This is internal, and his claim was that those individuals with a strong and favourable self-concept were best insulated against the drives and pulls towards criminality. A favourable self-concept might be illustrated by saying that the individuals view themselves in a positive way: as having values to live up to; as being law-abiding; and as having an idea of being of use and value to society and those in it. Parents affected an individual's self-concept most strongly, but other influences came from teachers and others in authority.

Reckless argued that this theory had a number of advantages—he claimed it could be applied to individuals; the various constraints could be measured; it could be applied to explain both conformity and criminality; and it could be used for the treatment and prevention of criminality. He carried out a number of studies which seemed to suggest that the theory was vindicated by being a good tool for predicting delinquency (Reckless (1967) and (1973)). However, one carried out in conjunction with Simon Dinitz (Reckless and Dinitz (1972)) found that of the boys the containment theory predicted would become delinquents, only 40 per cent had had contact with the police in the following four years.

Despite these doubts and assertions that the key terms are ill-defined and too general, strengthening people's self-esteem has been used to train them away from criminality. McGuire and Priestly (1985) claim that strengthening an individual's morals and feelings of altruism raises their feelings of worth and self-esteem, which decreases the likelihood of future criminality. This would involve using the learning techniques discussed in 10.2, and has been seen to achieve some success.

13.3 Individual control

Most of this chapter will be devoted to the social control theories. These are strongly based on external controls, often State or societal, as providing the impetus to legality, the bond to society which will tend to reinforce legal behaviours. In this the control is largely external and structural. Gottfredson and Hirschi (1990) have moved away from this towards a control theory based almost exclusively on individual aspects. It is interesting that Hirschi should be one of the leaders in this new move as he is also one of the central figures in the structural or social control theory.

The approach suggested by Gottfredson and Hirschi in their book, *A General Theory of Crime* (1990) and their re-discussion of it in 1993, unlike the ideas on individual control discussed earlier (Chapters Seven to Ten), does not propose a biological or genetic reason for criminality. Their focus is on self-control formed by early childhood socialisation, particularly in the family, and provides a wide theory of criminality, not dependent on legal definitions. It purports to explain all acts of 'force or fraud taken in pursuit of self-interest' (p. 15), which probably includes all property offences and acts of violence. There are two dependent aspects: the lack of self-control of the individual; and the opportunity for committing crimes. If the opportunity to commit a crime arises then the person with low self-control will commit it, whereas the person with high self-control will not. As they present their theory, low self-control is the central aspect, but will operate to give rise to criminal acts only if the opportunity arises.

By self-control they mean a subjective state whereby one individual is more vulnerable to the temptations of the moment than is another. It is an assessment of how restrained each individual feels about his or her actions. A person who lacks self-control will like quick, easy tasks where the outcome is clear and positive, will lack diligence and tenacity and will be impulsive; unable to postpone gratification; insensitive; self-centred and indifferent to the needs and sufferings of other people; risk-taking; short-sighted; non-verbal and short-tempered; easily frustrated; and physical, preferring physical activity to mental or cognitive experience. Furthermore, the traits arise at a young age, well before the usual age of criminal responsibility, and endure until death.

Although Gottfredson and Hirschi recognise that most crime is committed by the young and that the rate of offending declines as the age rises, they deny that there has been a change in criminality, arguing that the individual will still have low self-control but the problem may manifest itself in non-criminal activities. They also recognise that women commit less crime than men, but do not accept that women necessarily have greater self-control: they see the explanation in closer socialisation by their families when they are young. They also account for the sex difference by asserting that women may not get as many opportunities to commit offences as their male counterparts, and so their criminality may come out in non-criminal activities. The claim is thus that low self-control means criminality, but this may or may not manifest itself in criminal activity: the opportunities open will be the strongest factor operating on how criminality will manifest itself. If it does not lead to offending, it will come out in other imprudent activities such as heavy drinking or smoking, unemployment, a bad work record, failure in marriage, unwanted pregnancies, and even a greater likelihood of being involved in road and other accidents. Low self-control, when it coincides with opportunity, is supposed to predict all of these. If valid, this theory would explain differences in offending over time (for the same offender and for different offenders), in different locations, and between individuals.

In their theory the low self-control is not learned: no class or racial group intentionally teaches it. On the contrary, almost all socialisation is designed to teach self-control. The implication would appear to be that lack of self-control must be inherent. This would send us back to the earlier discussions but Gottfredson and Hirschi are very careful to exclude this possibility. Instead they state that any person can be effectively socialised but that individual differences can influence the prospects of effective or adequate socialisation. But this simply shifts the ambiguity. They attempt to resolve this by asserting: that the object of offending is always to maximise immediate pleasure; that without socialising most individuals would try to maximise pleasure; and thus teaching self-control is an essential precondition for law-abiding behaviour. The adequacy or otherwise of the socialisation— monitoring the behaviour of the child, recognising deviant or unacceptable behaviour and punishing such behaviour—determines how well self-control is developed. This aspect of the theory is therefore external, the self-control is externally shaped by socialisation or the lack thereof, but once the level of self-control is formed it is internal. In their view most of this socialisation occurs in the family, relegating other frequently cited socialising influences, such as peer groups and school, to peripheral roles in the formation of self-control. Peer pressure comes after self-control is formed and is merely confirming: school can only reinforce (not replace) the family socialisation because those with already low self-control are ill-equipped to learn new skills. The heavy stress on the family has been attacked by some feminists because it tends to blame the mother, often in reality the foremost socialiser, as the person at fault for improper socialisation (see Miller and Burack (1993)). However, the link to family and early attachments has recently been given a boost by the suggestion (Hayslett-McCall and Bernard (2002)) that disruptions in relationships with primary carers in early childhood, particularly that of boys, causes problems in the development of the masculine gender role. This gives rise to low self-control, which they posit as an explanation of gender differences in crime rates.

The second requirement for an offence to be committed is that the opportunity be present. Gottfredson and Hirschi (1990) say very little about opportunity, other than asserting that: it must clearly maximise immediate pleasure; involve simple mental and physical tasks; and involve a low level of risk or detection. The first two of these fall in with the definition of low self-control and so are unsurprising; the last is rather odd and appears to contain a contradiction. In defining self-control, being impulsive, shortsighted and enjoying risk are mentioned, and yet opportunity is maximised when risk is minimised. In the 1993 piece written by Hirschi and Gottfredson, there is a little more explanation of opportunity. Using the example of driving under the influence of drink, they argue that people of low self-control will do so when there is easy access to alcohol and a car is available, but when alcohol sales are restricted there may be no risk of such activity even for those of low self-control—the opportunity has been removed by a situational construct. In some cases this situational construct may depend on the offender: embezzlement from a bank requires one to be an employee and/or to have the necessary computer skills. These examples demonstrate a partial recognition that there are social and structural aspects to opportunity but even these are represented as depending on the individual's situation and level of self-control.

Another attack came from Grasmick et al. (1993) who tested the theory and found partial support for it, particularly the opportunity element. They then argued that the explanation of low self-control needed supplementation by variables which might increase the desire to commit a criminal act. For example, strain theory would allow recognition that the motivation for crime is not equal for all. Gottfredson and Hirschi both in 1990 and 1993 reject this call and state that it is fundamental to their theory that people are not more or less prone to criminality, not more or less desirous of its ends. They wholly reject any deterministic explanation claiming that they merely set out what factors increase a probability to offend not a propensity to do so. Criminality is equally attractive to all. They also attribute the failure of Grasmick et al. (1993) to discover a stronger correlation with low self-control to a faulty methodology using a self-report approach instead of direct observation of behaviour to assess self-control as had been done by Keane et al. (1993). However, their preference—direct observation—would appear to take the very behaviours the theory is trying to explain in order to test it. Gottfredson and Hirschi do not see this as problematic but others do: certainly Ackers (1991), who attacked the theory for being tautologous, would see this as a problem. Gottfredson and Hirschi respond that as long as criminal behaviour is not used as one of the indicators of low self-control when searching for a link with criminality there is no difficulty. It is legitimate to look for:

whining, pushing, and shoving (as a child); smoking and drinking and excessive television watching and accident frequency (as a teenager); difficulties in interpersonal relations, employment instability, automobile accidents, drinking, and smoking (as an adult). None of these is a crime. They are logically independent of crime. Therefore the relation between them and crime is not a matter of definition, and the theory survives the charges that it is mere tautology and that it is nonfalsifiable.

This is plausible, but not fully convincing and adds to the other questions about an approach which otherwise has strong possibilities for explaining behaviour. Thus Geis (2000) asserts that the data are excessively manipulated to accommodate the theory. Although Hirschi and Gottfredson (2000) respond forcefully, areas of uncertainty remain. Perhaps Tittle's control theory (see 13.5) will eventually carry more weight.

The similarities between Gottfredson and Hirschi's theory and cognitive learning theories is very marked (see 10.2.6). Both base the criminality heavily on certain learned behaviour and attitudes; both accept that there is a rational choice made to offend, both would recognise a heavy input from the family. There are also powerful differences. The cognitive learning theorists recognise differences in motivation; and are ready to accept that these could be learned, not only through cognitive learning, but also through other methods of acquiring motivation such as the strain theories or deprivation. The cognitive learning theorists also consider that an individual continues to learn and develop all through life. Gottfredson and Hirschi reject the notion of differences in motivation and claim that low self-control is fully shaped very young and that it is not really altered by later experience.

Apart from other inferences, these differences would point towards different ways of treating convicted criminals. One example would be over the efficacy of punishment. For example, Keane et al. (1993) briefly discuss how punishment could be used to deter criminal action through its likelihood, its severity and the rapidity of its application. The certainty of punishment has usually been claimed to be the strongest deterrent, but in empirical tests has not been found to be very effective. Keane et al. argue that one reason is that deterrence theory depends on offenders making rational choices, weighing up the possible gains against the possible losses, including detection and punishment. Some people do not act in such a rational manner: indeed, the very definition of low self-control (immediate gratification etc.) would exclude such calculating behaviour. If this is correct then punishment is almost never likely to deter, no matter how certain, severe or quick (unless it is so inevitable as to negate the opportunity, like the presence of a police officer at a house to be burgled). In any event true reading of Gottredson and Hirschi would not lead to severe punishment or to other limits on freedom; if the control is not present in the child it will not be induced in the adult. Their theory would rather suggest an emphasis on long-term initiatives designed to support and augment family control structures.

The theory may therefore have a useful place in assessing punishment. It may also be relevant in assessing treatment or alteration of behaviour. Gottfredson and Hirschi's suggestion of low self-control being formed early and more or less permanently implies that after a certain stage it can never be altered. The only ways of preventing criminality would then seem to be either to remove opportunity (for some discussion of this see Chapter Eleven), or to remove the individual (see dangerousness in Chapter Eight). The possibility of intervening before criminality is fully formed seems impractical if this takes place at a very young age, whilst a programme of educating everyone in good parenting skills to ensure appropriate family socialisation seems even more forlorn. In this control theory the essential element may seem to be beyond control! The only bright possibility would seem to be widespread provision of nurseries with a caring socialising programme.

13.4 Sociological control theories

One of the earliest sociological control theories was Durkheim's theory of anomie (see 12.1.1), but the more modern study of this area is often connected to Hirschi (1969). He argues that human beings are born with the freedom to break the law and will only be stopped from doing so either by preventing any opportunities arising, which would not be possible, or by controlling their behaviour in some way. Law-breaking is natural, and we need to explain law-abiding behaviour. This looks very like the starting point of the classical writers like Beccaria and Hobbes, but Hirschi is not arguing that criminality is an expression of free will, only that it occurs and is normal behaviour. Control theory does not mean that people who perform criminal activities lack morality; they just exhibit a different morality. Nor is it argued that people are born wicked; that people are born criminals. Instead, it is asserted that at birth they know nothing about acceptable and unacceptable behaviour, and will just follow their natural desires. Of course each individual might learn, by a process of trial and error, their own standards for behaviour, but where humans live together in a community they generally feel the need for a little more order than this would produce. Each new member, whether it be a newborn child or a person who previously lived in another community, is socialised into the activities which the community finds acceptable by use of carrots and sticks, rewards and punishments. Classical theorists only recognised fear as the agent of conformity; people could only be deterred if they feared a nasty punishment: control theorists recognise both punishments and rewards. The implication is that the amount of crime is partly constrained because people are reluctant to cause pain to those who love them, and are unwilling to risk losing their possessions and, often more importantly, their reputations. People are not permanently law-abiding or permanently law-breaking. Depending on the controls in their lives they may, at some time, become willing to take part in criminal activities or may turn away from criminality to a law-abiding lifestyle.

Law-abiding citizens are seen to have four elements: their attachments with other people; the commitments and responsibilities they develop; their involvement in conventional activity; and their beliefs. The first of these elements, and some have said the most important, is attachment, the strong social and psychological attachments with other people and institutions in their community. Strong attachments make criminality less likely, especially as they make individuals sensitive to the opinions of others. The first and strongest attachments are seen to be with the family, although others will be formed with those in authority, for example, teachers and employers as well as the looser friendships and other personal relationships. Note that here Hirschi is referring to strong attachments to non-criminal aspects of society, strong attachment to a criminal gang would, in Hirschi's view, presumably lead to criminality. Hirschi links this concept of attachment with the ability and likelihood of empathy with the group and therefore commitment to activities which help rather than harm the group, here he means the non-criminal group. For this reason Schinkel (2002) attacks his theory as being tautological—sensitivity is to non-criminal 'others' and attachments are to non-criminal aspects of society.

The second element is that of commitment—the more social investments an individual makes to spouse, children, education, job, financial commitments, property investment etc., the less likely that individual is to risk losing all or some of this by a delinquent act. It is a cost–benefit sort of argument. If commitments lose importance for the individual, or if they never make what they consider to be important commitments, then they are relatively free to perform delinquent acts. It is not only those who objectively have no commitments who may be able to commit crimes, but also those who do not value what others might assess as important. Furthermore, as shown in 13.7.3, commitments of this sort can sometimes lead to criminality.

The third element is involvement, and refers to the amount a person's life has been given over to a particular legitimate activity. Do they take part or involve themselves in the extra-curricular activities of a school? Do they have many friends, and does most of their social life revolve around a group of friends from work? Criminal acts are less likely if participation in conventional or legitimate activity is important to the individual. Schinkel (2002) questions this arguing that it may just alter the place for the criminal act.

The final element is the individual's beliefs. This is used as a sociological rather than a psychological term. Hirschi does not see beliefs as a set of deeply held convictions, but rather as something the individual chooses to accept. Unlike deeply held convictions, acceptance of a particular stance can be changed quite easily by being subjected to different arguments; therefore these beliefs need constant social reinforcement. For example, a person may not believe that it is morally wrong, or at least not criminal, to blaspheme, but may refrain from doing so to avoid upsetting others. As Hirschi puts it, 'delinquency is not caused by beliefs that require delinquency, but is rather made possible by the absence of (effective) beliefs that forbid delinquency' (1969, p. 26). Learning and understanding moral issues can help to promote a situation where criminality is less likely (see 13.2 and 10.2).

All four control elements interrelate and are, theoretically, given equal weight: each helps to prevent criminality in most people. However, to present Hirschi's four elements as if they were generally accepted would be to give too great a feeling of consensus. Other writers posit slightly different elements. As an example, the seven sources of control listed by Roshier (1989) will be quoted. He claims that these seven factors can be used as rewards to persuade us to conform or, by their denial, as punishments to threaten us. The seven sources are as follows:

1. *Affection*—The human need for affection is very strong and almost universal. Therefore, many people will refrain from criminality in fear of losing it.

2. *Status*—The way people outside the family view us, e.g., colleagues and peers. Individuals need to elicit feelings such as respect and admiration from others. In most cases, fear of a bad reputation will act as a barrier to criminality. Equally,

if the other person or group admires lawbreaking, it can militate towards criminality.

3. *Stimulation*—Many obtain this directly through a job or from leisure activities; or vicariously through friends; or through fiction and the media. Punishment, whether by fines, community service or prison, removes or reduces these possibilities.

4. *Autonomy*—Most people need to feel their independence and power over their own destiny; (see 12.4). If law-abiding ways of self-expression are not present, then it may be that people will resort to criminality.

5. *Security*—a desire for comfort and physical safety. Punishments often threaten this security by threatening the discomfort of prison, or by removing from us the money which can provide these comforts.

6. *Money*—This is necessary for what it can obtain. Wealth may bring with it status, autonomy and security, and can be used to increase the number and types of stimulation available. It is therefore very important to conformity and control, which has meant that the fine is the most frequently used punishment in developed societies. The desire to obtain money is, of course, also a major stimulus towards criminality, one way of controlling this is to remove the profits of crime, e.g., by confiscating monies on conviction of certain offences.

7. *Belief*—This is very similar to Hirschi's last element of conformity (see 13.4).

All these elements can act towards conformity, but several can also encourage criminality. The outcome in any individual case will be discussed below. An interesting analysis of these control theories and one of many discussions in 'modernist' criminology comes from Schinkel (2002). Generally these theories all support an idea that there is society—which is good and non-criminal and then 'other' criminal or deviant groups which are somehow external and need to be re-socialised or controlled to become a part of the conventional society. Schinkel asks where these deviant groups go—what are they part of? Are they not still part of society? He sees the main difficulty with this approach to be its implication that these rejected people are in some way individually problematic and that policies are thus needed to help to 're-integrate' these individuals into conventional society. Against this he argues that these members are a part of society: the problem is with society as a whole and any remedy has to address social and structural aspects. This analysis is close to what true restorative justice should be about but what restorative justice programmes in practice rarely live up to.

13.5 Control balance

Control balance was first mooted by Tittle (1995, and modified in 1997, 1999 and 2000) and provides the control area with a general theory to explain deviance. Tittle defines deviance as any activity which the majority find unacceptable or would disapprove of; it is thus a much wider concept than those of crime and offending, and it occurs when a person has either a surplus or a deficit of control in relations to others (perhaps it comes closer to the new field of zemiology, the study of harm, than it does to crime; see Hillyard and Tombs (2001)). Those whose position in society allows them to exert more control over others and their environment than is exerted over them, enjoy a control surplus. A control deficit arises in people whose position in society means that they are more controlled by others than they are able to control. Tittle suggests that any control imbalance (surplus or deficit) will be likely to lead to deviance which may be criminal in nature. A deficit of control may lead to resentment, envy, loss of any stake in society removing the need to conform, and humiliation. Each of these has been frequently linked to criminality, the link here being the attempt, through crime, to redress the deficit by increasing control and autonomy. At the other end of the spectrum a surplus of control is said to be corrupting, and may lead to a desire to extend that surplus which will enhance autonomy and feed a desire to dominate. The link with criminal activity rests in the belief that the subservience of others largely removes the risk of being caught: a more specific claim is that any break-down of subservience provokes angry outbursts which can explain some domestic violence (see Hopkins and McGregor (1991)). This dual aspect seems to provide explanations both of street crime (most likely to be associated with a control deficit) and corporate or white-collar crime (most likely to be associated with a control surplus). The approach may be of use in analysing sex differences in offending.

Tittle does not assume that an imbalance alone will lead to criminality, recognising the importance of rational choice in any human behaviour, but he puts great stress on the drive to extend autonomy. For deviance or criminality to occur the motivation has to be triggered by provocation and facilitated by both opportunity and the absence of constraint. Moreover, internal moral controls (see Chapters Eight and Ten) may mitigate against criminal behaviour even when all these factors favour it.

Linking crime with power and its acquisition is not new. Many see violent crime as involving an element of control or power over the victim, and sex crimes have often been analysed in this way (see Lansky (1987) and Scheff and Retzinger (1991)). It is also possible to analyse property offences in this manner—burglars have a sort of power over their victims, the power to decide what to take and leave, how much mess and upset to cause etc., and for some this may be part of the attraction (see Katz (1988)). Tittle (1995) originally made an ambitious attempt to predict the type of deviance/offending behaviour by reference to the amount of control deficit or surplus: since then (1999), 2000) he has withdrawn a little and relies more on identifying offence seriousness (Table 13.1). The exact boundaries between the types of deviance are difficult—perhaps impossible—to establish in the absence of any clear measures of degrees of control. This greatly reduces the practical utility of the categorisation: perhaps all that can be claimed is that the more serious the control imbalance, the more serious the outcomes for the individual and the community.

Nonetheless, the control balance theory does help with some of the more complex problems which vex criminologists: for example, it could be used to explain sex differences in deviance. There is still a tendency for women to be controlled to a greater degree than men, and in more spheres of their lives. Because of this women suffer control deficits more frequently than do men, and those deficits tend to be large so they would fall into the range of submissive deviance (see Table

Table 13.1 Offending behaviour/offence seriousness by reference to the amount of control surplus or deficit

Control surplus	Examples of deviance from original theory (Tittle (1995))	Seriousness of deviance from recent revisions (1999 and 2000)
Small	Exploitation—price fixing; bribery; protection rackets; blackmail.	Least serious.
Medium	Plunder—destruction of the environment for personal gain; destruction caused to the community by organised gangs controlled by others.	Less serious.
Large	Decadence—large-scale flaunting of wealth.	Most serious.
Control deficit		
Small	Predation—theft; burglary; violence (basic street crimes)	Most serious acts.
Medium	Defiance or escapism—protest against control (could include the above); or withdrawn (escapist) deviance such as drug abuse, suicide, mental illness or alternative cultures or political movements.	Less serious acts.
Large	Submissive deviance—compliance with everything because one is too frightened to exhibit any challenge.	Least serious acts.

13.1: subordinating themselves entirely and without thinking of complaint) or defiant/escapist areas and far less frequently into the predatory area. Fewer women are presumed to have a control surplus so they would be under-represented in the areas of exploitation, plunder and decadence. Tittle suggests that males, on the other hand, tend more to inhabit the centre of the spectrum, many being in balance and then successively reducing in numbers as they move out to the edges of the spectrum. They would thus be more heavily represented in the predation and exploitation areas of the continuum and less so in the submissive and defiant/ escapist areas. This would explain the low level of predatory criminal activity which every measure of female crime has always discovered. Such an interesting analysis of offending and general deviance is illuminating and at the least deserving of attention.

If it could be operationally established, Tittle's theory offers immense possibilities for a greater understanding of crime in general: it offers the possibility of being able to view all types of offending (deviance) and all types of offender (rich and poor; male and female; powerful and weak; racially discriminated against and racially dominant) as similar, and as equally destructive of community and equally damaging to victims. Such a universal approach has obvious attractions.

Braithwaite (1997) takes the theory further by proposing a policy approach which, he claims, would minimise the destructive effect of control imbalances. His solution is seen to be in an approach which bases policies on the need to redistribute control. A more egalitarian society, he claims, will reduce control surplus and control deficit, and so help to reduce deviance generally and offending in particular. It is recognised that some control will be necessary to an ordered society, but this should be exercised in a way which respects those subjected to the control. The optimistic conclusion is that such evenhandedness, both in the exercise and in the distribution of control, will ensure its willing acceptance. The prospects of such harmony would certainly recede still further if the generalised approach was converted into specific suggestions.

13.6 Facilitating and choosing criminality

If these control elements break down, it explains why a person may be free, on an individual level, to participate in criminal activity, but it does not explain why such a choice might be made.

13.6.1 Facilitating criminality

Some forms of criminal behaviour involve particular and necessary skills. Other crimes may require essential specialist tools. But for most crimes neither of these constraints is absolute. A more general restriction might result from the fact that some crimes may be possible only if the opportunity arises. For example, to defraud the Inland Revenue it is normally necessary to earn money, and it may be feasible only if you are self-employed or if your employer at least acquiesces in the crime by not telling the truth.

Some people might refrain from committing crimes until they are given some sort of social support to offend. They may deviate only when they are in a group which encourages it, or when they have friends who would support the activity. This is not the same as the peer group pressures of the last chapter, as the group does not cause the criminality, does not necessarily push otherwise law-abiding people to commit crimes. The group simply provides the supportive atmosphere in which those who already lack social controls might find that they can commit crimes. Some individuals who are sufficiently free of the social controls to allow them to take part in criminal activity may none the less wish first to be able to justify this to the wider community; social support can provide this justification. The justifications often take the form of one of the techniques of neutralisation discussed in 12.4.

Possibly the oldest and often most important element to be considered by potential lawbreakers is the likelihood of getting caught. A secondary consideration is the possible punishment which might be faced, and especially the probability of that punishment being administered. Thus many motorists break traffic regulations knowing what the penalty is, but will drive within legal limits when they are aware there is a police car in the vicinity. The activity is only deterred if the individual believes that the criminality is likely to be detected. This belief may be wholly erroneous, but it leads the potential criminal to ask: is the benefit worth the risk of being caught and the punishment to be faced if I am caught? In control theory this analysis will only lead to criminality if the individual perceives detection to be low and is otherwise willing to perform a crime—unlike the classical theorists, it is not postulated that everyone is bad and will only be deterred by fear of detection and punishment. If a law is unjust (e.g., an edict that no red-haired person should drive), or is seen to operate unjustly, it may encourage people to ignore or evade its application. Differential application of the laws, even to people who are guilty, can give rise to disrespect for the law (see 13.8.2).

13.6.2 Choosing criminality

Despite the factors which affect the ability of the individual to commit a crime, the individual still needs to choose to turn to criminal activity. In classical criminology this was not a problem, as all people were naturally evil and therefore crime was inevitable unless it was controlled by deterrence. In modern control theories man is not naturally either evil or moral, but needs a reason for choosing criminality. The theory predicts that this choice will be made when lawbreaking behaviour is more attractive than law-abiding behaviour. Lawbreaking may offer the possibility of more money or more goods. It may act as a way of satisfying physical desires, which most people manage to satisfy through willing participation in legally recognised activities, or to control or suppress. It may permit people better to meet what they see to be their roles: a man to show his masculinity by being tough; or a provider to feed or clothe his or her dependants. In some groups, criminal acts may bring with them recognition and position, and this is often a motivation. Again, the person may be encouraged into criminality by a peer group which is supportive of such behaviour. Criminal activity may be seen to be, and may prove to be, exciting or meet a desire to take risks. This is especially attractive to those who cannot afford to, or are not given the chance to take part in legitimate and possibly dangerous or exciting, but often expensive leisure activities. Lastly, an individual may find criminality useful in order to take control over something and make it happen.

13.7 Community-based origins of conformity

In this section some of the many possible origins of conformity will be considered. Much of the work in this area has been done with juvenile offenders, but consideration will also be given to adults. A number of the earliest control theorists tended to concentrate on psychological controls, giving particular importance to interpersonal relationships, especially those of family, close friends or peer groups. Control theorists who have a more sociological view would also add things such as race and sex divisions (sex will be discussed in Chapter Fifteen), as well as giving more attention to the institutional control agents.

13.7.1 Family

The most commonly quoted control factor is the family, which includes consideration of the effects of family breakdown (particularly early maternal separation), and the quality of the family relationship.

The effects of a family breakdown, whether it occurs naturally through the death of one of the parents or arises from traumas such as desertion or divorce, has long been considered a factor affecting the criminality of the children of the family. Haskell and Yablonsky (1982) assessed eight studies which researched the relationship between crime and broken homes, finding that between 23.9 and 61.5 per cent of delinquents came from broken homes while only 12.9 to 36.1 per cent of non-delinquents came from broken homes. Murray (1990 and 1994), without much supporting evidence, causally linked both criminality and the underclass to single-parent families, which he saw as a source of moral decline and lawlessness. Some have used these ideas to suggest that single parents should have to have their children adopted in order to be eligible for benefits (Muncie (1999)), whilst in the USA some States require proof of contraception before allowing benefits to single women. These ideas have never been adopted as policy in the UK. However, whilst not embracing Murray's ideology concerning single-parent families the 1997 Labour government did accept a strong link between bad parenting (whether of one or two parents) and criminal activities of youngsters, and introduced parenting orders, requiring parents to participate in weekly counselling to teach them to control their children. As some parenting orders have been successful, the government in 2003 wishes to see more emphasis on them, particularly in dealing with anti-social behaviour and truancy. With this in mind there are new draft guidelines (**http://www.crimereduction.gov.uk/antisocialbehaviour22.htm#wnloads**) for their use and for the use of voluntary contracts between parents and Youth Offender Teams. Each of these is intended both to offer/require parents to attend a counselling or guidance programme on parenting and to agree/be required to keep their children under control.

Two studies in Britain reported that broken homes and early separation predicted convictions up to age 33 (Kolvin et al. (1990)) where the separation occurred before age 5, and also predicted self-reported delinquency (Farrington (1992a)). Morash and Rucker (1989) found that although it was single-parent families who had the children with highest deviancy rates (used in the wider context), these were also the lowest income families: the nature of the problem—broken home, parental supervision, low income—was unclear and could have been structural (see Chapter Eleven). Altogether, the evidence from this wide range of studies is confused and conflicting. Wells and Rankin (1991) tried to reach some sort of conclusion by using a careful method called meta-analysis to compare 50 studies concerning broken homes and delinquency between 1926 and 1988. The result seemed to be that officially recorded delinquency had a stronger relationship with broken homes than did self-reported delinquency and that broken homes had a significantly higher prevalence of delinquency than did two-parent homes (10–15 per cent higher). The relationship was constant over sex and racial connections, but this fairly strong relationship was only true for minor offences and did not hold as strongly for serious offences. Some have recently suggested that the factor of broken homes is less important than the quality of the relationship between the child and parent or parents. In 1982 McCord claimed that the real link between broken homes and offending turned around whether the mother was loving: for males brought up in broken homes with unloving mothers the prevalence of offending was 62 per cent against 22 per cent in similar homes with loving mothers. Similar differences were found in non-broken homes which suggests that it is the relationship with the mother which is crucial rather than the status of the home. There are a number of problems underlying much of this research: for example, some of it may test conviction rates and these may be unconsciously skewed by decisions on prosecution or conviction (see Wells and Rankin (1991), above). The only firm conclusion is the need to be wary of the interpretation to be placed on any correlation between criminality and broken homes (see labelling, 14.2).

In part, the proposed connection with maternal affection relates back to the suggestion, reported earlier, that mothers may be primarily responsible for the relationship between families and criminality. Given without qualification the implication is that much of the blame for offending rests with the failure of women to adopt the appropriate relationships with their children. This rather simplistic connection needs to be questioned. Why is the relationship with the mother of such great importance? Should the implication be that power relationships in homes should be altered so that the burden of primary carer should be shared? As Morash and Rucker (see above) would suggest, the statement also ignores possible structural reasons—low income etc.—which may affect the ability of a mother (or other primary carer) to show affection and to have time for parental supervision (see Chapter Eleven).

There is also a problem because much of this research was conducted a long time ago or is reporting on longitudinal studies where the family break-up occurred well into the past and might since have changed. The concept of family is itself not unproblematic, particularly today. In the past in Britain it was basically defined by white Western society to mean two heterosexual adults, of different genders, married to one another, together with any children which were biologically theirs. However appropriate it may have been in the past, this definition is now much too restrictive when we have large numbers of single-parent families, extended families, unmarried parents, single-sex parents, adopted children etc. As society comes to accept these different families as 'normal', the effects of family breakdown or difference may be far less traumatic on the children and thus perhaps be less connected to criminals and deviant behaviour. In other words it may not be the families themselves but the way in which they are affected by external assessment of them that is crucial to offending.

The second way in which family has been related to criminality is in the quality of the relationship between parents and children. In this area, delinquency is connected to low levels of supervision by adults in the family, less affectionate relationships within the family, low levels of interaction between the parents and the children, less family harmony, and to the way in which discipline is carried out. There is general agreement that delinquents are less attached to their parents than are non-delinquents: they do not identify with their parents as closely, they care less about them and what they think, do not interact as much with them and are less likely to ask their advice. Many theorists link these factors with criminality, for example Boswell (1995); and Graham and Bowling (1995). This is confirmed by the

Youth Lifestyle Survey conducted in 1998–9, which also cofirmed the importance of parental supervision: boys aged 12 to 17 who were poorly supervised were three times as likely to offend as those who were better supervised (Flood-Page (2000), pp. 32–4).

A close relationship with parents only tends to produce a low rate of criminality if the relationship is used to supervise the child's behaviour to ensure conformity with conventional standards. This does not necessarily mean that middle- and upper-class parents are likely to perform these tasks better than lower-class, unemployed or black parents. Neither the way in which this task is performed nor its success simply depends upon the social position of the family. It may, however, be related to certain social facts within the family: such as the time available for parenting; individual attention; large family size; and social pressures. Although Sampson and Laub (1993) suggested that poverty and deprivation had little direct effect on criminality, they had a substantial indirect effect by making it more difficult for families to operate without conflict and coercion. Similarly Smith et al. (2001), while suggesting that poor family functioning is a powerful predictor of delinquency also noted that this was a feature more common in deprived and disorderly communities than in more affluent areas.

Farrington (1992b and 1994) has claimed that both juvenile and adult convictions are related to poor parental supervision, and also that offenders—then or later—had poor relationships with their partners. What was important was the whole relationship, including discipline, parental disharmony, low parental involvement, encouragement and supervision. It must also be noted that although the parents may perform all these functions well and although there may be strong ties of affection between parent and child and the parent may try to use these to teach law-abiding behaviour, if the child does not view that parent with prestige, then they will be less likely to learn from them (see differential association, 10.2.3).

Asserting a direct effect of the traumas of family disruption on delinquency may be too simple. One suggestion is that life course theories may offer a more sophisticated interpretation (see Juby and Farrington (2001) at end of this section). But in any event the link is unlikely to be due to genetics or biological factors. The implication is rather that the children learn the behaviour and attitude patterns of their parents.

Official acceptance of the controlling power of the family is not new. In the Victorian workhouse the children were separated from their parents partly to try to break the effect of poor parenting and the example of a 'bad' family. Similar ideology underlay reform schools and borstals. It is also partly the ideology behind care orders used when the family failed to produce responsible citizens (or looked as if it would). Care orders are possible even if the child has not committed any offence. More recently similar, if less drastic, measures have been introduced which accept the link between bad parenting and criminality. Sections 8 and 9 of the Crime and Disorder Act 1998 introduced parenting orders which require parents to participate in weekly counselling or guidance sessions for a period of up to three months. These sessions are intended to help them control their children better. Whatever the past connections between parenting and criminality the orders are intended to show parents that they have a duty to prevent further criminal activity. In this the Act embraces a link between families and criminality. All these measures—workhouse segregation, reform schools, borstals, care orders and parenting orders

—have and will be focused on poorer families. The official responses thus suggest that parenting amongst poor families is more likely to be sub-standard. Is it therefore poverty or parenting that is the real link?

In the more modern, post-positivist control theories, the relationships within a family are seen as dynamic, and therefore their effects on criminality may alter. This factor may help to explain the differential criminal involvement at different ages and stages of development. Generally, one would expect the ties to be stronger at very young ages when the child is most dependent upon its parents and when it is least likely to question them. Also, at this time the parental relationship controls most other contacts, for example with friends and others. As the child reaches adolescence, the parental bond and power may recede, and the child is likely to form closer bonds with peers which might then influence their behaviour more strongly. Furthermore, in adolescence the frustration from feelings of lack of autonomy may be greatest and the desire to take charge of some part of their lives might become powerful. After adolescence, family ties—perhaps with a spouse and children as well as parents—may once more become more important.

Family structures have also been used to examine sex differences in criminality. Thus some explain the lower crime rates for women by the fact that they are far more closely controlled and watched, as well as more severely punished for minor transgressions of societal mores. Another sex-based consideration of family socialisation arises from the observation that the power balance within the family is important—hence power–control theory (Hagan (1989) and Hagan et al. (1990)). The argument is that in patriarchal families girls will be socialised as home-makers and diverted away from risks, whereas boys will be socialised towards the outside world, be prepared to take risks and to enjoy the challenge of so doing. Where sons and daughters are given equal treatment in upbringing, it is the daughter's outlook which shifts towards a greater propensity for risk-taking, thus increasing the likelihood of turning to crime. These studies are useful in recognising the sex-based nature of much socialisation within the family, but are flawed in being too simplistic. For example, Hagan assumes that egalitarian families take the traditional male upbringing as the norm rather than borrowing from both traditional forms of rearing. The latter might still have the effect of creating more equal crime rates for males and females, but it would be less likely to increase the overall crime rate and might actually decrease it if the greater control over daughters was also used for boys and the greater self-control inculcated in girls was also taught to boys.

Most of this is based on the assumption that families will normally try to socialise their children towards law-abiding behaviour and that it is rare for any family intentionally to socialise its children towards criminality. Offending by the child is seen to be the result of a mistake or incapacity by parents to perform this function properly. There are, however, activities of the family which have been very closely related to criminality and have sometimes been said to have a socialising effect towards such behaviour. Such accusations are usually made against families in which there is abuse or neglect. Zingraff et al. (1994) refer to a number of studies where such a link is discovered although the link is not explained. They also note that other studies suggest that these effects can be altered by other positive socialising input. On this basis the family, although seen as highly important in both the positive and negative effects it may have, is not the one unique factor which shapes the control theory.

A further consideration is the possible effect which stable partnerships (especially marriage) might have in helping to settle people (particularly men) into law-abiding lifestyles. Most research suggests that such changes have been linked with a dropping off of criminality. Sampson and Laub (1993) view marriage along with obtaining employment and similar stabilising events as positive because of the controlling effect these have. Warr (1998), whilst accepting the link, proposed a different interpretation: that marriage in particular (but also other changes) leads to less time spent with criminal friends and it is the differential association which has had the stabilising effect. Farrington and West (1995) had earlier proposed that it was possibly the quality of the relationship, rather than the simple fact of marriage, which decides whether there is a change in behaviour. Whether it is control or association clearly these life changes have a profound effect on criminal patterns. In fact Juby and Farrington (2000) now suggest that the life patterns have a greater effect on criminality than just formal family relations.

13.7.2 School

The effects of school have long been associated with criminality. In earlier chapters the position of intelligence and criminality was discussed (10.1), as was the connection between school and criminality as part of the strain theories (Chapter Twelve). Here, the effect of attachment to school on the behaviour of the pupil will be considered.

The suggestion that school affects criminality was upheld in two famous pieces of research: one carried out by Hargreaves and reported in 1967. He claimed that streaming by ability, with low expectations and rewards for the lower streams, led to pupils in these streams becoming disillusioned with school and therefore failing to form bonds with teachers. Such pupils tended to form close peer group bonds with those who had similar feelings of hostility, which freed them to participate in delinquent activity.

The second study was carried out by Rutter et al. (1979) who compared 12 large comprehensive schools in London and discovered that problems associated with schools tended to arise together: schools with high delinquency rates also had high truancy rates and low academic success rates. Such schools also tended to have large numbers of pupils drawn from families of low social class, but even after allowing for the class differences there was still a difference in delinquency and truancy. These factors were more responsive to differences in the relative amounts of punishment and praise used by teachers than by the physical surroundings: much of the effect thus turned around the way in which children were controlled and encouraged. Agnew (2000) found similar results but based his analysis on the theory of strain rather than that of control. Although neither of these studies is conclusive, they each find a connection between school and offending, and each connects it with discipline and reward. They may thus be important for control theory since if schools reward only a small number of very bright children (usually for academic achievement) and they discipline others harshly (even for fairly small transgressions) they may, by alienating some pupils, negate the otherwise controlling and socialising environment of the school.

Often, the willingness to submit to, or become attached to, the authority of school may be strongly affected by the perceived utility of the school. If the pupil views the school as being instrumental to their career or success, they are more likely to invest time in school activities. Adolescents who do not consider that the skills they may learn in school are going to be of use to them may become antagonistic towards it, especially in the year or so leading up to their leaving school. During this period, they feel the futility of school more sharply than before and may also find the low streaming increasingly difficult to accept because of the low esteem in which they are viewed by others, and which they feel for themselves. This may all lead towards criminality and in times of recession this alienation is even more likely (see Box (1987) and Young (1999)). Low job prospects reduce the normal restraint of not wishing to jeopardise the chances of employment after leaving school.

Although it was not directed towards providing reasons, the Youth Lifestyle Survey, already mentioned, fully confirmed the importance of school and education. It found, for example, that boys who disliked school were three times as likely to be offenders, and girls four times as likely (Flood-Page (2000), p. 36). Thus it seems probable that school does have a large role to play in teaching children conforming behaviour, and in providing bonds or reasons for remaining law-abiding. If schools are sufficiently welcoming and encouraging they may be able to help to counter some of the negative aspects of socialisation elsewhere such as in the family. Hansen (2003) found that those in school had lower crime rates but this was based on good family relationships, whilst Zingraff et al. (1994) found that children who suffered abuse and/or neglect in the home were not necessarily more likely to be delinquents because of the influence of other socialising processes, such as school. This suggests that schools, when they operate well, can help to reduce the possibility of offending by providing a strong control link with conformity. If schools are to do this effectively, some prior socialisation is essential: and since, as already seen, it cannot always be assumed that this has already been provided by the family, there is a strong case for universal nursery education. This would greatly enhance the ability of schools to perform their socialising task: equally their ability in this respect will obviously be greatly reduced if pupils feel rejected by the school. The relevance to all this of the political priority given to education since the late 1990s is as yet unclear, especially as the success of such policies are largely defined in terms of academic results.

13.7.3 Peer groups, colleagues and neighbourhood

Peer groups have already had a large amount of attention given to them in Chapter Twelve, and neighbourhoods were discussed in Chapter Eleven. Their relevance to control will be considered here.

In the last chapter, peer groups, usually gangs, were used to explain why young people turn to criminality. In control theory, they are not necessarily gangs, and can be loose groupings of friends or just single companions. (See also Flood-Page et al. (2000).) Furthermore, in control theories peer groups can, like all other attachments, act for or against law-abiding behaviour. If a strong attachment is formed with a peer group for whom conventional behaviour is very important, this can be a strong pull towards conventional, law-abiding behaviour. There are, however, certain peer groups whose members clearly support delinquency, or who at least do not censor such behaviour. In these groups, it may be that some types of criminality are actively encouraged and given prestige, or merely that they are tolerated and not actively discouraged. In either situation, if individuals become attached to such a group they may feel freer to commit criminality if there are other motivations for wishing to do so. It is important to note that contact with a criminal peer group may only arise because the individual is willing to commit crimes. In this case the group only facilitates the activity by, for example, teaching the skills required.

Box (1987) took these ideas and applied them to adults in one of the few books in which this is done. He referred to corporate crime as being committed partly because colleagues encourage each other. They discover that certain activities, though unacceptable in all other areas of their lives, might be perfectly acceptable and even expected as part of their working lives. Company loyalty and the corporate requirement to make a profit both set up an environment in which it might not make good business sense to remain entirely within the law. Also, certain accepted business practices, for which people might gain acquiescence, or even prestige from their colleagues, may be illegal or near the edge of the law. As long as they succeed in the business objective and are not caught, they will be accepted and might even gain promotions. In most cases, the chances of being caught committing a corporate crime are very slim. Furthermore, if caught they rarely face any great stigma or penalty: they are often fined only a small amount and their peers do not ostracise them, nor do their careers necessarily suffer. A number of commentators have suggested that because these people have a very great stake in conformity, they could be easily controlled if detection were more certain, and punishment—monetary, social, professional—greater (see especially Nelken (2001), Slappec and Tombs (1999) and Braithwaite (1995)). Heckathorn (1990) adds that group disapproval (such as the disapproval of colleagues) could provide a further effective measure of control. It is clearly an area where a great deal could be gained by greater controls on these people's activities and by encouraging ethical working practices.

The adult effects of peer groups also enter other areas of the work environment. In some jobs certain violations against the employer may be seen as a 'perk of the job'. In offices, colleagues generally accept that local telephone calls are acceptable on the employer's phone bill as is use of the Internet for shopping etc., unless they are officially banned. In some labouring jobs certain items may be fair game, and the employer actually includes their loss in any estimates submitted. In adult peer groups as well as youth peer groups, especially in work, certain activities might be acceptable and, in some cases, actually encouraged.

The effect of the neighbourhood on criminality was largely discussed in Chapter Eleven. In some areas this was seen as a force towards criminality. Very often the reasons given for this were similar to control theories—a lack of community to watch over children, mobility and therefore anonymity. Neighbourhood watch schemes have been seen as one counter, both by increasing control and by cultivating mutual concern. Similarly, Coleman (1988) suggested changes in building design to make criminality less likely. The big difference is that in control theory, the area is seen as being more criminologenic not because these factors cause criminality, but because they fail to persuade the inhabitants towards conformity. This may appear to be merely semantic, but it has some important effects. One of the main problems with the Chicago School and other neighbourhood theories was that they predicted too much criminality. This problem is avoided in control theory, because if the control constructs in an area are weak it means only that a person would be free to commit crime; it does not mean that they will, or will want so to do.

Bursik (2000) makes a further connection between theories of social disorganisation and those of control. He claims that solving poverty without also addressing the underlying control features of such neighbourhoods can only ever be partially successful. Some of the same impetus lies behind the antisocial behaviour orders introduced in s. 1 of the Crime and Disorder Act 1998. These built on s. 4A of the Public Order Act 1986, concerning abusive language and signs, and the Protection from Harassment Act 1997, which introduced civil action and/or an injunction. The antisocial behaviour orders last a minimum of two years and carry a sentence of up to six months' imprisonment for breaches. They can be used against any individual over the age of 10 but are aimed primarily against youths who are misbehaving and disturbing others in a neighbourhood. The idea is that they will teach these individuals to respect the rights of others. The orders are available when a person has caused or is likely to cause distress, alarm or harassment to one or more people (not part of his or her household), and may be awarded to protect people from further antisocial acts. They are also intended to be used in cases where witnesses may be frightened of giving evidence in a criminal court or where the behaviour falls short of criminality but is disturbing, such as littering, excessive noise, obstruction and abuse. The application comes from the police or local authority (and there must be consultation between these bodies). It is designed to address a local problem and will normally apply within a particular local authority area. There is no evidence that the orders have been effective. They are rarely used. People can move to avoid them and youths can shift to slightly different locations to engage in the same activities and annoy another section of the public. Thus far these formal controls have not helped neighbourhoods to strengthen their natural control mechanisms. Despite this experience the government in 2003 is again promoting these orders in the hope that they will be both more widely used and more successful.

Informal stable social controls may have an effect in countering otherwise expected criminal and antisocial behaviour. Sampson and Laub (1990) set out to discover whether adults who might be predicted to have high rates of criminality might be controlled by secure and stable adult bonds. They used stable marriage and job security as indicators of adult bonds and chose to study a cohort of adults who had exhibited childhood behavioural problems and often also indicated juvenile criminality. As was seen in Chapters Eight and Ten, there is a strong continuity from childhood delinquency to juvenile crime and adult crime antisocial behaviour (as measured by items such as alcohol abuse, divorce etc.). Sampson and Laub claimed that this expected continuity could be broken by the informal social controls of stable marriage and job security. Shover (1996) agrees, noting that the forging of new stable relationships was a powerful factor in the ending of a criminal career. If these stabilising aspects could counter the behavioural problems of childhood, they might be able to counter other negative indicators such as living in a disorganised community or an upbringing which accepted criminal behaviour. Policies which encourage high levels of secure employment and stable and enduring marriages may therefore have a place in countering criminality.

Last in this section we will consider the effect of religion on criminality. Many theorists have noted that an attachment to religion may well help to reduce criminality and deviance (see, e.g., Cochran and Ackers (1989) and Grasmick et al. (1991)). The claim is that religion positively increases the desire for law-abiding and conforming behaviour and, negatively, fosters the fear of damnation. Others, such as Cochran et al. (1994), whilst admitting a strong correlation between religious practice and conformity, have none the less questioned the place of religion in controlling behaviour. They attempted to test the causal connection shown by the negative correlation between religion and offending and discovered that it did not hold for assault, theft, vandalism or illicit drug use. Two explanations were offered. Either those who commit crimes have low boredom thresholds which makes religion unattractive to them: thus it is not that religion promotes conformity but that those who are likely to be religious are likely to be conforming. Or that religion provides the backdrop in which the individual will form relationships with other individuals and it is these relationships, not the religion itself, which form the social bond for conformity (social control theory).

13.7.4 Race

Race has already been addressed at a number of points in the book. The connection between race and intelligence was addressed in 10.1, and the possibility of race being connected with criminality was considered again in Chapter Eleven. Here its connection with control theories and crime will be briefly considered.

The official statistics for England and Wales suggest that certain racial groups commit more crimes per head of their population than others. The West Indians are generally seen as the group with the highest crime rate, while the whites, Asians and Chinese have much lower rates. These statistics are not entirely representative of the real crime rates, but even taking account of all bias and of self-report studies, it does appear that some groups are more crime-prone. Control theory may offer an explanation of this. The higher West Indian crime rate relates only to those born and brought up in this country and not to the original immigrants who have a low crime rate while these differences in recorded crime rates are only fairly recent, despite there having been a sizeable black population in Britain for over a hundred years. These considerations should make anyone cautious about any assertions of an inherent link between any particular race and criminality: we need to look more closely at social circumstances. The Asian community tend to have a higher number in the business or professional classes and, as will be seen in the next section and Chapter Fourteen, these classes appear less in the crime figures, perhaps because they are less closely policed. The West Indians often live and work in the worst areas of Britain and, as was mentioned above, will therefore be in neighbourhoods where control over children is most difficult to perform and where the institutional control structures are least strong. They may also be sent to schools where scholastic achievement is low, and be in the lower streams. This low streaming may have more to do with social influences than with innate intelligence.

A further element which is likely to play a part in the race differentials in crime committal is racial prejudice. Prejudice in the general population makes it harder for these groups to secure good employment, especially in times of recession. This may lead to feelings of rejection, anomie, loss of self-esteem, low status, poverty, lack of autonomy, and insecurity both of person and property. The last is exacerbated by the conviction of many blacks, whether warranted or not, that the police are less than zealous in dealing with racially motivated attacks by whites on blacks. All these lessen the strength of many of the control mechanisms of society.

A detailed consideration of race and crime (Smith (1997)) found a number of these factors to be present. First, the hostile treatment by the authorities has an effect on the apparent criminality rates of young blacks, who tend to have a strong antagonism towards authority. These two aspects can lead to a vicious circle amplifying criminality. However, Smith concludes that this alone does not explain their higher rates of criminality: that the actual rate of offending is higher in blacks than in other racial groupings. Nor can all the difference be put down to poverty as other racial groupings, such as the South Asian Muslims, suffer greater social deprivation and yet portray much lower rates of criminality. Part of this he attributes to the fact that they are much newer immigrants: as they become second and third-generation British their criminality may rise. However, he believes the criminality of blacks may have been increased because on arrival they tried to integrate in the white community but were rejected. Such a problem is less likely to arise in the case of the South Asian Muslims who are far more inward-looking. This difference in integration may also mean that they retain more powerful control mechanisms within their own community so mitigating against criminality. As Tonry (1997) shows, it is not a question of particular ethnic types as similar findings are discovered amongst different groups of immigrants in different countries and times. Possibly Smith underplays both the level, nature and effect of official discrimination or 'institutional racism' (see the Lawrence Inquiry, MacPherson of Cluny (1999)) and the wider societal rejection suffered by this group in his analysis. But it could also be that control from within society has broken down both in the actions of this group and in the way they are thought of and treated by others.

Control theory writers thus imply that racial differences in crime rates may, like other crime, be explained by the level of control mechanisms.

13.8 Official or institutional control agents

The criminal justice system is a composite of a number of the main institutions or means of social control. The ones which will receive consideration here are the police and punishment, but others such as prisons, Customs and Excise or factories inspectorate could have been added. It is worth noting that, on top of the official State control agencies, there are unofficial control agencies such as private security firms, debt collection agencies, store detectives and other private detectives. These will not be considered here, although they may have an effect on the level of crime. It would be interesting to question where these agencies get their legitimation as control agents.

In an ideal society coercive State control systems would be unnecessary. Each individual would feel constrained to live within the rules because that is best for the society as a whole, and therefore for each individual within that society. The reality falls somewhat short of this, and therefore central or State control systems are seen as necessary to deal with the cases where the less formal controls have failed. They are based on a coercive type of control. Rather than persuading individuals to conform and thereby earn acceptance in society, they threaten them with what might occur if they do not. If they do not comply with State rules, individuals are threatened with punishments, which are meant to be sufficiently unpleasant to deter people from certain forms of behaviour (for an historical analysis, see Cohen and Scull (1983)). They are administered against those who have committed unacceptable criminal acts because they have committed those acts, and are chosen and administered by people who are empowered under the law of that State to perform such functions. They are intended to show society's displeasure at the acts which have been performed by the individual who is being punished.

Seemingly, most of the agents of criminal justice are centred on bringing transgressors to justice and punishing them. Before any of the agents of social control are considered, it is worth noting that it is possible to have a State control agency which is not centred on the use of coercive power—the factory inspectorate generally see their role as one of education, persuasion and promoting law-abiding behaviour rather than one of prosecuting and punishing for non-compliance. This, however, is not the role of most of the State agents of control.

Indeed, in effect most agencies have been moving towards more draconian and evasive measures. This is not entirely surprising: it is generally accepted that as less formal, community based, social controls such as family, school etc. weaken or are perceived to weaken so legal social controls expand and gain power to take their place. One reason for this is the common perception that crime is increasing because crime control is too lax. This leads to calls for a stronger system. As was suggested in 13.7 community-based controls have been less effective in recent years and there has been a corresponding increase in legal controls. The efforts can be seen in changes to the law, policing, and punishment (prison and community). The process can be illustrated by: the creation of new crimes or the extension of old offences; the introduction of CCTV surveillance; zero tolerance policing; increased emphasis on victims; increased emphasis on public protection and the management of risk; the introduction of severer punishments (longer prison sentences, greater use of life imprisonment, more minimum sentences, more extended sentences); even greater use of and severity in community punishments (the number sentenced to probation has increased by 50 per cent over the past decade and probation is becoming ever more intensive). Whether all this is appropriate and effective is an unsettled question. Certainly, there is discussion (see Triplett et al. (2003)) of all aspects of the control system, legal and community-based to try to find a balance for a lower crime society.

There are alternative ways of analysing these changes without linking them exclusively to the control nexus. Garland (2000 and 2001) adds a heightened use of emotion in punishment. He argues that the criminal justice institutions have to come more open to the emotions of fear, anger, vengeance and even hatred exhibited by traumatised victims and communities. Karstedt (2002) and Williams (2004) argue that emotion has permeated even the law and law making itself, especially in relation to morality and to the protection of children. Others have noted the ever more powerful and passionate calls for greater security. This use of emotion to explain the modern moves in the system permits more of the pieces of the jigsaw to be considered and therefore may help to further our understanding of the modern system and why it is developing in its present direction. For example, in the past 10 years restorative justice has become one of the most powerful voices in the penal reform. There are probably more books written about this area in the UK, US,

Australia, New Zealand and Canada than any other single issue. It is also a factor which has been embraced by the authorities, political and crime control, to a greater or lesser extent in each of these States. This may not seem to fit within the heightened punitive paradigm suggested in the previous paragraph, but the use of restorative justice can be analysed within the ascendance of emotional aspects in crime and punishment. As Van Stokkom (2002) indicates, guilt, shame and remorse are central to restorative justice. One might add that for true restorative justice there also needs to be forgiveness, understanding and an embracing of the offender back into the fold of the community. These too are powerful emotional aspects, largely ignored by Van Stokkom as they are by many who write about and practice restorative justice.

13.8.1 Police

The police are one of the last and most drastic elements of social control. They will only be required to intervene to control social behaviour if other, less severe and less formal, agents of social control have failed. They are intended as an objective and rational legal authority whose function is to control those who are a threat to society and to other people. They are seen as necessary because any control system has to have sanctions in order for it to function. In the case of the criminal justice system, the sanction is punishment.

Punishment will only act as a deterrent if it is likely to be used. Box (1983) suggests that the low possibility of being detected, prosecuted and punished is one of the factors which leads to high rates of corporate crime. If all crimes were detected and cleared up, one could therefore expect a large drop in the levels of criminality. Unfortunately, this is not the case. As was seen in Chapter Four, many crimes are never reported to the police, and for many of the others the police never catch the perpetrator because: no-one is found; the perpetrator is found but not convicted; or the wrong person is convicted. These all lead to higher rates of criminality. To be an effective deterrence of a particular type of behaviour, detection needs to occur at least more often than non-detection. For the individual, undiscovered criminal behaviour acts as positive reinforcement of that behaviour, making it more likely to be repeated. Detection and punishment act as negative reinforcements, making the behaviour less likely. Detection is essential to control.

As a result, control theorists have recently given some attention to detection. In general, they see actual detection rates as being less important than perceived detection rates; if people believe they are likely to be caught, they will be less likely to commit the act than if they believe that their deed will go undetected. Modern control theorists have therefore concentrated on increasing the risk of being caught. In an effort to increase detection rates, the police and local communities have sometimes chosen to use technical surveillance devices such as Closed Circuit Television (CCTV) to deliver control and deterrent effects—people will think twice because of the possibility of a rapid response by the police. This is a policy move away from dealing with crime through treatment and rehabilitation of offenders towards a 'new behaviourism' where the State is less interested in the causes of crime than in its prevention, and is less concerned with trying to change social conditions than with the more modest aim of 'changing behaviour sequences' by reducing the opportunity to commit crime with impunity (Cohen (1985)). CCTV therefore works at the level of deterrence, not crime causation. As already indicated (11.2.4), these surveillance techniques raise problems concerning civil liberties and do not necessarily produce a safer society. For an informed discussion of the theories of surveillance see Mathiesen (1997). As well as increased use of technical surveillance devices the police have also tried to increase detection and prosecution by more efficient policing. Such endeavours are not easy to implement, however, and in some instances have been found to be counter-productive. Thus, in the early 1980s, police used saturation policing in certain high crime rate areas in Britain: the purported object was to prevent crime by achieving high detection rates. Unfortunately, the detection rates, relative to the man-power expended, were not high and, more seriously, the locals viewed the policy as very unjust: the policy, indeed, was seen as one of the main factors in sparking off the 1981 riots in Brixton (London), Liverpool and Bristol (see Scarman (1981)). Similarly, police practice was an instigating factor in the riots in Liverpool, Brixton and Broadwater Farm (London) in 1985 (see Gifford (1986)). Each of these was also tied up with the appalling relations between the police and the black community. Where policing practice is, whether rightly or wrongly, seen to be unacceptable to the locals, the ensuing conflict is a constant threat to law and order and reduces their effectiveness in crime detection (see Reiner (1985); Institute of Race Relations (1987); Gifford et al. (1989); and the MacPherson Report (1999) which introduced the phrase 'institutional racism'). Also, some other police methods, such as those used in the 1980s and 1990s for the policing of marches and strikes, and certain uses of the computer and other technology, have been seen as being intrusive into the civil liberties and freedoms of law-abiding citizens to a degree unacceptable in a democratic society.

Finally so called 'zero tolerance' policing which has been introduced from New York into some British police forces centres on the policing and charging of all activities, even, or especially, low-level public order activities such as dropping litter, drinking alcohol in public and urinating on the street (see Innes (1999)). The post-1997 Labour administration backed this type of policing saying that the impact of low-level disorder causes fear on the streets and must be dealt with. As has been seen, the Crime and Disorder Act 1998 introduced anti-social behaviour orders to deal with anybody who is likely to cause 'harassment to the community'. It also introduced powers for exclusion zones and curfews of all youths, even those below 10, if the local community requested it. All this prompted some concern since it is open to the sort of racial abuse found from saturation policing in the 1980s. It also represents an intrusive interference with civil liberties without necessarily producing a safer community or higher clear-up rates.

Such reactions tend to lead to the alienation of the police from the community they are supposed to protect, reducing the ability of the police to fight crime. This suggests that the effectiveness of the police as agents of social control has been blunted and methods such as area targeting need critical re-examination.

Other types of policing may be more productive and get the backing of local residents, as has been the case with community policing. That is proactive policing, a system whereby the police consult with and work with the local community, often to help rebuild informal social controls. Using such methods, the police are acting more in an enabling role than in a coercive control role. Unfortunately, the manpower necessary to keep community policing going is thought to be prohibitive for some forces, where it is therefore viewed as inefficient. The essence of community policing is that community and police are equal partners in assessing how best to address the problems faced by the community as a whole. This suggests that the police should be willing to take directions from the community. Community policing also assumes active participation on the part of the community in engaging with the problems and how to address them but also sometimes in being more vigilant. Herbert (2001) suggests that this is never likely to become the most used method of policing as it goes counter to the culture of the police in taking control of situations and being the professionals in crime control (what he terms as a masculine bias) and an unwillingness to deal with all aspects of the community including those who may be causing the problems (he calls this their moralism, a wish to deal with the bad and protect the good). Other ideas which have been mooted are the increasing of police powers to improve the possibility of detecting crime, or raising efficiency by greater professionalism to enhance their powers of detection. Each of these might increase the detection rates of the police, but their effectiveness might vary in different parts of the country. It may be best to allow local communities more say in the way they are policed by increasing the accountability of the police to them. Methods of attainment are matters of dispute and debate, but there is no doubt that the ability of the police to detect crime is an important factor in the control of individuals in a society.

At a more national level, as indicated in 11.2.4, the Crime and Disorder Act 1998 aims to address many of the problems by pressing the need for multi-agency collaboration and, specifically, by placing a statutory requirement for the police to work with local authorities to put into effect community safety strategies. However, as indicated earlier the partnerships are problematic and the police tend to retain their operational control. The Act seems to have worked more towards the other partners acting to aid the police than to involve the police in altering their working practices, except where required to do by law. This latter requirement may in future be much increased under the Home Secretary's 2003 proposals for enforcing greater police response to local perceptions of the crime problem.

Police can also help in strategies designed to decrease criminal opportunity. Some of the initiatives in this area were discussed as part of the consideration of the neighbourhood in 13.7.3 above. Recently, the police have enhanced the work they do in preventing crime and in teaching individuals how to avoid being victimised, for example, visiting schools and talking to children, giving advice on locks and safety features, and by the support of neighbourhood watch schemes. Each of these can help in preventing crime and has a part to play in control, but the central police role in our society remains that of coercive control.

This does not necessarily need to remain the case and some recent initiatives would, if implemented, reduce the present emphasis on coercion. Most present policing reacts either to calls from the public or to situations they discover on the street. A drawback of reactive policing, especially when the police no longer live in the areas which they police, is that they often do not really get to know and understand their areas—they get to know the criminogenic parts but not necessarily the neighbourhood or district as a whole. Their whole lives are separate from those they control most. In reacting to incidents or to problems they may implement apparently logical policies which backfire because of inadequate understanding. This was seen in the riots in the early 1980s (see Scarman (1981)) and still happens in some areas, often those with high minority populations (see Gifford et al. (1989)). To remedy the problem it has been recognised that this does not need to be the shape of policing in the future. Police could be involved in society in a more proactive way.

Such a development would, however, require drastic changes. This is clear from the proposals of its leading advocate (Goldstein (1990)) in the US where it is termed 'problem-oriented policing'. A great deal is involved in a move from simply reacting to immediate problems and becoming involved in the community in a rounded way. It means much more than seeking out those who violate the law and bringing them before the courts for justice. It requires large-scale data collection which needs then to be broken down to be applied to more manageable problems. The deconstruction of the wider problems is only possible if the police understand the structural, personal and interactionalist difficulties of their communities as well as those elements of the equation which impact on the crime problem. For example, police could: work closely with those who have been victimised to see whether they can help themselves to avoid repetition and in areas with high offence rates try to alert all inhabitants (for problems associated with this see Chapter Five and 11.2.4); target particular environments or work with architects to prevent building designs which are favourable to offending (see 11.2.4); help to reinforce the less formal institutions of social control such as the family, school and neighbourhood (see above); work with local government and other agencies such as the welfare and medical agencies to try to resolve disputes and conflicts before they escalate into serious criminal problems requiring the intervention of the criminal justice system. The implication is that the police would not be fully tied to the criminal justice system and would use their powers in this domain only when that was of utility to the community as a whole, preferring the proactive use of less formal control aspects to reduce crime. Such a programme would certainly require a very different training programme for officers, and possibly a different sort of officer. It takes ideas like community policing, foot patrols, consultation with local people etc. to its logical and fully developed conclusion, which is probably several steps too far for its full application.

Nonetheless, partial implementation is possible: some British examples already in operation were discussed in 11.2.4. In addition, particular policing problems have also been approached from this wider perspective. One such is domestic violence where some police forces work hand-in-hand with social services and with treatment programmes, offering counselling and trial separation to try to prevent repetition. In this way they sometimes approach domestic violence from a less criminal justice oriented mode than many other crimes. This is often attacked by feminists as an indication that domestic violence is not being treated seriously. This suggests that where a problem-oriented solution is introduced only for certain crimes it may lose credibility. Other forces have prosecuted the offenders, but then used the punishment system to treat them, sometimes in an enclosed prison environment and sometimes in the community. There have also been attempts to divert some offenders, particularly the young, away from the full rigours of the criminal justice system. These efforts have recently been attacked as failures, but it may simply be that these policies have not addressed the full problems faced by the youths and the communities from which they come. Perhaps to work they need a fuller adoption of the ideas of problem-oriented policing such as in the projects described by Heywood et al. (1992) and discussed in 11.2.4. It is not a question which will be easily resolved.

Such a solution, if solution it be, has to confront the fact that it invests the police with a much greater control role. Communities need to decide whether they wish to embrace it in the hope of discovering answers to the crime problem. For it to operate the police would need the complete trust of the communities and this would involve changing a number of aspects of modern policing and the control of the police. First it necessitates much more open policing than at present, providing information both about their policies and individual actions. It would also require strong local and legal accountability which should extend to both individual and operational decisions. Lastly, it requires a more open recognition of some of the problems to be discussed in Chapters Fourteen and Fifteen so that sections of the community do not become isolated. One of the central themes of Goldstein's project is that minorities and the weak in society should not become marginalised and alienated. With all these caveats, policy-oriented policing is one of the brightest possibilities to have been suggested.

A major problem with any interventionist State model comes from the possibility of targeting whole groups and categories (see Mathieson (1983)) by the use of TV cameras, development of advanced computerised systems holding sensitive information for control purposes, and new covert intelligence and surveillance techniques which pry deeply into certain people's lives (see also Chapter Nineteen). Goldstein finds this unacceptable but some in society may consider that some such measures are vindicated as being necessary to prevent greater evil. At the moment large sections of society seem passively to accept the sacrifice of their freedom and privacy in order to try to achieve greater security. What may be necessary is a wholesale review of the nature of crime control and the way in which it engages with community, society, safety and privacy. The outcome needs to be a balance between societal interests, smaller-group interests, and the individual interest in privacy etc. That the problem-oriented policing model could foster such interventionist measures should not be ignored.

13.8.2 Punishment

In classical criminology it was thought that a system of punishments set to fit the crime would, through fear, prevent crime (Beccaria). It is generally assumed that this model entails universally harsh punishments. This is not strictly necessary to the theory: all it logically requires is proportionality of sentence for the crime committed. In practice, however, punishments based on this viewpoint tend to be fairly harsh, both to dissuade the potential offender, and to ensure that the law-abiding individual has not lost out to the criminal.

It is generally recognised that there needs to be an idea of justice involved—criminals should not be allowed to gain, materially or psychologically, from their criminality nor should they be punished more than necessary. This leads to a cost-effective type of punishment system. The State needs to decide how much punishment is necessary in each particular case to gain the desired end—reform of that criminal. Furthermore, each criminal has to decide whether the costs of criminality —punishments—are worth the benefits of crime. On this basis, it is considered important to remove from the individual the profits of the crime. Such action will reduce the plus side of any calculation a criminal might make, and can mean that the blow of any punishment is not softened by the knowledge of a large sum available for a prisoner to come out to.

Such an approach suggests that the level of punishment should be related to the crime, but in almost all societies the punishment is also individualised. Most courts ask not only what punishment is applicable to this offence, but also what should *this* offender suffer or, often, what does *this* offender need. Our system takes account of the offender's physical, mental and, especially, social situation. If this individualised system is seen as working unjustly in favour of particular groups, particularly in favour of otherwise advantaged groups, the ability of punishment to deter, and thus to control, is diminished. More recently the physical and emotional effects on the victim have come to the fore. These may be made known to the judge through victim personal statements whilst the emotional vengeance of victims is now strong within the shaping of punishments at a parliamentary level. Whether it is also in the minds of judges when sentencing is impossible to assess. However, if in any individual case punishment is perceived to be unfair, then its control element may be lost. Suppose A, B and C all commit the same crime: A gets away with it; B is convicted and faces a very severe sentence; and C is convicted but is only very lightly sentenced. It would be unsurprising if B were to feel aggrieved and lose respect for the law, unless B could be shown that there was good reason for the treatment of the other two—A had left the country, perhaps, and C was a minor. But if the difference is seen by B to be arbitrary—A was not suspected because she was a woman, and C was dealt with leniently because he was more articulate— then the way in which the law dealt with B may have an effect opposite to that intended. For this reason, the courts in sentencing, and the probation service in making out social inquiry reports, need to ensure that they are seen to be acting in an even-handed manner. Failure to do so gives substance to the common claim that individualised dispositions of the court, such as probation and discretionary life imprisonment, as well as strong mitigation, sometimes go too far and lose sight of the need for punishment to deter and ensure that people 'pay' for their crimes.

One of the elements of this individualised sentencing which is often applied by judges is that the previous character of the offender, in so far as there is no previous criminal record, should be taken into consideration in mitigating the sentence. As well as this mitigation of sentence Parliament has put in place a large number of cases where sentencing needs to be more severe because it is a second or third occurrence, especially of a sexual or violent offence. This may be counter-productive. To give greatest effect as a control mechanism, punishment should be inflicted early on in the behaviour. Someone who has committed numerous acts before being detected has already acquired a criminal habit, making the punishment less effective than if it had been administered after the first criminal act. Similarly, a first offender who does not receive very harsh punishment may conclude that the criminality is worth it: by the time severe punishment is forthcoming, the behaviour may be too entrenched for the punishment to have an effect. Arguably, our system of using mild punishments first may reduce their effectiveness as controls.

All the above assumes that there is a deterrent element to most punishment, but, as will be seen in Chapter Fourteen, in labelling individuals as offenders one may actually precipitate their further involvement in crime: for example, by reducing their chances of providing for themselves through legitimate means. In 1988 Braithwaite put forward a theory of the notion of reintegrative shaming (see 10.2.4) which suggests one way of avoiding this. Offenders are, through shaming, made aware of the suffering they have caused, but are then eased back into social acceptance.

It can be seen that in choosing any system of punishment the intended effects need to be considered very carefully. Unfortunately, there is almost never one desired effect of punishment towards which any system is leading, making a clear policy difficult to obtain and making it difficult to assess success. Any system tends to be an amalgamation of a number of ideas and objectives, which often prevents any one of them being successful.

The part played by official control agents is therefore quite complex. For their intervention to act as a deterrent, it is necessary to use the controls fairly and reasonably firmly.

13.8.3 Diversion and its net-widening control effects

One of the quickest-spreading control factors in Britain has arisen in the last 20 years or so and has blossomed largely out of the processes of diversion. Diversion is now an enormous industry and it occurs at all levels of the criminal justice system. Before a court appearance it takes two forms: first, the police or other primary law enforcement agency (such as factory inspectors, Inland Revenue inspectors or Customs and Excise) can unofficially or officially divert individuals away from the full rigours of the criminal justice system by cautioning them or, in the case of children and young people, using reprimands and warnings. In these instances the offender has to admit the offence, and some may do so even when they are innocent to avoid a court appearance or to get it over and done with. Similarly, the prosecution may decide not to prosecute, or agree to prosecute for a lesser crime to which the individual is willing to plead guilty. In Britain these forms of diversion are usually complete in themselves, but there is a form of diversion called 'diversion plus' where the individual may be asked to do something extra (normally, in the case of Customs and Excise or the Inland Revenue to make an extra payment over that actually owed). Systems of 'diversion plus' have been used more and more frequently in normal cautions and youth reprimands and warnings. These frequently involve a form of restorative justice, with the offender performing some function either for the victim or for the community. They may also involve a form of reintegrative shaming, with the offender apologising and possibly then agreeing to do something. In return the offender is then accepted back into the community and may be helped with personal problems. For discussion of some of these points see Maxwell and Morris (2001), Dignan (1999) and Young and Goold (1999).

There is also diversion at the court stage where again there may be a willingness to plead guilty to some of the lesser offences hoping for a lesser sentence (again this is not the formalised US system of plea bargaining: judges here are not allowed to make promises). Finally, there is diversion at the sentencing stage, away from a punishment model towards a treatment or community model. This may be in the form of a mediation and reparation scheme. One, the Leeds Reparation Scheme, has involved serious offences but most are concerned only with minor offences. More normally it involves probation with or without some counselling or other intervention such as community service, supervision order, curfew order or attendance centre order. Each of these appears to be more helpful to offenders than to victims. Each has been vigorously attacked by some authors and politicians as encouraging increased criminality by an excess of liberal permissiveness.

Other attacks suggest that such systems, far from keeping individuals outside the criminal justice system in fact suck more and more within their control. The most notable proponent of this 'net-widening' effect is Cohen (1985), who argues that community programmes and social diversion suck children in at a younger age, often before they have offended but are merely 'at risk'. The Crime and Disorder Act 1998 introduces antisocial behaviour orders, curfews and, for those under 10, exclusion orders. One aspect of these is that they will bring individuals into the police network much earlier. Something similar also arises at the sentencing stage. On pure punishment grounds a sentence of say six months might be appropriate, but by deciding on diversion a probationary sentence may be passed which might remain in force for one or two years. This, too, increases the numbers controlled at any one time. Moreover, those who offend whilst on probation may, in some circumstances, be sentenced not only for the most recent offence but also for the initial offence, which again leads to more people being contained in the criminal justice system.

There is also a difficulty of what Cohen terms 'thinning the mesh' whereby not only are the numbers controlled increased but the level of intervention in their lives is increased. In older probationary systems the level of intervention was fairly low: to ensure that the offender tried to live an industrious life, he or she would be recommended to pursue certain types of activities. Newer schemes, such as the community rehabilitation orders are more punitive and demanding: they require the offender to reflect on his/her activities and to consider their impact for others; offenders are required to attend counselling and training sessions and any breach will be reported and dealt with in a punitive fashion. Probation is no longer the gentle option: arguably aspects of it are more punitive than incarceration. Furthermore, there are now other additions which the court can choose to attach to the sentence. Requirements can include: residential requirements; community service (now community punishment); an order to take part in certain activities, especially those of a probation centre; treatment for mental conditions and drug treatment and testing. There are also specific requirements which may be used in cases of sex offenders and those suffering from drug or alcohol dependency. The control system is interfering to a much deeper level in the lives of individuals. Finally, in this respect, is the problem that most of the non-custodial interventions are used not as alternatives to incarceration, but have traditionally replaced the fine, the punishment which intervenes least in the lives of offenders.

The result, Cohen claims, is that there is a dangerous blurring of the formal and informal control system so that officially organised State intervention is becoming very wide and very controlling, especially of the poorer sections of society, as well as penetrating deeply into society. These wider control systems have not reduced the prison population but simply led to general increases in the numbers controlled and the extent of control. Cohen sees this as dangerous, unnecessary and unacceptable.

One newer method which tries to increase diversion from court without networking is the systems management approach, usually operated in connection with juveniles. This is intended to do for the criminal justice system what problem-oriented policing should do for the operation of the police. Basically systems management analyses all the elements of the criminal justice system—how the agencies interact, how and why particular suspects pass through the process—starting with detection and working through to final disposal. A knowledge of both how and why decisions are made could constructively affect final outcomes to secure diversion from court. Systems management schemes constitute an elaborate series of processes: the first diversion is taken by the police, the next level is a non-statutory multi-agency panel, now called a youth offending team (YOT). The panel has representatives from the police, probation, social and educational services and any other important local bodies dealing in child care. These panels try to divert as many juveniles as is safe either by use of a simple reprimand or the warning, sometimes with social work intervention or reparation to the victim. The panel is thus another gate through which the case has to go before a prosecution is arrived at, but any case not diverted then goes to the Crown Prosecution Service for its decision on whether to prosecute.

Following the Crime and Disorder Act 1998 the main aim of YOTs now is to ensure law-abiding behaviour. They work to support families from a very early stage and encourage voluntary contracts between parents and YOTs, they look for new ways of coping with and containing prolific offenders and, possibly their most innovative move, is their embracing of restorative justice as a means of dealing with youth offending. All this shows a real change from earlier approaches but it is still too early to measure success. There are some who are negative about the approach (Goldson (2000)) and the present author whilst supportive of the ideal of using restorative justice for young offenders questions whether their practical application undermines their true potential. They do however seem to demonstrate a real intention for a new approach on the part of politicians and senior practitioners.

If all this shows some possible ways of improving the criminal justice system, it also illustrates the complications of pursuing them. In particular, the proposed remedies will themselves have side-effects which are difficult to foresee and some of which will be unwelcome. An awareness of the dangers should not, however, inhibit the search for improvements.

13.9 **Evaluation of control theories**

The concepts which make up the control theory are based on logical connectors which have been linked with crime for a long period. They have therefore received much research. Grasmick and Bursik (1990), in an interesting study, tried to test the various elements of control theory to ascertain which had most validity and was most likely to produce conforming behaviour. Shame (or the internal deterrence of conscience) had the strongest deterrent effect: that is, if an individual believed something was wrong and would be ashamed of doing it, this factor was most likely to pull him or her back into conformity. This finding is supportive of socialisation processes such as those discussed in 13.7 and in Chapters Eight, Ten and Fourteen, and also lends support to policies based on shaming (13.8.2) as well as cognitive learning programmes (see 10.2.6). Legal punishments, if believed to be fairly certain, were another strong inhibitor of criminal activities. Surprisingly, disapproval of 'significant others' was least important, perhaps because the respondents thought it unlikely that 'significant others' would find out. At all events, there is now a substantial body of research based on control theory which lends some support to its use as a means of understanding and influencing conforming behaviour. Policies based on these findings could play a constructive role.

Of course, control theories cannot explain all types of criminality or delinquency, but no theory could ever do that, since crime is too disparate a feature of human behaviour. Nonetheless control theory remains a useful approach, perhaps especially if Tittle's control balance theory is adopted. There will always be crimes which people are willing to commit no matter how great their stake in conformity, because the potential gain is very high. There will also be a small number of criminals who commit criminal acts because they are suffering from some sort of mental or physical problem.

Further criticism has come from writers such as Agnew (1993) who claim that the social control model ignores aspects of motivation which they see as crucial to offending. The model would, they urge, be improved by taking account of theories of strain and differential association or social learning. Thus critics claim that, even in the absence of strong controls, there may be no offending if the motivation is insufficiently strong; and even in cases where the social control is strong, there may be offending if the motivation is sufficiently strong. They would contest, not the theory itself, but its claim to be so all-embracing and to stand alone. Tittle's theory aims to incorporate this criticism by using both control and motivation to explain criminality.

A more practical difficulty is that the qualities of the social controls which promote or nurture law-abiding behaviour and those which promote and nurture law-breaking behaviour have not yet been properly identified. As a result, the practical utility of the theory is somewhat lessened. Until the theory can pin-point more accurately the specific types of attachments, commitment, and involvement that will encourage law-abiding behaviour, and suggest how they can be promoted, the theory is only of limited help to our understanding of criminality. The insistence of its advocates that each of these variables is subjective further reduces its usefulness. It is not possible to generalise from a substantially subjective theory. It was in an attempt to meet some of these objections that 13.7 above discussed the way in which a few of the more important social constructs, such as family and school, affect criminality.

Despite these shortcomings, control is possibly one of the most promising intellectual developments yet to emerge in the struggle to understand and explain criminal behaviour.

Many policy suggestions arise from this field. In particular, the ideas support policies which will assist families, schools and other socialising organisations to carry out their functions. These might involve State-financed family and marriage counselling; more financial support for families; greater funding for schools, including funding to support extra-curricular activities; and efforts to develop closer ties between schools and families. There are also implications for the way the State sector deals with offenders. Control theories suggest that cognitive learning processes should be carefully considered in sentencing decisions (particularly involving probation) and in prisons and other institutions where offenders are held. This would involve a new belief in treatment/psychosocial processes and the willingness to invest in them. The approach also suggests broader policy goals: if, for example, real and stable employment was more readily available, more adults would be tied into more conventional lifestyles and diverted from criminality.

In the area of State control, policy is more difficult to delineate. This chapter suggests that the police and other agencies of control should be more closely integrated with each other, with agencies of social support and with the community they are there to serve. This would involve more consultation and accountability than is presently the case. The approach also indicates that, in relation to punishment, very tough measures could lead to feelings of resentment and rejection which in the long run could exacerbate offending (see also Chapter 14). At the very least, the studies examined suggest that the law and order rhetoric of the past 20 years or so needs careful analysis and assessment (see Currie (1996) and Raup (1996)). Policy based on reintegrative shaming or on cognitive learning might be more appropriate and effective.

Overall, the kind of policies prompted by control balance theory lean towards 'liberal' or 'progressive' solutions. They point to moving towards the equal distribution of control and of being controlled; to control being exercised with respect for others; and to State encouragement of and support for strong social bonds, strong communities and social support within the community. These ideological leanings will be sufficient for some to reject them out of hand. This, however, is to refuse to consider the evidence of the studies and—more fundamentally—to lose sight of the fact that all these policy suggestions assume that the *status quo*, the present middle-class values etc., are worth upholding and should be heavily inculcated into the whole population. The 'progressive' texture is seen by some as disguising an element of persuasive mind control which depends heavily on the ethics of the values being supported. These values are heavily attacked in the next two chapters.

SUGGESTED READING

Braithwaite, J. (1997), 'Charles Tittle's Control Balance and Criminal Theory', *Theoretical Criminology*, vol. 1, p. 77.

Hirschi, T. (1969), *Causes of Delinquency*, Berkeley, CA: University of California Press.

Hirschi, T. and Gottfredson, M.R. (2000), 'In Defence of Self-Control', *Theoretical Criminology*, vol. 4, p. 1.

Schinkel, W. (2002), 'The Modernist Myth in Criminology', *Theoretical Criminology*, vol. 6(2), p. 123.

Tittle, C.R. (1997), 'Thoughts Stimulated by Braithwaite's Analysis of Control Balance', *Theoretical Criminology*, vol. 1, p. 99.

QUESTIONS

1   Compare the essence of control in social and self-control sections of control theory. Which provides a better explanation of deviance and criminal behaviour? What policy might arise out of these theories and how has each been used in shaping policy in the past?

2   Carefully consider Tittle's Control Balance theory and its power as a theory to explain deviance and criminal behaviour. Does Braithwaite's analysis of it aid in this or rather move it

more towards a theory of predation? Does Braithwaite's more emotion-based analysis add or detract from the theory?

3 Which social control structures in today's society do you view as strong and which weak? Is the present balance between official and informal control healthy?

REFERENCES

Ackers, Ronald, L. (1991), 'Self-control as a General Theory of Crime', *Journal of Quantitative Criminology*, vol. 7, p. 201.

Agnew, Robert (1993), 'Why do they do it? An Examination of the Intervening Mechanisms between "Social Control" Variables and Delinquency', *Journal of Research in Crime and Delinquency*, vol. 30, p. 245.

Agnew, R. (2000), 'Strain Theory and School Crime', in S.S. Simpson (ed.), *Of Crime and Criminality*, Thousand Oaks, CA: Pine Forge.

Beccaria, Cesare (1964), *Of Crimes and Punishments* (first published 1776 as *Dei delitti e delle pene*), 6th edn trans. Fr. Kenelm Foster and Jane Grigson with an introduction by A.P. D'Entreves, London: Oxford University Press.

Boswell, G. (1995), *Violent Victims*, London: The Prince's Trust.

Bowlby, John (1973), *Separation: Anxiety and Anger*, London: Hogarth Press.

Box, Steven (1983), *Power, Crime and Mystification*, London: Tavistock.

Box, Steven (1987), *Recession, Crime and Punishment*, London: Macmillan.

Braithwaite, John (1988), *Crime Shame and Reintegration*, Cambridge: Cambridge University Press.

Braithwaite, J. (1995), 'Corporate Crime and Republican Criminological Praxis', in F. Pearce and L. Snider (eds), *Corporate Crime*, Toronto: University of Toronto Press, pp. 48–72.

Braithwaite, John (1997), 'Charles Tittle's Control Balance and Criminal Theory', *Theoretical Criminology*, vol. 1, p. 77.

Bursik, R.J. (2000), 'The Systematic Theory of Neighbourhood Crime Rates', in S.S. Simpson (ed.) *Of Crime and Criminality*, Thousand Oaks CA: Pine Forge.

Cochran, John K. and Ackers, Ronald L. (1989), 'Beyond Hellfire: an Exploration of the Variable Effects of Religiosity on Adolescent Marijuana and Alcohol Use', *Journal of Research in Crime and Delinquency*, vol. 26, p. 198.

Cochran, John K., Wood, Peter B. and Arneklev, Bruce J. (1994), 'Is the Religiosity-Delinquency Relationship Spurious? A Test of Arousal and Social Control Theories', *Journal of Research in Crime and Delinquency*, vol. 31, p. 92.

Cohen, Stanley (1985), *Visions of Social Control: Crime, Punishment and Classification*, Cambridge: Polity Press.

Cohen, Stanley and Scull, Andrew (eds), (1983), *Social Control and the State: Comparative and Historical Essays*, Oxford: Basil Blackwell.

Coleman, Alice (1988), 'Design Disadvantage and Design Improvement', *The Criminologist*, vol. 12, p. 20.

Currie, Elliot (1996), *Is America Really Winning the War on Crime and Should Britain Follow its Example?* NACRO, 30th Anniversary Lecture, London: NACRO.

Dignan, J. (1999), 'The Criminal Justice Act and the Prospect for Restorative Justice', *Criminal Law Review*, p. 48.

Farrington, D.P. (1992a), 'Juvenile Delinquency', in J.C. Coleman (ed.), *The School Years*, 2nd edn, London: Routledge.

Farrington, D.P. (1992b), 'Explaining the Beginning, Progress and Ending of Antisocial Behaviour from Birth to Adulthood', in J. McCord (ed.), *Advances in Criminological Theory*, vol. 3, New Brunswick, NJ: Transaction.

Farrington, D.P. (1994), 'Childhood, Adolescent and Adult Features of Violent Males', in L.R. Huesmann (ed) *Aggressive Behaviour: Current Perspective*, New York: Plenum.

Farrington, D.P. and West, D.J. (1995), 'Effects of Marriage, Separation, and Children on Offending by Adult Males', in Z. Smith Blau and J. Hagan (eds), *Current Perspectives on Ageing and the Life Cycle*, vol. 4, Greenwich: JAI Press.

Finnis, J. (1968), 'Old and New in Hart's Philosophy of Punishment', *Oxford Review*, vol. 8, p. 73.

Flood-Page, C. (2000), *Youth Crime: Findings From the 1998/99 Youth Lifestyles Survey*, London: Home Office.

Francis, P. and Faser, P. (1999), *Building Safer Communities*, London: Centre for Crime and Justice Studies.

Garland, D. (2000), 'The Culture of High Crime Societies: Some Preconditions of Recent "Law and Order" Policies', *British Journal of Criminology*, vol. 36, p. 445.

Garland, D. (2001), *The Culture of Control: Crime and Social Order in Contemporary Society*, Oxford: Oxford University Press.

Geis, G. (2000), 'On the absence of self-control as the basis for a general theory of crime: a critique', *Theoretical Criminology*, 4.1, February, p. 35.

Gifford, Lord (1986), *The Broadwater Farm Inquiry*, London: Karia Press.

Gifford, Lord, Brown, Wally and Bundy, Ruth (1989), *Loosen the Shackles: First Report of the Liverpool 8 Inquiry into Race Relations in Liverpool*, London: Karia Press.

Goldson, B. (2000), 'Simple Toughness Meets Tough Complexity', *Criminal Justice Matters*, vol. 41, p. 4.

Goldstein, Herman (1990), *Problem-Oriented Policing*, New York: McGraw-Hill.

Gottfredson, Michael, R. and Hirschi, Travis (1990), *A General Theory of Crime*, Stanford, CA: Stanford University Press.

Graham, J. and Bowling, B. (1995), *Young People and Crime*, Home Office Research Study 145, London: HMSO.

Grasmick, Harold G. and Bursik, Robert J. (1990), 'Conscience, Significant Others, and Rational Choice: Extending the Deterrence Model', *Law and Society Review*, vol. 24(3), p. 837.

Grasmick, Harold G., Bursik, Robert J. and Cochran, John K. (1991), 'Render unto Caesar What Is Caesar's: Religiosity and Taxpayers' Inclinations to Cheat', *Sociological Quarterly*, vol. 32, p. 251.

Grasmick, Harold G., Tittle, Charles R., Bursik, Jr, Robert J. and Arneklev, Bruce J. (1993), 'Testing the Core Empirical Implications of Gottfredson and Hirschi's General Theory of Crime', *Journal of Research in Crime and Delinquency*, vol. 30, p. 5.

Hagan, J. (1987), *Modern Criminology: Crime, Criminal Behaviour and its Control*, New York: McGraw-Hill.

Hagan, John (1989), *Structural Criminology*, New Brunswick, NJ: Rutgers University Press.

Hagan, J., Gillis, A.R. and Simpson, J. (1990), 'Clarifying and Extending Power-Control Theory', *American Journal of Sociology*, vol. 95, p. 1024.

Hansen, K. (2003), 'Education and the Crime-Age Profile', *British Journal Criminology*, vol. 43, p. 141.

Hargreaves, David, H. (1967), *Social Relations in a Secondary School*, London: Routledge & Kegan Paul.

Haskell, Martin R. and Yablonsky, Lewis (1982), *Juvenile Delinquency*, 3rd edn, Boston: Houghton Mifflin.

Hayslett-McCall, K.L. and Bernard, T.J. (2002), 'Attachment, Masculinity, and Self-Control: A Theory of Male Crime Rates', *Theoretical Criminology*, vol. 6(1), p. 5.

Heckathorn, Douglas D. (1990), 'Collective Sanctions and Compliance Norms: A Formal Theory of Group-Mediated Social Control', *American Sociological Review*, vol. 55, p. 336.

Herbert, S. (2001), 'Policing the Contemporary City: Fixing Broken Windows or Shoring up Neo-Liberalism?', *Theoretical Criminology*, vol. 5(4), p. 445.

Heywood, Ian, Hall, Neil and Redhead, Peter (1992), 'Is There a Role for Spatial Information Systems in Formulating Multi-agency Crime Prevention Strategies?', in David J. Evans, Nicholas R. Fyfe and David T. Herbert (eds), *Crime, Policing and Place: Essays in Environmental Criminology*, London: Routledge.

Hillyard, P. and Tombs, S. (2001), 'Criminology, Zemiology and Justice', Paper presented to the Socio-Legal Studies Association Annual Conference in Bristol, April 2001.

Hirschi, T. (1969), *Causes of Delinquency*, Berkeley, CA: University of California Press.

Hirschi, Travis, and Gottfredson, Michael, R. (1993), 'Commentary: Testing the General Theory of Crime', *Journal of Research in Crime and Delinquency*, vol. 30, p. 47.

Hirschi, T. and Gottfredson, M. (2000), 'In defence of self-control', *Theoretical Criminology*, 4.1, February.

Home Office (1990), *Crime, Justice and Protecting the Public: the Government's Proposals for Legislation* (Cmd 965), London: HMSO.

Hopkins, Andrew and McGregor, Heather (1991), *Working for Change: The Movement Against Domestic Violence*, Sydney: Allen & Unwin.

Innes, M. (1999), 'An Iron Fist in an Iron Glove? The Zero Tolerance Policing Debate', *Howard Journal of Criminal Justice*, vol. 39, p. 397.

Institute of Race Relations (1987), *Policing Against Black People*, London: Institute of Race Relations.

Juby, H. and Farrington, D. (2001), 'Disentangling the Link between Disrupted Families and Delinquency', *British Journal of Criminology*, pp. 22–40.

Karstedt, S. (2002), 'Emotions and Criminal Justice', *Theoretical Criminology*, vol. 6(3), p. 299.

Katz, Jack (1988), *The Seductions of Crime: Moral and Sensual Attractions in Doing Evil*, New York: Basic Books.

Keane, Carl, Maxim, Paul S. and Teevan, James J. (1993), 'Drinking and Driving, Self-control, and Gender: Testing a General Theory of Crime', *Journal of Research in Crime and Delinquency*, vol. 30, p. 30.

Kolvin, I., Miller, F.J.W., Scott, D.M., Gatzanis, S.R.M. and Fleeting, M. (1990), *Continuities of Deprivation?*, Aldershot: Avebury.

Lansky, M. (1987), 'Shame and Domestic Violence', in D. Nathanson (ed.), *The Many Faces of Shame*, New York: Guilford.

MacPherson of Cluny, Sir W. (1999), *The Stephen Lawrence Inquiry: Report of an Inquiry by Sir William Macpherson of Cluny*, Cm 4262, London: HMSO.

Mathieson, T. (1983), 'The Future of Control Systems: the Case of Norway', in David Garland and Paul Young (eds), *The Power to Punish: Contemporary Penalty and Social Analysis*, London: Heinemann.

Mathiesen, Thomas (1997), 'The Viewer Society: Michel Foucault's "Panopticon" Revisited', *Theoretical Criminology*, vol. 1, p. 215.

Maxwell, G. and Morris, A. (2001), 'Putting Restorative Justice into Practice for Adult Offenders', *Howard Journal of Criminal Justice*, vol. 40, p. 55.

Miller, Susan L. and Burack, Cynthia (1993), 'A Critique of Gottfredson and Hirschi's General Theory of Crime: Selective Inattention to Gender and Power Positions', *Women and Criminal Justice*, vol. 4, p. 115.

Moore, C. and Brown, J. (1981), *Community Versus Crime*, London: Bedford Square Press.

Morash, M. and Rucker, L. (1989), 'An Exploratory Study of the Connection of Mother's Age at Childbearing to her Children's Delinquency in Four Data Sets', *Crime and Delinquency*, vol. 35, p. 45.

Muncie, J. (1999), *Youth and Crime: A Critical Introduction*, London: Sage.

Murray, C. (1990), *The Emerging British Underclass*, London: Institute of Economic Affairs.

Murray, C. (1994), *Underclass: The Crisis Deepens*, London: Institute of Economic Affairs.

Nelken, D. (2002), 'White-Collar Crime', in M. Maguire, R. Morgan and R. Reiner, *The Oxford Handbook of Criminology*, 3rd edn., Oxford: Oxford University Press.

Raup, Ethan (1996), 'The American Prison Problem, Hegemonic Crisis, and the Censure of Inner-City Blacks', in Colin Sumner (ed.), *Violence, Culture and Censure*, London: Taylor & Francis.

Reckless, Walter, C. (1967), *The Crime Problem*, 4th edn, New York: Appleton-Century-Croft.

Reckless, Walter, C. (1973), *The Crime Problem*, 5th edn, New York: Appleton-Century-Croft.

Reckless, Walter C. and Dinitz, Simon (1972), *The Prevention of Juvenile Delinquency*, Columbus, OH: Ohio State University Press.

Reiner, R. (1985), *The Politics of the Police*, Brighton: Wheatsheaf.

Reiss, Albert J. (1951), 'Delinquency as the Failure of Personal and Social Controls', *American Sociological Review*, vol. 16, p. 196.

Robins, L.N. (1979), 'Sturdy Childhood Predictors of Adult Outcomes: Replications from Longitudinal Studies', in J.E. Barrett, R.M. Rose and G. L. Klerman (eds), *Stress and Mental Disorder*, New York: Raven.

Roshier, Bob (1989), *Controlling Crime: The Classical Perspective in Criminology*, Milton Keynes: Open University Press.

Rutter, M., Maughn, B., Mortimore, P., Ouston, J. and Smith, A. (1979), *Fifteen Thousand Hours: Secondary Schools and their Effects on Children*, London: Open Books.

Sampson, Robert J. and Laub, John H. (1990), 'Crime and Deviance Over the Life Course: The Salience of Adult Bonds', *American Sociological Review*, vol. 55, p. 609.

Sampson, R.J. and Laub, J.H. (1993), *Crime in the Making*, Cambridge, MA: Harvard University Press.

Scarman, Lord (1981), *The Brixton Disorders, 10–12 April 1981* (Scarman Report), Cmnd 8427, London: HMSO.

Scheff, Thomas and Retzinger, Suzanne (1991), *Emotions and Violence: Shame and Rage in Destructive Conflicts*, Lexington, VA: Lexington Books.

Schinkel, W. (2002), 'The Modernist Myth in Criminology', *Theoretical Criminology*, vol. 6(2), p. 123.

Shover, Neal (1996), *Great Pretenders: Pursuits and Careers of Persistent Thieves*, Boulder, CO: Westview Press.

Slapper, G. and Tombs, S. (1999), *Corporate Crime*, London: Longman.

Smith, D.J. (1997), 'Ethnic Origins, Crime, and Criminal Justice in England and Wales', in M. Tonry (ed.), *Ethnicity, Crime, and Immigration: Comparative and Cross-National Perspectives*, Chicago, IL: University of Chicago Press.

Smith, D.J., McVie, S., Woodward, R., Shute, J., Flint, J. and McAra, L. (2001), *The Edinburgh Study of Youth Transgressions and Crimes: Key Findings From Sweeps 1–2*. At **http:// www.law.ac.uk/cls/esytc**.

Taylor, Ian (1997), 'Crime Anxiety and Locality: Responding to the "Condition of England" at the End of the Century', *Theoretical Criminology*, vol. 1, p. 53.

Tittle, Charles R. (1995), *Control Balance: Towards a General Theory of Deviance*, Boulder, CO: Westview Press.

Tittle, Charles R. (1997), 'Thoughts Stimulated by Braithwaite's Analysis of Control Balance', *Theoretical Criminology*, vol. 1, p. 99.

Tittle, Charles R. (1999), 'Continuing the Discussion of Control Balance', *Theoretical Criminology*, vol. 3, p. 344.

Tittle, Charles R. (2000), 'Control Balance', in R. Paternoster and R. Bachman (eds), *Explaining Criminals and Crime: Essays in Contemporary Theory*, Los Angeles, CA: Roxbury.

Tonry, M. (ed.) (1997), *Ethnicity, Crime, and Immigration: Comparative and Cross-National Perspectives*, Chicago, IL: University of Chicago Press.

Triplett, R.A., Gainey, R.R. and Sun, I.Y. (2003), 'Institutional Strength, Social Control and Neighbourhood Crime Rates', *Theoretical Criminology*, vol. 7(4), p. 439.

van Stokkom, B. (2002), 'Moral Emotions in Restorative Justice Conferences: Managing Shame, Designing Empathy', *Theoretical Criminology*, vol. 6(3), p. 399.

Warr, M. (1998), 'Life-Course Transitions and Desistance from Crime', *Criminology*, vol. 36, p. 183.

Wells, L.E. and Rankin, J.H. (1991), 'Families and Delinquency: a Meta-Analysis of the Impact of Broken Homes', *Social Problems*, vol. 38, p. 71.

Young, J. (1999), *The Exclusive Society*, London: Sage.

Williams, K.S. (2004), 'Immoral Behaviour meets Immoral Law: Does Child Pornography Protect Our Children?' (Forthcoming).

Young, R. and Goold, B. (1999), 'Restorative Police Cautioning in Aylesbury—From Degrading to Shaming Ceremonies', *Criminal Law Review*, p. 126.

Zingraff, Matthew T., Leiter, Jeffrey, Johnsen, Matthew C. and Myers, Kristen A. (1994), 'The Mediating Effect of Good School Performance on the Maltreatment—Delinquency Relationship', *Journal of Research in Crime and Delinquency*, vol. 31, p. 62.

14

Labelling, phenomenology and ethnomethodology

14.1 Introduction

'The New Criminologies' is rather a misnomer. The ideas upon which much of this school is based are by no means new: they are drawn from the works of Plato and Aristotle, Machiavelli, Hobbes, Alfred Schultz, Karl Marx and the Chicago School. In any event, since the theory began to appear some 40 years ago it is perhaps no longer 'new'. In many texts the approach is referred to as radical criminology, conflict criminology, Marxist criminology or symbolic interactionism. Whatever the label, the contents are much the same. They first began to be propagated at the end of the 1950s and, although they are still frequently drawn on, writers of this school were most active and directly influential in the limited period between 1960 and 1975. Since that time their influence has been less direct but nonetheless powerful, often as points of reference and checks and balances for policy initiatives and for other theories. They will be discussed in this chapter and Chapter Fifteen though they have already been drawn upon to analyse other theories presented in this text.

It is unsurprising that they arose during this period, which was generally a time of questioning authority and the *status quo*. The 1960s are known for their campus conflicts in both Europe and America, as well as the wholesale rejection of many of the values of the immediate post-war years. The human rights movement began to become more popular and stronger; the young began to question the conventional way of life and conventional values; in America there was protest over the Vietnam war, and both here and elsewhere there was a growing pacifist movement; in Britain the Northern Ireland problem grew from a civil rights campaign into a violent conflict; and the women's rights movement and feminist arguments began to arise. Just as most of these movements or trends were reactions against the accepted values, explanations and ways of life, so the new criminologies were, to a large extent, a reaction against the positivism which had arisen in and taken over criminology. To understand the new criminologies, it is important to understand some of the theoretical, empirical and institutional elements against which these people were working.

As has already been seen, positivists believe that criminality is caused by something outside the control of the offender: it is the result of a biological, psychological or social fault. They therefore reject, or at least severely limit, the idea of a rational man able to exercise free will and to choose and direct his actions. In doing this, they cease to describe the world and the activities of a society by means of those who participate in it. Instead, they seek out what they consider to be the profound and compelling causes which subconsciously direct the participants' behaviour. The cause of the behaviour makes the individual choose to act in a particular way, and so the cause becomes the choice. As has been evident in many of the preceding chapters, if a particular factor arises markedly more frequently in criminals than in non-criminals, then the positivists tend to see that factor as a cause of that criminality (see Chapters Six to Twelve). In criticism, the new criminologists point out that it merely indicates seeming contacts between criminality and the various factors. They claim that it is not sufficiently supported by theoretical explanation to establish whether the connection is causal and how the causation works in practice.

If the positivist tradition is so obviously flawed, why was it accepted, and is still accepted, by so many people? Much of its appeal rests on its claim to be 'scientific'. The links between crime and the various factors seemed to be scientifically tested, and thus as 'objective': the presumed freedom from political or other bias made them more acceptable. These general considerations are reinforced by particular institutional traditions. For example, in Britain the judiciary is used to being asked to interpret and apply the law objectively without questioning its validity or fairness. A scientific and objective basis for explaning criminality is thus especially acceptable to it, the more so if it is postulated by other professionals. The positivist approach also appeals to substantial sectors of the general public: it makes them feel safe from becoming criminal themselves, whilst not simply condemning the individual who is criminal. 'Unlike myself, a criminal is not normal, or has experienced an upbringing/environment different from mine: they need help and I need to be protected against them.'

New criminologies reject this stance. Some of the reasons for this rejection will gradually emerge from our discussion, but others can immediately be made explicit. One argument against the positivist school is that it is too simplistic. It seems to treat the criminals as if they exist almost in a vacuum. Most criminal activities involve, either directly or tacitly, the cooperation or at least knowledge of many people or even groups, such as purchasers of stolen goods. When a member of a corporation does some illegal act within that institution, it is generally done with the knowledge and often the blessing or even direction of supervisors. A criminal act is not an isolated act, so the new criminologist would argue that to explain most criminality in positivist terms is neither realistic nor illuminating.

A second argument against positivism can be found in the rejection of the idea that criminal behaviour can be reduced to a purely scientific or technical question. The criminal act was seen as an abnormal act, and it was necessary to bring the criminal back to normality, either by correcting some psychological defect, or by teaching how to cope with some biological or social problem and become law-abiding. The implicit assumption was that crime is not really a rational choice, and therefore anyone making that choice must be different and need help (for a very strong questioning of this stance see Foucault's views, reproduced in Kritzman (ed.) (1988), pp. 125–51). Furthermore, positivists seemed to assume that if something was called a crime, it was necessarily wrong because the State said it was wrong. New criminologists probe behind this claim, and argue that many acts are defined as crimes largely to protect and reflect the interests of the powerful and to retain a political and ideological *status quo*. In the 1960s much of this was brought into question: many faced criminal charges for what they saw as oppression, and notions of 'helping' them back to normality seemed irrelevant. At a time when the *status quo* was being questioned in all other fields of life, it would have been surprising if it had not been challenged in the sphere of criminality. For the new criminologies, crime is related to the law-abiding, especially the powerful, as well as to those who violate the law.

The new criminologies largely agree on the basis for rejecting positivism, but they differ over what should replace it. The new criminologies, as the plural suggests, embrace different ideas and schools of thought. Here the study will be split into four areas or 'schools', namely: labelling or interactionism; phenomenology and ethnomethodology; conflict; and radical criminologies. It is not claimed that this is the only, or the correct, way to present the materials, but it is hoped that it will make them easier to follow. It is, however, important to emphasise that these areas are interlinked and do not constitute separate theories. Two of these perspectives (labelling or interactionism, and phenomenology and ethnomethodology) will be dealt with in this chapter, and two (conflict, and radical criminologies) in the next.

14.2 Labelling or interactionism

Labelling theories and interactionism were the spring-board for many of the proponents and ideas of the new criminology. Two preliminary points need to be noted. First, labelling or interactionism represents, not a single theory, but rather a number of different ideas drawn together under one method. This method is sometimes also called social reaction theory and, as this term suggests, it looks towards society's reaction to the deviant more than to the person of the deviant. Secondly, and possibly more important, its proponents never claimed that it caused criminality in a direct way. They saw it rather as widening the area to be considered in criminological theories, in particular to include the actions and positions of those around the criminal, and the effect these may have upon the criminal.

Although the ideas of labelling theory only took root in British criminology in the 1960s, they have a fairly long history. In 1936 Frederick Thrasher, in his work on juvenile gangs, recognised that the official label of 'deviant' had potentially negative effects upon the youths. Two years later, Frank Tannenbaum (1938) argued that calling someone criminal might result in him living up to the description.

Labelling, or interactionism, is a derivative of the widely used sociological idea of interactionist social theory. Interactionist theory analyses the way social actors, usually individuals, have conceptions of themselves and of the others around them with whom they interact. This gives meaning to the behaviour of individuals, as it places their action in their understanding of the world. Of course, many conceptions which each person holds will be drawn from their culture or position in society, but the interactionists attach importance to the meanings which the individual places on various occurrences. Labelling theory is drawn from this, but centres its study on how symbols, namely labelling someone, can be used, or can be seen, to influence someone's action.

In the traditional criminology the researcher is concerned with why a person commits crimes and how one can prevent criminality, or further criminality. In interactionist criminology the researcher, must take at least two perspectives. First, to look at the problem from the perspective of society and ask under what circumstances does a person get set aside and called criminal. How does the labelling come about? How does the label affect the actions of others towards the individual? What value do they put on the fact of deviance? Secondly, to look at the problem from the perspective of the person labelled and ask how they react to the fact of being labelled. Do they adopt the criminal role set for them by others? Does it affect the circles they live in, and alter their self concept to take account of the deviant role assigned to them?

This sets out two facets of the interactionist or labelling perspective, but it clearly has more. We shall briefly comment on these two facets, and add a third. Thus we shall ask: what behaviour should attract the label of 'crime', and why? This is the third question to add to the two already indicated: how do official agencies and society use and apply these labels, and what effect does labelling have on the individual?

14.2.1 Labelling behaviour: societal reaction

Howard Becker (1963 and 1973) pointed out that no behaviour is deviant or criminal until it is so defined and thereby labelled by a section (the section in power) or by the whole of the society. To call something a crime is therefore only a reaction to a particular type of behaviour, a reaction that marks the behaviour out as unacceptable to other members of society. Each society creates deviants and criminals by making rules whose breach will constitute deviance or criminality. The rules of any particular society at any particular time are not inalienable. For example, abortion was generally illegal in Britain up until 1967; now in certain defined circumstances it is legal and acceptable. Rules differ from society to society. Thus the proponents of labelling or interactionism consider that the conventional morality of rules (even criminal laws) should be studied and questioned, not merely accepted as self-evident truths. This covers a wide range of approaches to the criminal justice system, from reform to left realism to anarchic abolitionism. A more usual view is that nothing is criminal until someone reacts to it in such a way as to define it as such and treat its transgressors as criminal: there is no such thing as an act which by its very nature is criminal and reprehensible. Even the most commonly recognised crime, murder, is not universally defined in the sense that anyone who kills another is, everywhere and always, guilty of murder. Some killings are excused on the grounds of extreme provocation or of self-defence. Some are actively condoned and glorified—killing in war. Therefore the same act—killing—cannot be understood without reference to other people's reactions. In this theoretical analysis, the creators and enforcers of rules need to be subjected to a critical scrutiny which should not be confined to those who violate the rules.

This perspective on the setting of criminal laws goes against the more traditional normative idea under which an activity is a crime if it breaches the norms of behaviour accepted by those in the society. The problem with the normative idea is the idea of a consensus of all people in a society, since normative theory assumes that the views of all persons carry equal weight. In interactionism, this assumption is challenged by scrutinising the reactions of individuals and groups to see whose reactions are given most weight.

It is often argued that if actions are performed by powerful people, there is a reluctance to define the action as criminal, although it may be criticised. Even if the activity is made illegal, it may be defined as an administrative infraction rather than a crime. This can most clearly be seen in the area of corporate or white-collar crime, where very often morally reprehensible and damaging activity is not defined as criminal. This tendency arises not only because of the power of the person carrying out the acts, but also because of the proximity of the actor and the person who is setting out the reactions of the society. The closer these two are, the more likely the action is to be excused and explained away as fairly normal. The further apart they are, the more likely the action is to be classified as criminal and a harsh penalty set for those who transgress.

It is not only the powerful who fight for certain legal positions. All sorts of pressure groups argue for all manner of legal changes. For example, although in 1967 abortion was legalised in certain situations, there have always been pressure groups who argue for changing this. On the one hand, many groups may fight for the woman's right to choose, and therefore for abortion on demand and up until 28 weeks; other groups will be arguing for the rights of the foetus or, as they would call it, the child, and either push for no abortion at all, or for much tighter regulation of the laws. Each is arguing to protect rights: one the rights of the mother and the other the rights of the foetus (or child). Any changing of the law results in some redistribution of benefits. One or more type of person loses by being prevented from doing as they want or being criminalised for their behaviour, and others gain by having their rights protected. The group that wins is the one which is successful in obtaining the support of those in a position to decide.

Some behaviours become criminalised due to fairly small pressure groups or interest groups, but later become so accepted as criminal that almost all in a particular society would accept them as inherently bad. One of the best examples of this is the regulation of drugs. Until early this century, almost all drugs were legally available on demand. Many were used in the treatment of fairly minor ailments, and were commonly given to children. A small but strong international group led, in 1912, to the Hague Conference calling for the possession, sale etc., of such drugs as opium, morphine and cocaine to be made illegal. In 1920, under the Dangerous Drugs Act, they became illegal in Britain. Many in the country at the time would have opposed such a law, but now the possession of these substances for other than medical purposes is generally regarded as bad or wrong in itself. This clearly illustrates how general social perceptions can change over time. Beyond that we should always be aware and critical of how social problems are defined as crimes and how crime prevention can have unforeseen effects which may increase negative activities rather than purely control individuals. Thus, as Ekblom (2002) argues, unjust laws may be socially harmful and give rise to social disobedience, so that the criminal law and its control can cause greater insecurity. Communities should examine activities such as business crime which are traditionally sidestepped and should recognise the devastating effects these may have on individuals and communities. His call is for policies which will address social and structural problems rather than just controlling people.

The approach of interactionism has its own problems. The researchers are often effectively placing their own values on others. For example, they often assert that the powerless would draw the line defining criminality in a different position, which is not necessarily the case. In some respects this is as problematical as assuming a normative structure, but in the case of interactionism the theorists are at least more aware of the problematic position of labelling certain behaviour as criminal and other behaviour as non-criminal. This awareness is significant: it should make them less willing to condemn people for their behaviour and less willing to assume that something is wrong or bad *per se*. Because they do not view crimes as different in kind from other behaviours, the proponents of this school tend to study deviance rather than crime. They have looked at activities, some criminal, some not, which have led groups in society to view the perpetrators in a bad light.

Recently a new, more holistic, questioning of definitions of crime has been launched: zemiology (Hillyard and Tombs (2001)). Rather than assuming different values would be accepted, these theorists question the prioritisation of certain harms over others. They begin with a broad concept of harm; any physical, psychological, financial acts which have negative consequences for an individual, a family or a community; many would also include cultural harms caused by exclusion: reduction (or removal) of autonomy, the denial of cultural and informational resources which are generally available or which should be available. An implication is that all harm causes suffering and that the suffering may be greater from a harm caused by a non-criminal act than by a criminal act: not all socially harmful acts fall within the criminal law. To an extent therefore the focus on crime as our defining concept around which sympathy, justified anger and retribution and action to redress the harm should be hung is mistaken. Inadequate health care, unemployment, overcrowded housing, insufficient educational opportunities, inequalities in opportunities and treatment, natural disasters, accidents, legal emissions from factories are all harmful, all serious for those who suffer them but cannot and should never all be included in the definitions of criminal behaviour. To this extent the criminal law is centrally about controlling behaviour rather than about protecting citizens from harm. From this perspective the new central positioning of victims is thus possibly misplaced unless we are, as a society, willing to sympathise with and redress all victimisation, howsoever caused. As will be seen in Chapter Twenty more citizens are calling for greater security from these other harms and it may be pertinent for States to consider addressing harm rather than merely centring on a small number of harmful activities while evading responsibility for the broader level of harms being suffered. In this environment a concept of social harm has some advantages in that it enables the criminological gaze to go beyond legal and State definitions of injurious practices (Tifft (1995) and to recognise certain legal behaviours as harms in themselves. However, much caution is needed: what is 'good' or 'harmful' for both individuals and society is not always self-evident.

14.2.2 Labelling the individual

The main early proponents of this area were Lemert (1951) and Becker (1963 and 1973). Lemert saw the main problems arising when a label attaches and the individual identifies with that label. Becker (1963) took the view that in making rules or crimes, society created deviance and by applying the rules to particular people and labelling them as criminals and outsiders, society creates the criminals. In this section we are concerned with how society decides who to label; in the next we will consider the effects of such a label on the individual.

The question is: 'who do we label as criminal'? The trite answer is 'those who transgress the criminal law'. Such a response requires enormous qualifications. As should have been clear from Chapter One almost everyone has transgressed a criminal law but many have never been punished for so doing. Therefore the answer might be that we label and punish only those who are caught. This is partially true, and can explain some of the concentration on street as opposed to boardroom or domestic criminality. One of the factors affecting societal reaction to a particular activity is the visibility of the offence. If an offence is obvious and committed on the street, both the public and police are going to be more aware of it than if it happens in the home or in boardrooms. For this reason, its negative effects will be more obvious, and it is more likely to be officially controlled. Where this street activity becomes particularly prevalent and established as a 'problem' these factors are even stronger, as can be seen from the reaction to football hooligans. The types of crimes which are targeted in this way, and the public fear of them, can be artificially controlled. As was seen in Chapters Three and Five the media may build up a particular crime as being more important and more prevalent than the facts would suggest. This may alter its perception by society and therefore influence the reaction of society to it. Similarly the police, by deciding to target particular crimes, may make it appear that there is a problem in a particular area. For example, when Anderton took over as chief constable in Manchester in 1976 he began a crusade against homosexuality and used his police to seek out and prosecute this group. Manchester, which had hitherto believed it had an insignificant homosexual problem, suddenly discovered a large problem. The activity had always existed, but only now was it was being policed and reacted against. Similarly there may be a decision on the part of the police to patrol certain areas more closely. They are then likely to discover more crime there, which may justify their initial judgement that this is a high crime rate area; or it may simply mean that the apparently lower crime rate of other areas reflects a less intense level of policing.

Even this is too simple an answer, because many people who are caught committing a crime are either not reported to the police or have no action taken against them. Therefore, the label 'criminal' is only put upon someone in fairly rare circumstances, and their criminal activity is only a small part of the process. The way in which actions which have been defined as criminal are policed and controlled is at least as important.

In some cases the police are not the enforcement agency. This has already been seen for corporate crime. Here the control agencies, such as the factory inspectors, mostly use persuasion and rarely press criminal charges. In most offences, however, the enforcement agencies are the police, the courts, judges, probation officers and prisons. There are claims by labelling theorists that the police show sexual, racial, religious and/or class bias in performing their duties (see Macpherson (1999) and Commission for Racial Equality (2003)). On figures produced by the Home Office there is a clear difference in racial and sexual inclusion in the criminal justice system which is at least suggestive of bias (Home Office (2002 a and b)). On figures produced by the Commission for Racial Equality, or on their behalf, the bias is even more evident and exists at a number of levels in the system (see Commission for Racial Equality (2002) Hood (1992). Like other agents of the criminal justice system, the police are, not surprisingly, likely to be influenced by a variety of external circumstances, such as the attitude (respectful or aggressive) and the appearance of juveniles stopped in the streets.

Finally, the wrong person may be arrested, accused and eventually even convicted. This may happen if those in power decide to punish a scapegoat, that is, knowingly punish the wrong person, or if there is a mistake. At all stages of this 'mistake' there may be effects for the wronged individual, who may be treated differently by others on the basis that there is 'no smoke without fire'. All these areas of bias can again become important in the court appearances and the encounters with probation officers and other officials. The use of the word 'criminal' perhaps has as much to do with the reaction of society to the behaviour and to the individual as it does to the fact of an offence having been committed.

14.2.3 Social reaction: the individual and self-concept

The third part of the social reaction theories is that if someone is subjected to a label, this may be internalised by the person labelled, and this might affect behaviour. Becker (1963 and 1973) and many other labelling theorists who expound this idea are not saying that this caused deviance. Labelling theorists have never argued the simplistic misrepresentation that they are sometimes accused of —they have never said: if you catch me stealing, call me a thief and convict and sentence me for theft, I will internalise the label and will call myself a thief and act accordingly. They were seeking to comprehend a situation by taking account of all the participants, and of their interactions. How others treat and view people affects the way they view themselves (see Matsueda (1992)). A person may have a particular self-image, but unless this becomes accepted by others in the society it is difficult to sustain and may have to be relinquished. This is seen as crucial because each individual conducts his or her life according to their self-image.

This part of the labelling theory is possibly the best documented and most widely discussed. Most writers use the concepts of primary and secondary deviance. The former is seen as rule breaking, and generally has nothing to do with labels because the deviant act is neutralised, normalised or denied. Neutralisation involves justifying the action in some way, possibly by saying that the employer owes him the money; or he is only borrowing the money; or that the violence was committed in self defence. (For a fuller discussion of neutralisation, see 12.4.) It could be normalised if others around them also commit similar acts, making them seem slightly disreputable rather than criminal. For example, a worker may see that everyone pilfers a little from work, or a youth may see that most of his peers shop-lift. They come to see such acts as normal rather than criminal, and believe that they have a reasonable defence or justification (the employer or the shop can afford the loss etc.). Even people who have committed many crimes may fit into this category of primary deviance, especially if they have not been convicted and have therefore been able to maintain their self-image.

Primary deviance is not featured in many labelling explanations because those concerned have not yet changed their self-image in response to societal reaction to their behaviour. When the label criminal is officially applied to someone who is still a primary deviant, many labelling theorists say that the individual is falsely so defined. By this they do not mean that the individual is innocent, but rather that the individual has not accepted the view of society that it is not only the activity which is wrong, but also that the individual offender is a criminal. That is, society now views the person as less worthy and as the type of person who will get into trouble; but the term primary deviance implies that the person concerned does not share this view. They see criminality as neither part of their character nor of their lifestyle. However, calling them criminals may change this.

Secondary deviance is behaviour which results, at least in part, from the problems of self-identity and societal reactions. Secondary deviance may have a number of causes, but these writers suggest that it can be better understood through the effects of labelling which may have made it more likely. Those covered by the concept of secondary deviance are generally those who persistently break the law, both as a way of making a living and as a way of life. In fact, most of the criminological studies so far carried out, by positivists as well as by the proponents of labelling, have concentrated on this group because the examples of criminals are mostly drawn from prisons and similar institutions. One strength of the labelling school is that they are more aware that their findings mostly apply only to secondary deviants.

It is the members of society, and particularly the police, courts and other agents of social control, who are responsible for giving an individual a label. It is also society, largely through the same agents, which can determine the effects that label will have on the individual. The individuals so labelled are treated differently from others, and the effect of this depends partly upon their ability to deal with the consequences and how they then view themselves. The individual accepting the label becomes a secondary deviant. For some, this acceptance may arise after only one transgression and label; for others it may take a number of transgressions and penalties. Secondary deviance may also, but rarely, arise when the perpetrator, although undiscovered, believes that if caught he will be labelled and accepts that self-inflicted label. Becker calls this secret deviance (Becker (1963 and 1973)). No one of these types covers the whole of deviance, and therefore each is important to our understanding of the social interaction involved.

The effects of being labelled a criminal, and especially whether this is accepted as a self-image, depend upon two factors: first, the way the person is treated as a result of the deviance; and secondly, the way the person manages to handle these effects. It is important to note that labelling theorists see the act of labelling only as a first step in the process; the fact of being officially labelled is often not sufficient to affect the individual. For any stigmatisation to give rise to a deviant identity it must be disseminated through society, or a part of society which is significant to the person concerned.

If people know about the criminal label it is likely to affect the way in which they treat the individual. For many, the criminal label is likely to be the overriding identifying label. A person previously known mainly as a parent or a schoolchild, or whatever, is now primarily known as a thief. The individual may then start to wonder whether the conception of him as bad or as a thief is actually more real than the perception he had of himself previously.

Many people have a stereotype of offenders as less worthy than others, and often reject them because of their criminality. For example, offenders may be refused work because they have been convicted. This may be rational (e.g., being rejected as a child-minder because of convictions for child abuse) or irrational (e.g., if a conviction for child abuse results in rejection for a job as a cashier, despite excellent qualifications). Such people are considered less worthy or in some other way different from others in society because they are criminal. The same reasoning may also cause them to be treated differently in other spheres of their lives, cutting them off from friends and even relatives, and from the law-abiding sectors of society. This may force them into association with other law-breakers, which may further consolidate the criminal label as well as providing an opportunity to learn new crimes and criminal values. So an occasional drug user may, after the intervention of official agencies of control, become separated from the legal and acceptable sections of society and, by associating with others in the same predicament, learn the attitudes, aspirations and activities of this new subculture, becoming more inclined to use drugs and perhaps becoming involved in other illegal activities. Furthermore the police may help to consolidate the criminality by visiting them when crimes similar to those they committed arise in their area—'if they did it once, they may well do it again'. All of these effects are amplified if the State incarcerated them for their crimes. But, as the repeated use of the word 'may' indicates, there is nothing unavoidable or deterministic about such reactions. Indeed, some become determined to 'learn from the error of their ways' and to win back their reputation. The argument of the interactionists is, however, that many do internalise the label, and thus criminality arises out of the reaction of society to them.

The incarceration of offenders is generally seen as the most vehement societal condemnation and constitutes the strongest case for labelling theorists. Prisons are often referred to as the breeding-grounds for criminals, and the labelling perspective on this is a part of that claim. Prisons give people the opportunity of learning how to commit other crimes, but more important from our viewpoint is that they provoke criminality by reinforcing the alienation of these people from society. Many prisoners accept the label, see no possibility of change, and on release commit further crimes: prompting the question of whether these further crimes arise as (in part) a consequence of the label and the punishment. Others do not accept that their actions were genuinely criminal and so will never accept the label: still others will try to return to as normal an existence as possible and probably will not re-offend.

Such reformist intentions are made the more difficult to implement because, on release from prison, the stigma follows the individual into the community. All the problems with acceptance into a community, finding a job and police surveillance are amplified in the case of an ex-prisoner. They stem from the label, and they all keep the individual slightly apart from law-abiding society, which it becomes difficult to rejoin. The paradox is that the processes and means of social control which in the last chapter were said to lead to law-abiding behaviour are the very same processes that the labelling theorists argue lead to further criminality—the control and labelling leads to a redefinition of the self, resulting in an acceptance of a criminal self-image.

A similar conclusion can be drawn from the school of thought which applies social reaction theories to groups. By a process known as deviancy amplification, one group labels another as deviant, leading to the societal alienation of the deviant group. As the excluders reinforce their action against the deviant group, excluding them from normal social interactions, it leads to more crime by the deviant group. This heightened criminal activity merely re-affirms the original label, apparently confirming the initial alienation and justifying even less tolerance of the deviants. Basically, the postulate here is that crime increases, not because controls have failed, but because they are working, creating something like a vicious circle. Such a process could help to explain the extreme problems which have arisen at particular times in certain communities. For example, police action in stopping and searching youths suspected of street robberies in Brixton in 1981 was widely blamed as a central factor in causing the very much more serious crime which arose during the weekend of riots. If the allegation is true, this might be said to be an instance of amplification causing criminality, but it might also be explained by means of a wider conflict theory (see Chapter Fifteen). The argument is not that the way society viewed them caused all their unacceptable behaviour, but rather that the intense focus of media and official attention caused a panic in the rest of the population. The result was that even if their actions were not unduly harmful, they met harsh reactions from the control agencies (police and courts) which may then have helped them as individuals along the road to acquiring a negative self-image.

14.2.4 Relevance today

A slightly modified labelling theory may be useful in considering both the way in which we view criminality today and the attempt to control its apparent rise. In the late 1980s Link and others used labelling theory to study the way in which we view and treat the mentally ill (Link (1987), Link et al. (1987 and 1989)). They claimed that in America public attitudes had been conditioned to see the mentally ill in negative and devalued ways. As a result many of those who need mental help and those who care for them will either try to hide this fact from family friends, colleagues and their employers, or will withdraw from groups or people who they think might reject them, although a few will be open and actively try to educate people into changing their attitudes. In general they found that the prevalent attitudes affected the social ties, promotion, earning capacity and, possibly most important, the selfesteem of the people concerned.

Such findings along with those of the earlier labelling theorists may help to understand the problems of criminals and the ways in which these might be addressed. A number of recent papers have suggested that the criminal justice system and the public in Britain and elsewhere are increasing the stigmatisation of offenders, particularly juveniles, thus heightening the adverse effects of labelling (see Triplett (2000) and De Haan (2000)). De Haan notes that levels of violence appear to be rising, even in the Netherlands where it has tended to be low, and attributes this partly to re-labelling, making certain acts more serious than previously. The whole area of violence is being more harshly treated and less tolerated. Indeed, Triplett claims that in the US an increase in violent offences in the 1980s and early 1990s had been accompanied by changes in the criminal justice system moving less serious offences (particularly status offences such as truancy) up the sentencing tariff and, more importantly, by a change in the way in which (especially young) violent offenders are viewed as evil. Both the severe judgment and associated fear have a tendency to be transferred to all youth criminals, and even to collections of youths more generally. The effect is to isolate and segregate these youths from the rest of society, escalating the criminalising effects of labelling.

Meossi (2000) argues that this demonising of offenders as constituting a threat to the social fabric goes hand in hand with economic downturns. He notes its existence in both Italy and America. It is also asserted (Halpern (2001)) that a rise, or a perception of a rise, in crime leads to calls for harsher treatments of offenders. Again, the devaluing of people through such labelling can itself trigger more crime.

Whatever the reason for this demonising of individual offenders or groups of people this American view can be readily applied to the UK. Minor acts of public order are being more closely controlled; youths have antisocial behaviour orders against them, and are the subject of curfews. These restraints tend to apply not just to the criminals but to all youths. Furthermore it has become more common to classify the offender by the risk they pose rather than the crime they have committed, so analysing and punishing the person rather than the crime. Thus the probation service is now expected to advise the court in sentencing reports as to the risk posed by the individual, and similar processes are used in the application of community rehabilitation orders. One of the tools being designed is a central and uniform assessment of risk but the press and public are more ready to view wide groups of offenders as evil. There is a constant tendency to increase those viewed as 'folk devils', most of whom are young people—hooligans, muggers, youth subcultures, youth gangs (usually just groups of youths hanging out together, not structured gangs), football hooligans, teenage mothers, drug users and so on (Hall et al. (1978) and McRobbie (1994)). The widespread and damaging use of hate speech throughout public life further exacerbates the problem (see Whillock and Slayden (1995)). Young people are being labelled, feared, avoided and excluded to a greater extent than might arise simply from their social position or even from the amount of criminality committed. As in the US there have been discussions concerning their lack of socialisation (see 13.7.1 and the intention to address this by parenting orders). An associated issue is the discussion of the need to exclude dangerous people with severe personality disorder, where definitions including their assumed lack of socialisation and compassion tend to bring more categories within this group (see 8.4). The elements of this labelling perspective are thus present in the UK tending to produce negative and fearful attitudes against these individuals and groups. Youths in particular can feel discriminated against in social and employment terms as well as by the legal system.

In such an environment labelling suggests that it is almost inevitable that many young people are moved to socialise with different, less judgemental (or differently judgemental) groups and may be attracted to elements involved in antisocial and criminal activities.

14.2.5 More positive uses of labelling

In 1988, John Braithwaite suggested that labelling as discussed up until then, and as indicated in the preceding section, was too negative a concept and suggested instead a positive application, which he called 'reintegrative shaming'. Basically offenders should be shamed not to stigmatise them but to make them realise the negative impact of their actions and then to encourage others to forgive and to accept them back into society. There are two essential elements to the idea (Braithwaite (1994)): first, that the offender needs to be confronted with victims to provide the shaming necessary for the process; secondly, the process needs to take place in front of those who care about the offender (usually family) who can then provide the reintegration into society. Both these are necessary to make the shift from stigmatising and towards reintegration. This claimed positive effect is the intention behind reparation and caution plus; the offender admits guilt, is made to face up to his or her victim and to agree action which will then allow the affair to be forgiven. The idea has been used in New Zealand (see Morris et al. (1993)), Australia (see Strang (1993), Forsythe (1994) and Hudson et al. (1996)) and in parts of America (see Alford (1997)). It has been tested in various forms in Britain and since the Crime and Disorder Act 1998 has been used nation wide as part of reparation (see Maxwell and Morris (2001), Dignan (1999) and Young and Goold (1999)).

It is usually used as part of the early cautioning system but it could be important at a number of points: part of a caution (warning or reprimand); taken into account at bail decisions; considered when reports are prepared; and as part of sentencing, decisions as to release, and post-release intervention. Furthermore some (e.g., Simpson et al. (2000)) see this as a useful way of approaching some white-collar and corporate violations of the law. These often escape entirely unscathed: shaming and reintegration would be an advance on the normal tendency to ignore such activities. If all of these facets are true the policy could have very wide appeal.

Since the beginning of this century this approach has probably spawned more writing on a single topic than any other area in criminology or criminal justice. To name but a few: Miers et al. (2001); Miers, D. (2001); Morris and Maxwell (2001); Strang (2002); Strang and Braithwaite (2002); Walgrave (2002); WeiteKamp and Kerner (2002); Johnstone (2003); WeiteKamp and Kerner (2003); von Hirsch et al. (2003). It has also attracted political approval and that of practitioners. There is some reason to question whether its application always includes all the important aspects of the theory: shame, empathy (both of offender for victim and vice versa) and reintegration into the community. It does not always embrace the shame and recognition of wrongdoing on the part of the offender but this is not always accompanied by the forgiveness and acceptance back into the 'law abiding' community. Nor is the process always performed in an environment which is free of coercion and power: it cannot always be said that the expression of feelings and the reconciliation of the dispute reflect the honest feelings of the participants. Such considerations may impair the success of reintegrative shaming in its use in the community.

There is also a wider theory, republican theory, based on labelling (see Braithwaite and Pettit (1990) and Braithwaite (2000b)). This encompasses the definition of crime; how prisons and other criminal justice agencies should be run and used; the consequences caused by the decisions and shape of the criminal justice system; the need for the system to maximise individual rights and freedoms. Thus the legal system should not be unnecessarily intrusive, nor simply become a slave to crime prevention: the ultimate aim is to increase freedom and what the theory calls dominion. Besides the general links with labelling theory, Braithwaite (2000a) argues the need to connect reintegrative shaming with a strong individualist cultural paradigm where rights are important as well as to a more communitarian ideology which also stresses responsibilities. Communitarian arguments are given a similar weight by Rose (2000), who sees the potential of shaming as a control mechanism but questions its possible dangers for a free society. Some still believe that if rights and responsibilities are given equal weighting there may be a use for this approach. Both come to the fore in the process that sees both victim and offender as individuals, requiring respect as individuals but also as parts of a social whole.

14.2.6 **Evaluation**

It cannot be disputed that interactionism has had profound effects on later criminologists who have used some of its methods. Despite this, the central claims of
the theory have faced significant criticism.

First, they are accused of perpetuating the same sin of determinism as does positivism. The charge here is that interactionism seems to assume that, given certain
factors there will be a certain outcome. They are thus said to fall into the trap they
are trying to escape. The usual answer is that labelling is not a theory of causation,
but rather a method of interpreting what happens. It is not claimed that labels
create certain types of behaviour, but rather that they and the effects that they have
may be one of the factors considered in any offender's decision to choose criminality. Some may view this as a somewhat unsatisfactory answer but, in view of the
fact that it was never claimed as a causative theory, or even a theory at all, it is
perhaps acceptable.

A second difficulty with these theories is that they tend to class the offender
almost as the victim, and one loses sight of the fact that there are victims of their
crimes. When they remove the normative element of the offence, they make the
act appear morally neutral. It is made to seem that the disapproval of the act is
confined to those in authority. However, many in society would argue that certain
things are bad in themselves (e.g., violence). If the moral elements of actions are
removed, the person who suffers the crime is deprived of the status of victim. They
are not really victims, but only constructed victims.

Thirdly, as was mentioned above (14.2.3), the processes which interactionism
marks out as possibly adversely affecting those labelled criminal can have a positive
effect on the law-abiding. In terms of numbers, the positive effects it may have in
preventing law violation in others may outweigh any negative effects on the
offender (see Vold and Bernard (1986)). In any event, the effects of labelling are not
easily predicted. A study of the labelling effect of the impact of arrest in cases of
domestic violence (Sherman (1992)) found that those with steady jobs were
deterred but the reaction of the unemployed was, if anything, to increase the violence against their partners following an arrest. Perhaps, however, these findings
are more relevant to the power relations embodied in control balance theory
(see 13.5) than they are to labelling.

A fourth criticism often levelled at the labelling theory is that it does not with-
stand empirical testing. Far from stating a fact which existed, it could be said that
labelling was conveying a social and sometimes a political message. The assertion
that social reaction to a label may encourage a person's criminal career is very
difficult to test. Indeed, the proponents of labelling themselves argue the criminality is often a deep-rooted problem before people are officially labelled. None
the less, attempts at testing have been made. The results are ambiguous and
indecisive.

Lastly, the radical criminologists have attacked interactionism for not going far
enough. They say that it ignores the fact that the criminality and the use of labels
are rooted in the unfair system of capitalism. Thus, although the labellers argue
that those in power will tend to construct and apply the rules, they ignore the full
impact and political importance of this use of power. This is a standpoint which
will be expanded in considering radical criminology in Chapter Fifteen.

Whatever validity there is in the idea that labelling affects behaviour, it has had a number of positive effects. It has shown that the perspective of the various actors is essential to understanding criminality, and that the criminal law is not a given and unchallengeable set of rules. These insights need to be included in discussions of causes of deviance. The stress on the mutability of the criminal law has given more force to arguments for change. Thus, since the beginning of the 1960s there has been discussion about what some writers see as unnecessary criminal laws, often called (some would say mis-called) victimless crimes. In a few cases these offences have been decriminalised, for example, abortion within certain bounds, and homosexuality between consenting men over the statutory legal age and in private. Others have been seriously considered for decriminalisation, such as the use of certain so-called 'soft' drugs (for further consideration of this area see Chapter Two).

Similarly, the individual aspect of labelling theory has been one of the elements which has led to a greater use of measures to divert people from criminal actions. This has had a profound effect throughout the criminal justice system where diversion appears at many levels. We have already (Chapters Eleven and Thirteen) discussed some general preventative measures, but labelling directs attention to more individualised methods of diversion, such as cautioning and diversion from custody. Each of these is attractive to the authorities because it reduces labelling, but also because it is cheaper to deal with people in less formal ways and to punish them in the community rather than incarcerate them. Cautioning is a logical extension of the labelling theory: the individual no longer becomes heavily involved in the criminal justice system and is no longer labelled by others as an offender. Official cautioning demonstrates that offending will not escape official control whilst allowing the individual a second chance of averting a public and stigmatising label.

Despite its positive intention of diverting offenders, particularly young and new offenders, away from the system, diversion of this sort has major problems for any criminal justice system. First, it is secret and so it is very difficult to be sure that non-discriminatory reasons are being used for decisions. The Macpherson report (1999) suggested that such prejudice might be endemic in the decision-making processes of official agencies. However, many of these decisions as they affect young offenders are taken by Youth Offender Teams where a number of agencies are represented leaving less space for prejudice and at least an objective reason must be found for the decision and all facets aired. Secrecy also raises uncertainty that the individual, who must admit the offence before a caution can be used, has done so freely. Pressure may be brought, even if only that with the admission the individual will be released and very little else will be done. Moreover, it is not always clear why one offence is diverted and another is not, which, together with wide differences in diversion rates from one force to another, makes for unacceptable inconsistency. The final problem is that diversion, far from preventing individuals from being officially treated, has actually widened the net of the criminal justice system: many who would previously have been dealt with on the street are now brought into the station for official recognition (for a full consideration see 13.8.3 and Cohen (1985)). On this analysis a process which was intended to reduce the numbers of those officially recognised and labelled has led to more people being involved and labelled.

Similarly, the intention of diversion from custody was to avoid the heavy stig-matising effect of incarceration (and also perhaps to save money because punish-ment in the community is a cheaper alternative). Various alternative punishments have been made available: community service (now community punishment) for those who are 16 and over; probation (now community rehabilitation) for those who are 16 and over (now a sentence of the court). In addition there is: the attendance centre order for those between 10 and 20; supervision orders for those between 10 and 17; drug abstinence orders; and drug treatment and testing; cur-few orders with or without electronic monitoring (tagging). Each of these allows the offender to be diverted away from incarceration which in theory would reduce the stigma and labelling. Unfortunately many commentators suggest that they have had the opposite effect. The reason is again net-widening (see 13.8.3)). Although these measures may divert the individual from the most controlling aspects of the criminal justice system they have led to deeper intrusion over much greater periods resulting in more people being controlled at any one time. At the same time, there has been almost no reduction in the incarcerated population, suggesting that those who are being punished in the community may be those who would previously simply have been fined. Again the effects are not promising.

There may be other more positive effects. The labelling perspective should encourage careful consideration not simply of the characteristics of offenders but of society more generally, and the social, economic and physical aspects causing these problems. More importantly if the factors in 14.2.4 are to be accepted then it should lead to an alteration in the way in which people are conditioned to think about young people generally and those who carry out antisocial and criminal acts in particular. It may be that the wider society is, if not causing the problem, at least exacerbating it and that we should address this issue before turning to harsh punishments and defining individuals as evil.

Finally reintegrative shaming shows a concrete way in which the theory might find expression. Possibly even the embracing of republican theory would bring a more positive outcome. One of the most important elements of labelling theory is its recognition of the danger in pigeon-holing people rather than recognising and respecting their individuality.

14.3 Phenomenology and ethnomethodology

14.3.1 Introduction

These theories provided a drastic critique of established sociological views. They undermined positivist ideas by challenging the basis on which they sat, and replacing them with something totally different. They rejected virtually all socio-logical ideas which had to that date been used, and almost all methods of socio-logical study. In fact, many argued that the shift went too far and was therefore of little use. Nonetheless, it seemed to hit a nerve because it made many people question the limits to the extent that sociology can be objective and scientific in character.

14.3.2 **Phenomenology**

Of these two theories, ethnomethodology relates more directly to criminology, but since it was largely derived from phenomenology a brief treatment of the latter can help our understanding. Phenomenology was a concept developed by the German philosopher Edmund Husserl (1859–1938). Although quite complex (Kolakowski, 1974, provides an accessible account) the essentials for our limited purpose can be briefly stated. In philosophy, it is the study of the psychic awareness that accompanies experience and which, it is claimed is the source of all meaning for the individual. It is a study of that which appears to be the case. Phenomena are the experiences which are available to people as they explore the world around them with their senses and their imagination, thought and consciousness. It thus examines the way in which things are grasped by an individual's consciousness.

Phenomenology sees all action as intended, that is to say, that people choose their behaviour in terms of goals, projects, reasons, motives, purposes etc., which they have in their minds. This means that a person's mind or consciousness is intended; in other words, it is conscious of or about something. In its simplest form, then, we can always say what it is we are conscious of; we can put a name to it. Even if we only say it is uncertain or muddled, we have named it, and in this sense can always name the object of our consciousness or of our intention. The intention of the mind or consciousness is necessarily very closely related to the actions, which it substantially controls. It is also related to, and influenced by, the society within which the person lives. The intentions of individuals are modified, endorsed or defeated by others in that society with whom they have contact.

Phenomenology takes these intentional objects and, firstly, tries to define the intentions or meanings experienced by individuals and to relate them to the objects which gave rise to them. For example, if the intention or meaning is fear, then the intentional object is that which is feared. Secondly, phenomenology uses this description to construct or constitute the process by which the specific meanings arise in the person's mind or consciousness. If an individual performs any action, theft for example, then the phenomenologist relates that action or theft back to the views and meanings held by that person at each stage of the process which leads up to the theft.

From this it can be seen that the phenomenologist is trying to do something very different from that done by most sociologists. He is trying to question the whole process of sociological theorising. He tries to comprehend how people come to have the experiences they do have. The phenomenologist intends to put into language the typical experiences of the everyday world experienced by typical people for typical reasons.

14.3.3 **Ethnomethodology**

Ethnomethodology draws upon these phenomenological concepts and methods in order to describe social occurrences. Rather than a theory it is a general method, used in criminology and all other areas of sociological study. It does not purport to give explanations of criminality, although application of its methods may lead to greater understanding of the area. It seeks to give an accurate account of what has occurred or is occurring in any social interaction, and to provide a sense of structure for the interaction itself. Essentially, it is concerned with the sociological study of everyday activities by concentrating on the methods used by individuals to report their common-sense practical actions to others. Its interest is centred on how the individual experiences and makes sense of social interaction. For ethnomethodology, the experience of the person actually involved in the activity is essential: my world as I see it is the one which will allow an understanding of what I do.

Unlike phenomenology, where everything has to be questioned rather than accepted, ethnomethodology starts from how things are viewed by the ordinary person, whose perceptions are thus accepted as they appear, and not questioned. There is an assumption that if another person could swap places with me, and have exactly the knowledge I have, then they would see the world as I see it, share my interests and understandings and, more importantly, act as I do and *vice versa*. This is not to argue that there is no structure to life, but rather that the structure can only be understood in its context and by taking account of the thoughts, actions and knowledge of the participants.

The ethnomethodologists, unlike other earlier criminologists, view the social structure as part of the understanding of the activity. They generally accept that there is a basic structure to everyday life, and that most people's activities in any day are largely predictable or taken for granted. Nonetheless, they argue that since the social structure is understood slightly differently by each individual, no real understanding can come of what has occurred until the social structure which exists for that person, how they view the world, is also understood. These meanings they see as being essential to an understanding of human behaviour. For example, murder is always the same action, but rarely do two murders have the same meaning. If John kills Mary, he may do it in order to escape from the scene of a crime; he may do it to prevent her escape from a crime (a police officer); he may do it as an act of passion; he may do it as a drunken driver; he may do it as a freedom fighter or a terrorist; he may do it as a soldier. In all these instances he may perceive his act in one way; the control authorities may perceive it in another; and different sectors of society may perceive the act in still different ways.

To ignore these perceptions, particularly that of the actor, is to rob the act of its meaning and possibly to misunderstand or fail to understand the crime. Take a seemingly wanton killing where the parties are unknown to one another. It may be that if we ask the perpetrator he or she will explain that the crime was committed for political reasons and was justly done to undermine an unjust system. The dead person is then a casualty in the war, a necessary loss to obtain a greater good. The control agencies in the State in which the crime was committed, or against which the crime was committed, may term it an act of terrorism, an assassination, or treason. They will probably also claim that there is no reason for the violence and that its perpetrator is a common criminal, not a political prisoner or a prisoner of war (the situation in Northern Ireland). By such denials, the meaning of the act for the perpetrator is also denied, and the criminal is portrayed as a vicious and dangerous person who kills for no rational reason. Others, either individuals or States, may wholly support one of these meanings or accept partial explanations from each. For example, they may understand and accept the meaning given by the criminal, i.e., the political nature of the act, but deny the use of violence to support it. All this gives a crude idea of the intentions of the ethnomethodologists especially: in the example, the different positions are easily defined; normally they would not be so obvious. To criminology, the most important element of the ethnomethodologists' work is practical and involves clear interpretations of the positions, actions and thoughts of the actors in the crime.

The above description only covers the part of the method of the ethnomethodologist known as indexicality—any human activity is interpreted differently depending upon the context in which it is seen or the position of the viewer. A specific illustration of the use and implication of the approach is seen in its profound questioning of criminal statistics. It had long been accepted that the statistics did not represent the full criminal population or even the full catalogue of criminal incidents; that there was a large and worrying dark figure of crime statistics. Nonetheless, these statistics had been portrayed as reasonably objective and able to act as a reliable basis for indicating trends in crime and suggesting associations. Phenomenology and ethnomethodology questioned this interpretation of the statistics, which they saw as the result of interpretation by those in authority and of social organisation. If, in the past, the statistics had been treated as clear and unquestionable indications of such matters as the crime rate, they were now to be viewed as just one interpretation of the world. It is therefore important to follow the numbers back to see how they are constructed. For example, criminal statistics partly record and reflect the routine occurrences in the courtroom or in the police station. Thus, in the courts the staff will categorise and standardise their work so that the cases are more predictable and more easily dealt with. They will try to force all cases into categories. To understand the statistics is to understand the people who made them as much as their subject matter. To accept them without this questioning is to miss a very important element of their make-up. Indexicality requires that a similar process be entered into in most other studies of human behaviour, including the criminological.

Ethnomethodologists press beyond this, recognising, for example, that some interpretations given by actors may not give meaning to the act if they are constructed after the event, after the individual has reflected upon the action. They may be constructed for the audience or to help the individual to accept the action himself. Criminals often construct self-deceiving reasons for their actions in order to neutralise the action and perhaps to hide the real reason even from themselves.

Ethnomethodologists also question the interpretation of certain actions as typical of certain patterns of behaviour or structures. Garfinkel (1967) called this documentary interpretation. Many theorists, researchers and control agents have tended to make a leap from superficial appearances to identifying someone as a trouble-maker, a delinquent etc. By thus earmarking him they diminish the importance of the difficult and possibly conflicting social, political and economic factors which may be involved. In this way, criminal identities are imputed to individuals by various control agencies. The ethnomethodologistis interested to discover and describe how such imputations are arrived at.

The other area of interest in this context is that of rules or social norms. The argument here is that there is no such thing as a rule outside its social setting or its social interaction; it needs that interaction to give it meaning. As people in various social contexts come together, their interactions form into patterns which are then recognised as having a life of their own. By this understanding of the world, social order is people in a social context giving meaning to otherwise meaningless situations and thus making order out of chaos. One consequence is that phenomenology and ethnomethodology recognise that there is not one social order but many—schools, hospitals, courts, prisons, peer groups, families, communes etc., as well as many smaller social interactions such as that between prostitutes and clients, or between police and accused. The setting in which a thing occurs may be vital to the way in which it is viewed: in one it may be deviant while in another it is normal. From this viewpoint, behaviour outside the general pattern is difficult to interpret: its perpetrators may be ignored or avoided as harmless; or they may be seen as threatening, and so be labelled as dangerous and deviant. If A knocks B to the ground with a punch in a boxing ring, A is the winner and, in some people's eyes, a hero; if it occurs on the streets as part of a pub brawl, it is a crime, and A is a criminal to be punished. If it occurs in the home between husband and wife, then again it is a crime, but A is far less likely to be convicted and punished, and he, and many others, will consider it is a private incident between himself and his wife; and the police may be reluctant to get involved both for this reason and because they suspect that the wife will refuse to give evidence or will change her statement in court. The setting is important. It is argued that in this way the building up of rules can be studied, and the categories of deviant and criminal might be better understood.

In the criminal law some of these methods can be used to question the justice of what goes on at each stage of the proceedings. For example, suppose a person pleads guilty at trial to assault involving actual bodily harm. He may accept that he did hit the victim and is therefore technically guilty. At this point the court is only interested in the facts for the purposes of sentencing, and will call on the police to state the circumstances of the offence. The police may give a set of 'facts' about the incident quite different to the incident as seen by the offender, and may not give evidence which may reduce the blameworthiness of his action. At this point the offender generally has no opportunity of setting the record straight, as it is assumed that the guilty plea is to the facts as seen by the police. The defence lawyer is given the opportunity to speak, but often does not say what the offender wants laid before the court. He usually only addresses mitigating factors and not the facts, and although the judge can invite the offender to speak, this is rare. The law, or the legal players in the court, have denied the offender the opportunity of setting his or her perception of events before the court. This may distort the court's actions in sentencing the offender. The criminal justice system is neater without this complication; after all, the offender is guilty.

14.3.4 Evaluation

In this area of study the way in which individuals make sense of their own world and actions is of paramount importance. But in everyday life there is not normally time, nor is there the need, for people fully to examine or recognise their thought-processes, nor would they necessarily recognise any description of these. The fierce difficulties of validating or testing the description is a major obstacle to the widespread use of this approach.

The methods of the phenomenologists and ethnomethodologists could still be used by other sociologists to test their own work for personal and subjective weighting. They could be particularly useful in delineating the way in which certain words and phrases are used. Sociologists tend to use words such as rules, norms, delinquent, or criminal without always defining exactly what they mean by those words. The reader is left to use commonsense (or perhaps prejudice) to perceive the concept, and this perception may not match the author's intentions. Even if readers successfully hit on the intended usage, their construction of it may be different from that of the author. Properly applied, the approach can give more precision to empirical sociological study. For example, is the phrase 'labelling process' a term that those studied would use, or is it a sociological construct? If it is a construct, then do all sociologists use it in the same way, and what phenomena were referred to by the people in the study that the sociologist subsumed under this phrase?

Traditional criminology has largely ignored ethnomethodology and phenomenology because the practical ends are not obvious, and because the reflexive need to question their own research is both awkward and timeconsuming. The most that is usually done is to warn of the dangers of taking, for example, official statistics at their face value; and often the writers then go on to do just that. For these reasons, phenomenology is usually thought of as interesting but irrelevant. Many traditional criminologists would argue that there is a reality which can be discovered from a study of society and that constantly to question this is both unnecessary and unproductive. Each time it was done it would need to be re-tested in, logically, an endless process. Some deduce from this that if we are interested in such questions as who becomes criminal and why, then, for practical reasons, it is necessary to start from the world as it is. To this, the ethnomethodologists would reply that there is no such thing as one real world or one social reality; it depends upon the person, context, time and place.

The two views seem to be totally incompatible, and yet each has some element of truth. Accepting the absolutist view strips each occurrence of its particular facts and each actor of his particular reasons. The object is to search for general explanations, but this can distort the actual activity and force too much explanation under one head. Accepting the ethnomethodologist makes impossible any general understanding of particular actions; each must be described in its particular context and from the particular view of one person. It therefore makes it difficult to look at issues in their generality, to typify them and to study their distribution. Neither is a perfect method, but each has something to offer, so it is perhaps unfortunate that the phenomenological method has been almost totally ignored in favour of the simpler and more obviously practical absolutist methods.

As indicated earlier, the time when it is most dangerous to deny the individual position, and therefore to deny ethnomethodology, is when it should be used to challenge the way in which those in authority use their power to force individuals and actions into categories without giving full weight to the meaning and explanations of the people who actually carry out the activity.

14.3.5 **Phenomonology, symbolic interactionism and emotion in crime**

One of the foremost writers in this newly emerging field is Jack Katz and this section will focus on his work. In the *Seductions of Crime* (1988) Katz questions the approach of most theories of the causes of crimes, which he claims tend to concentrate on the background to offences and fail to understand the immediate issues of the drives to criminality at the time it is committed. He seeks to tease out the meaning in the activity of crime at the time and place at which it is committed, and particularly the meaning the crime has for the criminal at that point, using materials produced by the criminals themselves, (biographies, autobiographies, journalistic accounts as well as participant observation studies) he seeks to discover the immediate and, he believes, true explanation for the activity. This, and the nature of the material, involves him in comments on emotional meaning although as most of his data is produced after the criminal activity there is likely to be some unintentional alteration in emotional representation from that actually felt by the offenders at the time. He seeks to explain the drive or emotion in five offence groups: youthful property offences; gang violence; persistent robbery; murders of passion; and cold blooded murder. In each of these types of offence he suggests that the offender is trying to accomplish something (task) by committing the crime and that the task is tied in with morality—right and wrong, justice and injustice. The morality is tied to emotions such as humiliation, ridicule, arrogance, shame due to perceived incompetence, cynicism, vengeance, arrogance, righteous anger which are felt by the offender at the time of the crime and the crime is an attempt to transcend the moral emotional feeling and take back moral equilibrium. The act of restoring moral equilibrium is accompanied by an emotional thrill whilst performing the crime—this may manifest itself as sensual, as a high, as fulfilment but is always strong and compelling, satisfying.

Put briefly, he sees that property offenders, particularly shoplifters, often engage in the activity to escape the shame of perceived incompetence and to prove they are capable. Those who engage in persistent robbery are taking control of their lives in an aggressive way as a reaction to large areas of their lives where they lack control. In passion killings the killer reacts to humiliation and is filled with righteous anger. Cold-blooded murderers feel that they have been denigrated and/or defiled by members of society and not given protection: eventually they murder one member as an act of vengeance or to restore some justice—making the community/society pay through the death of one of its numbers. Each of the emotional triggers might be said to be bedded in shame of one kind or another. The later work (e.g., Katz (1999) and (2002 b)) both develops this and argues a more complex thesis where shame alone is not necessarily a sufficient trigger for criminal behaviour, which requires complex emotions.

On first reading these appear to be associated with Tittle's (1995) suggestion that the underlying reason for the offence is the control each offender experiences and the crime is a bid to escape that control, the emotions arise due to the control being forced onto the offender. Although this is an important and central aspect in Katz's thesis another central focus of his work is the phenomenological aspect. He attacks other theorists because they suggest causal elements which cannot be verified by or linked to the observable behaviour and, in particular, are not linked to the phenomenon, the particular criminal act, involved. From this phenomenological approach he set up a theory in which firstly, strong emotions arise as a result of symbolic interactionism (labelling, maybe internal, but which often denigrates the individual for powerlessness); secondly, the crime becomes a project or task, a practical course of action; and thirdly, there is the action, the corporeal processes, the interactions of individuals with others and with their surroundings, For the criminal the crime often represents a search for right and justice for themselves.

His explorations of meaning necessarily leads to individualised interactions of sets of causal connectors, most of which are bedded in emotion and played out against a backdrop, which is moral for the individual. In this he posits a genuinely phenomenological approach and explanation. His centring of emotion should not be allowed to suggest that he sees the criminal activities as uncontrollable acts, nor even that those who feel over-controlled will necessarily see criminal activity as a way of securing more control. He also explores the management of emotion and other (artistic or aesthetic) uses for emotions. Interestingly in doing this he puts less stress on social regulations which might arise through laws, social mores, manners etc. and more on their management by and for the individual.

The exploration of the emotion is an area that needs extended criminological exploration and should be used to question deeply some facets which are shaping practice and driving policy. For example, fear of crime is an assumed and seemingly measurable element which has been used to drive through more control and harsher punishments but what is it? How does it manifest itself and why? When is it felt and by whom? Is it something that is suggested and caused by the researcher asking the questions or bringing crime to the fore? Similarly we might visit shame in more detail, asking how and when it arises, its relation to the commission of, and what sort of, crime. How does it impact on the reporting and giving of evidence? Does it cause the 'story' to be altered or the meaning or truth as understood by the witness to be altered, maybe subconsciously, in order to hide or reduce the shame? How do we cope with all the different facets of shame, anger etc? (see also Stanko (2002) and Katz (2002b)). How are the emotions and their responses tied up with media and the market (see Ferrell et al. (2001)? There are many unanswered questions on the impact of emotions on crime and its control.

14.4 Left idealism

Left idealism has grown out of labelling perspectives, and to a lesser extent the phenomenological movement, which had began and largely flourished in the USA whereas left idealism is a largely European movement (see Cohen 1998)). Rather than claiming that there is a labelling perspective shaping the criminal law and its implementation these theorists see the influence of those in power in a far more all-encompassing way. The State and those who shape it touch not only the criminal justice system but all aspects of life and do not just set out the rules but influence the way of thinking of all those in a society. By shaping the way of thinking they also structure the behaviour of the people. The criminal justice system is there to deal with those who fail to conform, to coerce them into conformity. The reason that there are more poor than rich in the system is the result, first, of defining lower-class behaviour as criminal and, secondly, because of biases in arrest and other aspects of the criminal justice system.

On this reading all the agencies of the State and the powerful—government, schools, the media—are utilised to convince the masses that capitalist, patriarchal and racial protectionist perspectives are necessary to their well-being and to the survival of society and of themselves. Images are constructed of how 'normal' members of society should behave: compliant, contented and accepting their position in society. These images are deemed to be excessively simple, ignoring the pluralistic reality of cultural diversity, sexual difference, diverse family models, racial and class difference. Attempts to undermine this conformity are rejected by labelling any variation as deviant and investing the State agencies of social control with the job of ensuring that all conform either by persuasion (the media and the school) or by coercion (the criminal justice system).

Left idealists see no real causes of crime, but certain types of behaviour are constructed as criminal by the powerful in society. The behaviours so labelled will tend to be those most commonly associated with the less powerful in a society. The criminal law is here constructed not in order to prevent crime but to discover it amongst the lower classes who will be divided against themselves and fear crime from amongst their own number. The powerless will be persuaded to attack crime as the most important evil, leaving the powerful to their own activities, however unjust, unhindered by constraints (Cohen (1998)). The function of the criminal justice system is then not to solve crime but to unite the people against certain individuals, defined as deviant, and so to retain the legitimacy of the underlying social order. Prisons are not there to reform criminals but rather to stigmatise them and cause them to be viewed as the enemy (see Foucault (1980)). Police are not there to prevent and apprehend criminals but rather to retain the social order, being used to control strikes, demonstrations or any other activities which threaten to undermine the community as defined and constructed. They are also used to widen the net of social control so that it captures more of those who are seen as possible deviants. Finally, in order to do this, the authorities, particularly the police, will need to be invested with the necessary powers and relatively free of control: accountability to local and national governments is otiose when it is their interests which are being served (Van Swaaningen (1997)).

This view of social order, of law and of the criminal justice system seems all too simplistic and focused. It denies the reality which most people experience. The individual nature of criminality is not just a construction by the State and most criminal behaviour is not directed against the constructed social order. Similarly the criminal law is not just directed at keeping the less powerful in their place. Most of this group need the criminal law for protection. They are commonly the victims as well as the perpetrators of criminal activity. They use the criminal law and enforcement agencies to protect them. The left idealists ignore the fact that most in a society would support the prohibition of most of the behaviour which is defined to be criminal. All this is not to deny that there are definitions of illegality which show social control by the powerful and a reluctance to control their own activities. It is the fundamentalism of left idealism which is in question.

Left idealism picks up on labelling theory and tries to invest it with a single-minded construction of society as a whole. In this it fails but it does usefully draw attention to the possibility that labelling might be part of a wider interest, intended rather than accidental. It is thus likely to be more illuminating in discussions about particular aspects of the criminal justice system rather than as a guide to the nature and origin of the system as a whole.

SUGGESTED READING

Becker, H. (1963), *Outsiders: Studies in the Sociology of Deviance*, New York: The Free Press.

Farrell, J. and Hamm, M. (1998) (eds), *Ethnography at the Edge: Crime Deviance and Field Research*, Boston, MA: Northeastern University Press.

Johnstone, G. (2003), *A Restorative Justice Reader: Texts, Sources, Context*, Cullompton: Willan Publishing.

Katz, J. (1988), *Seductions of Crime: Moral and Sensual Attractions in Doing Evil*, New York: Basic Books.

Plummer, K. (1979), 'Misunderstanding Labelling Perspectives', in D. Downes and P. Rock (eds), *Deviant Interpretations*, Oxford: Oxford University Press.

QUESTIONS FOR REVISIONS

1   What role do lawmakers and those who work in the criminal justice system play in deviance and criminality?

2   In what way does the 'truth' and reality of institutions differ from that of individuals who are caught up in crime?

3   How might repressive and/or overly punitive regimes increase deviant and criminal behaviour rather than reduce it?

4   What are the key elements of reintegrative shaming? Are these elements respected when it is applied? How might reintegrative shaming be linked to labelling theory?

5   Why is it important to take account of the way in which individuals and communities interpret and socially construct their world? What might the criminal law, evidence and crime control learn from such an approach?

6   Consider how Katz's theory helps to expand understanding of crime and its commission. Is the study of emotion important in law-making, commission of crime, crime control, punishment, media representations and learning how to better adapt society so as to gain lower levels of crime? Is it only useful in some of these aspects?

REFERENCES

Alford, S. (1997), 'Professionals Need Not Apply', *Corrections Today*, vol. 59, p. 104.

Becker, Howard, S. (1963 and 1973), *Outsiders: Studies in the Sociology of Deviance*, 1st and 2nd edns, London: Macmillan.

Braithwaite, J. (1988), *Crime, Shame and Reintegration*, Cambridge: Cambridge University Press.

Braithwaite, J. (1994), 'Conditions of Successful Reintegration Ceremonies', *British Journal of Criminology*, vol. 34, p. 139.

Braithwaite, J. (2000a), 'Restorative Justice', in M Tonry (ed.), *The Handbook of Crime and Punishment*, Oxford: Oxford University Press.

Braithwaite, J. (2000b), 'Republican Theory, The Good Society and Crime Control', in S. Karstedt and K.D. Bussman (eds), *Social Dynamics of Crime and Control: New Theories for a World in Transition*, Oxford: Hart Publishing.

Braithwaite, J. and Pettit, P. (1990), *Not Just Desserts: A Republican Theory of Criminal Justice*, Oxford: Oxford University Press.

Cohen, S. (1998), 'Intellectual Scepticism and Political Commitment: The Case of Radical Criminology', in P. Walton and J. Young (eds), *The New Criminology Revised*, Basingstoke: Macmillan.

Commission for Racial Equality (2002), *A Plan for Us All: Learning from Bradford, Oldham and Burnley*, London: Commission for Racial Equality.

Commission for Racial Equality (2003), *A Formal Investigation by the Commission for Racial Equality into HM Prison Service of England and Wales—Part 1: The Murder of Zahid Mubarek*, London: Commission for Racial Equality.

De Haan, W. (2000), 'Explaining the Absence of Violence: A Comparative Approach', in S. Karstedt and K-D Bussmann (eds), *Social Dynamics of Crime and Control*, Oxford: Hart Publishing.

Dignan, J. (1999), 'The Criminal Justice Act and the Prospect for Restorative Justice', *Criminal Law Review*, p. 48.

Ekblom (2000), 'The Conjunction of Criminal Opportunity', in S. Ballintyne, K. Pease and V. McLaren (eds), *Secure Foundations: Key Issues in Crime Prevention, Crime Reduction and Community Safety*, Southampton: Institute for Public Policy Research.

Ferrell, J., Milovanovic, D. and Lyng, S. (2001), 'Edgework, Media Practices, and the Elongation of Meaning: A Theoretical Ethnography of the Bridge Day Event', *Theoretical Criminology*, vol. 5(2), p. 177.

Forsythe, Lubica (1994), 'Evaluation of Family Group Conference Cautioning Program in Wagga, NSW', Conference Paper Presented to the Australian and New Zealand Society of Criminology 10th Annual Conference.

Foucault, Michel (1980), 'On Popular Justice', in *Power/Knowledge*, trans. and ed. C. Gordon, Brighton: Harvester.

Garfinkel, Harold (1967), *Studies in Ethnomethodology*, New Jersey: Prentice Hall.

Hillyard and Tombs (2001), *Criminology, Zemiology and Justice*, Paper presented to the SLSA Bristol 4–6 April 2001.

Halpern, D. (2001), 'Moral Values, Social Thrust and Inequality', *British Journal of Criminology*, vol. 41, p. 236.

Hood, Roger (1992), *Race and Sentencing: A Study in the Crown Court*, Oxford: Clarendon Press.

Hudson, J., Morris, A., Maxwell, G. and Galaway, B. (1996), *Family Group Conferences*, Annandale, Australia: Federation Press.

Husserl, E. (1964), *The Paris Lectures*, The Hague: Martinus Nijhoff.

Johnstone, G. (2001), *Restorative Justice: Ideas, Values and Debates*, Cullompton: Willan Publishing.

Johnstone, G. (2003), *A Restorative Justice Reader: Texts, Sources, Context*, Cullompton: Willan Publishing.

Katz, J. (1988), *Seductions of Crime: Moral and Sensual Attractions in Doing Evil*, New York: Basic Books

Katz, J. (1999), *How Emotions Work*, Chicago, IL: University of Chicago Press.

Katz, J. (2002a), 'Social Ontology and Research Strategy', *Theoretical Criminology*, vol. 6(3), p. 255

Katz, J. (2002b), 'Response to Commentators', *Theoretical Criminology*, vol. 6(3), p. 375.

Kolakowski, Lesek (1974), *Husserl and the Search for Certitude*, New Haven, CN: Yale University Press.

Kritzman, Lawrence D. (ed.), trans. Alan Sheridan and others, (1988), *Michel Foucault: Politics, Philosophy, Culture, Interviews and other Writings 1977–1984*, London: Routledge.

Lemert, Edwin M. (1951), *Social Pathology*, New York: McGraw-Hill.

Levi, M. (2000), 'Shaming and the Regulation of Fraud and Business Misconduct: Some Preliminary Explanation', in S. Karstedt and K.D. Bussman (eds), *Social Dynamics of Crime and Control: New Theories for a World in Transition*, Oxford: Hart Publishing.

Link, B. (1987), 'Understanding Labeling Effects of Mental Disorders: An Assessment of the Effects of Expectations of Rejection', *American Sociological Review*, vol. 52, p. 96.

Link, B., Cullen, F., Frank, J. and Wozniak, J. (1987), 'The Social Reaction of Former Mental Patients: Understanding Why Labels Work', *American Journal of Sociology*, vol. 92, p. 1461.

Link, B., Cullen, F., Struening, E., Shrout, P. and Dohrenwend, B. (1989), 'A Modified Labeling Theory Approach to Mental Disorders: An Empirical Assessment', *American Sociological Review*, vol. 54, p. 400 (1987).

Mackay, R.E. and Moody, S.R. (1994), *Neighbourhood Disputes in the Criminal Justice System*, Edinburgh: Scottish Office, Central Research Unit, HMSO.

Mackay, R.E. and Moody, S.R. (1996), 'Diversion of Neighbourhood Disputes to Community Mediation', *The Howard Journal*, vol. 35(4), p. 299.

Macpherson of Cluny, Sir W. (1999), *The Stephen Lawrence Inquiry: Report of an Inquiry by Sir William Macpherson of Cluny*, Cm 4262, London: HMSO.

Matsueda, R.L. (1992), 'Reflected Appraisals, Parental Labelling and Delinquency', *American Journal of Sociology*, vol. 97, pp. 1577–611.

Maxwell, G. and Morris, A. (2001), 'Putting Restorative Justice into Practice for Adult Offenders', *Howard Journal of Criminal Justice*, vol. 40, p. 55.

McRobbie, A. (1994), 'Folk Devils Fight Back', *New Left Review*, vol. 203, p. 107.

Meossi, D. (2000), 'Changing Representations of the Criminal', *British Journal of Criminology*, vol. 40, p. 296.

Miers, D. (2001), *An International Review of Restorative Justice*, London: Home Office.

Miers, D., Maguire, M., Goldie, S., Sharpe, K., Hale, C., Netten, A., Uglow, S., Doolin, K., Hallam, A., Enterkin, J. and Newburn, T. (2001), *An Exploratory Evaluation of Restorative Justice*, London: Home Office

Morris, Allison, Maxwell, Gabrielle M. and Robertson, Jeremy P. (1993), 'Giving Victims a Voice: A New Zealand Experiment', *Howard Journal of Criminal Justice*, vol. 32, p. 304.

Morris, A. and Maxwell, G. (2001) (eds), *Restorative Justice for Juveniles: Conferencing, Mediation and Circles*, Oxford: Hart Publishing.

Musto, D. (1973), *The American Disease: Origins of Narcotics Control*, New Haven, CN: Yale University Press.

Rose, N. (2000), 'Government and Control', *British Journal of Criminology*, vol. 40, p. 321.

Sherman, P. (1992), 'The Variable Effect of Arrest on Criminal Careers: The Milwaukee Domestic Violence Experiment', *Journal of Criminal Law and Criminal Justice*, vol. 83, p. 1.

Simpson, S.S., Lyn Exum, M. and Smith, N.C. (2000), 'The Social Control of Corporate Criminals: Shame and Informal Sanction Threats', in S.S. Simpson (ed.), *Of Crime and Criminality: The Use of Theory in Everyday Life*, Thousand Oaks CA: Pine Forge.

Stanko, E.A. (2002), 'Symposium Discussion of J. Katz, *How Emotions Work*', *Theoretical Criminology*, vol. 6(3), p. 366.

Strang, Heather (1993), 'Conferencing: A New Paradigm in Community Policing', Paper delivered to the Annual Conference of the Association of Chief Police Officers.

Strang, II. (2002), *Repair and Revenge: Victims and Restorative Justice*, Oxford: Clarendon Press.

Strang, H. and Braithwaite, J. (2002) (eds), *Restorative Justice and Family Violence*, Cambridge: Cambridge University Press.

Tannenbaum, Frank (1938), *Crime and the Community*, New York: Colombia University Press.

Thrasher, Frederick (1936), *The Gang*, 2nd edn, Chicago, IL: University of Chicago Press.

Tifft, L. (1995), 'Social Harm Definitions of Crime' *Critical Criminologist*, vol. 7(1), p. 9.

Triplett, R. (2000), 'The Dramatisation of Evil: Reacting to Juvenile Delinquency During the 1990s', in S.S. Simpson (ed.), *Of Crime and Criminality: The Use of Theory in Everyday Life*, Thousand Oaks CA: Pine Forge Press.

van Swaaningen, R. (1997), *Critical Criminology: Visions from Europe*, London: Sage.

Vold, George, B. and Bernard, Thomas, J. (1986), *Theoretical Criminology*, 3rd edn, New York: Oxford University Press.

von Hirsch, A., Roberts, J., Bottoms, A.E., Roach, K. and Schiff, M. (eds) (2003), *Restorative Justice and Criminal Justice: Competing of Reconcilable Paradigms?*, Oxford: Hart Publishing.

Walgrave, L. (ed.) (2002), *Restorative Justice and the Law*, Cullompton: Willan Publishing.

Walker, Nigel (1973), 'Caution: Some Thoughts on the Penal Involvement Rate', in Louis Blom-Cooper (ed.) (1974), *Progress in Penal Reform*, Oxford: Clarendon Press.

WeiteKamp, E.G.M. and Kerner, H-J. (eds) (2002), *Restorative Justice: Theoretical Foundations*, Cullompton: Willan Publishing.

WeiteKamp, E.G.M. and Kerner, H-J. (eds) (2003), *Restorative Justice in Context: International Practice and Directions*, Cullompton: Willan Publishing.

Whillock, R.K. and Slayden, D. (eds) (1995), *Hate Speech*, Thousand Oaks, CA: Sage.

Young, R. and Goold, B. (1999), 'Restorative Police Cautioning in Aylesbury—From Degrading to Shaming Ceremonies', *Criminal Law Review*, p. 126.

15

Conflict theories and radical criminologies

15.1 Introduction

Mainstream or traditional criminology which, as has been seen, had dominated criminological study up until the 1960s, is largely rejected by the conflict and radical criminologists who will be discussed in this section. Traditional criminology was pragmatic, had little theoretical discussion, a strong correctional bias, a pathological interest in criminals and a weak reformist interest. Its proponents tended to be drawn from psychologists, psychiatrists and forensic scientists with a few conventional sociologists drawn in, and the work centred around clinical positivist studies. All this was to be questioned and often rejected by the conflict theorists, and wholly rejected by the early radical criminologists. But although they broke with the old or traditional criminology, their perspectives were not entirely new and drew upon earlier theorists, such as Marx, who will be considered here. Others, some of whom we have looked at in earlier chapters, had anticipated or suggested much of what was to come. For example, Mays (1954) and Morris (1957) both studied the confrontation between working-class values and the structure of middle-class authority (see 11.4), and could be seen as forerunners of the new criminologists.

Many of the writers to be discussed in this chapter were heavily influenced by the interactionist and phenomenological perspectives (see Chapter Fourteen) which had also challenged mainstream criminology. Radical and conflict criminologists drew on their rejection of the consensus model, on their focusing of discussion on the meaning of crime, and on their move away from a study of the individual pathology of convicted criminals. However, they rejected the interactionist tendency to accept the class *status quo*, as well as what they saw as the interactionist failure to deal with the use of power to control people. The new criminologists went on to suggest a possible alternative, which they argued would be more humane.

15.2 Conflict theories

15.2.1 Introduction

Most theories so far considered are based on the order, or consensus, idea—social order is the consensus of the people in that society. The conflict view gives more recognition to the fact that within any sizable society there are groups with conflicting needs and values. From this emerges a general discussion of the struggle which may arise over power, status and the desirable, but often scarce, resources of society. The conflict may be between individuals and/or groups. For reasons of exposition we have stressed the difference between views which emphasise conflict and those which emphasise consensus, but at the outset we need also to remind ourselves that there are dangers in attempting to draw too firm a distinction between these two models. It is important not to forget that each has an important place to play in the understanding of society and social interactions.

Conflict theories have a long history. Their most famous exponent was possibly Karl Marx, but the ideas of conflict go back much further. In the fourth century BC, Plato and Aristotle wrote of social disorder and conflicts within Greek politics: parts of the theories of Hobbes and Machiavelli also centred on this concept. It is obviously misleading to refer to this as a 'new' idea or perspective, but the theorists of the 1960s gave the ideas new lease of life. The present purpose is to consider certain theories which seek to describe how conflicts within society may lead to criminality, or more exactly how they explain the type of criminality which will occur. This will not involve studying the older texts, though reference will be made to some of them where they illuminate later writings.

15.2.2 **Marx, Engels and Bonger**

In the first half of the nineteenth century Marx and Engels were already predicting a collapse of the existing idea of an accepted social order (see Marx and Engels (1848), Marx (1904), and Engels (1971)). They further saw this decline as an inevitable aspect of a capitalist society. The unfair division of labour and capital would eventually lead, through conflict, to the overthrow of capitalist ideals. The State was based upon capitalism and it would have to be replaced by communism. conflict was inherent in capitalism, which promoted an unfair distribution of desired and scarce resources (housing, wealth and particularly property); that this unequal distribution would worsen over time; and that one consequence would be social conflict. For Marx and Engels such discord had a political basis: the oppressed would seek a revolutionary solution and overthrow the political oppressors. Crime was one of the means of opposing the oppressors but, for Marx in particular, it was a most imperfect form of opposition to the system.

There is an implication that if capitalism is overthrown there would be no conflict. This ignores the oppression which in the twentieth century has been committed in the name of communism. Their interpretation has other weaknesses. For example, it implies that the criminal activities of oppressed people reflect a positive, purposive, conscious and political reaction against the powerful in capitalist society. Apart from other considerations, this ignores the fact that, as was seen in Chapter Five, many victims come from the same class as the criminals. It also requires too great a political awareness and motivation from the common criminal. If there are serious drawbacks to the Marxist perspective, this should not obscure his innovative use of the concept of conflict, nor the fact that some later writers have constructively used it to suggest a cohesive basis for criminological explanation.

For example, Bonger (1969, originally published in 1916) believed strongly in the social instincts of humans. Left to themselves, people would naturally form into communities and live in social harmony, but once a system of exchange arises, people have to compete with their neighbours. In the ultimate system of exchange, capitalism, the process leads to the means of production being controlled by a few people, leaving most deprived and their economic position controlled by others. The poor are taught to seek material pleasures and are encouraged to compete against each other for this purpose. Such acute self-interest which can be expressed lawfully or through criminal action, only arises because of the capitalist State and would disappear if society were run upon other grounds. The poor might then commit crimes to address their poverty, either out of need or because of the injustice of the system. Bonger also recognised that the rich would commit crimes which might be related to a 'necessity' to protect their business or personal interests; or be related to their power, either because the power presented them with the opportunity or because it enabled them to commit crimes with relative impunity.

Bonger thus attributed many different and often quite surprising crimes to economic determinism. Clearly crimes such as theft, other property offences, political crimes (designed to obtain political power) could plausibly be related to this economic struggle. Prostitution or soliciting were similarly attributable because of the low economic status of women. Low status and their powerlessness in capitalist societies was also used to explain crimes committed against women, such as rape. Other crimes which could be included on similar arguments were infanticide, violence and domestic violence. Interestingly, the economic subjugation of women did not mean that the female crime rate was very high, and in fact Bonger argued that the economic and social liberation of women would give rise to an increase in their crime rate relative to men. As will be seen in the next chapter, recent official figures lend support to this claim, although it cannot be accepted unquestioningly.

Basically, Bonger attributed criminality to an economic determinism. He did not rule out the possibility that other factors might have some effect on it, but asserted that they could not have a causal basis in the absence of this economic determinism.

15.2.3 **Sellin**

As was seen in 10.2.3, Sutherland's theory of differential association was built on the concept of differential social organisation. It is possible to relate this to a conflict theory in that it does not assume that society is built on a consensus. Sellin's conflict theory has a similar basis. In 1938 he wrote about culture conflict which was based on the conflict of conduct norms, where each separate culture set out its own norms (rules of behaviour) and instilled them into its members. The norms learnt by any individual were therefore dictated by the culture in which that person was situated. He argued that, in a healthy homogeneous society, these were enacted into laws and upheld by the members of that society because they accepted them as right; they represented the consensus view. Where this did not occur, culture conflict would arise, and could take, Sellin saw, two forms: primary and secondary.

Primary conflicts were those which arose between two different cultures, because of border conflicts, territorial extension or, most typically, through migration.

Secondary conflicts are those which arise within one culture, particularly when it develops subcultures, each with its own conduct norms. The laws would usually represent the rules or norms of the dominant culture. The norms of other groups may even be criminal under the law, so that by living within their subculture's rules of behaviour, they may be breaking the criminal rules of the dominant culture. Note that, unlike the subcultural theories considered earlier (see 12.3), the norms of the subculture do not arise in order to question the middle- or upper-class values, or to represent a different means of achieving the cultural goals of the middle and upper classes, but rather they represent intrinsically different values and norms (see 11.4, 11.4.1).

15.2.4 Vold

Like Sellin's secondary conflicts, Vold's ideas are based on the conflicts within a culture, but instead of subcultures Vold looks at conflicts between interest groups which exist within the same cultures (Vold (1958)).

He argued that people are naturally group oriented, and those who have the same interests come together to form a group in order to push for these interests in the political arena. Unlike subcultures, these are likely to be transient, only coming into existence and only continuing in existence for as long as is required to reach their desired ends. Members become psychologically attached to groups, especially as they invest more of their time and effort in them. If the end is achieved, members will probably lose their allegiance to the group, and it may dissolve. Vold's theory thus comes from a social-psychological perspective.

Central is the idea that different groups have different and often incompatible interests which give rise to conflicts. Where groups are of a similar strength, then often these conflicts are resolved by compromise, lending stability to a society. Where they are of differing strength, one may win by using the full power of the State to enforce their interest. Where this involves the passing of a criminal law, the dominant group is backed by the police, lawyers and courts to protect its interests, whilst these same forces are used against the interests of the politically weaker groups and in some cases actually criminalise such interests. Crime is not the result of an abnormality, but rather is the natural response to an attack on their way of life, or on a way of life in which they believe.

Vold gives a number of illustrations of this type of conflict, and includes particularly crimes of political movements aimed at political reform. The ultimate example of this is a revolution in which whoever loses is the criminal—if the revolution succeeds, then the previous government is criminalised: if it fails, then the revolutionaries are criminals. From this it can be seen that such criminality has little to do with who, if anyone, is right, and more to do with winning. In the struggles to obtain the suffrage for women, many were punished as criminals. They are now more commonly seen as martyrs for the cause, in that their 'crimes' were justified because of the ends. A second category which Vold includes concern labour conflicts, either between management and labour unions which might involve certain illegal behaviours on the part of one or other—the legality of each side's actions will depend upon how successful they have been in getting their interests legally protected—or between labour unions. The final area which he mentions as giving rise to such criminal tensions is racial conflict, where there may be violence involved in the challenge to racial segregation and institutional prejudice.

Vold claims that a significant amount of criminality results from group conflicts; the crime is justifiable to reach a greater good. This approach only claims to explain this type of criminality, and does not explain individual criminality, which Vold sees as far less rational. This restriction limits the usefulness of the theory, as most criminality does not arise out of any clearly defined group interest.

15.2.5 **Dahrendorf and Turk**

Both of these writers look at the relationship between authorities and their subjects. For Dahrendorf, power is the crucial factor; whereas for Turk it is based on social status.

Dahrendorf (1959) attacked the Marxist idea for taking account of only one form of power, namely property ownership. Marx located conflict in an unjust economic system and saw it as something which could be eradicated. Dahrendorf, in contrast, saw it as located in the power differences, and especially in the distribution of authority, in a State, and as being necessary to a healthy society. All healthy societies need a difference in the levels of power or authority of the individuals, so that the cultural norms or rules can be enforced. If one is to have rules, one needs sanctions to enforce them, and to ensure that the sanctions are effective someone has to have the power to use them. This is bound to lead to conflict.

Turk (1969) also recognised that social conflict was a real and inescapable part of social life, and that someone had to be in authority. For Turk, if there was no conflict in a social order it was unhealthy. It might indicate either that there was too great a consensus in the community, or that individuals were being excessively controlled or coerced by those in power. Too much conflict would also be undesirable, as no society can be healthy without a fairly high level of consensus. Turk therefore saw social order as being based on a coercion-consensus model, and the authorities must ensure that the balance between the two is not lost.

Turk was interested in the conditions under which the cultural and social differences between authorities and subjects result in conflict. In doing this, he first distinguished between cultural norms and social norms. Cultural norms set out verbally what behaviour is or is not expected; the social norms represent what is actually being done, what the actual behaviour is. For the authorities, the cultural norms are usually laws, and the societal norms are the enforcement of those laws. For subjects, the cultural norms may be subcultural and the social norms the actual behaviour patterns of the individual. Clearly, the cultural and social norms of the authorities may differ from those of the subjects, but Turk also envisaged the possibility that within each group cultural and social norms might not correspond. He therefore saw four possible situations:

1. Authorities actually enforce the laws (so the cultural norms and social norms correspond) and the beliefs and the behaviour of the subjects are very close (again, cultural norms and social norms correspond). In this case, the cultural norms of each group are the same and there is no conflict; if they are different, there is a high degree of conflict. For example, if the State believes in banning alcohol and actually tries very actively to enforce that ban, but many of the subjects believe that it should be freely available and actively use it, then there is a very high likelihood of conflict. This is substantially what happened during prohibition in the United States of America (1920–33).

2. The authorities are very lax in their law enforcement (so that although the cultural norms exist, they are not acted upon, i.e., the social norms do not

correspond) and subjects do not act on their beliefs (again, although the cultural norms exist, the social norms do not correspond). In such a situation, the conflict potential would be very low. Until recently, this was the situation with the blasphemy laws. Although blasphemy is an offence, the authorities do not actively enforce it, and although many people do not believe in the Christian religion, they do not actively try to breach the law. If a situation does not give rise to tensions between the groups, the conflict level is low.

3. Authorities actually enforce the laws (so the cultural norms and social norms correspond) but subjects, although holding different cultural norms or beliefs, do not act upon them (although the cultural norms exist, the social norms do not correspond). Suppose the authorities imposed and enforced laws against 'soft' drugs but the subjects, although not opposed to soft drugs, made little use of them: conflict would be limited to that minority of cases where subjects did use the drugs.

4. The authorities are very lax in their law enforcement (so that although the cultural norms exist, they are not acted upon, i.e., the social norms do not correspond) but the beliefs and the behaviour of the subjects are very close (the subjects' cultural norms and social norms correspond). The State may, for example, have legislated against 'soft' drugs but does not enforce the law; and the subjects oppose the law and actively participate in the use of 'soft' drugs. The result is still lower potential for conflict than 3 above, because subjects found using the drugs are unlikely to be prosecuted.

The disjuncture between cultural and social norms is not the only factor which may induce conflict; the organisation and sophistication of both authorities and subjects also affects the degree of conflict. Authorities, other than mobs, must by their nature be organised to obtain and retain power. On the other hand, subjects often lack organisation; but those which are organised—by, for example, being members of a close-knit gang—will be better able to resist the power of the State. Turk argued that if those who were acting illegally were organised, there would be a greater conflict between them and the State. Interestingly, in sentencing an individual, the court always treats organised crime more severely, which suggests that the State sees it as more of a challenge to its authority, and therefore more threatening and worrying.

Sophistication exists when one side understands the behaviour of the other and uses that knowledge to manipulate them. If authorities are sophisticated, they will be able to persuade subjects that acting within the law is in their best interests, and hence reduce the need to rely on coercion in order to achieve obedience to the law. Sophisticated criminals will be able to hide their criminality, pretending to be law-abiding whilst acting in a criminal way; the less sophisticated will be in frequent conflict with the State. The conclusion would seem to be that the more sophisticated are both State and criminals, the less conflict would arise.

In the case of criminals Turk suggested four groupings representing four levels of conflict:

1. *Organised and unsophisticated*—for example, youth gangs. These would give rise to most conflict.
2. *Unorganised and unsophisticated*—for example, vagrants or careless individual thieves, whose crime was obvious but not threatening, and therefore less of a conflict.

3. *Organised and sophisticated*—for example, corporate criminals and some organised crime, where the crimes are less visible and the criminals less obvious. In such cases, conflict arises less often and is less likely, but the crimes are threatening and carry the potential for conflict.
4. *Unorganised and sophisticated*—for example, a lone embezzler or a con artist, where the crime has low visibility and where the threat from a single criminal is low. The conflict is the lowest in these situations.

These seem fairly logical but may not be borne out by actual study, that is, criminalisation may be upon different lines. Turk suggests that three other factors also affect whether a person is criminalised, and these might also affect the above analyses.

First, different enforcement agencies may have different views. Turk divides them into first-line enforcers, such as the police and factory inspectorate; and higher-level enforcers such as prosecutors, juries and judges. If none of these believe that the behaviour should be criminalised, enforcement is very unlikely. If they are all committed to the prevention of the behaviour, then enforcement will be high, with the likelihood of high arrest and conviction rates, and severe sentences. If the first-line enforcers are committed but the higher-level enforcers are not, then there will be high arrest rates but low conviction rates and lenient sentences. If the first-line enforcers are not committed but the higher-level enforcers are, then arrest rates will be low but when a person is arrested, they are likely to be convicted and receive a heavy sentence. Turk saw the police and other first-line enforcers as the most important element determining criminalisation.

Secondly, the relative power of enforcers and resisters is important. If the authorities and enforcers are powerful but the resisters, those who have behaved in a criminal way, are powerless, then the authorities are more likely to arrest, convict and harshly sentence them. If, however, the enforcers and resisters are of approximately equal power, then the enforcers may be more reluctant officially to label the individuals as criminals, making their criminalisation less likely. If the power of the resisters becomes sufficiently strong, they may be able to persuade the authorities to decriminalise the activity.

Finally, Turk said that the 'realism of the conflict moves' affected the likelihood of criminalisation. If those who broke the law were realistic, making their crime less visible; avoiding antagonising the enforcers by accusing them of being corrupt, unjust or violent; and not upsetting or alarming the public, the offensiveness of the activity would be reduced. If they behaved less 'realistically', they would provoke calls for the strengthening of the enforcement agencies. On the other hand, the enforcers should be realistic by refraining from doing anything which might reduce public support; they should make their procedures fair, and follow due process; they should not punish so severely as to evoke public sympathy for the criminals; and they should ensure a high level of consensus for both their cultural and their social norms.

Turk's conflict theory can be applied to a wide range of 'criminal behaviour' occurring in different social structures. It recognises that many laws are political and not purely legal constructs; nor do they represent any absolute morality, but are invented by those in authority or in power. He also deals with the political nature of enforcement, and how, at each stage, all the factors which have been discussed affect the level of conflict in a society and the criminalisation of individuals. In this way it is a broader and possibly more useful conflict theory.

15.2.6 **Quinney**

15.2.6.1 *Quinney's social reality of crime*

Quinney's writings change quite dramatically over time. He began in 1970 by postulating a social reality of crime which was based largely on phenomenological ideas (see 14.3), moved on, in 1974, to a Marxist theory based on materialism, and then, in 1980, postulated ideas which clearly show a theological base. Each will be dealt with here, but from a conflict perspective, the most important is his social reality of crime.

Quinney (1970), expressed this in six propositions:

1. Crime is a definition of human conduct that is created by authorised agents in a politically organised society (1970, p. 15).

2. Criminal definitions describe behaviours that conflict with the interests of segments of society that have the power to shape public policy (1970, p. 16).

3. Criminal definitions are applied by the segments of society that have the power to shape the enforcement and administration of the criminal law (1970, p. 18).

4. Behaviour patterns are structured in segmentally organised society in relation to criminal definitions, and within this context persons engage in actions that have relative probabilities of being defined as criminal (1970, p. 20). Some segments may be organised and strong, such as employers or unions; others may be more loosely organised, such as racial and religious groups or the women's movement; and others have virtually no organisation or power, such as the young, neighbourhoods and prisoners. Those with least power in any society are least likely to have their interests represented in law making, and are most likely to find their activities criminalised.

5. Conceptions of crime are constructed and diffused in the segments of society by various means of communication (1970, p. 22). For example, those who have property will wish for property protection to be seen as a high priority on the list of crimes; environmentalists, consumer groups and unions may see some of the activities of large companies and businessmen as the most dangerous crimes, and promote the control of such behaviour. The successful dissemination of these various views requires the segment of society promoting them to be able to ensure strong media coverage and acceptance of their views.

6. The social reality of crime is constructed by the formation and application of criminal definitions; the development of behaviour patterns related to criminal definitions; and the construction of criminal conceptions (1970, p. 23). The previous ideas can be summarised in this final element. The powerful segments of society successfully create and communicate their construction of reality, so it becomes condoned or sanctioned by others. They then use that to argue that they are selflessly protecting others for the common good, whilst they are really serving their own ends and their own interests.

The theory can be best summed up in Quinney's own concluding remarks:

The reality of crime that is constructed for all of us by those in a position of power is the reality we tend to accept as our own. By doing so, we grant those in power the authority to carry out the actions that best promote their interests. This is the politics of reality. The social reality of crime in a politically organised society is constructed as a political act.

15.2.6.2 *Quinney and Marxism*

Quinney sees the capitalist State as causing a criminalogenic society but, writing from a Marxist standpoint, he is not satisfied with explaining the criminality. He adds that it is important to work towards changing the establishment and replacing it with a socialist society in which individuals would have a more fulfilling and authentic existence, which would lead to crime reduction (Quinney (1974)). To this end, Quinney set out six propositions:

1. American society is based on an advanced capitalist economy.

2. The State is organized to serve the interests of the dominant economic class, the capitalist ruling class.

3. Criminal law is an instrument of the State and ruling class to maintain and perpetuate the existing social and economic order.

4. Crime control in capitalist society is accomplished through a variety of institutions and agencies established and administered by a governmental elite, representing ruling-class interests, for the purpose of establishing domestic order.

5. The contradictions of advanced capitalism—the disjunction between existence and essence—require that the subordinate classes remain oppressed by whatever means necessary, especially through the coercion and violence of the legal system.

6. Only with the collapse of capitalist society and the creation of a new society, based on socialist principles, will there be a solution to the crime problem. (Quinney (1974), p. 16)

The influence of the writings of Marx, Engels and Bonger is very clear in these propositions. One of the main differences appears to be that, whereas the older Marxist view depicted crime as an unsatisfactory response to a political problem, Quinney politicised crime by seeing it as the only available response of the powerless to the small and elite section which used its control of power for its own ends. Later, in 1977, he moved closer to the idea that crime, though natural, was an imperfect and irrational response to oppression unless it amounted to rebellion. For example, he pointed out that a capitalist economy naturally generated a surplus work force, the unemployed, which it had to support through the Welfare State while still making a profit. Those thrown into this position may find that welfare does not adequately provide for their needs, so they turn to crimes in order to survive. He argued that nearly all crimes of the working class were carried out in order to survive. This was a natural, but imperfect and irrational, choice: what they should be doing was overturning the capitalist system and replacing it with democratic socialism.

In 1977 Quinney set out a typology of crimes. There were crimes of domination which would be committed by those in power, and crimes of accommodation and resistance which were most likely to be committed by the oppressed. Crimes of domination included physical domination, such as police or other official brutality; crimes of economic domination, such as corporate crime and organised crime; and crimes of governmental misuse of power, such as sanction-breaking or Watergate. Crimes of accommodation include predatory crimes, such as theft and embezzlement, and personal crimes, such as murder and rape. Crimes of resistance generally involve a political struggle against the State, for example, terrorism (see Chapter Nineteen).

15.2.6.3 *Quinney's theological conflict ideas*

Although he retained a socialist perspective, Quinney began, in 1980, to place importance upon the spiritual as well as the social and political predicament of people under capitalism. He argued that a capitalist society taught people to be cold and calculating, and to have and show less feeling and less compassion. A genuinely just society would need to consider the divine and sacred meanings of existence; otherwise the essence of humanity would be ignored. Even a turn to socialism would not be sufficient if it ignored this divine element of justice.

15.2.7 **Chambliss and Seidman**

Chambliss and Seidman (1971) began with the argument that as society becomes more complex, the interests of individuals within the society begin to differ, and they are more likely to be in conflict with one another and need help to resolve these disputes. According to them these differences arise because people's values are affected by the conditions of their lives, which become more varied as societies become more complex. Initially, the resultant disputes may be resolved by reconciliation or compromise, but as society becomes more complex, more reliance is placed on rules enforced with sanctions against those who violate them. This form of normative society requires formal institutions with the power to make and enforce sanctions provided by the most powerful. The powerful groups would then have an interest in perpetuating their supremacy by using coercion if necessary. Although this is not a clear Marxist analysis, it is not counter to many who put forward such ideas.

In even more complex societies, there would be an increasing need for bureaucratic organisations to apply these sanctions. These bureaucracies would have their own interests, which might differ from those of the sanction-makers. They therefore saw the law in action reflecting the interests of both these groups.

These authors were interested in whether the power of the State was used in a fair and even-handed way merely to resolve disputes in an attempt to reduce conflict (as was suggested in most of the more traditional legal explanations based on a consensus model), or whether the power of the State, being used to protect certain interests, actually causes the conflicts (as suggested in conflict models such as the one they postulated). Their conclusion is that in State law-making it is the views of interest groups or pressure groups which are heard, not the public interest. The groups with greatest power and wealth will be most reflected in the law.

Turning to judges' decisions, they examined the space where the law was uncertain and it was left to judges to decide upon its meaning. Judges claim that they are drawing upon unquestionable ideas of justice as embodied in other laws or legal decisions: and therefore that they are not making laws. However, as Chambliss and Seidman point out, many judicial decisions are not unanimous, and the dissenting judgments are equally based on pre-existing legal rules and are equally valid. They assert from this that what the judges do, mostly unconsciously, is to decide a case on their own personal values and then fit their decision into a legal rule. Their assertion that they are deciding in the public interest only means that they decide in what they see as the public interest, which again is an application of their own value system. As people's values are affected by their life conditions, those of judges will reflect their position in society—affluent, successful, influential—and have more sympathy towards those with similar values. Indeed, Chambliss and Seidman claim that lawyers with views which are less in keeping with the powerful are less likely to be promoted, and therefore again the power base is protected. A similar view of the judiciary may also explain why corporate and white-collar criminals generally obtain relatively low sentences, despite having committed what some might consider very serious crimes, and despite the fact that severe sanctions may have more of a rehabilitative effect upon these people than upon other criminals.

Chambliss and Seidman also studied the workings of the police as the first enforcement agency, and one of the most important elements of the bureaucratic machinery. They were charged with the job of law enforcement and had an interest in obtaining reputations for fighting crime, but with as little difficulty for themselves as possible. Furthermore, law enforcement agencies depend for their resources upon those with most power. The authors deduced what they considered to be logical implications from the facts. For example, the more powerful an individual, the more problems they could cause for any enforcement agency; it is thus prudent for the agencies mostly to process those who are politically weak and powerless, and refrain from processing those who are politically powerful. In addition some criminals are useful to the police as informants and may gain immunity in return for information. The suggestion was that an amount of crime is tolerated because the police need it in order to deal with other criminals.

The general conclusion from Chambliss and Seidman is that both the structure and the enforcement of the law favour the powerful in society, and that the public interest is only of importance if it agrees with the well-being of these groups. The law and its enforcement are therefore against the powerless, and actually form a source of conflict. They conclude that the conflict perspective is the one which is upheld by empirical study.

15.2.8 Conflict and explanations of criminality

In the 1960s many theorists had ceased to search for an explanation of the cause of criminality and had focused on other elements. Control theories explained conformity; labelling said it was a question of how and why names became attached; ethnomethodology tried to restore the view of each individual in the event; and even conflict theory is primarily a theory of the behaviour of the criminal law.

However, conflict theorists do also address the issue of crime causation. Bonger argued that it arose out of the dehumanising effect of capitalism. Turk considered it to be explained by the existence of different cultural and social norms within a society, which makes the actions of some necessarily criminal. Quinney spoke of the way in which crime was politicised so that crime was the way in which the powerless could express their dissatisfaction with the political *status quo* and as the natural, if irrational and pointless, reaction to being oppressed. Finally, Chambliss and Seidman saw it as a natural reaction to exploitation; people's actions were directed by their positions and conditions.

Conflict theory in itself has a causative side. In saying that States tend only to regulate the damaging behaviours which are most likely to be carried out by the powerless, they are basically saying that powerlessness can be viewed as a cause of criminal behaviour. The powerless group is often poor, but it is important to note that they are not saying that the poor are criminal because they are poor, but rather because they suffer a relatively strong deprivation of both wealth and power. This idea of crime causation was considered in 12.2 under relative deprivation where the argument was postulates that individuals who felt that they were badly off relative to others were likely to join with others to seek a political solution, or to better their own position in a non-political and selfish way which might actually victimise others who cannot afford it. The problem grows as people are more marginalised through things such as unemployment and depression. Conflict balance theory might also be interpreted as supporting the main elements of this argument (see Tittle (1995 and 1997) and 11.5).

In Marxist conflict theory the existence of an unemployed group, the 'reserve army of workers', was seen as a necessary part of a capitalist society. Creating such a deprived group is bound to cause tensions and conflicts to arise and, as the group is the least powerful in society, they are least likely to have their views listened to, and are under most strain to become criminal. Youths, whilst still at school, will relate the hopelessness of the situation to themselves and come to see school as irrelevant to their position, and refuse to conform. They may get involved in a delinquent subculture or a criminal subculture and become alienated from school life. This prepares them for accepting the manual jobs or dole queues which await them on leaving. The hopelessness of their situation again leads them into conflict with authority.

15.2.9 Evaluation

Most of the conflict perspective is about the behaviour of the criminal law—that is, official crime rates depend on the enactment and enforcement of criminal laws. They particularly turn on the idea that the behaviours of the powerless in any society are more likely to be criminalised, and this same group is more likely to be arrested, convicted and harshly sentenced.

The first part of this assumes that it is only the interests of the powerful which are protected. This invites the riposte that most of the criminal law actually protects individuals and society in general from potentially very harmful behaviour, such as murder and personal violence. The conflict theorists would point out, however, that many acts which are as injurious as those criminalised are in fact perfectly legal, and that these tend to be behaviours which would be carried out by the powerful in society.

There is also an assumption that, if the power structures were altered, then the new powerful group could pass laws to protect its interests or values. For example, if drug users and distributors became more powerful they might be able to legalise the use of drugs, and so alter the criminal laws to protect their enjoyment and interests.

As non-smokers become much more powerful, they succeed in preventing smoking in public places and so increase their freedoms at the expense of smokers. If paedophiles became powerful, they might be able to legalise sexual encounters with children. In each case there would be a shift in the criminal laws, and either certain behaviours presently criminalised would be decriminalised, or certain behaviour presently legal would be criminalised. In each case the changes would benefit those who had become powerful enough to push them through, whilst being to the detriment of some other less powerful sector of society.

The second basic idea of the conflict theorist dealt with the enforcement of the criminal laws. As was seen in 14.2.3, there is conflicting evidence about the level of differential enforcement of the criminal laws, but it is likely that it has some part to play in law enforcement.

Conflict theories see two ways of changing the emphasis of the distribution of criminality. First, new interest groups could be formed which would promote their own welfare or, secondly, there could be a complete revolt which overthrows the present legal order and replaces it with something different. Generally, the Marxists are arguing for the second, which will be addressed in the next section. On the first, the rise of new interest groups, there is no inherent reason for expecting that the changes in the law which they introduce will necessarily lead to a reduction in the final number of criminals. They might simply replace present crimes with different ones, redistributing criminality by making criminals of those whose behaviour is presently legal, and vice versa. Whether any particular individual views it as fairer will, by definition, depend on their values, which in turn depend upon their social and structural positions in society. Possibly their most important contribution to criminology is this realisation. It leads to the questioning of the previously accepted methods which relied on acceptance of the criminal laws as objectively defined and has thus had a significant effect upon the whole area of crime and crime causation.

15.3 Radical criminology

15.3.1 Introduction

The most recent of the 'New Criminologies' is radical criminology, which has been described variously as Marxist, socialist, left-wing and critical. Whatever the label used, it generally encompasses similar ideas. It is important to note that it is not Marx's criminology, although it has clearly been influenced by Marx and sometimes reflects his views (see especially Bonger in the last section). More often, they expound a more contemporary radical view which is only fairly broadly grounded in Marxism. Nearly all are very critical of the systems in what are, or were until recently, socialist States in Eastern Europe and the USSR. Such States, although drawing upon a Marxist base, have their focus on correctionalism and personal pathologies, and in many ways are closer to traditional criminology.

Radical criminology has evidently also been influenced by conflict theories. Conflict theorists, however, do not generally go as far as radical theorists. They recognise a range of interests and power bases, whereas radicals recognise only capitalism. Furthermore, conflict analysts stop short of rejecting the need for a legal order and for legal definitions of crime; they generally fight for policy reforms rather than revolution. Having said this, radical and conflict theories and theorists do overlap, making it difficult to draw clear lines between the two.

15.3.2 **Early radical criminology**

Section 15.2.2 above introduced the basic ideas of Marx and Bonger. Briefly, they proposed that human nature itself is not criminal. Capitalism causes people to become criminal. Capitalism teaches individuals to be greedy, self-centred and exploitative. The law and legal systems are the tools of the owners of the means of production, and are used to serve their interests in keeping their activities legal even if they are harmful, brutal or morally unacceptable. They are also used to control the activities of the people, so that they do not challenge the position of the owners of the means of production. The people are made to compete for an inadequate number of jobs, pushing them towards self-interest in order to survive. Some turn to crime in order to survive, but this was seen as an irrational and unsatisfactory form of rebellion against the system; the only true and worthwhile action is revolution. This over-simplified statement of the position is clearly rather unsatisfactory, but will serve our purposes. Modern radical criminologists have reached varying conclusions based on these ideas.

It is useful to begin with a consideration of the early radical ideas as expounded in America by Quinney (1974) and in Britain by Taylor, Walton and Young (1973). Quinney's ideas on radical criminology developed from the conflict model, and were considered briefly in 15.2.6.2. He saw the unequal economic situation which exists in a capitalist State related to an equally unequal power and political basis, both of which grow out of the economic base. The economically powerful are also the politically powerful, and criminality grows out of this power base in order to protect it. A complete overhaul of the present system was needed, and its replacement with a new set of social realities based on equal power distribution. He particularly argued that the law and the legal system were illegitimate, as they served the interests of a few in the name of everyone. The law, far from being an inevitable part of our society, was unnecessary and oppressive, and should be abandoned in favour of a popular ideal of justice and right. On this analysis the very concept of law, not just the present legal rules, is illegitimate.

One of the many problems with this was that both the law and the legal system claim general support from most members of society. Accepting this, Quinney argued that the government and the powerful manipulate the people through propaganda disseminated via education, the media, State departments, the courts, and through academic disciplines such as traditional criminology which lends legitimacy to the State and owes its existence to the same State which pays for the research. Street crime, being visible and frightening, merely lends legitimation to this manipulation and draws attention away from the crimes of the powerful. As Quinney saw the law as illegitimate, he also saw the need to obey the law as being questionable, and certainly viewed crime as a natural choice in many instances.

Taylor, Walton and Young (1973 and 1975) arrived at similar conclusions to Quinney, but they did so via the different path of interactionist criminology. They started with the idea that all human behaviour should be considered normal and natural and not seen as a pathology. In this, deviance and criminality are simply diverse human behaviours. Criminality was therefore a social construct invented by the powerful to protect themselves; in reality it was unnecessary. If crime is only needed due to the types of social and political structures we live in, then, they believed, the abolition of crime was a real possibility under certain, socialist, arrangements. If inequalities of wealth, power, property and life-chances were abolished, their abolition would also remove correctionalism, which was an evil, as it assumed that deviation or different ways of living were caused pathologically. They wished to move towards a time when human diversity would be tolerated and not subjected to the control of the criminal law.

These theories have been widely criticised. To rid a society of all laws makes the weak into prey for the strong, possibly in a different way from a capitalist regime, but in ways which are for most as marked and unpleasant as those attributed to capitalist regimes. The disintegration of the so-called socialist States of Eastern Europe was a rapid demonstration of this. Radical theorists seemed to view crime as a rational choice for the oppressed, and often ignored the fact that the criminal was frequently preying upon those equally disadvantaged. Most people, whether in a socialist or capitalist State, would wish to be protected from certain harmful behaviour, especially that which is physically harmful. Possibly the worst indictment of these theorists is that they often argue for the wholesale destruction of existing systems, but offer little but rhetoric for their replacement. Despite these very heavy drawbacks, they do force criminologists to consider the legitimacy of the very heart of their science, not just its make-up but its very existence.

15.3.3 Recent radical criminology

Radical criminology has lately become a more disparate area of study which can only be briefly sampled here to give a flavour of the present radical perspective.

In 1975 Chambliss began to give his earlier conflict ideas (see 15.2.7) a more radical perspective. He argued that acts are only defined as criminal to protect the ruling economic class which can harm others with impunity, whilst these others are punished by the law. As the disparity between them widens, so the coercion is strengthened. In 1978, Chambliss added to this theoretical model an in-depth study of criminality in Seattle. In his results he claimed that the high levels of crime and racketeering in American society were related to the distinctive features of its capitalism. He concluded that crime and corruption were rife throughout American society, and entitled his work: *From Petty Crooks to Presidents*. Much of this criminal activity he traces to the Marxist oppression he had earlier documented.

In British criminology, Hall et al. (1978) studied the concept of mugging and how it was constructed. Mugging does not exist, in the sense that there is no offence defined as such. It is an idea invented by the media to encompass a collection of violent and property offences which occur on the street. The researchers noted that these offences had come to be associated with black youths, and these people came to be portrayed as unacceptable and dangerous. They then attempted to trace the origin of the concept of mugging, and maintained that it was artificially constructed in an overtly political way in order to divert attention from other problems. They depicted the real problems as lying in conflicts over power, wealth, the economy, class struggles, racial tensions and Northern Ireland. It is the politicised explanation of the construction of the concept of mugging which gives this study its radical perspective. In so far as it is valid, this is interesting. Unfortunately, the authors offer little proof of such a conspiracy.

Another British study which draws on the radical perspective in a number of respects is that of Box (1987). He linked crime with recession and the effects of income strains. Marx had predicted that capitalism would lead to a reduction of the propertied producers and an increase in the number of workers, and to large-scale unemployment. Box's study is interesting because it attempts to document the effects that the strains of an economic squeeze might have, not only on the worst off in society, but also those whose position is worsening, including large corporations. He identifies a process which narrows the productive base and widens unemployment, and relates this process to crime as a rational choice. He also considers income inequalities and links them to criminality; in a recession they are visible.

The radical elements in this are easy to see, but two factors are worth mentioning. First, he sees the strains caused by recession as affecting many sections of society. The effects will not be limited to property crimes committed by those most in need, but also lead to apparently less rational outbursts of violence, frustration and anger in reaction to the brutalising effects of the severity of capitalism during a recession. The harder times will also influence the extent to which workers 'fiddle' from both their employers and clients. Such crimes are committed by all sections of the workforce, ranging from fiddling small amounts through to high level embezzlement and frauds on shareholders. Box also thought that recession increased crimes of domination committed by the powerful as the pursuit of profit became more difficult. Lastly, Box argues that recessions lead to repressive crimes committed by agencies of the State, particularly the police and prison officers in confrontation with criminals, protesters and strikers. He postulates that at times of economic crises there is a greater need to control the oppressed classes. Box noted a similar rise in corporate criminal activity at these times, but in this case, the first-line enforcement agencies—the factories inspectorate—actually decreased. This does suggest some sort of control decisions made on grounds other than actual needs. His ideas therefore cover a number of areas, and although he falls well short of suggesting a wholesale rejection of law, his critique does have radical elements.

Radical criminology and conflict theories have spawned an important abolitionist debate. This perspective emerged out of calls to abolish the prison system claiming that it intensified, rather than ameliorated the social problem of crime. It has widened out into an abolitionist approach to all the penal or criminal justice system and sometimes even to the abolition of criminal laws. More constructively, it also suggests other, less socially destructive and often radical means of addressing the problems presently subsumed under the criminal justice and penal systems (see De Haan (1991), Davies (1998), van Swaaningen (1997)). The claim is not that there is no problem but that it is wrongly constructed within the limits of legal concepts of crime and punishment. There are errors in arguing that the problem of crime is one which can be blamed on an individual; that crimes are caused by individuals who 'go wrong'; that the States should address the problem through crime control; that individual punishments are the correct ways to address these issues. Instead crime is seen as a social event, resulting from complex social interactions. The dominant view of crime and punishment obscures these complexities and the real issues which need to be addressed. These include destructive aspects of society such as those noted by Box (strain) and Hall et al. (treating some groups as external to society) or the MacPherson report (1999) (the destructive effect of hate) as well as damaging results of negative life events such as abuse (Swanston et al. (2003)). A system based on blame, hate and avoidance of social responsibility can never hope to solve the problems. They suggest approaches built on the resolution of individual disputes and problems through reconciliation (ideas such as restorative justice would be welcomed) but also the importance for communities and society to face up to the destructive nature of some of its practices. Imprisonment is often very destructive of the individual, resulting in suicide, attempted suicide, self mutilation (all of which are more common in youth offender and female institutions), and aggression and conflict within the institutions, and often angry and damaged people on release. These approaches are not supported by all other radical theorists. A number of feminists have questioned how one would protect women against violent men and those bent on sexual violation. Abolitionists may argue that these violations result from abuse of power and the objectifying of women in today's culture but feminists point out that women need to be protected whilst these matters are being resolved. Abolitionists would also point out that other dangers and harms exist in society which are either not addressed or not analysed as dangerous (see also zemiology).

Not all Marxist and radical criminologists wholly reject law as a tool of social order. What they do is to suggest that in its present form it is merely used to repress certain factions, the poor whose criminality can be seen as an expression of frustration at their position and the class inequalities of the system, whilst leaving the rich and powerful largely unregulated. These theorists attack two main aspects of crime: first, the areas defined and controlled; and secondly, the whole structure of capitalist societies which they argue need to be dismantled. It is only through remedying the structural unfairness that crime might be remedied: full employment, workplace equality, wage equality, welfare, health, education and social services for all on an equal footing. For radical criminologists, without addressing the crimes of the rich, the use of power through the criminal law to control the poor and the structural inequalities within society, crime will always be a problem.

The preceding discussion might seem to imply that radical criminology has only a historical interest. At the end of the twentieth century there was a renewal of attention. A recent survey sees a strong future for the radical approach because it performs some crucial functions. It tests the limits of other theories, by questioning dominant ideas and 'truths' about society and crime. It aims to ensure that people rather than markets are prioritised, thus questioning the labelling of weak groups by the powerful. Theories based on positivist explanations of criminality, which ignore the socio-economic structures underlying individual activities, are challenged. Indeed the radical theorists' willingness to question, to address contradictions in present theory, and to re-examine ideas to take account of realities which may not be as accepted in dominant cultures, has provided essential support for the emergence of approaches giving attention to the struggles of such minority aspects as victimology, feminism and various kinds of legal discrimination. Seeing issues from different perspectives and giving voice to others is essential. Radical and critical approaches question the usually accepted 'realities' and present alternative approaches, often giving voice to those previously silenced and opening up the possibility of futures founded on a different basis.

These elements and others have already been used by some. For example, the notion that justice should only ever be envisaged as an inclusive concept immediately raises questions about power structures (Young (1998)). The exercise of power and its claimed ends has also been challenged: for example, the use of CCTV as simply being a weapon against crime whereas part (perhaps a major part) of the motive for its use is that it acts as a tool of exclusion to protect markets (see Williams et al. (2000)). Critical voices are now heard in most areas of criminology. One fruitful approach has been that of the zemiologists who look at levels of harm and try to address the most serious in order to deliver community safety whilst not being judgemental about the causes of harm (see Hillyard and Tombs (2001)). These, unlike some other radical writers, are not arguing to abolish crime or deviance but to view it in its relevant context and perspective. Other research which helps to do this might be centred on 'other crimes', such as those of the powerful or those suffered out of sight and by marginalised groups, crimes based on hate and those of the State. All these have received greater coverage in recent years (see, e.g., Walton and Young (1998)). Other writers (Taylor (1999)) have concentrated on issues of political economy by mapping out the way in which market societies generate crime and how crime operates as its own market. Still others (Young (1999)) have raised the wider issues arising out of exclusion: exclusion from normal societal patterns of work; exclusion through popular acceptance of demonising labels which affect personal interactions; and exclusion through the responses of criminal justice systems. The argument is in part that some of the sources of crime would be reduced in a society built on citizenship and inclusion.

These few modern examples of the theory in action show it not only to be alive and well but being revived and more frequently used in order to challenge the very authoritarian approaches to criminal justice and crime control which have tended to be prevalent in the recent past.

15.4 Conclusion

It is important to give space to these writers, as one of their effects has been to widen the study of criminology. Although many of the objects of their concern and comment fall outside the scope of this work, the wide-ranging questioning conducted by these radical theories provided, amongst other things, a basis for challenging the whole criminal justice system. Two examples out of many will be chosen here. The work of Cohen (1985) studies the way in which control agencies are essential to the modern State as we know it, but emphasises that theories of control must encompass the problems set out by critical and radical criminologies and, to retain conviction, must be able to answer some of the accusations presented by radical writers. Cohen is largely critical of the new criminologies, but he accepts their importance in any modern study of criminology. In a book edited by Carlen and Cook (1989), various essays point to the inequalities engendered in our present punishment system, especially in the use of the fine as a punishment. Without wholly denigrating the punishment system, they use new criminological ideas to question the present practice. Again, the criminal justice system is placed in the dock and questioned from the viewpoint of the less privileged.

An interesting practical example is also worth noting. It arose in Liverpool in a number of cases between 1987 and 1988, although similar cases have been heard elsewhere. The cases involved the policing of Liverpool 8 (Toxteth) and some incidents which arose out of it. Over a two-year period, a number of black youths were arrested for violent disorder arising in a few different incidents. Here, only one example will be followed. On this occasion, as on many others, a stolen car came into Granby Street in the Liverpool 8 district. This gave rise to trouble, partly because the locals felt that this occurred too frequently and could not be a coincidence. They felt that chases were engineered to culminate in this district, and could have been stopped before their arrival. Trouble ensued between some of the local youths and the police, during which a brick was put through the window of the police car. There were no arrests at the time. Two days later three youths were arrested. Before the arrests took place, one of the youths arrested had made a complaint about the behaviour of the police at the incident; he was cited by the police as leading the trouble which they alleged ensued. This particular youth had been previously convicted of other offences, including violent disorder. On these occasions he had always been unhappy with the way in which his defence had been conducted, as the lawyers had always refused to attack the police, and had ignored the racial elements which were involved in the cases. On this occasion again, the lawyers he spoke to in Liverpool advised him against bringing up these factors, as they explained that, in attacking the police, his own record would come to light and then, they felt, he would be convicted. As a result of this advice he felt that his case would not be represented in the way in which he wished, and therefore he brought up black lawyers from London to conduct his defence (all the other youths similarly believed that the only way their cases would be conducted in the way they wished was by using these same black lawyers from London). These lawyers brought evidence both about his complaint against the police which they felt was relevant to the case, and about the type of policing which occurred in the district (Margaret Simey, who chaired the Merseyside Police Authority from 1981 to 1986, gave evidence about this). There were nine or ten prosecution witnesses (mostly police officers) who all refuted the allegations about the policing on that night. During the trial, the defendants took a very active part in their own defences, interrupting proceedings to get their lawyers to ask the relevant questions or to explain something to them. They were acquitted.

Some of the factors which the defendants brought forward many traditional lawyers would have claimed were irrelevant to the legal issues before the court, but the defendants, and clearly the jury who acquitted them, felt that they were of the utmost importance to what happened and why. Had they been denied the representation that they viewed as essential to their case and to presenting what they viewed as all the relevant facts, they would probably have been convicted. A strict interpretation of the legal rules and traditional legal practice involved would have denied them their full hearing and a chance to have the facts as they saw them placed before the court. This and other cases are referred to in the Gifford Report (1989). They show how the law and practice have been used to deny some sections of the community, the less powerful sections, a proper hearing. They show what can happen when this practice is broken. They show that a radical approach to the problem can have positive results.

All these examples show that the various cultures which exist within a society are in conflict, and that neglecting this conflict leads to unfair outcomes and a perpetuation of the difficulties. Radical criminology is designed to highlight these problems and bring them to the fore.

Conflict and radical criminology have both had important effects on the way in which criminologists later theorised about crime, offender, victim and State. They raised questions which ought to be considered in any serious criminological debate, but they have had little effect on social or penal policy, at least in Britain. Mainstream criminology could not avoid addressing the challenge from the radical and critical criminologists. The mainstream tended to accept the law as given and then look for some sort of pathological explanation for offending behaviour (biological, psychological, ecological or social). Implicit in this approach was the notion that the *status quo* was essentially satisfactory, while it also started from the presumption that offenders were 'different' or that offending behaviour was 'different'. Against this, radical criminologists claimed that many of the problems lay in the artificial construction of the law and the biased way in which it was administered. When mainstream criminology, particularly the positivist school, replied that it was taking a scientific stance and dealing with factual data, the riposte was that the data were tainted with a specific moral and structural bias: by ignoring this the positivists were not the objective scientific observers they claimed, but were—probably unconsciously—actively upholding a particular set of subjective values. By questioning the fundamental assumptions of mainstream thinking, radical theorists encouraged criminologists to look more closely at the definitions of the criminal laws, to think more carefully about why punishment was administered, and to examine the power basis of punishment and the politics of punishment. Some of the work on social exclusion and social problems has led to policy suggestions and impacted on other aspects of political and social inquiry.

At the same time, many of the abuses raised by the radical school remain unaltered: in July 1997 a case was brought before the court following an identity parade which had been set up using white people, blacked up to have dark faces, to sit in with a dark skinned suspect; and none of the officers who were involved in the wrongful conviction of the Guildford Four or Birmingham Six have ever faced trial for their alleged brutality and perjury. The list could be extended. It could reasonably be argued that the legal system has failed to deal with the real issues brought up by radical and critical criminology, and there is some substance to Steinert's (1997) point that State and mainstream criminologists have more or less deliberately silenced the radical school of thought. The new millennium brings a renewed interest in radical analysis which promises a better balance. The best defence for existing values is to uphold them by reasoned debate. To deal with Steinert's assertion that ' "Progress" in criminology has meant breaking through the limits of the discipline' does not require the acceptance of the theoretical or political positions of the critical and radical school: it does require reasoned engagement with such views.

SUGGESTED READING

de Haan, W. (1991), 'Abolitionism and Crime Control: a Contradiction in Terms', found in K. Stenson and D. Cowell (eds), *The Politics of Crime Control*, London: Sage.

Pavlich, G. (2001), 'Critical Genres and Radical Criminology in Britain', *British Journal of Criminology*, vol. 41, p. 150.

van Swaaningen, R. (1997), *Critical Criminology: Visions from Europe*, London: Sage.

Walton, P. and Young, J. (eds) (1998), *The New Criminology Revisited*, Basingstoke: Macmillan.

QUESTIONS

1   How is law and the criminal justice system described by radical criminologists? Do all radical criminologists reject law as a tool of social control?

2   Is the attack these authors make confined to the law or does it encompass a wider critique of modern societies?

3   Although radical and conflict theories have not been central to the formation of laws or criminal justice policy they have contributed to criminology in a very positive way. What has their contribution been and why are they such important theoretical tools?

REFERENCES

Bonger, Willem (1969) (originally published in 1916), *Criminality and Economic Conditions*, Bloomington: Indiana University Press.

Box, Steven (1987), *Recession Crime and Punishment*, London: Macmillan.

Carlen, Pat and Cook, Dee (eds) (1989), *Paying for Crime*, Milton Keynes: Open University Press.

Chambliss, William J. and Seidman, Robert B. (1971), *Law, Order, and Power*, Reading, MA: Addison-Wesley.

Chambliss, William J. (1975), 'Toward a Political Economy of Crime', *Theory and Society*, vol. 2, p. 152.

Chambliss, William J. (1978), *On the Take: From Petty Crooks to Presidents*, Indiana: Indiana University Press.

Cohen, Stan (1985), *Visions of Social Control*, Cambridge: Polity Press.

Dahrendorf, Ralf (1959), *Class and Class conflict in Industrial Society*, London: Routledge & Kegan Paul.

Davies, A. (1998), 'Radicalized Punishment and Prison Abolition', found in J. James (ed.) *The Angela Y. Davies Reader*, Oxford: Basil Blackwell.

De Haan, W. (1991), 'Abolitionism and Crime Control: a Contradiction in Terms', in K. Stenson and D. Cowell (eds), *The Politics of Crime Control*, London: Sage.

Engels, Fredrick (1971) (original 1844), *The Condition of the Working Class in England*, trans. and ed. W.O. Henderson and W.H. Chalenor, Oxford: Basil Blackwell.

Gifford, Lord, Brown, Wally and Bundy, Ruth (1989), *Loosen the Shackles: First Report of the Liverpool 8 Inquiry into Race Relations in Liverpool*, London: Karia Press.

Hall, S., Cutcher, C., Jefferson, T. and Roberts, B. (1978), *Policing the Crisis*, London: Macmillan.

Hillyard, Paddy and Tombs, Steve (2001), 'Criminology, Zemiology and Justice', Paper presented to the Socio-Legal Studies Association Annual Conference in Bristol, April 2001.

MacPherson of Cluny, Sir W. (1999), *The Stephen Lawrence Inquiry: Report of an Inquiry by Sir William Macpherson of Cluny*, Cm 4262, London: HMSO.

Marx, Karl and Engels, Frederick (1848), 'Manifesto of the Communist Party', in *Marx-Engels Selected Works*, vol. 1, London: Lawrence & Wishart.

Marx, Karl (1904) (originally published 1859), *Critique of Political Economy*, New York: International Library.

Mays, John Barron (1954), *Growing Up in the City*, Liverpool: University of Liverpool Press.

Morris, Terence P. (1957), *The Criminal Area: A Study in Social Ecology*, London: Routledge & Kegan Paul.

Pavlich, G. (2001), 'Critical Genres and Radical Criminology in Britain', *British Journal of Criminology*, vol. 41, p. 150.

Quinney, Richard (1970), *The Social Reality of Crime*, Boston, MA: Little, Brown.

Quinney, Richard (1974), *Critique of Legal Order: Crime Control in Capitalist Society*, Boston, MA: Little, Brown.

Quinney, Richard (1977), *Class State and Crime: On the Theory and Practice of Criminal Justice*, New York: McKay.

Quinney, Richard (1980), *Class State and Crime: On the Theory and Practice of Criminal Justice*, 2nd edn, New York: McKay.

Sellin, Thorsten (1938), *Culture, Conflict and Crime*, New York: Social Research Council.

Steinert, Heinz (1997), '*Fin de Siècle* Criminology', *Theoretical Criminology*, vol. 1, p. 111.

Swanston, H.Y., Parkinson, P.N., O'Toole, B.I., Plunkett, A.M., Shrimpton, S. and Oates, R.K. (2003), 'Juvenile Crime, Aggression and Delinquency after Sexual Abuse: A Longitudinal Study', *The British Journal of Criminology*, vol. 43, pp. 729–49.

Taylor, I. (1999), *Crime in Context: A Critical Criminology of Market Societies*, Cambridge: Polity Press.

Taylor, Ian, Walton, Paul and Young, Jock (1973), *The New Criminology*, London: Routledge & Kegan Paul.

Taylor, Ian, Walton, Paul and Young, Jock (1975), *Critical Criminology*, London: Routledge & Kegan Paul.

Tittle, Charles, R. (1995), *Control Balance: Towards a General Theory of Deviance*, Boulder, CO: Westview Press.

Tittle, Charles, R. (1997), 'Thoughts Stimulated by Braithwaite's Analysis of Control Balance', *Theoretical Criminology*, vol. 1, p. 99.

Turk, Austin, T. (1969), *Criminality and Legal Order*, Chicago, IL: Rand McNally.

van Swaaningen, R. (1997), *Critical Criminology: Visions from Europe*, London: Sage.

Vold, George, B. (1958), *Theoretical Criminology*, New York: Oxford University Press.

Walton, P. and Young, J. (eds) (1998), *The New Criminology Revisited*, Basingstoke: Macmillan.

Williams, K.S., Goodwin, M. and Johnstone, C. (2000), 'Closed Circuit Television (CCTV) Surveillance in Urban Britain: Beyond the Rhetoric of Crime Prevention', in J.R. Gold and G. Revill, *Landscapes of Defence*, Harlow: Prentice Hall.

Young, J. (1998), 'From Inclusive to Exclusive Society: Nightmares in the European Dream', in V. Ruggiero, N. Smith and I. Taylor (eds), *European Criminology*, London: Routledge.

Young, J. (1999), *The Exclusive Society: Social Exclusion, Crime and Difference in Late Modernity*, London: Sage.

16

Criminology and realism

16.1 **The birth of realism**

The ideas, analyses and explanations already surveyed might seem sufficiently comprehensive and all-embracing to exclude any significant additions. Yet recent years have seen the emergence in Britain and the USA of an approach which is considered to be sufficiently distinctive and covering a sufficient scope as to be given its own title: realism. The genesis of realism lies essentially in the perception that crime *rates* have tended to rise remorselessly in advanced societies, and that established policies for dealing with crime have failed to stem this increase. Realism accepts these perceptions and aims to analyse the position in ways which will lead to more effective solutions.

Given so ambitious a project, it is not surprising to find that those starting from realism's basic presumptions have not all arrived at the same analysis and solutions. Broadly there are two main schools of realism: one which draws its philosophic stance from the politics of the right, and one drawing on leftist political values. The left realists, influence so far seems to have been stronger in Britain, and the central writers (Jock Young, Roger Matthews, Pat Carlen and John Lea) are British. The right realists have their greatest effect in the United States where the strongest proponent of these views was James Q. Wilson.

As indicated, the realist approaches have originated in a restatement of the object of criminology as the need to explain not just crime, but its apparent long-term increase. From this altered perspective, there are substantial difficulties with all the ideas discussed in preceding chapters. Most of these have turned around two basic concepts: the criminal either is seen as choosing criminality, or is seen mainly as an instrument. Theories which emphasise the choice by an individual attribute the criminal decision to a wide variety of possibilities such as a lack of moral fibre; a failure to make a proper internalisation of basic standards; or antagonism towards the oppression of the State. Those who see the criminal as merely the tool, stress that the criminal actions are preordained either by internal biology or by external forces of society or circumstance. They all have in common a desire to explain criminality, the aetiology of crime. Most commentators are now agreed that any plausible explanation would have to contain a mixture of causes, sometimes a biological/social mix, sometimes a psychological/social mix and sometimes a mixture of different social theories. As has been seen in preceding chapters this has sometimes led to mixed responses. So in Britain in the last two decades or so there has been what can be seen as a strange *mélange* of policies. The Conservative governments from 1979 first tried to impose a 'get tough' policy to crime and enforcement.

Punitive approaches were central and involved, amongst other things, a 60 per cent increase in the budget for the police (whose performance—crime clear-up rate—nonetheless dropped) and a massive prison building programme at a time when the rise in prison population was slowing down. The government also tried to implement a 'privatisation' of certain aspects of the system, sometimes with apparently perverse effects (Group Four). And yet at the same time, all this has been accompanied by a massive increase in the use of cautioning, especially for the young, and of a less intrusive and less punitive system for youths generally. The continuation of tough measures was signalled early by the new Labour government in 1997 and further endorsed when that government was re-elected in 2001: and is embodied in the Criminal Justice Act 2003.

What does seem to be irrefutable is that the level of criminality has altered radically upwards since the war. The existing theories also seem unable to provide an explanation. For example, unless there has been a vast biological change, theories in biology, even if it is accepted that they can explain some crime, cannot explain the increase. Nor, without some grave and widespread difference in the psychological health of individuals in a community, is it possible to explain it on this factor. The existing biological and psychological theories in criminology do not refer to such general physical and mental changes. There is more plausibility in some of the other ideas which have been examined. Thus social theories are often concerned with deprivation and other social ills which, at least in real terms, have become more apparent in the past 40 years. But although social background and upbringing may have altered, it is questionable whether they could explain the increase in criminality. It could be said that the ideas examined in earlier chapters can reasonably claim to give an insight into the aetiology of crime but none can begin to understand the recent changes. Nor do they, either separately or together, suggest an appropriate policy initiative or series of initiatives which might be useful for tackling the problem. Policies are either too expensive, too narrow or absent. Moreover, almost all of these theories are relevant only, or largely, to men. They rarely try to explain why women living in similar conditions or with similar biological make-up do not offend as frequently as men.

There have been various responses to these shortcomings. As the crime problem could not be fully explained some theorists and politicians called for greater State intervention in the form of greater numbers of police and a firmer criminal justice approach. These measures were predicted to be of minimal utility (Heal et al. (1985)) and when introduced they had almost no discernible impact.

A more fundamental response has been to deny the existence of the rise. It is argued that the increase is only an aspect of the official rate rather than a reflection of actual crime. Official statistics are officially constructed and do not necessarily give a true view of the problem. It is claimed that there is bound to be an increase as the result of a number of official responses: the authorities making new laws (if there are more laws to obey there are more to break); the authorities altering the way crimes are recorded; the authorities increasing enforcement and so including individuals who were not originally included but who had always committed crimes; the authorities increasing the awareness of and fear of crime leading to an increase in reporting and hence the appearance of greater criminality; more enforcement officers leading to greater numbers of crimes being detected; increased opportunity due to more affluent lifestyles and more goods to steal. There is obviously some substance in these claims, as seen in the preceding two chapters, but they are not sufficient to explain away the rise. They explain only a part of the rise.

This analysis of the shortcomings of existing theories and policies signalled a need for new approaches and new realistic goals. These have been provided by the two new theories: right and left realism. Realism of both types is intended to denote an acceptance that there is a real crime problem; a recognition that it has destructive effects on communities; that there is a need to discover realistic policies to counter the crime problem; and recognition that no miraculous solutions will ever be found. Both approaches also recognise the need to monitor the success of interventions so as to guarantee their cost-effectiveness and are critical of the present approach of the police. The similarities stop there.

16.2 Right realism

16.2.1 The basic concepts of the theory

Right realism is occasionally referred to as neo-conservatism and is strongly linked with administrative criminology and rational choice theory. James Q. Wilson was its foremost proponent (see Wilson (1985)) and wrote about criminology from the standpoint of new right philosophy and politics. Two broad consequences follow; right realism does not challenge the criminal law as currently defined by the State (i.e., the relatively powerful in society), and it centres its efforts on attacking 'street crime' to the exclusion of all other offences.

Wilson accepted that there was a real rise in the crime rate. Although he suggested that some of this could be explained by the greater number of young males, the most criminalogenic group, he recognised that this alone could not explain the rise. He thus turned to other aspects, and has been instrumental in pressing for a substantial shift in the terrain of discussion.

The right realist debate does not abandon aetiology altogether, rather it centres on certain aspects, especially the behavioural and conditioning theories. Wilson worked with Herrnstein (Wilson and Herrnstein (1985)) to devise a bio-social approach to crime. They recognised that circumstances do not cause everyone to participate in crime and so use individualistic biological and psychological explanations to explain why some are more prone to criminality. The biological section of their reasoning returns to body-type theories and to genetics. (Others in this school make links to psychological or biosocial ideas, see Chapters Six to Ten.) The psychological aspects seem to centre on learning, particularly conditioning within the family. It is unclear exactly how they see these as interacting but it seems that both the conditioning and the biological predisposition play a part in the ability of individuals to assess rewards and punishments. By punishments they do not mean the very uncertain actions of the State as it is likely that the activity will go undetected and, even if detected, punishment is not guaranteed. Instead they refer to the internalised conscience of the individual which is learned from the family and other social interactions. From this basis, the approach attacks certain types of family, particularly the single-parent family, for ineffective socialisation. At the same time, the ability to learn is affected by the constitution of the individual and the effectiveness of the input from family, peers, school, work etc. The conclusion is that biology sets the population who are at risk of becoming criminal, whilst socialisation, or its failure, helps to decide whether this will be realised. The possible punishments will then be assessed and balanced against the potential gains. As affluence increases the available opportunities for lucrative offending, so the choice to offend also becomes more likely.

Wilson thus used biological and conditioning factors in his initial analysis but then largely abandons them. This is justified, not because they are not important, but because they do not offer reasonable policy suggestions for moving forward with the debate. It is not, or not yet, possible to alter the biology of an individual in the way which would be necessary were his assumptions in this area correct. Nor is it possible rapidly to improve the socialisation offered by families, or quickly rid society of single-parent families (although both in Britain and the USA the New Right have seen this as a policy objective and one which should be tackled as part of a welfare problem). Nor can other socialisation influences which may militate towards criminality—the freedom, materialistic and individualistic nature of society—be easily altered. Therefore, despite having acknowledged broad causes of criminality, right realism does not propose to tackle these. Instead the aim is to reduce the problem via pragmatic intervention, accepting that this can be of only limited benefit, but stressing that it is feasible and ought to work. Wilson also saw no gain in merely increasing policing or other strictly law enforcement measures—this is merely costly and has never produced strong positive results.

His solution did, however, partially rest on the policing function. He and Kelling (Wilson and Kelling (1982 and 1989) and Kelling and Cohen (1996))) argued that the main and most effective use of police is not as law enforcers but rather as a body to keep order within society. As Kelling later summarised it: 'you ignore minor offences at great cost' and 'disorder not only creates fear but . . . is a precursor to serious crime' (1999). On the other hand, the maintenance of order by the police allows community control mechanisms to flourish, encouraging the maintenance of both order and law-abiding behaviour. The constructive function of the police is then seen to be not reducing crime, but providing the environment in which criminality is not able to flourish. To do this they have to be less centrally concerned with breaches of the criminal law and more interested in regulating street life in a wider perspective. They should centre on behaviour which may not seem to be the most criminalogenic but which reduces respect in the area and reduces the desire of the locals to enforce controls—behaviour such as soliciting, gang fights, drunkenness, disorderly conduct and pornography. In themselves these may not be harmful, but they harm the community and therefore need to be controlled. Right realists, far from legalising these behaviours, call for them to be more stringently controlled. Similarly, in fighting drugs they suggest no increase in activities against the dealers and the addicts who are beyond help: the effort should be concentrated on enforcement against small users, the least culpable and harmful in themselves but the ones identified as attacking the fibre of the community. Lastly, in calling for a restoration of order Wilson and Kelling saw no problem in allowing police to interfere even where the behaviour was not strictly criminal. Here they advocated action against empty properties, rowdy children, groups of teenagers on the streets, litter, noise, harassment and intimidation which falls short of criminality and other indicators of social decline. Such action was justified because these conditions lead to high crime rates. Right realists do not therefore argue for structural alterations but rather for the individual behaviours to be controlled whether or not these are strictly criminal. They do so by arguing that these non-criminal behaviours are often those which interfere most with the enjoyment of life for many people, particularly many poor people. Essentially the argument is that it is individuals, not society, who are at fault and the solution is to clamp down upon the individual behaviour of those at risk.

These measures to restore order, as those to control crime, should be most directed against the areas which are just beginning to turn into high crime rate areas. Areas which have gone so far that they are beyond saving should not have money and resources devoted to them: the focus should be on those which can be altered. Where the community controls are just beginning to lose their force there is still a possibility of restoring order.

In the less hopeful areas, and for those already criminals, the strategy involves a more direct attack on crime itself. In areas where there is already an irrevocably high crime rate there should be a more crime-orientated approach. The police should detect and prosecute offenders. Similarly, at an individual level, recidivists should be harshly treated. They should be punished not on the seriousness of the crime they have just committed, but on the weight of their criminal record. This is very similar to the old extended sentences (abolished by the Criminal Justice Act 1991) for those repeating serious offences and has given rise to the 'three strikes and you're out' policy in the US, whereby on a third offence—however trivial—an individual is removed from society for an extended period. A number of similar provisions have been introduced in the UK since 1997 where sentencing has been made more severe. Where it is a second or third occurrence, especially for sexual or violent offences, (a sentence of life or extended imprisonment is required (see, e.g., Crime (Sentences) Act 1997, Part V, chapter III and parts of chapter II of the Powers of Criminal Courts (Sentencing) Act 2000).

As already indicated, a major part of the right realist's thesis is that crime is the result of an individual choice and can be prevented or contained by pragmatic means which make the choice of criminal behaviour less likely: reducing the opportunity; increasing the chances of detection; raising feelings of being detected partly through close policing, especially of disorder; and, most importantly, definite punishment—the threat of severe, certain and swiftly imposed punishment. Imprisonment is seen as especially effective in neutralising or incapacitating offenders and terrorising others into lawabiding lifestyles. In the US, where this policy has been most enthusiastically followed, the prison population, in the early twenty-first century was well over 2 million. The stress on prisons simply as punishment goes alongside a belief in the need to move away from treatment and training, which, it is asserted, does not work. The move away from treatment to a punitive model in prison and the rest of the criminal justice system is lent support in detailed research by Garland (2000) and (2001). This rejection of the previous prison ideals has meant that it is easier to apply the simple economic drive of efficiency and cost-cutting and hence has made prisons more amenable to the application of market forces in the guise of private prisons. All of this fits well with the right realist ideal of simple punishment to disable present offenders and deter others. It also renders possible the distancing of government ministers from responsibility for the prisons, especially the operational aspects of containment, and makes it more difficult to employ any other initiatives in the institutions. It returns to the right realist belief that crime, responsibility and family are all inter-related (Young (1996)).

Under this type of approach much criminological enquiry turned towards a species of administrative criminology, the message is that one should focus on what constitutes the problem of crime and what will make a difference in terms of its reduction or reducing the debilitating results of criminal activities. This approach is heavily supported by right realism and has spawned fields of study and policy which have been used in the UK, such as the rational choice theory, situational crime prevention and pragmatic 'what works' criminal justice responses. The best known UK exponent of most of these is Ronald V. Clarke (see, e.g., 1997), a senior researcher at the Home Office, who takes a very pragmatic view. He ignores theoretical criminology and, like Wilson, considers individual problems too complex to solve: the State cannot resolve issues of desire and personality. Instead he claims that most criminal acts are the result of a rational choice on the part of the offender and can therefore be tackled by increasing the risks involved in offending—increasing the likelihood of detection—decreasing the rewards which are likely to result from the offending and increasing the effort/skills necessary to successful offending. This led to policies which would reduce the available opportunities and increase the chances of being caught (some of these have been discussed in Chapter Eleven). Over time his approach has been so widely adopted as a policy in crime prevention that many have come to view opportunity as one of the root causes of crime.

In policing this has given rise to 'zero tolerance' policing used mainly in USA but also evident in the UK. Police vigorously pursue minor transgressions to prove to both offenders and the law-abiding that the police are both able and willing to control all facets of disorder. This was energetically applied in New York by William Bratton, the Commissioner of the New York Police Department in the 1990s and claimed great successes (Bratton (1998)). These successes are powerfully supported by Fagan and Davies (2001) and equally powerfully questioned and contradicted by Sampson and Raudendusch (1999), Eck and Maguire (2000), Greene (1999) who argues that other policing methods are equally successful, Manning (2001) who suggests that the 'success' may largely be a media event and Taylor (2001) who claims that disorder only very rarely leads to crime.

In penology this has been complemented by an actuarial approach (see Simon and Feely (1995))—calculations of risk and probability of harm and statistical assessments of groups of individuals. Rather than concentrating on individuals the system should target certain groups or types of offender who are most likely to cause most harm (often violent and sexual offenders). Assessment is through statistical methodologies. In its less punitive guise this may be seen as neo-liberal but also embraces the harsh extra terms of imprisonment to protect the public (Crime (Sentences) Act 1997, Part V).

Implicit in these approaches is a neo-conservative politics, whereby traditional (middle-class) values and norms of morality, work ethic, obedience, responsibility and family are carefully protected and preserved or resurrected (self-expression, sexual promiscuity, rights and subjective values and goals are rejected) and technocratic tactics (management of the problem of crime by use of technology, and pragmatic solutions) are suggested. This approach also belittles or rejects the causative links between crime and social or economic factors and deems them, and individual factors, to be less relevant to the pragmatic technocratic approach. At an individual level the goal is to inculcate the correct moral values and to teach self-control. Here neo-conservatism accepts and embraces the technological, economic, managerial and actuarial aspects of modernity but rejects its moral, ethical and cultural aspects calling instead on facets, usually romanticised, of these from earlier times. This linking of moral and normative structures to control the poor and economically marginal and the use of technological, actuarial and managerial crime control means of achieving it are all powerfully present in this whole area. The criminological approach is coupled with State interference into the private sphere because of the negative effect this has on society: drugs; disorderly behaviour; single parents; children's upbringing.

16.2.2 Criticisms of the theory

First, the theory is very limited in the area of behaviour in which it is interested: street crime. This excludes any consideration of corporate or white-collar offences and is likely to exclude more powerful offenders from the arena. Furthermore, right realists accept official definitions of crimes as given, and fully concur in the validity of official priorities and assessments of seriousness. This presupposes that these assessments are not politically constructed and that most people's experience of crime is limited to harm caused by street crime; both of these assumptions are obviously open to challenge. Such criticism does not deny the importance and impact of street offences. All realist approaches recognise that these are the areas of offending which most visibly and directly affect individuals.

Secondly, in searching for explanations of criminality it ignores all social economic, structural and materialistic ideas and concentrates solely on the individual and the behavioural conditioning which is most strongly connected with the family. These criteria are not arrived at after careful empirical analysis and they ignore many pieces of research which undermine the claims; the individualistic nature is not strongly proved. For example, Matthews (1992) found little support for the hypothesis that there is a connection between crime and incivilities or order. Incivilities seemed to be marginal to the process of urban decline. Far more important were other social indicators and the general level of services available to an area. As many writers have noted the decline of such areas is far more dependent on structural, socioeconomic and other similar factors. To put the blame on incivility and increases in single-parent families, ignores the wider social issues. If this is so, solving these minor disorder problems would not solve criminality and in fact the limited targeting of areas suggests that what is far more likely to occur is not a lowering of criminality but a displacement of this activity to areas which Wilson and Kelling write off as being beyond help. This outcome is even more likely if one were to accept the individual nature of criminality which Wilson and Herrnstein claim.

This displacement of crime is more interesting, and more worrying. Wilson and Kelling admit that there are certain areas which are beyond helping, and their proposals seem likely to move the offending into these areas and away from those which still have some control mechanisms and, in their terms, are better equipped to deal with the difficulty. Thus the worst areas are written off, and the underclass and extremely poor who live in these areas are further marginalised and disadvantaged. They are to be heavily penalised when they step out of line (as in the 'three strikes and you're out' policy in the USA) and left to rot in high crime rate areas even if they do not. Their plight is seen as of their own making because they have not been sufficiently condemning of minor transgressions, they have not inculcated discipline into their offspring and used controlling, often physically controlling (corporal punishment), mechanisms to condition behaviour. Wilson and his colleagues ignore the social aspects, preferring to blame people. It is an approach which conveniently allows them to escape from financial investment in improvements for these areas. There is, in any event, a basic contradiction in their approach. Their central tenet is that criminality is a choice—a rational choice and a wrong choice which must be punished. The choice must be punished because it is an individual choice not affected by the social, political or cultural environment. It is thus inconsistent for them to argue that such choices are likely to arise, or more likely to arise, only in certain environments: if crime is an individual internal choice, how can more policing of 'order' within particular areas help to control behaviour?

In addition, de Haan and Vos (2003) argue that rational choice fails fully to explain or contain the phenomenon of crime which needs also to take account of impulsivity, expression, moral ambiguity and shame: it fails to take account of the meaning of the activity. Rational choice offers a necessary antidote against assuming that negative background elements necessarily lead to criminality but it goes too far in seeing individuals only as decision makers. In any event, it assumes too much real choice. For most people choice is constrained and for many, driven by a materialistic culture and street culture but limited by their poverty, there may seem to be little choice. They see offending as the only means to address the 'need': in this context can offending be seen as a genuine 'choice'?

This policing of order not of crime allows intervention on grounds which would not be entirely legal, or necessarily just. Moving towards an order model reduces the possibility of making reasonable assessments of police efficiency. It moves performance away from clear-up rates of crimes reported to them, and makes it possible to hide bad performance in figures on order. More worryingly, if the police are allowed on such a loose mandate to control all manner of activities, it is very difficult to make them accountable and ensure they act with integrity. It also opens the possibility of discriminatory decisions by police officers, or at least of claims of such by members of the public. Some of the areas which Wilson and Kelling portray as being merely instances of the maintenance of order are in fact cases of law enforcement—fights between youths, domestic disputes, soliciting, drunk and disorderly. It may be that what they are advocating is to treat them as problems of order and so to try to stamp them out without recourse to the courts and official mechanisms. This, too, could endanger the system of criminal justice. On the other hand, if crime is caused by the lack of order in these neighbourhoods, the negative impacts may be worth suffering in order to achieve a lower crime rate.

Although these policies have an immediate commonsense attraction, they could be very damaging to society as a whole. The acceptance by right realists of crime merely as an issue of a decline in moral values and pure rational choice obscures the associated social problems and inequality and brings with it intrusive, punitive and 'law and order' responses by the State (see Hogg and Brown (1998)). It punishes transgressors but does nothing to encourage conformity. It also permits the dominant group(s) within society to devalue criminals and the social groups from which they come into something almost subhuman, dangerous and demonised. The tendency then is to include within this group a plethora of different types of people—criminals, hooligans, terrorists, feminists, homosexuals, eco-warriors, atheists, New Age travellers, drug users, groups of young males (often referred to as marauding or predatory)—all of which are thought of as the 'enemy within' ready and willing to contaminate everyone and promote moral degeneracy. They are portrayed as so different from 'us' that the dominant culture will countenance, if not call for, severe and intrusive, vindictive punishments. As a total approach this is surely unacceptable.

16.3 **Left realism**

16.3.1 **Introduction**

The previous two chapters (Fourteen and Fifteen) concerned the response, mostly from the left, to existing deterministic theories. An important part of this response was to emphasise the role played by the powerful in society. These persons, it was asserted, also committed crimes; but in addition it was largely they who shaped the criminal laws, criminalising types of behaviour which were more common amongst the less powerful. In much of this, often called left idealism, the theorists presented the criminal almost as the 'victim' of society rather than as the positive and cognitive offender. More positively, they widened the scope to point out that the study of crime, like that of all social activities, should encompass all the actors: the criminals and lawbreakers, the enforcers, the police and the other organs of State control. Many of the theories considered crime at societal level, shaped by wide social aspects (a macro level) and not just the immediate micro level, shaped by smaller local social aspects. Left realism aims to look at the micro and macro levels. It considers crime as it would be perceived by many, either through their own experiences or through those of family and friends and through media images. It then tests these feelings about criminality and tries to include them in its explanations. Left realism also widens the plane of the debate to the plight and situation of victims and to the informal, community systems of social control.

Part of the impetus for this whole school came from feminist writing concerning victimisation, particularly of women but also more generally the victimisation of the disadvantaged, often by the disadvantaged. Each of these victim studies exposed the conflicts within the working class. Hitherto radical and critical criminologists had seen the working class as a unified whole, victimised by the powerful. Recognition of intra-class and sex-based victimisation was a major force in moving critical and radical criminologists towards a consideration of the realist debate. This rooting of the school also leads us to one of its central tenets—crime is a real problem, often a problem for the poor and the marginalised.

The most important writers in this field are British, e.g., Jock Young, Roger Matthews, Pat Carlen and John Lea. Two books are invaluable to the discussion of this subject; each is a collection of essays published in 1992: *Rethinking Criminology:*

The Realist Debate, edited by Jock Young and Roger Matthews; and *Issues in Realist Criminology*, edited by Roger Matthews and Jock Young.

16.3.2 **The essence of left realism**

In the author's judgement the essential element in left realism is its holistic approach to the question of criminology. The ideal is to identify the links between all facets and all the actors. The recognition of all aspects and actors in the subject is then used both for a macro and micro study of the subject. It is this approach which marks the school out from all others. This is not to devalue other aspects of the school but to recognise that many of these flow from the holistic approach: this is the strong theoretical aspect at the centre.

Left realism thus starts from the proposition that crime, like other social events, involves various subjects (offenders, victims etc.) who are engaged in a variety of social actions and reactions. Most earlier theories concentrated on just one or two aspects: the criminal, or the criminal and the victim, or the criminal and the State, particularly the control agencies. Left realism takes over some of the ideas which emanate from these theories, but rejects any notion that crime can be studied from a narrow range. Left realism is unwilling to compartmentalise the debate in this way and insists that there is a multiple relationship which should not be severed. More specifically, it recognises four main aspects: offenders; victims; formal control (the police and other agencies of social control); and informal control (the public). These four facets are posited as the points of a square. The essence is to study the interrelationships between them: the approach is sometimes characterised as 'the square of the crime'.

Positivist criminology has tended to centre wholly on the criminal and the reasons why he or she committed offences, whether these be social or biological. Labelling theory and radical criminology centred on the State as constructing both the area of behaviour to be delineated as criminal and the way in which actors would become embroiled in the system, as well as the reaction of the State to certain behaviours. Whilst recognising the worth of each of these approaches, left realists accept neither because they are too restricted. Full understanding requires consideration of: why people commit crimes; why the State delineates certain activities as unacceptable; why it controls behaviour in certain ways; the interaction between all the actors, offender, victim, enforcement officer etc.; how moral and social approval and disapproval interplay both with offending and with the definitions of offending; social interaction of groups in society and their impact on offending; structural aspects of offending; reasons for administrative decisions. All these questions interlink to give a full and meaningful comprehension of crime. Such totality of knowledge is beyond our reach but approximations can, at least, be sought. In pursuit of this the importance of the square of crime will be considered in relation to various aspects of the issue.

16.3.3 **The reality of crime rates and fear of crime**

Like those on the right, left realists recognise the rise in crime. They also accept that there has been a rise in the fear of crime. However, neither of these is seen as unproblematic or to have only a single, or narrow, dimension. Thus the notion that the crime rate has risen may be simple, but its significance for an under-standing of the reality of crime is highly complex. In part, this is because the crime rate is affected by the way in which the four corners of the square develop and react, the way in which the various aspects come together to provide a fuller understanding of the intricate social relationships between the poles of the square.

Officially recorded crime rates are affected by changes in the points of the square. So an increase in the normal offending group, young males, is likely to lead to an increase in offending. Similarly a change in the number of people who own desirable goods, or who are on the streets at high crime rate times will increase the number of potential victims and again is likely to increase the number of offences. A change in activity by members of the public can also alter the situation. For example, if there are fewer non-offenders on the streets there is a lower level of surveillance and hence a lower level of control. The figures will be similarly altered by changes in the official agencies of enforcement: an increase in policing, for example, is likely to give rise to an increase in officially recorded crimes. It should be noted that the last of these examples differs from the rest because it refers only to officially recorded offending whereas the others referred to actual levels of crime.

It is more significant to note, however, that to consider the effects in this dis-jointed way loses the force of left realism. It is important to register the impact of each point of the square, but it is essential to attempt to see how they fit together to form a social whole, a social relationship. The explanation for the crime rate must try to include all these considerations and the way in which they interact.

The texture of what is meant can be illustrated from a very brief consideration of burglary. Suppose that the official statistics registra a rise in the levels of burglary over time. This may be partly a product of changes in the social behaviour; or there may simply be more burglaries because there are more youths, or because there are more desirable goods owned by more potential victims. Or more burglaries can arise because of a more general acceptance of a consumerist society where people's worth is measured by the level of their ownership constituting a sort of pressure towards property-based offending. Or it may be partly a product of the way in which the behaviour is defined, policed and reacted to by official agencies. It may also be partially a product of an increased sensitivity to crime on the part of the public, which could be described as unofficial reactions to behaviour.

The last of these can be briefly expanded to suggest some of the more subtle possible interactions and also to show how it interacts with the others. Thus society may, over time, become less tolerant of certain activities. The shifts in attitudes towards drug use can illustrate the point. To look first at opiate use; although it was popularly accepted and widely practised in the nineteenth century, it became officially defined as criminal (unless prescribed by a physician) early in the twen-tieth century and fairly quickly became popularly rejected and defined as unacceptable behaviour. Today such activity is very widely rejected but still prac-tised by many individuals. The level of use may or may not have altered; certainly the reasons for the use today and in the nineteenth century are likely to be very different, and so are the main users. But it is largely the changed reactions of soci-ety, both officially and unofficially, which makes problematic any apparent increase in use. Certainly, until recently, there has been a marked increase since the

Second World War although, as the British Crime Survey has shown, it is not as widespread as popular opinion suggests and there is some suggestion that this is now levelling out (Sharp et al. (2004)), although cocaine use amongst 16–19-year-olds rose during the 1990s. There is as yet no comparable levelling out of the fear and intolerance.

The area of soft drugs is somewhat different. Again use was accepted and practised in the nineteenth century and became labelled criminal early in the twentieth century, leading to some rejection of it. However, today tolerance of use and possession in small quantities has risen; the official definition has not altered, but control both by enforcement agencies and the public is less interfering and more accepting. Use since the Second World War has risen very markedly (South (1997)) but is now more tolerated and cannabis has now been moved down to a class C drug. Interestingly, the official figures do not necessarily show this difference in tolerance; enforcement is statistically more common against soft drugs like cannabis than against hard drugs (May et al. (2001)), but the stronger penalties are reserved for the opiates and other hard drugs.

Changes in crime rates are thus normally the result partially of an increase in the behaviour itself, and partially as a change in the reaction to that behaviour. Also important are the social control constructs of both State and people: what people define as crime both as a community and officially. It is the way in which these fit together to form the pattern of offending which shapes the crime rate.

It seems that today we have a situation in which most of these factors are pulling together, that is, there is an increase in criminal behaviour as well as an increased intolerance of such behaviour. Thus the officially recorded rise in crime rates to some extent mark an actual rise in the activity, but they also mark a difference in what individuals will tolerate. There is both a rise in the recognition of the activity (whether official or not) and an increase in the official definitions of crimes (both in new crimes and in interpretations of, and willingness to record, crimes which are already in existence). These tendencies were seen in the discussion of drugs above, but there will also be slight differences in their application to various areas: it is necessary not only to study the general interactions but also how these come together in an explanation of the change in statistics for particular activities over time and in particular environments.

As well as the need to study tolerance and the activity, account needs to be taken of control. Again, as shown in the discussion concerning drugs, there may be a difference between the tolerance either officially (in defining crime) or unofficially (in reporting, complaining about, or being fearful of it) and in the control of the activity (the level of control which occurs for any particular offence, either official or unofficial). An activity may be less tolerated than it was in the past but that does not mean that its control will be more certain: control may remain constant or even decrease. As a consequence the agents of control—police (and other official agents), the family, school, media, peer group etc.—are less able to exert pressure or influence to persuade against offending behaviour. The criminal justice system may be less capable, through detection and punishment, of persuading individuals against offending than it was in the past. Similarly, the unofficial control system can decline or increase in its efficiency which will affect the actual rate of criminal activity.

16.3.4 The fear of crime

At the start of this section it was noted that left realists also acknowledge that rising crime rates have a destructive effect. Part of that effect occurs because of the fear to which the increase gives rise. As was noted in Chapter Five, there is a strong claim that some of the fear of crime is irrational in that the groups least likely to suffer victimisation are most fearful of it. Again as was noted earlier, the fear felt by these groups may not be as illogical as it first appears; it may be partly because of their fear that they conduct their lifestyles in ways which tend to reduce their victimisation (see 5.4 and Pearson (1993)). Furthermore, although they are not victimised by street crimes as readily as are their male and young counterparts, they are more frequently victimised in more hidden ways: domestic violence, rape, harassment and sexual violence or street crimes which are for various reasons less likely to be reported (see the special edition on violence of *Criminal Justice Matters* (2000/2001) No. 42).

More important for left realists is the different impact which crimes have on various people. An attack on one person or group may have very different effects from that on other groups. A woman who is attacked may suffer greater physical and psychological effects merely because of feeling unable to defend herself and so being made aware of her physical vulnerability. Women and the old lack power generally in society and their victimisation furthers this experience, reinforcing their believed impact of the criminal victimisation. In addition, if women are less tolerant of interference they will view minor infractions as more intrusive: the impact of the crime is thus more marked than is indicated by the bald rate of the crime figures.

In left realism, the notion of impact goes wider than this, because certain groups, particularly the poor and often racial minorities, are seen to be most at risk of high levels of victimisation. Victimisation tends to be focused geographically into the poorest areas and also on certain groups, for example, minority races. These groups are often least able to cope with the impact of such victimisation, because they have no financial or other resources: due to their poverty they are less likely to be insured and so unable to replace goods stolen. They are also the groups which suffer most from other social ills such as poverty, physical and mental illness, bad housing, unemployment, racism. Adding criminal victimisation to these other problems extends their generally negative experience and enhances its impact.

Victimisation, fear and the impact of crime are as complex as the relations which are at play in the discussion of the crime rate. The impact and the destructive effect of criminality, together with the fear of crime, are largely affected by internalised feelings. They are also influenced by the support structures both in the community and from the State, which can help in handling the victimisation. All these factors converge to give rise to the destructive nature of victimisation.

16.3.5 Causes of crime

Views on the causes of crime constitute a central element for left realism. Writers from this school often give priority to the need to remove or reduce the causes of crime, over the need for investment in dealing with offending after it has occurred. The causes they emphasise rest on viewing the wider social context of the offending behaviour. The immediate causes thus need to be studied in relation to their wider social placing, the reactions of State and informal control systems to social problems, and the behaviour of the offender and the impact on the victim.

Left realism accepts that many factors help to cause crime, and that no one explanation of any individual's choice to offend is likely. This said, the main cause which is recognised by left realists is social and relative deprivation. As was seen in Chapters Eleven and Twelve, this is very different from single causative factors like unemployment or absolute poverty. By relative deprivation what is meant is not the simple situation of having nothing but rather the injustice to which it gives rise —especially the injustice compared to others, and especially if it is felt that the problem could have been avoided. Relative deprivation is also different from absolute poverty in other ways—it can occur at any level in the economic chain and will be discernible whether the State is relatively poor or relatively affluent. Clearly the poor, particularly those who are unemployed or otherwise marginalised from the material benefits of society (racial minorities, single-parent families and others), are most strongly affected by deprivation and therefore may be most prone to criminality as a result of this factor. The more a State is economically divided the stronger will be their relative deprivation, and the more likely it is that offending will result. They are not, however, alone in this: the very wealthy may aspire to even greater riches and through greed be moved to criminality. A further complication which attaches to relative deprivation is that it is not possible for an outsider to state categorically whether someone is experiencing deprivation in a way which will lead to criminal behaviour: it is the individual's own subjective assessment of his or her position which is the essential aspect.

The way in which relative deprivation affects crime thus rests, to an extent, on anomie. Either the available opportunities are insufficient to meet the desires (which may be a factor in the crimes of the poor) or the community has failed to persuade people to internalise limits to their desires (the pure greed which ensues can explain the crimes of both rich and poor). The more a society stresses the desirability of having certain goods, the more people are encouraged to acquire, not just basics but the luxuries, the more pressure is placed on everyone to acquire these indicators of success and merit. It is not relevant that such success is illusory (as it often is): relative deprivation is felt if the socially approved targets are not attained. One result of this is to increase criminality. To take one example, the pressure on the young to conform to certain fashions is very strong. They are told to obtain not just certain clothing but brand-named clothing. They will turn to crime to obtain it. In the United States there are recorded instances of youths committing murder to secure a pair of Nike trainers. In Britain some left realists (see Young (1999) and Taylor (1999)) see an organic connection between a high crime rate and the encouragement given to self-help, self-interest and material success.

Most of the above would suggest that relative deprivation may be a good explanation for property offences but that it has nothing to offer in accounting for other types of offending. This is mistaken. Strain theory, discussed in Chapter Twelve, can help to explain the connection. This suggests that relative deprivation leads to frustration, creating a State where criminal activity is more likely to occur. The injustice suffered, or believed to be suffered, as a result of relative deprivation raises feelings of unfairness. These are exacerbated if there seems to be no possibility for a person lawfully to act to correct the injustice; if there is no legal way of addressing the problem there is a temptation to act in a criminal fashion. The feeling of injustice and strain is particularly strong where there is a belief that the deprivation was avoidable. For example, it may be believed that with investment jobs could be available, or that the State could act to reduce income inequalities: again this feeling could operate where the object is to relieve relative, rather than absolute, poverty. This injustice may thus be felt even by the rich where measures taken by government adversely affect their position, and in a way which they perceive as unfair. The strain may also be heightened if there is no end in sight to the unfairness, no end to the relative deprivation. This may have been particularly relevant in the 1990s when many of those who were most economically and politically marginalised saw no pending amelioration to their position and therefore possibly viewed criminality as their only sensible option. The usual controls which might otherwise mitigate against such action are weakened if they can offer no positive alternative. This points to a final element in strain. The immediate problem of losing a job or failing to obtain goods which are desired may be insufficient to move someone to criminality. Immediate deprivation may be insufficient unless the feeling of anger at the injustice is particularly strong. In many cases the relative deprivation, anomie and strain will take some time to work towards a choice to offend.

One other element which may be necessary is an environment in which criminal activity is made more possible, a place to sell stolen goods, to sell drugs, and peers with whom to share the experience. For left realists social structures and subcultures are crucial not only in determining whether criminality is chosen, but also the type of criminality. In other words, the relative deprivation, anomie and strain set the scene and the subculture helps to shape which solution is chosen. In this interpretation, subcultures do not cause crime *per se*, they facilitate it once the individual is facing problems. Understanding the phenomenon requires an understanding of both the reasons for the predicament and the structural facilities available. Any idea which ignores one part of this is unlikely to be of utility, and any solution which is so based is unlikely to succeed. One implication is that both causes and solutions need to be focused on particular problems and particular areas; ideas cannot simply be mechanically imported across international boundaries, possibly not even across city or neighbourhood boundaries. There is no one solution for all crime, not even for all crime of a particular type.

As indicated, left realists do stress the social and structural factors. But if biological factors are thus marginalised, they are not ignored. The final choice may rest, to a very limited extent, on biology: is the individual sufficiently strong to carry out the offence, sufficiently confident to break the law? Biology is essentially a limiting factor here. The relative deprivation, anomie and strain cause the climate in which an individual may choose criminality but negative biological factors may prevent offending.

16.3.6 The fact of crime

Realists have noted that offenders are not simply predators, nor are victims and the public simply innocents. There is what they describe as a shape to crimes—each offence or group of offences is seen to have a particular structure. For example, drug dealing is usually seen as a pyramid. One central and important dealer sends materials out on a large scale to a chosen few, each of whom passes them on to a few more. The chain expands until the drugs arrive with the large number of users at the base of the pyramid. Each person within the pyramid is an offender. Each relies on others for some desired purpose. There is a strong consensus in each of the relationships and in the structure as a whole. Adding an international dimension complicates the shape: the main dealer will pay certain parties to arrange for the production of the drugs and there may well be a double pyramid shape (a bow tie). Drug offences are largely consensual. Other groups of offences are partially consensual and partially predatory or coercive. Property offences rely on the public being willing to buy or handle stolen goods—this section of the relationship is consensual—but there is also a predatory or coercive element when the goods are actually taken from the victim. The hidden economy which exists in the distribution of stolen goods is usually local to the offenders, but the more general inference is that property offences occur because there is a fairly large number of people willing to participate. Without this such offences would become less attractive. There are then offences which are wholly predatory or coercive; most offences of violence fall into this category. In order to tackle crime in the most effective and efficient way much more needs to be understood about these relationships, which section of the chain might be easiest to tackle, and whether this might prevent the offending.

Over time the fact that a crime or crimes have occurred can have an effect on the interrelationships between the four aspects of the square. Victimisation can have profound effects on people's lives causing very real shifts in behaviour. Repeated victimisation is particularly debilitating in this way. Repeated burglaries can undermine the quality of life for a whole family. Repeated violent or sexual attacks can cause one of a number of psychological syndromes: rape trauma syndrome, battered woman syndrome, child sexual abuse accommodation syndrome, child abuse syndrome, parent abuse syndrome, post-traumatic stress syndrome. Each of these affects the victim in extreme ways. Whether such effects materialise will, to an extent, depend on the official and unofficial response to the victimisation once it is reported.

Similarly, once an individual has offended, whether the offending is repeated may depend on the response to the initial action. Official, administrative and community responses will all be factors and interact to change the experience, and possibly the behaviour, of the offender. In particular it may depend on whether the offender is detected and, if so, how his or her rationalisations concerning the action are treated. Such detection may be by peers in which case their response, rationalisations and acceptance are likely to be very different from those which would arise were the police to detect the offending. The end result might be very different.

As seen above, realism views all offenders as having chosen to offend. Offending is not determined by circumstance, situation, biology or psychology—left realists reject positivism. They also reject an organised and wholly rational decision to act against the system—the left idealist stance. This moral choice may alter over time. The causes of crime, too, alter over time and are affected by their relationship with the other aspects of the square of crime.

As well as a temporal, left realists also recognise a spatial, dimension to criminality. Some aspects of crime may be very wide-ranging—drug trafficking is an international offence, top-level dealing may be distributed throughout the country—while other aspects, such as street selling, will be largely located within certain defined areas, often small areas of a city. Burglary and handling usually share a spatial area. Violent attacks are often centred on particular areas. Some of these areas converge to give high crime rate districts where offending, particularly predatory offending, is common. Many people then avoid these districts, making offending still easier as it reduces surveillance.

All that has been said might suggest that left realists accept the present boundaries of the criminal law. This is not the case. They see nothing intrinsic in most behaviour which renders it necessarily criminal; even killing is not always against the law. The way crime is and should be defined should reflect the important aspects of the relations between the points of the square of crime. Left realists neither unquestioningly accept present definitions of crimes, nor do they take the relatively simplistic stance of left idealism or critical criminology. They do not assume that there is always a power analysis: official and unofficial interests have to be considered as does the fear of crime. They would also wish to split criminal activity down into its many constituents and assess its nature and its impact upon each facet of the square of crime before arguing either to criminalise or decriminalise any behaviour. Here the complexity of human activity is given full weight and all discussions are assessed in a wide social context. Thus some drugs might be passed over to regulatory agencies whilst others need tight control by the criminal law. Again, discussions about legalising soliciting and brothels must confront a possible need to protect the women who appear to enter these markets consensually, but their participation may have been coerced by their socioeconomic deprivation. White-collar and corporate crimes have only relatively recently been addressed by left realists.

16.3.7 Control of crime

Like other aspects, the control of crime will be unsuccessful unless it addresses the problem from all sides. It must involve action being taken to resolve problems at each point of the square—changes in policing, better community involvement, empowering and supporting victims, and dealing with the causes of offending.

The policing role must prioritise justice, which is the opposite of the suggestions made by the right realists who place the retention of order above justice in policing. Left realists view justice as essential as otherwise communities or sections of them will become further alienated from society, which would enhance feelings of relative deprivation, and increase the strain on individuals both of which left realists associate with criminality. Factors such as this were documented as causes of the Brixton riots in the early 1980s where Scarman (1981) stated that interventionist and saturation policing had been the factor which had tilted the balance towards riotous behaviour. Similarly in the 1990s the Macpherson report (1999) pin-pointed major problems with the policing of ethnic minority communities as being one of the issues underlying racial tensions and hence some criminality. This was again the issue underlying the Bradford riots of 2001 (see Commission on Racial Equality (2002)).

It is also recognised that any intervention by the State is bound to carry with it costs to victims, offenders and the community. The aim is to reduce the harmful effects, both those of the criminal activity and of control. This does not mean that policing should necessarily be removed or reduced, merely that it should be made more accountable, particularly accountable to the needs of the local area and to the law. It also means that enforcement should be more fairly distributed. Some areas are perceived as being targeted for too much control. Street crime in certain inner-city areas is often policed in this way and it is particularly unacceptable when the targeting is of particular groups or of minor transgressions, minor drugs offences or youth status crimes. It will be recalled that this is exactly what the right realists would focus on: here it is believed to be the source of the problem rather than the solution. Other areas are perceived as being too little policed: crimes such as white-collar or corporate offences fall into this category. Seeing these offenders more controlled would also add to the feelings of justice in the system and further enhance its effectiveness. Other activities which might benefit from closer State control include racial violence and harassment, child abuse and domestic violence. Again policing of these areas would enhance the quality of life of some of the population and imbibe an element of justice into the control system.

It follows that policing and other official control should be mindful of a number of factors: exactly what it is trying to achieve; the financial costs of intervention; the costs of its action to both the local community and to the criminals and victims; the costs of the criminal activity to the quality of life of the community and victims; and whether the likely outcome would justify the costs. In all of this the interests and desires of the community should be paramount. Once justice is carefully provided for, any State intervention needs to be carefully tailored to the problems faced in various areas because, without public support and willingness to provide information, the job of policing would become impossible. Herbert (2001) set out the elements in the community policing which would be essential to left realism but argues that they are unlikely ever to be fully and effectively implemented due to their conflict with police culture and organisation, and because of the attitudes to crime held by, especially, the press. In both cases the need to involve the whole community, including those who break the law, clashes with moralistic black and white views on crime.

Community control is the second limb of the fight against crime. This has two aspects, one is the informal control mechanisms such as those discussed in Chapter Thirteen, the other is the willingness of the public to cooperate with the official control agencies in order to solve crimes and catch offenders. Again each of these is most likely to flourish where there is justice in the system of official control. Left realists argue that the problem with this system is that it is least effective where it is most needed. In areas of high crime rate the informal systems of control are least evident and least able to exert any impact on the situation of offending. Left realists also attack some of what is done to bolster up the self-help systems. Many of these involve monetary input to make the targets less easy to attack, but such investment is least available where it is most needed. Indeed, it is noted that investment in more affluent areas serves to reduce crime in those locations but all too frequently causes an increase in other districts, particularly in the poorest areas. Right realists do not consider this to be a problem as they suggest heavier policing and sentencing tactics in such areas: a solution not possible for left realism which relies on justice. The private techniques which are employed in some areas are thus questioned on the basis that they further marginalise the least powerful, economically and politically. Left realists argue for different schemes which can unite society in a common cause, not further marginalise some whilst protecting the better off. This often means that they would support much greater community involvement in crime prevention and policy development.

The victims of crime are held to deserve special treatment. Their plight needs to be recognised both by the criminal justice system giving them the respect they deserve, and by society providing the social support which they may need. Their concept of the victim is wide, including social as well as criminal victimisation. Here it seems they believe that if the social rights which victims can expect are reinforced together with their position in society, they would cooperate and perform the social duty of giving evidence etc. There is therefore a payoff for the extra value given to victims. It may also mean that we can expect certain standards of care from the population to avoid being victimised.

Last, but in the eyes of left realists most important, is the need to address the causes of crime. Relative deprivation is the central element. Crime occurs when there are no legal means of addressing this problem or when those legal means are less pleasant and less likely to meet with success. On this reading, society needs to provide the more deprived with jobs, housing, and such community facilities as hostels, youth clubs, drop-in centres, clinics, nurseries etc. However, beneficial provision will not immediately give rise to an alleviation of the problem. Changing deep-seated attitudes like relative deprivation takes time measured in decades rather than days. Even then it depends on the nature of the positive input and on the make-up of the area in age, sex, race and in long-term unemployed, structural unemployment, and youths who have never worked. Many factors will bear upon recovery, just as many have a bearing on criminality and the choice to offend.

16.3.8 Assessment of left realism

Left realists claim that their theory is strongly based on the social reality of crime and on providing realistic, affordable and acceptable solutions to the problem. It is therefore in this vein that they should primarily be assessed. It is thus pertinent to note that their reality, despite embracing the four aspects in the square of crime, is largely constructed from victimisation studies (for a full discussion of these see Chapter Five). Moreover, left realists stress local rather than national studies on the grounds that these record not only the description of crimes but also explanations of the reality of crime. They ask more questions concerning issues such as: racial harassment and domestic violence; age, sex, ethnicity; the full impact of crime on particular victims; other disadvantages which people feel they suffer (a class situation); criminal activities of the interviewee. Local surveys also focus on a small geographical area encouraging the claim that they are better placed to understand the specific nature of a community's problems.

On this basis left realists have attempted to dispel claims that fears of crime are either irrational or that they are constructed outside the realities recognised and experienced by people. Their essential criticism of earlier views which dismissed the irrationality of a widespread fear of crime is undoubtedly well-founded, but their own tendency to replace this by establishing the rationality of fear is open to a similar comment. The assumption seems to be that fear can be assessed as lying on a linear continuum between rationality and irrationality: this represents too simplistic a view of fear (Sparks (1992)). On the one hand, it could be said that most people harbour fears which appear to be irrational—fears of spiders, flying, open spaces etc. But this is not to deny or remove the reality of the fear. On the other hand, attempting to establish rationality by measuring the risk of victimisation ignores the fact that most people have neither the information nor the capacity accurately to calculate the risks: their fear is not the product of some sort of actuarial assessment. The demand to know more than is practicable is part of modernity's desire for certainty and for control of the extended world. In this sense left realism, by putting too much stress on measures of crime, understates the importance of other influences which are not necessarily irrational. These would include: awareness of the political or economic marginalisation of an area; attack on, or control over, a group or groups; media, especially local media, comment; and the extent to which crime is discussed in a particular area or amongst particular groups. Left realist writers would not deny much of this, but in striving to place too much weight on the rational (in the sense of reasonably calculated) basis of fear they expose themselves to doubts and criticism. This could undermine the acceptance of their basic point: that, contrary to earlier views, the fear of crime is not irrational, and is a reality for many groups in society.

However, in trying to tie the rationality of fear to risk and behaviour the thesis becomes again problematic. We do not entirely live our lives in relation to how much we may suffer from particular dangers, and we are quite willing to accept some dangers while rejecting others which may be far less serious. Some parts of socialisation actually encourage 'living on the edge' and the taking of risk. This last may be a very sex-based aspect of our society, male socialisation accepting and encouraging risk-taking where the socialisation of women does not, or does to a lesser extent. Although perhaps declining, this is still an important aspect of our society and one not considered by the left realists (see also Chapter Thirteen, especially the section concerning control within the family).

In any event, victimisation studies are necessarily limited. Some of these limitations are recognised by the left realists when they argue that they take account not only of the reality as understood by victims but also of factors of which they are unaware. The effect is to take the impressions of the victims seriously (as being real) but then to superimpose a degree of structural analysis (the material conditions within which that reality is experienced) which the victims would probably not recognise. The approach empowers and disempowers victims within the one theory.

Left realism empowers because it presumes that by democratic process the community can participate in policies concerning their local policing and deterrence. This presumes sufficient interest for communities to become involved, and also presumes a level of understanding and knowledge of the crime problems of the area which may not always exist. Left realists reasonably justify the empowering of the public since more than 90 per cent of serious crimes of which the police become aware are reported by the public and most of the information necessary to a solution of such crime is also gained from the public. They then argue that such public support might not be forthcoming if people do not believe that the policing is for them, rather than of them, and if they are not able to see justice in the system: without public support the police could not operate. The conclusion is that the best policy for the police is to cultivate relationships with the public. For left realists this can be best achieved by fairly strict legal control of powers, limiting areas of individual discretion; minimal police-initiated activity and maximum public-initiated activity; a recognition of the inherently political nature of policing; and some accountability at a local political level.

There are problems with all items of this programme. To begin with, a legally controlled system will not in itself remove unfairness: the level of the injustice will then depend on the formulation of the rules. It is, in any event, not possible—as the left realist writings seem to imply—to remove all exercise of discretion. The real problems with misuse of discretion probably occur at the lowest ranks, are undocumented and are notoriously difficult to control. This problem is carefully illustrated by social interactionist considerations (see Chapter Fourteen). The initial contact between the police and criminals, victims and the public, takes place out on the street and much of this behaviour remains hidden from legal controls. Furthermore the impact of any policies, however accountable, may be thwarted because they are decided by the prejudices and personal approach of the individual officers on the street. This is not to argue that political accountability should not be used to control the police, nor even that it will be ineffective, but to recognise its limitations. The left realists are open to attack as having too simplistic an approach and not recognising the limitations of the utility of their suggestions.

Similarly, the equation that fairer policing will give rise to wider acceptance of police and control is questionable. It belies the complexity of these relationships and thus exaggerates the left realist case. Increasing the justice felt by a community might increase the general willingness of the community to impart information but this does not necessarily mean that there will be an increase in the type of information necessary to effective policing or that it will flow from those who hold most information about this social phenomenon. Much information now arises from informants whose information is affected by very different interests, often financial. There is undoubtedly truth in left realist claims concerning justice and the cooperation of communities, but this should not be overstated. Furthermore, left realists largely argue for a minimalist approach to policing and presume that this will be the type of policing chosen by communities. In reality this may not be the case. Many in the community might wish to have more proactive and interventionist policing. Presumably left realists, with their preferred democratic ideals, are not really arguing that they will impose the minimalist approach on society and that only within this would communities have discretion or have a democratic voice.

A policy largely directed by local democratic needs would tend to be heavily based on victims' real understanding of their position. The likely outcome is that, like most other theories, left realism would be largely concerned with street crime as this visible face of offending is the element most likely to be prioritised by any community. This is not quite so intense a problem as it used to be: but corporate crimes, especially as the offenders are likely to be outside the locality, or even the country, will never be as sharply seen as immediate street crimes. In any event, corporate violations also show some of the problems which may be associated with minimal intervention. In regulatory offences such as environmental pollution and breaches of factory legislation, much of the offending takes place over a period of time and, is perhaps most effectively detected and controlled by interventionist action by police or other agencies. These considerations have led some left realists to suggest that in the area of corporate crime the best approach is through a proactive control policy coupled with encouraging the public to report such offences or suspected offences (Slapper and Tombs (1999)). If the agencies which police these crimes actively responded to such public participation this might alter the power base between public and capital, enhance the feelings of justice with in the whole system, and increase the efficiency of the wider criminal justice system. However, such a solution probably rests on abandoning the strict calls for minimalist interventions in all crime control, an issue which is not embraced by all left realists.

Nor do left realist writings sufficiently confront some of the ambiguity of democracy. It could, for example, be said that their form of democracy and devolved power simply means more local responsibility for crime control and law and order, while real power is held and policy set at central government level. This problem is addressed in Chapter Twenty. Moreover, left realist reliance on a democratic basis might permit the largest groups to dominate the minority groups in any area, or a more powerful group to dominate a less powerful group. For example, if there is minimalist policing based on policies formed by the local community, this might lead to issues such as domestic violence and child abuse remaining marginalised: they are both less visible and may also conflict with the perception of crime held by most of the community. Thus although left realists espouse an understanding of the marginalisation of women, it would seem that their policies are unlikely to protect them. Similar difficulties may exist in racial and other issues. Perhaps these are areas and issues where policy is best set from outside the community and which are not most effectively addressed by the minimalist interventions espoused in most left realism.

Nonetheless, the call for greater community say in the management and control of crime is one element which has taken root in recent years. It has spawned all manner of suggestions—Neighbourhood Watch, mediation conferencing, restorative justice (see Chapter Five), the Safer Cities Programme (see Tilley (1992) and Sutton (1996)) and more recently the close partnerships required between local authorities and the police under the Crime and Disorder Act 1998. These bring with them immense difficulties and few certainties. Many of the suggestions of the left realists imply or openly suggest the need to move towards a criminal control system based partially in the community (a form of Communitarianism) where the community is the provider and upholder of social justice. The idea most left realists seem to have is that in this way democracy and justice are better served for all, but it is important to note that this does not always herald a fairer or more egalitarian society. The democratic aspects were discussed above, but it needs to be recognised that much communitarian thinking and motivation stems from the conservative right. Thus Murray (1990) suggests the removal of centralised welfare provision, leaving such functions to communities. He argues that local communities will provide the necessary welfare, housing, and education and crime control, but this effectively denies the differential needs of various communities dependent on whether they are affluent or poor. Such an approach would seem certainly to serve to increase the divide between rich and poor.

A left realist approach would need to confront these dangers as well as the democratic attractions of locating crime problems and solutions at the level of the community. One such danger, as Lacey and Zedner (1995) point out, is romanticising the past: for example, Murray from the right has an idealised version of simple,

crime-free communities of days gone by. There are thus two questions to be confronted: what is a community; and might empowering them for criminal purposes carry broader social risks? On the first issue there is a problem of whether a
community is a geographical or a social construct. The spatial element has often
been seen as central to criminal studies, but, as an examination of some of
this research indicates, the notion of community which was used was fluid.
There were:

two estate-based projects; two neighbourhood anti-burglary projects; an area-based street
offences project; a town-wide anti-cycle theft initiative; a borough-wide racial harassment
project and a drug-related crime prevention project. (Crawford (1995) note 3)

Currie (1988), Crawford (1995), Gardiner (1995) and Gilling (1997), amongst
others, see spacial community as problematic and have all considered not just
geographic ideas of space but also more abstract concepts of community. These
have included unified sets of attitudes or values; the presence or absence of a structural or institutional basis; and a social or economic homogeneity. Of course, if all
that is involved is an exhortation to encourage the informal social control of
neighbourhoods then we are back to pure control theory and a definition is less
important. But more is generally expected here (see Graham and Bennett (1995)). If
significant power is to be placed in communities it is necessary to define them. In
present criminal justice policy the political unit of the local authority is chosen
(Crime and Disorder Act 1998) but this may not fit well with broader social concepts of community. Nor, as Herbert (2001) notes, does the Act do anything to
involve presently excluded groups, including offenders, in setting of criminal
justice agendas.

It then becomes much more questionable whether definition of the social order
should be done by reference to crime. Certainly, this carries with it particular
difficulties from the point of view of left realism. If crime is the central defining
concept then issues such as health (see 9.5.6) may be reduced in importance, or
communities may be constructed from their views on crime rather than from
other social aspects, such as unemployment, housing, racism or the need for
social amenities. Even within the area of crime control such moves could be
socially divisive. Affluent areas may opt for private policing, making them
reluctant to contribute to official law enforcement agencies; those who refused—
or who were unable—to contribute to the private forces would be left without
protection; and crime might simply be driven from these areas into other, less
select areas. Such approaches would also do little to promote—might indeed
inhibit—action on domestic violence, corporate crime and white-collar offences.
The emphasis of private community schemes is overwhelmingly on control
(within their area and social group): if traditionally important issues, such as
prevention, are also to be addressed, communities would have to be given the
power and finance to alleviate social problems which often accompany crime.
Some of this may be achieved under s. 17 of the Crime and Disorder Act 1998,
which requires community safety to be considered in all local authority provision
of services.

If the sentiment in this is given broad interpretation by the local authorities, it
could go far to addressing some of the social problems that often accompany crime.
Ballintyne and Fraser (2000) argue that if properly implemented it should ensure

community safety in local authority services, deliver policing by consent, and tackle social exclusion (with help from the initiatives of the Social Exclusion Unit, in some areas). Although some initiatives such as the work of the Social Exclusion Unit and efforts to facilitate more people into the job market take a wider perspective those linked to criminal justice and the Crime and Disorder Act do seem to have been rather more focused simply on the problems which result from crime. A good example is the movement of drug treatment issues from Health to the Home Office and the resultant strong links with solving crime problems rather than addressing health needs (see 9.5.6). However, as Wiles and Pease (2000) note the issue might have been better addressed as a wider community safety issue rather than one of crime, perhaps taking the zemiological stance of assessing social harm rather than judging the cause of that harm (see Hillyard and Tombs (2001)). Even in dealing with crime critical awareness needs to be retained of how social problems are defined as crimes and how crime prevention can intersect the causes of crime rather than purely controlling individuals (Ekblom (2000))

One of the strengths of left realism is that it does recognise the importance of State agencies other than the police—agencies such as the social services; schools; medical agencies; factory inspectors; Inland Revenue; Customs and Excise; local authorities. These may be called upon in official capacities to deal with particular offences, offenders or victims. For example, in drug abuse the medical profession may be called on, or the Customs and Excise may be involved; in child abuse both the medical profession and social services will play a large role; sexual and physical assault will include medical as well as police agencies; corporate offences may involve factory inspectors or environmental agencies etc.; and local authorities might be involved in policies to help reduce crime in particular areas. Left realists argue that where more than one agency is logically involved the local authority should play a coordinating role to ensure an accountable and logical approach to crime. The partnership initiatives of the Crime and Disorder Act 1998 and later legislation are moves in this direction. In addition to these State bodies, a role is seen for less formal organisations such as the family, media, religious organisations and youth clubs which help to facilitate moral standards. All this sounds very acceptable but the precise role for these agencies, and the balance between them, is not clearly stated or addressed. As with policing, it presumably depends on local accountability which, as already seen, is not without its associated problems.

In any event, most of these agencies are primarily concerned with the areas of detection, prevention and decisions to prosecute. Left realism rather neglects many of these aspects of the criminal justice system. This is a serious drawback, especially when one of left realism's strongest attacks on other criminological theories is that they fail to take account of the whole picture. Left realism thus falls foul of one of its own testing criteria for an acceptable approach to crime. It may be that one of the reasons for this gap in attention arises because centring on later stages of the criminal justice system would necessitate a less local approach and could not be resolved by use of local political controls: being forced to confront the later stages of the criminal justice system might usefully force these writers to reconsider the all-embracing utility and acceptability of local political accountability over and above other forms of control.

Lastly, the central aspect of the approach is a call for the need to reduce relative deprivation through a package set to decrease feelings of marginalisation. However, the realists have not fully explained how the discontent which may arise out of relative deprivation may lead individuals to choose criminality. They have centred on subcultural aspects, but the only way in which relative deprivation, discontent and subculture appear linked to crime is through some sort of predisposition, something they attack in the theories of others. Furthermore, all the suggestions to attack relative deprivation etc. are based on structural and economic factors of absolute deprivation, although it is not fully explained how attacking these has an impact on feelings of relative deprivation. Presumably part of the hope is that attacking the physical problems might lead to structures which will encourage stronger ties in the community, moving the subculture slowly towards being more supportive of legal as opposed to illegal activities. But this, like other aspects of left realism, could be said to place too much belief in the idea of community without really defining what is meant by this concept. How small an area? Who is included? Will it simply further alienate those not included?

Some, such as Steinert (1997), bemoan the willingness of earlier critical and radical criminologists to move to left realism, which they see as insufficiently focusing on crime because of its concern with broad social issues. Others welcome the school as including alternative analytical accounts of State-defined aspects of crime and criminal justice (see Garland (1997)), and it is probably true that the left realists do posit one of the most convincing and potentially most useful approaches to date. The approach does, however, have its problems and an uncritical acceptance of their solutions would be counter-productive. As one response to criticisms some of its early central protagonists have moved on to a form of left realism which is married to a closer understanding of the negative effects of political power, market forces and other more radical issues (Young (1999)). Whilst the early rejection of these elements by left realists has been attacked by Cottee (2002) as being insufficiently rigorous in its analysis, perhaps as the theory matures, more of these difficulties will be addressed.

SUGGESTED READING

Kelling, G.L. and Coles, C.M. (1996), *Fixing Broken Windows: Restoring Order and Reducing Crime in Our Communities*, New York: Touchstone Books.

Matthews, R. and Young, J. (1992), *Issues in Realist Criminology*, London: Sage.

Wilson, J.Q. and Kelling, G. (1982), 'Broken Windows: the Police and Neighborhood Safety', *Atlantic Monthly*, March, p. 29.

Young, J. and Matthews, R. (1992), *Rethinking Criminology: the Realist Debate*, London: Sage.

REVISION BOX

	Right Realism	Left Realism
Political positioning	Politically right wing—society is basically healthy and crime needs to be dealt with before it renders society unhealthy.	Politically left—crime is seen as endemic in the class and patriarchal nature of society.

Basic tennet	Protects traditional (middle-class) values and norms of morality, work ethic, obedience, responsibility and family.	Crime is serious and needs to be tackled. Understanding crime and its causes within the normal operation of societies. Promotion of justice, rights, self-expression and community based resolutions to offending.
Main thesis	Minor disorder causes problems of fear etc. for society and therefore needs to be addressed before it undermines basic values.	Studies causes, methods of intervention, effects (on victim etc.). Looks at all aspects of the square of crime: offenders; victims; formal control (the police and other agencies of social control); and informal control (the public).
Policies	Law and order campaigns. Strict and harsh punishments, policing of minor disorder as evidenced in zero tolerance policing. Based firmly on rational choice it holds the individual responsible for their behaviour (blaming them) so possibly ignoring the effect of external factors.	Involves a multi-agency approach to solving crime problems. Also assumes a community or communitarian link. Crime prevention should focus on attacking the social causes of crime, though there might be some place for ideas such as situational crime prevention or deterrence. The ideal is to address the social order to reduce crime but also have policies which will protect individuals from unacceptable risks.

QUESTIONS FOR REVISIONS

1   Explain the social, legal and theoretical context within which zero tolerance policing and 'three strikes and you're out' policies have arisen. Using the critique of others consider how effective these policies have and might be in reducing crime.

2   Does rational choice adequately explain offender behaviour? Do offenders weigh up the costs and benefits of offending before acting and if so what aspects may be counted as costs and what as benefits? What practical applications might come out of an application of rational choice theory?

3   Explain left realism and consider how it differs from the more radical criminologies from which it evolved.

4   Critically explore the broad policy implications which might arise out of left realists policies.

5   What similarities are there between right and left realism? What are the essential differences?

REFERENCES

Ballintyne, S. and Fraser, P. (2000), 'It's Good to Talk, But it's Not Good Enough', in S. Ballintyne, K. Pease and V. McLaren (eds), *Secure Foundations: Key Issues in Crime Prevention, Crime Reduction and Community Safety*, Southampton: Institute for Public Policy Research.

Braithwaite, J. (2003), 'What's Wrong with the Sociology of Punishment?', *Theoretical Criminology*, vol. 7(1), p. 5.

Bratton, W. (1998), *Turnaround: How America's Top Cop Reversed the Crime Epidemic*, New York: Random House.

Brown, David and Hogg, Russell (1992), 'Law and Order Politics—Left Realism and Radical Criminology: a view from Down Under', in Roger Matthews and Jock Young, *Issues in Realist Criminology*, London: Sage.

Clarke, R.V. (1997), *Situational Crime Prevention: Successful Case Studies*, 2nd edn, New York: Harrow & Heston.

Commission for Racial Equality (2002), *A Plan for Us All: Learning from Bradford, Oldham and Burnley*, London: Commission for Racial Equality.

Cottee, S. (2002), 'Folk Devils and Moral Panics: "Left Idealism" Reconsidered', *Theoretical Criminology*, vol. 6(4), p. 387.

Crawford, Adam (1995), 'Appeals to Community and Crime Prevention', *Crime Law and Social Change*, vol. 22, p. 97.

Criminal Justice Matters (2000/2001), Special Edition exploring violence, *Criminal Justice Matters*, vol. 42.

Currie, Elliott (1988), 'Two Visions of Community Crime Prevention', in T. Hope and M. Shaw (eds), *Communities and Crime Reduction*, London: HMSO.

de Haan, W. and Vos, J.M.C. (2003), 'A Crying Shame: The Over-Rationalized Conception of Man in the Rational Choice Perspective', *Theoretical Criminology*, vol. 7(1), p. 29.

Eck, J. and Maguire, E. (2000), 'Have Changes in Policing Reduced Violent Crime? An Assessment of the Evidence', in A. Blumstein and J. Wallman (eds), *The Crime Drop in America*, Cambridge: Cambridge University Press.

Ekblom, P. (2000), 'The Conjunction of Criminal Opportunity', found in S. Ballintyne, K. Pease and V. McLaren (eds), *Secure Foundations: Key Issues in Crime Prevention, Crime Reduction and Community Safety*, Southampton: Institute for Public Policy Research.

Fagan, J. and Davies, G. (2001), 'Street Stops and Broken Windows', *Fordham Urban Law Review*, vol. 28(4), p. 457.

Gardiner, Simon (1995), 'Criminal Justice Act 1991—Management of the Underclass and the Potentiality of Community', in Lesley Noaks, Michael Levi and Mike Maguire (eds), *Contemporary Issues in Criminology*, Cardiff: University of Wales Press.

Garland, David (1997), ' "Governmentality" and the Problem of Crime: Foucault, Criminology and Sociology', *Theoretical Criminology*, vol. 1, p. 173.

Garland, D. (2000), 'The Culture of High Crime Societies: Some Preconditions of Recent "Law and Order" Policies', *British Journal of Criminology*, vol. 40, p. 347.

Garland, D. (2001), *The Culture of Control: Crime and Social Order in Contemporary Society*, Oxford: Oxford University Press.

Gilling, Daniel (1997), *Crime Prevention: Theory, Policy and Politics*, London: University College London.

Graham, J. and Bennett, T. (1995), *Crime Prevention Strategies in Europe and North America*, Helsinki: European Institute for Crime Prevention and Control.

Greene, J. (1999), 'Zero Tolerance: A Case Study of Police Policies and Practices in New York City', *Crime and Delinquency*, vol. 45, p. 171.

Heal, K., Tarling, R. and Burrows, J. (eds) (1985), *Policing Today*, London: HMSO.

Herbert, S. (2001), 'Policing the Contemporary City: Fixing Broken Windows or Shoring up Neo-Liberalism?', *Theoretical Criminology*, vol. 5(4), p. 445.

Hillyard, Paddy and Tombs, Steve (2001), 'Criminology, zemiology and Justice', Paper presented to the Socio-Legal Studies Association Annual Conference in Bristol, April 2001.

Hogg, R. and Brown, D. (1998), *Rethinking Law and Order*, Sydney: Pluto Press.

Kelling, G. (1999), 'Broken Windows, Zero Tolerance and Crime Control' in Francis, P. and Penny, F. (eds), *Building Safer Communities*, London: Centre for Crime and Justice Studies.

Kelling, G.L. and Coles, C.M. (1996), *Fixing Broken Windows: Restoring Order and Reducing Crime in Our Communities*, New York: Touchstone Books.

Lacey, N. and Zedner, L. (1995), 'Discourses of Community in Criminal Justice', *Journal of Law and Society*, vol. 22, p. 301.

Macpherson of Cluny, Sir W. (1999), *The Stephen Lawrence Inquiry: Report of an Inquiry by Sir William Macpherson of Cluny*, Cm 4262, London: HMSO.

Manning, P.K. (2001), 'Theorizing Policing: The Drama and Myth of Crime Control in the NYPD', *Theoretical Criminology*, vol. 5(3), p. 315.

Matthews, Roger (1992), 'Replacing "Broken Windows": Crime, Incivilities and Urban Change', in Roger Matthews and Jock Young (eds), *Issues in Realist Criminology*, London: Sage.

Matthews, Roger and Young, Jock (eds) (1992), *Issues in Realist Criminology*, London: Sage.

May, T., Warburton, H., Turnbull, P.J. and Hough, M. (2001), *Times they are A-Changing: Policing of Cannabis*, London: YPS in conjunction with the Joseph Rowntree Foundation. See http://www.jrf.org.uk/bookshop/details.asp?pubID=421.

Murray, C. (1990), 'Underclass', in Murray, C. (ed), *The Emerging British Underclass*, London: Institute of Economic Affairs.

Pearce, Frank and Tombs, Steve (1992), 'Realism and Corporate Crime', in Roger Matthews and Jock Young, *Issues in Realist Criminology*, London: Sage.

Pearson, G. (1993), *Hooligan: A History of Respectable Fears*, London: Macmillan.

Sampson, R. and Raudendusch, S. (1999), 'Systematic Social Observation of Public Spaces', *AJS*, vol. 105, p. 603.

Scarman, Lord (1981), *The Brixton Disorders, 10–12 April 1981*, Cmnd 8427, London: HMSO.

Sharp, C., Baker, P., Goulden, C., Ramsey, M. and Sondhi, A. (2001), *Drug Misuse Declared in 2000: Key Results from the British Crime Survey*. Findings 149, London: Home Office.

Slapper, G. and Tombs, S. (1999), *Corporate Crime*, London: Longman.

South, Nigel (1997), 'Drugs: Use, Crime and Control', in Mike Maguire, Rod Morgan and Robert Reiner (eds), *The Oxford Handbook of Criminology*, 2nd edn, Oxford: Clarendon Press.

Steinert, Heinz (1997), '*Fin de Siècle* Criminology', *Theoretical Criminology*, vol. 1, p. 111.

Sutton, Mike (1996), *Implementing Crime Prevention Schemes in a Multi-Agency Setting: Aspects of Process in the Safer Cities Programme*, Home Office Research Study No. 160, London: HMSO.

Taylor, I. (1999), *Crime in Context: A Critical Criminology of Market Societies*, Cambridge: Polity Press.

Taylor, R. (2001), *Breaking Away from Broken Windows: Baltimore Neighbourhoods and the Nationwide Right Against Crime, Grime, Fear and Decline*, Bolder, CO: Westview Press.

Tilley, Nick (1992), *Safer City and Community Safety Strategies*, Home Office Police Research Group, Crime Prevention Paper 38.

Wiles, P. and Pease, K. (2000), 'Crime Prevention and Community Safety: Tweedledum and Tweedledee', in S. Ballintyne, K. Pease and V. McLaren (eds), *Secure Foundations: Key Issues in Crime Prevention, Crime Reduction and Community Safety*, Southampton: Institute for Public Policy Research.

Wilson, James Q. (1985), *Thinking about Crime*, 2nd edn, New York: Vintage Books.

Wilson, James Q. and Herrnstein, Richard J. (1985), *Crime and Human Nature*, New York: Simon & Schuster.

Wilson, James Q. and Kelling, G. (1982), 'Broken Windows: the Police and Neighborhood Safety', *Atlantic Monthly*, March, p. 29.

Wilson, James Q. and Kelling, G. (1989), 'Making Neighborhoods Safe', *Atlantic Monthly*, February, p. 46.

Young, Alison (1996), *Imagining Crime: Textual Outlaws and Criminal Conversations*, London: Sage.

Young, J. (1999), *The Exclusive Society: Social Exclusion, Crime and Difference in Late Modernity*, London: Sage.

Young, Jock and Matthews, Roger (1992), *Rethinking Criminology: the Realist Debate*, London: Sage.

Young, Jock and Matthews, Roger (1992a), 'Questioning Left Realism', in Roger Matthews and Jock Young, *Issues in Realist Criminology*, London: Sage.

17

Positivist explanations of female criminality

17.1 Introduction

In the past, women were virtually invisible in the literature on crime. Until recently, the problems posed by female criminality were generally ignored in most textbooks or were added as a footnote to the discussion of male criminality. In these accounts the experience of women has generally been marginalised, and their criminality has been distorted to fall in with whatever male theory was being expounded. In such accounts criminality was assumed to be a male characteristic, and therefore explaining male criminality explained all criminality. This chapter will deal with these areas and discuss their inadequacy as explanations for female criminality. The second chapter on women and crime (Chapter Eighteen) will discuss the newer explanations, some of which are said to be linked with greater freedom and more rights for women, others with feminism generally or with a clear gendered analysis of crime. Accordingly, this book discusses two main explanations of female crime. The present chapter will consider the more traditional positivist theories; the next chapter will concentrate on the thesis which has developed out of 'feminism', and its alleged link to female criminality.

In both these areas, until the last 30 years, the lack of literature on female criminality is often astounding. One reason given for this lack of interest is that females have traditionally been seen as being intrinsically law-abiding. It is certainly true that, from the statistics available, crime appears to be a largely male, and young male, activity. Although sex crime ratios (the proportion of men and women offending) differ depending on what crimes one is considering, men are generally represented more frequently than women. Even in shoplifting, a crime which is traditionally linked with women, there are more males than females convicted. In Britain, of those convicted of serious crimes 80 per cent are male, and women make up only about 5 per cent of the prison population, suggesting that their offences tend to be less serious. In the early 1990s the figure would have been about 3 per cent so this is a significant rise. A change in sentencing is noted by the Home Office: 'Between 1993 and 2001 the average population of women in prison rose by 140 per cent as against 46 per cent for men, reflecting sentencing changes at the courts' (Home Office (2002)) (the difference is even more marked for young offenders where between 1992 and 2002 female imprisonment increased by 250 per cent and male by 50 per cent). The magistrates' courts imprison women five times more frequently in 2001 than in 1992 (for a full consideration of this see Hough et al. (2003)). The change has occurred even though there has not been such a marked change in either the nature or the extent of female offending. And, as already indicated, despite the change only a small proportion of those in prison are women. The figures of sex ratios in the United States are similar to those for Britain. Indeed, these sorts of figures are fairly global, indicating the law-abiding behaviour of most females, making gender possibly the easiest predictor of criminality. If one were put into a room with 20 people chosen at random, half male and half female, and were told that ten of them were convicted criminals, the best single predictor would be sex.

It could be that female crime remains undetected vastly more frequently than male crime. This seems unlikely, as the two largest areas of hidden crime are white-collar and corporate crimes, which women have less opportunity to commit, and domestic crimes such as spouse battering and child physical and sexual abuse, both of which are more commonly carried out by men than by women. It is true, however, that when women do commit crimes of violence these are often committed in the home.

The different involvement in crime of men and women is one of the most striking and consistent criminological truths, and it is therefore surprising that it has not been more widely studied in order to ascertain what causes this difference. As we shall see in this chapter, the female is generally overlooked in the explanation of criminality, and even in the explanation of conformity—where one would expect women to be the central consideration—they are often marginalised in favour of discussion from a purely male perspective.

17.2 Biological, hormonal and psychological theories

17.2.1 Introduction

Physiological and psychological theories subsume a number of explanations which basically attribute female criminality to individual characteristics (physiological, hormonal or psychological) which are either unchanged or only marginally affected by economic, social or political forces. These theories often conclude that criminality is due to the inherent nature of particular 'abnormal' women who are bad and begin their life with a propensity for criminality; that is, in everyday language, they are considered to be 'born criminals'.

Because these theories are centred upon the individual, they all suggest a 'cure' based upon adjustments to the individual. These 'cures' range from sterilization in order to prevent crime in future generations through to psychoanalysis. Little, if any, consideration is given to the role, status or socio-economic position of women in society. The neglect of social factors has an immediate attraction for anyone wishing to retain the *status quo* in society, helping to explain the popularity of these theories amongst the better-off sections of the community. Such an approach also lent support to the idea that the penal system should 'reform' prisoners whilst in custody. Criminals were thought of as persons who suffered from something which could be 'cured'. It takes time to 'cure' or to 'help' people, and so it is necessary to incarcerate them for long enough to have the desired effect. In this way, these theories also influenced the lengths of prison sentences.

Nonetheless, it is important to bear in mind that at the time they were written they represented novel and innovative thinking. For our purposes, the study of female criminality will begin with the work of Lombroso (see Chapter Six for his thesis on male criminality), whose writing on this topic started in 1895. At that time, little had been done to study the criminal individual, whether male or female, and merely to begin such work was innovative. His theories were topical, as they could be seen to have their basis in the then relatively new and still controversial arguments of Darwinism. It is therefore not surprising that they became popular and widely accepted. With hindsight it is now all too easy to point out flaws in his rather simplistic arguments, but it is not possible wholly to discount his ideas on physiological reasons for female criminality. Because of the importance of the issue, the discussion of Lombroso's work will be followed by a selection of the work of other writers to illustrate the way in which physical and psychological explanations of female crime have progressed to the present day.

17.2.2 Lombroso

Although Lombroso's work on female criminality is now largely discredited in its pure form, its relevance continues because several infuential later writers base their ideas upon it. Lombroso is also a good starting-point because he states explicitly what is only implied by later theorists.

His basic idea is that all crime is the result of atavistic throwbacks, that is, a reversion to a more primitive form of human life or a survival of 'primitive' traits in individuals. He argues that the most advanced forms of human are white males, and the most primitive are non-white females. He studied the physiology of both criminal and non-criminal females (this is one of the few occasions on which he studied a control group). Any traits found more commonly in the criminal group he described as atavistic: large hand size; low voice pitch; having moles; being short; having dark hair; being fat, and so on. All his tests were carried out in Italy, and some of the so-called characteristics can be seen to be particularly prevalent in certain areas, most markedly in Sicily. He gave little consideration to the fact that within Italy Sicilians were generally poorer than other groups and that their social conditions rather than their physical appearance may have led to their criminality. In later writings he did compromise by admitting that the 'born criminal' accounted for only 35 per cent of criminals, and that some crime was committed by pseudo-criminals who might be pushed into crime by adverse environment, passion or criminal associations. But his main arguments explaining persistent criminals were based on atavistic traits.

On this basis, women portraying certain 'atavistic' characteristics would become more criminal than others. However, if crime was to be explained merely by primitive traits, female crime would be greater than male crime because, according to Lombroso, all females are less advanced than males. Lombroso's theory therefore seems to point towards a higher female than male crime rate, whereas the female rate was, and is, according to the statistics, lower. He explains this apparent anomaly partly by maintaining that prostitution was the female substitute for crime and partly by attributing the lower female crime rate to women's proximity to lower life forms. He claimed that women had a smaller cerebral cortex which rendered them both less intelligent and less capable of abstract reasoning. This, he argued, led to a greater likelihood of psychological disturbance (see Freud, 17.2.6 below) and was also more likely to lead to sexual anomalies than crime. He further maintained that because females are more simplistic than males, women, like lower animal life, are more adaptable and more capable of surviving in unpleasant surroundings. This might explain why he largely ignores the poverty of the environment in which criminal women often lived. In his view, with this ability to adapt, they can survive male manipulation and male control and, in this respect, are seen as a stronger though less well-developed sex. This ability to survive evidences an inability to feel pain and a contempt of death, making them insensitive to the pain and suffering of other people. However, in most women the coldness is controlled or neutralised by pity, weakness, maternity, and, he argues, most importantly by underdeveloped intelligence and lack of passion. On the other hand, criminal women, and all men, possess passion and intelligence. So criminal women have a cranium closer in size to that of men, and have more body hair and other masculine physical traits which are not signs of development in women. He argues that passion and any over-activity in women must be a deviation from normal, as their nature is normally passive. The more passive a woman, the more highly developed she is, and the further from being a 'born criminal'.

Lombroso was not himself consciously race- and class-biased, but the whole idea of a passive female gives rise to criticism of his theory being prejudicial. A racist criticism arises because Lombroso's atavistic traits are necessarily more prevalent in certain races, particularly the non-whites (traits such as large cranium, square jaw and dark hair). Such traits necessarily appear more commonly in certain races and although five characteristics had to be portrayed before a person was labelled a 'born criminal', the possession of one of these traits by a whole race puts every member of that race closer to the category of 'born criminal'. His approach can also be said to be rooted in class because in order to have a wholly passive female, devoted only to family and home, it is necessary to have a society in which some-one works in order to support these women. Of course, when Lombroso wrote, this was the way much of society was structured, and was seen as normal, acceptable and just. Both the racist and class bias can be illustrated by looking at the applica-tion of his traits to Italy. There was a distinct prevalence of 'atavism' amongst the Sicilians, who were both darker skinned and poor.

Lombroso's ideas re-appear as threads in theories right up to the present day. Partly this is because he and his followers provided the basis of the positive school of criminology (see Chapter Six), but Lombroso also infuenced at least two main areas of criminological thought, namely, the notions that crime can be explained by reference to biological and inherited characteristics; and that crime is caused by a pathological or chemical abnormality which needs to be treated. Later writings based on Lombroso tend not to express these ideas quite so directly, but they often make similar assumptions.

17.2.3 Later biological writings

In seeking to explain differences between male and female criminality most writers in the physiological or psychological arena have remarked on the passivity and basic lack of aggression on the part of females, asserting that this explains their lack of criminality. In a more specifically biological approach it has been suggested

(Money and Erhardt (1972), and Rose et al. (1971)) that the genetic passivity of females is related to the different brains of men and women and the difference in hormones between men and women. Clearly, it is difficult to experiment on hormonal change in humans, so all tests have been done on animals, mainly rats. Soon after birth a rat's brain becomes either male or female. If there is a predominance of female hormones (oestrogens), the brain becomes female; if a predominance of male hormones (androgens), the brain becomes male. If, early in life, a female is injected with androgens, she becomes aggressive and indistinguishable from a male, and an early castrated male will be more passive later in life. It has been claimed that these tests, and some rather more complex ones involving monkeys, show that the same may well be true for humans.

The extrapolation of any finding from rats or monkeys to humans is necessarily very risky. It remains unclear what, if any, the effects are of hormones, particularly in early life. Behaviourists try to claim that differences between the sexes are purely a result of socialisation. It could be argued that upbringing over many generations has actually over-emphasised what was originally a negligible difference between the sexes. It is very difficult to ascertain which, if either, of the social or the genetic has had the greater effect.

17.2.4 'Generative phases' of women

This biological theory is based on changes connected with the menstrual cycle. Although it is unclear whether women generally are involved in a higher incidence of criminality during their generative phases, it is clear that the law takes account of these elements in deciding some cases. Menstruation has been used as a partial defence plea, and both menstruation and menopause have been accepted as factors which should reduce sentences (see also 7.1.1). Here the case of menstruation will be considered, but similar factors apply to menopause. Although both these 'generative phases' have been commonly used in such relatively minor cases as shoplifting, more serious cases will be considered here. Susan Edwards (1988) notes that in the nineteenth-century pre-menstrual tension (PMT) was frequently discussed as being an important element of a defence in cases of violence, killing, arson and theft. Both she and Luckhaus (1985) refer to cases in the early 1980s where PMT was successfully pleaded. In one of these, the woman faced a murder charge which was reduced to manslaughter due to diminished responsibility attributed to PMT, and had received a probationary sentence with a proviso that she undergo hormone treatment (*R v Craddock* [1981] CLY 476). Only a few months after the first offence, the same woman was charged with threatening to kill a police officer and of possessing an offensive weapon. Although convicted, PMT acted as a factor to reduce sentence and she was again placed on probation and required to undergo an increased hormone dose (*R v Smith* [1982] Crim LR 531; Craddock and Smith are the same person). In another case a woman, charged with murder, was convicted only of manslaughter due to diminished responsibility; there was no custodial sentence, not even the requirement of hormonal treatment (*Christine English, The Times*, 12 November 1981 and see also Rose (2000)). Clearly, in the cases of these women the law accepted that PMT, although not amounting to a full defence, was the most important reason for the behaviour. PMT was accepted as a partial excuse and as a reason for lenient sentencing; the total effect was the acceptance of the controversial idea that PMT amounted to a causative explanation. This is an inter-esting acceptance in the light of the fact that medical evidence is divided about the existence of such a syndrome and its effects. If there are effects, they appear to be mainly psychological, such as tension, irritability, depression, tiredness, mood swings and feelings of loneliness, although Dalton (1984) has included some rele-vant physical effects such as epilepsy, fainting and even hypoglycaemia. Rose (2000) would wish to see women receiving treatment at an early stage to avoid both the later criminal behaviour and the need to admit this type of evidence in court.

In the case of post-natal depression there is, of course, the special case of infanti-cide (see generally 7.1.1 and 9.2.4 for a definition of this defence). Again, in this instance the law accepts as a partial excuse the fact that a woman's mind and behaviour are affected by the hormonal changes in her body. If a mother kills her child within its first year as a result of post-natal depression or lactation, she would have a partial defence to murder which would render it infanticide. This is clearly only a defence open to women, and is the only sex-specific defence recognised in the criminal law. Some of these killings may possibly be the result of exhaustion through caring for the child, guilt through not feeling affection for it, or the effect of other social pressures, all of which could equally well be suffered by a man if he was the person primarily in charge of the care of the child (for a full discussion of this see Wilczynski and Morris (1993)). The Law Commission's Draft Criminal Code 1989 suggested (clause 64(1)) that these social reasons for infanticide be recognised but only in the case of women (see Mackay (1993)). But a man cannot rely upon the same defence and would have to argue that his mind was unbalanced in some other way in order to plead diminished responsibility. Perhaps there is scope for extend-ing this defence: in the case of women to include 'circumstances consequent on the birth' as suggested by the Law Commission in the draft Criminal Code Bill; and in the case of men for severe stress caused by the birth and care of a child.

As was seen in Chapter Seven the hormonal imbalances suffered by men do not normally affect either their conviction or their sentence. Women, however, can successfully plead such imbalances even in the most serious cases where they take the life of another person (see also (9.2.4)). For the individual women involved, this is probably an advantage as they will either elude an unpleasant label or an unpleasant sentence, or both. For women in general, its effects are not so positive. It allows the continuation of the idea that women are incapable of controlling themselves and that their actions can be explained through medical reasoning—they are mentally or physically sick, or both. Widely used, the implication of this reasoning would be that women should be treated for this 'sickness' rather than punished. It removes from women the idea that they may choose the criminality, that it might be a rational decision arising out of a social, economic or political situation. In many cases these factors are merely used as pleas in mitigation, to be taken into account in sentencing. In the case of a murder charge there is no discre-tion in sentencing, and therefore to allow the judge any discretion PMT must be used to reduce the charge to manslaughter.

17.2.5 **Thomas**

The work of Thomas (1907, 1967 originally publisher in 1923) acts as a stepping-stone between physical and psychological explanations. Thomas moves away from

Lombroso's idea of female criminality being due to masculine tendencies towards saying that, for civilised cultures, female criminality is an unacceptable use of female traits. Female criminals are considered to be amoral, that is, without morality, not immoral, which implies loss of morality. They are described as being cold, calculating people who have not learned to treat others with pity and concern. They use the less developed and colder sides of their natures in order to gain something for themselves through sexual promiscuity, soliciting, prostitution, or other 'unacceptable' and sometimes illegal means.

For Thomas, there are four basic wishes which drive every individual: the desire for new experience (for example, hunting or dangerous sports); for security (the fear of death); for response (maternal and sexual love); and for recognition (dominance within the group). Thomas argues that for females generally, it is the response wish which is most marked. In 'normal' lawabiding women, this wish for response is fed by retaining her chastity as a good way of obtaining a devoted husband who can give her security and a family to love. For 'amoral' women the need for love drives her to commit any act in order to gain affection; her own sexual and other feelings take a minor role. Female criminality is thus largely seen as being based on sexuality, leading Thomas to emphasize prostitution and soliciting to explain all unacceptable and criminal behaviour. If the 'amoral' and generally lower-class female was controlled and taught the same standard as her 'normal' middle- and upper-class counterpart, she would be law-abiding. Social conditions are ignored: if women adhered to their model role in society, there would be no female crime. Re-educating those who failed to come up to the conventional role was the change advocated by him. These ideas were common at the time and were extensively used in the control of women by the authorities. Women were channelled, both culturally and by the State correction system, into female roles.

17.2.6 Freud

The next milestone on this road is the writings of Sigmund Freud (1973, originally written in 1925 and 1931). Where Lombroso distinguished between born criminals and other people, Freud saw everyone as a potential criminal in the sense that all human beings are born with immoral and anti-social instincts. The other main difference is that for Lombroso the criminal was a product simply of hereditary factors, whereas for Freud it was a mixture of inherited factors and the effect of external experiences. So, Freud recognises that although all humans are born with criminal designs, most will learn to control them; it is those who do not learn such control who end up as criminals. For Freud, the inability to learn social habits is partly hereditary and partly related to upbringing. His successors often argue the human personality is shaped by its social environment alone and that heredity plays no part (see Chapter Eight for a discussion of this), but Freud places a large part of his argument on heredity. Here, it is intended to focus upon Freud's theory of female criminality.

As with a large portion of Freud's work, the central tenet of his theory tends to be sexual; that is, that the explanation or motivation for the female criminal is largely sexual neurosis. Due to the lack of a penis the female feels, and often is, inferior, better suited to the less demanding destiny of being wife and mother rather than breadwinner. He says that a woman, whilst she is still a child, recognises that she has inferior sexual organs and believes this to be a punishment. She then grows up envious and revengeful. The feminine behaviour of most women can be traced to their lack of a penis. They become exhibitionist and narcissistic, and so try to be well-dressed and physically beautiful in order to win love and approval from men. Freud argues that the genetic differences between men and women lead to a difference in sexual functions which make women passive and masochistic, as their sexual role is receptive:

It is perhaps the case that in a woman on the basis of her share in the sexual function, a preference for passive behaviour, and passive aims is carried over into her life to a greater or lesser extent . . . (p. 149)

He further argues that women generally do not develop a strong conscience. Men develop one as a result of controlling their Oedipal complex. An Oedipal complex is a man's or boy's incestuous love for his mother which is repressed due to a fear of a jealous reaction from his father. The fear is that the father may ultimately castrate the son—this is the most feared punishment. As a result, boys generally by the age of about 5 develop a very strong super-ego or conscience. As girls and women cannot be castrated, they do not possess the fear necessary to overcome the Electra complex (their desire for their father and hatred of their mother). Normally this would lead to a higher crime rate for women, but due to the passivity (mentioned above) and their very strong desire for love and affection, particularly from their fathers or other men, they are controlled. They do not break men's laws, for to do so would lead to disapproval and a withdrawal of male love and affection.

In Freud's world, deviant women are those who attempt to become more like men, those who compete or try to achieve acclaim within the masculine spheres of activity, or those who refuse to accept their 'natural' passivity. These women are driven by the desire to claim a penis, which leads to aggressive competition. This ultimate desire is, of course, hopeless, and they will end up by becoming 'neurotic'. Such women need help to enable them to adjust to their intended sex role. The birth of a child would be seen as particularly therapeutic as the baby is seen as a substitute for a penis, according to Freud.

Like Lombroso, Freud mostly ignores social, economic and political factors: unlike Lombroso, who centred his theory on physical characteristics, Freud's theory uses psychology and mental disease to explain female criminality. Nevertheless, the concept of a well-adjusted woman is based very much on traditional ideas of sexuality and society. It thus suffers from the same sex and class problems as the earlier theories, but was probably more demanding because of its 'scientific' basis.

17.2.7 **Pollak**

Pollak's theory (1950), was also sex-based. He was doubtful that women commit as little crime as the official statistics showed. He thus advanced a theory of 'hidden' female crime. Pollak follows Freud in explaining female crime by reference to sexual neurosis. Women are traditionally shy, passive and passionless, but can simulate a sexual orgasm to hide their true feelings. They can take part in sex without any physical passion, and they can learn to hide their monthly menstruation. All this means that within the sexual sphere they learn to manipulate, deceive and conceal—this, he claims, decides the inherent nature of women, making them likely to be the instigators of crime which is then actually perpetrated by men. Where they do themselves commit crimes, these are related to their feminine nature and explained either on psychological (mental) grounds (e.g., shoplifting is the result of kleptomania, an uncontrolled urge to steal), or on sexual grounds (for example, soliciting for prostitution or sexual blackmail). Other crimes committed by women can be hidden and underhand, for example, poisoning or infanticide. In so far as this description of female crime is valid, he seems not to have considered the possibility that lack of social, political and economic power may have forced women into taking an underhand or manipulative way to enforce change, and so better their position and standing in society.

Lastly, Pollak claimed that women appeared less before, and were more leniently treated by, the criminal justice system because they were differentially treated by all officers of the law. This preferential or, as he saw it, chivalrous treatment arose from the fact that men generally had a protective attitude towards women. Men thus disliked making accusations against women because they did not want women to be punished. This chivalrous treatment, he claimed, stretched from police through the jury to the judge, and thus resulted in a great under-conviction of female criminals. This is a thread picked up by much later writers, although in rather more refined form.

17.2.8 Modern applications

Each of the above theories seems to assume that women are more or less totally different from men in every respect: biology; psychology; needs; desires; motivations. They often link criminality in women to old, unquestioned popular assumptions about problem women—usually associated with their breach of the societal norm of wife, mother and homemaker. Implicit in such views are concepts of women as sources of evil, causing the downfall of mankind: their criminality is then represented as more destructive of social order than anything man could do. This almost pathological fear of female non-conformity and criminality is reminiscent of the 'witch-hunts' of history, which, as Heidensohn (1996) suggests, is a powerful and recurring popular image of 'deviant women as especially evil, depraved and monstrous . . . used by "scientific" criminologists . . . as the basis of their theories, theories which . . . not only had a stigmatising effect, but have also had unfortunate consequences for the treatment of women offenders'. However, Heidensohn may provide us with one of the reasons why female criminality is so feared: women are relied upon to maintain order and to continue present societal structures, so deviance from this role is seen as especially threatening. The socialising role of women in the family and in society is also limiting on them, because it means that they are expected to, and often do, have a far greater stake in conformity. In addition, since the pressures of these roles limit their opportunities to offend, such action by women becomes viewed as more peculiar, and hence less acceptable, than it would be for men.

In studying male criminality, it was clear that mental illness or strong psychological problems were useful explanations only in rare cases where the mental problem was clear. In female criminality, it has been assumed that a wide range of crimes can be explained by such mental factors and that the sexual basis of the mental problem is strong, whereas it was absent in explanations of male criminality. In male criminality, even sex crimes are generally explained on some basis other than the sexual. Even rape is very rarely associated with an incomplete resolution of the Oedipal complex; more often it is said to be a crime of power or violence which just happens to assume a sexual element. In court it is often ascribed to sexual frustration (usually caused by the female dressing or behaving in a 'provocative' manner) or to drink, and is thereby more understandable. Female criminality is, however, often explained in a clinical or sexual way. Shoplifting, traditionally a female crime (although in fact more males than females commit it), has frequently been connected with both mental problems and sexuality. The sexual nature is interesting, as it is a crime which does not obviously possess any sexual elements. Female shoplifting has often been attributed to kleptomania despite the fact that such a mental disease is very rare (see 9.3.4), whilst women are supposed to obtain sexual excitement from the act; or perform the crime to still repressed sexual desires; or in order to be punished for such feelings. The prevalence of these ideas, until at least the 1960s, partly continued because of the number of single, divorced or widowed women who performed such acts; the possibility was ignored that this particular group faced unusually harsh economic and social stresses.

Several psychologically based pleas have now emerged for the legal defence of women. The most interesting addition to this catalogue is the use of post-traumatic stress syndromes; the one most applicable as a defence is the battered woman syndrome; whilst the rape trauma syndrome has been used as a tool to back up both the defence and the prosecution cases. Similar syndromes have been clinically discovered in both men and women but are more frequently used in the courts in cases involving women. In the case of the battered woman syndrome the defence is to a charge of murder and the claim is that what may look like a premeditated crime —or at least one in which self-defence and provocation as presently defined would be difficult to use—can be psychologically explained. Some have attacked the use of, and the need to use, such defences and suggest that the traditional defences such as self-defence should be forced to take account of women's culture and experience (see Lacey et al. (2003) and Law Commission (2003)); or that in assessing the reasonableness of the accused's actions and beliefs they should be explicitly subjective (how would a person in her circumstances and with her emotional condition assess the situation?). If these approaches were taken there would be less need to use psychological defences, particularly the syndromes which rather stretch and alter the legal concepts which they are used to prove. Some of these matters may be addressed as a result of the Law Commission 2003 consultation relating to partial defences to murder.

The resurgence of women's sex roles and their treatment by the criminal justice system is evident in the treatment which women obtain from the application of the criminal law. Downes and Rock (2003) conclude that contrary to the belief of many positivist writers there is no chivalry towards women in the criminal justice system. The feminist claim is much the reverse of this: female offenders are often viewed as having breached the idea of the female role and are therefore subjected to harsher sanctions for relatively less serious crimes (see Carlen (1983) and Kennedy (1992)). In the early 1990s a number of studies purported to have refuted these claims (see Heidensohn (1996) and Daly (1994) and the Home Office, Hedderman and Hough (1994)). At about this time there was some talk of ending female imprisonment but by the end of the century female imprisonment had risen spectacularly (see

p. 447 above). Although there were more cases of violence by women these were almost all fairly low in seriousness, (see Gelsthorpe and Morris (2002) but a lot more women got custody; and prison sentences, especially for drug trafficking, were for longer). Carlen ((1999) and (2002)) reiterated her claim that courts were more punitive towards female offenders, particularly those who are economically and socially marginalised. Gelsthorpe and Morris (2002) though not refuting this were less convinced of a gender bias but rather as the result of increased punitiveness generally. Interestingly, as will be seen in Chapter Twenty women are largely missing from the risk and governance debates but clearly these figures show that either there is gender bias within the system or that the effects of recent criminal justice and sentencing strategies (such as less tolerance of drug offending; the 'gender-blind' focus on risk rather than offender needs; and 'gender-blind' mandatory sentencing, which is as yet mainly a US practice) impacts more severely on women than on men. Neither of these possibilities should be acceptable in a criminal justice system.

The new sentences proposed in the Criminal Justice Act 2003 will probably further exacerbate the situation. Most women serve either community sentences (usually community treatment) or short prison sentences. The latter are to be replaced by three new approaches: custody plus, which involves custody of between 2–13 weeks followed by a community programme on licence of between 26–49 weeks; custody minus, which is similar to custody plus except the prison sentence is suspended for between six months to two years; and thirdly, intermittent custody, the custodial part is served on an intermittent basis, e.g., weekends rather than as a block of time. Each of these combines a short prison sentence with a community sentence designed to alter the offender's behaviour in the future, in this way they address the problem of the short prison sentence. However, they may well lead to more women being imprisoned; custody plus may retain short sentences and just add on the programme; custody minus might well be used for those who presently face community sentences in order to increase the threat if the order is breached; and intermittent custody might be used instead of community sentences as it will be seen as less destructive of family life whilst being genuinely punitive. Again women's imprisonment is likely to rise without any change in female criminality.

From the above, it should be clear that clinical and sexual reasons for female criminality have been accepted even where those crimes have no clear sexual basis. In the case of male criminality, such explanations were rejected even where the crime appeared to have a very real sexual link. There would appear to be different standards being applied to explaining male and female criminality. At the same time, recent changes in sentencing seem to have impacted particularly harshly on women: this is neither helpful in reducing offending nor necessary to protect the public.

17.3 Learning theories

In Chapter Ten the idea that criminality was the result of differential learning theories was mooted. This claim that criminality is not innate, but is learnt from interaction with other persons; the learning process includes both the motives for its commission and the methods of carrying it out. Criminality will result if the definitions favourable to law-breaking outweigh those unfavourable to it. In modern industrial societies, people are encouraged to pursue self-advancement and are not inculcated with a sense of social responsibility. As a result, although some still learn that the pursuit of aims by legitimate means is the morally acceptable way to behave, many at all social levels will learn that the achievement of the goal is the only important factor: they thus learn both legitimate and illegitimate modes to this end. Sutherland and Cressey maintain that their theory is of general application and applies to rich as well as to poor, and to women as much as to men. The class equality continues throughout the book, but gender equality wavers under the need to explain why the male crime rate is so much higher (see Sutherland and Cressey (1966), pp. 138–43). Sutherland does this by excluding females from this absorbed pursuit of self-interest. He argues that females of all classes and ages are socialised into the same sex role: they are taught to be nice rather than egotistical. Women, on this interpretation, seem to be excluded from the pursuit of wealth which pervades the rest of society.

Although not referring to any innate trait in women, Sutherland implies that women are more law-abiding because they are excluded from the dominant and, he seems to say, male culture. He avoids the potential clash between this and his claim to disprove innate criminality by arguing that differences of gender explain different socialisation of males and females. Because of their sexual difference, girls and boys had different capabilities and interests which are channelled and developed through different training and education, which leads to differential behaviour. Sutherland removes from women the education necessary to criminality or to competitive law-abiding behaviour. He only allows them learning which fits their perceived roles as mothers and carers; any criminality has to arise out of this. More recently Giordano and Rockwell (2000) have revisited the link between differential association and female crime and concluded that this is a decisive factor. Although many women have suffered social deprivation or physical abuse without turning to criminality, they suggest that all female criminals had firm associations with positive depictions of deviant lifestyles. From a young age many of the women were 'immersed' in these definitions, from mothers, fathers, aunts, cousins and siblings who might be caught up in these activities. From this Giordano and Rockwell contend that learning theory and differential associations may explain much female criminal activity.

17.4 Sex role theories

17.4.1 Introduction

After the Second World War, this general line of thought is further developed through what are often referred to as the masculinity (or masculinity/femininity) theories. These centre not on sex itself, but on a recognised and accepted role for each sex. Under this approach, proper socialisation is explained purely as a function of the individual's physical sexual nature: maleness gives rise to masculinity and femaleness to femininity. It is only when this 'natural' process breaks down that women become criminal. These writers generally portray women as passive, gentle, dependent, conventional and motherly, a picture of woman that is not different from that painted by many of the biological determinant theorists. In these later writings, similar behaviours are being considered, but the role is learned. Gender roles are among the strongest learnt social roles in our society and, although not entirely static, they remain fairly constant although they may vary widely between different ethnic groups.

17.4.2 Masculinity/femininity theories

The American sociologist Talcott Parsons (1947 and 1954) explained the different levels of delinquency between males and females as being due to the basic structure of American society and families. The father is the breadwinner, and he works outside the home in order to provide for the family. The mother is involved with the care and upbringing of the children and looking after the home. Boys see the different functions performed by each sex and realise that they are expected to emulate the father, who is largely absent during their upbringing. They feel that they need to prove independence from the mother and act as unlike her as possible. Parsons argues that her role is clearly less prestigious than that of the breadwinner and therefore the boy, wishing to become important, assumes that passivity, conformity and being good are behavioural traits to be avoided. This leads to an aggressive attitude which can lead to anti-social, rebellious and criminal activities. Girls, on the other hand, have a close adult model, the mother, to emulate which allows them to mature emotionally and to learn slowly and surely to become feminine.

Grosser (1951, in Gibbons (1981), pp. 239–41) uses this analysis and applies it to explain juvenile delinquency. Boys see they must become future breadwinners and so become interested in power and money, which might lead them to steal to provide, and to fight to obtain power and prestige. Girls see they must become the home-makers, and so close relationships are more important to them. Girls are more likely to participate in sexual promiscuity than criminality; any criminality will be committed to win the affection of men, such as theft of clothes and make-up which may make them more attractive to the opposite sex.

This thesis was taken up by Cohen (1955), first to formulate his theory on male delinquency with which we have already dealt in 12.3.2, and secondly to argue that, although it is true that girls are essentially law-abiding, there are some who will break the law. He further argued that such law-breaking, when it did occur, was related to their feminine role in that it was either sexually promiscuous or directed at the task of finding an emotionally stable relationship with a man. He argued that women would avoid masculine aggressive behaviour.

Reiss (1960) similarly claims that the sexual activity of females may lead to criminality. Young girls may be willing to participate in sexual activity, both because by having a close relationship with a male they obtain prestige among their peers, and because they consider it necessary to maintain a close relationship with the boy. However, if complications, such as pregnancy or sexually transmitted diseases develop, the young girl will lose all prestige both from her male and female peers. Loss of prestige in this way may lead to criminal activity. Here, criminality is the result of sexual behaviour which arises due to the need to fulfil a particular sex role

—that of having a relationship with a male, which may also involve other types of criminality such as stealing clothes and make-up.

Dale Hoffman Bustamante (1973) notes that females are rewarded for conforming behaviour, whereas males, although being taught to conform, are often rewarded when they breach the rules. She argues that this teaches men, but not women, that though conformity is generally desirable, it can be rational to breach the rules in some cases. Women are shown that the only way forward is by conformity. She notes that media images can also be influential: male heroes can be portrayed as rule-breakers or benders (cowboys in western movies, police in adventure films); heroines, at least until recently, have generally been pictured as girlfriends, mothers and housewives. She says that sex role skills are important as they dictate what type of crime an individual will be capable of committing. Women are less likely to use weapons because they rarely learn how to use them, but they may use household implements to threaten their victims. This is also consistent with the fact that female crimes of violence are often committed against family members or close friends. Property crimes, she argues, often take the form of forgery, counter-feiting or shop-lifting which may arise from the stereotyped role of women as paying the bills and doing the shopping. She notes that amongst children and teenagers in America, girls are more likely than boys to be arrested for the juvenile crimes of 'breach of curfew' (which is an offence in some states in America) and 'running away'. This she explains by saying that girls are more likely to be noticed if they are out alone than are boys, and parents are more likely to worry about their daughters than they are about their sons.

The sex-role stereotyping is so strong that in some cases even where a theory is being postulated which runs counter to this idea, a feeling of the sex role may be present. Smart (1976) proposes a feminist critique of explanations but at points she lapses into a sex role orientation. For example, she explains receiving stolen goods, when committed by women, in terms of a passive act carried out for a loved one, and the goods are likely to be hidden somewhere in the house. The offence is thereby ascribed to relationships and to passivity, both of which fit in with sex-role stereotypes.

Masculinity/femininity theories are based upon behavioural theories (see earlier 17.2), social learning theories (see earlier 17.3), control theories (see below 17.6), and they are sometimes related to biological theories (see earlier 17.2).

17.4.3 Evaluation of masculinity/femininity

In the 1970s three studies (Cullen et al. (1979); Widom (1979) and Shover et al. (1979)) aimed to provide an empirical test of masculinity/femininity theories, but the results were inconclusive. They neither prove nor disprove the hypothesis that increased 'masculinity' leads to crime. While there is some suggestion that the female crime rate is inversely related to femininity, this is by no means proven, nor is it necessarily a causative relationship. Because the male is so much greater than the female crime rate, any tests which seem to suggest that masculin-ity leads to crime and femininity leads to law-abiding behaviour are understand-ably attractive at first glance. But the tests all confront the difficulty that, both theoretically and empirically, there seems to be no unexceptional criterion by which to measure 'masculinity' and 'femininity'. At most it could be cautiously claimed that the tests cast doubt on any correlation between masculinity and crime, but found some inverse relationship between crime and femininity. The implication is that masculinity is an unreliable indicator but that a very 'feminine' woman may be less likely to commit crime than is her less feminine counterpart.

Many doubt whether even such tentative implications have much validity. The constructs of masculinity/femininity are themselves seen as patriarchal and are rejected by many feminists. In particular, their use as an explanation of crime is challenged because one of the defining elements of femininity is usually given as conformity. Partly as a result of early radical feminist writings, a newer field studying masculinity and its connection to criminality is beginning to emerge (see Jefferson and Carlen (1996)). This links crime, particularly violent crime to masculinity. The question they posed was: what is it that makes men more criminal and more violent than women? Feminists began to claim it was masculinity and the greater power men systematically enjoy. But it then becomes necessary to explain why so many men are law abiding. One approach has been to differentiate between kinds of masculinity. Messerschmidt (1993) applied the concept of masculinities within three structures: labour; power (control and violence); cathexis (relationships and desire), and he suggested that crime permitted some men at certain times to attain masculinity in one of these areas. Hall (2002) suggests that in postmodernity the insecurity fear and removal of ability to compete or be useful suffered by many marginalised male groups may release or encourage powerful and aggressive forms of masculine identities to arise as a power issue. Similar claims are made by Young (1999) and Hall and Windslow (2003) where the violence and other criminality are seen to arise in order to secure some self-respect or to achieve something within the market economy. This might be seen as a construction of masculinity. The implication is that gender/masculinity alone is of little use but when related to other social and particularly economic aspects may help to refine explanations. Possibly the main problem in this line of academic analysis remains the lack of agreed conceptions of masculinity or femininity. Some are linked to outward behaviours (Messerschmidt (1993, 1997 and 2003)) and might be seen to merely describe what they are claimed to explain, others (e.g., Jefferson (1992 and 1998)) present a more psychic or psychoanalytical aspect of the concept but with little precision. It seems that a more useful conception may be in building self-image and therefore a personal and internal image of self.

Some have explored the idea that girls who partake in violence are enacting masculine portrayals. Miller (2001 and 2002), writing largely about young women in US gangs, challenges this and disputes the validity and reliability of treating masculine/feminine as merely oppositional. She argues that women's violence needs to be seen in a more complex light and associated with severe insecurities. Similar findings have been replicated by Burman (2003) and Phillips (2003) both of whom note the functionality of such aggression and violence to the lives of the women who perpetrate it. Despite this the criminality of female offenders is often viewed as resulting from their failure to embrace their femininity and their female and conforming role. Bosworth (2000) argues that in the past prisons were one of the social methods of restricting women and trying to teach them 'good' and 'bad' femininity. Similarly, Erricson (1998) discusses the role of child welfare work in trying to curb boys' criminality whilst not subduing their masculinity but working

462 Positivist explanations of female criminality

to alter girls back to the path of 'virtuous' femininity. It may be difficult to establish identities of femininity and masculinity, and even harder to establish whether, if any exist, they are innate or socially learnt, but it does seem that punishment regimes have been using such a distinction to try to socialise females back into accepted feminine roles whilst leaving masculinity unaltered and merely trying to persuade men and boys back to law-abiding behaviour.

17.5 **Strain theories**

The strain theory as applied to men was discussed in Chapter Twelve, which described the anomic theories of Durkheim and the way they were adapted and almost completely altered by Merton to explain the American way of life. In Merton's analyses, individuals are taught to desire certain things such as material success, but the legitimate means of achieving this—education and thence employment—are either not available or have only a limited relevance for the bulk of the American people. Those with limited opportunities were then frustrated into committing criminality to obtain the goals. This formulation was adopted by Cohen to explain male lower-class and youthful criminality but, as seen above (17.4.2), females were excluded from this form of strain: the only thing which they ought legitimately to desire was a mate or male companion, and therefore their criminality would revolve around that aim. In Cohen's scheme the whole of American culture is basically gendered; ambition, wealth, rationality and control of the emotions are the outward signs of a successful person, but only a male person. For women, success is to form a close relationship with a successful man. A lack of ambition, inactivity, irrationality and emotional instability are signs of a failed and defective male; they are the very identity of women. The other main proponents of the strain theory, Cloward and Ohlin, also relegate women to a position which excludes them from the main masculine culture. Because women are not subjected to financial pressures, they do not suffer strain in the same way and so have no need of criminal gangs or cultures to redress the balance.

The basis for such analyses has been eroded by some broad modern trends. Thus females have increasingly become economically less marginalised. More women are now the only, the major, or the joint breadwinner, and therefore the pressures or strains of economic requirements are increasingly placed upon them especially as women often inhabit low paid and insecure areas of employment, or are unemployed. Within this context it is instructive to note that women are more likely than men to be poor. From the official social security statistics over a number of years it is clear that two-thirds of adults supported by the social assistance income support scheme are women; while the Family Expenditure Survey reveals that women are over-represented in the lowest deciles, both on the basis of their individual incomes and when taking account of the incomes of other household members. In the latter case, two-thirds of adults in the poorest households are women. This is not a peculiarly British situation: in the whole of Europe (except the Netherlands) Eurostat figures show that female-headed households suffer much higher rates of poverty—this is particularly so in the UK, Ireland, Portugal and France. These increased strains may help to explain some of the modern increase in female criminality, especially in the traditionally male criminal areas. Applying strain theory to females could, however, predict too much criminality since they are the most economically marginalised so if they were also to enter the competition for success one might expect their criminality to exceed that of men. Some of the reasons for the lack of such an immense increase in female criminality may be found in Tittle's control balance theory (see 13.5). However, there are certain offences which have risen dramatically and which are associated with female poverty: evasion of payment for television licences is probably the most dramatic example (see Pantazis and Gordon (1997)).

There is no doubt that to view the criminality of women as related only to their desire for a partner is too narrow. Clearly, women play a real role in society in general, and often fall under similar strains to those suffered by men. If there is a vast difference in their criminality, it must be ascribed to some other reason.

17.6 **Control theories**

Theorists in this school claim that it is not necessary to explain criminality, as this activity is natural. What is to be explained is conformity: why don't more people break the law? This question was addressed in Chapter Thirteen; here its specific relation to female criminality needs to be considered.

Hirschi (1969) set out the main thesis of control theories, whereby society controls people by means of four methods: attachment to conventional and law-abiding people; commitment to conventional institutions such as work, school or leisure activities; involvement in these same activities; and belief in the conventional rules of behaviour. These should lead to conformity. This idea is set out as a gender-neutral idea, but Naffine (1987) suggests that for a number of reasons it remains a male-gendered theory. First, she notes that if Hirschi was really interested in conformity he would have studied females, as the largest and strongest conforming group, to see why they were law-abiding, and yet he studied men. Secondly, Hirschi sets out as factors of conformity the traditional male role idea of breadwinner, such as responsibility, hard work, commitment to employment and making a rational decision to remain law-abiding rather than risk all of that. Conformity in males is thus depicted as positive, but females are said to conform because of their passive natures—conformity has become negative.

Control theory does not necessarily involve this strong gendering and negative view of the female. Some more recent studies have attempted to incorporate into control theory changes in patterns of family upbringing. Thus Hagan (1989, see also Hagan et al. (1990)) sees family socialisation as important, but notes that in some respects upbringing has altered and that this may explain changes in crime rates for women: in patriarchal families, girls, in contrast to boys, will be socialised as home-makers and away from risks; whereas egalitarian families increase the propensity of girls for risktaking and so of their likelihood of turning to crime (see 13.7.1). Similarly McCarthy et al. (1999) found that girls brought up in less patriarchal homes were more involved in common forms of criminality whilst boys in such homes are less involved in criminality. Where the power—control relationship between parents was more equal it thus had a beneficial effect on boys and a detrimental effect on girls. Interestingly Hagan and McCarthy (1997) suggest that in young people living on the streets where the controlling influences had been removed, the crime involvement by gender was similar, though they might be involved in differing forms of criminality (young women in prostitution, young men in stealing food and serious theft).

It has been suggested (Braithwaite (1989)) that the greater family control exercised over women not only makes them less likely to be criminal but easier to reintegrate into society and conformity if they do stray into criminality. Hagan and McCarthy (2000) state that they replicated this in a re-analysis of their data concerning street youths. If this holds true for most female offenders, it would seem that they would be most likely to respond positively to reintegrative and community punishments. It is thus particularly unfortunate that as noted by Worrall (2000) and McIvor (1998) these sentences are considerably under-used in the case of female offenders. McIvor found that the underuse meant women were unnecessarily sent to prison, albeit for short periods. Worrall suggests that because of under-use by the courts, community service for women is more difficult to organise, Hannah-Moffat (2003) found a similar problem in Canada. Worral (2003) argues that women's needs are not being prioritised and therefore not met by community sentences. The 140 per cent increase in the female prison population between 1993 and 2001 points in the same direction. It is against this background that it seems a reasonable judgment to argue that the disposals most likely to lead women away from further criminality, reintegrative and community punishments, are vastly underused.

Heidensohn (1985 and 1996) proposes control theory as offering the best account of female criminality or, more particularly, female conformity. She argues that women are controlled in the home by their caring role of mothers and wives. She sees this role as being reinforced by social workers and health visitors stressing the rights and welfare of the child, through the idea of community care for the elderly and disabled, and through the way society assumes dependency of women in certain areas. She notes that although it is obviously a simple fact that many women are dependent, the legitimation of the position by the State helps both to perpetuate this position and to control their behaviour. Even if they are at work, their free time is often constrained by having to perform the household tasks as well as their jobs, while because they are often in the least secure employments they are deterred from behaviour which might jeopardise their position. Lastly, male violence also acts as a very real control; domestic violence may keep them in their place in the home, while street violence also tends to keep women in the home. Heidensohn (1996), does also consider the changes that have and may come about as women attain positions of control in criminal justice.

The already mentioned work of Tittle (1997, 1999 and 2000) concerning control balance might also be used to analyse gender differences in offending (for a full discussion see 13.5). He notes that in most areas of their lives women are controlled, often very heavily. As he sees control deficit as one aspect of deviant behaviour, this would appear to predict that women would be heavy offenders, but he notes that large control deficits result in submissive behaviour rather than predatory offending. Also, as women's lives less frequently motivate them towards deviance they tend to be law-abiding. This theory and its possible use in explaining gender differences in offending needs to be more closely considered.

The way in which controls act in our society generally means that females have less opportunity to take part in criminal behaviour and are possibly more at risk if they so do. This makes criminality a less rational and available choice in the case of females than it is in the case of males. The argument here is that it is not women's natures which make them more conforming; it arises rather in the way others control them, together with fewer opportunities. This will be discussed again in connection with female emancipation and its effects on criminality.

17.7 Conclusion

Unfortunately, no conclusive scientific tests have been found to ascertain what link, if any, psychological and physiological factors have with crime. Thus, although theories based upon these ideas can be very strongly attacked, they cannot be wholly discounted. Behavioural scientists and those involved in social sciences have tried to offer other explanations for criminal behaviour and so have largely displaced biological differences; the claim is that either upbringing or environment have emphasised what was originally a very small or non-existent biological difference. As was shown above, a theory (in this case the masculinity/femininity theory) can be said to arise either from upbringing or from biological factors, but both arguments may be questionable if their central tenet is not sound. The only definite conclusion is that biological arguments have been largely discounted as major reasons for crime. The more socially based theories seem to offer more plausible explanations.

However, social explanations of criminality have not provided very plausible answers to the question of why women commit crimes, nor do they satisfactorily explain why females are more conforming than their male counterparts. It may be that the tendency to see male crime as normal necessarily overshadows the study of the much less common female offending. Female criminality is, in any event, most directly damaging to people they know and live with rather than to the wider society, so that theories based on societal conflict seem less immediately relevant. Studies which are implicitly based on masculinity and on presumptions that the offenders will be male, mean that the behaviour of women, if included at all, is—unconsciously—seen through a masculine prism. Even in more recent research where there has been an attempt to include feminism, this remains predominantly the case. The most promising ideas so far come from control theories, and from strain theories as long as these are applied in a gender-neutral manner. Each of these theories suffers from the idea that they are basically determinate, that is, that if certain factors arise, criminality will occur, or if others arise, law-abiding behaviour will result. This will be questioned in the next chapter.

SUGGESTED READING

Carlen (2002), *Women and Punishment: The Struggle for Justice*, Cullompton: Willan Publishing.

Heidensohn, F. (1996), *Women and Crime*, London: Macmillan.

Miller, J. (2002), 'The Strengths and Limits of "Doing Gender" for Understanding Street Crime', *Theoretical Criminology*, vol. 6(4), p. 433 and the reply by Messerschmidt 461 and her reply to his critique 477.

QUESTIONS

1   Why did physical and psychological explanations of female criminality become so accepted in the mid-twentieth century? Are they still accepted by some and do they still affect policy and decisions in the criminal justice system?

2   How have theories based on masculinity and femininity informed criminology? Do they help to explain the differentials in offending between men and women and if so how?

3   Do women suffer from similar strains to those of men and if so why do they not offend as regularly? How does strain theory explain this?

4   Can control theory help to explain differentials in behaviour as between men and women?

REFERENCES

Bosworth, M. (2000), 'Confining Femininity: A History of Gender, Power and Imprisonment', *Theoretical Criminology*, vol. 4, p. 265.

Braithwaite, J. (1989), *Crime, Shame and Reintegration*, Cambridge: Cambridge University Press.

Burman, M. (2003), 'Girls Behaving Violently?', *Criminal Justice Matters Special Issue concerning Gender and Crime*, vol. 53, p. 20.

Carlen, P. (1999), *Sledgehammer*, Basingstoke: Macmillan

Carlen, P. (2002), *Women and Punishment: The Struggle for Justice*, Cullompton: Willan Publishing.

Cohen, A.K. (1955), *Delinquent Boys: The Culture of the Gang*, Glencoe: The Free Press.

Dalton, Katharina Dorothea (1984), 2nd edn, *The Premenstrual Syndrome and Progesterone Therapy*, Droitwich: Heinemann Medical.

Edwards, Susan (1988), 'Mad, Bad or Pre-Menstrual?', *New Law Journal*, p. 456.

Erricson, K. (1998), 'Gender, Delinquency and Child Welfare', *Theoretical Criminology*, vol. 2, p. 445.

Freud, Sigmund (1973), 'Femininity', from papers originally written (1925) and (1931), reproduced in J. Strachey and A. Richards (eds), *New Introductory Lectures on Psychoanalysis*, Harmondsworth: Penguin.

Gelsthorpe, L. and Morris, A. (2002), 'Women's Imprisonment in England and Wales in the 1990s: A Penal Paradox', *Criminal Justice*, vol. 20(3), p. 277.

Giordano, P.C. and Rockwell, S.M. (2000), 'Differential Association Theory and Female Crime', in S.S. Simpson (ed.), *Of Crime and Criminality*, Thousand Oaks, CA: Pine Forge Press.

Grosser, George H. (1951), quoted in Don C. Gibbons (1981), *Delinquent Behaviour*, 3rd edn, Englewood Cliffs, NJ: Prentice Hall.

Hagan, John (1989), *Structural Criminology*, New Brunswick, NJ: Rutgers University Press.

Hagan, J., Gillis, A.R. and Simpson, J. (1990), 'Clarifying and Extending Power-Control Theory', *American Journal of Sociology*, vol. 95, p. 1024.

Hagan, J. and McCarthy, B. (1997), *Mean Streets: Youth Crime and Homelessness*, Cambridge: Cambridge University Press.

Hagan, J. and McCarthy, B. (2000), 'The Meaning of Criminology', *Theoretical Criminology*, vol. 4, p. 232.

Hall, S. (2002), 'Daubing the Drudges of Fury: Men, Violence and the Piety of the "Hegemonic Masculinity" Thesis', *Theoretical Criminology*, vol. 6(1), p. 35.

Hall, S. and Winlow, S. (2003), 'Rehabilitating Leviathan: Reflections on the State, Economic Regeneration and Violence Reduction', *Theoretical Criminology*, vol. 7(2), p. 139.

Hannah-Moffat, K. (2003), 'Getting Women Out: The Limits of Reintegration Reform', *Criminal Justice Matters Special Issue concerning Gender and Crime*, vol. 53, p. 44.

Hedderman, C. and Hough, M. (1994), *Does the Criminal Justice System Treat Men and Women Differently?*, Home Office Research Findings No. 10, London: Home Office. **http://www.homeoffice.gov.uk/rds/pdfs2/r10.pdf**.

Heidensohn, Frances (1985), *Women and Crime*, London: Macmillan.

Heidensohn, Frances (1992), *Women in Control?*, Oxford: Oxford University Press.

Hirschi, Travis (1969), *Causes of Delinquency*, Berkeley, CA: University of California Press.

Hoffman Bustamante, Dale (1973), 'The Nature of Female Criminality', *Issues in Criminology*, vol. 8, p. 117.

Home Office (2002), *Statistics on Women and the Criminal Justice System: A Home Office Publication Under Section 95 of the Criminal Justice Act 1991*, London: Home Office. **http://www.homeoffice.gov.uk/rds/pdfs2/s95women02.pdf**.

Hough, M., Jacobson, J. and Millie, A (2003), *The Decision to Imprison: Sentencing and the Prison Population*, London: Prison Reform Trust.

Jefferson, T. (1992), 'Theorising Masculine Subjectivity', in T. Newburn and E. Stanko (eds), *Just Boys Doing Business*, London: Routledge.

Jefferson, T. (1998), ' "Muscle", "Hard Men" and "Iron" Mike Tyson: Reflections on Desire, Anxiety and the Embodiment of Masculinity', *Body & Society*, vol. 4(1), p. 77.

Jefferson, Tony and Carlen, Pat (eds) (1996), 'Masculinity, Social Relations and Crime', *British Journal of Criminology*, vol. 36(3), Special Issue.

Lacey, N., Wells, C. and Quick, O. (2003), *Reconstructing Criminal Law: Texts and Materials*, 3rd edn, London: Butterworths.

Law Commission (1989), *Report and Draft Criminal Code Bill*, Law Com. No. 177, London: HMSO.

Law Commission (2003), Consultation on Partial Defences to Murder. **http://www.lawcom.gov.uk/files/cp173apps.pdf**. The summary can be found at **http://www.lawcom.gov.uk/files/cp173sum.pdf**.

Lombroso, Cesare (with Ferrero, G.) (1895), *The Female Offender*, London: Unwin.

Luckhaus, Linda (1985), 'A Plea For PMT in the Criminal Law', in Susan Edwards (ed.), *Gender, Sex and the Law*, London: Croom Helm.

Mackay, R.D. (1993), 'The Consequences of Killing Very Young Children', *Criminal Law Review*, p. 21.

McCarthy, B., Hagan, J. and Woodward, T.S. (1999), 'In The Company of Women: Structure and Agency in a Revised Power-Control Theory of Gender and Delinquency', *Criminology*, vol. 37, p. 761.

McIvor, G. (1998), 'Jobs for the Boys?: Gender Differences in Referral to Community Services', *Howard Journal of Criminal Justice*, vol. 37, p. 280.

Messerschmidt, J. (1993), *Masculinities and Crime: Critique and Reconceptualization of Theory*, Lanham, MD.: Rowman and Littlefield.

Messerschmidt, J. (1997), *Crime as Structured Action: Gender, Race and Class and Crime in the Making*, London: Sage.

Miller, J. (2001), *One of the Guys: Girls, Gangs and Gender*, Oxford: Oxford University Press.

Miller, J. (2002), 'The Strengths and Limits of "Doing Gender" for Understanding Street Crime', *Theoretical Criminology*, vol. 6(4), p. 433.

Money, John and Ernhardt, Anke, A. (1972), *Man and Woman: Boy and Girl*, Baltimore: Johns Hopkins University Press.

Naffine, Ngaire (1987), *Female Crime: The Construction of Women in Criminology*, Sydney: Allen & Unwin.

Parsons, Talcott (1947), 'Certain Primary Sources and Patterns of Aggression in the Social Structure of the Western World', *Psychiatry*, vol. X, p. 167.

Parsons, Talcott (1954), *Essays in Sociological Theory*, Glencoe, IL: The Free Press.

Phillips, C. (2003), 'Who's Who in the Pecking Order?: Aggression and "Normal Violence" in the Lives of Girls and Boys', *British Journal of Criminology*, vol. 43, p. 710.

Pollak, O. (1950), *The Criminality of Women*, Philadelphia: University of Pennsylvania Press.

Reiss, Albert, J. (1960), 'Sex Offences: The Marginal Status of the Adolescent', *Law and Contemporary Problems*, vol. 25, p. 309.

Rose, N. (2000), 'The Biology of Culpability: Pathological Identity and Crime Control in a Biological Culture', *Theoretical Criminology*, vol. 4, p. 5.

Rose, R.M., Holoday, J.W. and Bernstein, S. (1971), 'Plasma testosterone, dominance, rank and aggressive behaviour in male rhesus monkeys', *Nature*, vol. 231, pp. 366–8.

Ryan, Christopher and Scanlan, Gary (1991), *Swot: Criminal Law*, 3rd edn, London: Blackstone.

Smart, Carol (1976), *Women, Crime and Criminology: a Feminist Critique*, London: Routledge & Kegan Paul.

Smart, Carol and Smart, Barry (eds) (1987), *Women, Sexuality and Social Control*, London: Routledge & Kegan Paul.

Sutherland, Edwin H. and Cressey, Donald R. (1978), *Criminology*, 10th edn, Philadelphia: Lippincott.

Thomas, William, I. (1907), *Sex and Society*, Chicago, IL: University of Chicago Press.

Thomas, William, I. (1967) (first published 1923), *The Unadjusted Girl*, New York: Harper & Row.

Tittle, Charles R. (1995), *Control Balance: Towards a General Theory of Deviance*, Boulder, CO: Westview Press.

Tittle, Charles R. (1997), 'Thoughts Stimulated by Braithwaite's Analysis of Control Balance', *Theoretical Criminology*, vol. 1, p. 99.

Tittle, Charles R. (1999), 'Continuing the Discussion of Control Balance', *Theoretical Criminology*, vol. 3, p. 344.

Tittle, Charles R. (2000), 'Control Balance', in R. Paternoster and R. Bachman (eds), *Explaining Criminals and Crime: Essays in Contemporary Theory*, Los Angeles, CA: Roxbury.

Worrall, A. (2000), 'Community Sentences for Women: Where Have They Gone?', *Criminal Justice Matters*, vol. 39, p. 10.

Worral, A. (2003), ' "What Works" and Community Sentences for Women Offenders', *Criminal Justice Matters Special Issue Concerning Gender and Crime*, vol. 53, p. 40.

Young, J. (1999), *The Exclusive Society*, London: Sage.

18

Feminist theories

18.1 Introduction

In the previous chapter, it became obvious in the 1970s that one of the most striking features about female criminality and conformity was the lack of research and information available. Female and gender issues were ignored, and attention focused on male criminality and the male. The exclusion of half the population from study is very likely to lead to distortions even, perhaps especially, if that half is likely to be much less represented in the behaviour studied.

When the female was considered, she was generally seen as being inferior to the male. Although conformity was generally to be appreciated, when women conformed, it showed their inferiority. This inferiority was of the same type, whether it was seen as arising out of biological, psychological or social reasons. The male was seen as independent, autonomous, intelligent, active, assertive, rational, unemotional, competitive, achieving and objective. The woman was seen as dependent, passive, uncompetitive, immature, unachieving, unintelligent, emotional, subjective and irrational. The male qualities were portrayed in a positive manner even when they led to negative outcomes such as criminality, and the female attributes were portrayed as negative even when they led to positive outcomes such as conformity to the legal rules.

This view of women has been challenged by feminists in various ways. Some have tried to prove that second wave feminism has made women more like men and more able to compete on an even footing. Others have attempted to force established theorists to rethink their ideas by taking into consideration a feminist perspective and allowing a more gendered approach to the whole question of criminology. Much of the research in these areas is in its infancy.

18.2 Female liberation

18.2.1 The proposition

In the last chapter, some of the theories suggested that people are not born criminal, but learn criminality or conforming behaviour from associates and from the environment in which they are brought up. Some writers, although recognising that in-born characteristics play a part, attach most importance to the society in which a person is brought up. If one accepts that it is through close conditioning that a woman learns to conform, and that it is this close supervision which prevents criminality, then any lessening of the control would lead to increased criminality. The 'women's liberation' movement or early second wave feminism of the 1960s is one obvious source of a lessened control: we should look first at studies made in the 1970s and 1980s to assess the effects of this on female criminality, before turning to look at more general feminist theories.

Adler (1975) claimed that the increase in female criminality (although she assumed, rather than established, that there was an increase) was the proof of the success of second wave feminism: it proved women were free to behave more like men both in legitimate and illegitimate spheres. Simon (1975) claimed this to be true of an increase in property offending and many others at the time linked assumptions of increases in female offending to second wave feminism. Any assessment of these arguments requires a prior examination of the assumption of increase.

18.2.2 Crime statistics

The question here is whether there was a rise in female offending following second wave feminist of the 1960s. There were undoubtedly large percentage increases in female offending: Smart (1979) noted a 100 per cent increase from 1965 to 1975 but also drew attention to the very low base of female crime such that small increases in numbers appeared as large percentage increases (e.g., murder went up by 500 per cent, but this reflected a jump from just one to five cases). Smart suggests that one should look at increases over a number of decades. Table 18.1 shows a fluctuation in crime figures over the period 1935–99. It portrays a general increase in female compared with male crime over this substantial period. More significantly for the present purpose, it shows that the period immediately preceding the 1960s wave of feminism generally shows a higher increase in female crimes than the later period when emancipation was presumed to be leading to the greater involvement of women in criminal activity. Indeed, on this measure there is an actual decrease in female criminality in the 1980s and 1990s. The effect is seriously to question, if not to refute the claim that there have been more increases in female crime as a result of feminist activities.

The area is clearly full of statistical traps for the unwary. One of the fullest British discussions on the numerical increase in female crime and the question of whether or not it is linked with women's emancipation came in 1983 from Steven Box and Chris Hale. They attack the whole idea of a link between female criminality and feminism, and reject most previous arguments on the grounds that earlier writers commit one or more of the following errors:

1. A failure to take into account changes in the number of females available to

Table 18.1: Number of males and females found guilty of indictable offences per 100,000 of the male and female population respectively

	1935	1945	1955	1965	1975	1980	1985	1990	1995	1999
Male	370	512	502	971	1,694	1,850	1,805	1,382	1,199	1,292
Female	47	86	69	149	278	303	260	193	162	209

Source: Calculated from figures provided by *Criminal Statistics, England and Wales*.

commit crimes in each particular year. Most researchers look at the numbers of crimes committed in various years without looking at whether the number of women has changed, and particularly without discovering whether the number of women between 15 and 65, that is, those likely to commit crimes, has changed.

2. Failure to take into account the change in male crime. If this is also increasing, then although female crime may be increasing *absolutely* (i.e., when compared with female crime in previous years) it may not be increasing *relative* to male crime. If both increase at the same rate then, although there may be a need to be concerned about crime in general, it is uncertain whether there should be concern about female crime in particular.

3. Failure to break down the broad categories of crime recorded in the criminal statistics into different types of crime, particularly into those which are more theoretically relevant.

4. Failure to specify theoretically and measure rigorously the other dependent or independent variables which may have had an effect on the statistics. This would include, for example, changes in the law, or in the recording of statistics or in court practices.

5. Failure to apply relevant statistical tests to the data so that significant changes and relationships between the independent and dependent variables can be identified. That is, they do not try to test how much of an effect each of the factors may have had.

In an analysis of statistics Walklate (1995) concluded that men and women commit similar types of crimes although women offend at a much lower rate and commit serious offences far less frequently than do men. Women tend to commit theft and handling, this accounts for 60 per cent of female offenders, and drug offences (see Home Office (2002)). Violence against the person only counts for about 10 per cent of their criminal activities, and it is this low level of violence that is of most significance. In self-report studies women always report far lower rates of criminal activity than do men, while female offending peaks at an earlier age (14 or 15) than for male crime (18, see Home Office (2002)), and thus before feminism is likely to be a major influence.

These surveys of statistical data cast serious doubt on the notion that there is a causative correlation between female crime and feminism. If, however, the arguments based on criminal statistics are left to one side for a moment, there are still those who propose that the activities of the 1960s must have affected female crime. They say it has led to an increase in legitimate opportunities for women, allowing them even after marriage to leave the home and go out to work, which necessarily leads to increased criminal or other socially unacceptable opportunities for women.

18.2.3 The women's movement

The women's movement is not wholly or even largely concerned with women's positions and standing in the working environment. Nonetheless it seems that popular opinion sees this as their main area of concern, and it is in any event plausible to consider whether their clearly important efforts in this area are likely to have affected female crime. Smart (1979) argued that if criminal opportunities are directly related to the release of women from the home environment and into work, the results would show up in increases in specific crimes. In particular, the increases would fall into the area of white-collar crime rather than that of violence, robbery or burglary. Yet it is not white-collar crime which appears to have increased. It is difficult to know what to make of this since, as was seen in earlier chapters, white-collar crimes remain largely hidden. Its relation to female crime is further obscured, because it appears to be only the middle-class professional or clerical worker whose employment opportunities have been noticeably improved by the so-called liberation movement. Lower down the social scale the main change has been in the number of women (often married) doing mostly part-time, low-paid work. Otherwise, working-class women have always had to go out to work, and in fact the working position and opportunities of these women in the last 30 years has in some respects been worsening as Smart found in the 1970s by increased unemployment amongst working-class women. Yet, Smart argued, it was the working-class women who were increasingly appearing in the criminal statistics.

If Smart is correct in her analysis, then it is difficult to detect any direct causative connection between feminism and the level of female crime. It may have had an indirect effect by shaping the way in which law enforcement agencies perceive and treat women. It may have made them more likely to suspect, charge, prosecute, convict and sentence women than was previously the case. Her conclusion, that in order to study the real effect of the women's movement we must look wider than pure statistical analysis or its direct effects, seems difficult to refute.

There have been some attempts to test the links in both America and Britain. Josefina Fiqueira-McDonogh's 1984 American study tested three hypotheses about the importance of feminist aspirations on behaviour:

1. *The 'equal opportunity' hypothesis:* a high level of feminist aspirations (for example, equality between the sexes) will press women towards a greater involvement in the male's sphere of activities, both legitimate and illegitimate (Adler (1975); Simon (1975); see above).

2. *The frustration hypothesis:* a high level of feminist aspirations under conditions of *lagging* opportunities will lead to a greater involvement of women in illegitimate behaviour (Austin (1983); see above).

3. *The competitive hypothesis:* a high level of feminist aspirations will lead females to high levels of legitimate activity to compete with males for available legitimate opportunities.

She obtained her data from male and female high school students who completed self-administered questionnaires. The groups chosen had been drawn from a variety of social and economic backgrounds. The subjects were born in 1964 and so were brought up in an environment which was likely to be aware of the women's movement and of women's rights generally. As well as collecting figures on criminal activity, the study was based on: feminist orientation or the effects of feminism; on class, race and social aspirations: on school involvement, grades and social activities; and on sexual activity. She states in her conclusion:

The findings support best a subcultural deprivation explanation of delinquency. Lower-class position depresses aspirations leading to lower school performance and high social activity which strongly predict delinquency. *The contribution of feminist orientation to the predominant explanatory path is minimal.* (our emphasis)

Support of sexual equality in public opportunities and private life showed no effect and a negative effect respectively. Only where there was a personal identification with feminist attitudes was there any slight positive effect on delinquency. All three original hypotheses received some confirmation. Feminist orientated girls had higher career aspirations, performed better in school and were less involved in sex. They fell within the competitive hypothesis which predicted no extra crime as a result of feminism. This hypothesis was most strongly supported by the results. The equal opportunity and frustration hypotheses drew some support from aggressive and success-orientated girls. The overall results showed that the feminist movement had given rise to a number of positive effects and very few negative effects. It also suggested that the best way of curbing the small negative results is by encouraging high school performance and reinforcing career and/or conventional aspirations rather than by trying to curb the aggressive, success-orientated aspect.

This empirical study gives rise to quite strong results which seem to disprove a correlation between women's liberation and the female crime rate.

The 1983 British study by Steven Box and Chris Hale (18.2.2) looked at crime in general and used a very careful breakdown of the official statistics. Box and Hale found that, taking the female population which is available to commit crimes, then between 1951 and 1979 female offending increased overall at a somewhat higher rate than that of males. Recognising the difficulties in making and explaining such comparisons they used changes in four broad social factors in on attempt to assess the effect of the women's movement on crime.

These factors were:

1. fertility;
2. female undergraduates plus graduates;
3. female labour force participation; and
4. unattached women (single/divorced/widowed).

(1) and (4) were used as indicators of female release from family ties; (2) and (3) show their entry into other spheres of activity. They also attempted to test for the lower economic groups by looking at the rates of female unemployment, but this may be rather misleading as many eligible women do not register, and their willingness and ability to do so almost certainly changed over the period covered (1951–79).

Box and Hale found no statistical relationship with crime in any of the four indicators of feminism in the 29-year period. They did, however, find that crime was affected both by the number of registered unemployed and by the level of employment of women police officers. Thus over the three decades studied there was a fourfold increase of women in the police force, which indicated the extent to which the force has increasingly recognised demands for sex equality, and this recognition probably extended to the routine processing of female suspects.

This account squares quite well with Brown and Heidensohn (2000), who observed that the increases in female police officers were prompted more by general liberal ideas of equality rather than notions of social justice or to change policing practices. Female police officers were expected to do the job like men, which leads, as both Box and Hale and Brown and Heidensohn suggest, to an equal application of male values to female offenders. However, Brown and Heidensohn (2000) found that female police officers were still assessed and analysed as sexual beings, just as female offenders are still punished and controlled through conceptions of female roles. The role of policewomen was and, to an extent, still is seen as one to 'control the sexuality' of other women, which tends to push female officers into certain types of roles or jobs: perhaps rising female criminality is to be expected as women are being more closely controlled. On the other hand, this facet of policing is also linked with the discovery of higher rates of female victimisation, especially of violence which is often committed in the private domestic sphere.

These studies point towards the absence of any strong direct causative link between the women's movement and women's criminality, either amongst juveniles or amongst adults. Recent developments in control balance theory (see 13.5) also support these views. They suggest that, even if the women's movement has made a difference in the power or control of women, particularly in the opportunities for paid employment, this would not necessarily lead to a large difference in female crime rates because other traditional socialising aspects may remain, or because women may be less likely to choose such behaviour. However, it is probable that feminism has affected the consciousness of women. This was the conclusion reached by Heidensohn (1994) after a survey and analysis of studies stretching over 30 years. Women were seen now as more aware of their ascribed status, more willing to resist that expected role and more willing to voice that dissent. Women's positions and expectations had altered and there was no going back. The change does not necessarily result in more criminality, though it should impact on explanations of offending, both those applying to women and to men. Another study (Tomsen (1997)) gave a different twist suggesting that women who actively seek equality may suffer higher rates of victimisation, being seen as a threat to masculinity and male power. The overall implication is that to assume that feminism would necessarily lead to greater female criminality is both too deterministic and too simplistic. A fuller discussion is thus necessary.

18.3 Feminist theories

18.3.1 Old ideas re-assessed

In the last chapter, many of the theories which have been posited for explaining male criminality were studied to discover how they fitted female criminals into the picture. Most of them viewed male criminality in a far more positive light than they did female criminality, and applied very negative explanations to both female criminality and female conformity. Here, it is proposed to re-assess some of these ideas and discover whether there is anything more positive which they may have to offer to explain female criminality.

Sex-role socialisation theories of criminality have been found to be very unreliable predictors of criminality (see 17.4 and 18.2). The assumption that masculinity leads to criminality because of its aggressive, positive, rational and objective qualities is not found to be the case where women are concerned; in fact some of the women with high masculinity factors seemed to have a lower tendency towards offending. Similarly, femininity, when portrayed by women in the form of a passive and pliant female, does not reliably predict conformity. The simple negative view of femininity as compliant and passive is a stereotype which can no longer be credibly employed. It can be argued that there are positive values attached to feminism: against the positive male value of rights, it is possible to see a positive female ethic of responsibility, that is, consideration of others before oneself, consideration of relationships and feelings, kindness, compassion and an idea of mutual dependence and attachment. Although to test whether these revised masculinity and femininity factors made better predictors of criminality and conformity would be interesting, there is a major prior question. Are these personality variables inherently connected with male and female, or are they merely constructed that way by society? Is femininity just a product of the exploitation of women within the society?

In Chapter Twelve sub-cultural gang theories, largely of the 1950s and 1960s, were considered. But, these were then applied only to young males: male researchers empathised with male offenders (Heidensohn (1996)) and presumed that women did not participate in such activities. More recently, feminist literature has forced virtually all criminological areas at least to acknowledge its existence so that more recent work in these areas has tried to include females and feminism or gender. Thus when Bourgois (1996) looks at gangs of crack dealers in Spanish-Harlem and at their environment, he takes gender and feminism as one of his analytical tools but is still drawn to explanations based on economy more than feminist interpretations (thus when one gang member beats his pregnant wife this is explained as frustration at not being able to provide for his family, ignoring the possible power and gender aspects which might be present). Despite stated intentions, the voice of women and feminism is still muted in such studies. Other research centres on female gangs or subcultures. Both Campbell (1993) and Joe and Chesney-Lind (1998) argue that these female peer groupings (or gangs) are used to support non-criminal ways of coping with victimisation or marginalisation, and that where offending occurs it is mostly of a very minor nature. In this interpretation these gangs are constructive: Campbell even suggests that they help to sustain, rather than subvert, communities. However, Messerschmidt (1995) discovered female gangs of girls from ethnic minorities connected with other (usually) female gangs in a way similar to that which had been documented for some male gangs. These women defined and pursued their own ideas of femininity, claiming that their criminality was consistent with these ideas as it allowed them to experiment and take part in exciting activities which they chose for themselves and within boundaries which they set themselves. This may not be mainline feminism but it recognises constructs of gender similarities and differences being created by boys and girls on the street. Here then there may be a place for masculinity/femininity and gang cultures, but on very different grounds to those discussed in the largely male-orientated literature (see Messerschmidt (1993, 1995, 1997 and 2003), Jefferson and Carlen (1996), Hall (2002), Hall and Wilmslow (2003), Miller (2001 and 2002), Burman (2000 and 2003) and Phillips (2003) and the discussion in 17.4.3. This is an interesting example of the way in which feminist perspectives permit a broader and more inclusive academic debate than has hitherto been possible within the strict confines of mainstream criminology. In this way feminist theories have helped to emphasise how both masculinity and femininity could well form a central area of research for criminologists.

Later work in the UK suggests a rather different link with both gangs and violence. Press coverage in the UK through the 1990s and beyond has suggested a growing and major problem with girl violence, reporting 'girl gangs' on the streets attacking innocent victims. As with most press coverage of criminality much of this is misleading. Batchelor (2001) states that in their lengthy discussions with 800 teenage girls none of them was in a gang nor knew of any other female who was a gang member. Burman et al. (2000 and 2003) in the summary report of their full research discovered close-knit groups of girl friends; the girls describe these friend-ships as the most important things in their lives. They were reported as supportive structures but also as sources of conflict and insecurity because of the permanent fear of falling out, and falling out with a friend was a 'devastating' experience. Girls also reported family and the home and the wider peer group as being very import-ant to them and generally supportive even though most violence suffered by the girls took place in the home (mostly between siblings). Almost all the girls had witnessed physical violence, usually in familiar settings. Four out of ten had suffered physical violence, normally between siblings. The girls themselves thought that verbal abuse, experienced by over 90 per cent of them, was more destructive and victimising. Only 10 per cent described themselves as violent: these were the most likely to be involved in other criminal behaviour and had suffered the highest levels of physical victimisation. Burman (2003) concludes that female vio-lence among young girls permitted the perpetrators to get reputations of being 'hard' which brought status and respect and feelings of empowerment, the violence was not 'irrational, hysterical or pathological' but committed for reasons and tangible gains.

This research suggests that girls do not form genuine gangs though they do form very close-knit friendships of a supportive nature (as suggested by Campbell (1993) and Joe and Chesney-Lind (1998)). It also shows that girls learn to manage and avoid violence both as receivers and givers. It bears out the criminal statistics that show low levels of female violence (in 1990 4,400 women offenders were convicted of violence against the person, in 1995 the figure had dropped to 2,800, by 1999 it was 3,600 and by 2001 it was 3,400; the respective figures for men were 48,100, 26,400, 32,100 and 31,800). More importantly it shows the peripheral place of physical violence in their daily lives and the importance of supportive friendships and other structures and the fear of losing these. Nonetheless, as Heidensohn (2000 and 2000/2001) points out, we should never lose sight of the fact that women have the potential for violence which can be seen in their participation in terrorist groups, their active involvement in military service, even in police work as well as in certain, usually notorious crimes. These crimes may be rare but they demand study and understanding: much, but not all, female violence is retaliatory, after suffering violence at someone else's hands. Heidensohn agrees with Burman et al. (2000) that women often learn strategies to control aggression and refers to Heimer and De Coster (1999), who used differential association and feminist theory to consider young male and female violence and concluded that socialisation and position within the peer group and society both fed into violent behaviour. While violence was more likely (both as offenders and victims) for those who suffered social disadvantage, the gender roles caused females to be more controlled and turn to violence less frequently.

Much of this work reflects feminist claims of giving voice to different views of the world. In contrast, as we have seen (17.5), strain theorists initially dismissed women from serious consideration by claiming that a woman's only role was as a seeker of a partner and a family. This was questioned by the more feminist approach of Box and Hale (1983) when they pointed to the economic marginalisation of women which clearly placed them under great strain (see 17.5). Steven Box (1987), after reviewing fifty American and British studies linking crime and unemployment, concluded that the most plausible explanation for the increase in conventional crimes committed by females is that more women become economically marginalised during a recession. This economic element of their plight has also been addressed by Pat Carlen (1988). In an intricate study of thirty-nine women she discovered that poverty (a desire or need for money) was a frequent reason for their criminal behaviour. Of the thirty-nine women interviewed, thirty-two were poor and had been so for all but brief interludes in their lives, and five others had been poor at some time. Most had only achieved short periods of prosperity from their criminality. But the women themselves did not attribute their crimes to poverty. Although over 80 per cent admitted being poor and 95 per cent had been poor at some time, only 30 per cent saw it as the main reason for the criminality, and only 50 per cent mentioned it as one of the factors leading to criminality.

No doubt economic marginalisation does cause a certain amount of criminality amongst women, and a proper application of the strain theory may well be useful in describing these cases, but it is only of limited use. Thus in the 1980s when economic disparity and marginalisation was increasing, especially for women, their criminality declined. If this indicates (Pantazis and Gordon (1997)) that poverty and strain are not generally linked to female crime, the more important issue might be quite different. Since women are generally economically worse off than men, how can we explain female conformity? The problem that the strain theory needs to address is why females, despite being more economically marginalised, are less criminal than males. If an answer is found to this problem, it will not only benefit explanations of female criminality but also explanations of male criminality.

Various refinements to strain theory have been suggested which may be of assistance. One is that, as with male criminality, the strain might be caused by feelings of relative, rather than absolute, deprivation. Or that relative deprivation may be less strongly experienced by women than by men. This is possible since feelings of relative deprivation are necessarily subjective, and reflect social and cultural values. And many would say that social structures affect men and women in different ways and to different degrees. It may be that some combination of relative deprivation, subcultural theories and strain may help not only to explain the rate of female offending but also to explain some of the differences between male and female rates of offending.

In any event, it needs first to be further clarified exactly what needs to be explained. All writers on criminality are agreed that male and female crime rates are very different. But how different? Over the 1980s, 1990s and 2000–1 official statistics show that women were responsible for only 16 per cent or less of indictable (more serious) offences but are more frequently involved in offences of handling or of theft. On the other hand, self-report studies suggest that the discrepancy is much less, perhaps that one-third of offences are committed by women but again they tend to be less serious offences (see Home Office (2001) and Graham and Bowling (1995)). There are also areas where the involvement of women looks more serious. The NSPCC suggest that in the early 1980s, where children were physically injured, natural mothers accounted for more cases of suspected abuse than did natural fathers (33 as opposed to 29 per cent) although fathers were more implicated when account was taken of the parent with whom the child lived (Creighton and Noyes (1989)). The figures all show that there is a discrepancy, but it may be neither as simple nor as great as the official statistics suggest, and that there may be some offences where women are more evident. Explanations must take account of all these factors.

In Chapter Seventeen the effects of differential association on women were also discussed (17.3) and were seen in the light of their different socialisation. One indicator was involvement in gangs. Carlen (1988) discovered that over half of her sample had been members of mixed gangs involved in antisocial and criminal activities. Clearly, the criminality of their peers had strong effects upon the criminality of these women. Furthermore, Campbell (1981 and 1984) has produced two lengthy works which indicate that women do join gangs and participate in violent behaviour. The findings suggest the possibility that a straight application of the differential learning theories might be as useful to explaining female criminality as it is to male criminality (see 10.2). Interestingly, Campbell found that the girls in the gang were very conventional in their outlook and their aims—to find a stable relationship with a man, have a family, and live happily (see also the earlier discussion concerning the rationality of female violence within certain circles, Burman (2000 and 2003)).

Following on from this is the question of the control theories in which conformity is both learned and based upon the investment made in conformity. As was seen in section 17.6, this can be seen as a male gendered theory. However, as pointed out by Hindelang (1973), Box (1981), Heindensohn (1985 and 1996) and Tittle (1995, 1997, 1999 and 2000), this is not necessarily so and control theory may be as, or more, useful in explaining female criminality and conformity. Women in modern society are as committed and responsible in their public lives as are men and, because of their differential socialisation, they are also more concerned than their male counterpart about the effects of their behaviours on those close to them, particularly dependent children.

Most working-class women, Carlen (1988) claims, are controlled by two mechanisms. First at work, where the rewards of employment outweigh the rewards of crime. Secondly in the home, where their parents or husbands keep fairly close control over them. They have a psychological commitment to a family, and so remaining in the family would be more important than the rewards which might be gained if they were to turn to crime. Women who have been brought up in care (particularly if this occurs from their early childhood) lose this commitment, or never fully gain it. They see themselves as having little or nothing to lose by engaging in criminality, and so the temptation of criminality is not so well controlled as for other women. The effect of residential care on women was strong in Carlen's study (second only to poverty) and might be said to have come about from a change in the control of these women.

Carlen also claims that once they are brought before the courts for their first offence then, if they are already in care, the authorities often see the only possible punishment as custodial, particularly if they have been difficult to control whilst in care. Moreover, once released from care the women are badly equipped with the skills necessary to cope with an independent existence. This inadequacy, she claims, may cause these women to engage in acts of criminality either because other deviants are the only easy form of companionship available, or because they feel that they only need to consider themselves and are willing to enter into almost any activity to enhance their own position. Ironically, many of the women had been taken into care in order to provide greater control of their upbringing and to teach them conformity, particularly sexual conformity. Yet just this type of attempt to inculcate conformity and traditional values actually led to criminality.

If female conformity is seen as arising out of the way in which women are controlled, then this may be used by some as a cogent reason for opposing more freedom for women. It may result in some people arguing that women should be made to face their responsibilities in the home, particularly in child-rearing. This type of attitude can be seen in the reasoning of the Conservative government in the late 1980s for not providing greater nursery and child care facilities—women should face their responsibilities in these areas, and so keep themselves in conformity and teach their children conformity. Right realists, as we have seen, would go still further, placing the blame for the general rise in crime on parents, particularly mothers and especially single mothers (see Wilson (1985) and Murray (1990 and 1994)).

Possibly if there is a lesson to be learnt from the association of the greater conformity of women with their being more closely controlled, it is that it might better be used to control men. From study of the victims and criminals on the street, many victims are female and are victimised by men (male victims are, of course, also victimised by men). It would seem logical to socialise men and boys in a more controlled way, teaching them conformity. Such a crude application of these ideas would carry with it clear dangers. One of the most obvious might be that it would merely increase domestic violence against wives, sisters and children. Less crude controls, such as inculcating in boys stronger ideas of caring and responsibility and weaker ideas of self, might, however, lead to some reduction of male violence and male criminality.

As already indicated (13.5), control balance theory may be relevant in this respect. In particular, Tittle's notion that deviance will occur when a person either has a surplus or a deficit of control in relations with others would be useful if it could be made operational. Women have traditionally been seen as falling into the latter category, as suffering a severe control deficit. This can be seen in their general treatment in society, especially in terms of harassment, being regarded as objects, the lack of support by authorities, and typically having little control in all kinds of situations (see Warner (2000) (sentencing in rape); Conagham (2002) (rape, harassment and harm); Martin (1999) (sex and harassment); Brooks Gardner (1996) (harassment on the street); Dobash and Dobash (1992) (domestic violence); Hanmer et al. (1989) (rape and other violence); Smith (1989) (rape); Smart (1977) (female victims of violence are often on trial as much as the male perpetrators); Binney (1981) (domestic violence and lack of support by authorities); Hagan (1989) and Hagan et al. (1990) (gendered social control)).

In domestic violence in particular, the rationale for non-intervention has probably been that the family is a private place where the male has power and can choose which methods are necessary to assert his control; a clear illustration of the traditional view of women as being in substantial control deficit and often unprotected by the State. But, as Tittle points out, to assume from this that women will turn to criminality is to accept a deterministic aspect to behaviour: he sees a place for motivation and other concepts of choice. The imbalance in control is not seen as being itself sufficient to predict deviance: the individual must also be motivated, provoked and criminality must be facilitated by both opportunity and the absence of constraint. Of particular importance here may be a commitment to moral ways of behaving which may constrain deviant or criminal activity. At present, because of the very heavy control deficit women suffer, it is argued that they would tend to choose defiant or submissive behaviour which may be destructive, particularly of themselves, but which need not be criminal. Defiant activity may be positive, as can be seen from women collecting together: to redress the balance (see the suffragette movement); to help each other against male control (see women's refuges); to change control bases (see how women have helped to change the criminal justice approach to the way rape and domestic violence are dealt with); or to defy male violence in more open ways (see the Greenham Common protests against US nuclear bases in Britain). Cook and Kirk (1983)). More destructive deviance may also arise—drug or alcohol abuse, suicide, mental illness or forms of activity which challenge the dominant culture: 40 per cent of women sentenced to prison report drug dependency in the year before prison (see above the discussion of female gangs). As their control imbalance is corrected because of changes—brought about in part by feminist pressures but also by other changes in society—they may move into an area where, if they choose deviance, they are perhaps more likely to commit predatory types of behaviour which will often be criminal. This is still not to be taken for granted: the other influences of motivation, opportunity and moral constraint may still be decisive. The important point is that deterministic outcomes should not be assumed: control balance and alterations in the power bases are the backdrop against which individuals may feel a need to deviate or offend, but they will do so only if they choose such behaviour.

From this it can be seen that careful use of male-orientated theories of criminality may be appropriate in explaining women's criminality, and may also help to focus on the strengths and weaknesses of these areas. Adding a feminist or gendered perspective may then further illuminate both female and male behaviour, conforming and offending. Feminist research in these areas needs to be expanded, perhaps particularly the sort which is sympathetic to women's own views of their behaviour.

18.3.2 Feminisms and gender

There are a number of different strands of feminism, each of which has impacted on criminology in different ways. Radical feminism has probably had the most profound effect and is considered in the following section. Other types will be considered more briefly here. They all to a greater or lesser extent assume that the problem is one of men, masculinity and patriarchal control and social relations.

Liberal feminism views women as an equal part of society. It centres on rights and non-discrimination. Laws should be altered to ensure equality in all areas of life—equal work rights, equal pay. Within criminology much of the work of this group has been associated with a study of the discriminatory practices of the criminal justice system, whether these be in favour of, or, more likely, against women. This involves consideration of the ways in which the criminal law itself (crimes and defences), whilst claiming to be gender neutral, in fact works more favourably for one gender or other. It also embraces analysis of discriminatory application of the law: arrest; decisions as to whether to prosecute; believing victims; willingness to get involved in the 'private' domain; acceptable types of evidence; acceptable ways of giving of evidence; rights of defendants and victims; findings of guilt and sentencing. Liberal feminism is interested in discrimination of offenders, witnesses and victims. It also helped to unveil the long absence of women in much criminological research. There had been some consideration of women, particularly as innately more law abiding and as being unwell (physically or psychologically) if they offended, but there was very little sociological work concerning female offending and they were and are absent from many of the major studies. Against this background the work of the early liberal feminists has been fruitful as it has shown the need for broader perspectives.

The separate strand of socialist feminism is interested in the effects of both patriarchy and capitalism on criminality. It notes the exploitation and oppression of women in both their public and private arenas but analyses these issues as exacerbated by capitalism. It studies the effect of power on crime and generally would consider that misuse of power is probably the most harmful element within society. The constructs of class and gender power interact to create different opportunities for different groups to engage in both legitimate and illegitimate activities. Here the motivation for criminality is often seen as being structural rather than allowing humans to choose their own actions, whilst the analysis explores how power differentials in class and gender impact differently on men and women both as victims and offenders.

Cultural feminism explores and often celebrates differences between men and women. It is interested in women's culture and socialising qualities. It paints the gender essence of women in positive colours. The caring and community or social attributes of women are seen as valuable attributions especially when set against the individuality, egotism and desire for power of men.

Finally post-modern feminism celebrates difference in a distinctive way. Its intention is to give a voice to any element that may have been silenced in the past, attacking any theory that tried to place people in constraining categories. Its proponents tend to be critical of any broad-sweep social policies in criminal justice or any other sphere. They make heavy use of deconstructionist tools, questioning standard and accepted categories, expressing as subjective much that had previously been presented and accepted as natural, and constructing alternative ideologies, social lives and truths. It is epitomised by alternative living styles such as New Age travellers, and by new forms of protest such as eco-protests (see Lane (1998)). Some theorists in this area have questioned feminist approaches which have allowed research into female criminality to remain on the periphery of mainstream criminology and be basically sidelined rather than forcing the whole discipline to address factors that are presently missing from their analysis. The post-modern propensity to question all essentialist thinking more or less unavoidably leads post-modern feminism to undermine the all-embracing claim that many feminists make concerning patriarchy and even to question the existence of 'women' as a unified group whose social and other interactions can be explained by a single formula. It forces theorists to recognise difference and to avoid general theories that can never fit with complex, fragmented, late modern, social experience. Gender is treated as just one aspect of social and individual identity: class, race, ethnicity, linguistic group, age, sexual orientation etc. should all also be considered by criminologists. These factors have to be addressed as part of the powerlessness, poverty and racial difference which is apparent in female offending and the control of women.

If feminist criminology just looked at why women offend, aiming to establish alternative theories of offending for women than for men, it would be based on a premise which may be entirely erroneous—that women break the law for entirely different reasons from those of men. For example, in Miller's (2000) work on robbery it was found that the reason or motive for the offending was often very similar, even if the methods of operating were different because of different opportunities or power structures. Feminists have performed a valuable service to the law by making criminology re-evaluate its whole foundation and way of theorising. One summary of the main elements has been defined by Daly and Chesney-Lind (1996) as: gender is a complex construct which is related to but never defined by biology; gender and gender relations regulate social relations and the working of institutions and are centred around the fact of the social, political and economic dominance of men; knowledge generally reflects men's 'truth'; and possibly most important, women should be central to all knowledge discovery, on an equal footing with men.

18.3.3 Radical feminists

Many radical feminists take a similar stance to the radical criminologists discussed above (see Chapter Fifteen), except that they consider the position on a gender rather than a class basis. They are concerned with what they see as the failure of the law and legal system to protect women, particularly from violent crimes. They connect this to the patriarchal nature of societies and to power relations, especially within the family, and they try both to explain the domination and to find ways to end it. From this point of view crime must be studied in relation to the general position of women in society, and the involvement of women, whether as victims or criminals, cannot be understood outside its social context. Some have proposed that crime should be deconstructed into its essential components which could then be related to the particular social aspects which seem best suited to explain the behaviour so that, for example criminology would study rape and child sexual abuse in the social context of sexuality. Such deconstruction can be misleading (thus rape and sexual abuse may really be acts of power) and is also unnecessary since the general position only requires an understanding that crime is related to the sexual, economic and political powerlessness of women in society.

Klein (1995) suggests an even more radical recreation of crime and how to study it—'commitment to women's lived experiences and concerns' rather than the mere building and testing of academic criminological theories. Women, and all people to be studied, should be treated with dignity and respect; they should be included as participants not just objects. This type of study requires more than just quantitative studies, it needs qualitative accounts (Daly and Stephens (1995)). It involves a critical questioning of the presumption that justice is an objective ideal or value, and raises the possibility that the system of criminal justice is heavily inclined towards particular types of order. The implication is that equal access to the presently defined concept of justice does not necessarily guarantee justice so far as certain groups are concerned, requiring reconsideration of the nature of justice in the light of feminist and other, particularly racial, constructs.

Some radical feminists view the very nature of law as necessarily gendered and patriarchal, and question both its validity and the enforcement mechanisms which are used (Smart (1989 and 1990)). The suggestion is that the essential nature of criminology represents an attempt at social engineering and continued patriarchy, leading to a belief that, whatever the intentions, there is something inherently dangerous about both law and the study of its social control in the form of criminology. This is obviously similar to the Marxist attacks on the nature of law being an attack on certain classes, and it suffers from similar problems. First, it ignores the fears and control over women that come out of their victimisation which would exist even without laws to control it and might even exist in a non-patriarchal society. Secondly, it assumes that the State is patriarchal in all its endeavours and must always stay so.

Other writers, although accepting the essentially patriarchal nature of the State, would still choose to use the law for their own ends, to protect women. Many of these have fought passionately for the alteration of the law in various guises. To take but one example, MacKinnon and Dworkin have argued hard for the protection of women by the further criminalisation of pornography, a form of expression which they view as degrading to women, whom it portrays as submissive, as subjects, and as second-class citizens. Its criminalisation they see as necessary to restore to women their dignity, equality and power (MacKinnon (1993 and 1994); Moore (1993)). Similar arguments can be found in other claims to alter the law (see Radford et al (2000) and Nicolson and Bibbings (2000), as well as section of Lacey et al. (2003)). Through altering the criminal law and the focus of control one might be able to empower women and so increase their position in society.

Another strand of radical feminist criminology looks generally at crime from the perspective of women. This includes how they experience victimisation (much of this has informed left realist criminology), how they experience their own criminal conduct, how they experience law enforcement and sentencing. It is a politicised approach which questions one of the main bases of our present society, patriarchy.

Radical feminism is centrally concerned not with crime but with the way in which men treat women and does not always sit neatly with either criminology or the concept of crime in what they see as a patriarchal society. Socialist feminism is often linked to radical feminism but takes on another dimension, that of the structural aspects which may impact differently on each gender. Basically it is linked with a broader call to social justice on race, class and sex grounds. Postmodern feminists try to tease out all the ways in which criminality/normality interface with male/female to give a more complex and textured approach but they often ignore the other structural aspects of the equation and thus cannot normally resolve the issues they raise.

18.3.4 Gender issues

A side-effect of focusing on female criminality has been that the whole area of crime, both male and female, has become a gender issue. To some degree all aspects of the criminal justice system are being re-assessed from a gender perspective. Much of the work centred on the police (see above) and on the use of sentencing powers.

Discriminatory sentencing of women became an issue in the 1980s and early 1990s (see the discussion in 17.2.8). More recently it has again arisen as an issue because, as noted earlier, general female imprisonment rose by 140 per cent between 1993 and 2001; that for young offenders by 250 per cent between 1992 and 2002; and magistrates imprisoned five times more women in 2001 than they did in 1992. Yet there were not that many more convictions and the offences were not more serious. Over the same period male imprisonment only rose by 46 per cent. As already seen Carlen ((1999) and (2002)) claims that courts were more punitive towards female offenders, particularly those who are economically and socially marginalised. Gellsthorpe and Morris (2002) interpreted the data differently, as the effect of increased punitiveness rather than gender bias; the result of a move from sentencing of the offender and the offence towards assessment of risk (see Chapter Twenty). It seems that women tend to have more needs than men and, if these are not addressed, the assessment is that they will continue offending, labelling them as high risk and sentenced more severely. Against this the ratio of men to women in prison is 30:1.

The reasonable conclusion is that, although it may seem that women are dealt with leniently there are instances of very hard treatment of women (see Kennedy (1992)). More recently there may be more evidence of harsh punishment for women. Although the number of offences committed by women decreased in the 1990s (see table 18.1) as did violent offending by females (see discussion in 18.3.1), Carlen (1999/2000) noted a doubling of the female prison population between 1990 and 1998. Although this was a time when all sentencing was becoming more punitive the rate at which women were being more harshly treated is particularly marked, especially as women are frequently imprisoned for very minor infringements. This last point is not convincingly addressed by Gallsthorpe and Morris (2002). These general findings are supported by Worrall (2000 and 2003) and McIvor (1998) when they witness that community sentences are considerably underused in the case of female offenders so that women were unnecessarily sent to prison, albeit for short periods. Worrall explores why community sentences are underused, suggesting that both the probation service and courts are at fault (if too few community sentences are awarded for women then there are no or insufficient programmes set out for dealing with them). Horn and Evans (2000) explore another reason: they found that female offenders were disproportionately allocated to female probation officers for the preparation of pre-sentence reports and that female officers were more punitive than their male colleagues (see also Nash (1995)).

Worrall sees the escalation of sentencing not only in the prison sector; she reports that women have been given community punishment more frequently in recent years (in 2003 they make up 1:8 of all such orders whereas 10 years ago they were only 1:18). This has been done without addressing issues of 'child care, inappropriate work, insufficient female supervisors and sexual harassment' (Worrall (2003) at p. 40). She also reports that community rehabilitation programmes are rarely specifically designed for women, and those designed for men are often inappropriate. The different needs of women are not so much addressed as used to argue that they are more likely to re-offend, and thus to increase the severity of treatment. The programmes therefore do little to help women to take control of their own lives and instead teach them that they are responsible for their offending and need to alter their behaviour. It seems likely that the new sentences in the Criminal Justice Act

2003 will further exacerbate the situation (see Player (2003) and the discussion towards the end of 17.2.8).

What is clear is that the position of women is often very problematic, and that the criminal justice system seems less clear about how to deal with them. When women are punished by being imprisoned the impact of this on many women is greater than on men: there are fewer facilities for education and training; fewer female prisons means that many are kept at long distances from their families; prison is more likely to lead to the break-up of the family in the case of women than men; women exhibit their disquiet with their predicament in ways which are less serious for the authorities. They do not riot but there are higher levels of self-mutilation, and more tranquillisers are used in women's prisons than in men's. In fact the way in which women are treated within the punishment system is still very old-fashioned. Over the past 300 years or so prisons and houses of correction have been used to teach women 'good' and 'bad' female roles and femininity (see Bosworth (2000)). More recently this type of intervention has occurred from a very young age, for example, child welfare work with girls has been used to bring them back to the path of 'virtuous' femininity (see Erricson (1998)). Prisons still tend to attempt to inculcate ideas of female roles in society, although there was through the 1990s a tendency for women's prisons to become more brutalising (perhaps to punish them for the double deviancy of criminality and behaviour unacceptable for a woman). However, Carlen (1999/2000) who noted this also saw a more recent positive change to take more account of the needs of women (and to reinforce their roles as wives and mothers). Later still Carlen (2003) fears that this has developed in a less helpful way and it is likely to fail as all it does is to teach the women that they are responsible but fails to address their needs such as a roof over their heads on release. Without attending to practical issues she claims all the good intentions will fail to alleviate offending. Similar needs-based strategies are reported in Canada but some writers there have claimed that they are very much used to reinforce the already existing male power structures (see Hannah-Moffat (1999 and 2000)).

Interestingly other aspects of the criminal justice system also still treat women differently. As noted in Chapter Seventeen women still use psychological factors as defences more frequently than do men. Almost all women, but only 30 per cent of men, used this defence in UK cases of child killing. Much of this is in response to suggestions from their defence lawyers, who may have found such strategies successful in the past. Such psychological strategies may be used when there is no other defence, in situations where it would not be tried for a male client. Similarly, some social inquiry reports still try to explain away female offending, particularly serious offending, as the result of a psychological problem or even portray the offender as a person so controlled by others that she is not fully responsible, and thus should not be fully punished, for her actions (Allen (1998)).

Another area where women's experience of the system is different from that of men is in their victimisation. In victimisation their experiences at the hands of men has come out into the open more frequently than was previously the case. This has led to some changes in women's position and highlighted some major problems. The two areas most frequently studied are rape and domestic violence.

In the case of rape, the feminist view of the victim has led to some improvement in her position: first, she was theoretically allowed anonymity and protection from having her character tested, although in practice few women actually were protected (see Adler (1982)) until, following pressure from feminist groups, the Youth and Criminal Evidence Act 1999 excluded most evidence about the complainant's previous sexual history (see Kibble (2000)); secondly, by setting up more sympathetic units in police stations for her to attend (rape suites) and generally altering the police response to a rape victim. These changes have encouraged some improvement in reporting, although the incidence of rape is still far higher than is officially recorded, as any rape crisis centre will confirm. The new rules on excluding evidence of previous sexual history go a long way to answering feminist calls for greater protection and understanding of the needs of women. The law is extremely controversial, though if our experience is similar to that in the USA it may actually have little effect on trials and be more important in the symbolic message which it sends out in respect of rape (see Horney and Spohn (1991)). Feminist calls, particularly those of radical feminists, go further and attempt to expose rape as the epitome of male power.

In the case of domestic violence, again there have been some improvements. There are some provisions aimed at protecting women and children (e.g., the Domestic Proceedings and Magistrates' Courts Act 1978, ss. 16–18). But some critics contend that these Acts have worsened matters: they allow these offences to be less seriously dealt with than would be the case in street violence. More recently the position of women who have fallen victim to domestic violence may have been improved by new programmes involving cognitive learning strategies which are designed to force men to face, manage and control their aggression (see Diamond and Wong (2000/2001) and Heery (2000/2001)). Though these are to be welcomed the provision is patchy (Hague (2000/2001)) and often does not respond appropriately to the needs of ethnic-minority victims (Siddiqui (2000/2001)). Despite these improvements women still feel that their voices are not being sufficiently heard (Hague (2000/2001)). More recently the Home Office Women's Policy Team (2003) has been developing the Women's Offending Reduction Programme (WORP) which will run (initially) from 2003 for three years and is designed to coordinate and implement strategies to address women's offending. Their intention is to address both practical aspects such as 'substance abuse, mental and physical health, housing, child-care issues, histories of abuse, poverty and education, training and employment' (Home Office Women's Policy Team (2003)). Probation have also recently recognised the need for change (Home Office (2003)) although their timeframe and paper suggest that they still do not view this issue as either essential or a major priority.

The separate study of women and their experience in crime has had a threefold effect. First, it has led to different explanations of female criminality and conformity. Secondly, it has led to a general gendering of crime and therefore gendered explanations of certain male criminality. It is important that gender issues are seen as relevant to both male and female criminality and are not relegated to a narrow relevance in female issues. In some significant respects men have also been sex-stereotyped in criminological theories, creating a need to study gender for both males and females. Thirdly, it has led to a recognition of a different 'experience' of crime, victimisation, and the criminal justice system. Recent realisation of this led left realists to base much of their research and many of their proposals on victim studies which are tailored to discovering women's experience of crime. This has been achieved because of the work of feminist criminologists. More generally, feminist research has still not been widely accepted nor has its potential in address-ing both male and female criminality. Partly for this reason the feminist agenda now is to bring its concerns within mainstream criminology rather than having it sidelined by treating women as a separate issue.

18.4 Conclusion

A number of studies have shown that female emancipation is likely to have some indirect effect upon officially recorded cases of female criminality. These studies suggest a correlation between changing perceptions of women by bodies who enforce the criminal law and the increase in recorded female crime. Thirty years ago women were less likely to be suspected of crime; when suspected they were less likely to be charged and prosecuted; and finally, when prosecuted they were less likely to be convicted, than they are today. Today they are more generally seen as being equally capable of committing both legitimate and illegitimate activities. In other words, belief in the constitutional idea that women are somehow, physically or psychologically, incapable or unlikely to be criminal is weakening. This is reflected in the more than proportionate increase in the number of women in prison, albeit often for minor offences (see 18.3.4).

Clearly, neither psychological/physical factors nor 'women's emancipation' is going to explain female crime satisfactorily. Other reasons will have to be postu-lated. For these it may be necessary to draw upon the studies so far applied to male criminality. Most types of crime committed by women are also committed by men and, to a large extent, both sexes live in the same environment and are subject to the same types of peer group pressures and effects on upbringing. From this stand-point, crimes by each should be explicable along similar lines. It is also true, how-ever, that the causative effect of each factor may differ for men and women as it does for men from different backgrounds or with different peer groups.

To understand female criminality fully it is first essential to study all explanations of crimes. Women are as likely as men to be primarily affected by their environ-ment, their peers, their upbringing, labelling, general social interactions, anomie, and all the other factors that were mooted in earlier chapters. Beyond this, there are explanations of women's crime (and especially of some particular crimes) which are based on factors peculiar to, or predominant amongst, women (such as reasons argued for infanticide and theories based on the menstrual cycle and other typic-ally female body functions). But, in contrast to the view of earlier generations of legal theorists, present analysis suggests that specifically feminine characteristics (whether biological, psychological or behavioural) do not constitute the main explanation of women's crime. It may prove more fruitful to apply to women explanations previously used to explain male crime.

From the above it is clear that feminist studies have had some impact. They have influenced left realism, altered some experiences of women in the criminal justice system, and ensured more consideration for women, feminism and gender in gen-eral criminological theories. These effects have been limited, however. Mainstream criminology remains largely sexist, in that it is focused on crime and criminal justice, areas which are for the most part still defined and inhabited by men (Young

(1996)). Although it is recognised (Heidensohn (2000)) that many writers accept the impact of feminism on their work, employ the tools of feminism and acknowledge the need to examine the gender aspect of both offending and victimisation, the full theoretical integration of gender into all aspects of criminology is still some way off. Work in this area has nonetheless opened up fresh topics for study (see, e.g., Comack (1999)). Thus Heidensohn (2000) argues an important issue for the new century is the breaking down of the barriers between public and private. In its application to crime and justice, feminists have had much to do with this process in the fields of both domestic violence and child abuse. The trend can also be seen in the parenting classes for those whose children offend and of anger management classes for men (usually but also women) who abuse their partners and children. These examples illustrate the broader point that gender approaches and theories can have much to offer to social science generally and criminological discourse in particular.

SUGGESTED READING

Criminal Justice Matters Special Issue concerning Gender and Crime, vol. 53.

Heidensohn, F. (1996), *Women and Crime*, 2nd edn, Basingstoke: Macmillan.

Heidensohn, F. (2000), *Sexual Politics and Social Control*, Buckingham: Open University Press.

Walklate, S., *Gender, Crime and Criminal Justice*, Cullompton: Willan Publishing.

REVISION BOX

As in all other fields of social knowledge or history women have been largely absent. Feminist discourse has begun to correct this blind spot in knowledge and this is probably its greatest contribution—it has laid bare the ignorance concerning the criminal and conforming activities of almost half of the population. At the very least it has forced criminologists to ask new questions and to examine more carefully earlier findings.

The opening up of questions as to who commits crime, who is victimised and the reasons and effects of these differences has been illuminating. The feminist approach has also raised such issues as domestic violence (suffered by adults, usually women, and children) and areas such as rape leading to far greater scrutiny than had previously been the case. It has provoked the possibility that masculinity may underlie or explain some offending though the assumption that it underlies all crime is as distorting as ignoring it. The last point serves as a reminder that although feminist agendas and the area of gender may help to illuminate some issues a blind faith that it is always an issue or can be a main element of all offending needs to be treated with scepticism.

Interestingly even the government has had to take account of gender and the need to tackle the causes of crime from a gendered position. One of the few pillars of society still left claiming neutrality whilst still using a largely male view of the world is the law—judges, magistrates etc.

However, one might question whether a gendered difference approach to the world is really the most useful—might it be better to search for a holistic human approach that takes account of gender, race, age, class, economic position etc. simply when these factors are important and relevant? Would this not be more likely to lead to true equality and social justice, the ideals claimed by most feminist groups? But is it attainable?

QUESTIONS FOR REVISIONS

1 What is a feminist approach to criminality? How does it differ from other explanations of crime?

2 What is the relationship between patriarchy and crime? Would the elimination of patriarchy give rise to more or less crime?

3 Does feminist criminology have more to do with victimology or criminology?

4 Do feminists look more at sex differences or gender differences? How do these approaches differ? Are either of these the most important difference faced by society or should we be looking at other differences either instead or as well?

5 How has feminist thought impacted on policy and practice within the criminal justice system?

REFERENCES

Adler, Freda (1975), *Sisters in Crime: The Rise of the New Female Criminal*, New York: McGraw-Hill.

Adler, Zsuzsanna (1982), 'Rape—The Intention of Parliament and the Practice of the Courts', *Modern Law Review*, vol. 45, p. 664.

Allen, H. (1998), 'Rendering Them Harmless: The Professional Portrayal of Women Charged with Serious Violent Crimes', in K. Daly and L. Maher (eds), *Criminology at the Crossroads: Feminist Readings in Crime and Justice*, Oxford: Oxford University Press. First printed in P. Carlen and A. Worrall (eds), *Gender, Crime and Justice*, Buckingham: Open University Press.

Batchelor, S. (2001), 'The Myth of Girl Gangs', *Criminal Justice Matters*, vol. 43, p. 26.

Bosworth, M. (2000), 'Confining Femininity: A History of Gender, Power and Imprisonment', *Theoretical Criminology*, vol. 4, p. 265.

Bourgois, Phillippe (1996), *In Search of Respect: Selling Crack in El Barrio*, Cambridge: Cambridge University Press.

Box, Steven (1981), *Deviance Reality and Society*, 2nd edn, London: Holt, Rinehart and Winston.

Box, Steven (1987), *Recession, Crime and Punishment*, London: Macmillan.

Brooks Gardner, Carol (1996), *Passing By: Gender and Public Harassment*, Berkeley, CA: University of California Press.

Brown, J. and Heidensohn, F. (2000), *Gender and Policing: Comparative Perspectives*, Basingstoke: Macmillan.

Burman, M. (2003), 'Girls Behaving Violently?', *Criminal Justice Matters Special Issue concerning Gender and Crime*, vol. 53, p. 20.

Burman, M., Brown, J., Batchelor, S. and Tisdall, K. (2000), *A View from the Girls: Exploring Violence and Violent Behaviour*, Glasgow: University of Glasgow. A copy of the Summary Report is available at **http://www.gla.ac.uk/girlsandviolence/findings.htm.**

Campbell, Anne (1981), *Girl Delinquents*, Oxford: Basil Blackwell.

Campbell, Anne (1984), *The Girls in the Gang*, Oxford: Basil Blackwell.

Campbell, B. (1993), *Goliath: Britain's Dangerous Places*, London: Methuen.

Carlen, Pat (1988), *Women, Crime and Poverty*, Milton Keynes: Open University Press.

Carlen, P. (1999/2000), 'Women's Imprisonment at the Millennium', *Criminal Justice Matters*, vol. 38, p. 20.

Carlen, P. (2003), 'A Strategy for Women Offenders? Lock them up, programme them . . . and then Send Them Out Homeless', *Criminal Justice Matters Special Issue concerning Gender and Crime* 53, p. 34.

Comack, E. (1999), 'Producing Feminist Knowledge: Lessons from Women in Trouble', *Theoretical Criminology*, vol. 3, p. 287.

Conaghan, J. (2002), 'Law, Harm and Redress: A Feminist Perspective', *Legal Studies*, vol. 22(3), p. 319.

Creighton, S.J. and Noyes, P. (1989), *Child Abuse Trends in England and Wales 1983–1987*, London: NSPCC.

Daly, K. and Chesney-Lind, M. (1996), 'Feminism and Criminology', in P. Cordella and L. Siegal (eds), *Readings in Contemporary Criminological Theory*, Boston, MA: Northeastern University Press.

Daly, Kathleen and Stephens, Deborah J. (1995), 'The Dark-Figure of Criminology: Towards a Black and Multi-Ethnic Feminist Agenda for Theory and Research', in Nicole Hahn Rafter and Frances Heidensohn (eds), *International Feminist Perspectives in Criminology: Engendering a Discipline*, Buckingham: Open University Press.

Diamond, A. and Wong, K. (2000/2001), 'Violence Against Women: The Crime Reduction Initiative', *Criminal Justice Matters*, vol. 42, p. 16.

Erricson, K. (1998), 'Gender, Delinquency and Child Welfare', *Theoretical Criminology*, vol. 2, p. 445.

Fiqueira-McDonogh, Josefina (1984), 'Feminism and Delinquency', *British Journal of Criminology*, vol. 24, p. 325.

Graham, J. and Bowling, B. (1995), *Young People and Crime*, Home Office Research Study No. 145, London: HMSO.

Griffin, S. (1971), 'Rape: The all American Crime', *Ramparts*, vol. 10, p. 3.

Hagan, John (1989), *Structural Criminology*, New Brunswick, NJ: Rutgers University Press.

Hagan, J., Gillis, A.R. and Simpson, J. (1990), 'Clarifying and Extending Power-Control Theory', *American Journal of Sociology*, vol. 95, p. 1024.

Hague, G. (2000/2001), 'The Voices and Views of Women Experiencing Domestic Violence', *Criminal Justice Matters*, vol. 42, p. 18.

Hahn, P., Rafter, Nicole and Heidensohn, Frances (eds) (1995), *International Feminist Perspectives in Criminology: Engendering a Discipline*, Buckingham: Open University Press.

Hall, S. (2002), 'Daubing the Drudges of Fury: Men, Violence and the Piety of the "Hegemonic Masculinity" Thesis', *Theoretical Criminology*, vol. 6(1), p. 35.

Hall, S. and Winlow, S. (2003), 'Rehabilitating Leviathan: Reflections on the State, Economic Regeneration and Violence Reduction', *Theoretical Criminology*, vol. 7(2), p. 139.

Hannah-Moffat, K. (1999), 'Moral Agent or Actuarial Subject: Risk and Canadian Women's Imprisonment', *Theoretical Criminology*, vol. 3, p. 71.

Hannah-Moffat, K. (2000), 'Prisons that Empower: Neo-Liberal Governance in Canadian Women's Prisons', *British Journal of Criminology*, vol. 40, p. 510.

Heery, G. (2000/2001), 'Preventing Violence in Relationships: the PVR Programme', *Criminal Justice Matters*, vol. 42, p. 21.

Heidensohn, Frances (1985), *Women and Crime*, London: Macmillan.

Heidensohn, F. (1994), 'From Being to Knowing: Some Issues in the Study of Gender in Contemporary Society', *Women in Criminal Justice*, vol. 6, p. 13.

Heidensohn, F. (2000), *Sexual Politics and Social Control*, Buckingham: Open University Press.

Heimer, K. and De Coster, S. (1999), 'The Gendering of Violent Delinquency', *Criminology*, vol. 37, p. 277.

Hindelang, M.J. (1973), 'Causes of Delinquency: A Partial Replication and Extension', *Social Problems*, vol. 20, p. 471.

Home Office (2002), *Statistics on Women and the Criminal Justice System: A Home Office Publication Under Section 95 of the Criminal Justice Act 1991*, London: Home Office. **http://www.homeoffice.gov.uk/rds/pdfs2/s95women02.pdf.**

Home Office (2003), *The Heart of the Dance: A Diversity Strategy for the National Probation Service for England and Wales*, London: Home Office.

Home Office Women's Policy Team (2003), 'Women Offenders: The Case for a Distinct Response', *Criminal Justice Matters Special Issue concerning Gender and Crime* 53: 32.

Horn, R. and Evans, M. (2000), 'The Effect of Gender on Pre-Sentence Reports', *Howard Journal of Criminal Justice*, vol. 39, p. 184.

Horney, J. and Spohn, C. (1991), 'Rape Law Reform and Instrumental Change in Six Urban Jurisdictions', *Law and Society*, vol. 25, p. 115.

Hough, M., Jacobson, J. and Millie, A. (2003), *The Decision to Imprison: Sentencing and the Prison Population*, London: Prison Reform Trust.

Jefferson, Tony and Carlen, Pat (eds) (1996), 'Masculinity, Social Relations and Crime', *British Journal of Criminology*, vol. 36(3), Special Issue.

Joe, K.A. and Chesney-Lind, M. (1998), ' "Just Every Mother's Angel": An Analysis of Gender and Ethnic Variations in Youth Gang Membership', in K. Daly and L. Maher (eds), *Criminology at the Crossroads: Feminist Readings in Crime and Justice*, Oxford: Oxford University Press. First published in 1995 in *Gender and Society*, vol. 9, p. 408.

Kennedy, Helena (1992), *Eve Was Framed*, London: Chatto & Windus.

Kibble, N. (2000), 'The Sexual History Provisions: Charting a Course Between Inflexible Legislative Rules and Wholly Untrammelled Judicial Discretion?', *Criminal Law Review*, p. 274.

Klein, Dorie (1995), 'Crime Through Gender's Prism: Feminist Criminology in the United States', in Nicole Hahn Rafter and Frances Heidensohn (eds), *International Feminist Perspectives in Criminology: Engendering a Discipline*, Buckingham: Open University Press.

Lacey, N., Wells, C. and Quick, O. (2003), *Reconstructing Criminal Law: Texts and Materials* London: LexisNexis Butterworths.

Lane, P. (1998), 'Ecofeminism meets Criminology', *Theoretical Criminology*, vol. 2, p. 235.

McIvor, G. (1998), 'Jobs for the Boys?: Gender Differences in Referral to Community Services', *Howard Journal of Criminal Justice*, vol. 37, p. 280.

MacKinnon, Catherine (1993), 'On Collaboration', in Stevi Jackson (ed.), *Women's Studies: a Reader*, London: Harvester Wheatsheaf.

MacKinnon, Catherine (1994), *Only Words*, London: HarperCollins.

Messerschmidt, James W. (1993), *Masculinities and Crime—Critique and Reconceptualisation of Theory*, Lanham, MD: Rowman & Littlefield.

Messerschmidt, James W. (1995), 'From Patriarchy to Gender: Feminist Theory, Criminology and the Challenge of Diversity', in Nicole Hahn Raften and Frances Heidensohn (eds) *International Perspectives in Criminology: Engendering a Discipline*, Buckingham: Open University Press.

Messerschmidt, J. (1997), *Crime as Structured Action: Gender, Race and Class and Crime in the Making*, London: Sage.

Messerschmidt, J. (2003), *CA Mystery in Broad Daylight: Adolescent Gender, the Body, and Violence*, Boulder, CO: Westview Press.

Miller, J. (2000), 'Feminist Theories of Women's Crime: Robbery as a Case Study', in S.S. Simpson (ed.), *Of Crime and Criminality*, Thousand Oaks, CA: Pine Forge.

Miller, J. (2001), *One of the Guys: Girls, Gangs and Gender*, Oxford: Oxford University Press.

Miller, J. (2002), 'The Strengths and Limits of 'Doing Gender' for Understanding Street Crime' *Theoretical Criminology*, vol. 6(4), p. 433.

Monti, G. (1999), 'A Reasonable Woman Standard in Sexual Harassment' *Legal Studies*, vol. 19(4), p. 552.

Moore, Wendy (1993), 'There Should Be a Law Against It . . . Shouldn't There?', in Stevi Jackson (ed.), *Women's Studies: a Reader*, London: Harvester Wheatsheaf.

Murray, C. (1990), *The Emerging Underclass*, London: Institute of Economic Affairs.

Murray, C. (1994), *Underclass: The Crisis Deepens*, London: Institute of Economic Affairs.

Nash, M. (1995), 'Aggravation, Mitigation and the Gender of Probation Officers', *Howard Journal of Criminal Justice*, vol. 34, p. 250.

Nicolson, D. and Bibbings, L. (2000), *Feminist Perspectives on Criminal Law*, London: Cavendish.

Pantazis, C. and Gordon, D. (1997), 'Television Licence Evasion and the Criminalisation of Female Poverty', *Howard Journal of Criminal Justice*, vol. 36, p. 170.

Phillips, C. (2003), 'Who's Who in the Pecking Order?: Aggression and "Normal Violence" in the Lives of Girls and Boys', *British Journal of Criminology*, vol. 43, p. 710.

Player, E. (2003), 'Reducing Women's Imprisonment: An Unlikely Prospect', *Criminal Justice Matters Special Issue concerning Gender and Crime*, vol. 53, p. 36.

Radford, J., Friedberg, M. and Harne, L. (eds) (2000), *Women, Violence and Strategies for Action: Feminist Research, Policy and Practice*, Buckingham: Open University Press.

Siddiqui, H. (2000/2001), 'Domestic Violence and Black/Minority Women: Enough is Enough', *Criminal Justice Matters*, vol. 42, p. 14.

Simon, Rita J. (1975), *Woman and Crime*, Lexington, MA: Lexington Books.

Smart, Carol (1979), 'The New Female Criminal: Reality or Myth?', *British Journal of Criminology*, vol. 19, p. 50.

Smart, Carol (1989), *Feminism and the Power of Law*, London: Routledge.

Smart, Carol (1990), 'Feminist Approaches to Criminology, or Postmodern Woman Meets Atavistic Man', in Lorraine Gelsthorpe and Alison Morris, *Feminist Perspectives in Criminology*, London: Routledge.

Smith, L.J.F. (1989), *Concerns about Rape*, Home Office Research Study No. 106, London: HMSO.

Tittle, Charles R. (1995), *Control Balance: Towards a General Theory of Deviance*, Boulder, CO: Westview Press.

Tittle, Charles R. (1997), 'Thoughts Stimulated by Braithwaite's Analysis of Control Balance', *Theoretical Criminology*, vol. 1, p. 99.

Tittle, Charles R. (1999), 'Continuing the Discussion of Control Balance', *Theoretical Criminology*, vol. 3, p. 344.

Tittle, Charles R. (2000), 'Control Balance', in R. Paternoster and R. Bachman (eds), *Explaining Criminals and Crime: Essays in Contemporary Theory*, Los Angeles, CA: Roxbury.

Tomsen, S. (1997), 'A Top Night: Social Protest, Masculinity and the Culture of Drinking Violence', *British Journal of Criminology*, vol. 37, p. 90.

Walklate, S. (1995), *Gender and Crime: An Introduction*, Hemel Hempstead: Prentice Hall Harvester.

Warner, K. (2000), 'Sentencing in Cases of Marital Rape: Towards Changing the Male Imagination', *Legal Studies*, vol. 20(4), p. 592.

Wilczynski, A. (1997), 'Mad or Bad? Child-Killers, Gender and the Courts', *British Journal of Criminology*, vol. 37, p. 419.

Wilson, James Q. (1985), *Thinking about Crime*, 2nd edn, New York: Vintage Books.

Worrall, A. (2000), 'Community Sentences for Women: Where Have They Gone?', *Criminal Justice Matters*, vol. 39, p. 10.

Worrell, A. (2003), ' "What Woks" and Community Sentences for Women Offenders', *Criminal Justice Matters Special Issue concerning Gender and Crime*, vol. 53, p. 40.

Young, Alison (1996), *Imagining Crime: Textual Outlaws and Criminal Conversations*, London: Sage.

Young, J. (1999), *The Exclusive Society*, London: Sage.

19

Terrorism and State violence

19.1 Terrorism: introduction

Terrorism is a part of the human condition in the sense that, like the poor, it is always with us. It seems that whenever and wherever we break into the historical record some form of terrorist activity is likely to be found.

Naturally we know about more activities which seem to be terrorist—and generally know more about them—as we approach recent times. Nonetheless there are well-authenticated cases which go back into quite ancient times. Thus the Assassins emerged nearly 1,000 years ago (c.1090) to defend and propagate a particular version of Islam. Their tactics included the use of stealth, surprise and suicide killings aimed at intimidating opponents. The organisation behind this movement (the Order of Assassins) lasted for about 150 years. Even more persistent was the Thuggee cult which operated in India for some 600 years before being eventually eliminated by the British in the nineteenth century. The Thuggees too were sustained by religion as worshippers of the Hindu goddess Kali, the destroyer. They were also heavily engaged in robbery, especially of travellers, which was justified as necessary to provide the funds to secure the protection from rulers which partly accounts for the long life of the cult. The distinctive method of killing was through strangulation which again stemmed from the object of offering homage to Kali. The use of the Inquisition by the Catholic Church to suppress heresy and discourage challenges to the authority of the Church and its hierarchy was a similar exercise in religious terrorism. Comparable tactics were inspired by secular and political aims. These were often operated by the State, or those who controlled the power of the State, in order to suppress or intimidate opposition, whether legitimate or illegitimate. A classic case would be the operation of the activities of the Committee of Public Safety during a few early years (1791–3) of the French Revolution. This was unusual in being widely and explicitly described as 'the Terror' even at the time: compared to what came later the scale of the executions was relatively modest and, it is often overlooked that after the fall and execution of Robespierre the process proceeded under the counter-revolutionaries. Parts of what came later were epitomised by the twentieth-century experiences of the Stalinist regime in the Soviet Union and the Nazi regime in Germany. Torture, disappearances, summary arrests and executions were widely used to terrorise groups and individuals into obedience to the dominant ideology. The so-called 'dirty war' waged by the Argentine military junta against left-wing dissidents in the late 1970s would be just one more instance of a phenomenon that has become unfortunately commonplace over the last century.

There are also recurring attempts at intimidation from below for political and social ends. One such area of focus has centred around the attempts by workers to secure recognition of the right to unionise. Employers, both directly and through their control or influence over the use of State power, have habitually resisted demands of this sort, frequently by victimising those joining or organising trade unions. Whether such methods were legal or not varied in different countries and at different times but they constituted a form of intimidation (terrorism?) which sometimes provoked a terrorist response. Thus in south Wales in the 1820s and 1830s coal miners in Monmouthshire used force, or the threat of force, to ensure that workers showed solidarity at times of industrial disputes. Since virtually any form of resistance was illegal and would be suppressed by the authorities, such actions were secret and clandestine. Known as the 'Scotch Cattle' they sent lurid warning notes to men working during a strike. If such men continued to blackleg they were visited at night by a gang (from a distant village) with the masks and horns of cattle and their property and sometimes their persons were roughly dealt with. The use of some such tactics is not uncommon in industrial relations especially when the law, or the way it is interpreted, seems to deny workers the right to organise and withdraw their labour: in the United States the activities of the so called 'Molly Maguires' in the Pennsylvania coalfield in the 1870s was similar to those of the Scotch Cattle.

More generally political minorities, especially (but not only) if they are denied the expression and exercise of their views, often turn to more violent methods. Unable to secure their aims or to overthrow the existing, established order by other means terrorism and disruption are adopted to force a change or acceptance of their demands. This can take many forms and have different objects: much of the widespread, more or less continuous, and largely nihilistic dissidence in nineteenth-century Russia was aimed at overthrowing the existing Tsarist State; the Basque movement in Spain is aimed at securing separation from the State; the anti-Vietnam protests in the US (in 1969 there were 298 explosive and 243 incendiary bombings in America (Select Committee on Government Operations reported in Martin, G. (2003)) were directed towards securing a fundamental change in a major government policy. This last could be said to fall into the same category of other single-issue campaigns of intimidation like those on anti-abortion in the US or the more violent animal rights campaigners on both sides of the Atlantic.

Terrorism is also a common and effective weapon for those engaged in straightforward mercenary activities. Every organisation running a 'protection racket' necessarily backs up its demands with violent punishments for any who fail to comply or 'join'. Groups exercising control over the illegal trade in drugs, like the 'Yardies' in London, protect 'their' territory by violently intimidating would-be interlopers. And some form of terrorism is essentially the hallmark of any 'Mafia-type' organisation.

19.2 Definitions, types and causes

These issues will be treated very briefly here. It should be made clear, however, that they raise the questions (what is terrorism? how does it manifest itself? why does it arise?) which would be at the heart of any comprehensive treatment of the overall problem of terrorism. The justification for their terse treatment here is that the topic of terrorism in this text is being dealt with from the specific and narrower perspective of its relation to, and implications for, criminology and the criminal justice system. This perspective will be given fuller examination in the succeeding sections of this chapter.

19.2.1 Definitions

Terrorism is an abstract noun, the practical application of which is painfully concrete. It might therefore be thought that, like the elephant, it is difficult to describe but easily recognised when seen. Defining terrorism is, however, further complicated by two sources of ambiguity which are inherent in the concept. In the first place there is the difficulty of distinguishing terrorism from several similar animals. Thus it would not generally be thought of as being the same as conventional warfare, but there is obviously some overlapping: the conduct of wars can involve specific acts aimed at terrorising the enemy. President Bush gives explicit expression to the ambiguity by declaring war on terrorism. It is even more difficult to separate from guerrilla warfare where a central aim for both sides is to secure the support or acquiescence of the general population and intimidation is often seen as an effective means to this end (in most guerrilla warfare the combatants engage with another army, seize and hold territory and usually have sovereignty over some land; all of these are absent in the case of the terrorist). Much terrorist activity is also difficult to distinguish from straightforward criminal behaviour. Not only is it difficult to distinguish terrorism from other clearly violent acts but at times it is difficult to distinguish it from legal and/or acceptable means of action such as legal protest; or protest which should be legal in order to guarantee freedom of expression. Furthermore the line between resistance and terrorism may be difficult to draw with precision.

A second broad source of ambiguity stems from the very different ways in which particular acts of violence might be seen. At the very time that its perpetrators are being generally denounced for a callous and wanton attack on innocent citizens, they may be being seen by others, if the motivation was to defend a fundamental religious or political principle, as commendable or even as heroic and noble (freedom fighters). It is possible for both sides to share a definition but, from their different perspectives, to see its application being relevant to quite different people or groups or institutions. In November 1974 Yasser Arafat in an address to the United Nations General Assembly succinctly explained that the '. . . difference between the revolutionary and the terrorist lies in the reason for which each fights. For whoever stands by a just cause and fights for the freedom and liberation of his land from the invaders, the settlers and the colonists, cannot possibly be called terrorist . . .' By this measure terrorists and terrorism can never be objectively defined as there will always be the subjective question of the 'just' cause.

It is not surprising to find nuanced differences in some of the official and academic definitions as quoted in Martin (2003), pp. 31–2. There an official British definition is given as: '—the use or threat, for the purpose of advancing a political, religious or ideological cause, of action which involves serious violence against any person or property'. The Office of the Constitution of the European Union provides: '. . . terrorism is . . . the use, or the threatened use, by a cohesive group of persons of violence (short of warfare) to effect political aims'. As an illustration of a difference in emphasis the brief definitions offered by two scholars may be cited: '. . . the deliberate creation and exploitation of fear through violence or threat of violence in the pursuit of change' (Bruce Hoffman), and 'A strategy of violence designed to produce desired outcomes by instilling fear in the public at large' (Walter Reich).

An indication of the elusive nature of the definitional problem can perhaps be gained from the fact that one study (Schmid and Jongman (1988)) was—well before the Twin Towers focused so many minds on the issue—able to offer 100 definitions. The proliferation is partly explained by the variety of forms in which terrorism is manifested. There seem to be a few generally accepted elements:

Firstly it is political in that it intends to alter the political order or to influence political decisions or actions (note that this does not mean that the intention must be to replace the present order with something specific it may just be to overthrow the status quo.

Secondly it is about power: sometimes the acquisition of power but almost always the use of power or violence, or its threatened use, to attain that political change.

Furthermore, terrorism is planned and calculated to achieve the ends set out.

Although, as with many of the other concepts of terrorism this may help to focus the mind on the area under discussion this may not be sufficient.

For political and social discourse the lack of a definition is not a major stumbling block, in fact this flexibility and the constant search for new ways of conceiving of the concept permits terrorism and our understanding and approach to the topic to be constantly refreshed and re-evaluated. However, if one is to use State or international agencies to control or punish perpetrators it is essential to have a clear understanding of what activities and people are caught within the law. For this reason one might have expected international law to have defined terrorism so as to delineate the area to be controlled but although there are a number of conventions dealing with terrorism each defines it in a way specific to the issue being controlled under that convention (e.g., from the United Nations: the Convention against the Taking of Hostages 1979; the Convention for the Suppression of Terrorist Bombings 1997 and the Convention for the Suppression of the Financing of Terrorism 1999). There is as yet no global internationally accepted definition: the international community has even questioned the need for a definition and debated the issue in the Security Council of the United Nations in September 2001. Some have argued that terrorism is not really a separate aspect of international law, there is no international law of terrorism but just international laws which deal with the specific problem posed by terrorism. As Higgins says, 'Is . . . terrorism the study of a substantive topic, or rather the study of the application of international law to a contemporary problem?' (p. 13). Although recognising this viewpoint the Security Council clearly backed the need for a definition. There is therefore the will to construct an international concept of terrorism. Although there is work being done to prepare a general Convention concerning terrorism none has yet been agreed. It is therefore necessary to look to the work of individual States. At certain times in history many States have defined activities which might be thought of as terrorism. In modern times possibly one of the most sophisticated is that emanating from the UK. Due to the terrorist activities in Northern Ireland the authorities in the UK have continuously had to deal with the issue of terrorism and its impact on the population over more than 30 years. Until recently they had almost always opted for a relatively simple definition such as that found in the 1989 Prevention of Terrorism (Temporary Provisions) Act:

20(1) . . . 'terrorism' means the use of violence for political ends and includes any use of violence for the purpose of putting the public or any section of the public in fear.

This was very similar to earlier definitions used but in 1996 Lord Lloyd in his review of the terrorism legislation suggested that it was rather too narrow, he thought that it might not catch single issue or religious terrorism and expressed approval for the wider concept used by the FBI which in 1999 read:

There is no single, universally accepted, definition of terrorism. Terrorism is defined in the *Code of Federal Regulations* as '. . . the unlawful use of force and violence against persons or property to intimidate or coerce a government, the civilian population, or any segment thereof, in furtherance of political or social objectives.' (28 C.F.R. Section 0.85) (found in '*Terrorism in the United States*' (1999))

The FBI use this for purely administrative and budgetary purposes and it was insufficient as a legal term where more precision is necessary to guarantee that rights are respected. The definition was thought to be too broad in certain respects as it might include blackmail as an act of terrorism and yet too narrow in others, it limited terrorism to criminal acts. The UK did not want to be fettered from acting merely because a particular terrorist activity was not a crime in another State and considered that certain terrorist activities in the UK might not be classified as crimes; the refusal to perform a duty may not be a criminal offence but it may cause terror. Lord Bassam gave an interesting example:

. . . an employee may advance a political cause and deliberately omit to update a vital computer programme or omit to put cleansing agent in a sewage system . . . (HL Debs. Vol. 614 col. 1448)

All this has led to a very wide definition in s. 1 of the Terrorism Act 2000:

(1) In this Act 'terrorism' means the use or threat of action where—
  (a) the action falls within subsection (2),
  (b) the use or threat is designed to influence the government or to intimidate the public or a section of the public, and
  (c) the use or threat is made for the purpose of advancing a political, religious or ideological cause.

(2) Action falls within this subsection if it—
  (a) involves serious violence against a person,
  (b) involves serious damage to property,
  (c) endangers a person's life, other than that of the person committing the action,
  (d) creates a serious risk to the health or safety of the public or a section of the public, or
  (e) is designed seriously to interfere with or seriously to disrupt an electronic system.

(3) The use or threat of action falling within subsection (2) which involves the use of firearms or explosives is terrorism whether or not subsection (1)(b) is satisfied.

(4) In this section—
  (a) 'action' includes action outside the United Kingdom,
  (b) a reference to any person or to property is a reference to any person, or to property, wherever situated,

(c) a reference to the public includes a reference to the public of a country other than the United Kingdom, and

(d) 'the government' means the government of the United Kingdom, of a Part of the United Kingdom or of a country other than the United Kingdom.

(5) In this Act a reference to action taken for the purposes of terrorism includes a reference to action taken for the benefit of a proscribed organisation.

It is interesting to note that this broader definition predates the twin towers incident on 11 September 2001 and occurred when the terrorist activities in Northern Ireland had largely subsided. A further point of interest is that the definition is different from that of many crimes as it refers to the intention and therefore partially includes the motive for the activity, the desire to influence government or cause fear for a political, religious or ideological cause. Arguably the inclusion of fear of the public without any intention to influence government or political action might be seen as broadening the definition unnecessarily though the intention to elicit fear in the population in order to attain the desired outcome might be seen as a normal part of the definition. Furthermore the inclusion of motive as to political, religious or ideological cause some see as unnecessary (see Sorel (2003)). If there is a desire to influence either the government or political decisions or actions then does it matter whether there is a political, religious or other ideological end?

Whether this definition would be of any help in building an international definition is questionable. It does not deal with the problem of 'freedom fighters'. According to s. 1 of the Terrorism Act 2000, therefore, any violent act intended to bring about interference with the legal order in any State is an act of terrorism. The section takes an international stance in that it applies to actions outside the UK and to those who wish to alter governments or politics in other States; the neutral language seems to suggest that it views all such actions as acts of terrorism. Therefore 'freedom fighters' would under this definition be dealt with as terrorists. As the wording merely gives the power to act presumably the UK authorities would not use these powers in cases where they believed that the actions were justified; being acts necessary to overthrow an oppressive and illegitimate regime. Interestingly, the definition is wide enough to encompass State terrorism, at least that committed by one State against other regimes or those living in other States and that of States outside the UK who use their power against their own people or a section of their community.

Sorel (2003) suggests a less precise definition should be adopted by the international community:

International terrorism is an illicit act (irrespective of its perpetrator or its purpose) which creates a disturbance in the public order as defined by the international community, by using serious and indiscriminate violence (in whatever form, whether against people or public or private property) in order to generate an atmosphere of terror with the aim of influencing political action.

All of this illustrates that even when one tries to alight on a legal and objective definition the task may be thwarted. First, the term 'terrorist' is loaded with many value laden ideas. If one calls a group terrorist then, certainly in most people's minds, one is usually depicting them as fanatical and often irrational, drawing attention to the unacceptable nature of their activities so as to convince the target audience of their threat and therefore often the need and right to use broader security devices to deal with them. The one word 'terrorist' sums up all of that. The media and politicians use the term in order to transmit all these meanings. Furthermore, present legal regimes are loathe to include within the legal concept of terrorism any act of State terrorism. They do not want their actions or those of their servants to be invested with all the negative connotations associated with the word terrorism. Therefore definitions often ignore acts conducted by a government on its own people. Thus the discussion within the rest of this chapter will not be limited to any particular legalistic definition of terrorism but rather will consider the activity in all its facets.

19.2.2 Types of terrorism

The introduction to this chapter has already suggested a number of different types. First amongst these is State terrorism. There are good reasons for giving this pride of place. It tends to get forgotten or overlooked perhaps partly because in most western democracies the State is seen as a, or the, main instrument for combating terrorism. In many countries, however, and at different times those who have controlled the power of the State have used it to intimidate other citizens or groups of citizens. Even more significant is the fact that State terrorism has been responsible for more killings, more tortures, and more disappearances than all other forms. This would still be true even without the spectacular examples of Stalin and Hitler: it largely reflects the greater power attaching to the State, and the greater difficulty of resisting that power if it is exercised for these purposes.

At all times, somewhere, some form of religious group has chosen the path of terror to secure their demands and the same is probably equally true of some of those seeking political change. On the other hand those using a type of terrorism to pursue a single issue, such as anti-abortion or animal rights, emerge comparatively rarely and are probably largely a phenomenon of the late twentieth and early twenty-first centuries. The label of terrorism to these single issue groups has at times been slow in coming, for example, in the USA the anti-abortion fighters who used terrorist tactics were until the early 1990s often not labelled as such, although their acts were condemned the media and government used language which failed to connect this to terrorist activity. Finally, terrorist tactics in the pursuit of greed is a more universal and predictable human characteristic so the use of these tactics for straightforward monetary gain is always likely to be found. In many instances the term is not used where personal greed is the main aim, these are seen as more mundane crimes but in instances where the activity is highly organised such as the Mafia, Chinese Triads and drug lords and cartels it is probably instructive to conceive of these as terrorists—they often use terrorist tactics and infiltrate or manipulate those in power to protect their organisations. Furthermore, increasingly the distinctions between organised crime, illegal trafficking (in arms, drugs, people or other commodities) and terrorist organisations has become blurred; crimes which appear to be for pure gain may be committed by terrorist organisations in order to finance their other activities, or such groups may be involved somewhere in the chain of events.

In one sense the differences of these varied types can be said to be largely superficial. This is because, thus far, they have all basically used the same methods (although perhaps State terrorism which can use means, such as arrest, which are largely peculiar to the State, would be a potential exception). Essentially this means more or less random killings; targeted assassinations; destruction of property, particularly public buildings; kidnapping and hijacking; mutilations (knee-capping) and other tortures. And these have thus far almost entirely been put into practice by the use of such long-established weapons as bombs and small arms. The use of more recent, rapid technological changes seems to have been substantially restricted to means of communication. They have been used to facilitate networking between groups or cells and to spread propaganda though, now, electronic systems are being shunned by terrorist groups for much of their frontline work as surveillance systems become ever more sophisticated. Computers and their networks have also been used as weapons through the manipulation of electronic systems to destroy communications or information, the so-called cyberterrorism. The activity is very new and is not considered in many books on terrorism but as the modern world is so dependant on information-systems these attacks will become more widespread; they could be used to paralyse vital infrastructures or critical safety systems, possibly killing many people, or they could freeze State computer systems and those systems necessary to the running of the transport and communications infrastructure so interfering with the ability to govern without causing death (is this then terrorism?). The use of more advanced technology in the form of hi-tech weaponry—biological, chemical, nuclear—has, perhaps surprisingly, been very restricted up to the present.

19.2.3 **Causes: motives**

For many the motivation behind acts of terror is inconceivable—they cannot conceive that any rational being could perform an act of terror. The actions, quite simply, defy belief. But terrorist acts are, in the final analysis, committed by individual human beings. In this sense the causes and motivations are, as is the case with 'ordinary' murders etc., almost infinitely variable. Terrorists, like other criminals, may occasionally suffer from personality disorders or be mentally different but most researchers are struck by their normality; they are not suffering from mental disorder nor are they psychopathic. Indeed some terrorist groups actively discourage those with such mental problems as they are a security risk.

Here the motives and causes of terrorism cannot be considered in depth but it is reasonable to point to a few more general considerations which are operative, and in most cases, dominant. These points need to be split into two distinct types: group and individual.

19.2.4 **Group motives**

Where the apparatus of the State is used to impose the tactics of terror it is almost certainly the case that this is being initiated by one person or a small group or class to maintain, enlarge or extend their personal power. The justification, however, is presented in terms of the need to maintain internal security and order which will benefit, and is to the advantage, of all the citizens. There is a similar appeal to necessity to account for acts of violence performed against the State. A minority group might argue that they are prevented from taking part in political activity or that being allowed to vote once in five years is irrelevant when what they see as their rights are being consistently overridden by the majority or by those who control the power of the State. Such minority groups are often welded together by an ethnic bond which, for example, drives the Basque campaign for autonomy or separation from Spain.

Other groups are driven more by ideology, secular or religious. Those acting on the basis of a political ideology are usually pressing for a fundamental change in the way the State and society is structured and operated. The nature of the change being sought will differ vastly depending on which of the political extremes is being drawn upon: from the left the call might be for a completely socialistic system; from the right for a restoration of aristocratic ascendancy. In either case a claim is being made to high moral values: to the overriding need for equality and justice, or to the respect for, and imposition of, earlier moral values. For those whose cause is founded on religious beliefs the moral considerations emerge still more starkly partly because they derive their force from an outside source (God, or the prophets, or sacred writings). Sharp distinctions are made between such explosive concepts as good and evil, whilst strict behavioural proscriptions are commonly laid down for the faithful.

It is, of course, clearly the case that most people with strong ideological convictions do not express them through terrorist activity: indeed, they are restrained in part by other aspects of their beliefs such as the importance of freedom of expression or the sanctity of human life. Those who are driven to use violence in the pursuit of their beliefs are likely to argue that they have the only truth and that those opposing its implementation must be immoral or even evil. The essential cause of their terrorist action can, given the brevity of our treatment here, be expressed in a kind of crude reductionism as the ends justifying the means, the over-arching justice and virtue of the cause providing absolution for the violence of the behaviour. In the extreme case, especially but not exclusively for religious terrorists, their own death is an acceptable sacrifice, which will be rewarded with the status of martyrdom and/or by eternal salvation.

Many terrorists groups begin as groups with a grievance, often they are a minority, or even a majority which is discriminated against. A social movement may begin to form whose end is to redress the situation; often they begin by the use of legal means but as these fail or opportunities are closed (possibly legal battles are lost or the constituencies for voting preclude their representation in the legislature, or marches and demonstrations are outlawed so that their legitimate voice is stifled) they may turn to illegal means. For most that may be a form of civil disobedience which is not violent, they may hold peaceful marches and risk being arrested. Most will be restrained by other moralities. But for a few the cause is too important and its success will excuse terrorist acts and so terrorist wings of movements are formed, often those for whom they purport to be fighting do not support their methods and may well suffer as a result of their actions.

Groups, even those with real fears and grievances may degenerate into the use of terrorist tactics very quickly. Usually they will fail to recognise their acts as those of terror and will continue to denounce what they perceive of as 'real' terrorism. Possibly one the clearest modern examples in the UK is the use of terrorist tactics against paedophiles living in communities which occurred in 2000. After publication of names and some addresses of paedophiles a number of mobs in various parts of the country rose up to terrorise these people. In the action innocent people, such as paediatricians were terrorised and a number of people were pin-pointed due to rumour rather than any proof. Their homes were under siege, missiles thrown and hate slogans chanted. The violence arose quickly and involved many otherwise law abiding and peaceful individuals. It is an indication of how we are all capable of such acts (see Evans (2003)).

The motivation for terrorist acts perpetrated for commercial purposes is less complex. Money is the aim and greed is the driving force. The desire for wealth and potential for greed are both deep-seated human characteristics but again it needs to be remembered that this makes very few into systematic practitioners of violence to achieve these ends.

19.2.5 Individual motives

Before considering the motives of the foot-soldiers of terrorism it is instructive to say a few words about its most significant proponents and leaders, those who have caused most deaths and suffering to be carried out; people such as Stalin, Hitler, Pol Pot, Idi Amin, the Ayatollah Khomeini, Saddam Hussein, Osama Bin Laden and similar leaders. Robins and Post (1998) suggest that these charismatic terrorists suffer from a paranoid personality disorder. They suggest that a part of this disorder is that they are unable to accept their own feelings of rage or hostility and they project them on to others. They have a damaged self-concept, cannot deal with the good and bad parts of themselves so they split them into the 'me' and 'not me'. They then need to find someone to blame for the 'not me' parts and this may be a section which becomes an enemy. So they deny their own feelings and then project them onto supposed enemies who they imagine are persecuting them and therefore need to be hunted down and either destroyed or rendered safe by being severely controlled. These authors link the paranoia with Freud and Klein's analysis of a failure to develop fully in child-hood and then document how it takes over the lives of these otherwise charis-matic individuals. Their analysis, though very reasonable and apparently logical, suffers from certain flaws. First, both Post, in almost everything else he has written concerning terrorists (see, e.g., 1998), and most other writers in this area argue that terrorists are mentally 'normal', not mentally ill. Secondly, the way in which they depict this type of paranoia, as being linked with delusions and split with accepted rationality might apply to many religious believers. This is not to deny that these leaders may project their own feelings onto others, or blame others for the ills of the world, e.g., Hitler's blaming the Jews or Osama Bin Laden blaming the Americans. It is to question whether this is the result of a mental illness, or whether it may be a purely rational way of ensuring that they continue in power. The actions of these individuals are in need of further analysis and explanation.

The leaders may be the cause of State terrorism but servants of the State actually carry out the atrocities. Why? In this area much of the activity may be explained on the basis of personal preservation or personal gain; in order to avoid persecu-tion, to do well or get on under that regime they may feel the need to perform cruel and inhuman acts. There is often no conviction on the part of these individuals. Sir Nigel Rodley, the UN's special rapporteur on terrorism from 1993 to 2001, stated:

When you meet torturers you realise that they're not doing it because they enjoy it, they torture people because it's a way of getting promotion and pay rises. They want to get confessions and convictions because they see that as meeting the wishes of the institution.

There is a process of culturisation, where torturers are made to stop seeing their victim as human. But if they didn't think they'd be rewarded, they wouldn't do it. (Quoted by Coughlan (2003))

Turning to those individuals, or to their followers, who form or join a movement which then may adopt terrorist tactics, what are their motives or what causes them to act? Motives may be split into three basic types: rational, performing terrorist acts as the only means to attain the goal; psychological, full identification with the group and its goals so that the group becomes the means of self-identity and the group is more important than the ends—the group is good and everything else evil so compromise is not an option; and cultural, violence may be a cultural norm and therefore resorting to it is simpler in some cultures than in others; or there may be a feeling that the culture is threatened at its roots and needs to be protected by any means. These are very general overviews which will be explained in more detail in particular situations.

A number of motives may be particular to terrorist activity. First, there may be very rational choices made that a cause is all important and that the risks are worth taking to try to attain the desired end. This type of recruit often starts at the level of a believer who through disillusionment with legal means of change is moved to believe that the only possible route is terror and that the action is justified by the 'moral right' of the cause, the cause is so just that it permits them to break the moral codes which might normally bind them. Secondly, recruits may arise to avenge the deaths or wrongs done to friends or members of their families, a personal crusade. Thirdly, there are religious fundamentalists who would do anything for their God or their belief. Most religions have had fundamentalist religious terrorists associated with them at some time in history. In some cases the terror comes from the heart of the Church, in others it arises in fanatical offshoots of the religious order. In all cases these fanatical believers are the most difficult to deal with, their belief and the reason for their actions arises out of their very identity. Despite the fact that their acts of terror are usually condemned or breach the teachings of the religion they purport to follow they believe that their actions are justified and even required by the religion as they believe them to be the direct will of their 'God' and will guarantee them and their family a better life after death. Post (2001) refers to a 1998 Fatwa which reads 'We with God's help call on every Muslim who believes in God and wishes to be rewarded to comply with God's order to kill the Americans and to plunder their money whenever and wherever they find it. Allah the merciful and the compassionate has ordered all religious Muslims to kill all the American civilian and military.' Finally, there may also be those who wish to protect their culture from outside interference or invasion, they act to preserve or protect the community. These true believers in a cause are often, though not exclusively, highly educated and drawn from the elite. In each of these instances it may be that the hatred grows slowly over time and through a failure of their cause to be recognised, or the hatred is taught by others (e.g., the teaching carried out by Osama Bin Laden in his camps in Afghanistan). Here the identity of the individual is often shaped by the cause, so what the cause calls just is seen as necessary.

Many recruits will not have this direct link with the cause, why do they join? Many terrorist groups recruit members as youths. As has been evident in earlier chapters adolescence has anyway been linked with a tendency to rebel against home, society and the established order. Their recruitment may be aided if the adolescents are marginalised or feel excluded from society or have suffered in poverty, from lack of educational achievements, have no jobs or are from broken homes. They may be suffering from a feeling of low self esteem or view their exclusion and failure as the fault of others so be ripe for joining a group. A number may also seek excitement and stimulation, they may even already practice aggression to attain what they want. Each of these has been studied in earlier chapters and will not be elaborated upon here.

In joining a terrorist organisation many of these 'problems' may be addressed. Bion (1961) noted that any group, be it a gang, a close community or presumably a terrorist organisation, will welcome individuals into its midst, support them and give them a sense of belonging. Individuals become subsumed into the whole; they are valued, given opportunities and become one with the group and its intentions and the decisions of its leaders. The group becomes all important to them and to their identity, they are unable to leave and are willing to perform acts which may have been unthinkable under the moral code leaned before they joined the group. Many, if not most, terrorist groups cannot allow individual members to leave and will kill their former colleagues rather than let them leave. This may be partly to protect their security but, as Post (2001) notes, also arises because allowing an individual to leave places the whole justification for the group into question—how can someone who used to be committed to 'good' or to 'the cause' now have tuned to 'evil' or have lost the message? To allow individuals to leave questions their very existence it puts into doubt the justification for their otherwise unacceptable actions. For a number, even once their cause has been largely met through negotiation or political changes the group is so important that they cannot or will not give up the struggle, they have to continue to terrorise. This can be seen in certain factions in Northern Ireland and it may be that it is necessary to find other paths for these individuals such that disbanding or leaving the group is possible. In other instances they may change enemies: at one time Osama Bin Laden fought against Russia in Afghanistan and was supported in that struggle by the US, once he had won that struggle and no longer had a single enemy he turned his attentions to the US military presence on Muslim sacred soil and later to the US and Western culture more generally. The fight for the supremacy of the cause of Islam continued throughout.

In addition Post (1998) whilst recognising that terrorists are mentally normal suggests that certain personality types may be more attracted to these groups than are other types. First, he notes that those who crave excitement and stimulation are heavily over-represented in this group, and also suggests that those who have a slightly damaged self-concept may be more likely to become involved in terrorism (see the discussion above).

19.2.6 Concluding remarks

In a general treatment of terrorism the aspects touched upon is this section would be more fully developed as central themes. The central objective of the present work is, however, different. It is to explore various elements of criminology. In this context terrorism is thus particularly interesting, as a type of criminal behaviour and in the way the criminal justice system has been influenced by terrorism and the perceived needs to adjust that system as a counter to such activities. These issues are taken up in the following sections.

19.3 Is terrorism criminal?

19.3.1 National controls

This may seem a rather strange question but what is really being questioned is whether terrorism should be thought of as separate from the 'normal' acts proscribed under State law. Most terrorist acts by dissidents or minority groups *within* a country will be offences against the normal (existing) criminal law (murder; kidnapping; torture; destruction of property; extortion). It might be argued that the use of the normal criminal law is inadequate to mark the denunciation society feels towards terrorists; it fails to mark the aims and motivations of the activities. Others might suggest that existing punishments are inadequate to mark the seriousness of the offending and/or that dealing with terrorists under the existing punishment regime will render it impossible to mark the seriousness of terrorist acts. Although at first sight these claims may be powerful there are a number of reasons why, where possible, terrorism should be controlled through the normal mechanisms. Firstly, standard criminal laws are there to protect society from unacceptable acts; they are constructed and applied so as to maintain the status quo and order in society. Whilst every society hopes that they will only need to be used against normal threats to that order clearly where the threat is greater, as in an act of terrorism, it is important that the 'normal' laws are able to operate against such a threat. The use of special legislative provisions plays into the hands of the terrorist: it marks them as different and makes it easier for them to claim that they are being punished for their beliefs not their deeds, it makes them into martyrs. The government, and many in society, often do not wish to recognise and give further voice to the political goals of terrorists, treating them as common criminals removes from them the political element and may be seen as the State undermining their believed justification for their terrorist activity.

Therefore most States deal with terrorism largely through their already existing criminal laws. This is clearly the group of activities the US wishes to constrain as they do not define terrorism within the anti-terrorist enactments such as the PATRIOT Act which leaves the definition to those used in the various government organisations all of which focus on acts which are already illegal. Similarly the UK whilst defining terrorism for the purposes of the use of extra powers does not have a separate offence of terrorism despite that having been suggested by the Lloyd Report. However, there may be a number of reasons why a State may criminalise extra activities and choose to extend their criminal laws. For example, first, as seen above certain terrorist activities in the UK might not be criminal under existing law: the refusal to perform a duty such as to refuse to perform a vital safety function may not be a criminal offence but it may cause terror and if it is intentional and arises in order to persuade the government of certain activities then it might be seen as terrorist activity. Secondly, there may be certain groups which are seen as so dangerous that membership should be an offence (in the UK Schedule 2 to the Terrorism Act 2000 proscribes 14 domestic groups, most of them Irish, and after being amended in February 2001 it also proscribes 21 international terrorist organisations, including Al-Qu'ida whose threat was recognised prior to the bombing of the trade towers). Thirdly, there are some acts which may not be offences under the normal order and which are particular to terrorism. In the UK these include: inciting terrorism overseas; weapons training (s. 54 of the Terrorism Act 2000); dangerous substances (now include chemical, biological and nuclear materials and threats under ss. 113 to 115 of the Crime and Security Act 2001); the directing a terrorist organisation (s. 56(1) of the Terrorism Act 2000); possession of otherwise legal substances for terrorist purposes, possibly the makings of a bomb (s. 57 of the Terrorism Act 2000); collecting information which might be useful to terrorists (s. 58 of the Terrorism Act 2000); offences required under international obligations, (such as hijacking, contained in many acts); offences to finance terrorism. Finally, States may wish to take jurisdiction over acts of terrorism committed outside their territory. The criminal law may not normally permit this but terrorist legislation may permit a State to treat activities as criminal even when committed outside their jurisdiction and even if they would not be criminal acts in the jurisdiction within which they are committed. Usually these special provisions refrain from marking any political element in the offence so as to make them as commonplace and similar to ordinary offences as is possible.

Therefore whilst most activities will be caught by and dealt with under the normal criminal legislation, acts of terrorism may occasionally require special offences especially as the focus has now been very sharply turned on terrorist acts and groups which transcend national frontiers. The one blind spot in the national laws is terrorist offences committed by the State. As indicated, State action has been responsible for more victims of terrorism than that of dissident groups. State terrorism may be international where it is used to promote perceived political, economic or ideological interests in other parts of the world (States may offer ideological, financial, military or operational support or may become directly involved in terrorist attacks). State terrorism may also be domestic, used to preserve an existing order and maintain State authority by demonstrating State power. Domestic terrorism may be overt as practiced by totalitarian regimes such as Nazi Germany, the Khmer Rouge in Cambodia or the Taliban in Afghanistan; or may be covert which is the secretive application of terror against a perceived domestic enemy and has often been used in countries with extensive police services such as Pinochet's Chile, Iran, Syria and Argentina.

Some States may have provisions to try to deal with terrorism from outside their border; although where they are committed by other States the opportunity to enforce them is much reduced. The US Department of State compiles a list of State sponsors of international terrorism, in 2001 the list, in order of degree of nuisance, read: Iran; Iraq; Syria; Libya; North Korea; Sudan (presumably North Korea would now be 'promoted'). Some States may try to ensure that they are not themselves perpetrating or funding terror outside their borders. A good example of State intervention and its control is the CIA funding of the Contras for guerrilla warfare against the Sandinista regime in Nicaragua between 1981 and 1983. The Contras were implicated in numerous and serious human rights violations, repeatedly denied by the Reagan administration. In 1982 Congress limited this intervention and in 1984 it forbade further US involvement. Reagan tried to circumvent this ban by various means of channelling money to the Contras, this policy led to the Iran–Contra scandal headed by Oliver North which finally ended all support for the Contras. Therefore vigilant democratic systems may prevent this type of intervention but it is difficult where a State is intent on a particular path.

Whilst States may act on the international arena they rarely protect their people against terror committed by themselves or their servants. Whilst the State is not generally above the law and its acts or those of its servants may well fall within the definitions, the apparatus of enforcement is rarely used against it. This failure is particularly marked when a State embarks on the use of terror as a tactic to enforce internal security and order, rather than less orchestrated State violence. In effect this means that any group or person controlling the State could be beyond the law. Of course constitutions, even unwritten ones, and human rights provisions are meant to indicate and provide legal restraint on State power but in many instances it may not be possible to enforce such constraints in the face of an emergency or when the State is intent on the use of terror to force its will. A good example of its open use in a free society is the series of US moves against communists within the US. The first of these arose in 1919 after a number of letter bombs were intercepted, the US conducted many raids (the Palmer Raids) against communist and radical left-wing groups, offices were shut down, leaders were arrested and tried and hundreds were deported. The second began in 1930 and went on into the 1940s and gave rise to the House of Un-American Activities Committee and many prosecutions and investigations of suspected communists. The last arose in the 1950s under Senator Joseph McCarthy who held 'McCarthy Hearings' to expose communists within government, industry and Hollywood. Hundreds of careers were ruined, many were 'blacklisted' to prevent them obtaining employment and many of the decisions were made on spurious evidence given by other suspects in order to protect themselves. Whilst non-governmental organisations or private agencies such as Human Rights Watch (founded in 1978) or Amnesty International (founded in 1961) monitor political abuses and report on them and groups such as Liberty in the UK may do this internally and may even bring or fund actions against the State to try to use the legal process to control State power their ability to prevent such abuses is very limited.

The conclusion would seem to be that in the normal situation national laws suffice and should be used. But in times of conflict, whether internal or international, the enforcement mechanisms are either not operated (governments and their control structures politically choose not to prosecute their own officers or officials as in the former Yugoslavia) or cannot be implemented (perhaps because national institutions may have collapsed as happened in Rwanda). Where is the protection in these situations?

19.3.2 **International controls**

What part does and should international law play in the defining of terrorism? There are many treaties in international law dealing with aspects of terrorism, to take just a few:

- Convention on the Prevention and Punishment of the Crime of Genocide 1948
- Convention for the Suppression of Unlawful Acts against the Safety of Civil Aviation 1971
- Convention for the Suppression of Unlawful Seizures of Aircraft (Hijacking) 1971
- Biological and Toxic Weapons Convention 1972
- Chemical Weapons Convention 1993
- Comprehensive Test Ban Treaty 1996
- UN Convention for the Suppression of Terrorist Bombings 1997
- UN Convention for the Suppression of the Financing of Terrorism 1999
- Convention on Cybercrime 2001

Each deals with a specific issue; there is no general control of terrorism though the UN is working to achieve this. Many of these definitions involve either acts of individuals against civilians and the international nature comes about because the offence is not fully committed in one State. These Conventions assume that States' parties will enforce these rules by use of internal laws. The other definitions involve agreements between States concerning, for example, the types of weapons which will be unacceptable in any conflict. These are enforced through political pressure between States or by recourse to courts such as the International Court of Justice at The Hague which handles cases between States, but does not try individuals. The international community has not defined terrorism.

Until recently the international community has done little to plug the gap left when a national court cannot or will not act against agents of the State who are committing acts of terror. There are three instances where the international community has acted: the Nuremburg trials following the Second World War; the International Criminal Tribunal for the Former Yugoslavia; and the International Criminal Tribunal for Rwanda. This means that most perpetrators of war crimes, crimes against humanity or crimes of terror committed by or for the State have gone unpunished. Examples from the last 50 years include the Khmer Rouge in Cambodia, armed conflicts in Mozambique, Liberia, and El Salvador whilst other countries have targeted the innocent as in the massacres in Algeria and the Great Lakes region of Africa. Most of those intent on the use of such tactics have rightly believed they will not be punished.

For the last 60 years the international community has been discussing setting up a court to remedy this situation. In July 1998 they adopted the Rome Statute of the International Criminal Court (see **http://www.icc-cpi.int/php/index.php**). In July 2002 this entered into force having achieved its 60th ratification. The Rome Statute sets up the International Criminal Court before which heads of State and commanding officers as well as foot soldiers or militia will be able to be tried and, if guilty, punished for acts of genocide, crimes against humanity and war crimes. This will catch genocide and those who incite genocide; ethnic cleansing (expulsion, killing, rape and intimidation of individuals due to their cultural or religious background); social cleansing (elimination of undesirable social elements such as street children, prostitutes, drug addicts, the homeless, homosexuals etc.); murder, rape and the brutalising of civilians caught in an armed conflict. Terrorism and State terrorism are only included if they fall into the categories of genocide, crimes against humanity or war crimes. States parties wanted to include acts of aggression but could not agree a definition. There was no discussion of the inclusion of a separate crime of State terrorism. Hopefully, once the Court is fully operational it will catch many acts of terror committed by agents of the State and so will deter people from being willing to take part in such activities. As with national laws it seems that the international community has chosen to prosecute for particular actions rather than to recognise a separate offence.

Having said that, the UN is presently discussing a definition for terrorism. At the moment this is intended to be used to determine what measures should be taken to control the activity, i.e., how to arrange anti-terrorism or counter-terrorism at an international level rather than to prosecute for a separate offence.

19.4 Mechanisms of control

Debate here needs to open with a discussion of the need for anti-terrorism legislation. Clearly where there is a State of emergency caused by terrorism most would admit the need for special powers to deal with that situation. The American Judge, Douglas J., stated that democracy is not a suicide pact and it permits action to be taken by a State when there is clear and present danger (*Terminielo* v *Chicago* (1949) 337 US 1 at p. 37). An example of a State using this authority would be the anti-terrorist legislation and powers which were used over more than 20 years of violence concerning the situation in Northern Ireland. During that period there was terrorist violence used by both factions in the dispute and there were extended powers given to the enforcement agencies in order to deal with that; the UK also had to declare a derogation under Article 15 of European Convention of Human Rights and Fundamental Freedoms (ECHR). Most of the powers and provisions enacted over this period were temporary and centred the powers on terrorism in, and concerning, the emergency situation in Northern Ireland. In *Brannigan & McBride* v *United Kingdom* (1994) 17 EHRR 539 the derogation was accepted as valid and necessary such that suspects could be detained for up to seven days. However this right of a State to protect itself in times of emergency has limits, it does not permit a State to use unreasonable force. Under the ECHR torture and inhuman or degrading treatment would still be unacceptable, see *Ireland* v *United Kingdom* (1978–9) 2 EHRR 25. In February 2001 the United Kingdom withdrew its derogation at least in so far as it applied to the United Kingdom. The government were of the opinion that the emergency situation no longer existed and that the anti-terrorist legislation they presently had was in conformity with the ECHR. Despite there being no emergency there is still anti-terrorist legislation in force, namely the Terrorism Act 2000 and the Anti-Terrorism, Crime and Security Act 2001. In the absence of any pressing threat or emergency are these necessary?

Arguably they are. Every State has a duty to protect its people from any violence including terrorist or political violence; furthermore States have a duty to protect the other rights and liberties of their citizens. These duties can be found in all the major international declarations of human rights. Furthermore most actions of terrorists are illegal and the State has an obligation to maintain law and order. As already indicated it can be argued that the State responsibility would be fulfilled by the usual powers of enforcement for all other crimes. However terrorism presents special difficulties to the enforcement agencies—its secrecy, the frequent international element, the fact that the command structure and planning may be far removed from the active terrorists possibly even out of the country. Terrorism is also rather different in kind from common crime: it is intended to cause the most damage and suffering so as to put the community in fear; it aims to cause political instability in the hope of bringing about a change in political policies if not politicians; it is organised; its perpetrators are trained; it often crosses national borders; and the perpetrators may be supported and assisted by parts of the community.

Therefore States, even liberal States, can, and arguably ought, to have in place special laws to empower and deal with a terrorist threat if it arises. As with the laws that should be permitted in case of emergency these should be reasonable and necessary to the service of democracy. To ensure the balance is correctly and fairly struck it seems sensible to debate and pass such legislation when there is no particular threat rather than to permit through ill-conceived and possibly too controlling a legislative provision in the face of a pressing emergency.

It is certainly the case that in times of stress States, even democratic States, often pass authoritarian laws or adopt unlawful practices—the greater good of protecting against the immediate danger is seen to outweigh suspension of civil liberties or constitutional rights. The argument is that this is necessary in order to obtain important information, confessions or to access terrorist cells and weapons caches. Two examples of such situations will be briefly discussed here. First, Northern Ireland has been problematic and has had the potential for terrorism since its formation in the 1920s. In the early 1970s terrorist violence once again became a serious and pressing threat in Northern Ireland. As a knee-jerk reaction regulations under the Civil Authorities (Special Powers) Act (NI) 1922 were passed which introduced quasi-martial law. These regulations permitted searches without warrant of civilian homes; temporary detention of people without charge; internment without trial of those suspected of serious terrorist activities but against whom there was not sufficient evidence to bring court proceedings; and questioning of those detained, interred and others. These provisions were, to some extent successful as they led to the seizure of thousands of weapons but this came at a high price. About a quarter of a million homes were searched. Hundreds of suspects were arrested and detained or interred. A number of those detained or interred were questioned using the 'five techniques':

- *Wall-standing*—spread-eagled against a wall with their fingers high above their heads and pressed against the wall, the legs spread apart with the feet back so as to place much of the body weight on the fingers. This position had to be held for long periods, hours at a time.

- *Hooding*—putting a black hood over the individual's head and face and leaving it there for long periods of time, possibly days, except when the individual was being interrogated.

- *Subjection to white noise*—when not being interrogated they were subjected to a continuous and loud hissing noise.

- *Sleep deprivation*—pending interrogation depriving them of sleep.

- *Deprivation of food and drink*—reduced diet and low levels of nutrition whilst detained and pending interrogations.

This was a form of quasi-torture, giving rise to weight loss and psychiatric symptoms though not to other physical pain (apart from that suffered from the wall standing). Many of these powers were tested in *Ireland* v *United Kingdom* (1978–9) 2 EHRR 25. The European Commission of Human Rights decided the use of the 'five techniques' was in breach of Article 3 of the ECHR and amounted not only to inhuman or degrading treatment but also to torture. However the Court decided that it was merely inhuman and degrading treatment and did not occasion the levels of suffering and cruelty implied by the word torture. There was also other evidence of physical brutality and ill-treatment by the British security forces which was also found to be inhuman and degrading treatment though not torture. As to the detention this was found to breach Article 5 of the ECHR but to be covered by the derogation lodged by the UK government. These techniques were largely withdrawn by the mid-1970s and replaced with slightly more balanced provisions, which showed greater respect for human rights. Possibly the most lasting and worst side-effect of the legislation is that it was thought to have enabled the IRA to recruit many more members and it removed the more moderate leaders and replaced them with individuals more ready to hit innocent civilian targets. In the long-term it may have had more negative effects than positive.

Secondly, the US following the attacks of 11 September 2001 (9/11) has taken a number of questionable measures. First, there are hundreds of prisoners being held in a sort of legal limbo in Guantanimo Bay, no-one quite knows what their status will be if they stand trial, no-one is sure what rights they are enjoying, if any, whilst they are detained, no-one can be sure that they or a few of them are not suffering inhuman and degrading treatment or even torture. The legalities of their detention are unclear and the mere fact that it is occurring may breach international standards. Unfortunately the ECHR does not apply and so it will not be tested in the same way as was that of the Northern Irish detainees. The situation may, however, be explored by the United Nations Human Rights Committee. Even if one accepts the claims that the inmates are not being tortured or otherwise badly treated the whole secrecy shrouding their detention sends a threatening message to the rest of the world, or to those who may sympathise with them, and may be tantamount to a form of quasi-terrorism. Added to this the US government passed the USA PATRIOT Act 2001, very shortly after the terrorist attack on the twin towers of the World Trade Centre. The acronym stands for the Uniting and Strengthening America by Providing Appropriate Tools Required to Intercept and Obstruct Terrorism Act. The Act has led to interference with many liberties the Americans thought they enjoyed. The Act was passed very quickly, it did attract fierce debate, especially in the Senate, and there were some concessions but it remains a large inroad on rights and freedoms. Among other things the Act provides for:

- Greater government surveillance including access to private records.
- Increased information sharing between domestic law enforcement and intelligence.
- Enhanced electronic tapping into e-mails, electronic address books and private records as well as a requirement on Internet Service Providers to provide government agencies with more private information concerning individuals.

- Legal use of 'roving wire-taps' to permit eavesdropping on telephone conversations or computer links of an individual wherever he or she may be. The taps can move between phones and computers without demonstrating that they are being used by a suspect or the target of an order. Wire-taps and pen-taps can be served even if the individual or entity is not named and without proving that the information may be relevant to a criminal investigation.

- Requiring banks to identify sources of money deposited in an individual's private account and requiring foreign banks to report on all large suspicious transactions.

- Introduction of nationwide search warrents.

- The deprotation of immigrants who raise money for any terrorist organisation.

- Detention of immigrants without charge for up to seven days if they are suspected of supporting terrorism.

To these can be added the fingerprinting of all immigrants from specified Arab and Islamic countries, this has already led to the collection of 44,000 records of individuals not suspected of anything, merely because of their origins. Interestingly no-one has proven that the previous civil liberties posed a barrier to the effective tracking or prosecution of terrorists, no-one showed that the ordinary powers were insufficient to investigate terrorism. Yet the PATRIOT Act has significantly undermined certain rights to free expression and privacy to an extent which would have been inconceivable prior to 11 September 2001. In 2003 Sutherland (*Guardian*, 1 September 2003) reported on the problems faced by students just to illustrate the problem.

Campus police are obliged, under the pretext of 'homeland security' to liase with the FBI. So, to their indignation, are college librarians ('What is Ali reading?'). The Immigration and Naturalisation Service (INS) requires universities to provide confidential information about their Middle Eastern and Muslim students—those suspecting of 'harbouring' al-Quida ('Who is e-mailing Ali?') . . . At the beginning of this month, American college officials were required to register all foreign students with federal authorites under the provision of Sevis, the newly established student and eschange visitor information service . . . In order to get into the Sevis system applicants must first be interviewed by US officials in the would-be student's home country. It can take a year to get through the necessary hoops and bottlenecks . . .

These two examples show what can happen when the response to an emergency is made in the context of panic. A more measured approach such as that above is suggested. This does not guarantee rights and liberties will be protected but at least the liberal voices of human rights groups and protectors and defenders of the constitution are more likely to be heard, maybe even heeded. It would perhaps be salutary if contemporary Americans also listened to a voice from their pre-revolutionary past. In 1759 Benjamin Franklin stated the essence with admirable economy: 'They that can give up essential liberty to obtain a little temporary security deserve neither'.

It is less likely that legislation will transgress the rights of citizens if it is fully debated in a calm atmosphere rather than passed frantically to deal with immediate difficulties. The Anti-Terrorism Crime and Security Act 2001 was fiercely debated, particularly in the House of Lords, and much altered to provide for more safeguards against abuse by the enforcement agencies. It provides for wide powers by State agencies but is more tempered than its US counterpart. Despite that many libertarians, even those who accept the need for such legislation, are still very scathing about it and feel that it goes too far and offers too few safeguards to the liberties of citizens in general or to those who fall suspect under the legislation. Its most controversial measure is the power to intern foreigners without trial. At least nine people are being held in this way and have very limited family visits or access to lawyers. In February 2002 The Committee for the Prevention of Torture and Inhuman or Degrading Treatment or Punishment made an emergency visit to investigate these internees. In July 2002 the Special Immigration Appeals Tribunal found that although there was a public emergency permitting derogation from Article 5 the provision was discriminatory as it only applied to foreign nationals. In October the Court of Appeal ruled that there was no discrimination. The detainees are still being held without charge: they should be released or given an open and fair trial and, if convicted, punished. Furthermore, there is concern over the way in which terrorist legislation, both the 2001 Act and the Terrorism Act 2000, might be employed by the police; to control not just those one might reasonably suspect of being terrorists but also those who are, or whose activities are, a nuisance or undesirable. In Spring 2003 hundreds of stop and searches were conducted under s. 44 of the Terrorism Act 2000 (legally only to be used as part of the prevention and investigation of terrorism); one 11-year-old school girl was even served with a s. 44 notice (see Liberty (2003a and b)). No terrorists were apprehended as a result of this activity. The suggestion seems to be either that peace protesters are a potential terrorist threat or that the powers are being misused. Walker (2002), sees the need to ensure that the extra powers are not used unless they are necessary and therefore suggests the inclusion of three safeguards to any anti-terrorism legislation: informed legislative debates setting clear and limited powers (to this I would add that all such debates should be free of the party whip); constant scrutiny of its operation and use as well as its compatibility with international provisions; and judicial control built into the law itself. Arguably the need for well balanced permanent anti-terrorism legislation sitting on the shelf ready to use if an emergency arises is even more necessary post-11 September 2001 due to the perceived increase in an international terrorist threat to the West. There is an additional problem which arises: once the State has powers of this sort and a number of agencies looking for terrorists and terrorist activities it is predictable that they will find some, or claim to find some. It is rather like the witch hunts of the fifteenth century. If you look hard enough and your *raison d'être* rests on discovery you are likely to discover something. States need to be particularly vigilant against this type of problem.

So what sort of measures is one considering? They fall into different categories. Counter-terrorism usually refers to pro-active policies that specifically seek to eliminate terrorist groups and the environments in which they can flourish. Its intended aims are to work proactively to prevent or decrease the number of terrorist attacks which occur. This might be achieved through diplomacy (persuading others of the right of ones position), financial controls (undermining terrorists, criminal money making ventures, confiscating funds and dissuading or criminalising individual donors), military force, intelligence (the constant collection and analysis of small, often seemingly unimportant pieces of information) and covert action; through legal (granting of powers to the authorities such that many of these actions are possible, e.g., extended stop and search, extra powers of detention, and the use of law to criminalise certain behaviours often associated with terrorism); repressive (use of asylum and refugee proceedings to detain suspected terrorists and to fingerprint others); conciliatory responses to terrorism; or through targeted and untargeted prevention (see Martin (2003)). On the other hand Anti-terrorism refers to target hardening (the use of very high security measures such as those at airports and on airlines, CCTV, protection for key politicians etc.), enhanced security (CCTV, port and border controls) and other measures seeking to deter or prevent attacks. Basically counter-terrorism is offensive (though not necessarily violent) or proactive in its approach whereas anti-terrorism is defensive or reactive in its approach. Each can involve interventions which will transgress human rights but with care each could also lead to heightened security without unnecessary or excessive interference with liberty.

Basically the State wants to 'spoil' or prevent terrorist action. They also wish to undermine terrorist organisations and gain as much information as possible about terrorists: aims; skills; operational capacities; tactics; sources of money and weapons; links with other individuals, groups or States. They want to be in a position to assess the level of risk within their territory and have the capacity to respond. Once they have the information and capacity there are then political choices such as whether to negotiate or not, whether to punish States or other organisations or individuals for helping or even tolerating terrorists. There are decisions concerning the legal powers to allow enforcement agencies to interfere with general rights and freedoms in order to deliver on the desired aims.

The important factor is to balance rights; to ensure that protecting the rights and interests of a State and a people against terrorist attack does not remove those very rights and liberties. To do so would in itself undermine the State: it would by law and the perceived need for security do what the terrorists want—alter the community beyond recognition. Arguably in both the US and the UK too many rights and freedoms have been sacrificed to protect against a supposed but unproven and badly assessed threat of terrorism.

In September 2003, two years after the destruction of the twin towers, the Attorney General, Lord Goldsmith, addressed the issue of balance in a speech to the International Bar Association conference in San Francisco (*Guardian*, 19 September 2003). After asserting that 'the goal of the terrorist is not only to kill, maim and destroy but also to undermine our societies', he added 'that aim is furthered if democratic governments place those suspected of terrorist crimes outside the law and compromise on their fundamental principles'. Acknowledging that many would find extreme difficulty in accepting that terrorists should be granted the protection of processes they had sought to destroy, the essential point remained:

We cannot allow our long established and hard-won system of justice and liberty to be swept away in the aftershock of a suicide bomb. Otherwise the terrorist will have robbed us of our freedoms and will have won. So those suspected of being terrorists are not outside the law, nor do they forfeit their fundamental rights by virtue of that fact.

Some imaginative flexibility was seen as being necessary. A British example was of laws allowing foreign nationals with no immigration rights to be detained indefinitely. But even then there were some safeguards in the right of judicial scrutiny by a body presided over by a senior judge and with a right of appeal to the highest court. Some flexibility, then, but 'without compromising either our respect for the rule of

law or the right to a fair trial—on which there can be no compromise'. Whether
these high standards have been (can be?) fully exercised, especially in times of fear
and panic, may be debatable but it is still important that the principles embodied
should be articulated and publicised.

19.5 State violence: introduction

State violence is very closely linked to terrorism and tyranny. Many issues are pertinent to both discussions. State violence is a less orchestrated and focused abuse of
power than is State terrorism or tyranny.

As was noted above State terrorism and tyranny has been responsible for more
killings, more tortures and more disappearances than all other forms. State violence
accounts for proportionately more violence than other forms (when one takes into
account the number of individuals who are in a position to commit such offences).
Furthermore State violence accounts for more serial offenders than are seen in
other criminal spheres.

19.5.1 How does State violence arise?

As with the causes of State terrorism more research is necessary into this area. Here
an interesting thesis which was aired in a BBC 2 documentary entitled *Five Steps to
Tyranny* in 2000 will be considered. As well as helping to understand State violence
this is particularly useful as an explanation of State tyranny and terrorism. The five
steps involve the following:

Step One— Creation of 'us' and 'them'

> Communities often create groups which are 'in-groups' and those which are 'out
> groups'. In our society we have many 'out groups' such as the homeless, asylum
> seekers, offenders, prisoners, beggars, paedophiles, the disabled etc. These groups
> are thought of as different and excluded from the dignity and humanity the 'in-
> group' enjoys. Leaders can exploit this difference and cultivate it to give rise to
> superior, dominant groups and inferior powerless groups. 'Out groups' may be
> portrayed as lacking intelligence, utility or morals such as occurred in Nazi
> Germany. They may also be portrayed as 'beasts' and as a threat to the dominant
> culture. The argument on the part of white supremacists that immigrants (usu-
> ally only black immigrants) are here to steal jobs from 'us' is a good example. An
> even more powerful example can be drawn from Rwanda where in 1994 the
> government, run by the minority Hutus, began a radio station to broadcast anti-
> Tutsi messages, portraying them as inferior and dangerous (saying they were
> cannibalistic and would eat the Hutu's children). This led to the massacre of over
> 800,000 Tutsis and moderate Hutus.

Step Two—Obedience to requests or orders

> To function smoothly all societies need most people to be obedient to the rules
> most of the time. Most of us therefore obey an authority figure without question,

almost without thinking. In most situations this is acceptable but there need to be limits; rebels who are willing to question why the rule or request is made are useful to prevent immoral or unacceptable rules or orders being given.

Step Three—Obedience to immoral orders of a perceived responsible individual

Professor Stanley Melgram at Yale University carried out an experiment as to whether people would administer lethal levels of electric shock to other individuals. He told the volunteers that they were investigating how to improve memory and asked them to administer ever increasing shocks for incorrect answers (the increases were small each time but eventually reached mortal levels). Of 900 volunteers over 600 were willing to administer the maximum dose of 450 volts. The researcher when challenged by the volunteers encouraged them to go on and stated that he would take full responsibility for the consequences. Where the learners were described as subhuman or beasts they were more willing to administer high levels of electric shock. This illustrates a number of factors: setting up an ideology or a reason for what is going to happen, something that allows people to make sense of it; obedience on the part of the volunteer; negative response to the portrayal of an individuals as 'other', as different from and inferior to the volunteer; the feeling that another is taking responsibility for the outcome, that the volunteer is just doing as he or she is asked and is absolved of blame and moral questioning. All of this is helped if the actions they are asked to perform start as only a little bit wrong and are slowly increased until they are torture. The usual reason given by ordinary individuals as to why they tortured or massacred individuals is 'we were only following orders'; this was used, though rejected, as a defence at the Nuremburg trials following the atrocities in Nazi Germany; it was used by the Serbs in the former Yugoslavia and by the Hutus in Rwanda.

Step Four—Stifling of free speech

Suppression of dissent is essential to tyranny or to torture. Most people will simply sit back and allow things to happen in their name. Most people are bystanders and do nothing, they are the most useful to tyranny or to terrorism as they pose no threat and will obey when necessary. Although they may see their action as passive they have actively decided not to get involved and therefore are tacitly supporting the tyranny. There are a few individuals who dissent and question, these are the ones who may be able to stop tyranny who will question what happens before the State goes too far. These people are few in number and are usually brutally treated and silenced by tyrannical regimes. Interestingly we are more likely to stand up for or help people if we feel that they are like us. The more we see them as falling into an 'out' group the more likely we are to ignore their plight. How many of us stand up for the asylum seekers who are portrayed by our media as 'other' and as 'bad' and who have systematically had their rights and interests reduced over the last 25 years?

Step Five—Dehumanising which leads to ethnic cleansing

In 1971 Professor Zimbardo of Stanford University carried out an experiment using 24 students. The students were drawn from one class and had much in common; they were seen as one community that cared for each other. Half of the students were assigned the role of prisoner and half the role of prison guards. They had cells, a communal area and a punishment area. The experiment was to last for 14 days. Within five days the experiment had to be called off as things had gone too far. The guards had become all powerful and lacking in compassion; they used physical and verbal aggression and even degraded the prisoners or treated them inhumanely for their own amusement. The prisoners had become totally powerless. The experiment showed how quickly humane and compassionate people could become changed and treat others inhumanely and act without morality. This suggests how ethnically mixed communities where people know each other and have lived together can be turned into communities of racial conflict as happened in the former Yugoslavia and in Rwanda. The atrocities committed in China as part of the Cultural Revolution and in Nazi Germany show how this can split families so that family members will act brutally to members of their own family.

These five steps can occur within weeks as was seen in Rwanda or it may take longer but all societies are vulnerable to these influences and most individuals (me?, you?,) might commit the atrocities if the environment were correct.

These steps demonstrate, or at least suggest, the ease with which States might be able to motivate ordinary individuals to tyrannise others. Similar steps, though less extreme, are used to release people to commit isolated acts of State brutality. Again in these instances the individuals who perform the acts gain no immediate personal benefit but may earn promotional opportunities if their actions lead to increased convictions, less troublesome prisoners or similar positive outcomes.

A further cause of State violence may perhaps lie in another frequent characteristic. In many environments where there is State violence the victim is from a group which is denigrated sometimes by the organisation, sometimes by sections of society: asylum seekers, refugees, illegal immigrants, suspects, offenders, prisoners, young black males, young males, the mentally or physically ill, those needing financial support from the State, the homeless. Some groups are particularly denigrated: those suspected or convicted of terrorism, sexual violence, paedophilia or child pornography. Sometimes they may jokingly be spoken of in negative terms either as a group or as a individuals, for example the elderly in health care when they are blocking a bed, the terminally ill or a particular patient on a ward or in a hospital, a particular suspect who always seems to elude the law but is 'known to be guilty', youths from certain areas of a city. The negative consideration of these groups may arise at work, in the press or media, in films, in discussions with family and friends but is likely to arise at some point. Once this negative image is fixed and the individual can see it is accepted by others, especially those he or she respects, they may feel and be able to act as if the individual or group were less deserving or less human than they are. This is particularly likely if they are in a position of power over the individual. This may start with their being less polite towards and tolerant of the individual or group but may then move on to their not according that person or group their full rights (possibly refusing or merely not bothering to protect them from racist violence or from attack from other prisoners), speaking to them in an aggressive manner and finally to physical brutality. In the experiment conducted by Professor Zimbardo of Stanford University in 1971 this is exactly what happened: the students who were guards began to see their colleagues in a very negative light and to treat them less humanely. The transformation took less than five days. Added to the negative views may be the fact that the individual or others from the 'group' have acted in a violent or disrespectful way to that public servant.

This evidence might raise an expectation of very high levels of State violence. Against this, many organisations work hard to try to contain the tendency. Others assume that as long as they do not condone the activity they have done enough. Assessing the problem is, however, complicated because levels of State violence are very difficult to ascertain. Admitting that members of a State organisation have committed violence towards members of the public, even if those actions would be condemned by the organisation as a whole and by most of its members, undermines the moral standing and therefore the authority of the organisation. It is therefore an area which is often shrouded in mystery. A film entitled *Injustice* (2001) which documents over five years the struggle for justice of four families whose relatives died in police custody states that between 1969 and 1999 1,000 people died in police custody in England and that no police officer has ever been convicted of any of these deaths. The film has attracted severe criticism from the establishment; the police have tried to censor the film and the Police Federation has threatened legal action against cinemas that show it, television channels have refused to show the film. However, it has ignited fierce debate whenever it has been shown, including at the European Parliament. Politicians have been forced to react, there have been some prosecutions and it has caused the State at least to look at the issue more carefully and was probably one of the catalysts to the setting up of a working group to consider how best to investigate deaths in custody (of both police and in prison).

In many societies police violence is a significant feature and failure to confront it can result in the intimidation of the population, or, more likely, sections of the population. This is not the case in Britain but even in such a society manifestations of police violence inevitably appear. Some of this may be racist as in the Lawrence case previously considered (see Chapter Thirteen) but there are a few studies identifying the additional use of excessive force by the police (Sherman (1980); Jacobs and O'Brien (1998); Phillips and Smith (2000)). One worrying aspect is the relative scarcity of statistics. The Police Complaints Board recorded for 2000–1 355 referrals of complaints concerning death or serious inquiry and 223 of actual bodily harm, but most incidents are unlikely to get so far as to be reported. This is even more likely of incidents in the prison service. A figure of 209 complaints (of which 19 were upheld) was obtained by direct request from the Office of Prison and Probation Ombudsman, but this is clearly only the tip of an iceberg (complainants need to exhaust all local remedies within the prison before appealing to the Ombudsman). The point is that even in relatively open democratic societies forms of State violence will occur and emerge: and that information about their scale and existence needs to be readily available to ensure that such practices are confronted and so do not become institutionalised.

19.6 **Conclusion**

Recent events in the US and elsewhere have necessarily thrust the issue of terrorism into prominence; the repercussions are naturally most evident in national and international politics and, given the particular flavour of some of the activities, in theological divisions. It is the basic contention of this chapter that these events also raise problems and questions, which justify their separate treatment in a book on criminology.

The chapter does not, therefore, purport to offer a general account of terrorism but to concentrate on a few issues more specific to the study of crime. However, these issues cannot be properly understood and appreciated unless they are placed in context. The early part of this chapter attempted to do this by briefly referring to a few more general points. One was to emphasise that the phenomenon of terrorism has a very long historical tail: it is essential to grasp that it is far from being a product of the new millennium. The chapter also surveys, but does not claim to solve, the issues raised by the questions: what is terrorism? how does it manifest itself? and why does it arise?

These influences have helped to shape the effects on the various elements of criminology which constitute the central theme of the chapter. These elements can be summarised under the two crucial questions: is terrorism criminal? and what legal issues are raised by the responses of governments to their sharply heightened perception of terrorism as a significant threat?

On the first question, it is argued that whilst most acts seen as terrorist can fall under, and be dealt with by normal criminal legislation, there are at least two large areas of complication and ambiguity. The current perception is that the most significant threats are those which transcend national boundaries where international criminal legislation is both less structured and less enforceable. The normal national criminal systems are also generally ill-fitted to deal with another major aspect of terrorism: that which is committed by the State itself. On the second question of the legislative responses aimed at controlling terrorism the chapter attempts to focus discussion on the extent to which, both nationally and internationally, it becomes impossible for governments to avoid confronting the crucial issue of balance. That is, in exercising its duty to protect its citizens from violence, including terrorist violence, the State also has a duty to safeguard the liberties and rights of its citizens. Recognising the difficulties, the argument here is that for democratic societies the responses must not be allowed to undermine established freedoms embodied in the rule of law and the right to a fair trial: indeed to do so is to cede too much to the aims of the terrorists.

SUGGESTED READING

Martin, G., (2003), *Understanding Terrorism: Challenges, Perspectives, and Issues*, Thousand Oaks, CA.: Sage Publications.

Whittaker, D.J. (2002), *Terrorism: Understanding the Global Threat*, Harlow: Pearson.

Whittaker, D.J. (2003), *The Terrorism Reader*, 2nd edn, London: Routledge.

WEBSITES

Amnesty International: **http://www.amnesty.org**

Co-ordinator for Counter Terrorism, Department of State: **http://www.staet.gov/www/ global/terroris**

Human Rights Watch: **http://www.hrw.org**

International Policy Institute for Counterterrorism (a private research organisation): **http://www.ict.org.il**

State Department. State Sponsored Terrorism 2001: **http://www.state.gov/s/ct/rls/pgtrpt/ 2001/html/10249.htm**

QUESTIONS

1 What, if anything, is new about terrorism in the twenty-first century?

2 Discuss the view that the State is the main defence against terror and violence but has also been the main perpetrator.

3 Why do particular groups and individuals resort to terrorist activities?

4 Are all terrorist acts crimes?

5 How far and in what way do recent attempts to combat terrorism endanger existing legal practises in the US and the UK?

REFERENCES

Bion, W.R. (1961), *Experiences in Groups and Other Papers*, London: Tavistock.

Coughlan, S. (2003), 'Do Human Rights Stand a Chance Post 9/11?', *The Times Higher Education Supplement* 29 August 2003.

Foucault, M. (1977), *Crime and Punishment*, Translated by Alan Sheridan, London: Penguin Books.

Higgins, R. (1997), 'The General International Law of Terrorism', in R. Higgins and M. Flory (eds), *Terrorism and International Law*.

Jacobs, D. and O'Brien, R.M. (1998), 'The Determinants of Deadly Force: A Structural Analysis of Police Violence', *American Journal of Sociology*, 103(4): 837–62.

Liberty (2003a), *Can You Spot the Difference?*, London: Liberty.

Liberty (2003b), *Casualty of War: 8 Weeks of Counter-Terrorism in Rural England*. Produced by Liberty, Gloucester Weapons Inspectorate and Berkshire CIA, London: Liberty.

Lloyd Report, Lord Lloyd and Sir John Kerr (1996), *Inquiry into Legislation Against Terrorism*, Cm 3420, London.

Martin, G. (2003), *Understanding Terrorism: Challenges, Perspectives and Issues*, Thousand Oaks, CA.: Sage.

Phillips, T. and Smith, P. (2000), 'Police Violence Occasioning Citizen Complaint', *British Journal of Criminology*, vol. 40, pp. 480–96.

Post Jerrold, M. (1998), 'Terrorist Psycho-Logic: Terrorist behaviour as a Product of Psychological Forces', in W. Reich (ed.), *Origins of Terrorism*, Baltimore: Johns Hopkins University Press.

Post Jerrold, M. (2001), *Washington Post*, Monday 22 October 2001.

Robins, Robert S. and Post, Jerrold M. (1998), *Political Paranoia: The Psychopolitics of Hatred*, New Haven, CO: Yale University Press.

Sherman, L.W. (1980), 'Causes of Police Behaviour: The Current State of Quantitative Research', *Journal of Research in Crime and Delinquency*, vol. 17(1), pp. 69–100.

Simon, J. (2001), ' "Entitlement to Cruelty": The End of Welfare and the Punitive Mentality in

America', found in K. Stenson and R. Sullivan (eds), *Crime, Risk and Justice*, Cullompton: Willan Publishing.

Sorel, J-M. (2003), 'Some Questions About the Definition of Terrorism and the Fight Against its Financing', *European Journal of International Law*, vol. 14, p. 365.

Sutherland, J. (2003), 'Nowhere has Post-9/11 Paranoia Struck More Deeply than in American Universities. Just Ask Ali', *Guardian*, 1 September 2003.

Terrorism in the United States 1999. FBI Counterterrorism Threat Assessment and Warning Unit, Counterterrorism Division. **http://www.fbi.gov/publications/terror/terror99.pdf**

Walker, C. (2002), *Blackstone's Guide to the Anti-Terrorism Legislation*, Oxford: Oxford University Press.

20

Governance, risk and globalisation theories

20.1 Introduction

As has been indicated at various parts of this book the broad social context within which the study of criminology takes place is both important and changes over time. The purpose of this chapter is to draw the attention of students to some very broad recent changes which are currently being reflected in the criminal laws, in their administration and in their interpretation. Two such changes are identified: shifts in the role and status of the State (governance); and an altered perception of the significance of risk. An attempt is made to place each of these within the prevailing context of neo-liberalism in economic and social affairs and the associated trend towards the so-called globalisation of much economic activity. Some of the implications of these developments to the study of criminology are then briefly indicated. It is hoped that this will alert students to the need to consider how, and to what extent, they impinge upon the discourse of criminology.

20.2 Governance—the changing role of the State in crime control from liberal social-welfare to neo-liberal ideals

20.2.1 Introduction to governance

From the mid-nineteenth century until the end of the 1960s it was generally accepted that the State would take responsibility for matters of law and order. Towards the end of the twentieth century this comfortable situation became increasingly questioned by theorists and undermined by Western liberal governments. One of the most quoted intellectuals of this period, Michel Foucault, studied the 'art of government' (1991) and stated that it involved addressing questions concerning the way in which people govern themselves, the way in which they should be governed, how they should govern others, by whom and in what way people will accept to be governed and how to improve and perfect governing skills. The claim was often that the means of government over the previous 50 years, possibly even 100 years, had been to control, pacify and render harmless the lower classes. This approach was questioned as it was often seen as exclusionary and that this was especially so in the case of crime policy (see Foucault (1978), Goffman (1961) and Garland (1985)). Pavlich, speaking about the changes to crime control and prevention in the past 30 years notes that it '. . . is not just a slight adjustment to political technique; rather, the very notions of who is governed, who governs and what governance entails are in the process of significant revision' (1999, pp. 103–4). The recent changes thus touch on the central ideas in the 'art of government' and are not exclusive to the area of crime.

20.2.2 Governance generally

In most Western States there has been a shift from government to governance (Garland (1996 and 2001); Crawford (1997); Smandych (1999); Braithwaite (2000)), meaning a shift away from government taking responsibility and authority for guaranteeing services and traditional State spheres of activity towards provision by other agencies, some private and some public, which, in a sort of partnership, provide what should be full cover. The State then merely orchestrates or guides the policy by retaining power over resources, policy decisions and/or regulations (the accounting and managerial aspects), whilst others (public, private and voluntary sectors) actually deliver the services. This helps government to reduce both its financial outlay and its accountability for failure in provision of services. As part of this change citizens need to be taught to take responsibility for themselves to a far greater extent than in the past (what in the ugly jargon is called 'responsibilisation'). All these changes allow the State to reduce in size whilst still retaining the appearance of controlling its traditional services. Its main functions become managerial and financial and its main advisers are 'experts' drawn from these fields.

Fragmentation of responsibility and accountability is a major problem with this type of government provision. If parts of a service are provided by a number of different agencies, they may have different agendas. Each organisation will be working, at least in part, towards its own ends rather than the broader good of society as a whole. This is a real problem even if all the agencies are in the public sector: it becomes especially marked where private organisations are involved because, in these cases, there is a clear responsibility first to the owners or shareholders and only secondly to society. Similarly where voluntary agencies are used, the body concerned may have a particular interest in a small section of the community that it has been set up to help, and only secondly to a broader constituency. Even within the public sector organisations will be answerable to different masters, some to central government, others to local authorities and now with devolution in Wales, Northern Ireland and Scotland there is yet another layer of control: in these countries local authorities are answerable to the devolved powers so any organisations working under their umbrella answer to the policy requirements of the devolved authorities rather than to Westminster. In crime this will become an issue because the police are answerable to Westminster, whilst health trusts and probation services in Wales and Scotland are at least partially accountable to the devolved powers, and local authorities are wholly answerable to them; private organisations and charities (the voluntary sector) have yet other masters. The result is many service providers trying to deliver different policy objectives. The capacity for Westminster directly to guide policy and to govern is thus reduced but within this new mode of government Westminster has to attempt to resolve the tensions and build partnerships between these factions.

One significant consequence of the complexity of this system is that accountability for any failure is difficult to ensure. Government can claim that it is not responsible for any problems but rather it is the responsibility of the service provider. Each service provider may be able to claim that the area where the failure has occurred does not fall within its remit. No one has the full power, no one takes the full responsibility. Furthermore the public cannot alter the position by replacing the government, because the next in power will not necessarily be in any better position to meet the need. Accountability, one of the main requirements of democratic government and its control, is lost.

A more speculative, but potentially serious, danger is that the credibility and legitimacy of the State over wide sectors is called into question. If the delivery of services is provided by other agencies, often in the private sector, people will become less inclined to contribute to the State either through taxes or through political involvement.

20.2.3 The shift away from social-welfare towards neo-liberal policies

In 1945, following the Second World War, the British people were ready to accept a large shift towards a Welfare State—free health and education, benefits for the elderly, sick and unemployed. They fully embraced the ideals of Beveridge (1942) for 'security from the cradle to the grave' for all. This was not the first move to improve the welfare of all citizens—there had been many earlier provisions on education, health and benefits—but it was one of the largest carried out in a relatively short period. The ideal was to try to ensure social happiness through social justice, rights for all and respect for all. Part of the education of the citizen was this idea that everyone was included and should be provided for, that everyone was important. This message was distributed through official education as well as through the media, advertisements, documentaries, news items and dramas. The ideals of this policy were widely internalised and through the 1950s and 1960s there was a period of consensus politics where all parties largely accepted this. The Welfare State brought with it a feeling that everyone's advancement was connected as everyone relied on the same services—there was a shared responsibility for and a State (collective) insurance against problems.

Through the 1970s this ideology became more and more questioned. Individuals, the media and the Conservative party all began to question how much this shared system cost. Those who could afford to pay for their own cover found out that they could buy better or preferential treatment privately. They also began to question their need or duty to pay for others, and to demand reduced taxes. Their desire to pay less tax was seen as natural, only wanting to hold on to what was rightfully theirs. Claimants of State benefits, legitimate as well as fraudulent, became scroungers or spongers, not citizens making just claims from an insurance system which they had paid into, or would pay into in the future. As more people bought their way out of the public system and political parties (particularly the Conservatives) encouraged and facilitated this, the public system became more run down. The tendency of the affluent, what has been termed 'the comfortable majority' (Galbraith 1992) was to see the less fortunate as having themselves to blame for their dependency. Those in need are often not a cause for concern for the many and are politically weak. So the 1980s and 1990s saw increased economic growth accompanied by both a rise in poverty, and by greater inequality. In 1994 the Commission on Social Justice stated that in 1979 the bottom half of the population received a third of the national income whereas by 1994 they received only a quarter; and that the gap in earnings between the highest-paid and the lowest-paid workers was greater in 1994 than it had been at any time since records began in 1886. The young have borne an ever-increasing burden of poverty—in 1979 only 10 per cent (which was still 1.4m) of those under 18 lived in households below the poverty line whereas by 1992 32 per cent were below that line—one-third of Britain's children were living below the poverty line.

By 1997 at a conservative estimate three to four million children were living in poverty, three times the rate in 1979. Between 1997 and 1999 this had increased by a further 100,000 despite the Labour administration stating that one of its central aims was to tackle child poverty. More recently policies have begun to address this situation, Sutherland et al. (2003) suggest that child poverty had dropped by half a million by 2001 and that it would probably drop by a further 800,000 by 2003/4, but they recognise that policies have not tackled other areas of poverty nearly as effectively and that most of the success arises out of increased employment and working families tax credits for families on low incomes. Howard et al. (2001) report rather less successful figures: first, they claim that by 2001 4.5 million children were in poverty and whilst they note some reduction by 2000 (200,000) and might agree with the figure of a further half a million by 2001 this only represents a net reduction of 400,000 from 1997 as the figures rose in the first two years; secondly, they note that single parents, the elderly, young people living away from their families and ethnic minorities still suffered high levels of poverty and little had been done to address these. They also assert that over the last 20 years (1980s and 1990s) whilst the income of the lowest 10 per cent saw only a 6 per cent rise in living (after housing costs) while the highest 10 per cent enjoyed a rise of 86 per cent. At the same time there has been a rise in homelessness and begging, particularly of young people. In the poorest areas of Britain death rates are back up to what they were 40 years ago. There was an enhanced feeling of insecurity not only for those who fell into this new poverty but also for those who feared they might do so through ill-health, unemployment or some other misfortune.

20.3 Risk and insecurity: new challenges or merely new political approach?

20.3.1 Risk and the 'risk society'

In many areas of social, political and academic debate the issues of risk and the 'risk society' have become important and taken on a surprising prominence. Two of the earliest proponents of this trend are Ulrich Beck (1992, 1994, 1998 and 2000) and Anthony Giddens (1990, 1994 and 1998). They note that many of the 'risks' resultant from modern technology either cannot be limited in their effects of time and space or in the number or groups of people they affect (e.g., a disaster at a nuclear installation such as happened in Russia at Chernobyl), or they cannot be traced back to one particular cause (e.g., many environmental problems such as breaking the ozone layer). In such cases the old orders which bound time and space have lost meaning or become disembodied. This new order is more difficult to define and control and can reasonably be seen by many as being less secure or more potentially dangerous. At the same time people are aware that they have less ability and power to control the safety of themselves and their dependants. For Giddens (1990) this disembodied order characterises high modernity. Within this order the term 'risk society' has been coined to collect together discussion concerning the social impact of modern technology and how best to tackle its often negative aspects.

In this context Giddens and Beck have both referred to a concept of 'manufactured uncertainty' where everyone is forced to live with unknown and incalculable risks. Most of these risks are caused by advances in science and technology whose overall effects are difficult to assess. Scientists cannot know the effects until after they have carried out the experiments, or indeed, until products have been introduced on to the market. But both scientists and producers need financial support that may lead them to play down possible risks. The heated debate over genetically modified (GM) crops provides a clear example. Politicians may then be forced to make decisions based largely on economic pressure and on the need to provide reassurance, particularly if the scientists are playing down, disagreeing or refusing to calculate the risks. No one takes responsibility for management of the 'manufactured uncertainty' and there is a void. As Beck says (1998, p. 16):

. . . dangers are being produced by industry, externalised by economics, individualised by the legal system, legitimised by the sciences and made to appear harmless by politics.

Although not necessarily more dangerous than previously, the risks are now manufactured in the sense that technology has altered the natural world extensively and in so many areas. One consequence is that past experience provides little guidance to future risks; another is that the risk becomes inescapable. Individuals have to make choices based on risk (to themselves, others and the environment) in all aspects of their lives—what to eat, whether to walk, drive, cycle or use public transport to get to work, whether to use e-commerce or go to the shops, how to provide for their retirement, and whether to allow children access to the Net. These choices are made against the backdrop of little certainty in scientific advice. It is thus unsurprising that people expect the State, through politicians, to minimise future risks and to provide compensation, or require companies to compensate, when they fail in this responsibility.

There is a range of significant issues where science and technology have created new uncertainties. These encompass health problems such as BSE; or the use of GM crops; economic problems such as the lack of control over the use and protection of pension funds (Maxwell and the Equitable) or the use of futures markets (Leeson); moral problems such as the control of criminals, or the risk of pornography on the Net; and security problems such as the danger of unknowingly having one's e-commerce transaction intercepted and information being made available to unknown individuals. These provide a fruitful source of stories that are naturally given broad media attention thus increasing feelings of personal insecurity, risk and danger. The dangers are too large for individuals to deal with and media reports commonly indicate that the State should have prevented the risk from surfacing; should be responsible for reducing or controlling its effects; and should ensure that compensation is forthcoming for those who have suffered.

It is necessary to stress that what is involved is not so much the creation of risk as a shift in its scale and scope. 'Risk' means a hazard, a chance of loss or injury or some other undesirable event occurring. It always involves an element of uncertainty and usually an element of chance, but these elements are calculable. People have always lived under the cloud of risks or chances of undesirable occurrences. The fresh aspects, which analysts of the 'risk society' such as Beck and Giddens are stressing, are that the risks are 'manufactured' by people or society usually through technological advances. Some of these risks are both global and 'democratic' in the sense that they threaten both rich and poor, powerful and powerless. Although the wealthy and powerful try to ensure that they are not as much at risk from these negative elements in some applications, their efforts are largely fruitless; rain holding nuclear material from Chernobyl does not respect wealth or power though the length of time it may affect the environment, the area likely to be affected and the numbers and extent of illnesses can all be calculated. The combination of the possibility of destructive events in the 'risk society' and its global nature makes the call on States to address the issues both understandable and pressing. Just as the proximity of the houses of employers and capitalists to the sewers of the nineteenth century brought medical and public health issues to prominence at that time, so the limited ability of the rich and powerful to avoid or control their own risk exposure is doing the same this century. This is largely a call for management of the problem, which therefore falls neatly within the new governance concept that has overcome Western States.

20.3.2 Insecurity

Insecurity is by its nature uncertain, usually incalculable. Chapter Nineteen in its examination of the recent concern with terrorism looked at one specific cause of instability. More generally, a number of commentators believe that it describes a facet of the past 20 to 30 years which affects people's physical and mental well-being but which is less predictable than the risks just considered. Insecurity has an opposite—security—and exploring its meaning illuminates what its absence conjures up. Security usually means an individual has a sense of well-being, of stability personally and in those around and confidence in being able to ensure a positive life and lifestyle. Insecurity is a state where some or all of these are lacking; individuals feel vulnerable and that they have lost control of their future. Importantly insecurity imparts ideas of powerlessness and this is often marked in the writings of social scientists who explore this area.

According to Bauman (1994) today's world proliferates an environment which best serves insecurity because it is constituted of fragmentation, discontinuity and inconsequentiality, each of which leads to insecurity. Everything is transient. In the near past building materials were steel, concrete, glass, metal (designed for permanence), now we turn to transient materials such as plastic (preferably bio-degradable) so as to facilitate recycling once goods are no longer required. Information is not necessarily permanently recorded on paper but on the Internet which is always altering and is by its nature transient. Will historical records be endangered? The information itself has become more transient; yesterday's sensation or crisis crowded out by today's.

More importantly people's lives are being dismantled. Jobs are no longer for life; they may be removed at any time. To an extent this is not new—in the nineteenth century most labour was transient and casual. What is new? First, the work environments are now more transient: in particular the incessant activity over mergers and acquisition means that companies come and go, and in the process many jobs disappear and the locations of work are shifted. Companies, as dramatically illustrated by the widespread collapse of the new digital companies in the early 2000s, shed workers and physical ties swiftly when it is deemed commercially necessary. There is a move to short-term contracts; activities which used to be performed internally are commonly outsourced by subcontracting to firms (often small and relatively powerless) or individuals who bear the brunt of fluctuations in demand or decisions to move. With larger companies there are fewer core staff, less tenure for workers who have to accept flexible hours and be prepared to move if the firm moves. Power today is the ability to disengage without notice, to move to where the global economy is most favourable. Rulers also need to understand this and be flexible and able to respond quickly so as to create an attractive environment for business. As Mitchell states (1997, p. 303): '. . . capital is able to behave . . . like a plague of locusts circling the globe, touching down hither and yon, devouring whole places as it seeks even better comparative advantage.' Although, as always, the uncertainties bear hardest on the poor and least skilled, a modern feature is the increased extent to which skills and qualifications can themselves be made redundant, placing greater stress on a much wider range of employees.

As a sign of the general context Bauman (2000) indicated that the International Monetary Fund was critical of French and German efforts to get their people back to work as it ran counter to the ideal of a flexible labour market. A further insecurity, particularly for men, is born out of changes in gender relations. Women have moved into the labour force which many males see as part of their difficulty in obtaining employment. At the same time some young mothers choose to manage without adult male support which has also given rise to some male insecurity (Young (1999)).

More generally Lianos and Douglas (2000) suggest that the social, ethical and physical identities of individuals are of less importance due to the use of cards and passwords as marks of identity and passes into the worlds of credit, commerce, desirable spaces, work environments and technical markets. There is less need to prove oneself on a moral basis to individuals one knows and with whom one will have to have social ties. The main test is not one of moral worth but of safety to the employer, ability to pay etc. The market-induced insecurities also slide down the age range. Although the increased market power of the young has positive aspects, problems arise from the intensive targeting of teenagers, and now the 'tweenies' (7–12 year olds) by advertisers. They are seen as the ultimate consumers and sold 'freedom' and 'choice'. For many whose lives, personal finances or degree of antonomy deny them these benefits their insecurity is heightened (see the discussion in 12.2).

There is less permanence in relationships. As Giddens has suggested modern relationships tend to be entered into not for their own sakes but with an eye for what the individual can get out of them and once they cease to deliver this they can be easily terminated. This is increasingly true even of legally entered and traditionally binding relationships between adults, such as marriage. The modern ideal seems to be to avoid ties, be free to move on when satisfaction is diminished, to deny that relationships have a moral significance and to remove the security they might otherwise bring. These trends increase personal insecurity.

There are then other facets to security. Thus for many security is strongly dependent on the provision of a State-provided financial safety net. This links with the way in which money gives status and even legitimacy to people. Thus consumers with financial power are welcomed; those without are unwelcome and even their rights as citizens may be unrecognised and unprotected. They may be labelled the problem and the 'other' who is to be feared. As Chapter Three indicated the media may construct groups who are to be feared and seen as outsiders. Not only does their exclusion increase their insecurity but also everyone else feels more insecure because of the risk they have been told these groups pose. In the 1970s and 1980s prominent politicians such as Edward Heath (see Hall et al. (1978)) and Margaret Thatcher lent credence to labelling various groups as 'folk devils' who undermined the 'traditional British way of life'. To the list of criminals, scroungers, trade unions (Thatcher's depiction of miners as 'the enemy within') and marauding youths were added terrorists, 'subversives', drug users, single mothers, the homeless, homosexuals, hunt saboteurs, groups of young males, New Age travellers, abortionists, environmental campaigners etc. The rest of the population needed to be protected from these 'dangerous' people who should be controlled by fairly strong authoritarian State action. Politicians and the media helped to feed the fears of the populace and then suggested commonsense solutions for example, harsher punishments, zero tolerance and more police with greater powers. The greater population also felt less secure as they were constantly told that the new harsher powers had not worked, crime was ever rising and the groups of 'folk devils' were ever increasing.

There has also been a reduction in the degree of security that people derive from a secure social environment in which there is a general recognition of reciprocal ties between people. A secure physical environment, in which individuals feel safe and at ease, is a major prerequisite for a stable society. Related to the decline in these aspects is a tendency for political discourse to stress soundbites rather than principles or ideologies. It is a development which seems to foster cynicism and apathy amongst the electorate at large as indicated by the low turnout at elections. If so it undermines a vigorous and healthy political environment which is itself a source of insecurity.

All these aspects serve, for many people, to erode a sense of self. At all events there is much modern debate and concern over the problem of people's identity. It is argued that, compared to the more stable societies of the past based on land or class, the modern transience of work and relationships undermines security. There are of course benefits. There is a new freedom, new choices and rights, more social mobility. But for many these choices are illusory. Resources are needed both to lend reality to individual choices and to give substance to notions of equality of opportunity. The gap between the enticements held out to people and their actual experience can itself compound the problem. As Vail (1999, p. 7) states:

Insecurity is a feeling of hopelessness, a constrained sense of self and a belief in the futility of advancement. It is also a sense of powerlessness, an inability to realise one's goals or protect one's interests as well as a heightened awareness of vulnerability to events and forces over which an individual has no control.

It is not claimed that all this is unique: the past throws up plenty of instances, like the process of industrialisation, which created vast insecurities. The present stress on transience and flexibility does, however, seem to be particularly pervasive and to affect almost all levels of society. The global characteristics produce further instabilities when actions taken in one part of the world have quicker and larger consequences for other States and societies. Insecurity is seen as a major problem of the present age even compared with ideas of insecurity over the past 2,000 years or more.

One response has been to propose a form of social justice which Rawls (1971) would argue could flatten out the insecurities and vulnerabilities in life so that those at the bottom have a reasonable existence, possibly provided by those at the top. The idea is that it is the sort of just society that one would choose if one did not know what one's lot was to be—whether one would be one of the lucky ones or the unlucky ones.

Such notions are not, however, part of the present social reality where the apparent freedoms are mostly only available to those whose position allows them greater possibility to exercise the available freedom. For most people choices are limited to the lesser of two or more evils rather than what is really wanted. But notions of individual rights and freedoms are so much a part of the new era that they are unlikely to be retracted. To do so would mean forgoing some freedom (of mobility, for example) and putting constraints on the rights of the rich and powerful. It needs also to be acknowledged that the notion of community involves exclusion for others. Community depends upon this idea of bounded caring and morality. We care for each other but do not interest ourselves in the 'other' outside the community. This fact clarifies (but does not necessarily justify) the actions of the powerful concerning insecurity; they may act so as to limit their own insecurity and those of their own kind whilst increasing insecurity for 'others'. Those with real choices and power exercise them to ensure that their choices are, or feel as if they are, constantly expanding—by, for example, purchasing better (meaning private) health care, schooling and pensions. In the USA, and increasingly in Britain, this is taken to the extreme of 'gated communities' that keep out any insecurities and dangers that can be physically excluded. Within the community, schools, leisure activities, doctors and sometimes hospitals are provided for a fee. These people have removed themselves and often care little for the 'others' who cannot afford these benefits—they want lower taxes and fewer social benefits.

These attitudes are bolstered and justified by interpretations which run counter to much that has been implied in this section where the discussion has generally depicted the excluded as those who, often through no fault of their own, have suffered from insecurities and been excluded from parts of the larger social order. However, this is often not the way they are portrayed, especially by the affluent. Those in power will view and present the exclusion of groups and individuals as being of their own making or their own 'fault' (Bauman (2000 and 2001)). Thus they should not be surprised if they are castigated and excluded for their behaviour. In this version, controlling and policing these people is claimed as necessary to protect society and protect their own best interests.

20.3.3 Crime, insecurity and risk

Most 'risk society' literature ignores crime, but aspects of the 'risk society' are clearly part of the crime problem. Crime is entirely 'man-made', in fact in most instances this term is almost a literal description: it is created by humans and most of those who take part in criminal activities are male. More importantly for the 'risk society' literature the crime problem has grown, often out of the same unforeseen consequences of industrial or technological advances. Thus the car, whilst providing enhanced business possibilities and greater personal freedom for leisure activities, has also provided a target for crime as well as a means by which criminals can cover a wider geographical range, steal more and escape from the crime scene. Air travel and greater movement of both people and goods around the world have provided increased opportunities for moving illicit goods such as drugs. Technology has created more leisure items such as televisions, computers, sound equipment and mobile telephones which are valuable targets, have resale value, are easily carried from the scene of the crime and difficult to trace to their original owners. There is also a global nature to crime, both geographically as in the case of drugs, slavery, money laundering, and now terrorism, and where it affects a broader spectrum of people—rich, poor, powerful and powerless are potential victims and therefore feel more vulnerable, though to varying degrees.

Similarly few of those writing in the area of insecurity link it to crime. However, crime has a dual effect on insecurity, both as a cause of insecurity and as a means of countering it. For many the technological changes and the increase in personal freedom have increased feelings of insecurity that many associate with crime. First, as seen above, the technical changes have widened the spectrum of victims to include the middle classes and powerful classes to an extent not seen in the past. Secondly, increased freedom for the young has released them on to the streets, where they are often seen as frightening or threatening, not necessarily because they are taking part in crime but because they are not controlled. In addition people are constantly being told that they are free, but for many of the poor and powerless, the means of expression of freedom is very limited. Some may express their desire for freedom by indulging in graffiti or vandalism. Even if such activities are not meant as a specific criminal act, they cause others to feel more threatened and insecure. So one person's expression of freedom may make others less secure. This effect is not confined to the criminal sphere: for example, the enhanced freedom of employers to make money may make the workers less secure. For some, crime may be their means of countering their own insecurity, alleviating economic insecurity by providing money or a reassertion of self and of identity. The counter effect is to reduce the security of others. Here, as noted in Chapter Three, the media may well help to increase the feeling of insecurity from these occurrences by making them widely known and making them feel as if they are a part of everyday experience.

A prominent example of both insecurity causing crime and that of crime then increasing the feelings of insecurity of the wider population is seen in the case of black males. In the USA Taylor (1999, p. 31) states:

... the effects of these combined processes of racial discrimination, racialisation of neighbourhoods ('hyper-ghettoisation'), accelerating joblessness, poverty and inequality, and the masculinist culture of the black neighbourhood are unambiguous. Some 40–50 per cent of all serious crimes against the person (homicides, forcible rapes, armed robberies and aggravated assaults) in America in the early 1990s were committed by African-Americans.

Most of these offenders were between 15 and 19 years old. Most victims in the US appear also to be drawn from the Afro-American community which suffers a 25 per cent higher victimisation rate than society as a whole. In the United Kingdom unemployment rates among young black males have been consistently higher than their white counterparts since the 1970s. The major growth in jobs in the latter part of last century was in educated and skilled labour and the losers were young black males and young, very poor, white males. Over the past 25 years these two groups have been competing for an ever-decreasing number of jobs and the tribal animosity has been powerfully felt in terms of football hooliganism, pub brawls and racist clashes. These factors also probably explain the ever-increasing levels of racially motivated crime in the UK. There are also claims in the UK that young, black males commit a disproportionate number of crimes. In 1995 the then Metropolitan Police Commissioner, Paul Condon, stated that this group committed 70 per cent of street robberies in London. If the police believe this is true, it will lead to their targeting of the young, male, black community, which will enhance the disparity. The Commission for Racial Equality (1999) estimated that in June 1997 the incarceration rate per 100,000 population in England and Wales was 1,249 for black people, 176 for while people and only 150 for Asians. In 2001/2 blacks made up 12.1 per cent of the prison population but only 1.8 per cent of the population over 10 years old (Home Office (2002)). Their over-representation in prison feeds a public perception that they are more of a threat than is the true picture. The resultant social exclusion itself then generates criminal behaviour. This downward spiral is not helped by the fact that the opportunities open to these economically marginalised groups are narrowing, further enhancing their insecurity and exclusion in a largely economic and market-led society.

Many of the extra risks and insecurities induced by technology affect everyone in society, but the rich and powerful can often protect themselves by such means as buying private schooling, health care, pensions and unemployment benefits. Many of these then oppose taxes which leads to much lower levels of protection for the poor. Not only that: their legitimate decisions on such aspects as levels of employment, location of factories etc. can increase the insecurity of others. Such insecurities may affect more people, more deeply than those caused by activities we call crime, but they are both legal and usually supported by the State as 'necessary'. In this sense the political and business community largely control which insecurities are defined as socially necessary and which are criminal.

20.3.4 The effects in the area of crime and criminal justice

As Garland (2000) states about the new position of criminal justice in the UK:

... the field of crime control exhibits two new and distinct lines of governmental action: an *adaptive strategy* stressing prevention and partnership and a *sovereign State strategy* stressing enhanced control and expressive punishment.

This represents a substantial change from the mid-twentieth century when there were two parallel policies: 'controlling dangerous offenders' and 'rehabilitation or future avoidance of crime problems'. The first involved the incapacitation of very serious offenders to prevent them being a danger to the public. The second, more general approach, used rehabilitation of criminals hopefully to avoid future criminal activity. Although in the new terminology these might be referred to as 'risk control' and 'risk avoidance' the prominence of a risk ideology was not known at the time. Neither of these had blame as a central tenet. The focus was on the causes of crime, what caused an individual to commit offences, and attempting to neutralise these in order to achieve a safer society. Much of this policy was linked to the welfare system, which would provide basic needs, and to a just, equitable and inclusive society, which would itself reduce the need for crime. Many of the rehabilitative aspects were designed to befriend and help the offender rather than force change (so that probation was seen as wholly rehabilitative and the probation service's motto was that they would advise, assist and befriend), or they addressed behavioural disorders. Criminal justice policy was left to the professionals who used scientific reports and information to inform policy. Policing was largely seen as a welcome force designed to guarantee social justice and order in all communities in Britain. This view was helped as the 'bobby' on the street was often local, lived in the community, belonged to it and had a personal interest in the success of keeping the peace. Here criminology and the criminal justice and penal systems all centred on either the individual being ill in some way or on social or economic problems not of their own making. The system tried to help them by providing treatment and/or social or economic support. To some degree it ignored the criminal 'event', as well as victims and how the criminal opportunity arose (Garland and Sparks (2000)). These last elements were to become central to the new criminal justice and penal approaches and media reports have made a similar shift (see Reiner (2001)). Society has become obsessed with crime and the risks it poses. The general public, encouraged by parts of the media, have become less tolerant and less ready to sympathise with the offender. This has permitted enormous changes to the criminal justice and penal systems.

Since the late 1970s there has thus been an enormous shift in policy. There is now a three-pronged initiative: 'target hardening', 'risk removal' and 'risk management'. Each of these turns on blaming the offender, and carries with it the expectation that citizens should be more responsible for their own safety and that of their property. Crime control and criminal justice are no longer the preserve of the professionals, but are much more open to populist pressures produced by the media and soundbite politicians demanding harsher and more simplistic solutions (see Chapter Three). The general shift to a culture of blame implies that fault rests with the individual not the society. The criminal justice system is thus meant to impose on offenders acceptable moral and behavioural standards and to prevent them from causing 'risks' for the rest of us.

'Target hardening' was discussed in depth in Chapter Eleven but basically it involves management of the environment so as to deter criminals. This may be through potential victims being responsible about their own goods and person, not flaunting goods, keeping them safe and leading a lifestyle which reduces risk of personal victimisation. As the public internalise this role they expect more help in its fulfilment, so one sees campaigns such as calls for the public to be notified about the whereabouts of paedophiles. It may involve greater surveillance through something like CCTV in public spaces. Here the emphasis is on proactive prevention of crime rather than on catching and punishing offenders. The approach is often one of 'zero tolerance' towards petty transgressions but may also involve the exclusion of people who it is felt should not be in a particular place at a particular time despite the fact that no crime is being either committed or threatened (see Crowther (2000), Williams et al. (2000), and Williams and Johnstone (2000)). Many of these actions are taken not by the State but by others, local authorities, health services, voluntary agencies and individuals. This extra responsibility placed on the empowerment of individuals and communities may have hidden problems: it will only succeed where there is trust between the State and ordinary people in the community; it also assumes that if each is working to the same end such trust will be enhanced. However, this is not always how it works. Evans (2003) reports on the vigilante actions which arose in Portsmouth as a result of names of paedophiles being released and of rumours that certain individuals were paedophiles. She claims that the fear this group give rise to (fuelled by both the press and the government) coupled with the feeling that the State was not directly protecting the community (governance, or governing at a distance) caused the community to take matters into their own hands in a violent, destructive and one might argue terrorist way against a number of people they erroneously grouped together under the label paedophiles. The rhetoric is that there is a need to widen responsibility for crime control by enabling civil society to provide the services at the behest of and largely under the control of the State. Much of this involves rhetoric about 'empowering' local communities where people are told that they can take control over their own community and choose the crime prevention programmes most appropriate to them.

Ultimately local communities might be permitted to make all their own policing and crime-control decisions within a preset budget. They would then be free to buy in policing from the private or public sector and/or choose to pay for activities for their youths in the hope that this would discourage criminal activities (see Brogden and Shearing (1993)). Given current trends this would have to include the meeting of targets set by or at least agreed by the central State and the use of their monitoring guidelines. Britain has been slowly moving in this direction for the past 20 years and in 1998 the Home Secretary, Jack Straw, stated that the Crime and Disorder Act 1998 was 'the culmination of a long-held ambition to empower local people to take control of the fight against crime' and that local people should be 'invited to participate actively in the process of tackling local problems, not just passively consulted about them' (Introduction to the Home Office Guidance Notes). Under s. 6(2) of this Act local authorities are required to audit the levels of crime and disorder in their area, not just through police records but also local surveys of inhabitants' experience of crime (see Chapter Four) and consultation with local bodies. They are then required to use these to work with the police to provide strategies for crime prevention (s. 6(4)) that must include objectives and both long and short-term performance targets against which the authorities can be tested. Although the idea is that the police and local authority are then accountable to local people, the Home Office can, under s. 7, require reports on specific factors to be provided to central government. In Britain, therefore, crude geographical concepts are used to define 'community'. These geographical units do not necessarily represent real communities; they are after all designed for political rather than any other purposes. Community in general usage encompasses sociological ideas of inclusion and cohesion (Gardiner (1995); Crawford (1995); and Gilling (1997)). Nor is community necessarily a positive concept as it usually means that others are excluded and empowering 'communities' does not necessarily guarantee a more positive existence for all. Decisions are not necessarily democratic and those making them are often not drawn from the high-crime-rate areas nor do they include those who may have their freedoms curtailed by any resultant crime-control initiatives. All this means that it is a strategy which might increase rather than reduce exclusion (see Chapter Sixteen and Norris and Armstrong (1997, 1998)). In work the author has carried out into CCTV it was found that the police and local authorities do not work together, they each take responsibility for particular tasks whilst not becoming involved or even particularly interested in the tasks of the other. Other agencies from the voluntary sector or from other layers of government were excluded. The empowering of communities is thus questionable, partnerships are more apparent than real, and the shift has been from central to other governmental agencies where the lines of responsibility for various tasks are not clear (Garland (1998 and 2001) and Crawford (1997)). The State has retained overall power and still controls both policy and finances; it only shifts the means of delivery.

'Risk removal' involves the incapacitation and control of offenders through means such as imprisonment, electronic monitoring and drugs to control behaviour etc. It is the tough end of the idea that criminals will get what they deserve for the offences that they have committed—without much recourse to mitigating factors. Offenders are to take all the blame for their offending. This coupled with increasing maximum sentences and the greater use of minimum sentences, particularly minimum prison sentences, leads to wider incapacitation. The policies on 'three strikes and you're out' started in the USA, but, partly in the Crime (Sentences) Act 1997 (now in the Powers of Criminal Courts (Sentencing) Act 2000, part V, chapter III), something very similar was incorporated into the British penal system: offenders who repeat certain serious offences can be removed for extended periods of time.

The increasing prison population and the apathy of the public as to what happened to incarcerated individuals led Christie (1993 and 2000) to note that prisons were run with bureaucratic rationality which was, he claimed leading to harsh and often inhumane treatment—what he refers to as 'Gulags Western Style'. There is an amount of truth in this. The prisons are not filled with deliberate institutionalised violence such as would lead to deaths of inmates (though too many, mostly suicides, die within their walls): this encourages public complacency which sometimes spills over into claims that they are too 'soft'. However, prisons are often extremely degrading and brutal environments, and Christie is calling our attention to the abuse of those who are powerless to resist, the clear signs of totalitarian activity in our name. This brutality and removal of dignity is difficult to document as the institutions are secretive, whilst many newer prison buildings do not appear to be controlling and threatening. At all events the public are generally uninterested in the plight of prisoners; the concern is simply that the public is made 'safe' from offenders by having them removed into custody. There is truth in what he writes, possibly especially in the US system, but also in other Western systems. Indeed Pratt (2001) suggests that we may be moving beyond this, arguing that the public are becoming increasingly interested in crime and increasingly punitive as to the risks that it poses for them. They are becoming vociferous over being empowered to be able to protect themselves—we see this particularly clearly in the call to name and shame sex offenders. However, the greater empowerment of communities may well lead to widespread, popular, uncontrolled and unjust types of exclusion from or effective removal from society by social rejection, a form of extra-legal punishment and risk-removal which has a long history and is usually very unjust (see Bauman (2001) and Evans (2003)). Against all this, in the UK in recent years there have been some moves to control the worst elements of this tendency, for example, the instigation of a Prisons Ombudsman in 1995. There are also more progressive community based crime control options such as restorative justice (see Chapter Five) which may be used to counter the movement towards risk removal. Furthermore, both Christie and Pratt argue that higher human values, possibly some ideas of communitarianism of commitment to and caring for others, may be able to prevent both the continued spiralling of the 'Western style gulag' and the increase of community tyranny.

'Risk management and reduction' operate through what are often intrusive monitoring of individuals and the use of predetermined programmes designed to alter behaviour patterns so as to 'deliver responsible citizens'. The emphasis is on 'development' of certain 'acceptable' types of behaviour and ways of thinking, a sort of cloning of the ideal 'safe' citizen to remove risk and guarantee success. Here personal and professional expertise in areas like probation is less important than following correct procedures and using the accredited programmes. Before these are effective there needs to be an assessment of 'dangerousness' and the degree of interference should reflect the level of dangerousness of the offender. Throughout the punishment there are often re-evaluations of 'dangerousness' and the purpose of the punishment is to manage and neutralise the elements which render the person dangerous. The end result is intended to produce a person who is more controlled and fettered by standards of acceptable behaviour. This approach goes counter to what many see as the 'normal' position of individuals in late modernity: free, almost totally free to act as they want, to maximise pleasure and minimise pain (e.g., Bauman (2000) and (2001)). Even though this freedom does not necessarily deliver happiness, it is seen as 'normal'. Thus a system of crime control premised on teaching control of desire to ensure responsible citizens might be seen as training people to behave abnormally given the values of society. At all events the use of these programmes to alter behaviour are about to be extended as being useful after brief terms of imprisonment (see the Criminal Justice Act 2003).

Along with these have come changes in policing. The force is now less locally based, officers move between forces more frequently and, certainly in inner cities, officers rarely live in the community they police. Furthermore, through the 1980s and 1990s clear-up rates were declining and the central changes in criminal justice practice, decentralising and devolving service provision to others as well as encouraging individuals to be more responsible for their own safety (see Garland (1996 and 2001)), have led to a reduction in the central position held by the police. First businesses and thence homeowners have decided that they wish to embrace a private form of protection which will be directly answerable to them as the paymasters and will 'do their bidding' (within, one would hope, the law). It is not difficult to see that private policing will work well for the rich. All of this is unsurprising in a more market and self-interested social environment, and some (Shearing (1996)) see the general extension of private policing as both natural and desirable. Against proposals to strengthen official policing to provide equal protection in the poorer areas Shearing argues instead that taxes should be used to permit poor neighbourhoods broader decision-making in buying in private policing or other means of increasing their security. Hirst (2000) would go even further arguing that logically in a late modern era one should allow communities to set their own rules or standards of behaviour. As an indication of the perceived popular basis for such an approach, the Conservative Party Conference 2003 suggested some of these ideas as a basis for future policy. Only the universally agreed crimes should be centrally defined and enforced. It is clear that these trends not only carry sharply divisive potential at a broad social level, but have similar implications for the system of criminal justice.

20.3.5 Risk and crime: a preliminary assessment

It can thus be seen that the use of risk in criminal justice and penal systems has already had a number of interesting consequences. First, punishment has less and less to do with the event of the crime and more to do with possible future problems posed by the offender. The permission for the State to intervene comes about because of the criminal act, but the amount and nature of intervention have more to do with possible future actions and the nature of perceived dangerousness or risk posed by the perpetrator. In this respect the new approach, like the old system, has more to do with the individual offender (though in a different and less benign way) than with the offence. Now the offence does not even serve to limit the amount of punishment except by a very crude control in the form of an absolute maximum. Equality before the law is diluted when punishments depend on assessments of individual dangerousness—on the aim of societal safety. Although the UK has not wholly embraced this, many policies are moving in this direction. Secondly, although risk may well be a reasonably calculable quality in many contexts, it is a less secure guide when applied to many aspects of human behaviour, especially as the risk-assessment tools used in the criminal justice system are based on fairly simple numerical assessments. The likely degree of error in determining the future 'dangerousness' of an individual seems not to warrant the unnecessary and (perhaps) unacceptable extent of interference with the offender's liberty. Not only is it morally not justified, it seems to be based on inexact and therefore unfair criteria. Thirdly, the concept of risk is very unclear as shown by Hannah-Moffat (1999 and 2003) in her study of its use in a Canadian women's prison where they conflated ideas of risk of escape and danger with the risk of an inability to adjust to the prison regime: the last aspect thus brought in purely subjective items to the risk assessment (see also Hayman (2003)). Fourthly, the risk of dangerousness is, it could be argued, a very masculine concept. Thus applying the same criterion to female offenders should generally lead to greater leniency but this does not happen. It thus seems that when risk increases punitiveness it is followed, when it does not it is ignored. This forces the question: is this really a risk society or merely a punitive society looking for justifications to exclude and confine? Finally, in assessing risk and punishment very often the risk to family is ignored. For example, the use of tagging to confine a person to his or her home may protect society but increase the risk for the family. All these aspects of the use of risk in the criminal justice and penal system raise questions about acceptability on moral, ethical and even its own alleged 'scientific' basis. Nonetheless it is clear that it has helped to shape our criminal justice system.

20.4 **Conclusion**

The combined effects of changes in governance, technical developments and risk assessments have, with other factors, led to a very different criminal justice system than that which existed just 25 years ago. The public are more concerned about crime, they are being asked to take more responsibility for their own safety and the security of their goods. The greater publicity given to these issues has encouraged the public to take a greater interest in the system and its success. Crime has become one of the five most important factors in national and increasingly in local elections. It is one of the few areas where politicians can appear to have effect. As has been shown, however, neither the attention nor the concern is evenly distributed. Thus the pressure is mostly to tackle 'street crime' rather than the offences of the powerful which are often left untouched. This is despite the fact that corporations probably cause more harm than individual criminals to society at large (see Tombs and Whyte (2003); Braithwaite and Drahos (2000)). In this environment the views of criminologists, criminal justice professionals and even of judges have become frequently excluded from policy decision-making processes. Koch's (1998, p. 175) statement that Home Office policy decisions were 'political and irrational' and 'rarely based on research but on what [was] thought by the individual minister to be popular with *The Sun* readers' may be too sweeping but it broadly reflects what many criminologists feel. Feely (2003) writing about the US situation documents carefully the exclusion of most criminologists from the policy field and their replacement by those conversant in systems analysis and in the containment of risk. These specialists picked the criminological approaches which best fitted neo-conservatism and other approaches were excluded. They then fed information to the media and thence the public.

This central role of both the media and the necessarily ill-informed general population, is for most of those working within the area of criminology and criminal justice rather disturbing, not just for their personal egos but for the implications for such abstractions as justice and individual freedom. One possible consequence is that some of the carefully considered and well-researched criminological theories and approaches which have been surveyed in this book will be ignored because they cannot win popular, and thus political, support. It would be foolish to be too pessimistic about the trends recorded in this chapter. Such trends have tended to reflect broad social shifts that will continue to change and might well affect and soften some current approaches to crime. In Britain, for example, it is already evident that the faith of the general public in the superiority of private over public enterprise and management is shifting. Some academics are analysing the effect on lowering crime, particularly violent crime which arose out of State intervention in the delivery of economic stability to individuals, so helping to counter their feelings of insecurity and exclusion. Although a return to the systems by which this was achieved in the 1950s and 1960s is unlikely it may suggest that addressing risk and insecurity at a level outside the criminal would be more fruitful in delivering greater security and safety for all. For the more restrictive purposes of the present text it can more positively be hoped that some of the themes raised in this chapter and elsewhere will provide readers with an understanding of some of the larger social changes underlying choices made in the crime-control arena.

SUGGESTED READING

Garland, D. (2001), *The Culture of Control: Crime and Social Order in Contemporary Society*, Oxford: Oxford University Press.

Smandych, R. (ed.) (1999), *Governable Places: Readings on Governmentality and Crime Control*, Aldershot: Ashgate Dartmouth.

Stenson, K. and Sullivan, R.R. (eds) (2001), *Crime, Risk and Justice*, Cullompton: Willan Publishing.

REVISION BOX

This chapter notes a number of factors which have strongly affected the criminal justice system in recent years: the decline of the welfare State and the welfare ideal; the rise of governance as opposed to government which involves the government in setting policies which are largely delivered by others; and the rise of insecurity and risk politics as the guiding principles and facets in need of being addressed. These alongside the growth of crime and a popular obsession with crime and safety have led to a number of responses which have included:

- The decline of rehabilitation in the penal system;
- Decline of focus purely on the crime and more on future risk;
- Emergence of punitive sanctions and expressive justice in dealing with crime;
- An increase in the prominence of victims and their interests;
- The growth of areas of crime prevention and protecting the public and therefore concentration on risk removal and risk management;
- Less emphasis on tackling the problems which may give rise to risk;
- A greater tendency to blame individuals and therefore a call for individuals to be more responsible both to ensure that they and their property are safe and to refrain from endangering others;
- The fragmentation of crime control through a plethora of agencies;
- Partnership work to tackle crime;
- The increasing use of private agencies in crime control;
- The development of actuarial and bureaucratic management of the crime problem.

These have led to a very different society and a very different view of crime, justice and crime control.

QUESTIONS FOR REVISIONS

1   Are Western societies uniquely insecure? What are the main indicators of risk insecurity?
2   What, if any, are the links between crime and insecurity?

3 How has the notion of 'risk society' influenced policies on crime and the criminal justice system?
4 What damages do such trends entail?

REFERENCES

Bauman, Zygmunt (1994), *Alone Again: Ethics After Certainty*, London: Demos.

Bauman, Zygmunt (2000), 'Social Issues of Law and Order: A Panel Data Approach', *British Journal of Criminology*, vol. 40, pp. 205–21.

Bauman, Z. (2001), *Individualised Society*, Cambridge: Polity Press.

Beck, Ulrich (1992), *Risk Society: Towards a New Modernity*, Transl. Mark Ritter from a manuscript first published in 1986, London: Sage.

Beck, Ulrich, Giddens, Anthony and Lanash, S. (eds) (1994), *Reflexive Modernization: Politics, Tradition and Aesthetics in the Modern Social Order*, Cambridge: Polity Press.

Beck, Ulrich (1998), 'Politics of Risk Society', in J Franklin (ed.), *The Politics of Risk Society*, Cambridge: Polity Press.

Beck, Ulrich (2000), *World Risk Society*, Cambridge: Polity Press.

Beveridge, William (1942), *Social Insurance and the Allied Services*, London: HMSO.

Braithwaite, J. (2000), 'Republican Theory, The Good Society and Crime Control', in S. Karstedt and K.D. Bussman (eds), *Social Dynamics of Crime and Control: New Theories for a World in Transition*, Oxford: Hart Publishing.

Braithwaite, J. (2003), 'What's Wrong with the Sociology of Punishment?', *Theoretical Criminology*, vol. 7(1), p. 5.

Braithwaite, J. and Drahos, P. (2000), *Global Business Regulation*, Cambridge: Cambridge University Press.

Brogden, M. and Shearing, C. (1993), *Policing for a New South Africa*, London: Routledge.

Christie, N. (1993), *Crime Control as Industry: Towards Gulags Western Style*, London: Routledge.

Christie, N. (2000), *Crime Control as Industry: Towards Gulags Western Style*, 2nd edn, London: Routledge.

Commission for Racial Equality (1999), *Crimnal Justice in England and Wales: Factsheet*, London: Commission for Racial Euqlity

Commission on Social Justice (1994), *Social Justice: Strategies for National Renewal*, London: Vantage.

Crawford, Adam (1995), 'Appeals to Community and Crime Prevention', *Crime Law and Social Change*, vol. 22, p. 97.

Crawford, Adam (1997), *The Local Governance of Crime: Appeals to Community and Partnership*, Oxford: Clarendon Press.

Crowther, C. (2000), 'Thinking about the Underclass: Towards a Political Economy of Policing', *Theoretical Criminology*, vol. 4:2, p. 149.

Evans, J. (2003), 'Vigilance and Vigilantes: Thinking Psychoanalytically about Anti-Paedophile Action', *Theoretical Criminology*, vol. 7(2).

Foucault, Michel (1978), *Discipline and Punish, the Birth of the Prison*, transl. by Alan Sheridan, New York: Vintage Books.

Foucault, Michel (1991), 'Governmentality', in G. Burchell, C. Gordon and P. Miller (eds), *The Foucault Effect: Studies in Governmentality*, Chicago, IL: University of Chicago Press.

Galbraith, J.K. (1992), *The Culture of Containment*, London: Sinclair-Stevenson.

Gardiner, S. (1995), 'Criminal Justice Act 1991—Management of the Underclass and the Potentiality of Community', in L. Noaks, M. Levi and M. Maguire (eds), *Contemporary Issues in Criminology*, Cardiff: University of Wales Press.

Garland, David (1985), *Punishment and Welfare*, Aldershot: Gower.

Garland, David (1996), 'The Limits of the Sovereign State: Strategies of Crime Control in Contemporary Society', *British Journal of Criminology*, vol. 36, pp. 445–71.

Garland, David (2000), 'The Culture of High Crime Societies: Some Preconditions of Recent "Law and Order" Policies', *British Journal of Criminology*, vol. 40, pp. 347–5.

Garland, D. (2001), *The Culture of Control: Crime and Social Order in Contemporary Society*, Oxford: Oxford University Press.

Garland, D. and Sparks, R. (2000), 'Criminology, Social Theory and the Challenge of our Times', *British Journal of Criminology*, vol. 40, pp. 189–204.

Giddens, Anthony (1990), *The Consequences of Modernity*, London: Polity Press.

Giddens, Anthony (1994), *Beyond Left and Right*, Cambridge: Polity Press.

Giddens, Anthony (1998), *The Third Way*, Cambridge: Polity Press.

Gilling, D. (1997), *Crime Prevention: Theory, Policy and Politics*, London: UCL Press.

Goffman, Erving (1961), *Asylums*, New York: Doubleday-Anchor.

Hall, S., Critcher, C., Jefferson, T., Clarke, J. and Roberts, B. (1968), *Policing the Crisis*, Basingstoke: Macmillan.

Hannah-Moffat, K. (1999), 'Moral Agent or Actuarial Subject: Risk and Canadian Women's Imprisonment', *Theoretical Criminology*, vol. 3, pp. 71–95.

Hannah-Moffat, K. (2003), 'Getting Women Out: The Limits of Reintegration Reform', *Criminal Justice Matters*, vol. 53, p. 44.

Hayman, S. (2003), 'The Lessons of History: Prison Reform and Unintended Consequences', *Criminal Justice Matters*, vol. 53, p. 42.

Hirst, P. (2000), 'Statism, Pluralism and Social Control', *British Journal of Criminology*, vol. 40, pp. 279–95.

Home Office (1998), *Crime and Disorder Bill 1998: Guidance on statutory crime and disorder partnerships*, London: Home Office.

Home Office (2002), *Statistics on Race and the Criminal Justice System: A Home Office Publication under Section 95 of the Criminal Justice Act 1991*, London: Home Office. **http://www.homeoffice.gove.uk/rds/pdfs2/s95race2002.pdf.**

Howard, M., Garnham, A., Fimister, G. and Veit-Wilson, J. (2001), *Poverty: The Facts*, London: Child Poverty Action Group.

Koch, B. (1998), *The Politics of Crime Prevention*, Aldershot: Ashgate.

Lianos, M. and Douglas, M. (2000), 'Dangerization and the End of Deviance: The Institutional Environment', *British Journal of Criminology*, vol. 40, pp. 391–400.

Mitchell, D. (1997), 'The Annihilation of Space by Law: The Roots and Implications of Anti-homeless Laws in the United States', *Antipode*, vol. 29(3), pp. 303–35.

Norris, C. and Armstrong, G. (1997), *The Unforgiving Eye: CCTV Surveillance in public spaces*, University of Hull: Centre for Criminology.

Norris, C. and Armstrong, G. (1998), 'Introduction: Power and Vision', in C. Norris, J. Morgan and G. Armstrong (eds), *Surveillance, Closed Circuit Television and Social Control*, Aldershot: Ashgate.

Pavlich, G. (1999), 'Preventing Crime: "Social" versus "Community" Governance in Aotearoa/New Zealand', in Russell Smandych (ed.), *Governable Places: Readings on Governmentality and Crime Control*. Aldershot: Ashgate Dartmouth.

Pratt, J. (2001), 'Beyond "Gulags Western Style"?: A Reconsideration of Nils Christie's Crime Control as Industry', *Theoretical Criminology*, vol. 5(3), p. 283.

Rawls, John (1971), *A Theory of Justice*, Oxford: Oxford University Press.

Reiner, R. (2001), 'The Rise of Virtual Vigilantism: Crime Reporting Since World War II', *Criminal Justice Matters*, vol. 43, p. 4.

Safer Communities: The Local Delivery of Crime Prevention through the Partnership Approach (1991), report from an independent working group convened by the Home Office Standing Conference on Crime Prevention chaired by James Morgan, Home Office, London: HMSO.

Shearing, C. (1996), 'Rethinking Policing: Police as Governance', in O. Marenin (ed.), *Changing Police, Policing Change: International Perspectives*, New York: Garland Press.

Smandych, Russell (ed.) (1999), *Governable Places: Readings on Governmentality and Crime Control*, Aldershot: Ashgate Dartmouth.

Sutherland, H., Sefton, T. and Piachaud, D. (2003), *Poverty in Britain: The Impact of Government Policy Since 1997*, London: Joseph Rowntree Foundation.

Taylor, Ian (1999), *Crime in Context*, Cambridge: Polity Press.

Tombs, S. and Whyte, D. (2003), *Unmasking the Crimes of the Powerful*, London: Peter Lang.

Vail, John (1999), 'Insecure Times: Conceptualising Insecurity and Security', in John Vail, Jane Wheelock and Michael Hill (eds), *Insecure Times: Living with Insecurity in Contemporary Society*, London: Routledge.

Williams, Katherine S., Johnstone, Craig and Goodwin, Mark (2000), 'CCTV Surveillance in Urban Britain: Beyond the Rhetoric of Crime Prevention', in John R. Gold and George Revill, *Landscapes of Defence*, Harlow: Prentice Hall.

Williams, Katherine S. and Johnstone, Craig (2000), 'The Politics of the Selective Gaze: Closed Circuit Television and the Policing of Public Space', *Crime, Law and Social Change*, vol. 34, pp. 183–210.

Young, J. (1999), *The Exclusive Society: Social Exclusion, Crime and Difference in Late Modernity*, London: Sage.

21

Envoi

One trend which has been widely shared by most modern industrial countries in recent years has been a rising concern over crime. There is a widespread public perception that lives and property (and, some believe, organised society itself) are increasingly threatened by a seemingly irresistible tidal wave of lawlessness. 'Law and order' has become a significant political issue, made none the less important because it is so little specified and analysed in public debate. It is against this general atmosphere of concern that the survey of crime and criminology offered in this book has been undertaken. One objective has been to offer some perspective and understanding of the complex issues involved.

In part this can be done by indicating the extent of our ignorance on some of the most basic aspects. Thus, even the brief critique of the official crime statistics which was offered in Chapter Four makes it clear that in a quite literal sense we do not know how much crime is now committed in Britain. Problems of definition and the many problems over unrecorded, or misrecorded, crime make comparisons over time even more problematic. It can only be said that crime as revealed in the official statistics has increased (or decreased or altered) historically: but for most practical purposes this may be sufficient if, and it is a major qualification, *if* there is an awareness of the limitations and defects of the statistics. Unfortunately, neither the media nor many politicians, exercise such restraint. If the Home Office alter the recording of crimes statistics in the way discussed in Chapter Four this may preclude sensible historical comparisons and make for less transparency in assessment of the crime situation.

The judgement on the statistics may be said to constitute a negative conclusion: but the more general characteristic of the survey is that no conclusions have emerged. This should not be surprising. One impression which should have emerged with some clarity is that explanations in criminology have been, and still are, drawn from a wide variety of sources and disciplines. Biology, anthropology, philosophy, law, theology, psychology, sociology and social administration have all made their contributions. In attempting to assess these contributions it has been shown that each of the subjects could offer some justification for its involvement. Synthesising their approaches is, however, extremely difficult, if only because they often use different definitions and language, as well as having different methods and objects. No doubt what is needed is some generally accepted, overarching theory. Some integrated theories have, indeed, been forthcoming, e.g., Braithwaite's reintegrative shaming and Tittle's control balance, but these do not integrate all the disciplines involved and are far from being universally accepted so that it would be foolish to pretend that any such serious candidate is in sight. And would any single theory suffice to answer such different questions as, for example: what is the explanation of crime?; who are, or will become, the criminals?; and, what causes changes in the types of crime? One way forward is by decomposing the problem into its constituent parts. It is thus encouraging to see that many studies now focus on specific activities or groups.

If the study of the subject is confused by the Babel of discourses which it has attracted, a still more fundamental obstacle exists in the intractable nature of the basic subject matter. This is not crime as such, but human beings and human nature. The wide variety of human experience, and the motives, attitudes and behaviour which it produces (or is produced by it) necessarily makes generalisation elusive and unreliable. And there is a similar complicating variety in the forms of social organisation and cultures. It should again have emerged with some clarity from the rapid forays made in this book that it is wholly insufficient to relate crime simply to some presumed homogeneous national, institutional and cultural milieu. Many studies have indicated the importance of differences within societies and have identified a multiplicity of subcultures and social arrangements. There is a continuing need to recognise the forces which lie behind the control mechanisms, forces such as patriarchy, racism and class.

These reflections are not meant to indicate the impossibility of progress in this field. On the contrary, they are meant to give a realistic assessment of the task which still needs to be done as a prelude to considering where we have reached, and to suggest some possible ways forward. There certainly have been substantial advances made in what is still, in any systematic sense, a young area of study. One of the reasons for presenting this survey in a partially chronological way is to highlight the changes. If it is hardly in the nature of the subject and its material that it will ever become a science, there is no doubt that the approaches to it have become more 'scientific'. In most areas of interest, laboratory-type experiments are, and are likely to remain, out of reach; but there is a much greater awareness of the need to collect and use evidence more carefully through, for example, using control groups as a check on findings arising from studies of criminals or other social groups. There has also been a greater awareness of the value of using victim and local studies as ways of ascertaining the problems which crime causes for people.

One factor which has possibly retarded progress in the general field of criminology has been the relatively unsophisticated use of statistical methods. A number of the studies which have been looked at in this book derive their significance from attempting to measure one or other aspect of crime or criminals or victims. Yet, perhaps because of the academic background of the researchers, the statistical manipulations are relatively rudimentary, and the use of even common statistical techniques for testing the results largely nonexistent. In this respect we are now entered on a period of substantial change and progress from at least two directions. First, many of the people working in this area are now better equipped for making fuller use of their material in this way—one characteristic of the so-called New Sociology, for example, is its greater use of statistical, and even mathematical, methods. And secondly, technological advances—and especially the development of the computer—have revolutionised both the amount of material which can be collected and, even more, the ways in which it can be analysed and manipulated.

Such advantages are not without their problems. One set arises from the use of quantitative approaches to meet the need to provide policy changes to tackle the 'crime' problem. One consequence is that the more theoretical or conceptual work is being ignored. For example, feminist and much socially based research has given us an awareness of the limitations of purely quantitative studies: there will always be a need for qualitative research to give an understanding of people's lives, and as a reminder that it is people, and not just objects or concepts, which criminologists have to study. The increasing use of quantitative data is doubtless reflected in the present work, but it is hoped that students will seriously consider any theoretical suggestions which may give an insight into behaviour and society's need to control it.

In addition, many aspects of this book have tended to indicate that the area for study, crime and criminal justice, is not even stable or universally accepted. In Chapter Two it was pointed out that the criminal justice system was intended to make society safer for its citizens. However, it should now be clear that this is done on a narrow definition of what citizens need protection from, and what security means. Radical, critical and feminist research indicates the schisms in these areas— it sets a rigorous task for criminology: a recognition of the problematic areas of its discourse; the possibility that what we have at present is crime as defined by a few, mostly powerful, rich, white men; a criminal justice system which serves the interests of particular groups in society rather than the whole range of disparate groups; a narrow and traditional understanding of control etc. Criminology as manipulated by State agencies has tended to claim that it has addressed these issues by merely taking on board small aspects of this agenda—for example, by slightly altering the way police and courts deal with rape and/or domestic violence—rather than being willing to reconsider the whole area to be studied. Another indication of the narrow approach of the criminal justice system is the limited view it has of justice: in Chapter Two a number of seemingly very different models of justice were set out (see especially crime control and due process in 2.6), but each accepted justice as an objective or value-free concept. Criminology must now meet the challenge that such simplistic acceptance of the basic tools and concepts of its field of study is not always either useful or necessary.

All this is probably particularly true of British criminology, which takes a very pragmatic view of the area to be studied and the policies which this suggests. As a result, many policy alterations in Britain turn around controlling the opportunity for crime as being the simplest target—for example, by target hardening or removing from society those considered to be threatening. The wider consideration of the underlying social and psychological aspects tends to be down-played. It is an approach which beyond a certain point becomes too expensive, both in terms of freedom and finance. The growth of imprisonment is a case in point. Prisons are extremely costly and at a time of reduced finances for all other public services their continued growth should be questioned. Prisons are also negative institutions, particularly with the current reduced emphasis on rehabilitation. Situational crime prevention is similarly expensive, both in personal and financial terms. It may be possible for the richest in society ('gated communities' and other security devices) or in certain public situations where the State can, or has to, afford it, but again there will be large areas unprovided for. Besides being ethically questionable and invasive of privacy the overuse of both imprisonment and of situational crime prevention or management of risk will create large excluded and discontented sectors of society leading to greater insecurity and less safety in society generally. The unrestrained rhetoric of the 1980s and 1990s calls for law and order have moved us closer to this point and suggest the need to search for additional strategies, some of which will involve a more farreaching questioning of overall social structures. In late modernity it is probably not possible to return to the grand State structures of the mid-twentieth century. The State alone cannot protect its citizens from crime and it is tending to devolve power both to new national institutions of Scotland and Wales and local organisations and structures. Although the crucial issues of accountability, power and finances are not yet worked out criminologists need to recognise these changes and begin to explore the theoretical, practical and ethical implications of the new order of governance, for social justice and security. Part of this will involve a consideration of how to apply and adapt the theories set out in this book to the new structures. As a first step there is a need to challenge the obsession of the public and politicians with the need to be 'hard' on crime and educate them in more positive means of addressing crime and delivering safer communities.

It has not been a main objective of this book to examine specific policies, or to make explicit policy proposals, but towards the end of most chapters there is a brief section on policy implications. The immediate objective of this book is, and must be, more modest. It is to introduce students to the broad area covered by criminology and to convey some understanding of the development and present State of the subject. More ambitiously, it aims to convey some of the writer's enthusiasm and concern for problems which are both intrinsically fascinating, and of major significance for our times.

Useful websites

Acts of the UK Parliament and access to the devolved legislators
http://www.hmso.gov.uk/acts.htm

American Society of Criminology
http://www.asc41.com/
http://www.bsos.umd.edu/asc/four.html

American Society of Criminology—Division of Critical Criminology and the Academy of Criminal Justice Sciences (ACJS)
http://critcrim.org/

Association of Chief Police Officers
http://www.acpo.police.uk

Australian Institute of Criminology
http://www.aic.gov.au/

Bills before the UK Parliament
http://www.parliament.the-stationery-office.co.uk/pa/pabills.htm

British Journal for Sociology
http://www.lse.ac.uk/serials/Bjs/abstract.htm

British Society for Criminology
http://www.britsoccrim.org/index.htm
http://www.britsoccrim.org/journal.htm

Centre for Crime and Justice Studies
http://www.kcl.ac.uk/depsta/rel/ccjs/home.htm

Centre for Criminal Justice Studies, Leeds University
http://www.leeds.ac.uk/law/ccjs/homepage.htm

Coalition for an International Criminal Court
http://www.igc.org/icc

Colorado Centre for the Study of Prevention of Violence
http://www.colorado.edu/cspv/infohouse/databases.html

Community Justice National Training Organisation
http://www.cjnto.org.uk/index.html

Criminal Cases Review Commission
http://www.ccrc.gov.uk/

Crime Concern
http://www.crimeconcern.org.uk/

Crime Research Centre, University of Western Australia
http://www.aic.gov.au/

Criminal Justice Links
http://cjstudents.com/cj_links.htm

Criminology Links
http://www.prison.org.uk/

Crown Prosecution Service
http://www.cps.gov.uk

Department of Constitutional Affairs: Justice, Rights and Democracy (was the Lord Chancellor's Department)
http://www.dca.gov.uk/

DrugScope
http://www.drugscope.org.uk/home.asp

European Forum for Victim–Offender Mediation and Restorative Justice
http://www.euforumrj.org/

European Institute for Crime Prevention and Control, affiliated with the United Nations (HEUNI)
http://www.heuni.fi/

Her Majesty's Prisons Website
http://www.hmprisonservice.gov.uk/prisons/default.asp

Home Office
http://www.homeoffice.gov.uk/

Home Office Crime Reduction Programme Unit
http://www.crimereduction.gov.uk/training2.htm

Home Office Research and Development Statistics
http://www.homeoffice.gov.uk/rds/index.htm

Howard League for Penal Reform
http://web.ukonline.co.uk/howard.league

Innocent until proven guilty (website funded by the Persula Foundation and run by
the Prison Reform Trust)
http://www.innocentuntilprovenguilty.com/

Inquest
http://www.inquest.org.uk

International Centre for Prison Studies, King's College London
http://www.kcl.ac.uk/depsta/rel/icps/

Institute for Public Policy Reform—IPPR
http://www.ippr.org.uk/about/

International Victimology Website
http://www.victimology.nl/

Justice
http://www.justice.org.uk/

Justice for Kids and Youth
http://www.usdoj.gov/kidspage/

Kent Criminal Justice Centre
http://www.sentencing-advisory-panel.gov.uk/

National Association for the Care and Resettlement of Offenders—NACRO
http://www.nacro.org.uk/

National Criminal Intelligence Service
http://www.ncis.co.uk/

National Criminal Justice Reference Service
http://www.ncjrs.org/whatsncjrs.html

National Probation Service
http://www.homeoffice.gov.uk/cpg/nps/

Prison News
http://www.prison.org.uk/

Prison Reform Trust
http://www.prisonreformtrust.org.uk

Radzinowicz Library—Cambridge Institute of Criminology
http://www.crim.cam.ac.uk/library/

Rethinking Crime and Punishment
http://www.rethinking.org.uk/

Sentencing Advisory Panel
http://www.sentencing-advisory-panel.gov.uk/

Social Exclusion Unit
http://www.cabinet-office.gov.uk/seu/index.asp

Statewatch
http://www.cabinet-office.gov.uk/seu/index.asp

UK Criminal Justice Weblog
http://www.britsoccrim.org/index.htm

UK Government Criminal Justice System Website
http://www.criminal-justice-system.gov.uk/home.html

UK Government Drugs Prevention Website
http://www.drugsprevention.net/

United Families and Friends Campaign
http://www.uffc.org/

United Nations Crime and Justice Information Network
http://www.uncjin.org/

United Nations Interregional Crime and Criminal Justice Research Institute
http://www.unicri.it/index.htm

Victim Support
http://www.victimsupport.org.uk/

Webjournal of Current Legal Issues
http://webjcli.ncl.ac.uk/

Western Society of Criminology
http://www.sonoma.edu/cja/wsc/wscnetmain.html

Youth Justice Board
http://www.youth-justice-board.gov.uk/youthjusticeboard

Youth Policies in the UK
http://www.keele.ac.uk/depts/so/youthchron/about/

NAME INDEX

SUBJECT INDEX